Babingtonite

Triclinic

In a triclinic system, all three axes of the coordinate axis are different lengths. All the angles between them are oblique.

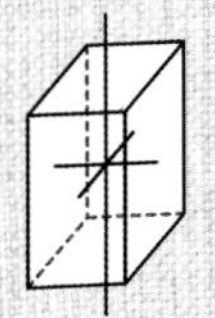

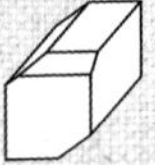

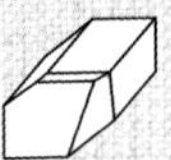

Rotational axes and mirror planes

The symmetrical properties of a specific crystal determine which crystal system it belongs to. The physical form of a crystal is considered symmetrical when it can be positioned in such a way by rotating or mirroring that it cannot be distinguished from the previous positioning. The axis on which it is rotated is called the rotational axis. A two-fold rotational axis means that the object returns again to its same starting position after two rotations of 180° each. In the case of a three-fold rotational axis, three rotations of 120° each are then necessary. In the case of a four-fold rotational axis, four rotations of 90° each and so on.

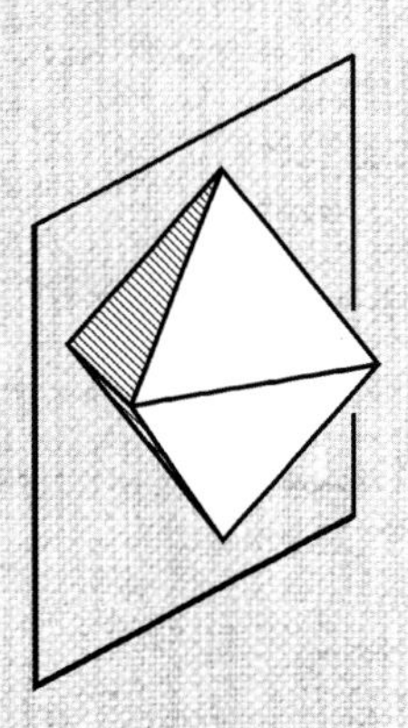
A mirror plane splits an object, even a crystal, into two inversely equal halves.

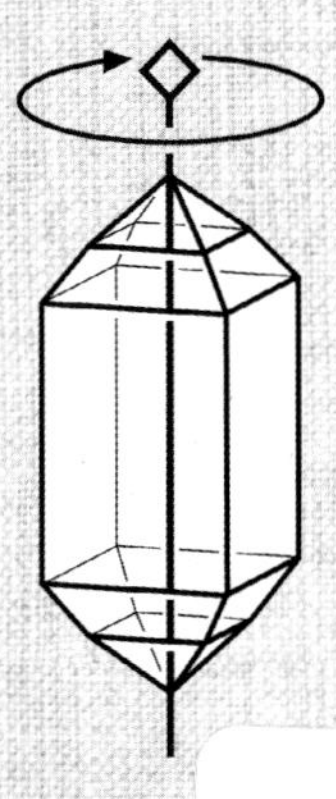
With a four-fold rotational axis, the crystal has the same appearance after each rotation of 90°.

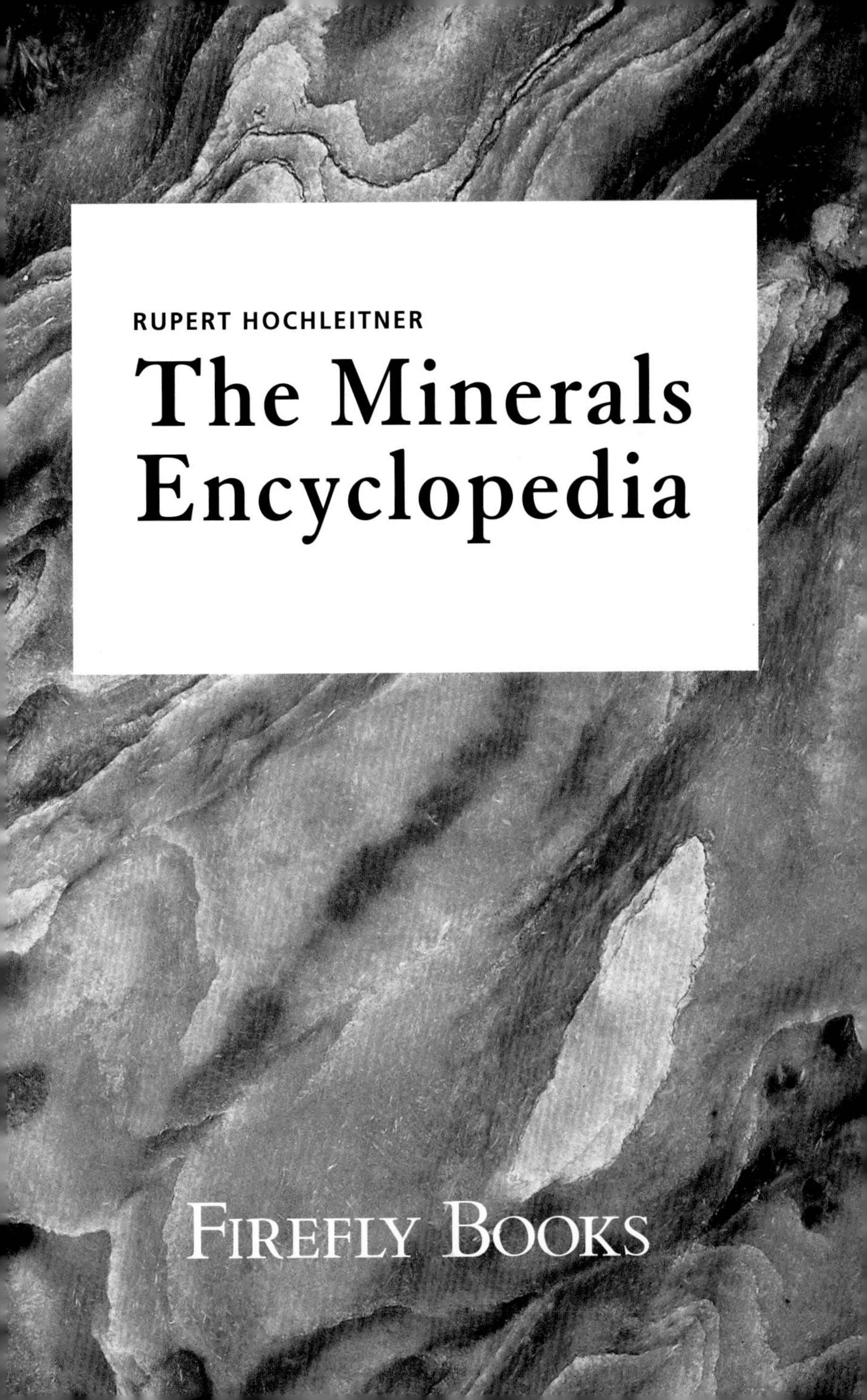

RUPERT HOCHLEITNER

The Minerals Encyclopedia

FIREFLY BOOKS

Contents

Rock profiles

What Stone is That?

This question occurs again and again, whether you pick up a pebble while walking, find a crystal in the mountains, find gold or silver shiny chunks in a spoil heap at an ore mine, trip over the curb or look at a beautiful piece of jewelry. Time and again, you want to know what that mineral is, what kind of rock lies before you, what type of gemstone glitters with such beautiful colors.

The purpose of this book is to answer such questions — as a constant companion when hiking, travelling, mountaineering, collecting minerals or when searching quarries and spoil heaps, at mineral fairs and even at the jeweler's.

There are a few basic points to keep in mind:

With the exception of mercury, **minerals** are always solids. No matter how good mineral water may taste, no matter how many minerals it shows on the label, it is still a liquid and therefore not a mineral.

Anything man-made, from window glass to the quartz crystal in a wristwatch to an artificial diamond, is not a mineral. A mineral must always be of natural origin.

The same cannot be said about **crystals**. Crystals are solid chemical substances; their atoms are arranged in a uniformly ordered structure. This ordered arrangement of atoms is characterized by the flat, even surfaces that form the outer edges of crystals. Unlike a mineral, a crystal does not necessarily have to be naturally formed to be classified as such. Crystals are produced industrially in large quantities. Even children can grow crystals for themselves — in a crystal growing box, for example. Thus, there are naturally formed crystals, which can also be referred to as minerals, and artificially produced crystals that cannot be classified as minerals.

Nearly all minerals are crystals, even if this is sometimes not readily visible from their appearance. These crystalline varieties of minerals have lost their smooth outer surfaces, possibly due to weathering or due to a stray hammer blow, yet they still

Japan Law Twin Quartz from the La Gardette Mine in France

possess their internal ordered arrangement of atoms and the crystal lattice. Thus, they are classified as crystalline. There are only a few minerals that have atoms which are not arranged in an ordered crystal lattice. These are classified as amorphous. The best-known example of an amorphous mineral is opal. Similar to quartz in its composition, it cannot form crystals although quartz does have this ability.

Gemstones are minerals that are cut for the production of jewelry. To be classified as a gemstone, a mineral must fulfill various criteria:

It must be beautiful; more precisely, it must meet aesthetic standards. This means that it should be splendidly colored and, when polished, should glitter and sparkle as much as possible. The latter point becomes all the more important if the mineral in question is normally colorless, as is the case with diamonds.

A gemstone mineral should have a hardness of at least 7. There is a very simple reason for this: a large portion of the dust-particles in the air that, by their very nature, constantly settle on gemstones are quartz. Quartz has a hardness of 7. If the gemstone mineral were softer, it would be scratched by these quartz grains, causing it to dull at a much quicker pace. By contrast, if the gemstone mineral is harder than quartz, it will remain a genuine gemstone — fully unchanged, shimmering and sparkling, in its original form.

Rocks can be described as large geological bodies comprised of many individual elements from one or more different mineral species. Marble, for example, consists solely of multiple grains of the mineral calcite. Granite, on the other hand, is composed of three mineral species: feldspar, quartz and common mica.

Considering their formation, rocks can be divided into four basic groups:

1) **Intrusive igneous rocks** are formed when molten magma (semi-fluid rock) solidifies below the Earth's surface, ultimately producing solid rocks before breaking through the Earth's crust.

2) However, if the molten magma comes to the surface, e.g. in a volcano, and only solidifies above the surface, a **volcanic rock** is formed.

3) Rocks formed by the deposition and resolidification of small particles, such as sand grains, are called **stratified rocks** or **sedimentary rocks**, often abbreviated to the term **sediments**.

4) If such sediments are transported below the Earth's surface, they then transform under rising temperature and pressure. At this stage, the **resulting rocks** are referred to as **metamorphic rocks** or, simply, **metamorphites**. This process is called metamorphism. Depending on the extent of the pressure and temperature, the occurring metamorphism is classified as low, medium or high-grade. Contact metamorphism occurs when rocks come into contact with hot magma.

If rocks are rapidly transported to great depths below the surface, causing high pressure to act on them immediately, and then quickly return to the surface so that the temperature cannot increase drastically, this type of metamorphism is called burial metamorphism.

The partial melting of rocks is called anatexis, and the resulting rocks are called anatexites.

The Properties of Minerals

In identifying minerals, it is necessary to determine their properties. Each mineral species has a series of properties which, when combined, are unique to a particular mineral. This means that to reliably identify a mineral, it is imperative to verify as many of its properties as possible. With some properties, such as hardness or streak, this is easy, as it requires no or only readily available aids; for others, such as chemical composition, a precise verification requires a great deal of equipment, which a layperson may not normally be able to operate.

For this reason, this field identification book places emphasis on those properties that are easiest to determine and which, under normal circumstances, can assist in the reliable identification of a mineral.

Streak

The streak is the color obtained by drawing a line with the mineral on an unglazed and therefore slightly rough porcelain tile (streak plate). The color of the mark thus obtained is characteristic of the mineral species. No matter how different the colors of various specimens of the same mineral species may appear, the streak always displays the same color. For instance, although fluorite samples may be colorless, yellow, green, blue, brown, pink or purple, its streak is always white.

A streak plate can be acquired for an affordable price from a mineralogy supplier. If, for whatever reason, a streak plate is not available, an old porcelain fuse or the unglazed lower edge of a plate or a cup will suffice in an emergency.

Therefore, the streak is a distinct characteristic of a mineral that is well-suited for classification. For this reason, all minerals in this field identification book are grouped together based on the color of their streak. This allows you to easily determine which part of the book you need to refer to.

Within the streak groups, the minerals are then arranged by increasing hardness.

Hardness

It is very easy to determine the hardness of a mineral. It is a well-known fact that you can cut glass with a diamond. In fact, diamonds are the hardest substance found on our planet. Other minerals, such as soapstone, are so soft that, like wood, you can carve figures out of it and even scratch it with a fingernail.

All minerals can be ordered according to their hardness, depending on whether one mineral can scratch another mineral or the mineral can scratch itself. Since this property is characteristic of every mineral, it is used in this book, alongside the streak, as the most important trait for identification and classification.

The easiest way to determine the hardness of a mineral being identified is to compare it with the Mohs scale of mineral hardness. This scale comprises a sequence of ten minerals, each of which can scratch those below it on the scale.

<table>
<tr><td>1</td><td>**Talc**</td><td rowspan="2">*Can be scratched with a fingernail*</td><td rowspan="5">*Can be scratched with a knife*</td></tr>
<tr><td>2</td><td>**Gypsum**</td></tr>
<tr><td>3</td><td>**Calcite**</td><td rowspan="3"></td></tr>
<tr><td>4</td><td>**Fluorite**</td></tr>
<tr><td>5</td><td>**Apatite**</td></tr>
<tr><td>6</td><td>**Feldspar**</td><td colspan="2" rowspan="5">*Scratches glass*</td></tr>
<tr><td>7</td><td>**Quartz**</td></tr>
<tr><td>8</td><td>**Topaz**</td></tr>
<tr><td>9</td><td>**Corundum**</td></tr>
<tr><td>10</td><td>**Diamond**</td></tr>
</table>

Hardness scales, i.e. a test kit containing the nine test minerals (as the hardest substance, the diamond is not necessary), can be purchased from specialist mineralogy suppliers.

In an emergency, e.g. in the field, you can also use your fingernail (about hardness 2), a pocket knife (about hardness 6) and a small piece of broken glass (harder than hardness 6) to identify minerals.

Hardness is determined as follows:

First, take a mineral of medium hardness,

for example apatite, hardness 5, and check whether the mineral being identified can be scratched by it. If this is the case, continue with the next softer mineral until you reach a mineral that cannot scratch the mineral being identified. Conversely, if the mineral being identified cannot scratch the mineral from the test kit, then both have the same hardness. You have reached your objective. If, on the other hand, the mineral being identified cannot be scratched by the first selected test mineral of medium hardness, then simply continue analogously with the next harder one.

With this method, the hardness of any mineral can be determined within the framework of the Mohs scale of mineral hardness.

Always check the hardness with sharp edges and on freshly broken areas! Always wipe away any dust after scratching to ensure that scratching has actually occurred as opposed to a case of a mere grating of the test mineral. With very fine-grained mineral aggregates, individual grains may break off during the scratch test. This can feign a lower hardness. With very smooth crystal surfaces, a hardness higher than the true hardness is often erroneously measured. This is because, in such cases, extra force must be applied to be sure that the mineral really cannot be scratched.

Tenacity

Tenacity describes a mineral's resistance to scratching or bending. Most minerals are brittle, which means that, when scratched, such as with a steel needle, the powder caused by scratching jumps off. If this is not the case, the mineral is said to be brittle (e.g. galena).

If a scratch mark can be made without creating any powder at all, in the same way as when cutting into butter with a knife, the mineral is said to be cuttable, or sectile (e.g., argentite, gold). Moreover, gold can also be hammered into flakes. Such minerals are said to be ductile.

On the other hand, other minerals are elastically flexible, such as mica, which means that when bent they return to their original position after bending. In contrast, inelastic flexible minerals, such as gypsum, remain in their new position after bending.

Important: During hardness testing, always perform a cross-check! If the test mineral scratches the mineral being identified, it must always be checked whether the test mineral cannot be scratched by the mineral being identified. This is the only way to be certain.

Color

At first glance, color appears to be the most useful characteristic of a mineral. However, it quickly becomes apparent that this is not the case. While there are indeed minerals for which color is very characteristic,

Gypsum crystals are inelastically flexible. Once bent, they retain their new shape.

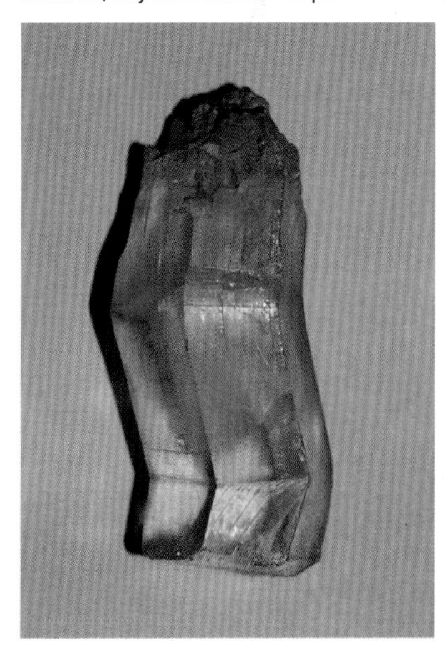

such as green malachite or blue azurite, a large number of minerals do not occur in just one color but rather in a wide range of colors. Quartz, for example, can be colorless, pink, purple, brown, black or yellow, while diamond occurs in the colors white, yellow, green, brown, blue and black. In addition, the exterior layer of some minerals changes color when exposed to air. For example, just after fracturing, the surface of bornite is a metallic pink hue, which is covered by an iridescent blue-red-green oxidation layer in a few hours. Therefore, the color of a mineral must always be checked on a fresh surface.

Luster

Every unprocessed mineral has a very specific luster, characteristic of the respective mineral species. However, this luster is very difficult to measure. It can only be described in comparison with objects from day-to-day life.

Vitreous luster corresponds to the luster of plain window glass. It is the most common type of luster.

Metallic luster corresponds to the luster of polished metal, such as aluminum foil.

Silky luster is a luster comparable to the undulating shimmer of light on natural silk.

Pitchy luster is the luster of pitch, comparable to that of the tar clumps seen in road repairs.

Greasy luster is similar to the luster of grease marks on paper.

Adamantine luster is the familiar brilliant luster of cut diamonds but also that of lead crystal glass.

Minerals with a **pearly luster** exhibit a luster similar to the insides of some mussel shells, which exhibit a whitish shimmer with a colored glimmer of light.

Density

Density is the weight of a mineral per volume unit (expressed in grams per cubic centimeter), while specific gravity (relative density) is the ratio relative to the weight of water and therefore unitless. Measuring density is not easy and requires accurate equipment. Nevertheless, density can be used as a determining characteristic. By simply weighing it in your hand, you can determine if a mineral is light (density less than 2), normal (density around 2.5), heavy (density greater than 3.5) or very heavy (6 or higher). An even better estimate can be achieved by holding a piece of the same size of a mineral of known density in the other hand and comparing.

Cleavage and fracture

If you shatter a mineral (e.g. with a hammer) or break it, fracture surfaces of varied appearance are created depending on the mineral species. The mineral can break into pieces with flat smooth cleavage faces or into geometric bodies that are always similar. Galena, for example, breaks into small cubes, and calcite breaks into small rhombohedra. In mineralogy, the former case is referred to as "cubic cleavage" and the latter case as "rhombohedral cleavage." On occasions, the angles made by the cleavage faces relative to each other are also important in identifying a mineral. For example, augite can easily be distinguished from the similar mineral, hornblende, due to the fact that its cleavage faces intersect at an angle of about 90 degrees. On the other hand, hornblende has a cleavage angle of about 120 degrees. Cleavage can have different qualities ranging from "perfect" to "indiscernible." The latter indication means that cleavage, although present, is not normally distinguishable using simple means.

All separation surfaces that are not cleavage faces are described under the heading "Fracture." Depending on the appearance of the surfaces, the fracture can be described as conchoidal (e.g. rock crystal), crystalline (e.g. calcite), uneven (e.g. feldspar) or hackly (e.g. gold).

Rock salt (left) breaks down into perfect cubes when cleaved, as does galena (right).

Fluorescence, Phosphorescence

If certain minerals are irradiated with ultraviolet light, they can exhibit a glow of varying intensity in a wide range of colors. If the UV light is switched off, some minerals will continue to glow for a few seconds. This phenomenon is called phosphorescence. Usually, neither property is characteristic of a mineral. Individual samples of the same mineral species may exhibit entirely different fluorescence colors, while some samples may not fluoresce at all. This is because fluorescence is not normally a fundamental property of a mineral but is usually only caused by minor impurities. An intense fluorescence is only seen as a viable characteristic in identifying scheelite. Some minerals containing rare earth elements, such as monazite or some zircons, give off a characteristic yellow-green colored glow in unfiltered UV light.

There are two different types of UV light: longwave UV light, also called black light, which is used, for example, in discotheques and is harmless under normal circumstances. There are special bulbs and fluorescent tubes that can be inserted into ordinary sockets to generate this light. Shortwave UV light is much more high energy; you need very special (and not very inexpensive) lamps with special filters to generate it. Many more minerals fluoresce under shortwave UV light and usually more intensively than under longwave light. Moreover, there are also minerals (for example, ruby) that fluoresce better or indeed only under longwave UV.

Caution when using UV light: UV light (especially shortwave) can harm the eyes. Always wear safety glasses! These are available from the UV light supplier for a reasonable price.

The Origin and Occurrence of Minerals

Minerals grow over periods of many thousands to hundreds of thousands of years.

The formation of minerals is divided into three different formation stages:

The *magmatic stage* includes minerals and rocks formed from a hot melt either in the Earth's interior (intrusive, or plutonic, igneous rocks) or at the Earth's surface (volcanic igneous rocks).

Intrusive igneous rocks are characterized by the fact that they are relatively coarse-grained, which means that even the individual grains of the groundmass can be observed with the naked eye.

Volcanic igneous rocks are very fine-grained; the individual grains of the groundmass cannot be seen with the naked eye or even with a magnifying glass.

The *sedimentary stage* consists of minerals that are primarily formed by the weathering of minerals or rocks which are then transported by water or wind and subsequently deposited.

Sedimentary rocks usually have distinct layers. The individual crystals of the rock components are indiscernible. Unlike all other rocks, sedimentary rocks frequently contain fossils.

In the *metamorphic stage*, minerals and rocks are formed by varying pressure and temperature conditions at a certain depth below the Earth's surface.

Metamorphic rocks often exhibit

recognizable layers and folds, and the individual crystals of the rock components are generally easily discernible.

Magmatic Formations

Intramagmatic deposits

Intramagmatic deposits are accumulations of minerals within intrusive igneous rock bodies.

The metals chromium, platinum and nickel, in particular, are extracted from such deposits.

A special type of the occurrence of minerals in igneous rocks is represented by kimberlite pipes. These are huge volcanic pipes filled with a unique rock called kimberlite. This kimberlite contains diamond crystals that developed within the rock and are brought to the surface by the molten magma, where high pressure and temperatures favor the growth of such crystals.

The oxidation zone is characterized by the prevalence of the iron mineral limonite. Therefore, it is also referred to as the iron hat.

Pegmatite

Pegmatites are very coarse-grained rocks that have filled the fissures in an older body of rock. They primarily consist of feldspar, quartz and mica. Feldspar is extracted as a raw material for the porcelain industry. Mica is used as an insulating material and, more recently, in the production of automotive paints.

In addition, pegmatites often contain a whole range of minerals, including gemstone minerals as well, that have formed large anhedral crystals in the rock, such as beryl, topaz, tourmaline and many others. These crystals, however, are almost always cloudy and opaque and therefore not useful as gemstones for jewelry.

Younger formations are found in vugs and cavities within the pegmatites and also contain beautiful euhedral crystals, that are often of cutting quality. In particular, the gemstones extracted from pegmatites are topaz, tourmaline, aquamarine and morganite. Pegmatites are the main sources of these gemstones.

Pneumatolytic Deposits

Pneumatolytic deposits are formed from hot gases in the depths of the Earth. Minerals possibly occurring in such formations include fluorite, topaz, tourmaline and cassiterite, or tinstone. Tin, in particular, and, more rarely, tungsten, are extracted from pneumatolytic deposits. One exception is the well-known topaz from the Schneckenstein rock formation in the Vogtland region. It occurs in a pneumatolytically altered tourmaline schist breccia and was mined for cutting purposes for several centuries.

Hydrothermal Veins

A "vein" refers to the filling of a fissure in a rock with minerals younger than the rock. Veins often contain open cavities in which crystals can grow freely, including gemstone minerals such as amethysts. Hydrothermal veins contain important ore minerals from which metals are extracted, e.g. copper, zinc, lead, silver or gold.

Alpine fissures exhibit a unique case of veins: these cracks and crevices in the rock contain beautiful and sometimes very large specimens of rock crystal, smoky quartz, citrine, hematite or feldspar.

Vulcanic Formations

During the cooling and solidification of molten lava, the gases contained in the molten mass are released. A portion escapes from the surface of the lava flow, but another portion also becomes entrapped in the rapidly solidifying rock in the form of "gas bubbles" and thus forms relatively round cavities that can be many centimeters, in rare cases even meters, wide in diameter. During the cooling process of the now solid rock, these cavities can be filled with mineral formations by invasive hot solutions. Giant deposits of such mineral formations in Brazil and Uruguay yield large quantities of amethyst and agate. Many zeolite minerals, such as phillipsite, chabasite or stilbite, are also mainly found in these cavities of volcanic rocks.

Sedimentary Formations

Copper phosphate turquoise, a very popular gemstone, can form in the fissures of silicate rock weathering formations with already low copper levels. During the weathering of silicic rocks, silica deposits in the form of the gemstone opal can form close to the groundwater table, especially in desert areas.

Oxidation and Cementation Zone

In areas where a vein deposit reaches the surface, its appearance and mineral content are significantly changed. The vein no longer contains sulfide ores. Its most common mineral is the iron hydroxide limonite. Oxidation minerals, such as malachite, azurite, wulfenite, vanadinite, zinc spar and many others, fuse with it or grow in its cavities. Some of the minerals that occur in the oxidation zone, particularly in copper deposits, are cut for jewelry.

These include chrysocolla azurite, and turquoise in addition to the most common mineral, malachite.

Placers

It is well known that gold can sometimes be found in the sands of streams and rivers. It is less well known that other minerals can also be found there. Predominantly, these are minerals characterized by their high specific gravity and chemical resistance, such as platinum, garnet, ilmenite, rutile, monazite, and numerous gemstone minerals, such as diamond, ruby, sapphire, chrysoberyl, topaz, spinel and many others.

Such deposits, known as placers or placer deposits, occur when minerals are exposed during the weathering of rocks or deposits, transported away with water, enriched in the process and then deposited again.

Metamorphic Formations

Ruby and spinal minerals typically occur in metamorphic rocks and, here particularly, in marbles. Sapphire also occurs rarely. Gneisses or mica schists sometimes contain deposits in which beautiful emerald crystals are found. The only European emerald deposit of this type, occasionally mined for gemstones, is located at the Leckbachscharte mountain saddle in the Habach Valley in the Austrian Alps. Garnet crystals from mica schists (mainly almandine) were also mined for a long time to make stones for Central European garnet jewelry.

Jadeite and nephrite are also formed by the transformation of basic rocks, frequently where large serpentinite bodies exist.

Classification of Rocks

Most rocks can be divided into three different groups based on how they are formed:

Igneous rocks (magmatites)

The igneous rock group contains intrusive igneous rocks and volcanic (extrusive igneous) rocks, which are all formed by a more or less rapid solidification of a molten rock.

Relatively large crystallites are formed because crystal growth is slow during solidification under the Earth's surface because the magma body, protected by the surrounding rocks, can only cool slowly. As a result, most intrusive igneous rocks are rather coarse-grained, so that it is normally easy to see the individual components with the naked eye. Sometimes crystals grow long before the main part of the molten mass solidifies; such crystals are called inclusions. These rocks are called porphyritic. Porphyritic intrusive igneous rocks are characterized by the fact that the components of the groundmass are still relatively coarse-grained as well. Porphyritic volcanic rocks also contain inclusions that are up to several centimeters in size. In contrast, their groundmass is so fine that at least a magnifying glass is needed to be able to identify individual components. This is the general characteristic of volcanic rocks, which are always — apart from inclusions or xenoliths (= foreign rock inclusions) — extremely fine-grained due to the rapid cooling of the molten mass at the Earth's surface. This can be so advanced that no crystal growth at all is possible. This is how volcanic glasses, e.g. obsidian, are formed.

Pyroclastites (volcanic tuffs) are rocks formed during volcanic eruptions. Material expelled from the volcano is deposited on the ground like sedimentary rock. They exhibit the typical layered structure of sedimentary rock but consist entirely, or almost entirely, of volcanic material. In this way, they form a transition, as it were, between these two rock groups.

Sedimentary Rocks (sediments)

Sediments or sedimentary rocks are formed by the prior destruction of already existing rocks, their dissolution into their individual components and the subsequent redeposition of the individual particles after a relatively long transport distance. Depending on the mineral content, sandstones with a wide range of binding mediums, clays, marls or conglomerates and breccias, are formed. Most limestones, consisting of biogenic (produced by living organisms) lime, are an exception. These are primarily formed from the shells or skeletal parts, calcified shells or calcified skeletons of living organisms. Much rarer is the direct inorganic precipitation of calcium carbonate from water which occurs, for example, in hot springs. Likewise, salt and gypsum rocks also owe their formation to inorganic precipitation from the evaporation of seawater. The various coals are formed by the conversion of organic matter (namely, wood and plant parts to, by and large, pure carbon), which thus represent a link between sedimentary and metamorphic rocks but, in this book, are still classified among the sediments.

Metamorphic Rocks (metamorphites)

If the pressure on a rock slowly increases with layering, the originally loose sediments solidify into solid rocks. Clay mud, for example, solidifies into argillite through the expulsion of water. This process is called diagenesis. The first chemical changes also take place during this process. For example, in limestones, finely distributed silicon or iron can concentrate around certain nuclei (mostly organic) forming flint or pyrite concretions. If the pressure and temperature continue to rise, many of the original minerals are no longer stable, and the mineral associations transform into those that are better suited to the changed conditions. Such rocks, transformed through pressure and temperature, are called metamorphic rocks or metamorphites. For example, as temperature and pressure increase, argillaceous rocks first transform into phyllites, then mica schists and finally gneisses. The type of rock formed always depends first and foremost on the source rock. This does not only affect sediments. Volcanic rocks or intrusive igneous rocks can also undergo metamorphism. For example, where gneisses are concerned, a distinction is made between orthogneisses formed by the transformation of an igneous rock, such as granite, and paragneisses which began as a sediment.

Depending on the geological situation and the relationship between the pressure and temperature change, different types of metamorphism are identified:

In **regional metamorphism**, large rock masses ("whole regions"), such as during orogeny, are transported to great depths over long periods of time. The rocks are exposed to a uniform increase in pressure and temperature. Typical rocks of regional metamorphism include mica schists, chlorite schists, amphibolites or gneisses.

Eclogites and granulites are archetypal of particularly high-grade regional metamorphism and, in exceptional cases, may even contain diamonds. If extremely high temperatures are reached, the rocks may melt partially or even completely. This process is called anatexis. The end products are molten masses, from which igneous rocks can once again be formed. Thus, the rock cycle comes full circle. Rocks in which the lighter rock components had already melted while the darker components still exhibit metamorphic structures are called migmatites or anatectites.

If molten magma penetrates other, already solid rock particles (sediments, but also all other rock types), then they are transformed through the effect of temperature, while the ambient pressure remains unchanged. Therefore, this metamorphism is caused solely by temperature and is therefore referred to as a thermometamorphism or **contact metamorphism**. For example, hornfels or knotenschiefer (spotted slate), garbenschiefer (caraway seed slate) and chiastolite slate, are typical rocks resulting from contact metamorphism.

If rock masses are transported very quickly into the Earth's depths where individual plates of the crust slide over each other, thereby pushing one into the depths (= subduction), the masses are immediately exposed to the high pressure there, while it takes a considerably longer time for the temperature to rise due to the poor thermal conductivity. If such rocks are brought back to the Earth's surface relatively quickly (e.g. by tectonic uplifts during orogeny), their mineral composition is entirely due to the high pressure. This type of metamorphism is called **burial metamorphism**; prototypical rocks are, for example, glaucophane schists.

Identifying Minerals, Rocks and Gemstones

How to identify a mineral

1. Check the streak. This will help you determine in which section of the book you need to search.
2. Determine the hardness. This leaves only a few minerals within the same streak group that it could be.
3. Check the other properties specified in the text. Under the heading "Similar minerals," you will learn which minerals are most likely to be confused with each other and which characteristics could help you to distinguish between them.

Once you have achieved your objective, you can find additional interesting information about your mineral under the headings "Origin and occurrence" and "Accessory minerals." Sometimes minerals that are not described in this field identification book are mentioned as accessory minerals. In this case, the specialized works listed in the For Further Reading page on page 437 will help you.

How to identify a rock

First, determine the rock group in question. To do so, use the descriptions on the back flap.

If you know which group the rock belongs to, try to determine the main mineral mixture elements. When distinguishing limestone from other similar looking rocks, diluted hydrochloric acid is often very useful. Once you have identified the main minerals, you can readily classify the rock as one of the rock types shown. Conspicuous secondary mineral mixture elements sometimes allow for a more accurate determination (e.g. hornblende-granite or garnet-peridotite).

How to identify a gemstone

The identification of gemstones is not exactly straightforward, since various mineral identification methods, e.g. hardness testing or fracture and cleavage testing, are inherently excluded. Aside from that, valuable stones must not be damaged. Nevertheless, there are far fewer gemstones than minerals and therefore far fewer opportunities for confusion.

Therefore, it is best to proceed as follows during identification:

If you have a gemstone in front of you, immediately determine its color and whether it is transparent or opaque. Now select any gemstone with these properties in the identification section. Under the heading "Differentiating," you can learn which gemstones have the same properties and how you can differentiate between them. This allows you to determine which gemstone you are in possession of as quickly as possible.

What are meteorites?

Meteorites are pieces of rock that originated at the beginning of the Solar System. They are either, as in the case of the iron meteorites, the remains of a planet developed during the formation of our planetary system and then immediately destroyed again, or, in the case of chondrites, matter from the solar cloud that was never part of a planet. They travelled through space on a path around the sun for 4.5 billion years before crashing into our Earth. The well-known shooting stars are tiny grains of dust that light up briefly when they enter our atmosphere and then immediately burn up. Much rarer are the larger pieces, which do not burn up completely despite the intense heat of the atmosphere but instead land as meteorites on the Earth's surface and can then be found. Very roughly, meteorites are divided into three groups:

1. **Iron meteorites**, which consist almost entirely of iron-nickel,
2. **Stony-iron meteorites**, which contain iron-nickel metal in which silicate crystals or crystal fragments are suspended, and
3. **Stony meteorites**, which consist mainly of silicate minerals, although they may still have a rather significant metal content.

Additionally, there are a very small number of meteorites that originate from other planets or moons, for example, lunaites from our Earth's moon and shergottites, nakhlites and chassignites from Mars as well as howardites, eucrites and diogenites from the large asteroid Vesta. They were all ejected into space during large meteorite impacts on their parent bodies (the moon or Mars) and travelled on their orbits around the sun until they crashed into our Earth after millions or billions of years in space.

With its characteristic drawing, the landscape agate is unmistakable.

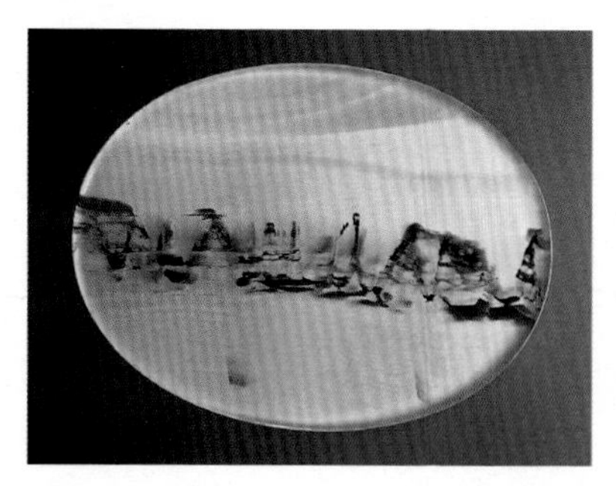

How can I recognize meteorites

Only specialists can reliably identify a found meteorite.

However, there are some clues that can make it recognizable, even for the layperson. Compare your find with the checklist below.

Meteorite checklist

1. *The find is quite different from any other stones within its vicinity.*
2. *The piece is dark or black. Its surface is relatively smooth, almost as though melted.*
3. *The piece is discernibly heavier than most other stones.*
4. *The piece has no bubble cavities.*
5. *The piece is magnetic, i.e. it is attracted to a magnet.*

If a majority of the statements apply to your find, there is a possibility, although still quite small, that it is a meteorite. If so, then you should present the piece to an expert in a museum or mineralogical institute for identification.

If a meteorite is recognized as such by the International Meteoritical Society, it is given a name. This is usually the name of the geographic entity nearest to the point of discovery. For example, the meteorite that landed in Bavaria in 2002 was given the name Neuschwanstein because it was found very close to the Bavarian Neuschwanstein Castle.

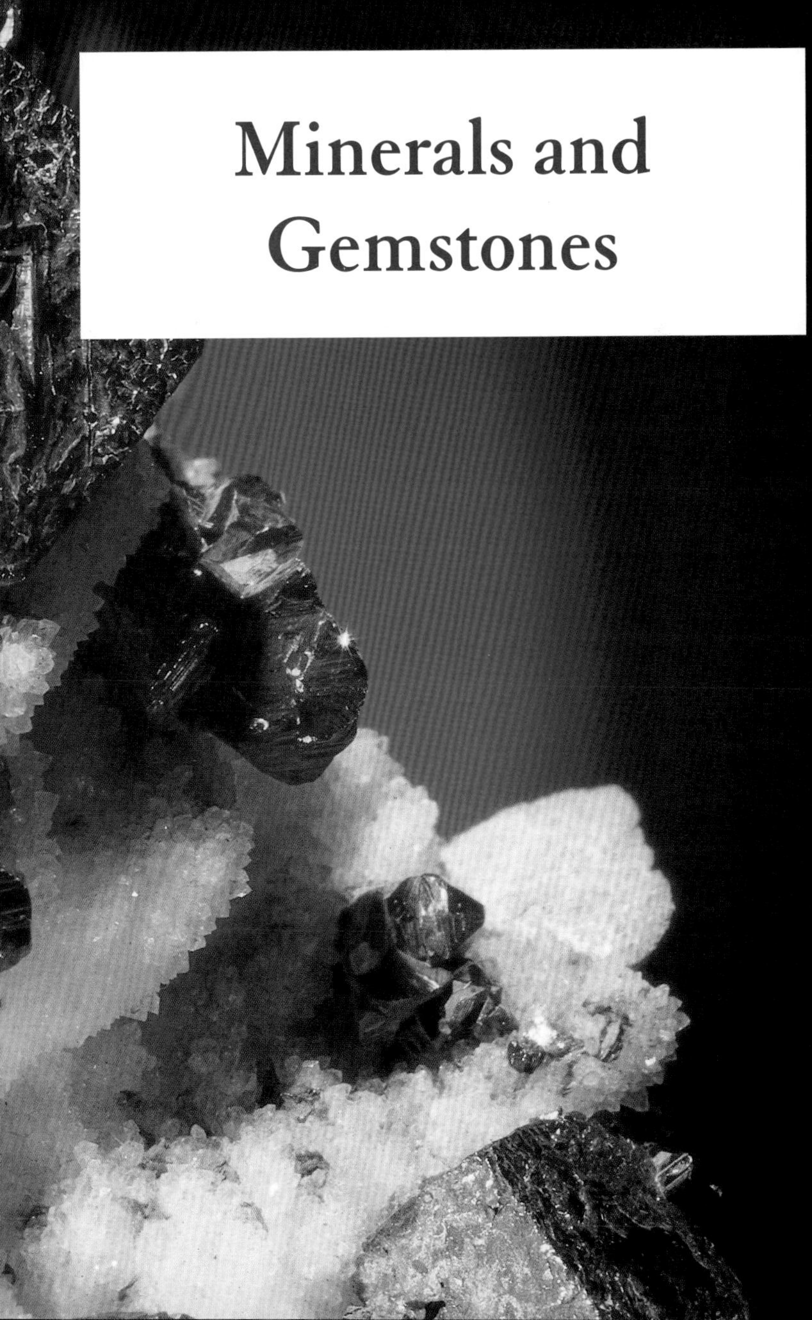
Minerals and
Gemstones

1 Chalcoalumite

Chem. formula $CuAl_4(SO_4)(OH)_{12} \cdot 3\,H_2O$
Hardness 2½, **Sp. gr.** 2.29
Color Light blue
Streak Blue-white
Luster Vitreous to dull
Cleavage Perfect
Fracture Foliated
Tenacity Brittle to non-brittle
Crystal form Monoclinic

Morphology Botryoidal aggregates, foliated crystal aggregates, drusy, uneven.
Origin and occurrence In the oxidation zone of sulfidic copper deposits, especially where aluminum-rich country rocks occur.
Accessory minerals Chalcopyrite, bornite, chalcocite, malachite, cuprite, brochantite, azurite.
Similar minerals Azurite is darker blue; gibbsite is harder; unlike chalcoalumite, chalcanthite is water soluble.

2 Chalcanthite *copper vitriol*

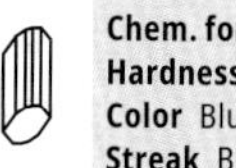

Chem. formula $CuSO_4 \cdot 5\,H_2O$
Hardness 2½, **Sp. gr.** 2.2–2.3
Color Blue
Streak Blue
Luster Vitreous
Cleavage Scarcely discernible
Fracture Conchoidal
Tenacity Brittle
Crystal form Triclinic

Morphology Rarely prismatic to lenticular crystals, stalactitic aggregates, drusy, uneven.
Origin and occurrence In the oxidation zone of sulfidic copper deposits, often formed from the intrinsically very low copper contents of pyrite deposits, formation is dependent on precipitation.
Accessory minerals Chalcopyrite, malachite, brochantite.
Distinguishing feature Chalcanthite is water soluble.
Similar minerals Azurite is a darker blue and, unlike chalcanthite, not water soluble.

3 Liroconite *Lenticular ore*

Chem. formula $Cu_2Al(AsO_4)(OH)_4 \cdot 4\,H_2O$
Hardness 2–2½, **Sp. gr.** 2.95
Color Blue to blue-green
Streak Blue to blue-green
Luster Vitreous
Cleavage Poor
Fracture Conchoidal
Tenacity Brittle
Crystal form Monoclinic

Morphology Crystals tabular, prismatic, lenticular, drusy, earthy, uneven coatings.
Origin and occurrence In the oxidation zone of copper deposits whose ores have some arsenic content, for example, from primary ores such as fahlore or arsenopyrite.
Accessory minerals Clinoclase, azurite, malachite.
Similar minerals Azurite and malachite have a different color and effervesce with hydrochloric acid; clinoclase has a characteristic lenticular crystal shape and is a much darker blue.

4 Linarite

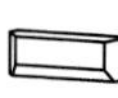

Chem. formula $PbCu[(OH)_2/SO_4]$
Hardness 2½, **Sp. gr.** 5.3–5.5
Color Blue
Streak Light blue
Luster Vitreous
Cleavage Good, distinct, however, only discernible in the larger crystals
Fracture Conchoidal
Tenacity Brittle
Crystal form Monoclinic

Morphology Prismatic to rarely tabular, often wide-area, drusy, earthy.
Origin and occurrence In the oxidation zone.
Accessory minerals Galena, chalcopyrite, brochantite, malachite, cerussite.
Distinguishing feature When dabbed with HCl, it turns light blue to white.
Similar minerals Azurite effervesces when dabbed with HCl and does not become lighter; caledonite is a lighter blue and exhibits a different crystal form.

Localities

1 Grandview Mine, Arizona, USA	**3** Wheal Gorland, Cornwall, Great Britain
2 Arkansas, USA	**4** Leadhills, Scotland, Great Britain

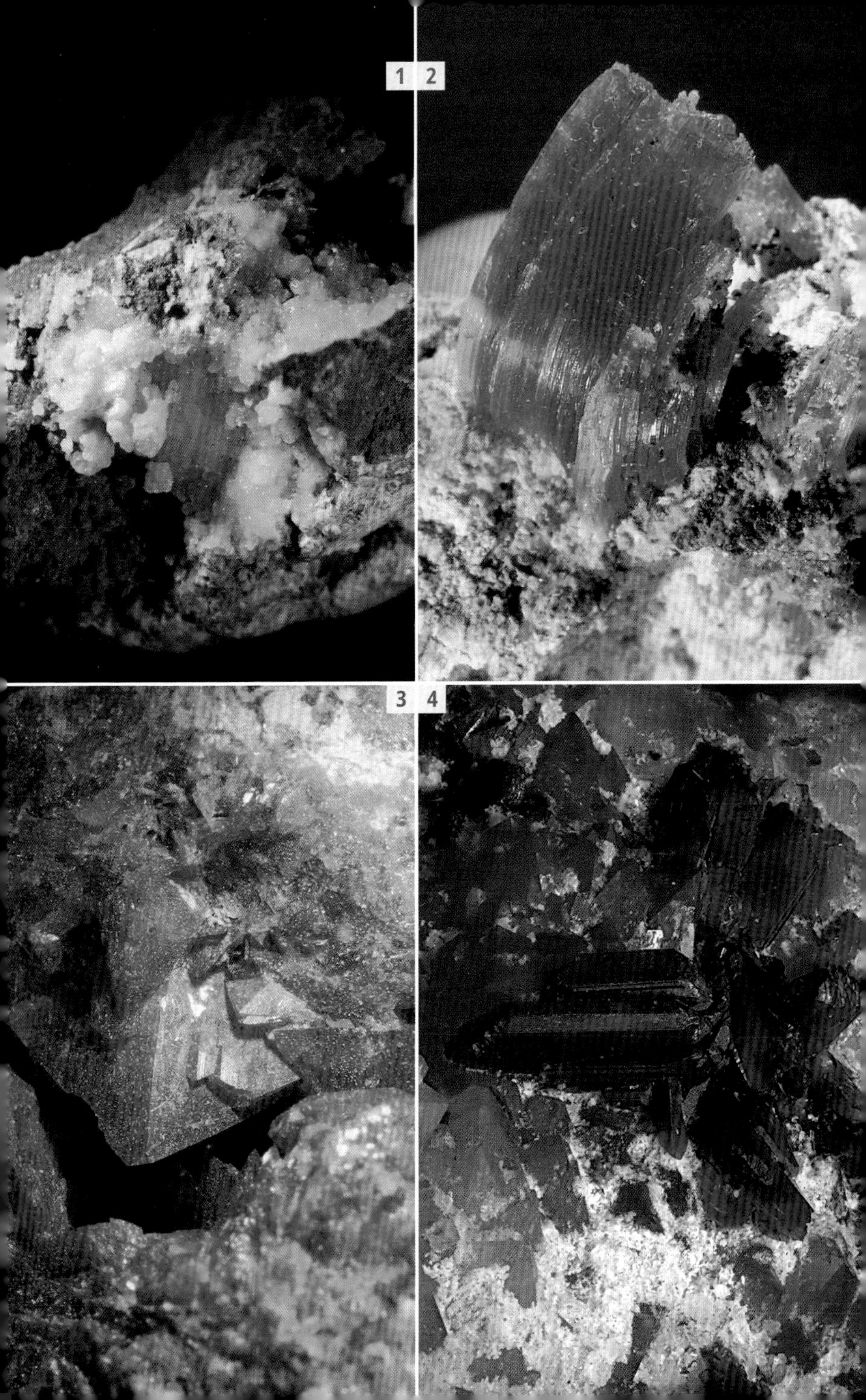
1
2
3
4

1 Caledonite

Chem. formula $Cu_2Pb_5(SO_4)_3CO_3(OH)_6$
Hardness 2½–3, **Sp. gr.** 5.6
Color Blue, blue-green
Streak Whitish-blue
Luster Vitreous
Cleavage Perfect
Fracture Uneven
Tenacity Brittle
Crystal form Orthorhombic

Morphology Prismatic, acicular, fibrous, crystals mainly euhedral, drusy.
Origin and occurrence In the oxidation zone of lead deposits, when copper ores are present in addition to lead ores.
Accessory minerals Leadhillite, anglesite.
Similar minerals Linarite has a different crystal form and turns white when dabbed with hydrochloric acid; azurite has a clearly different blue, a different crystal form, and effervesces when dabbed with hydrochloric acid.

2 Cumengeite

Chem. formula $Pb_{21}Cu_{20}Cl_{42}(OH)_{40} \cdot 6H_2O$
Hardness 2½, **Sp. gr.** 4.67
Color Blue
Streak Blue
Luster Vitreous
Cleavage Good
Fracture Foliated to conchoidal
Tenacity Brittle to non-brittle
Crystal form Tetragonal

Morphology Octahedral crystals, euhedral and anhedral single crystals, botryoidal crystal aggregates, encrustations.
Origin and occurrence In the oxidation zone of copper deposits and in ancient slags.
Accessory minerals Laurionite, cumengeite, anglesite, phosgenite.
Similar minerals Diaboleite and boleite have a different crystal form; linarite turns white when dabbed with hydrochloric acid; azurite has a different crystal form and effervesces when dabbed with hydrochloric acid.

3 Boleite

Chem. formula $Pb_9Cu_8Ag_3Cl_{21}(OH)_{16} \cdot H_2O$
Hardness 3–3½, **Sp. gr.** 5.10
Color Blue
Streak Blue
Luster Vitreous
Cleavage Perfect
Fracture Conchoidal
Tenacity Brittle
Crystal form Tetragonal

Morphology Octahedral and cubic, euhedral and anhedral single crystals, encrustations.
Origin and occurrence In the oxidation zone of copper deposits and ancient slags.
Accessory minerals Laurionite, cumengeite, anglesite, phosgenite.
Similar minerals Diaboleite and cumengeite have a different crystal form; linarite turns white when dabbed with hydrochloric acid; azurite has a different crystal form and effervesces when dabbed with hydrochloric acid.

4 Diaboleite

Chem. formula $Pb_2CuCl_2(OH)_4$
Hardness 2½, **Sp. gr.** 5.42
Color Blue
Streak Blue
Luster Vitreous
Cleavage Perfect
Fracture Foliated to conchoidal
Tenacity Brittle
Crystal form Tetragonal

Morphology Tabular to prismatic, mainly euhedral single crystals, encrustations.
Origin and occurrence In the oxidation zone of copper deposits and ancient slags.
Accessory minerals Laurionite, cumengeite, anglesite, phosgenite.
Similar minerals Boleite and cumengeite have a different crystal form; linarite turns white when dabbed with hydrochloric acid; azurite has a different crystal form and effervesces when dabbed with hydrochloric acid.

Localities	
1 Leadhills, Scotland, Great Britain	**3** Boleo, Baja California, Mexico
2 Boleo, Baja California, Mexico	**4** Lavrion, Greece

1
2
3
4

1 Likasite

Chem. formula $Cu_3[(OH)_5NO_3] \cdot 2\,H_2O$
Hardness 2–3, **Sp. gr.** 2.96–2.98
Color Blue
Streak Light blue
Luster Vitreous
Cleavage Perfect
Fracture Foliated to conchoidal
Tenacity Brittle
Crystal form Orthorhombic

Morphology Tabular crystals, foliated aggregates, encrustations.
Origin and occurrence In the oxidation zone of copper deposits.
Accessory minerals Cuprite, malachite, brochantite, buttgenbachite.
Similar minerals Boleite and cumengeite have a different crystal form; linarite turns white when dabbed with hydrochloric acid; azurite has a different crystal form and effervesces when dabbed with hydrochloric acid; buttgenbachite is always acicular.

2 Connellite

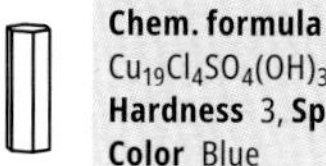

Chem. formula $Cu_{19}Cl_4SO_4(OH)_{32} \cdot H_2O$
Hardness 3, **Sp. gr.** 3.41
Color Blue
Streak Blue
Luster Vitreous
Cleavage Indiscernible
Fracture Conchoidal
Tenacity Brittle
Crystal form Hexagonal

Morphology Acicular crystals, often intergrown into sheaves, stellate aggregates.
Origin and occurrence In the oxidation zone of copper deposits.
Accessory minerals Azurite, malachite, olivite, liroconite.
Similar minerals Cyanotrichite is sometimes indistinguishable from connellite using simple means, but is usually a slightly lighter blue; azurite is a darker blue; agardite is somewhat greenish and does not have a blue streak; without chemical analysis, buttgenbachite is indistinguishable from it but is much rarer.

3 Langite

Chem. formula $Cu_4(SO_4)(OH)_6 \cdot 2\,H_2O$
Hardness 3–4, **Sp. gr.** 3.48–3.5
Color Blue with a slight tinge of green
Streak Blueish
Luster Vitreous
Cleavage Poor
Fracture Conchoidal
Tenacity Brittle
Crystal form Orthorhombic

Morphology Prismatic to tabular, skeletal crystal forming, euhedral crystals, encrustations.
Origin and occurrence In the oxidation zone of copper deposits, usually as a very young formation, often first formed on spoil heaps or excavation walls.
Accessory minerals Brochantite, malachite, azurite, tirolite, parnauite, antlerite.
Similar minerals Azurite effervesces when dabbed with hydrochloric acid and is a darker blue; linarite is a darker blue and turns white when dabbed with hydrochloric acid.

4 Buttgenbachite

Chem. formula $Cu_{19}Cl_4(NO_3)_2(OH)_{32} \cdot 2\,H_2O$
Hardness 3, **Sp. gr.** 3.41
Color Blue
Streak Blue
Luster Vitreous
Cleavage Indiscernible
Fracture Conchoidal
Tenacity Brittle
Crystal form Hexagonal

Morphology Acicular crystals, often intergrown into sheaves, stellate aggregates.
Origin and occurrence In the oxidation zone of copper deposits.
Accessory minerals Azurite, malachite, olivite, liroconite.
Similar minerals Cyanotrichite is sometimes indistinguishable from buttgenbachite using simple means, but it is usually a slightly lighter blue; azurite is a darker blue; agardite is somewhat greenish and does not have a blue streak; connellite is indistinguishable from it without chemical analysis.

Localities	
1 Kazakhstan	**3** Richelsdorf, Hesse, Germany
2 St. Just, Cornwall, Great Britain	**4** Almeria, Spain

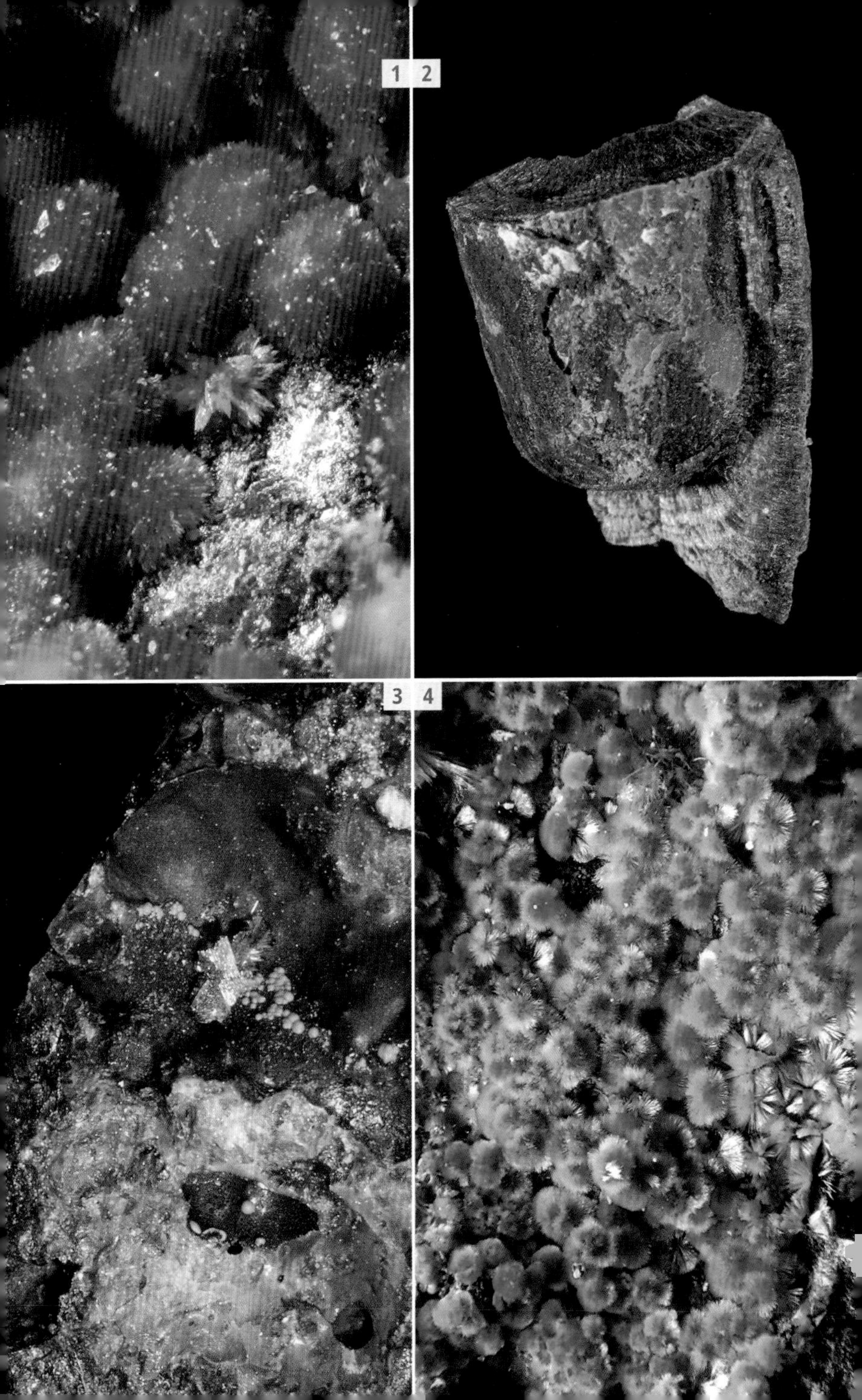
1
2
3
4

1 Azurite *Chessylite*

Chem. formula $Cu_3[OH/CO_3]_2$
Hardness 3½–4, **Sp. gr.** 3.7–3.9
Color Deep blue, uneven is somewhat lighter
Streak Blue
Luster Vitreous
Cleavage Perfect
Fracture Conchoidal
Tenacity Brittle
Crystal form Monoclinic

Morphology Columnar to tabular crystals, botryoidal groups and encrustations, stellate aggregates, uneven, earthy.
Origin and occurrence In the oxidation zone of copper deposits, especially those containing fahlore or other arsenical copper ores as the primary ore.
Accessory minerals Malachite, cuprite and many other copper oxidation minerals.
Similar minerals Clear differentiations from other minerals because of its dark blue color, effervescence when dabbed with hydrochloric acid and occurrence as erosion formation of copper ores.

2 Keyite

Chem. formula $Cu_3(Zn,Cu)_4Cd_4(AsO_4)_6 \cdot 2\,H_2O$
Hardness 4, **Sp. gr.** 5.10
Color Intense sky blue
Streak Pale blue
Luster Vitreous
Cleavage Good
Fracture Uneven
Tenacity Brittle
Crystal form Monoclinic

Morphology Prismatic to long tabular or acicular crystals, crystal sheaves, stellate or parallel-acicular aggregates.
Origin and occurrence In the oxidation zone of copper deposits.
Accessory minerals Malachite, cuproadamine, zeunerite, olivite.
Similar minerals Azurite and clinoclase have a different color; azurite foams when dabbed with hydrochloric acid; linarite is formed in a different paragenesis and turns white when dabbed with hydrochloric acid.

3 Cornetite

Chem. formula $Cu_3PO_4(OH)_3$
Hardness 4½, **Sp. gr.** 4.1
Color Greenish blue to dark blue
Streak Blue
Luster Vitreous
Cleavage None
Fracture Uneven
Tenacity Brittle
Crystal form Orthorhombic

Morphology Short prismatic, often rounded; encrustations, stellate, sun-shaped aggregates on parent rock.
Origin and occurrence In the oxidation zone of copper deposits.
Accessory minerals Malachite, pseudomalachite, brochantite.
Similar minerals Azurite and clinoclase have a different color; azurite foams when dabbed with hydrochloric acid; linarite is formed in a different paragenesis and turns white when dabbed with hydrochloric acid.

4 Cyanotrichite *Lettsomite, velvet copper ore*

Chem. formula $Cu_4Al_2[(OH)_{12}/SO_4] \cdot 2\,H_2O$
Hardness 3½–4, **Sp. gr.** 3.7–3.9
Color Sky blue
Streak Blue
Luster Silky to vitreous
Cleavage None
Fracture Uneven
Tenacity Brittle
Crystal form Orthorhombic

Morphology Acicular to long tabular, filiform, sheaf-like, stellate, often forms velvety coatings (=velvet copper ore) on the parent rock.
Origin and occurrence In the oxidation zone of copper deposits.
Accessory minerals Brochantite, smithsonite, malachite, azurite, cuproadamine, olivite.
Similar minerals Azurite is much darker; connellite is indistinguishable using simple means; agardite is slightly greenish and has no blue streak.

Localities	
1 Tsumeb, Namibia	**3** Mine de l'Etoile, Zaire
2 Tsumeb, Namibia	**4** Lavrion, Greece

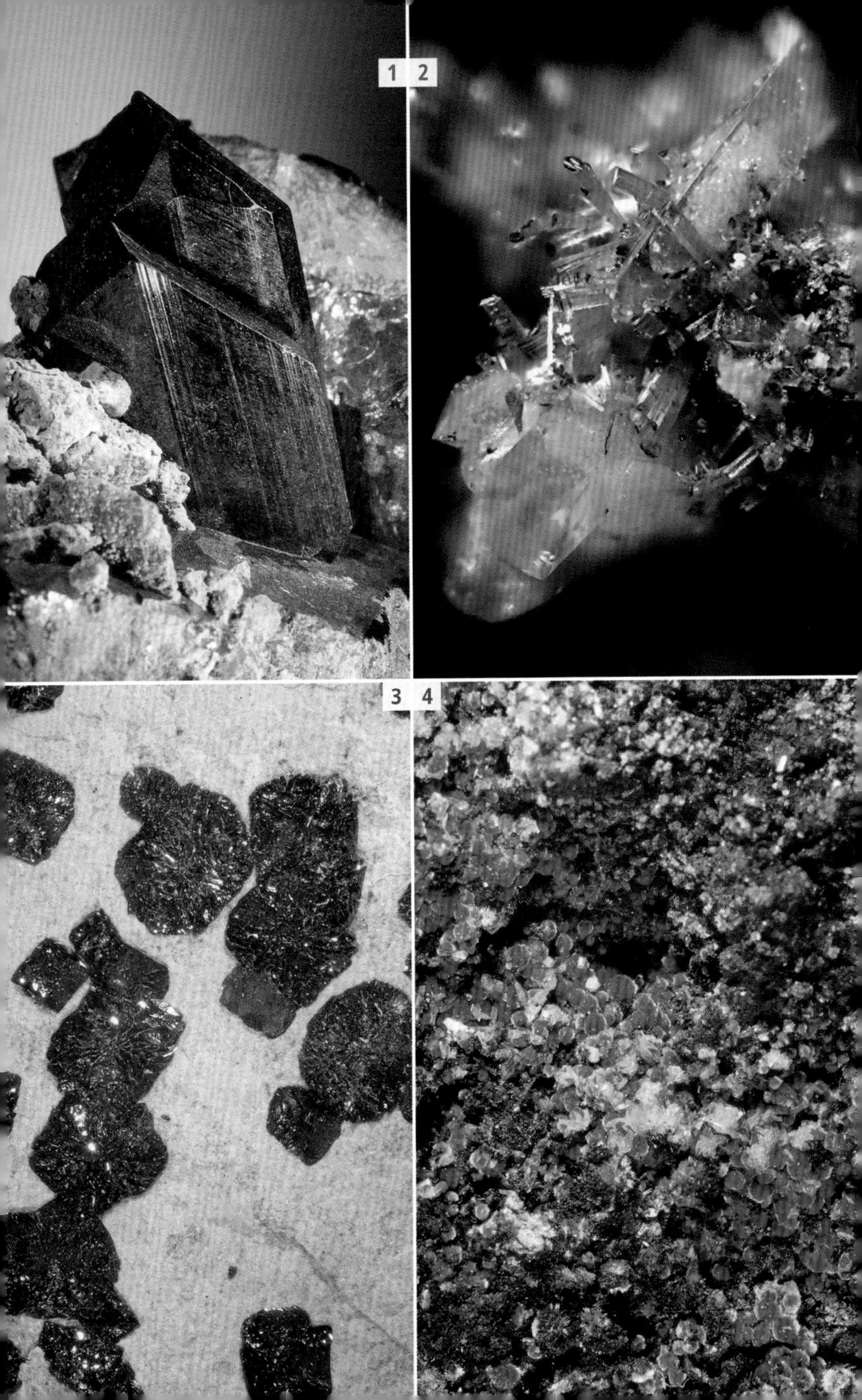
1
2
3
4

1 Lasurite *Lapis lazuli*

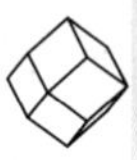

Chem. formula $Na_8[S/(AlSiO_4)_6]$
Hardness 5–6, **Sp. gr.** 2.38–2.42
Color Blue
Streak Blue
Luster Vitreous, on the fracture greasy
Cleavage Scarcely discernible
Fracture Conchoidal
Tenacity Brittle
Crystal form Cubic

Morphology Rarely anhedral rhombic dodecahedra, mainly uneven masses, granular, dense.
Origin and occurrence In sodium-rich marbles. Lasurite only occurs in a few deposits on Earth but is usually found in large quantities in such deposits.
Accessory minerals Diopside, pyrite, calcite.
Similar minerals Azurite effervesces when dabbed with diluted hydrochloric acid. Occurrence together with pyrite is extremely typical for lapis lazuli.

2 Lapis Lazuli

Gemstone

Color Blue, often with white (calcite) and gold (pyrite) inclusions, opaque
Luster Vitreous
Shape and Cut Cabochon cut, spheres

Usage Cabochons as ring stones and for brooches, pendants, spheres for stone necklaces, also often as handicraft items.
Treatment Non-beautiful blue lapis lazuli is frequently colored by placing it in dye solutions. However, this can be easily identified by rubbing with alcohol or acetone; dyed stones color the cotton pad blue.
Differentiation The essentially always present inclusions of pyrite and calcite are highly characteristic. They are always absent in other dyed stones.

3 Glaucophane

Chem. formula $Na_2Mg_3Al_2[(OH)_2|Si_8O_{22}]$
Hardness 6, **Sp. gr.** 3–3.1
Color Dark blue to gray-blue
Streak Gray-blue
Luster Vitreous
Cleavage Perfect
Fracture Conchoidal
Tenacity Brittle
Crystal form Monoclinic

Morphology Prismatic, tabular, fibrous, acicular, often radial masses, granular, dense.
Origin and occurrence In sodium-rich crystalline schists, typical of rocks occurring where rock material has been rapidly transported to great depths.
Accessory minerals Chlorite, muscovite, rutile, epidote, pumpellyite.
Similar minerals Azurite effervesces when dabbed with diluted hydrochloric acid and does not have perfect cleavage; pumpellyite and epidote are green.

4 Crossite

Chem. formula $Na_2(Mg,Fe)_3(Fe,Al)_2[(OH)_2|Si_8O_{22}]$
Hardness 6, **Sp. gr.** 3–3.1
Color Blue-gray
Streak Gray-blue
Luster Vitreous
Cleavage Perfect
Fracture Conchoidal
Tenacity Brittle
Crystal form Monoclinic

Morphology Prismatic, tabular, fibrous, acicular, often radial masses, granular, dense.
Origin and occurrence In sodium-rich crystalline schists, typical of blueschist facies, rocks that were rapidly transported to great depths.
Accessory minerals Chlorite, muscovite, rutile, epidote, pumpellyite.
Similar minerals Azurite effervesces when dabbed with diluted hydrochloric acid and does not have perfect cleavage; pumpellyite and epidote are green; glaucophane is indistinguishable using simple means.

Localities

1 Sar-e-Sang, Badakshan, Afghanistan	**3** Minas Gerais, Brazil
2 Sar-e-Sang, Badakshan, Afghanistan	**4** Brittany, France

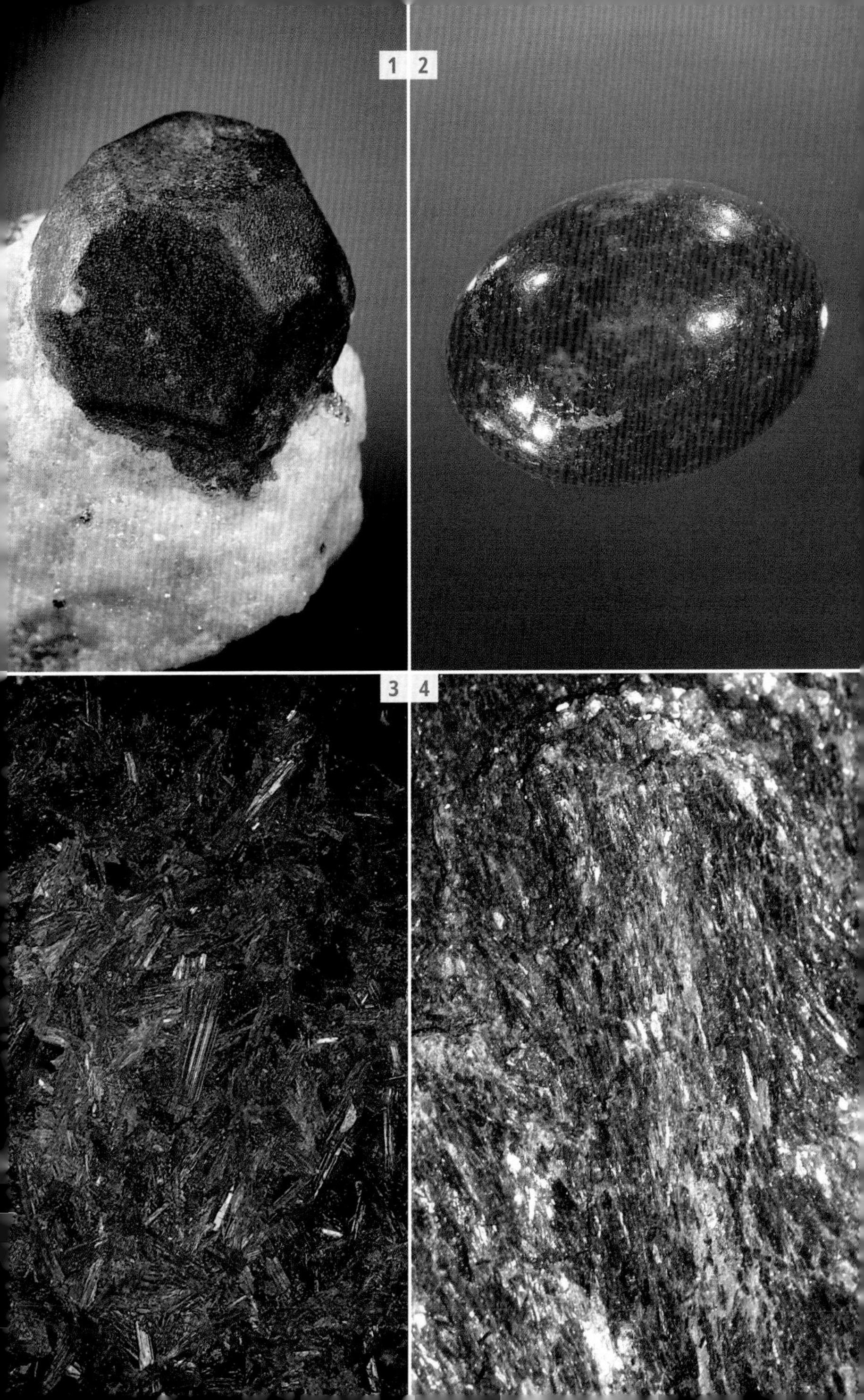
1
2
3
4

1 Kermesite *Red antimony*

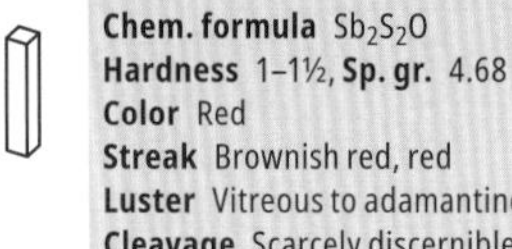

Chem. formula Sb_2S_2O
Hardness 1–1½, **Sp. gr.** 4.68
Color Red
Streak Brownish red, red
Luster Vitreous to adamantine
Cleavage Scarcely discernible
Fracture Fibrous
Tenacity Non-brittle
Crystal form Monoclinic

Morphology Rarely prismatic, almost always acicular crystals, filiform, stellate aggregates, as an uneven rough coating.
Origin and occurrence In the oxidation zone of antimony deposits.
Accessory minerals Stibnite, quartz, valentinite.
Similar minerals Considering the paragenesis with stibnite, kermesite is distinctive because of its red color; realgar has a yellow streak and usually does not occur quite as acicular; piedmontite is much harder; hematite is never as acicular.

2 Hutchinsonite

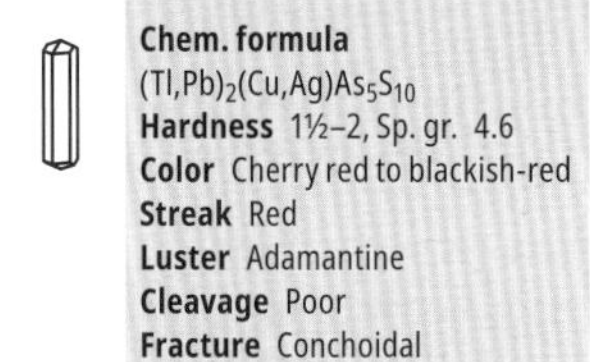

Chem. formula $(Tl,Pb)_2(Cu,Ag)As_5S_{10}$
Hardness 1½–2, Sp. gr. 4.6
Color Cherry red to blackish-red
Streak Red
Luster Adamantine
Cleavage Poor
Fracture Conchoidal
Tenacity Brittle
Crystal form Orthorhombic

Morphology Prismatic to acicular, fibrous, stellate, coatings.
Origin and occurrence In hydrothermal copper-silver deposits with high arsenic contents.
Accessory minerals Orpiment, enargite, pyrite, sartorite, realgar, quartz, dolomite.
Similar minerals Enargite and realgar do not have a red streak; miargyrite, proustite and pyrargyrite are harder.

3 Erythrite *Red cobalt*

Chem. formula $Co_3(AsO_4)_2 \cdot 8\,H_2O$
Hardness 2, **Sp. gr.** 3.07
Color Red, pink-purple, pink
Streak Red
Luster Vitreous, on cleavage faces pearly luster, in encrustations also earthy, dull
Cleavage Perfect
Fracture Uneven
Tenacity Non-brittle, thin flexible flakes
Crystal form Monoclinic

Morphology Acicular to tabular crystals, radial aggregates, often earthy, drusy, uneven.
Origin and occurrence In the oxidation zone of cobalt-bearing deposits.
Accessory minerals Safflorite, cobaltite, skutterudite, native bismuth.
Distinguishing feature The pink coatings of erythrite are always a clear indication of cobalt-bearing ores.
Similar minerals The characteristic pink-purple to pink color of erythrite prevents any confusion; roselite and wendwilsonite have a completely different crystal form.

4 Miargyrite

Chem. formula $AgSbS_2$
Hardness 2½, **Sp. gr.** 5.25
Color Gray to black
Streak Red
Luster Metallic
Cleavage Indiscernible
Fracture Conchoidal
Tenacity Brittle
Crystal form Monoclinic

Morphology Thick tabular to blocky crystals, radial aggregates, uneven ore.
Origin and occurrence In hydrothermal silver ore veins, especially in the cementation zone.
Accessory minerals Pyrargyrite, argentite, proustite, quartz, stibnite.
Similar minerals Stephanite and polybasite have a gray to black streak; proustite is deep red; pyrargyrite is at least reddish; hutchinsonite is significantly softer.

Localities

1 Bräunsdorf, Saxony, Germany	**3** Bou Azzer, Morocco
2 Quiruvilca, Peru	**4** Baia Sprie, Rumania

1
2
3
4

1 Cinnabar *Cinnabarite*

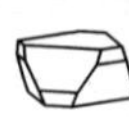

Chem. formula HgS
Hardness 2–2½, **Sp. gr.** 8.1
Color Light red, dark red, brown red
Streak Red
Luster Adamantine, fine-grained often dull
Cleavage Perfect prismatic
Fracture Splintery
Tenacity Non-brittle
Crystal form Trigonal

Morphology Thick tabular to rhombohedral crystals are rather rare; cinnabar is mainly uneven, granular, earthy, radial.
Origin and occurrence In low-temperature, hydrothermal veins, in the oxidation zone, especially as a weathering formation of mercury-bearing fahlore, at outlet points of volcanic gases on the country rock.
Accessory minerals Quartz, chalcedony, pyrite, fluorite.
Similar minerals Red sphalerite is considerably lighter and harder and has rhombohedral cleavage; hematite, cuprite and rutile are harder.

2 Proustite *Ruby silver ore*

Chem. formula Ag_3AsS_3
Hardness 2½, **Sp. gr.** 5.5–5.7
Color Scarlet to vermilion
Streak Scarlet
Luster Adamantine to metallic, sometimes tarnished dull
Cleavage Sometimes distinct rhombohedral
Fracture Conchoidal
Tenacity Brittle
Crystal form Trigonal

Morphology Prismatic to pyramidal crystals are usually euhedral, but proustite often occurs in an uneven form.
Origin and occurrence In subvolcanic gold-silver deposits and in hydrothermal veins.
Accessory minerals Argentite, stephanite, polybasite, native silver, calcite.
Similar minerals Pyrargyrite is darker and has a darker streak; cuprite has a different crystal form (usually octahedral, cubic or rhombic dodecahedral); hutchinsonite is much softer.

3 Pyrargyrite *Dark red silver ore*

Chem. formula Ag_3SbS_3
Hardness 2½–3, **Sp. gr.** 5.85
Color Dark red to gray-black, translucent red
Streak Cherry red
Luster Metallic
Cleavage Sometimes discernible
Fracture Conchoidal
Tenacity Brittle
Crystal form Trigonal

Morphology Rhombohedral and scalenohedral, sometimes prismatic, always euhedral, rarely unevenly anhedral.
Origin and occurrence In silver veins, especially in the rich ore zone together with other silver minerals.
Accessory minerals Proustite, argentite, stephanite, miargyrite, galena, calcite.
Similar minerals Proustite is dark tarnished, has a lighter red color and is distinguished from pyrargyrite by its lighter streak; miargyrite and hutchinsonite are softer.

4 Crocoite *Red lead ore*

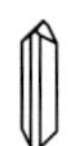

Chem. formula $PbCrO_4$
Hardness 2½–3, **Sp. gr.** 5.9–6
Color Red with occasional yellow tinge
Streak Orange-red
Luster Greasy to adamantine
Cleavage Discernible
Fracture Conchoidal
Tenacity Non-brittle
Crystal form Monoclinic

Morphology Acicular to prismatic, tabular, stellate, uneven, as bloom.
Origin and occurrence In the oxidation zone of lead deposits; at the contact point with chromium-bearing weathering solutions, usually from nearby serpentines.
Accessory minerals Cerussite, pyromorphite, embreyite, dundasite.
Similar minerals Cinnabar and cuprite have a different crystal form; realgar differs due to its typical paragenesis.

Localities	
1 Erzberg Mine, Styria, Austria	**3** St. Andreasberg, Harz, Germany
2 Schlema, Saxony, Germany	**4** Dundas, Tasmania, Australia

1
2
3
4

1–2 Copper, native

Chem. formula Cu
Hardness 2½–3, **Sp. gr.** 8.93
Color Copper red, often tarnished darker
Streak Copper-red, metallic
Luster Metallic
Cleavage None
Fracture Hackly
Tenacity Non-brittle, ductile
Crystal form Cubic

Morphology Cubic, octahedral, usually strongly distorted, also tabular, skeletal, plate-like, wire-like, uneven.
Origin and occurrence In the cementation zone of many copper deposits, there often in large masses and sheets (weighing up to several tons), in bubble cavities of volcanic rocks.
Accessory minerals Malachite, cuprite, copper glance, copper pyrite, epidote, datolite, native silver, calcite.
Similar minerals Silver has a different color and streak; the same is true for gold. Copper coated with malachite always displays its copper-red color when scratched. Nickeline has a different streak.

3 Wendwilsonite

Chem. formula $Ca_2(Mg,Co)(AsO_4)_2 \cdot 2\,H_2O$
Hardness 3½, **Sp. gr.** 3.5–3.74
Color Dark pink
Streak Reddish
Luster Vitreous
Cleavage Perfect, fracture uneven
Tenacity Brittle
Crystal form Monoclinic

Morphology Thick tabular crystals, uneven encrustations.
Origin and occurrence In the oxidation zone of cobalt deposits, especially in dolomitic gangue.
Accessory minerals Erythrite, roselite.
Similar minerals The crystal form of wendwilsonite is very characteristic, thus making confusion extremely unlikely; roselite, however, can only be distinguished by chemical analysis.

4 Roselite

Chem. formula $Ca_2(Co, Mg)(AsO_4)_2 \cdot 2\,H_2O$
Hardness 3½, **Sp. gr.** 3.5–3.74
Color Dark pink
Streak Reddish
Luster Vitreous
Cleavage Perfect, fracture uneven
Tenacity Brittle
Crystal form Monoclinic

Morphology Thick tabular crystals, uneven encrustations.
Origin and occurrence In the oxidation zone of cobalt deposits, especially in the cavities of ores and gangues.
Accessory minerals Erythrite, wendwilsonite, chloanthite.
Similar minerals The crystal form and color of roselite is very characteristic, thus making confusion extremely unlikely; wendelwilsonite, however, can only be distinguished by chemical analysis.

5–6 Cuprite *Red copper ore, chalcotrichite*

Chem. formula Cu_2O
Hardness 3½ –4, **Sp. gr.** 6.15
Color Deep red to brown-red
Streak Metallic brownish-red
Luster Metallic, adamantine, also dull in aggregates
Cleavage Octahedral distinct
Fracture Conchoidal
Tenacity Brittle
Crystal form Cubic

Morphology Octahedral, more rarely cubic, filiform (Chalcotrichite Fig. 5), granular, uneven.
Origin and occurrence In the oxidation zone of cobalt deposits, particularly at the border of the cementation zone.
Accessory minerals Native copper, malachite, limonite, calcite, chalcocite, chalcopyrite.
Similar minerals Hematite is harder; cinnabar has a different crystal form; a paragenesis with malachite is characteristic of cuprite.

Localities		
1 Keeweenaw, Michigan, USA	**3** Bou Azzer, Morocco	**5** Wolf Mine, Siegerland Region, Germany
2 Kausersteimel Mine, Siegerland Region, Germany	**4** Bou Azzer, Morocco	**6** Tsumeb, Namibia

1
2
3
4
5
6

1 Auricupride

Chem. formula Cu_3Au
Hardness 3–3½, **Sp. gr.** 11.5
Color Bronze yellow to copper red
Streak Metallic copper red
Luster Metallic
Cleavage None
Fracture Hackly
Tenacity Non-brittle, ductile
Crystal form Cubic

Morphology Anhedral grains, encrustations around other gold alloys.
Origin and occurrence Anhedral in serpentinites, formed by segregation of other gold-copper alloys.
Accessory minerals Gold, copper and other gold-copper alloys.
Similar minerals Silver has a different color and streak; the same is true for gold. Copper almost always occurs in other paragenesis, but it is otherwise difficult to distinguish by simple means.

2 Heterosite

Chem. formula $(Fe,Mn)PO_4$
Hardness 4–4½, **Sp. gr.** 3.4
Color Brown with purple shimmer, purple
Streak Pale purple-red
Luster Vitreous, slightly silky on cleavage faces.
Cleavage Good
Fracture Uneven
Tenacity Brittle
Crystal form Orthorhombic

Morphology Anhedral masses, cleavage pieces, uneven inclusions.
Origin and occurrence In phosphate pegmatites.
Accessory minerals Triphyline, feldspar, quartz, lithiophilite, ferrisicklerite, rockbridgeite.
Similar minerals The purple color is extraordinarily characteristic considering its occurrence in phosphate pegmatites. The purple color intensifies significantly when dabbed with hydrochloric acid. Many deep purple heterosites in the collections (often mistakenly called purpurite) have been "color-enhanced" using hydrochloric acid baths.

3 Lepidocrocite *Ruby mica*

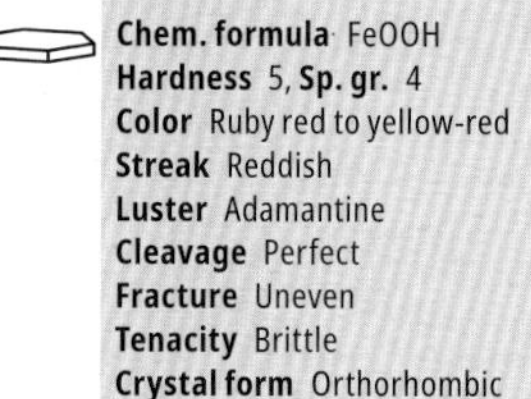

Chem. formula FeOOH
Hardness 5, **Sp. gr.** 4
Color Ruby red to yellow-red
Streak Reddish
Luster Adamantine
Cleavage Perfect
Fracture Uneven
Tenacity Brittle
Crystal form Orthorhombic

Morphology Tabular crystals euhedral, radial, foliated, uneven.
Origin and occurrence In the oxidation zone of iron deposits, much rarer than goethite.
Accessory minerals Goethite, pyrolusite.
Similar minerals Lepidocrocite differs from goethite in red color and red streak; jarosite, natrojarosite, and beudantite have a different streak; hematite is harder.

4 Piemontite

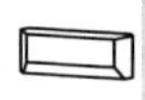

Chem. formula $Ca_2(Mn,Al)(Al_2[O/OH/SiO_4/Si_2O_7]$
Hardness 6½, **Sp. gr.** 3.4
Color Light to dark red
Streak Blackish red
Luster Vitreous
Cleavage Poorly discernible
Fracture Conchoidal
Tenacity Brittle
Crystal form Monoclinic

Morphology Prismatic to acicular crystals, fibrous, radial aggregates, anhedral and euhedral.
Origin and occurrence In metamorphic manganese deposits and vugs of pegmatites, on fractures of metamorphic rocks.
Accessory minerals Braunite, rhodonite, rhodochrosite, sursassite.
Similar minerals Very difficult to confuse with other manganese minerals when color, morphology and paragenesis are taken into consideration.

Localities	
1 Ural, Russia	**3** Ameise Mine, Siegerland Region, Germany
2 Sandamab, Namibia	**4** St. Marcel, Piemont, Italy

1
2
3
4

1–3 Hematite *Red hematite, micaceous iron oxide, red iron ore, bloodstone*

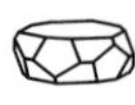

Chem. formula Fe_2O_3
Hardness 6½, **Sp. gr.** 5.2–5.3
Color Uneven aggregates (red iron ore) and thin red flakes, otherwise metallic black-gray, often exhibits variegated tarnishing
Streak Reddish-brown, but black with low titanium content
Luster Metallic to dull
Cleavage None, but often foliated
Fracture Conchoidal
Tenacity Brittle
Crystal form Trigonal

Red iron ore from Cumberland

Round cabochon from hematite (bloodstone)

Morphology Dipyramidal, reminiscent of octahedral, thick to thin tabular, rose-shaped (=iron roses, Fig. 1), often uneven, foliated, stellate, with smooth surface (red iron ore), earthy, drusy.

Origin and occurrence Microscopically in almost all rocks; there also larger deposits, especially metamorphic rocks; in pneumatolytic and hydrothermal veins, at exit points of volcanic gases (fumarole fissures), as a coloring component of many sedimentary rocks, in contact metasomatic deposits. Argillaceous rocks characterized by high level of finely divided hematite are called red chalk. Iron roses are beautiful crystals, specifically rose-shaped aggregates as well, that are found, in particular, on alpine fissures of the Austrian and Swiss Alps. Excellent well-shaped hematite crystals come from iron deposits on the Italian island of Elba and in Brazil.

Accessory minerals Magnetite, pyrite.

Distinguishing feature Rose-shaped aggregates are called iron roses; finely foliated silvery hematite is also called iron mica, or micaceous iron oxide.

Similar minerals Magnetite and ilmenite have a black streak although the latter is almost indistinguishable from titaniferous hematite. Brown iron ore (goethite) has a brown streak. Lepidocrocite, cuprite, miargyrite, cinnabar and realgar are softer. Hematite in the form of iron mica differs from mica and mica schists due to its more metallic luster and its red streak. Finely foliated hematite can even write with a reddish color on paper. This differentiates it from graphite and molybdenite, which write in black; both are also much softer and not as brittle.

4 Hematite *Gemstone*

Color Black, shiny metallic
Luster Metallic
Shape and Cut Cabochon cut, spheres

Use As a ring stone, in necklaces, brooches.

Distinguishing feature Especially beautiful hematite in the form of red iron ore comes from Cumberland. This material is also cut into gemstones and called bloodstone. The name is derived from the observation that when hematite is cut, its red streak stains the cutting fluid red, as if the stone were bleeding.

Differentiation For jewelry purposes, cheap magnetite is often cut instead of the more expensive hematite. This is clearly magnetic and exhibits a slightly brownish streak in its cut state.

Localities	
1 Fibbia, St. Gotthard, Switzerland	**3** Haardt Mine, Siegerland Region, Germany
2 Cumberland, Great Britain	**4** Siegerland Region, Germany

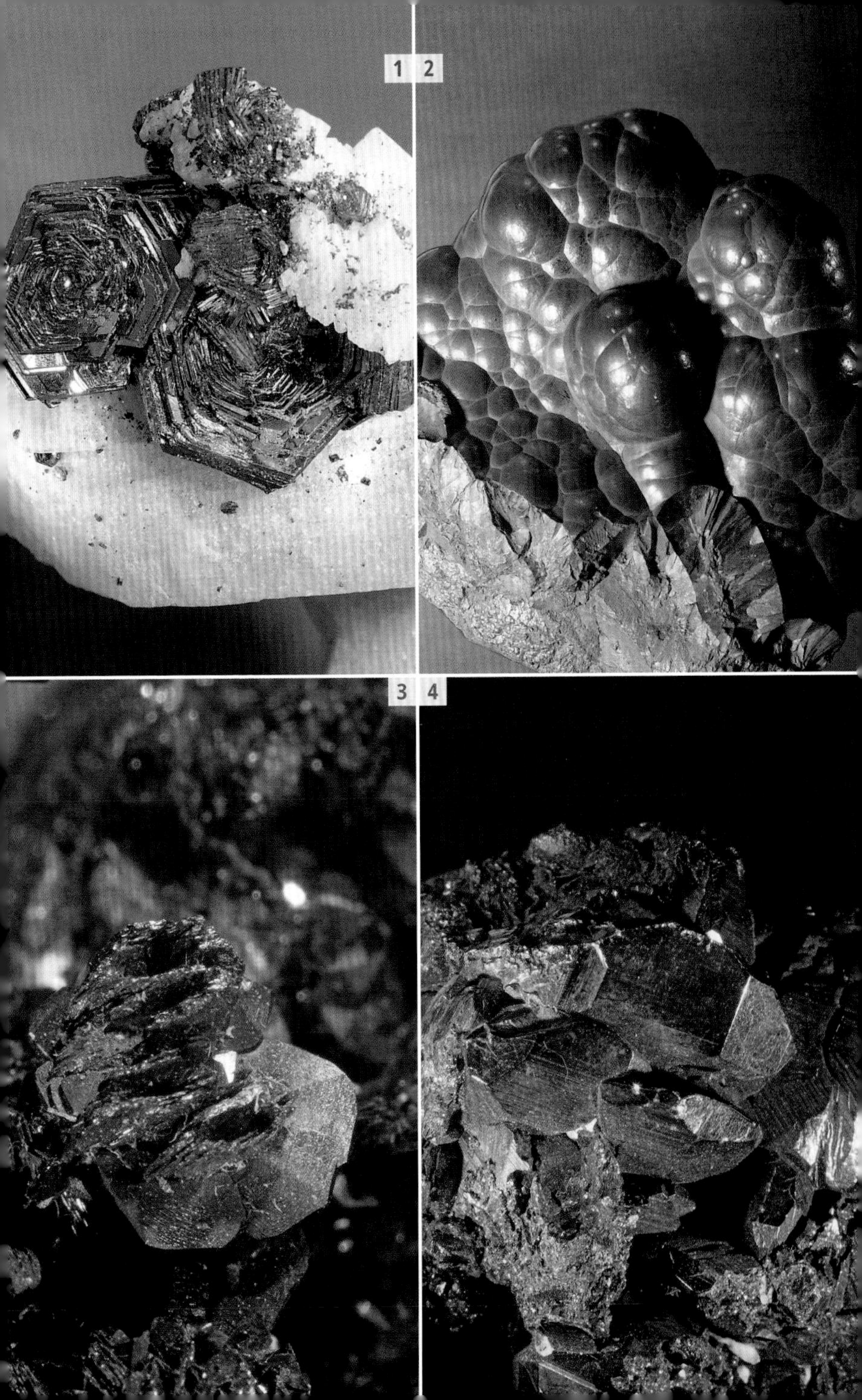
1
2
3
4

1 Realgar *Red arsenic*

Chem. formula AsS
Hardness 1–1½, **Sp. gr.** 3.5–3.6
Color Deep red, translucent to opaque
Streak Orange-yellow
Luster Adamantine to greasy
Cleavage Scarcely discernible
Fracture Conchoidal
Tenacity Thin flexible flakes, non-brittle
Crystal form Monoclinic

Morphology Prismatic, acicular, powdery, uneven.
Origin and occurrence In ore veins of low formation temperature, as precipitation from hot springs and volcanic gases, on clays and limestones, as a weathering product of arsenical ores.
Accessory minerals Orpiment, stibnite, dolomite, wakabayashilite.
Similar minerals Cuprite has a different crystal form and streak; cinnabar is much heavier and, in contrast to realgar, has perfect cleavage.

2 Karibibite

Chem. formula $Fe_2As_4(O,OH)_9$
Hardness 1–1½, **Sp. gr.** 4.07
Color Brown-yellow to orange
Streak Light yellow
Luster Vitreous
Cleavage Scarcely discernible
Fracture Fibrous
Tenacity Flexible needles
Crystal form Orthorhombic

Morphology Prismatic, acicular, sheaf-like, velvety coatings, powdery, uneven.
Origin and occurrence In the oxidation zone of ore veins of the cobalt-nickel-arsenic formation, in pegmatites as an alternation product of loellingite.
Accessory minerals Loellingite, schneiderhöhnite, scorodite, parasymplesite, quartz.
Similar minerals Goethite is much harder and inflexible; its paragenesis with loellingite and color are extraordinarily characteristic.

3 Carnotite

Chem. formula $K_2(UO_2)_2(V_2O_8) \cdot 1\text{-}3\,H_2O$
Hardness 2, **Sp. gr.** 4.7
Color Yellow
Streak Yellow
Luster Silky on crystal surfaces, otherwise dull
Cleavage Perfect
Fracture Uneven
Tenacity Brittle to non-brittle
Crystal form Monoclinic

Morphology Tabular crystals, mainly euhedral, drusy, earthy, powdery.
Origin and occurrence In the oxidation zone of uranium deposits, in uranium-bearing sandstones, in limestones.
Accessory minerals Torbernite, quartz, volborthite, uraninite, davidite.
Similar minerals Torbernite is green and does not fluoresce; it is often difficult to distinguish autunite and novacekite using simple means, but they are usually slightly more yellow.
Caution! Carnotite is radioactive!

4 Wakabayashilite

Chem. formula $(As,Sb)_{11}S_{16}$
Hardness 1½ –2, **Sp. gr.** 3.96
Color Lemon yellow to orange-yellow
Streak Orange-yellow
Luster Greasy
Cleavage Perfect
Fracture Foliated
Tenacity Non-brittle, sectile, thin needles are flexible
Crystal form Monoclinic

Morphology Crystals prismatic, acicular, fibrous, radial, uneven.
Origin and occurrence In hydrothermal veins and low-temperature arsenic deposits.
Accessory minerals Realgar, stibnite, orpiment, quartz, pyrite, calcite.
Similar minerals Greenockite has a different crystal form; its paragenesis with sphalerite is characteristic; orpiment is more foliated, and, when it is the same color, never as acicular as wakabayashilite.

Localities	
1 Hunan, China	**3** Radium Hill, Australia
2 Bou Azzer, Morocco	**4** Jas Roux, France

1
2
3
4

1 Orpiment *King's yellow*

Chem. formula As_2S_3
Hardness 1½–2, **Sp. gr.** 3.48
Color Lemon yellow to orange-yellow
Streak Light yellow
Luster Greasy
Cleavage Perfect
Fracture Foliated
Tenacity Non-brittle, sectile, thin orpiment flakes are flexible
Crystal form Monoclinic

Morphology Crystals prismatic, acicular, lenticular, stellate, foliated, radial, uneven.
Origin and occurrence In hydrothermal veins and on fissures and cracks in argillaceous rocks.
Accessory minerals Realgar, arsenic minerals.
Distinguishing feature Orpiment was used for a long time as an — albeit toxic — bright yellow painting pigment and sold under the name King's yellow.
Similar minerals Greenockite has a different crystal form; its paragenesis with sphalerite is characteristic.

2 Amarantite

Chem. formula $Fe_2O(SO_4)_2 \cdot 7\,H_2O$
Hardness 2½, **Sp. gr.** 2.19–2.29
Color Orange-yellow
Streak Yellow
Luster Vitreous
Cleavage Perfect
Fracture Uneven
Tenacity Brittle
Crystal form Monoclinic

Morphology Crystals prismatic, acicular, lenticular, radial, granular, uneven.
Origin and occurrence In the oxidation zone of ore deposits, particularly in desert climates.
Accessory minerals Chalcanthite, copiapite, coquimbite, sideronatrite.
Similar minerals Copiapite is a purer yellow; coquimbite is always slightly purple; goethite is not as vitreous as amarantite, and the brown is darker.

3 Nontronite

Chem. formula $Na_{0,33}Fe_2(Al,Si)_4(OH)_2 \cdot n\,H_2O$
Hardness 1–2, **Sp. gr.** 2–3
Color Yellow to green-yellow
Streak Yellowish
Luster Resinous to dull
Cleavage Perfect
Fracture Conchoidal to earthy
Tenacity Non-brittle
Crystal form Monoclinic

Morphology Uneven, earthy, as coatings.
Origin and occurrence As an alteration product of silicates during deep weathering.
Accessory minerals Opal, quartz.
Distinguishing feature Nontronite densely intergrown with opal is called chloropal.
Similar minerals Considering its paragenesis, nontronite is unmistakable; kaolinite is not yellow-green; carnotite is yellower and radioactive.

4 Saleeite

Chem. formula $Mg[UO_2/AsO_4]_2 \cdot 8\text{-}10\,H_2O$
Hardness 2½, **Sp. gr.** 3.6
Color Yellow with green tinge; Vitreous luster
Streak Yellowish
Luster Pearly on cleavage faces
Cleavage Perfect
Fracture Uneven
Tenacity Brittle to non-brittle
Crystal form Tetragonal

Morphology Tabular crystals, mainly euhedral, drusy.
Origin and occurrence In the oxidation zone of uranium deposits.
Accessory minerals Zeunerite, barite, quartz.
Special property Saleeite fluoresces with a distinct yellow-green color when irradiated with a UV lamp.
Similar minerals Torbernite and zeunerite are green and do not fluoresce; it is often difficult to distinguish autunite and novacekite using simple means, but they are usually slightly yellower.
Caution! Saleeite is radioactive!

Localities	
1 Quiruvilca, Peru	**3** Kropfmühl, Bavarian Forest, Germany
2 Chucquicamata, Chile	**4** Großschloppen, Fichtel Mountains, Germany

1 2
3 4

1 Novacekite

Chem. formula $Mg[UO_2/AsO_4]_2 \cdot 12\ H_2O$
Hardness 2½, **Sp. gr.** 3.5
Color Yellow with green tinge
Streak Yellowish
Luster Vitreous, pearly on cleavage faces
Cleavage Perfect
Fracture Uneven
Tenacity Brittle to non-brittle
Crystal form Tetragonal

Morphology Tabular crystals, euhedral, encrustations.
Origin and occurrence In the oxidation zone of uranium deposits.
Accessory minerals Zeunerite, barite, quartz, scorodite.
Special property Novacekite fluoresces with a distinct yellow-green color when irradiated with a UV lamp.
Similar minerals Torbernite is green and does not fluoresce; it is often difficult to distinguish autunite and uranocircite using simple means, but saleeite is greener.
Caution! Novacekite is radioactive!

2 Beraunite

Chem. formula $Fe_3[(OH)_3/(PO_4)_2] \cdot 2½\ H_2O$
Hardness 3–4, **Sp. gr.** 2.9
Color Yellow, green, brown, red
Streak Yellow
Luster Vitreous
Cleavage Good, but discernible only on larger crystals
Fracture Uneven
Tenacity Brittle
Crystal form Monoclinic

Morphology Crystals tabular, long tabular to acicular, stellate aggregates, encrustations.
Origin and occurrence In phosphate pegmatites as a weathering formation of primary phosphate minerals, in brown iron deposits.
Accessory minerals Cacoxenite, strengite, rockbridgeite, strunzite, laubmannite, kidwellite.
Similar minerals Yellow beraunite is sometimes indistinguishable from strunzite using simple means although the latter is usually more distinctly straw-yellow; laubmannite and kidwellite do not form tabular crystals.

3 Cetineite

Chem. formula $(K\ Na)_{3+x}(Sb_2O_3)_3(SbS_3)(OH)_x \cdot 2{,}4\ H_2O$
Hardness 2½, **Sp. gr.** 4.21
Color Red-orange
Streak Orange-yellow
Luster Greasy
Cleavage Good, but scarcely discernible
Fracture Uneven
Tenacity Non-brittle, sectile
Crystal form Hexagonal

Morphology Crystals prismatic, acicular, stellate, fibrous, radial, uneven.
Origin and occurrence In the oxidation zone of low-temperature antimony ore veins.
Accessory minerals Stibnite, senarmontite, klebelsbergite.
Similar minerals Klebelsbergite is yellower; valentinite is more likely white; stibiconite is yellowish. Cetineite differs from all other similar minerals in its typical paragenesis with antimony minerals.

4 Nealite

Chem. formula $Pb_4Fe[Cl_2|AsO_3]_2 \cdot 2\ H_2O$
Hardness 4, **Sp. gr.** 5.88
Color Yellow to slightly orange
Streak Light yellow
Luster Adamantine to greasy
Cleavage Scarcely discernible
Fracture Conchoidal
Tenacity Brittle
Crystal form Triclinic

Morphology Prismatic, acicular, rarely stellate aggregates.
Origin and occurrence In ancient lead slags resulting from the smelting of arsenical ores that were dumped into the sea.
Accessory minerals Georgiadesite, anglesite, phosgenite, laurionite, paralaurionite.
Similar minerals Typical crystal form, hardly possible to confuse it if the type of occurrence is taken into consideration.

Localities	
1 Wittichen, Black Forest, Germany	**3** Le Cetine, Italy
2 Cornwall, Great Britain	**4** Lavrion, Greece

1
2
3
4

1–2 Gold, native

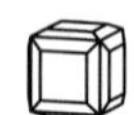

Chem. formula Au
Hardness 2½–3, **Sp. gr.** 15.5–19.3
Color Gold to brass yellow
Streak Metallic gold yellow
Luster Metallic
Cleavage None
Fracture Hackly
Tenacity Non-brittle, very ductile
Crystal form Cubic

Morphology Octahedral, cubic, rarely well formed, usually distorted, skeletal, plate-like, wire-like, often uneven, anhedral, unrolled nuggets.
Origin and occurrence In hydrothermal quartz veins of high to moderate temperature, in placers in rivers and streams.
Accessory minerals Quartz, arsenopyrite, pyrite, tourmaline, fluorite.
Distinguishing feature Gold can be hammered into flakes and drawn into long, thin wires.
Similar minerals Pyrite, chalcopyrite and marcasite have a black streak and are not ductile. They are also significantly harder. Siderite is sometimes tarnished golden yellow, but is distinguished by its cleavage and tenacity. When scratched, tarnished native silver immediately shows its silver-white color. Even low gold content (a few grams per ton) makes a gold deposit worth mining if it can be easily mined using open pit methods. However, this often entails major environmental degradation and is usually impossible in more populated areas with high environmental standards.

3 Walpurgite

Chem. formula $(BiO)_4UO_2(AsO_4)_2 \cdot 3\,H_2O$
Hardness 3½, **Sp. gr.** 5.95
Color Yellow to pale orange
Streak Yellow
Luster Greasy vitreous
Cleavage Perfect
Fracture Foliated
Tenacity Brittle
Crystal form Triclinic

Morphology Tabular crystals, euhedral, stellate, earthy, drusy.
Origin and occurrence In the oxidation zone of uranium deposits of bismuth-cobalt-nickel formations.
Accessory minerals Torbernite, zeunerite, bismutite, quartz, annabergite.
Similar minerals Autunite, saleeite and novacekite have a different crystal form.
Caution! Walpurgite is radioactive!

4 Cacoxenite

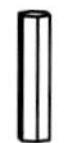

Chem. formula $Fe_4[OH/PO_4]_3 \cdot 12\,H_2O$
Hardness 3, **Sp. gr.** 2.3
Color Golden yellow to brownish
Streak Yellow
Luster Silky to vitreous
Cleavage Indiscernible because of its thin acicular to fibrous morphology
Fracture Fibrous
Tenacity Brittle
Crystal form Hexagonal

Morphology Acicular, filiform, mainly botryoidal, fibrous, stellate.
Origin and occurrence In phosphate pegmatites and brown iron deposits.
Accessory minerals Beraunite, strengite, rockbridgeite, goethite, strunzite, phosphosiderite.
Distinguishing feature The name caxoxene means "unwanted guest" because it indicates an undesirable phosphorus content in iron ores.
Similar minerals Strunzite is a pale yellow but is sometimes indistinguishable from cacoxenite using simple means.

Localities	
1 Eagle's Nest Mine, California, USA	**3** Wittichen, Black Forest, Germany
2 Beresowsk, Russia	**4** Svappavaara, Sweden

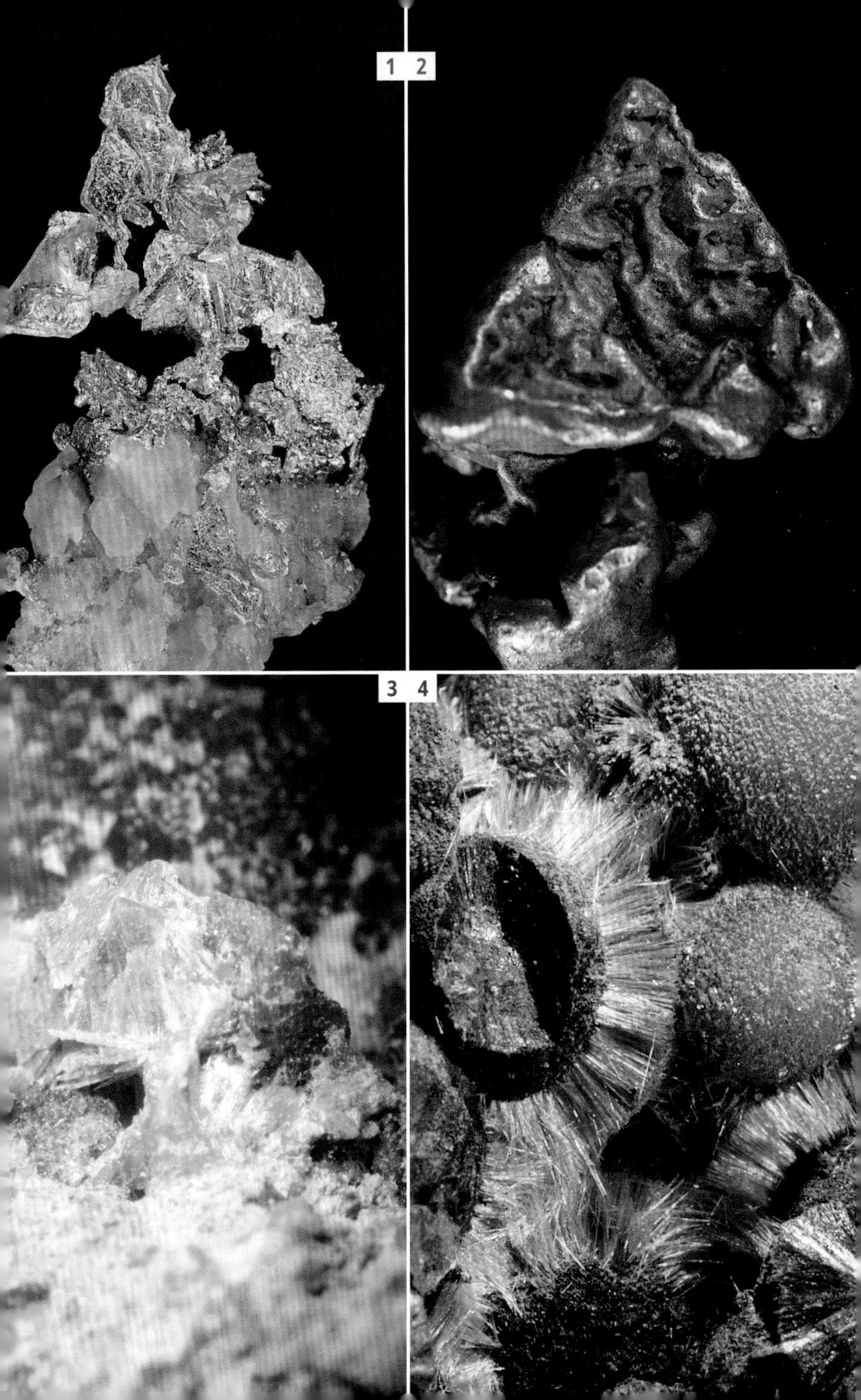
1 2
3 4

1 Kleinite

Chem. formula
$Hg_2N(Cl,SO_4) \cdot n\ H_2O$
Hardness 3–4, **Sp. gr.** 7.9–8
Color Yellow to slightly orange
Streak Sulfur yellow
Luster Adamantine to greasy
Cleavage Scarcely discernible
Fracture Conchoidal
Tenacity Brittle
Crystal form Hexagonal

Morphology Prismatic to isometric crystals, acicular, rarely stellate aggregates, encrustations, uneven.
Origin and occurrence In the oxidation zone of mercury deposits.
Accessory minerals Native mercury, cinnabar, calomel, calcite.
Similar minerals When considering the paragenesis with other mercury minerals, confusion is almost impossible because of the intense yellow color; orpiment is not brittle.

2 Natrojarosite

Chem. formula
$NaFe_3(OH)_6(SO_4)_2$
Hardness 3–4, **Sp. gr.** 3.1–3.3
Color Yellow to brown
Streak Yellow
Luster Vitreous
Cleavage Basal sometimes discernible
Fracture Uneven
Tenacity Brittle
Crystal form Trigonal

Morphology Tabular to rhombohedral, granular, powdery, drusy, as coating, earthy, botryoidal.
Origin and occurrence In the oxidation zone of hydrothermal deposits.
Accessory minerals Goethite, scorodite, arseniosiderite, pharmacosiderite.
Similar minerals Natrojarosite can only be distinguished from jarosite by chemical means; beudantite is slightly harder; goethite is harder and has a different crystal form.

3 Jarosite

Chem. formula
$KFe_3(OH)_6(SO_4)_2$
Hardness 3–4, **Sp. gr.** 3.1–3.3
Color Yellow to brown
Streak Yellow
Luster Vitreous
Cleavage Basal sometimes discernible
Fracture Uneven
Tenacity Brittle
Crystal form Trigonal

Morphology Tabular to rhombohedral, granular, powdery, drusy, as coating, earthy, botryoidal.
Origin and occurrence In the oxidation zone of hydrothermal deposits.
Accessory minerals Goethite, scorodite, arseniosiderite, pharmacosiderite.
Similar minerals Jarosite can only be distinguished from natrojarosite by chemical means; beudantite is slightly harder; goethite is harder and has a different crystal form.

4 Chiavennite

Chem. formula
$CaMn_2Be_2Si_5O_{13}(OH)_2 \cdot 2\ H_2O$
Hardness 3–4, **Sp. gr.** 2.65
Color Yellow to orange-yellow
Streak Pale yellow ocher
Luster Vitreous
Cleavage Perfect
Fracture Foliated
Tenacity Brittle
Crystal form Orthorhombic

Morphology Tabular, hexagonal crystals, foliated, drusy coatings, earthy, botryoidal.
Origin and occurrence In phosphate pegmatites, partially as coatings on beryl, in syenite pegmatites.
Accessory minerals Beryl, microcline, albite, bavenite, analcime, natrolite.
Similar minerals Micas are never so orange; association with beryl is very characteristic; stilbite and heulandite have a different crystal form.

Localities	
1 McDermitt Mine, Nevada, USA	**3** Barranco Jaroso, Nijar, Spain
2 Lavrion, Greece	**4** Tvedalen, Norway

1
2
3
4

1 Beudantite

Chem. formula $PbFe_3[(OH)_6/SO_4/AsO_4]$
Hardness 4, **Sp. gr.** 4.3
Color Yellow, brown, green, olive
Streak Yellow
Luster Vitreous
Cleavage None
Fracture Conchoidal
Tenacity Brittle
Crystal form Trigonal

Morphology Rhombohedral, pseudo-cubic, euhedral crystals, planar crystal intergrowth, tabular, drusy, earthy, uneven.
Origin and occurrence In the oxidation zone of lead-bearing deposits that also contain arsenic-bearing primary minerals.
Accessory minerals Mimetesite, jarosite, conichalcite, scorodite.
Similar minerals Jarosite and natrojarosite are somewhat softer and, unlike beudantite, exhibit cleavage; tsumcorite is somewhat harder and has a different crystal form.

2 Desautelsite

Chem. formula $Mg_6Mn_2^{3+}(CO_3)(OH)_{16} \cdot 4\,H_2O$
Hardness 2–3, **Sp. gr.** 2.1
Color Orange-yellow, brown
Streak Yellow
Luster Vitreous
Cleavage Perfect
Fracture Foliated
Tenacity Brittle
Crystal form Hexagonal

Morphology Hexagonal tabular crystals, planar crystal intergrowth, encrustations, coatings, earthy, uneven.
Origin and occurrence On fissures of brecciated serpentines, on fissures of ultrabasic rocks.
Accessory minerals Serpentine, artinite, magnesite, calcite, aragonite.
Similar minerals Aragonite is somewhat harder; serpentine is more yellow-green; artinite is never orange; brucite and hydrotalcite have different colors. The color is very typical when paragenesis is considered.

3 Pucherite

Chem. formula $Bi_2V_2O_8$
Hardness 4, **Sp. gr.** 6.25
Color Reddish brown to yellowish
Streak Yellow
Cleavage Perfect
Fracture Conchoidal
Tenacity Brittle
Crystal form Orthorhombic

Morphology Thick tabular, isometric, acicular, euhedral crystals, drusy, earthy, uneven.
Origin and occurrence In the oxidation zone of deposits of bismuth-cobalt-nickel formations.
Accessory minerals Bismuth, bismuth ochre, eulytine, quartz, scorodite.
Similar minerals Considering its paragenesis with bismuth minerals, it is not possible to confuse it with other minerals.

4 Zincite

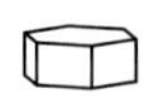

Chem. formula ZnO
Hardness 4, **Sp. gr.** 5.66
Color Yellowish, deep red
Streak Yellow-orange
Luster Vitreous
Cleavage Perfect
Fracture Uneven
Tenacity Brittle
Crystal form Hexagonal

Morphology Rare pyramidal crystals, hemimorphic (i.e., the two crystal ends are different), cleavage pieces, granular, uneven.
Origin and occurrence In metamorphic zinc-manganese deposits, in the oxidation zone of zinc deposits, in volcanic exhalations.
Accessory minerals Willemite, franklinite, calcite, smithsonite, hemimorphite.
Similar minerals Sphalerite and wurtzite are usually a darker brown and do not have a yellow streak.

Localities	
1 Tsumeb, Namibia	**3** Pucherschacht, Schneeberg, Saxony, Germany
2 San Benito County, California, USA	**4** Franklin, New Jersey, USA

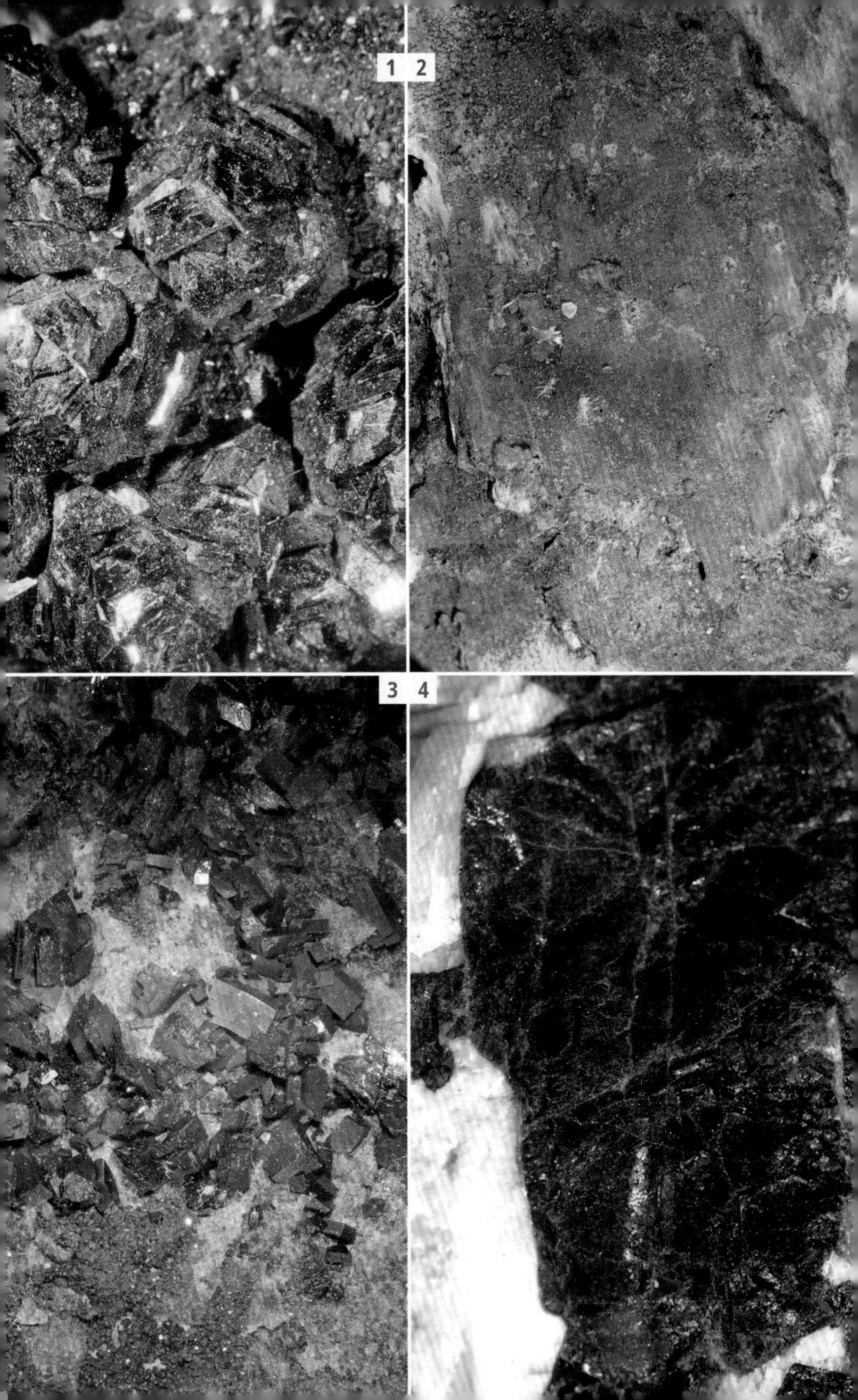
1
2
3
4

1 Tsumcorite

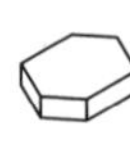

Chem. formula $PbZnFe(AsO_4)_2 \cdot H_2O$
Hardness 4½, **Sp. gr.** 5.2
Color Yellowish-brown to orange
Streak Yellowish
Luster Vitreous
Cleavage Indiscernible
Fracture Uneven
Tenacity Brittle
Crystal form Monoclinic

Morphology Short prismatic, tabular, foliated, stellate, earthy encrustations.
Origin and occurrence In the oxidation zone of lead- and zinc-bearing deposits.
Accessory minerals Malachite, cerussite, mimetesite, beudantite, quartz, calcite.
Similar minerals Mimetesite has a different crystal form; beudantite is usually rather brown, sometimes indistinguishable when using simple means.

2 Ojuelaite

Chem. formula $ZnFe_2^{3+}(AsO_4)_2(OH)_2 \cdot 4\,H_2O$
Hardness 3–4, **Sp. gr.** 3.39
Color Yellow, pale yellow
Streak Pale yellow
Luster Silky
Cleavage Scarcely discernible
Fracture Fibrous
Tenacity Brittle
Crystal form Monoclinic

Morphology Acicular crystals, planar crystal intergrowth, fibrous, velvety encrustations, euhedral, earthy, uneven.
Origin and occurrence In the oxidation zone of zinc-bearing deposits that also contain arsenic-bearing primary minerals.
Accessory minerals Mimetesite, smithsonite, paradamine, goethite, legrandite, scorodite.
Similar minerals Strunzite looks similar but only occurs in phosphate parageneses, legrandite is never so acicular-fibrous.

3 Saneroite

Chem. formula $NaMn^{2+}_5[Si_5O_{14}(OH)](VO_3)(OH)$
Hardness 4, **Sp. gr.** 3.47
Color Orange to orange-red
Streak Yellow
Luster Resinous
Cleavage Good, in two directions
Fracture Uneven
Tenacity Brittle
Crystal form Triclinic

Morphology Tabular crystals, rarely prismatic to isometric, mainly anhedral, granular, uneven.
Origin and occurrence In metamorphic manganese deposits.
Accessory minerals Aegirine, quartz, rhodochrosite, ganophyllite, sursassite.
Similar minerals Sursassite is more fibrous; tinzenite has a different crystal form; calcite effervesces when dabbed with diluted hydrochloric acid.

4 Durangite

Chem. formula $NaAl(AsO_4)F$
Hardness 5–5½, **Sp. gr.** 3.9–4.1
Color Orange to orange-red, orange-brown, red
Streak Yellow
Luster Vitreous
Cleavage Discernible
Fracture Uneven
Tenacity Brittle
Crystal form Monoclinic

Morphology Tabular crystals, rarely prismatic to isometric, mainly euhedral, granular, uneven.
Origin and occurrence In cavities of rhyolitic rocks, in tin deposits, in pegmatites.
Accessory minerals Tinstone, hematite, quartz, topaz, tridymite, cristobalite.
Similar minerals Considering paragenesis, confusion is almost impossible; topaz is much harder; quartz is harder and does not have such a red color.

Localities	
1 Tsumeb, Namibia	**3** Gambatesa, Piemont, Italy
2 Ojuela Mine, Mapimi, Mexico	**4** Durango, Mexico

1
2
3
4

1 McGovernite

Chem. formula $Mn_9Mg_4Zn_2As_2Si_2O_{17}(OH)_{14}$
Hardness 2–3, **Sp. gr.** 3.7
Color Ocher brown to chestnut brown
Streak Brown
Luster Vitreous
Cleavage Perfect
Fracture Foliated
Tenacity Brittle
Crystal form Hexagonal

Morphology Tabular crystals, foliated aggregates, mainly anhedral.
Origin and occurrence In metamorphic manganese deposits and manganese-zinc deposits.
Accessory minerals Franklinite, willemite, rhodonite, spessartine, zincite.
Similar minerals Micas are elastically flexible and not brittle; chlinochlore is green; rhodonite is red; spessartine has no cleavage.

2 Berthierite

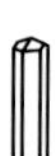

Chem. formula $FeSb_2S_4$
Hardness 2–3, **Sp. gr.** 4.6
Color Steel gray, often tarnished yellow
Streak Brown-gray
Luster Metallic
Cleavage Distinct, in the longitudinal direction
Fracture Uneven
Tenacity Brittle
Crystal form Orthorhombic

Morphology Acicular, fibrous, radial aggregates, rarely single crystals.
Origin and occurrence On antimony veins together with other low-thermal ore minerals.
Accessory minerals Quartz, stibnite, semseyite.
Similar minerals Stibnite is lighter colored and inelastically flexible; boulangerite and jamesonite have a different streak; the same is true for meneghinite. Millerite is more golden metallic.

3 Baumhauerite

Chem. formula $Pb_{12}As_{16}S_{36}$
Hardness 3, **Sp. gr.** 5.33
Color Steel gray, often deep red internal reflections
Streak Brown
Luster Metallic, sometimes dull
Cleavage Only poorly discernible
Fracture Conchoidal
Tenacity Brittle
Crystal form Triclinic

Morphology Prismatic crystals, mainly with rounded edges, unevenly anhedral.
Origin and occurrence In vugs in the dolomite marble and unevenly anhedral in these.
Accessory minerals Dolomite, realgar, scleroclase, jordanite, pyrite, tennantite.
Similar minerals Scleroclase has skewed end surfaces and has no red internal reflections; fahlore never has prismatic crystals; stibnite has a different streak and is not brittle. Emplectite and bismuthinite are not brittle and occur in different parageneses.

4 Sartorite *Scleroclase*

Chem. formula $PbAs_2S_4$
Hardness 3, **Sp. gr.** 5.05
Color Steel gray
Streak Brown
Luster Metallic
Cleavage Only poorly discernible
Fracture Conchoidal
Tenacity Brittle
Crystal form Monoclinic

Morphology Prismatic to acicular crystals, with oblique end surface, often longitudinally grooved, unevenly anhedral.
Origin and occurrence In vugs in the dolomite marble and unevenly anhedral in these.
Accessory minerals Dolomite, realgar, baumhauerite.
Similar minerals Baumhauerite has rounded crystal edges and red internal reflections; fahlore never has prismatic crystals; stibnite has a different streak and is not brittle.

Localities

1 Franklin, New Jersey, USA	**3** Lengenbach, Valais, Switzerland
2 Baia Sprie, Romania	**4** Lengenbach, Valais, Switzerland

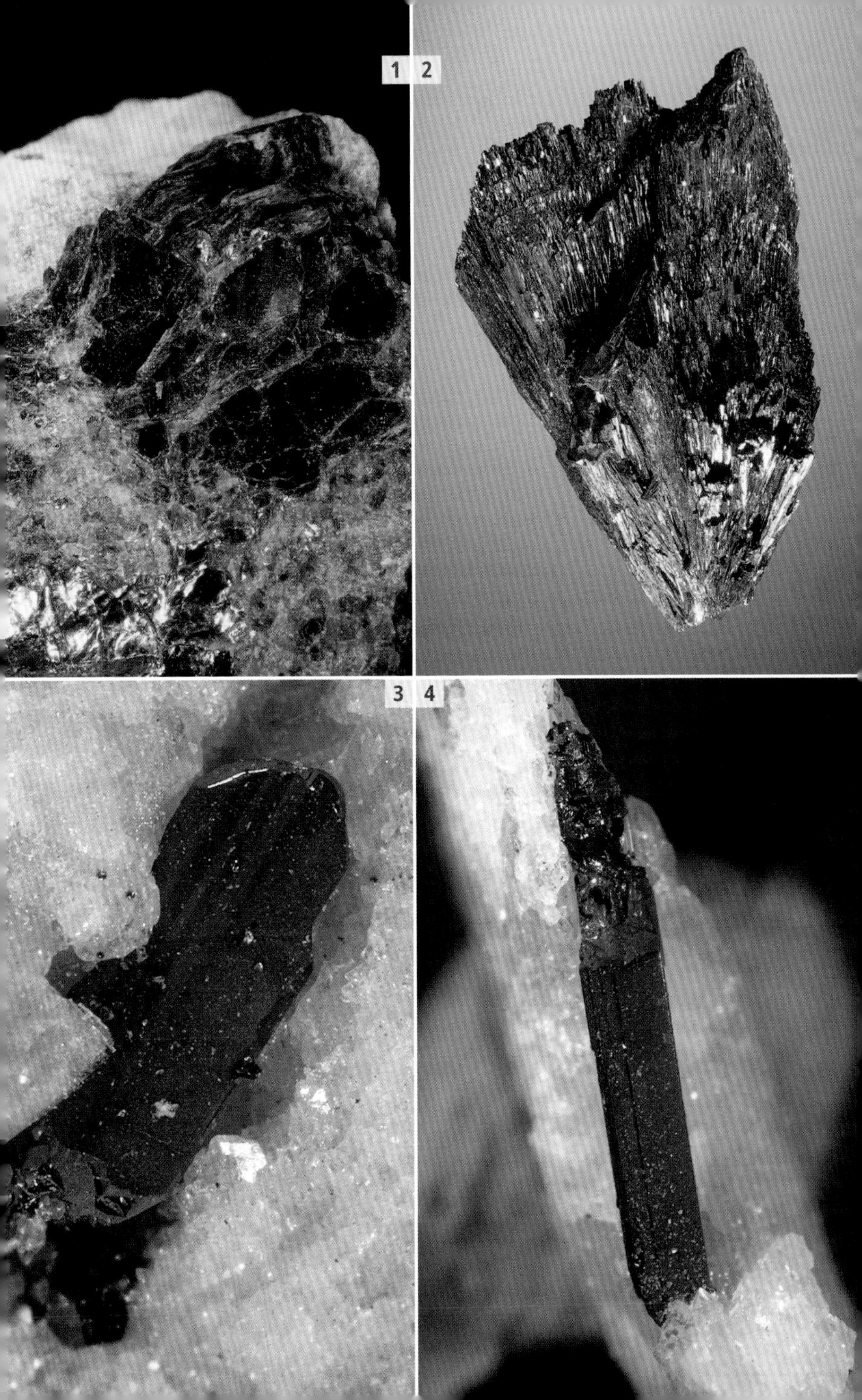
1
2
3
4

1 Descloizite

Chem. formula $Pb(Zn,Cu)[OH/VO_4]$
Hardness 3½, **Sp. gr.** 5.5–6.2
Color Brown, red-brown, yellow-brown, dark brown
Streak Light brown
Luster Resinous
Cleavage None
Fracture Uneven
Tenacity Brittle
Crystal form Orthorhombic

Morphology Crystals prismatic, rarely tabular, often dendritic, stellate, drusy, uneven.
Origin and occurrence In the oxidation zone of lead deposits. The vanadium originates primarily from black shales in the surroundings.
Accessory minerals Vanadinite, wulfenite.
Similar minerals Magnetite is harder; brown calcite or smithsonite are lighter and exhibit distinct cleavage; wulfenite has a different streak.

2 Jamesite

Chem. formula $Pb_2Zn(Fe^{2+},Zn)_2 Fe^{3+}{}_4(AsO_4)_4(OH)_{10}$
Hardness 3½, **Sp. gr.** 5.08
Color Brown, red-brown
Streak Light brown
Luster Vitreous to adamantine
Cleavage None
Fracture Uneven, fibrous
Tenacity Brittle
Crystal form Triclinic

Morphology Crystals prismatic, long tabular, often dendritic, stellate, drusy, uneven.
Origin and occurrence In the oxidation zone of lead-zinc deposits with higher arsenic contents.
Accessory minerals Duftite, tsumcorite, goethite, calcite, mimetesite.
Similar minerals Fibrous goethite is not as reddish brown and has a darker streak; it is also much harder; descloizite has a different crystal form and a distinct resinous luster.

3–6 Sphalerite *Zinc blende, fibrous blende*

Chem. formula ZnS
Hardness 3½–4, **Sp. gr.** 3.9–4.2
Color Yellow, brown, red, green, black, rarely colorless to white
Streak Light brown to brown
Luster Semi-metallic adamantine, in dense aggregates greasy
Cleavage Rhombohedral perfect
Fracture Conchoidal, splintery
Tenacity Brittle
Crystal form Cubic

Morphology Often euhedral crystals, mainly tetrahedral, rhombic dodecahedral, often octahedral due to a combination of two tetrahedra, surfaces often striated, often twinned, unevenly stellate, crystalline, granular.
Origin and occurrence In granites, gabbros as an accessory mineral; as an ore mineral in contact metasomatic deposits, hydrothermal veins and displacement deposits, sedimentary and resulting metamorphic deposits.
Accessory minerals Galena, pyrite, magnetite, marcasite, calcite, barite, chalcopyrite.
Distinguishing feature Red to orange-red translucent sphalerite can be cut into faceted stones. Because of their high light refraction, these stones have an extraordinary brilliancy, comparable to that of cut diamond. However, sphalerite is so soft and delicate that it is not possible to set and wear such stones. They are just an adornment in collections of cut and polished minerals.
Similar minerals Sphalerite differs from galena, garnet, fahlore and sulfur in hardness and cleavage.

Localities		
1 Berg Aukas, Namibia	**3** Rüdersdorf near Berlin, Germany	**5** Joplin, Missouri, USA
2 Tsumeb, Namibia	**4** Marburg, Hesse, Germany	**6** Wiesloch, Baden-Wuerttemberg, Germany

1
2
3
4
5
6

1 Wurtzite

Chem. formula ZnS
Hardness 3½–4, **Sp. gr.** 4.0
Color Light brown to dark brown
Streak Light brown
Luster Resinous
Cleavage Basal and prismatic
Fracture Uneven
Tenacity Brittle
Crystal form Hexagonal

Morphology Crystals spindle-shaped, pyramids with base, horizontally striated, radial, reniform, fibrous, dense.
Origin and occurrence In hydrothermal veins and zinc ore deposits.
Accessory minerals Sphalerite, galena, pyrite, marcasite, quartz, calcite.
Similar minerals Sphalerite has a different crystal form and cleavage, but can similarly be reniform and radial; however, as fibrous blende, it always has a concentric structure.

2 Manganite

Chem. formula MnOOH
Hardness 4, **Sp. gr.** 4.3–4.4
Color Brown-black to black
Streak Brown
Luster Metallic
Cleavage Distinct
Fracture Uneven
Tenacity Brittle
Crystal form Monoclinic

Morphology Long prismatic to short prismatic, rarely tabular, cruciform twins, stellate, earthy, uneven.
Origin and occurrence In hydrothermal veins, together with other manganese ores.
Accessory minerals Pyrolusite, limonite, braunite, barite, calcite, quartz.
Similar minerals Goethite has a different color; unlike manganite, pyrolusite has a pure black streak and is harder.

3 Arseniosiderite

Chem. formula $Ca_3Fe_4(OH)_6(H_2O)_3(AsO_4)_4$
Hardness 1½–4, **Sp. gr.** 3.6
Color Yellowish to brown
Streak Yellowish brown
Luster Silky to slightly metallic
Cleavage Poorly discernible
Fracture Uneven
Tenacity Brittle
Crystal form Monoclinic

Morphology Stellate, granular, uneven, often as a pseudomorph after scorodite.
Origin and occurrence In the oxidation zone.
Accessory minerals Scorodite, natrojarosite.
Similar minerals The typical occurrence and characteristic luster of arseniosiderite normally prevent any confusion. The pseudomorphs after scorodite crystals differ from fresh scorodite crystals due to their opacity and typical metallic luster.

4 Hausmannite

Chem. formula Mn_3O_4
Hardness 5½, **Sp. gr.** 4.7–4.8
Color Iron black, slightly brownish
Streak Brown
Luster Metallic
Cleavage Perfect basal
Fracture Uneven
Tenacity Brittle
Crystal form Tetragonal

Morphology Octahedral, often regular aggregation of five crystals (quintuplets), as shown, granular, uneven.
Origin and occurrence In metamorphic manganese deposits, on hydrothermal manganese ore veins.
Accessory minerals Braunite, manganite, barite, calcite, pyrolusite, psilomelane.
Similar minerals Magnetite has a black streak; braunite a mainly indiscernible cleavage; manganite and pyrolusite have a different crystal form.

Localities	
1 Oruro, Bolivia	**3** Romaneche, France
2 Ilfeld, Harz, Germany	**4** Ilmenau, Thuringia, Germany

1
2
3
4

1 Keckite

Chem. formula $Ca(Mn,Zn)_2Fe_3(OH)_3(PO_4)_4 \cdot 2H_2O$
Hardness 4, **Sp. gr.** 2.7–2.9
Color Yellowish to brown
Streak Yellowish brown
Luster Vitreous
Cleavage Good
Fracture Uneven
Tenacity Brittle
Crystal form Monoclinic

Morphology Prismatic crystals, stellate, fibrous aggregates, pseudomorphs after rockbridgeite fibers, drusy, granular.
Origin and occurrence In pegmatites, as an alteration product of rockbridgeite and other phosphates.
Accessory minerals Mitridatite, apatite, rockbridgeite, frondelite.
Similar minerals The minerals of the jahnsite group cannot be distinguished from keckite using simple means; however, the occurrence as pseudomorphs after rockbridgeite is very characteristic.

2 Frondelite

Chem. formula $(Mn,Fe)Fe_4[(OH)_5/(PO_4)_3]$
Hardness 4½, **Sp. gr.** 3.4
Color Brown
Streak Brown
Luster Vitreous
Cleavage Present, but only scarcely discernible
Fracture Uneven
Tenacity Brittle
Crystal form Orthorhombic

Morphology Prismatic to tabular crystals, often stellate aggregates, hematite-type, reniform, drusy, fibrous, uneven.
Origin and occurrence In phosphate pegmatites, it is an alteration product of primary phosphate minerals and in phosphorus-rich brown iron deposits.
Accessory minerals Beraunite, strengite, phosphosiderite, apatite.
Similar minerals Color and streak are highly characteristic. If the typical occurrence is also taken into consideration, confusion is rarely possible; its close relative, rockbridgeite, is always black to green.

3 Hauerite

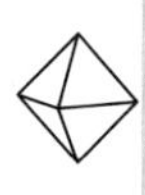

Chem. formula MnS_2
Hardness 4½, **Sp. gr.** 3.46
Color Black, brown-black
Streak Brown
Luster Vitreous
Cleavage Good
Fracture Uneven
Tenacity Brittle
Crystal form Cubic

Morphology Octahedral to rhombic dodecahedral crystals, stellate, botryoidal aggregates, uneven.
Origin and occurrence In sulfur deposits, often intergrown in clay, in decomposed extrusive rocks, in solfatara formations.
Accessory minerals Sulfur, realgar, gypsum, calcite, celestine, aragonite.
Similar minerals Pyrite is harder and golden yellow; pseudomorphs of limonite after pyrite are browner and harder.

4 Sursassite

Chem. formula $Mn_2(Al,Mn)_3[(OH)_3|SiO_4|Si_2O_7] \cdot 3H_2O$
Hardness 4½, **Sp. gr.** 3.25
Color Reddish brown
Streak Brown
Luster Vitreous
Cleavage Indiscernible
Fracture Fibrous
Tenacity Brittle
Crystal form Monoclinic

Morphology Fibrous, stellate aggregates, anhedral, granular, uneven.
Origin and occurrence In metamorphic manganese ore deposits.
Accessory minerals Rhodonite, rhodochrosite, spessartine, tinzenite, braunite, quartz, saneroite.
Similar minerals If its paragenesis is considered, confusion with other minerals is not possible; piedmontite is a much darker red; saneroite is not radial; actinolite is green and has a green streak; spessartine is not radial; the same applies to rhodonite.

Localities

1 Hagendorf-Süd, East Bavaria, Germany	**3** Tarnobrzeg, Poland
2 Minas Gerais, Brazil	**4** Gambatesa, Piemont, Italy

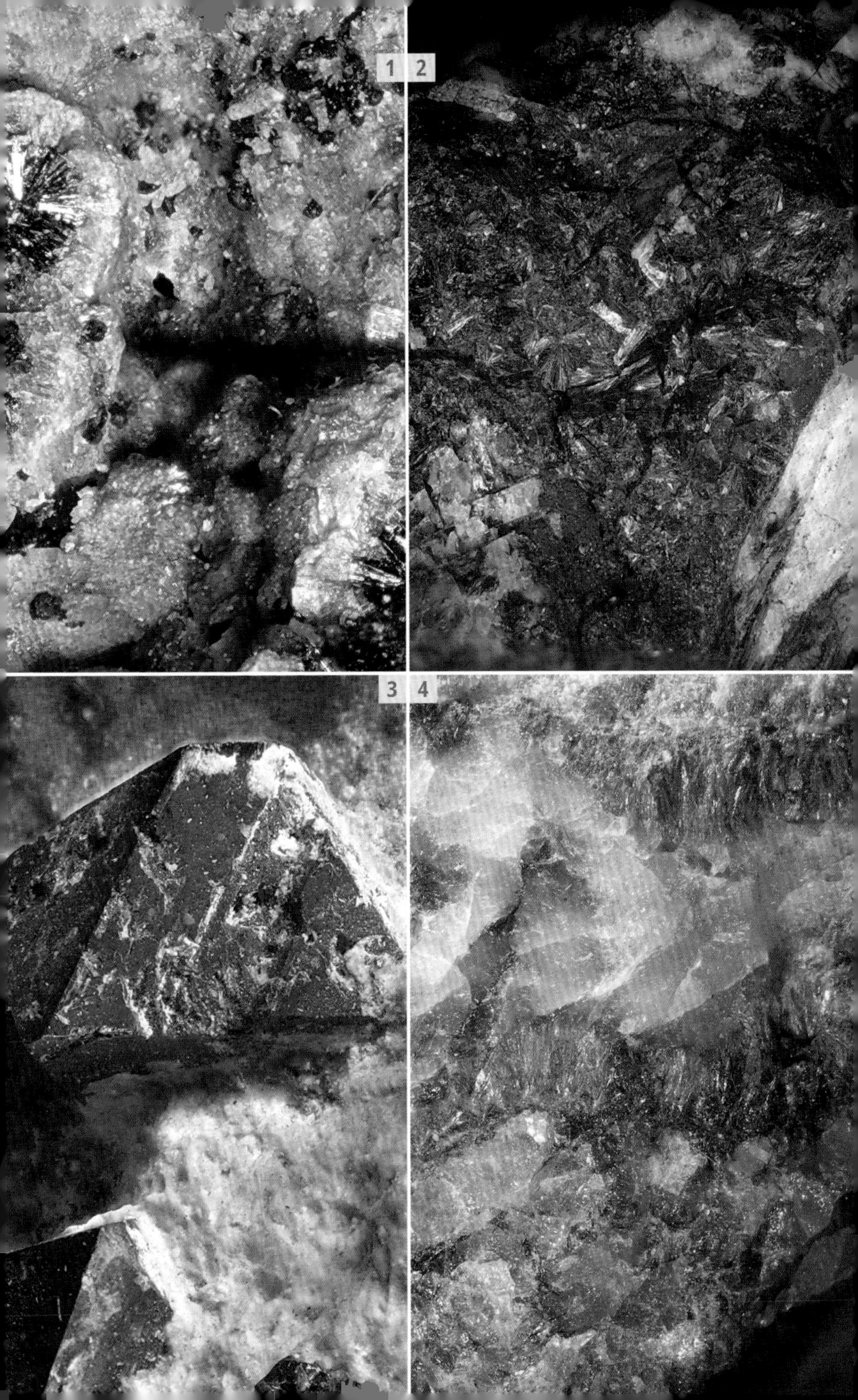
1
2
3
4

1–2 Goethite *Brown ironstone, brown iron ore, limonite*

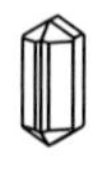

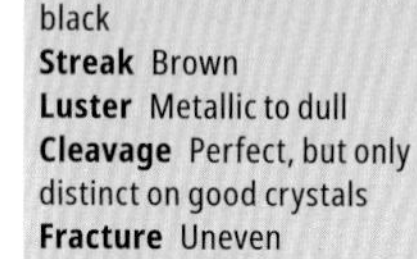

Chem. formula FeOOH
Hardness 5–5½, **Sp. gr.** 4.3
Color Light yellow, brown to dark brown, reddish brown, black
Streak Brown
Luster Metallic to dull
Cleavage Perfect, but only distinct on good crystals
Fracture Uneven
Tenacity Brittle
Crystal form Orthorhombic

Morphology Acicular, prismatic and long tabular crystals, radial, reniform with smooth surface (brown iron ore), uneven, earthy (limonite).
Origin and occurrence Crystals in bubble cavities of volcanic rocks, in the oxidation zones of various ore deposits. Here it forms the main mass of the oxidation zone. Many, usually colorful oxidation minerals are found in its cavities.
Accessory minerals Occurs together with an extraordinary large number of minerals, especially with oxidation minerals, malachite, cuprite, azurite.
Distinguishing feature Goethite often forms pseudomorphs after other minerals, for example, after pyrite crystals or marcasite crystals.
Similar minerals Lepidocrocite is clearly more reddish and mainly foliated; hematite has a red streak; psilomelane has a black streak.

3 Ferberite

Chem. formula $(Fe,Mn)WO_4$
Hardness 5–5½, **Sp. gr.** 7.14–7.54
Color Brown to black
Streak Yellow brown to dark brown, sometimes almost black
Luster Greasy metallic
Cleavage Very good
Fracture Uneven
Tenacity Brittle
Crystal form Monoclinic

Morphology Tabular to prismatic crystals, also acicular, radial, crystalline, uneven.
Origin and occurrence In granites, pegmatites, pneumatolytic and hydrothermal veins.
Accessory minerals Tourmaline, tinstone, quartz, fluorite, apatite, arsenopyrite, molybdenum glance.
Distinguishing feature Ferberite is a member of a mixture series with the two end members ferberite ($FeWO_4$) and hubnerite ($MnWO_4$).
Similar minerals Columbite is somewhat harder and does not have as good cleavage; tinstone has a different crystal form; hubnerite is discernably reddish; tourmaline has no cleavage and is always clearly trigonal.

4 Hubernite

Chem. formula $(Mn, Fe)WO_4$
Hardness 5–5½, **Sp. gr.** 7.14–7.54
Color Brown, translucent reddish (hubnerite), to black
Streak Yellow brown to dark brown, sometimes almost black
Luster Greasy metallic
Cleavage Very good
Fracture Uneven
Tenacity Brittle
Crystal form Monoclinic

Morphology Tabular to prismatic crystals, also acicular, radial, crystalline, uneven.
Origin and occurrence In granites, pegmatites, pneumatolytic and hydrothermal veins.
Accessory minerals Tourmaline, tinstone, quartz, fluorite, apatite, arsenopyrite, molybdenum glance.
Distinguishing feature Hubnerite is a member of a mixture series with the two end members ferberite ($FeWO_4$) and hubnerite ($MnWO_4$).
Similar minerals Columbite is somewhat harder and does not have as good cleavage; tinstone has a different crystal form; ferberite is dark brown to black and not reddish.

Localities

1 Siegen, Siegerland Region, Germany	**3** Tae-Wha, Korea
2 Freisen, Saarland, Germany	**4** Pasto Bueno, Peru

1
2
3
4

1 Chromite *Chromate of iron, chromic iron ore*

Chem. formula (Fe, Mg)Cr_2O_4
Hardness 5½, **Sp. gr.** 4.5–4.8
Color Brown-black to iron black
Streak Yellow-brown to brown
Luster Metallic to greasy
Cleavage None
Fracture Conchoidal
Tenacity Brittle
Crystal form Cubic

Morphology Rarely octahedral, mainly granular, uneven, often in the form of roundish grains grown into the rock.
Origin and occurrence Anhedral in grains and crystals in basic rocks such as peridotite, anorthosite, serpentinite; because of its high hardness and chemical resistance often also in placer deposits in the form of unrolled grains.
Accessory minerals Olivine, magnetite, anorthite, pyroxene.
Similar minerals Magnetite has a black streak and is clearly magnetic; augite has good cleavage.

2 Nickeline *Niccolite*

Chem. formula NiAs
Hardness 5½, **Sp. gr.** 7.8
Color Metallic pink, darker tarnished
Streak Brown to blackish brown
Luster Metallic
Cleavage Scarcely distinct
Fracture Uneven
Tenacity Brittle to non-brittle
Crystal form Hexagonal

Morphology Rarely pyramids and spindle-type crystals, crystals overall rare, almost always uneven, stellate, reniform aggregates.
Origin and occurrence In hydrothermal veins, in gabbros.
Accessory minerals Maucherite, barite, nickel bloom.
Similar minerals Maucherite is slightly lighter, otherwise nick-elite is unmistakable due to its color; pyrite is more yellow and harder; magnetite has a black streak.

3 Neptunite

Chem. formula $Na_2FeTi[Si_4O_{12}]$
Hardness 5½, **Sp. gr.** 3.23
Color Black to dark brown
Streak Brown
Luster Vitreous
Cleavage Mainly indiscernible
Fracture Conchoidal
Tenacity Brittle
Crystal form Monoclinic

Morphology Crystals prismatic, often wide-area, uneven.
Origin and occurrence In alkali pegmatites, anhedral crystals in natrolite veins.
Accessory minerals Benitoite, aegirine, natrolite, feldspar.
Similar minerals Tourmaline has a clearly different crystal form and is harder; aegirine has the typical cleavage with a 90° cleavage angle; the same applies to augite; hornblende has cleavage with a 120° cleavage angle.

4 Hypersthene

Chem. formula $(Fe, Mg)_2[Si_2O_6]$
Hardness 5–6, **Sp. gr.** 3.5
Color Black, brown, green
Streak Greenish to brownish, infrequently white
Luster Vitreous, often with a metallic glimmer
Cleavage Distinct, often foliated, cleavage angle about 90°
Fracture Uneven
Tenacity Brittle
Crystal form Orthorhombic

Morphology Tabular to prismatic crystals, foliated, granular, uneven.
Origin and occurrence In igneous rocks, on fissures also euhedral in metamorphic schists, in volcanic ejecta.
Accessory minerals Olivine, diopside.
Similar minerals Bronzite and enstatite are often indistinguishable from hypersthene by simple means; augite and hornblende have a different crystal form; hornblende also has a different cleavage angle.

Localities

1 Guleman, Turkey
2 Sangerhausen, Thuringia, Germany
3 San Benito County, California, USA
4 Summit Rock, Oregon, USA

1
2
3
4

1 Aeschynite-(Ce)

Chem. formula $(Ce,Th,Ca)(Ti,Nb,Ta)_2O_6$
Hardness 5–6, **Sp. gr.** 4.9–5.1
Color Brown to black (anhedral), translucent yellow to brown (euhedral)
Streak Yellow-brown
Luster Pitchy (anhedral), vitreous (euhedral)
Cleavage None
Fracture Conchoidal
Tenacity Brittle
Crystal form Orthorhombic

Morphology Tabular to prismatic crystals, euhedral and anhedral, uneven.
Origin and occurrence Anhedral in granite pegmatites; euhedral on alpine fissures.
Accessory minerals Xenotime, monazite, zircon, hematite, rutile, quartz albite, microcline.
Similar minerals Rutile exhibits tetragonal symmetry; orthite is more purple in euhedral and, like samarskite, has a different streak. Gadolinite is greener or at least has a greenish streak.

2 Pinakiolite

Chem. formula $Mg_3MnMn_2B_2O_{10}$
Hardness 6, **Sp. gr.** 3.9
Color Black
Streak Brown
Luster Metallic
Cleavage Good
Fracture Conchoidal
Tenacity Brittle
Crystal form Monoclinic

Morphology Long tabular, prismatic crystals, almost always anhedral.
Origin and occurrence Anhedral in regional metamorphic manganese deposits.
Accessory minerals Dolomite, hausmannite, braunite, manganite.
Similar minerals Crystal form and occurrence prevent any confusion between pinakiolite and other minerals; hornblende does not have such a reddish streak; actinolite has a greenish streak; tourmaline has a white streak.

3 Euxenite-(Y)

Chem. formula $(Y,Ce,U)(Nb,Ta,Ti)_2O_6$
Hardness 5½–6½, **Sp. gr.** 4.3–5.8
Color Black, often yellowish coating
Streak Yellowish, brownish
Luster Greasy
Cleavage None
Fracture Conchoidal
Tenacity Brittle
Crystal form Orthorhombic

Morphology Tabular, prismatic crystals, often parallel intergrowths.
Origin and occurrence In pegmatites, on alpine fissures in metamorphic schists.
Accessory minerals Monazite, feldspar, quartz, samarskite, beryl, columbite.
Similar minerals Monazite is not black; wolframite has good cleavage.
Caution! Euxenite is radioactive!

4 Bronzite

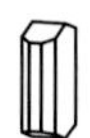

Chem. formula $(Mg,Fe)_2[Si_2O_6]$
Hardness 5–6, **Sp. gr.** 3.1–3.2
Color Brown, greenish
Streak Brown
Luster Vitreous, silky on cleavage faces
Cleavage Good
Fracture Conchoidal
Tenacity Brittle
Crystal form Orthorhombic

Morphology Rarely short prismatic or tabular crystals, often crystalline, radial, uneven.
Origin and occurrence As a constituent mineral in norites, gabbros, peridotites, andesites, melaphyres.
Accessory minerals Talc, apatite, serpentine.
Similar minerals Hornblende has a 120° cleavage angle, while the cleavage angle of bronzite is about 90°; olivine has a different crystal shape; augite is black; enstatite and hypersthene can often not be distinguished by simple means.

Localities

1 Birkelund, Norway
2 Langban, Sweden
3 Antsirabé, Madagascar
4 Bernstein, Burgenland, Austria

1
2
3
4

1–2 Hornblende

Chem. formula $(Ca,Na,K)_{2-3}(Mg,Fe,Al)_5[(OH,F)_2/(Si,Al)_2Si_6O_{22}]$
Hardness 5–6, **Sp. gr.** 2.9–3.4
Color Dark green, black
Streak Gray-green to gray-brown
Luster Vitreous to greasy
Cleavage Perfect, the cleavage faces form an angle of about 120°
Fracture Uneven
Tenacity Brittle
Crystal form Monoclinic

Morphology Prismatic crystals, with often trihedral end face, columnar, uneven, stellate aggregates, anhedral.
Origin and occurrence Anhedral in granites, syenites, diorites and many volcanic rocks; euhedral on their fissures, often in volcanic tuffs; partly large, loose crystals formed all around; anhedral in gneisses, mica schists and chlorite schists.
Accessory minerals Biotite, augite, magnetite, feldspar, chlorite, almandine.
Similar minerals Augite differs from hornblende in its cleavage angle; tourmaline has no cleavage; neptunite has a different crystal form and no cleavage.

3 Aenigmatite

Chem. formula $Na_2Fe_5TiSi_6O_{20}$
Hardness 5–6, **Sp. gr.** 3.74–3.85
Color Black
Streak Reddish brown
Luster Vitreous to pitchy
Cleavage Perfect
Tenacity Brittle
Crystal form Triclinic

Morphology Long prismatic, tabular crystals, usually anhedral.
Origin and occurrence Anhedral in alkali-rich igneous rocks, especially in trachytes and rhyolites and in alkali granites and alkali syenites, practically never euhedral.
Accessory minerals Sodalite, feldspar, quartz, biotite, nepheline, zircon.
Similar minerals Hornblende does not have such a reddish streak and has a cleavage angle of 120°; actinolite has a greenish streak and likewise a cleavage angle of 120°; tourmaline has a white streak; neptunite has a different crystal form and no cleavage.

4 Fergusonite

Chem. formula $Y(Nb,Ta)O_4$
Hardness 5–6½, **Sp. gr.** 4.7–6.2
Color Brown to black
Streak Light brown
Luster Greasy
Cleavage None
Fracture Conchoidal to uneven
Tenacity Brittle
Crystal form Tetragonal

Morphology Pyramidal to prismatic crystals, euhedral or anhedral, uneven.
Origin and occurrence In granite pegmatites, mainly anhedral, partly very large crystals; in volcanic ejecta and on alpine fissures, euhedral crystals, only a few millimeters large.
Accessory minerals In pegmatites: monazite, samarskite, aeschynite, feldspar, quartz; in volcanic ejecta: sanidine, rutile, titanite, allanite; on alpine fissures: rutile, hematite, synchisite, monazite, quartz, feldspar.
Similar minerals Samarskite, aeschynite have a different streak; monazite has perfect cleavage; the same applies to ferberite and hubnerite; synchisite always exhibits a hexagonal cross section.

Localities	
1 Daun, Eifel Mountains, Germany	**3** Naujakasik, Greenland
2 Zillertal, Austria	**4** Tsaratanana, Madagascar

1
2
3
4

1 Franklinite

Chem. formula $ZnFe_2O_4$
Hardness 6–6½, **Sp. gr.** 5–5.2
Color Black
Streak Red-brown
Luster Metallic
Cleavage None
Fracture Conchoidal
Tenacity Brittle
Crystal form Cubic

Morphology Mainly octahedral, uneven, anhedral, rarely euhedral.
Origin and occurrence In metamorphic zinc deposits.
Accessory minerals Zincite, willemite, calcite, jeffersonite, hardystonite.
Similar minerals Franklinite differs from magnetite in its paragenesis with zinc minerals; gahnite is always somewhat greenish in thin splinters.

2 Jeffersonite

Chem. formula $Ca(Mn,Zn,Fe)[Si_2O_6]$
Hardness 6, **Sp. gr.** 3.4–3.7
Color Dark brown, black
Streak Brown
Luster Vitreous
Cleavage Distinct, prismatic, angle between the cleavage faces (cleavage angle) about 90°
Fracture Conchoidal
Tenacity Brittle
Crystal form Monoclinic

Morphology Short prismatic to long prismatic, stellate aggregates, rarely euhedral, mainly anhedral, granular, uneven.
Origin and occurrence In metamorphic zinc-manganese deposits.
Accessory minerals Sphalerite, willemite, zincite, franklinite, galenite, calcite.
Similar minerals Hornblende has a different cleavage and a distinct hexagonal cross section in contrast to the distinct quadrilateral or octagonal cross section of jeffersonite; augite has a different streak. Jeffersonite cannot be distinguished from johannsenite using simple means.

3 Cafarsite

Chem. formula $Ca_{16}(Na,Fe^{2+},REE)(Ti,Fe^{3+},Fe^{2+},Mn^{2+},Al)_{16}(AsO_3)_{28}F$
Hardness 6, **Sp. gr.** 3.9
Color Brown, black
Streak Yellow-brown
Luster Vitreous to resinous
Cleavage None
Fracture Conchoidal
Tenacity Brittle
Crystal form Cubic

Morphology Octahedral to rhombic dodecahedral crystals, euhedral, uneven.
Origin and occurrence On alpine fissures in rocks with arsenic-bearing minerals.
Accessory minerals Asbecasite, titanite, synchisite, chlorite, quartz, feldspar, hematite.
Similar minerals Anatase has a different crystal form; pyrite is golden yellow; pseudomorphs of limonite after pyrite are normally lighter colored but sometimes may be difficult to distinguish.

4 Johannsenite

Chem. formula $Ca(Mn,Fe)Si_2O_6$
Hardness 6, **Sp. gr.** 3.4–3.6
Color Greenish, brown, black
Streak Brown
Luster Vitreous
Cleavage Good
Fracture Conchoidal
Tenacity Brittle
Crystal form Monoclinic

Morphology Short prismatic to thick tabular crystals, anhedral and euhedral, uneven.
Origin and occurrence In metamorphic manganese deposits.
Accessory minerals Rhodonite, bustamite, franklinite, willemite, zincite, spessartine.
Similar minerals Taking into consideration the manganese-rich paragenesis, confusion is almost impossible; johannsenite cannot be distinguished from jeffersonite using simple means.

Localities	
1 Franklin, New Jersey, USA	**3** Cherbadung, Valais, Switzerland
2 Franklin, New Jersey, USA	**4** Broken Hill, Australia

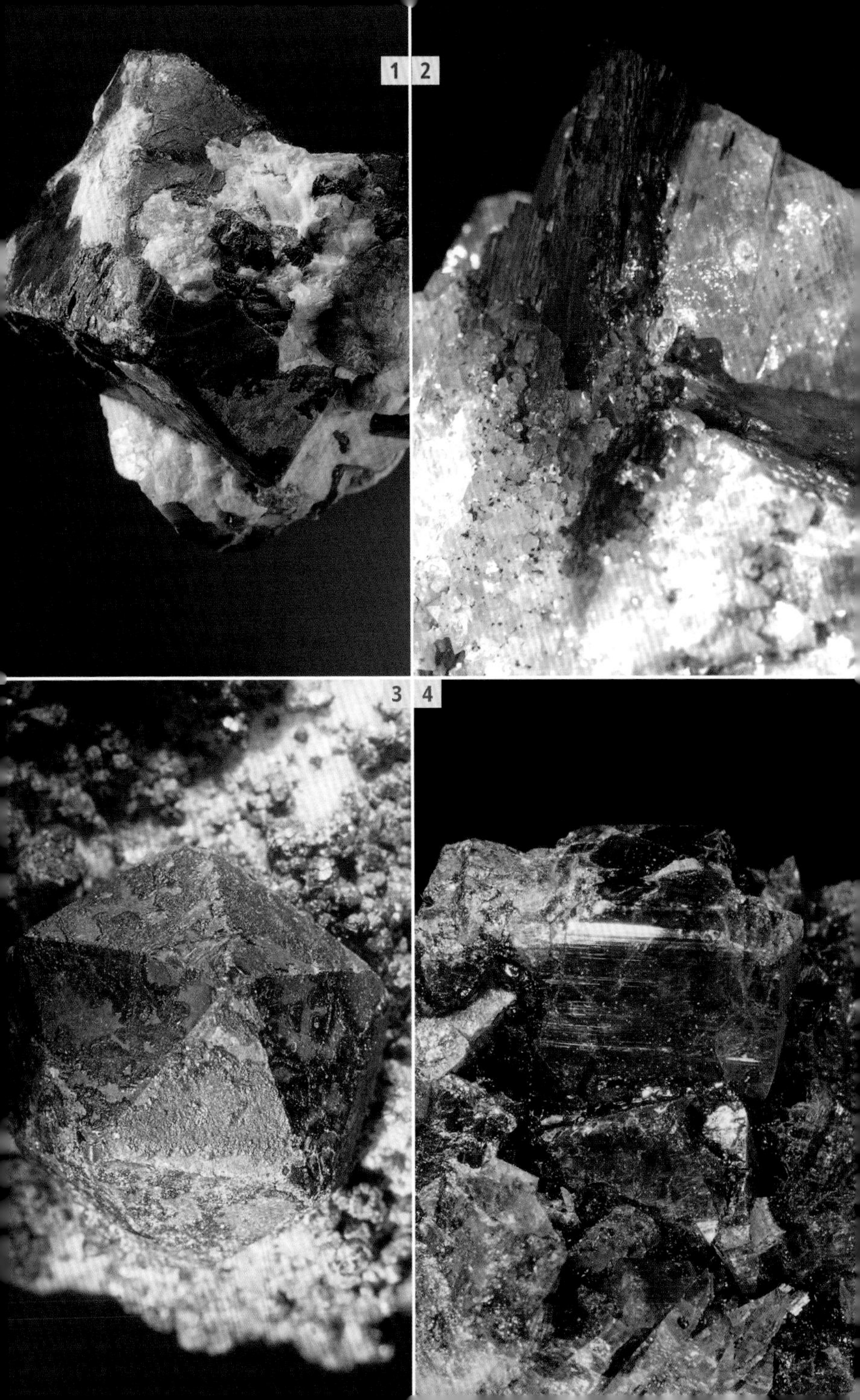
1
2
3
4

1 Babingtonite

Chem. formula $Ca_2FeFeSi_5O_{14}OH$
Hardness 5½–6, **Sp. gr.** 3.25–3.35
Color Black
Streak Black-brown
Luster Vitreous
Cleavage Perfect
Fracture Uneven
Tenacity Brittle
Crystal form Triclinic

Morphology Thick tabular to short prismatic crystals, mainly euhedral, rarely uneven.
Origin and occurrence On fissures in granite, in pegmatites and cavities of volcanic rocks.
Accessory minerals Epidote, quartz, prehnite.
Similar minerals Axinite has a different streak, is usually lighter colored and has distinctly sharper-edged crystals; in contrast to babingtonite, augite and diopside exhibit cleavage with a 90° cleavage angle; hornblende has a 120°cleavage angle.

2 Ardennite

Chem. formula $Mn_5Al_5(As,V)O_4Si_5O_{20}(OH)_2 \cdot 2\,H_2O$
Hardness 6–7, **Sp. gr.** 3.62
Color Yellow-brown
Streak Yellowish brown
Luster Vitreous
Cleavage Perfect
Fracture Uneven
Tenacity Brittle
Crystal form Orthorhombic

Morphology Radial, parallel radial, stellate, almost always anhedral.
Origin and occurrence In metamorphic manganese deposits as manganese and vanadium carriers.
Accessory minerals Quartz, calcite, spessartine, rhodonite, sursassite, rhodochrosite.
Similar minerals Sursassite and saneroite are more reddish; clinozoisite and zoisite are not so yellowish; the occurrence in a metamorphic manganese parageneses together with other manganese minerals is highly typical.

3 Lorenzenite

Chem. formula $Na_2Ti_2Si_2O_9$
Hardness 6, **Sp. gr.** 3.4
Color Brown to black
Streak Blackish brown
Luster Vitreous to greasy
Cleavage Poor
Fracture Uneven
Tenacity Brittle
Crystal form Orthorhombic

Morphology Thick tabular, acicular crystals, fibrous, radial aggregates.
Origin and occurrence Anhedral in alkaline rocks.
Accessory minerals Aegirine, nepheline, feldspar, astrophyllite, phlogopite.
Similar minerals Orthite, zircon have a different crystal form; monazite is never black; tourmaline has a different streak and a different crystal form. Hematite has a metallic luster and a red streak.

4 Helvine

Chem. formula $(Fe,Mn,Zn)_8[S_2/(BeSiO_4)_6]$
Hardness 6, **Sp. gr.** 3.1–3.66
Color Light yellow, reddish brown, dark brown-red
Streak Brownish
Luster Vitreous
Cleavage None
Fracture Conchoidal
Tenacity Brittle
Crystal form Cubic

Distinguishing feature Helvin belongs to a mixture series; the end members are called danalite (Fe), helvine (Mn) and genthelvite (Zn).
Morphology Tetrahedral, sometimes combined into octahedral crystals, rarely rhombic dodecahedral, euhedral, anhedral, granular, dense.
Origin and occurrence In skarn deposits.
Accessory minerals Fluorite, garnet.
Similar minerals The tetrahedral crystals of helvine are very characteristic; garnet has a white streak; sphalerite is softer and exhibits distinct cleavage.

Localities	
1 Pune, India	**3** Kola, Russia
2 Salmchateau, Belgium	**4** Schwarzenberg, Saxony, Germany

1
2
3
4

1 Polymignite

Chem. formula (Ca,Fe,Y,Th)(Nb,Ti,Ta)O_4
Hardness 6½, **Sp. gr.** 4.7–4.8
Color Black
Streak Brown
Luster Greasy metallic
Cleavage None
Fracture Conchoidal
Tenacity Brittle
Crystal form Orthorhombic

Morphology Long tabular crystals, radial aggregates, anhedral, uneven.
Origin and occurrence Anhedral in pegmatites, especially in alkali pegmatites.
Accessory minerals Feldspar, zircon, aegirine.
Similar minerals Thortveitite is not black; columbite has a black streak; aegirine has a greenish streak; tourmaline has a different streak and different crystal form.

2 Pseudobrookite

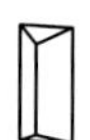

Chem. formula Fe_2TiO_5
Hardness 6, **Sp. gr.** 4.4
Color Red, black, red-black
Streak Brownish to reddish, yellow ocher
Luster Metallic
Cleavage Scarcely discernible
Fracture Conchoidal
Tenacity Brittle
Crystal form Orthorhombic

Morphology Prismatic to tabular crystals, euhedral and anhedral, acicular, euhedral sheaf-like and radial aggregates.
Origin and occurrence In vugs and cavities of volcanic rocks.
Accessory minerals Pyroxene, hornblende, tridymite, apatite, perovskite.
Similar minerals Taking the paragenesis into consideration, confusion is scarcely possible; enstatite and hypersthene have a different crystal form and do not have such a metallic luster.

3 Braunite

Chem. formula $MnMn_6SiO_{12}$
Hardness 6–6½, **Sp. gr.** 4.7–4.8
Color Black
Streak Dark brown
Luster Metallic
Cleavage Perfect, but normally poorly discernible
Fracture Uneven
Tenacity Brittle
Crystal form Tetragonal

Morphology Octahedral and cubic crystals, euhedral and anhedral, granular, uneven.
Origin and occurrence In metamorphic manganese deposits.
Accessory minerals Hausmannite, manganite, pyrolusite, psilomelane, barite, calcite.
Similar minerals Magnetite is clearly magnetic; hausmannite is often difficult to identify by simple means; typically, its crystal edges are usually folded; the formation of quintuplets is characteristic.

4 Rutile

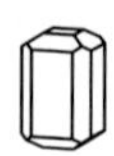

Chem. formula TiO_2
Hardness 6, **Sp. gr.** 4.2-4.3
Color Straw yellow, yellowish brown, brown-red, red, black
Streak Yellow to brown
Luster Adamantine to metallic
Cleavage Perfect prismatic but only discernible on thick crystals
Fracture Conchoidal
Tenacity Brittle
Crystal form Tetragonal

Morphology Prismatic to acicular, filiform, elbow-shaped twins, regular lattices (=saganite), together with hematite or ilmenite attractive stellate crystals.
Origin and occurrence In pegmatites, on alpine fissures, in metamorphic rocks and placers.
Accessory minerals Anatase, brookite, titanite, hematite.
Distinguishing feature Rutile often forms twins according to different laws, elbow-twinned with a flat angle and heart-shaped (geniculated) twins having an acute angle.
Similar minerals Tourmaline is harder and has a different luster; brookite and anatase have a different crystal form.

Localities	
1 Tjölling, Norway	**3** Langban, Sweden
2 Thomas Range, Utah, USA	**4** Itabira, Brazil

1
2
3
4

1 Tyrolite

Chem. formula $Ca_2Cu_9[(OH)_{10}/(AsO_4)_4] \cdot 10\,H_2O$
Hardness 2, **Sp. gr.** 3.2
Color Blue-green to light green
Streak Blue-green
Luster Pearly
Cleavage Basal perfect
Fracture Foliated
Tenacity Non-brittle, flexible flakes
Crystal form Orthorhombic

Morphology Thin tabular crystals, often intergrown to roses, botryoidal aggregates, uneven, drusy, as coating.
Origin and occurrence In the oxidation zone of copper deposits.
Accessory minerals Brochantite, langite, posnjakite.
Similar minerals Posnjakite is pure blue; brochantite is pure green; azurite is a darker blue; chalcophyllite has a different crystal form; clinotirolite is indistinguishable by simple means.

2 Clinotyrolite

Chem. formula $Ca_2Cu_9[(OH)_{10}/(AsO_4)_4] \cdot 10\,H_2O$
Hardness 2, **Sp. gr.** 3.2
Color Blue-green to light green
Streak Blue-green
Luster Pearly
Cleavage Basal perfect
Fracture Foliated
Tenacity Non-brittle, flexible flakes
Crystal form Monoclinic

Morphology Thin tabular crystals, often intergrown to roses, botryoidal aggregates, uneven, drusy, as coating.
Origin and occurrence In the oxidation zone of copper deposits.
Accessory minerals Brochantite, langite, posnjakite.
Similar minerals Posnjakite is pure blue; brochantite is pure green; azurite is a darker blue; chalcophyllite has a different crystal form; although it is much rarer, tirolite is indistinguishable by simple means.

3–4 Ktenasite

Chem. formula $(Cu,Zn)_3(SO_4)(OH)_4 \cdot 2\,H_2O$
Hardness 2–2½, **Sp. gr.** 2.9
Color Blue-green, green
Streak Greenish
Luster Vitreous
Cleavage Discernible
Fracture Uneven
Tenacity Brittle
Crystal form Monoclinic

Morphology Tabular crystals, planar crystal intergrowth, drusy, coatings, earthy.
Origin and occurrence In the oxidation zone of copper-zinc deposits.
Accessory minerals Glaucocerinite, serpierite, chalcanthite, azurite.
Similar minerals Glaucocerinite is softer; serpierite does not form tabular crystals but forms more acicular crystals; chalcantite is deep blue.

5 Chalkophyllite

Chem. formula $Cu_{18}Al_2[(OH)_{27}/(AsO_4)_3/(SO_4)_3] \cdot 36\,H_2O$
Hardness 2, **Sp. gr.** 2.67
Color Blue-green to emerald green
Streak Greenish
Luster Vitreous
Cleavage Perfect
Fracture Foliated
Tenacity Flexible
Crystal form Hexagonal

Morphology Thin tabular, hexagonal flakes, roses, encrustations.
Origin and occurrence In the oxidation zone of copper deposits that exhibit arsenical ore mineral content.
Accessory minerals Devilline, malachite, spangolite, tirolite.
Similar minerals Minerals with a green streak that could be confused with chalcophyllite do not form hexagonal small slabs; serpierite is more acicular; claringbullite has a white streak.

Localities

1 Brixlegg, Tyrol, Austria	**3** Rodalquilar, Spain	**5** Redruth, Cornwall, Great Britain
2 Molvizar, Spain	**4** Letmathe, Iserlohn, Germany	

1
2
3
5
4

1 Glauconite

Chem. formula $(K,Na)(Fe^{3+},Al,Mg)_2(Si,Al)_4O_{10}(OH)_2$
Hardness 2, **Sp. gr.** 2.4–2.95 (depending on iron content)
Color Green, yellow-green, blue-green
Streak Greenish
Luster Vitreous, pearly on cleavage faces
Cleavage Perfect
Fracture Foliated, earthy
Tenacity Non-brittle, inelastically flexible
Crystal form Monoclinic

Morphology Pseudomorphs after biotite, anhedral grains or nodules, uneven.
Origin and occurrence As an alteration product of biotite; formed in marine deposits under reducing conditions, in sandstones, in limestones.
Accessory minerals Quartz, feldspar, calcite, siderite, dolomite, glaucophane, ankerite, pyrite.
Distinguishing feature Glauconite is a coloring component of many types of colored clay, e.g. Bohemian green earth.
Similar minerals Micas are harder and elastically flexible; the paragenesis is absolutely typical.

2 Clinochlore

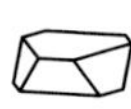

Chem. formula $(Fe,Mg,Al)_6[(OH)_2/(Si,Al)_4O_{10}]$
Hardness 2, **Sp. gr.** 2.6–3.3
Color Dark green to brown
Streak Green
Luster Vitreous, pearly
Cleavage Perfect
Fracture Foliated
Tenacity Non-brittle, inelastically flexible
Crystal form Monoclinic

Morphology Thick to thin tabular crystals, granular, sandy, foliated, uneven.
Origin and occurrence Rock-forming in metamorphic rocks (chlorite schist) and sediments, on alpine fissures, beautiful crystals here as well, partially forming roses.
Accessory minerals Grossular, almandine, rutile, muscovite, biotite, vesuvianite, diopside, quartz, adularia, pericline, apatite, magnetite, pyrite.
Similar minerals Micas are harder and, with the exception of margarite, elastically flexible.

3 Rhipidolite

Chem. formula $(Mg,Fe,Al)_6[(OH)_2/(Si,Al)_4O_{10}]$
Hardness 2, **Sp. gr.** 2.6–3.3
Color Dark green to brown
Streak Green
Luster Vitreous, pearly
Cleavage Perfect
Fracture Foliated
Tenacity Non-brittle, inelastically flexible
Crystal form Monoclinic

Morphology Thick to thin tabular crystals, worm-like curved aggregates, granular, sandy.
Origin and occurrence Essential mineral in metamorphic rocks (chlorite schist) and sediments, on alpine fissures, here also crystals, mainly worm-shaped.
Accessory minerals Grossular, almandine, rutile, muscovite, biotite, vesuvianite, diopside, quartz, adularia, pericline, apatite, magnetite, pyrite.
Similar minerals Micas are harder and, with the exception of margarite, elastically flexible.

4 Devilline

Chem. formula $CaCu_4[(OH)_6/(SO_4)_2 \cdot 3\,H_2O$
Hardness 2½, **Sp. gr.** 3.13
Color Blue to greenish blue
Streak Greenish
Luster Silky
Cleavage Perfect
Fracture Foliated
Tenacity Brittle
Crystal form Monoclinic

Morphology Foliated to long tabular crystals, sheaves, radial aggregates, foamy crystal encrustations, coatings.
Origin and occurrence In the oxidation zone of copper-zinc deposits.
Accessory minerals Gypsum, spangolite, serpierite, schulenbergite, aragonite, calcite.
Similar minerals In contrast to devilline, linarite turns white when dabbed with hydrochloric acid; serpierite is more acicular to prismatic; schulenbergite is foliated.

Localities

1 Bellegarde, France	**3** Zillertal, Austria
2 Val Casaccia, Switzerland	**4** Glücksrad Mine, Harz, Germany

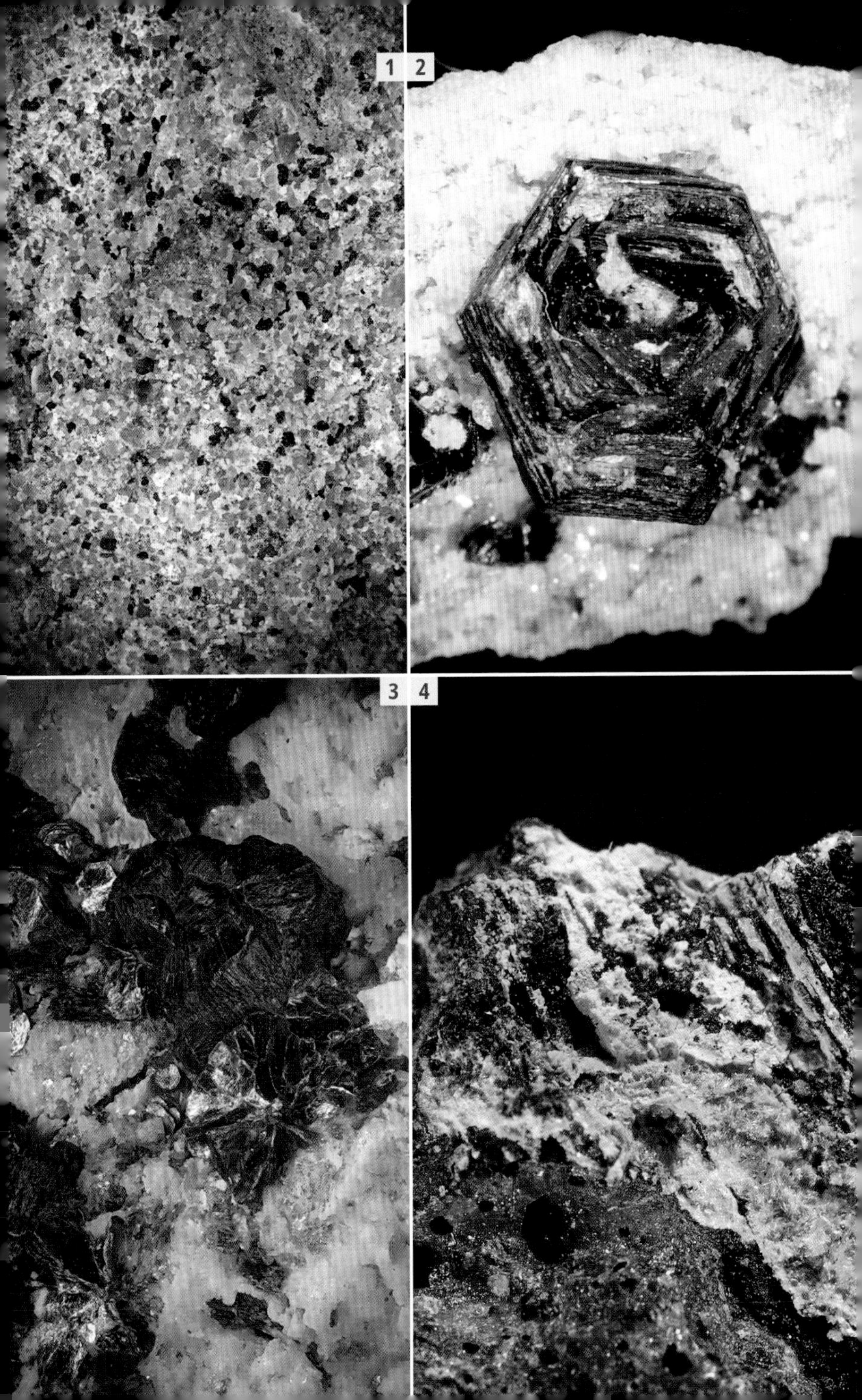
1
2
3
4

1 Torbernite

Chem. formula $Cu[UO_2/PO_4]_2 \cdot 8\text{-}12\ H_2O$
Hardness 2–2½, **Sp. gr.** 3.3–3.7.
Color Emerald green
Streak Green
Luster Vitreous, pearly on cleavage faces
Cleavage Perfect basal
Fracture Uneven
Tenacity Brittle to non-brittle
Crystal form Tetragonal

Morphology Thin to thick tabular crystals, bipyramidal, euhedral, earthy, drusy.
Origin and occurrence In the oxidation zone of copper and uranium deposits, on granite fissures.
Accessory minerals Autunite, uranocircite, fluorite, barite.
Similar minerals Unlike torbernite, autunite and uranocircite fluoresce when irradiated with UV light and tend to be more yellow; zeunerite cannot be distinguished by simple means although the paragenesis with arsenical minerals provides clues.
Caution! Torbernite is radioactive!

2 Zeunerite

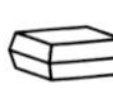

Chem. formula $Cu[UO_2/AsO_4]_2 \cdot 8\text{-}12\ H_2O$
Hardness 2–2½, **Sp. gr.** 3.79
Color Emerald green
Streak Green
Luster Vitreous, pearly on cleavage faces
Cleavage Perfect basal
Fracture Uneven
Tenacity Brittle to non-brittle
Crystal form Tetragonal

Morphology Thin to thick tabular crystals, bipyramidal, euhedral, earthy, drusy.
Origin and occurrence In the oxidation zone of copper and uranium deposits, on granite fissures.
Accessory minerals Autunite, uranocircite, fluorite, barite.
Similar minerals Unlike zeunerite, autunite and uranocircite fluoresce when irradiated with UV light and tend to be more yellow; torbernite cannot be distinguished by simple means although the paragenesis of zeunerite with arsenical minerals provides clues.
Caution! Zeunerite is radioactive!

3 Clinoclase

Chem. formula $Cu_3[(OH)_3/AsO_4]$
Hardness 2½–3, **Sp. gr.** 4.2–4.4
Color Greenish to dark blue
Streak Blueish green
Luster Vitreous
Cleavage Perfect
Fracture Foliated
Tenacity Brittle
Crystal form Monoclinic

Morphology Prismatic to tabular crystals, radial, reniform, drusy, as coating.
Origin and occurrence In the oxidation zone of copper deposits.
Accessory minerals Olivenite, azurite, malachite.
Similar minerals Azurite is a purer blue and has a blue streak; ktenasite is greener; chalcophyllite is not so dark blue.

4 Nissonite

Chem. formula $Cu_2Mg_2(PO_4)(OH)_2 \cdot 5\ H_2O$
Hardness 2½, **Sp. gr.** 2.73
Color Blue-green
Streak Greenish
Luster Vitreous
Cleavage Poorly discernible
Fracture Uneven
Tenacity Brittle
Crystal form Monoclinic

Morphology Tabular to long tabular crystals, mainly encrustations, coatings, uneven.
Origin and occurrence In the oxidation zone of copper deposits as an alteration product of copper ores.
Accessory minerals Turquoise, chrysocolla, azurite, malachite.
Similar minerals Chrysocolla is difficult to distinguish from course nissonite; malachite is distinctly emerald green; serpierite is bluer; schulenbergite is foliated; connellite is deep blue.

Localities

1 Rudolfstein, Fichtel Mountains, Germany	**3** Majuba Hill, Nevada, USA
2 Wittichen, Black Forest, Germany	**4** Panoche Valley, California, USA

1
2
3
4

1 Chrysocolla

Chem. formula $CuSiO_3$ + aq.
Hardness 2–4, **Sp. gr.** 2–2.2
Color Light blue, blue, green-blue
Streak Greenish white
Luster Vitreous, somewhat greasy
Cleavage None
Fracture Conchoidal
Tenacity Brittle
Crystal form Mainly amorphic

Morphology Botryoidal, reniform masses, stellate aggregates, drusy, stalactitic, uneven, often pseudomorphs after other copper minerals, for example azurite.
Origin and occurrence In the oxidation zone of copper deposits.
Accessory minerals Cuprite, malachite, azurite, limonite.
Similar minerals Malachite has a different color; turquoise is harder; azurite is always a darker and more intense blue; lapis lazuli and sodalite are harder.

2 Chrysocolla

Gemstone

Color Blue to blue-green, often with green and black intergrowths
Streak Greenish white
Luster Vitreous
Shape and Cut Cabochon cut, spheres

Use Cabochons as ring stones and for brooches, pendants, spheres for stone necklaces, also often as handicraft items.
Differentiation The practically always present intergrowths with malachite (green) make the stone very typical and unmistakable in appearance.

3 Olivenite

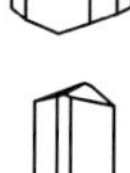

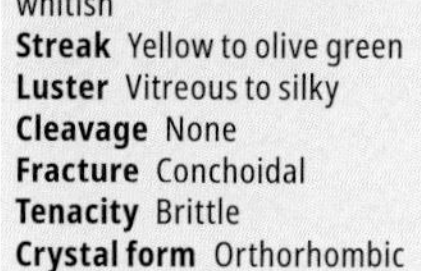

Chem. formula $Cu_2[OH/AsO_4]$
Hardness 3, **Sp. gr.** 4.3
Color Light green to olive green, black-green, brown, whitish
Streak Yellow to olive green
Luster Vitreous to silky
Cleavage None
Fracture Conchoidal
Tenacity Brittle
Crystal form Orthorhombic

Morphology Tabular to prismatic crystals, acicular, filiform, fibrous, stellate, botryoidal, reniform aggregates, earthy, uneven.
Origin and occurrence In the oxidation zone of copper deposits.
Accessory minerals Cornwallite, clinoclase, azurite, malachite, agardite, limonite.
Similar minerals Adamine is normally a much lighter green but is often difficult to distinguish in the copper-bearing variety cupro-adamine; the same applies to libethenite although the paragenesis with other arsenical minerals hints at the presence of olivenite.

4 Libethenite

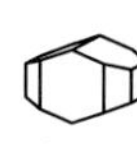

Chem. formula $Cu_2[OH/PO_4]$
Hardness 3, **Sp. gr.** 4.3
Color Light green to olive green, black-green
Streak Green
Luster Vitreous
Cleavage None
Fracture Conchoidal
Tenacity Brittle
Crystal form Monoclinic

Morphology Pseudo-orthorhombic, tabular to prismatic crystals, acicular, stellate, botryoidal, reniform aggregates.
Origin and occurrence In the oxidation zone of copper deposits.
Accessory minerals Pseudomalachite, azurite, malachite, chalcosiderite.
Similar minerals Adamine is usually a much lighter green but is often difficult to distinguish in the copper-bearing variety cupro-adamine. The same applies to olivenite, but the paragenesis with other phosphorus-bearing minerals hints at the presence of libethenite.

Localities

1 Eilath, Israel	**3** Wheal Gorland, Cornwall, Great Britain
2 Ajo, Arizona, USA	**4** Estremoz, Portugal

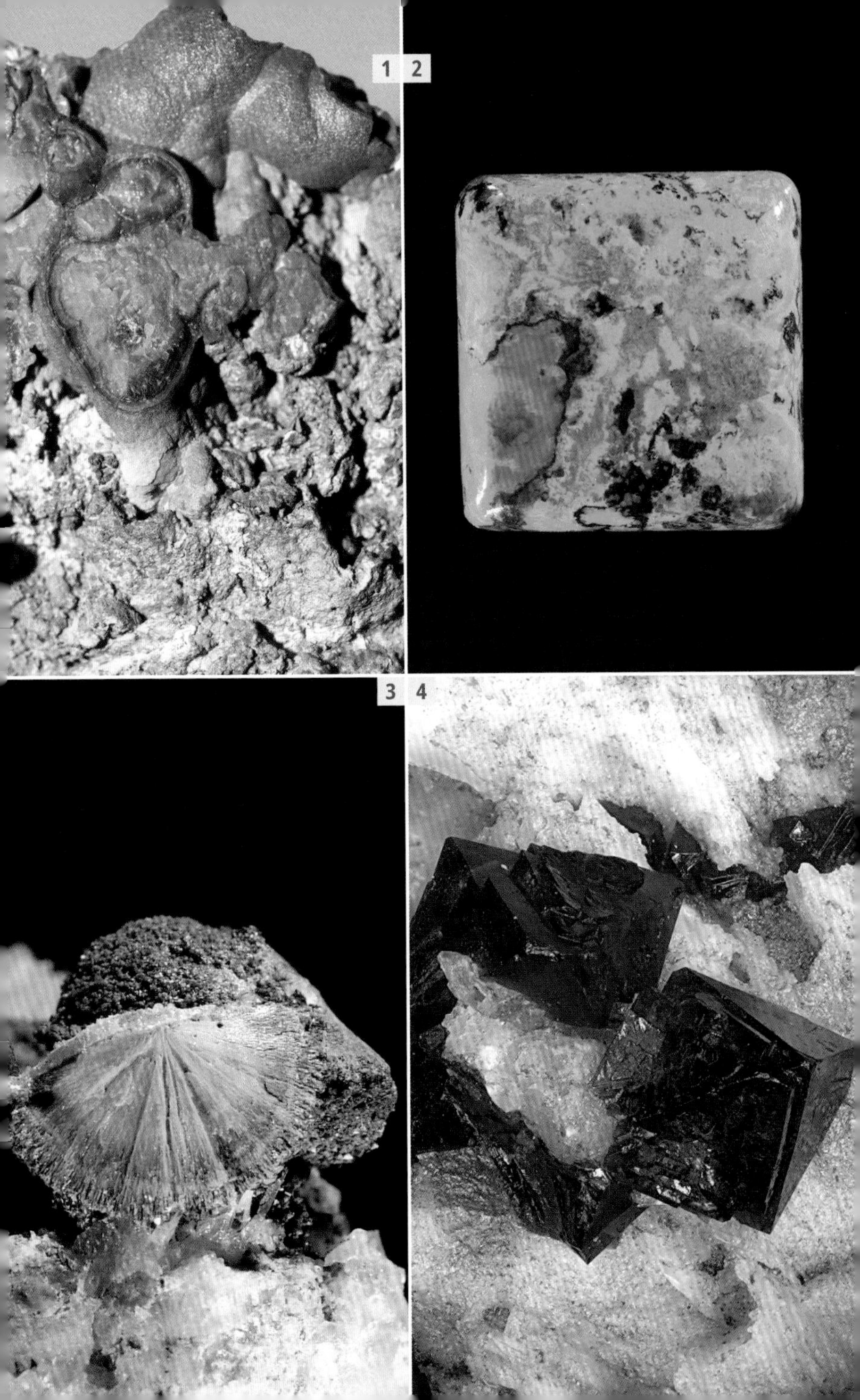
1
2
3
4

1 Atacamite

Chem. formula $Cu_2(OH)_3Cl$
Hardness 3–3½, **Sp. gr.** 3.76
Color Emerald green to blackish green
Streak Green
Luster Vitreous
Cleavage Perfect
Fracture Conchoidal
Tenacity Brittle
Crystal form Orthorhombic

Morphology Prismatic to acicular crystals, rarely tabular, radial, foliated, drusy, uneven as bloom.
Origin and occurrence In the oxidation zone of copper deposits, particularly in arid desert climates.
Accessory minerals Cuprite, malachite, native copper, claringbullite, connellite.
Similar minerals Malachite effervesces when dabbed with hydrochloric acid; brochantite is slightly harder and not as blackish green as atacamite.

2 Hagendorfite

Chem. formula $(Na,Ca)_2(Fe,Mn)_3[PO_4]_3$
Hardness 4, **Sp. gr.** 3.5–3.7
Color Black-green
Streak Green
Luster Vitreous to greasy
Cleavage Distinct in three directions
Fracture Crystalline
Tenacity Brittle
Crystal form Monoclinic

Morphology Rarely anhedral crystals, prismatic, usually uneven, crystalline masses, intergrown with other primary phosphates.
Origin and occurrence In phosphate pegmatites.
Accessory minerals Zwieselite, triphyline, wolfeite, pyrite, arrojadite, quartz, feldspar.
Similar minerals Confusion between hagendorfite and other phosphates is almost impossible: Rockbridgeite is always radial; hornblende exhibits distinct cleavage with a 120° cleavage angle.

3 Mottramite

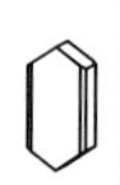

Chem. formula $Pb(Cu,Zn)[OH/VO_4]$
Hardness 3½, **Sp. gr.** 5.7–6.2
Color Olive green to black-green
Streak Green
Luster Resinous
Cleavage None
Fracture Uneven
Tenacity Brittle
Crystal form Orthorhombic

Morphology Rarely prismatic crystals, mainly radial, drusy, reniform aggregates, dendritic.
Origin and occurrence In the oxidation zone of vanadium-rich lead and copper deposits.
Accessory minerals Descloizite, azurite, malachite, vanadinite, mimetesite, calcite.
Similar minerals Descloizite is browner; malachite effervesces when dabbed with hydrochloric acid and is more emerald green; ktenasite is more bluish; brochantite is distinctly emerald green, as is atacamite.

4 Brochantite

Chem. formula $Cu_4[(OH)_6/SO_4]$
Hardness 3½–4, **Sp. gr.** 3.97
Color Emerald green
Streak Green to light green
Luster Vitreous, pearly on cleavage faces
Cleavage Perfect, but normally indiscernible because of the acicular crystals
Fracture Uneven
Tenacity Brittle
Crystal form Monoclinic

Morphology Acicular, rarely tabular crystals, stellate, fibrous, reniform aggregates, granular, earthy.
Origin and occurrence In the oxidation zone of copper deposits.
Accessory minerals Malachite, azurite, langite, posnjakite, atacamite, cuprite.
Similar minerals Malachite effervesces when dabbed with hydrochloric acid; atacamite is softer and normally somewhat darker; olivite is not so emerald green, nor are cornwallite or pseudomalachite. In contrast to brochantite, langite is bluer.

Localities

1 La Farola, Chile	**3** Tsumeb, Namibia
2 Hagendorf-Süd, East Bavaria, Germany	**4** Potrerillos, Chile

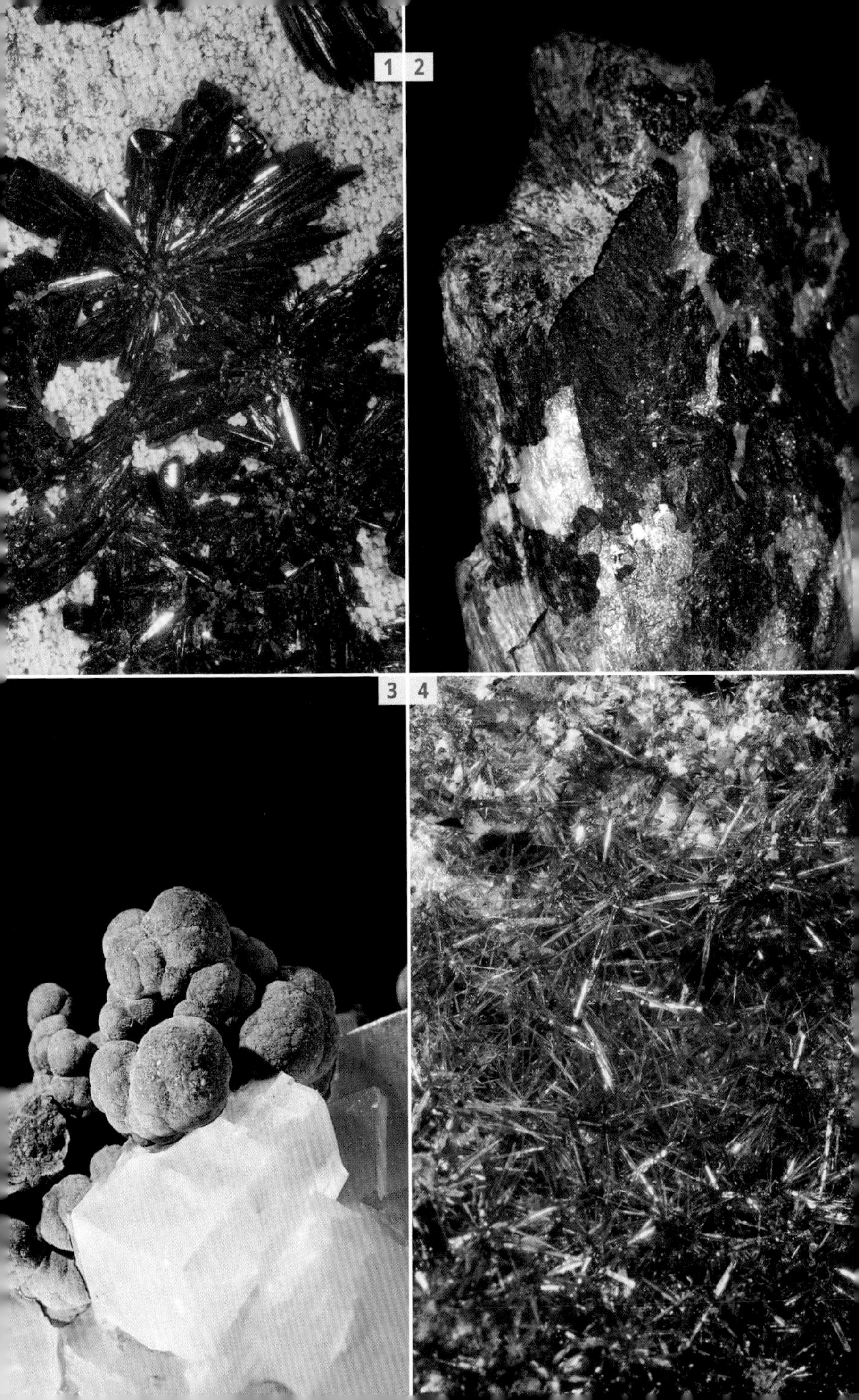
1 2
3 4

1 Euchroite

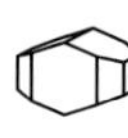

Chem. formula $Cu_2AsO_4OH \cdot 3\,H_2O$
Hardness 3½–4, **Sp. gr.** 3.45
Color Green
Streak Green
Luster Vitreous
Cleavage Indiscernible
Fracture Conchoidal
Tenacity Brittle
Crystal form Orthorhombic

Morphology Short prismatic to thick tabular crystals, usually euhedral.
Origin and occurrence In the oxidation zone of copper deposits.
Accessory minerals Libethenite, azurite, malachite, olivite, dolomite, calcite.
Similar minerals Olivenite and libethenite have a different crystal form; malachite and brochantite are mostly acicular and more emerald green; olivite is more olive green.

2 Zaratite

Chem. formula $Ni_3CO_3(OH)_4 \cdot 4\,H_2O$
Hardness 3½, **Sp. gr.** 2.6–2.7
Color Emerald green
Streak Green
Luster Vitreous
Cleavage None
Fracture Conchoidal
Tenacity Brittle
Crystal form Cubic

Morphology Uneven, drusy, thin glassy coatings, earthy, dense masses.
Origin and occurrence Euhedral in serpentine rocks on fissures, formed during the weathering of primary nickel minerals.
Accessory minerals Serpentine, chromite, millerite, asbestos, annabergite, garnierite.
Similar minerals If paragenesis and color are considered, it cannot be confused with other minerals; annabergite has a different crystal form and is not as glassy; antigorite serpentine is foliated.

3 Arthurite

Chem. formula $Cu_2Fe_4(AsO_4)_4(O,OH)_4 \cdot 8\,H_2O$
Hardness 3–4, **Sp. gr.** 3.02
Color Apple green to yellowish emerald green
Streak Greenish
Luster Vitreous
Cleavage Indiscernible
Fracture Uneven
Tenacity Brittle
Crystal form Monoclinic

Morphology Prismatic to acicular crystals, loose sheaves, fibrous, stellate or reniform aggregates, drusy, uneven.
Origin and occurrence In the oxidation zone of copper deposits.
Accessory minerals Pharmacosiderite, beudantite, olivite, malachite, jarosite, azurite.
Similar minerals Fine-fibered olivite is often not easily distinguishable from arthurite using simple means; however, arthurite is usually slightly more yellowish green; malachite and brochantite exhibit a purer emerald green.

4 Antlerite

Chem. formula $Cu_3SO_4(OH)_4$
Hardness 3½, **Sp. gr.** 3.8–3.9
Color Emerald green
Streak Green
Luster Vitreous
Cleavage Perfect
Fracture Uneven
Tenacity Brittle
Crystal form Orthorhombic

Morphology Thick tabular to short prismatic crystals, fibrous aggregates, flaky masses, acicular.
Origin and occurrence In the oxidation zone of copper-bearing deposits.
Accessory minerals Malachite, atacamite, chalcopyrite, chalcocite, calcite.
Similar minerals Unlike antlerite, malachite effervesces when dabbed with diluted hydrochloric acid; atacamite is a relatively darker green.

Localities	
1 Libethen, Slovakia	**3** Chovar, Spain
2 Lord Brassey Mine, Tasmania, Australia	**4** Bisbee, Arizona, USA

1
2
3
4

1 Agardite-Ce

Chem. formula $(Ce,Ca)_2Cu_{12}[(OH)_{12}/(AsO_4)_6] \cdot 6\,H_2O$
Hardness 3–4, **Sp. gr.** 3.6–3.7
Color Yellowish green to blueish green
Streak Pale green
Luster Vitreous
Cleavage Indiscernible
Fracture Uneven
Crystal form Hexagonal

Morphology Acicular, fibrous, felt-like.
Origin and occurrence In the oxidation zone of copper deposits, formed in the presence of small amounts of rare earth elements in the primary ores (for example, as xenotime).
Accessory minerals Adamine, olivite, limonite, malachite, azurite.
Similar minerals Differentiating the individual agardite minerals among one another and from mixite is impossible using simple means. Malachite effervesces when dabbed with diluted hydrochloric acid.

2 Agardite-Y

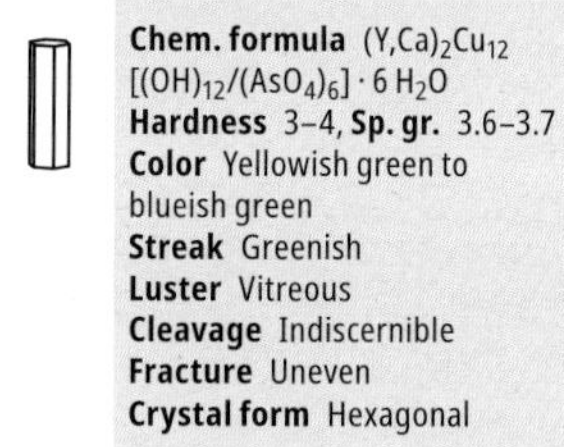

Chem. formula $(Y,Ca)_2Cu_{12}[(OH)_{12}/(AsO_4)_6] \cdot 6\,H_2O$
Hardness 3–4, **Sp. gr.** 3.6–3.7
Color Yellowish green to blueish green
Streak Greenish
Luster Vitreous
Cleavage Indiscernible
Fracture Uneven
Crystal form Hexagonal

Morphology Acicular, fibrous, felt-like.
Origin and occurrence In the oxidation zone of copper deposits, formed in the presence of small amounts of rare earth elements in the primary ores (for example, as xenotime).
Accessory minerals Adamine, olivite, limonite, malachite, azurite.
Similar minerals Differentiating the individual agardite minerals among one another and from mixite is impossible using simple means; malachite effervesces when dabbed with hydrochloric acid.

3 Agardite-La

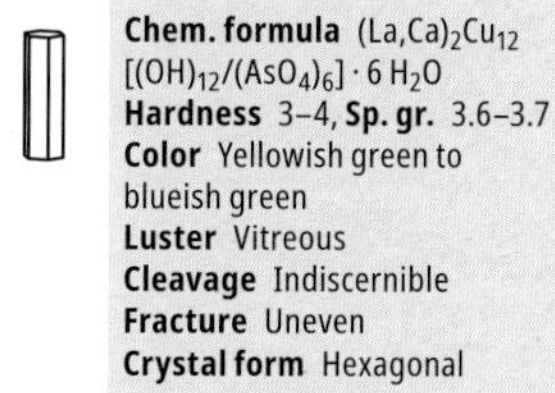

Chem. formula $(La,Ca)_2Cu_{12}[(OH)_{12}/(AsO_4)_6] \cdot 6\,H_2O$
Hardness 3–4, **Sp. gr.** 3.6–3.7
Color Yellowish green to blueish green
Luster Vitreous
Cleavage Indiscernible
Fracture Uneven
Crystal form Hexagonal

Morphology Acicular, fibrous, felt-like.
Origin and occurrence In the oxidation zone of copper deposits, formed in the presence of small amounts of rare earth elements in the primary ores (for example, as xenotime).
Accessory minerals Adamine, olivite, limonite, malachite, azurite.
Similar minerals Differentiating the individual agardite minerals among one another and from mixite is impossible using simple means; malachite effervesces when dabbed with hydrochloric acid.

4 Mixite

Chem. formula $(Bi,CaH)Cu_6[(OH)_6/(AsO_4)_3] \cdot 3\,H_2O$
Hardness 3–4, **Sp. gr.** 3.8
Color Blueish green to yellow-green
Streak Green
Luster Vitreous to silky
Cleavage Indiscernible
Fracture Fibrous
Tenacity Brittle
Crystal form Hexagonal

Morphology Acicular crystals, filiform, stellate, earthy, drusy, uneven.
Origin and occurrence In the oxidation zone of arsenic-rich bismuth-cobalt-nickel deposits.
Accessory minerals Pharmacosiderite, zeunerite, emplectite, wittichenite.
Similar minerals The minerals of the agardite group are not easily distinguished by simple means, but the paragenesis with bismuth ores often provides clues.

Localities	
1 Clara Mine, Black Forest, Germany	**3** Lavrion, Greece
2 Bou Skour, Morocco	**4** El Pinar, Spain

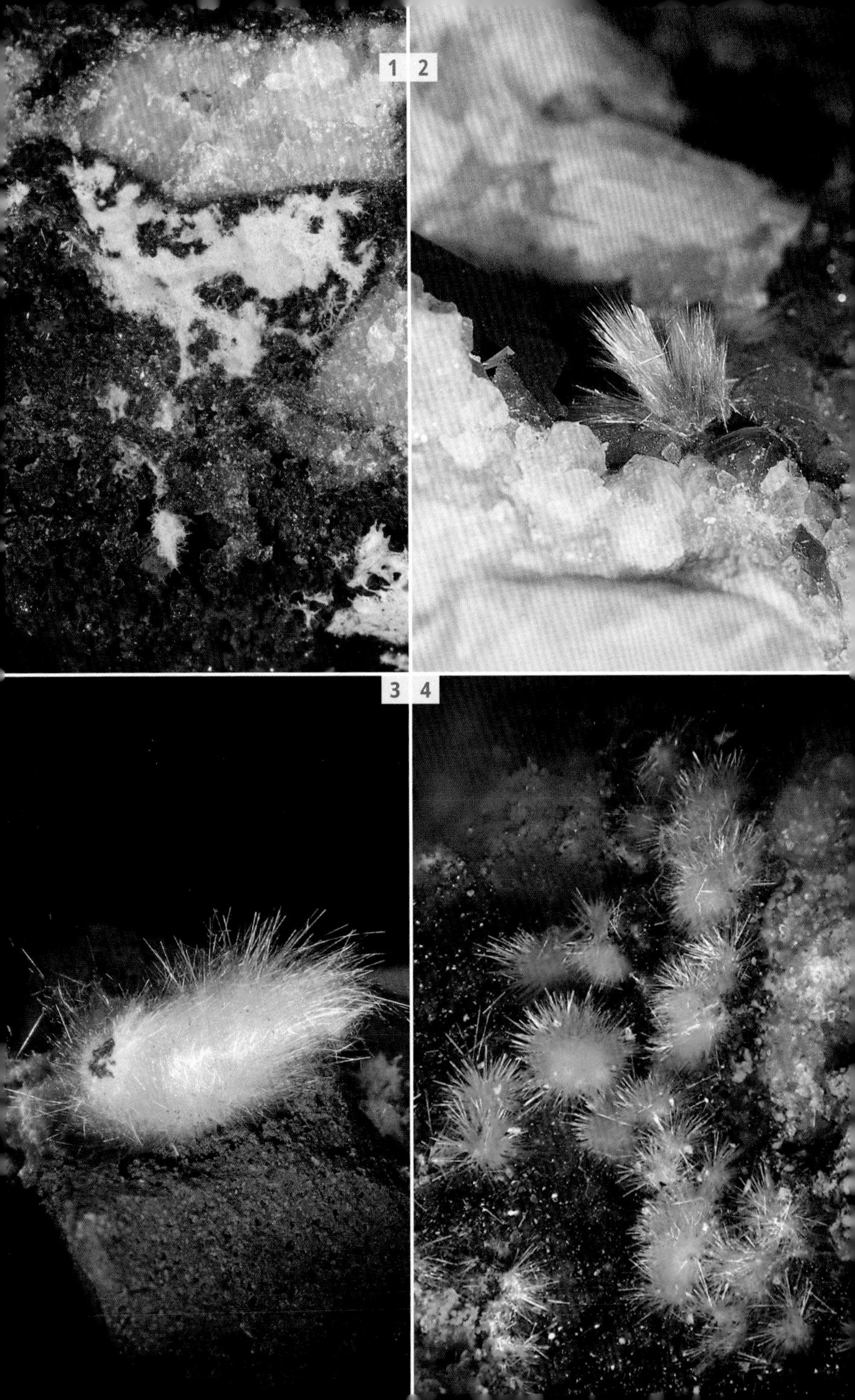
1
2
3
4

1 Spangolite

Chem. formula $Cu_6AlSO_4(OH)_{12}Cl \cdot 3\,H_2O$
Hardness 3, **Sp. gr.** 3.14
Color Dark green to blue-green
Streak Pale green
Luster Vitreous
Cleavage Perfect
Fracture Uneven
Tenacity Brittle
Crystal form Hexagonal

Morphology Short prismatic to thick tabular crystals, encrustations, coatings.
Origin and occurrence In the oxidation zone of copper deposits.
Accessory minerals Serpierite, brochantite, azurite, malachite, cuproadamine.
Similar minerals Chalcophyllite and devilline are always thin tabular crystals; serpierite forms more acicular to long tabular crystals; langite has a different crystal form; azurite has a blue streak.

2 Dufrenite

Chem. formula $Fe^{2+}Fe_4^{3+}(OH)_5(PO_4)_3 \cdot H_2O$
Hardness 3½–4, **Sp. gr.** 3.1–3.3
Color Yellow-green to black-green, brown due to oxidation
Streak Green
Luster Vitreous to dull
Cleavage Perfect
Fracture Uneven
Tenacity Brittle
Crystal form Monoclinic

Morphology Thick tabular crystals, clothespin-like twins, radial coatings, botryoidal aggregates, coatings, uneven masses.
Origin and occurrence In phosphate pegmatites through the alteration of primary phosphates, in phosphorus-rich brown iron deposits.
Accessory minerals Hureaulite, laubmannite, rockbridgeite, goethite.
Similar minerals Rockbridgeite is blacker; the clothespin-like twins of kraurite are highly typical.

3 Laubmannite

Chem. formula $Fe_3^{2+}Fe_6^{3+}[(OH)_3/PO_4]_4$
Hardness 4, **Sp. gr.** 3.3
Color Gray-green to olive green, yellow-green
Streak Green
Luster Vitreous
Cleavage Indiscernible
Fracture Fibrous
Tenacity Brittle
Crystal form Orthorhombic

Morphology Acicular to fibrous crystals, sheaves, stellate aggregates, botryoidal, reniform coatings and encrustations.
Origin and occurrence In phosphorus-bearing brown iron deposits.
Accessory minerals Rockbridgeite, beraunite, strengite, cacoxenite, kaurite.
Similar minerals Rockbridgeite is normally darker but sometimes difficult to distinguish from laubmannite; the latter may form acicular proliferations on rockbridgeite; cacoxenite is more golden yellow; strunzite is more straw yellow.

4 Kidwellite

Chem. formula $NaFe_9(PO_4)_6(OH)_{10} \cdot 5\,H_2O$
Hardness 4, **Sp. gr.** 2.5
Color Yellowish green
Streak Greenish
Luster Vitreous
Cleavage Indiscernible
Fracture Fibrous
Tenacity Brittle
Crystal form Monoclinic

Morphology Acicular crystals, fibrous, stellate encrustations, coatings.
Origin and occurrence As an alteration formation of primary phosphates in phosphate deposits.
Accessory minerals Rockbridgeite, strengite, kaurite, laubmannite, goethite.
Similar minerals Beraunite usually only forms single sheaves and no dense encrustations; laubmannite has a lighter colored streak, but is difficult to distinguish by simple means.

Localities

1 Lavrion, Greece	**3** Rothläufchen Mine, Giessen, Germany
2 Eleonore Mine, Giessen, Germany	**4** Polk County, Arkansas, USA

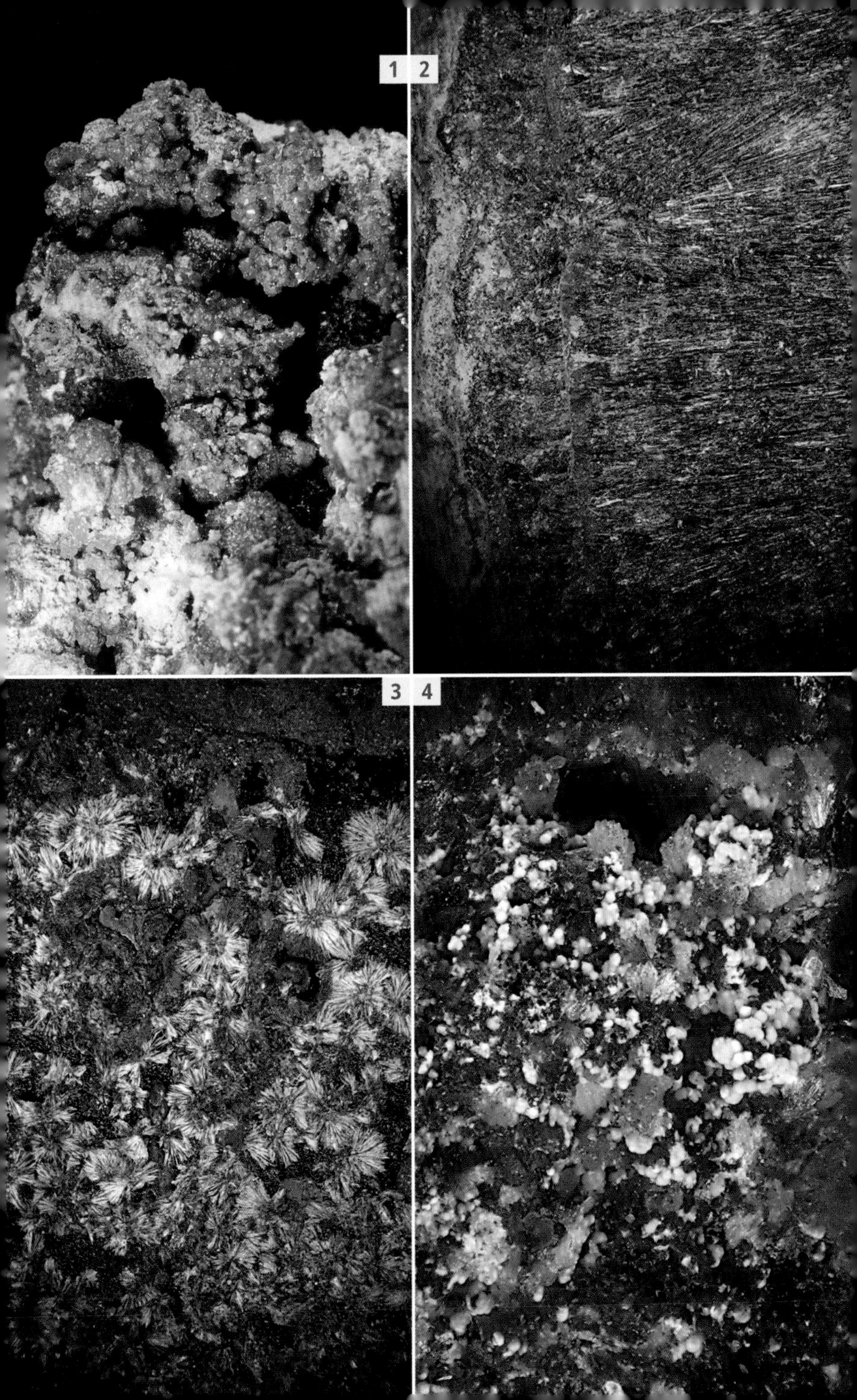
1
2
3
4

1–3 Malachite

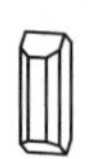

Chem. formula $Cu_2[(OH)_2/CO_3]$
Hardness 4, **Sp. gr.** 4
Color Emerald green to light green
Streak Green
Luster Vitreous, silky luster in aggregates, also dull
Cleavage Good, but practically indistinct due to mostly acicular or fibrous morphology
Fracture Conchoidal
Tenacity Brittle
Crystal form Monoclinic

Morphology Acicular sheaves, tabular to prismatic crystals, fibrous, radial, reniform encrustations, uneven, earthy.
Origin and occurrence In the oxidation zone of copper deposits; here it's the most common oxidation mineral.
Accessory minerals Limonite, azurite, brochantite, cuprite, native copper and many other copper oxidation minerals.
Distinguishing feature Malachite often forms pseudomorphs after azurite crystals. At the same time, the crystal form of the azurite remains the same, while the color changes to green.
Similar minerals Minerals that could be confused do not effervesce when dabbed with diluted hydrochloric acid.

4 Malachite

Gemstone

Color Green, mainly with typical lighter and darker stratification
Luster Vitreous
Shape and Cut Cabochon cut, spheres

Use Cabochons rarely as ring stones and for brooches, pendants, spheres for stone necklaces, also often as handicraft items. Moreover, malachite is very soft and dulls quickly with use. It is sensitive to acids and alkalis.
Differentiation The more or less always present stratifications make the stone very typical and unmistakable in appearance.

5 Pseudomalachite

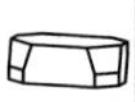

Chem. formula $Cu_5[(OH)_2/PO_4]_2$
Hardness 4½, **Sp. gr.** 4.34
Color Dark to blackish green
Streak Green
Luster Vitreous to greasy
Cleavage None
Fracture Conchoidal
Tenacity Brittle
Crystal form Monoclinic

Morphology Tabular crystals are rather rare, mainly stellate aggregates, reniform aggregates, drusy, earthy.
Origin and occurrence In the oxidation zone of copper deposits.
Accessory minerals Malachite, libethenite.
Similar minerals Unlike pseudomalachite, malachite effervesces when dabbed with diluted hydrochloric acid; cornwallite is indistinguishable by simple means, but the paragenesis of pseudo-malachite, together with phosphorus-bearing minerals, always provides clues.

6 Cornwallite

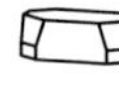

Chem. formula $Cu_5[(OH)_2/AsO_4]_2$
Hardness 4½–5, **Sp. gr.** 4–4.1
Color Emerald green
Streak Green
Luster Vitreous
Cleavage None
Fracture Conchoidal
Tenacity Brittle
Crystal form Monoclinic

Morphology Tabular crystals, botryoidal, stellate aggregates, drusy, reniform, earthy.
Origin and occurrence In the oxidation zone of copper deposits.
Accessory minerals Olivenite, chlorotile, clinoclase, malachite, conichalcite.
Similar minerals Unlike cornwallite, malachite effervesces when dabbed with diluted hydrochloric acid; pseudomalachite is indistinguishable by simple means but never occurs with arsenical minerals.

Localities		
1 Friedrich Mine, Siegerland Region, Germany	**3** Kamariza, Greece	**5** Nishni Tagil, Russia
2 Friedrich Mine, Siegerland Region, Germany	**4** Shaba, Zaire	**6** Clara Mine, Black Forest, Germany

1
2
3
4
5
6

1 Bayldonite

Chem. formula $PbCu_3[OH/AsO_4]_2$
Hardness 4½, **Sp. gr.** 5.5
Color Green to yellow-green
Streak Green
Luster Resinous
Cleavage None
Fracture Uneven
Tenacity Brittle
Crystal form Monoclinic

Morphology Thick tabular crystals, pseudohexagonal triplets, drusy, stellate, often as prismatic pseudomorphs after mimetesite (Fig. 1), which often still display interior mimetesite residues.
Origin and occurrence In the oxidation zone of copper-lead deposits.
Accessory minerals Mimetesite, azurite, malachite, cerussite.
Similar minerals Malachite is always acicular; olivite has a different crystal form, as do conichalcite, cornwallite and pseudomalachite.

2 Chalcosiderite

Chem. formula $CuFe_6[(OH)_8/(PO_4)_4] \cdot 4\,H_2O$
Hardness 4½, **Sp. gr.** 3.22
Color Dark green
Streak Green
Luster Vitreous
Cleavage Perfect
Fracture Uneven
Tenacity Brittle
Crystal form Triclinic

Morphology Short prismatic to thick tabular crystals, encrustations, coatings, uneven.
Origin and occurrence In the oxidation zone of copper deposits, in phosphate pegmatites.
Accessory minerals Malachite, olivite, libethenite, pseudomalachite, cacoxenite, turquoise.
Similar minerals Olivenite and libethenite have a different crystal form, as does pseudomalachite. Malachite and brochantite are almost always acicular.

3 Conichalcite

Chem. formula $CaCu[OH/AsO_4]$
Hardness 4½, **Sp. gr.** 4.33
Color Light green to apple green
Streak Light green
Luster Vitreous
Cleavage Indiscernible
Fracture Uneven
Tenacity Brittle
Crystal form Orthorhombic

Morphology Rarely prismatic crystals, mainly stellate, reniform aggregates, warty, drusy, uneven coatings.
Origin and occurrence In the oxidation zone of copper deposits together with other aresenate minerals.
Accessory minerals Cuproadamine, olivite, beudantite, scorodite, azurite, malachite.
Similar minerals The apple green color is very characteristic and distinguishes conichalcite from malachite, olivenite, cuprian adamite or cornwallite. Skorodite can be greenish but exhibits a different crystal form.

4 Rockbridgeite *Green iron ore*

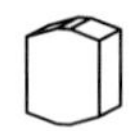

Chem. formula $(Fe,Mn)Fe_4[(OH)_5/(PO_4)_3]$
Hardness 4½, **Sp. gr.** 3.4
Color Black, black-green
Streak Green
Luster Vitreous
Cleavage Present, but only scarcely discernible
Fracture Uneven
Tenacity Brittle
Crystal form Orthorhombic

Morphology Prismatic to tabular crystals, often stellate aggregates, hematite-type, reniform, drusy, fibrous, uneven.
Origin and occurrence In phosphate pegmatites as an alteration product of primary phosphate minerals and in phosphorus-rich brown iron deposits.
Accessory minerals Beraunite, strengite, phosphosiderite, apatite, limonite.
Similar minerals Color and streak are highly characteristic. If the typical occurrence is also taken into consideration, confusion is rarely a possibility; the close relative frondelite is always brown.

Localities	
1 Tsumeb, Namibia	**3** Lavrion, Greece
2 Estremoz, Portugal	**4** Siegerland Region, Germany

1
2
3
4

1 Gormanite

Chem. formula $Fe_3Al_4(PO_4)_4(OH)_6 \cdot 2\,H_2O$
Hardness 4–5, **Sp. gr.** 3.1–3.2
Color Blue-green to green
Streak Greenish
Luster Vitreous
Cleavage Mainly indiscernible
Fracture Splintery
Tenacity Brittle
Crystal form Triclinic

Morphology Acicular crystals, crystal sheaves, stellate aggregates.
Origin and occurrence On fissures of phosphorus-rich sediments, on fissures of tonalites.
Accessory minerals Quartz, whiteite, lazulite, kulanite, baricite, siderite.
Similar minerals Vivianite is softer; azurite is a darker blue and occurs in a completely different paragenesis; it also has a blue streak. Blue beryl is considerably harder; kulanite is greener. Lazulite is not so acicular.

2 Dioptase

Chem. formula $Cu_6[Si_6O_{18}] \cdot 6\,H_2O$
Hardness 5, **Sp. gr.** 3.3
Color Emerald green
Streak Green
Luster Vitreous
Cleavage Basic rhombohdral distinct
Fracture Conchoidal
Tenacity Brittle
Crystal form Trigonal

Morphology Long to short prismatic crystals, acicular, radial aggregates.
Origin and occurrence In the oxidation zone of copper deposits, especially with silicic country rock.
Accessory minerals Malachite, azurite, duftite, wulfenite, cerussite, chrysocolla, quartz.
Similar minerals Malachite has a different crystal form and effervesces when dabbed with diluted hydrochloric acid; emerald is much harder and has a different crystal form.

3 Omphacite

Chem. formula $(Ca,Na)(Mg,Al)(Si,Al)_2O_6$
Hardness 6, **Sp. gr.** 3.3–3.4
Color Green, black
Streak Greenish
Luster Vitreous
Cleavage Good
Fracture Uneven
Tenacity Brittle
Crystal form Monoclinic

Morphology Rarely prismatic to tabular crystals, radial, uneven, granular, anhedral.
Origin and occurrencev Rock-forming in eclogites and some kimberlites, less common in blue schists.
Accessory minerals Pyrope, kyanite, muscovite, corundum, hornblende, epidote, scapolite.
Similar minerals Grossular and vesuvianite have a white streak; actinolite exhibits a different cleavage with a 120° cleavage angle; diopside has a different streak; olivine has a different crystal form.

4 Pumpellyite

Chem. formula $Ca_2MgAl_2[(OH)_2/Si_2O_7] \cdot H_2O$
Hardness 5½, **Sp. gr.** 3.2
Color Gray-green, black-green, dark green
Streak Gray-green to green
Luster Vitreous
Cleavage None
Fracture Conchoidal to uneven
Tenacity Brittle
Crystal form Monoclinic

Morphology Rarely prismatic crystals, mainly acicular, stellate, fibrous.
Origin and occurrence In metamorphic rocks, in bubble cavities of volcanic rocks, in vugs of pegmatites.
Accessory minerals Epidote, stilbite, chabazite, laumontite, heulandite.
Similar Minerals Epidote is not as acicular and relatively harder; actinolite exhibits a distinct cleavage with a 120° cleavage angle.

Localities

1 Rapid Creek, Yukon Territory, Canada	**3** Fichtel Mountains, Bavaria, Germany
2 Altyn Tyube, Kazakhstan	**4** Norilsk, Russia

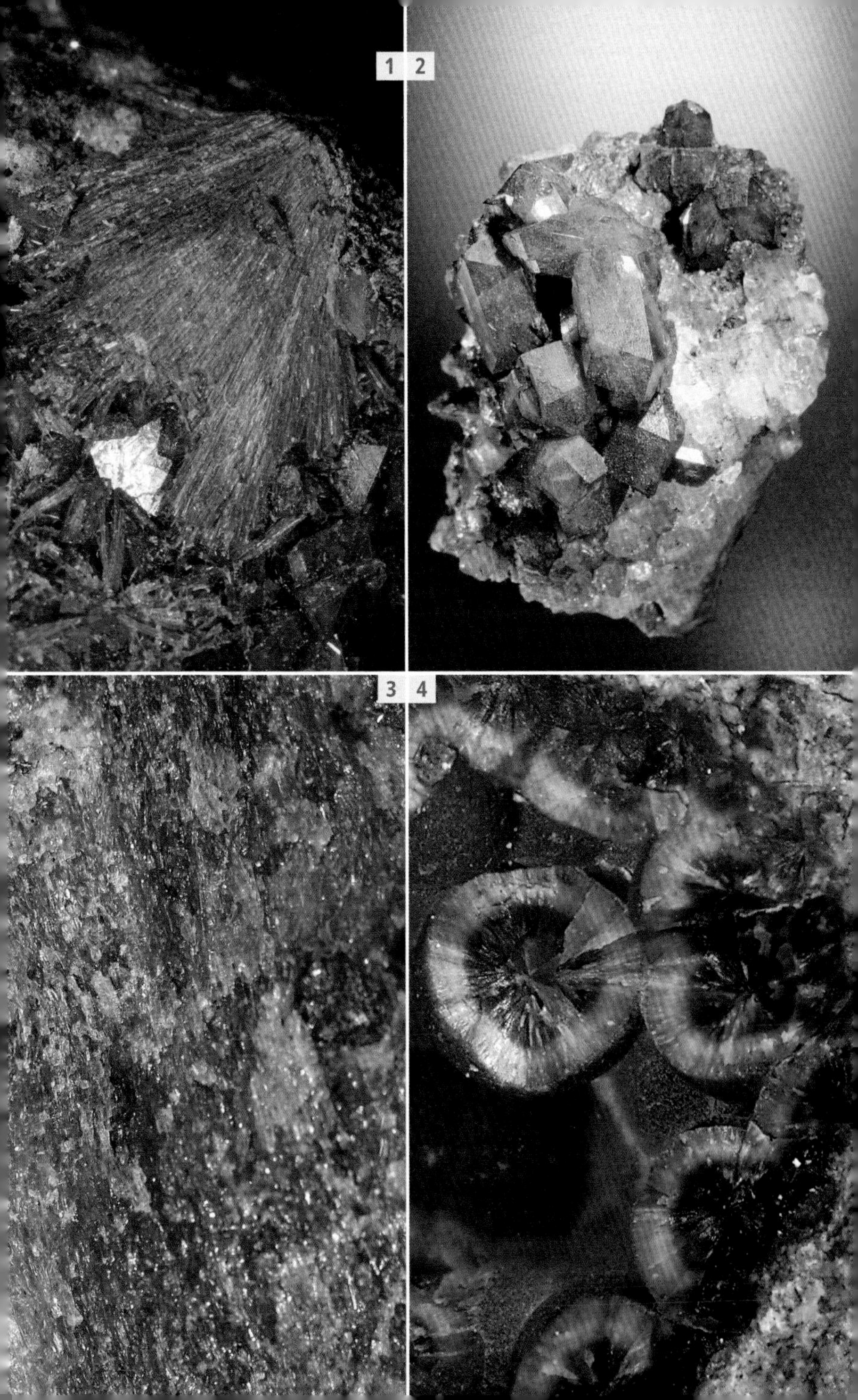
1
2
3
4

1–2 Actinolite *Stralite*

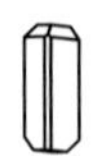

Chem. formula $(Ca,Fe)_2(Mg,Fe)_5[OH/Si_4O_{11}]_2$
Hardness 5½–6, **Sp. gr.** 2.9–3.1
Color Light to dark green
Streak Gray-green
Luster Vitreous
Cleavage Perfect, cleavage angle about 120°
Fracture Uneven
Tenacity Brittle
Crystal form Monoclinic

Morphology Columnar to acicular, prismatic crystals, radial aggregates are called stralite (actinolite); fine fibrous to filiform morphologies are called amiant or byssolite. Fine-fibered varieties are also called actinolite asbestos.
Origin and occurrence Anhedral in metamorphic rocks, particularly talc and chlorite schists, in eclogites, on alpine fissures (especially as amiant and byssolite here), in skarn rocks and contact metamorphic and contact metasomatic deposits.
Accessory minerals Albite, talc, muscovite, biotite, calcite, epidote, feldspar.
Distinguishing feature Particularly dense varieties are called nephrite and, similar to jade, are used in jewelry and in the production of art objects. However, nephrite is much less valuable than jade. To improve its salability, nephrite is also often given misleading location-based names, such as "Russian jade."
Similar minerals Pyroxenes exhibit a different cleavage angle; tourmaline has a different crystal form and no cleavage; hornblende is blacker; tremolite has a white streak; epidote does not form radial aggregates; wollastonite is whiter.

3 Fassaite

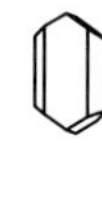

Chem. formula $Ca(Mg,Fe,Al)(Si,Al)_2O_6$
Hardness 6, **Sp. gr.** 2.9–3.3
Color Green, black
Streak Greenish
Luster Vitreous
Cleavage Good
Fracture Uneven
Tenacity Brittle
Crystal form Monoclinic

Morphology Prismatic to tabular crystals, radial, uneven, granular.
Origin and occurrence In contact metamorphic rocks and volcanic ejecta.
Accessory minerals Grossular, vesuvianite, gehlenite, spinel.
Similar minerals Grossular and vesuvianite have a white streak; actinolite exhibits a different cleavage with a 120° cleavage angle; diopside has a different streak; olivine has a different crystal form.

4 Enstatite

Chem. formula $Mg_2[Si_2O_6]$
Hardness 5–6, **Sp. gr.** 3.1–3.2
Color White, yellow, green, brownish
Streak Whitish to green-gray
Luster Vitreous
Cleavage Scarcely discernible
Fracture Conchoidal
Tenacity Brittle
Crystal form Orthorhombic

Morphology Short prismatic or tabular crystals, often crystalline, radial, uneven.
Origin and occurrence As a constituent mineral in norites, gabbros, peridotites, andesites, melaphyres, in cavities in volcanic ejecta.
Accessory minerals Talc, apatite.
Similar minerals Hornblende exhibits a different cleavage with a 120° cleavage angle, while the cleavage angle of enstatite is about 90°; olivine has a different crystal form; augite is black.

Localities	
1 Zillertal, Austria	**3** Monzoni, South Tyrol, Italy
2 Krimmler Tal, High Tauern, Austria	**4** Bamle, Norway

1 2
3 4

1 Aegirine

Chem. formula $NaFeSi_2O_6$
Hardness 5–6, **Sp. gr.** 3.5–3.6
Color Dark green to black
Streak Greenish
Luster Vitreous to greasy
Cleavage Perfect, cleavage angle about 90°
Fracture Uneven
Tenacity Brittle
Crystal form Monoclinic

Morphology Tabular to prismatic crystals, acicular, euhedral, often anhedral, columnar aggregates, stellate suns, botryoidal aggregates.
Origin and occurrence In alkali rocks and their pegmatites.
Accessory minerals Zircon, titanite, feldspar, nepheline, xenotime, astrophyllite.
Similar minerals Hornblende exhibits a different cleavage; augite occurs in completely different rocks.

2 Hedenbergite

Chem. formula $CaFe[Si_2O_6]$
Hardness 6, **Sp. gr.** 3.55
Color Dark green to black
Streak Light brown to greenish
Luster Vitreous
Cleavage Discernible, cleavage angle about 90°
Fracture Crystalline
Tenacity Brittle
Crystal form Monoclinic

Morphology Prismatic crystals, mainly stellate, columnar, uneven.
Origin and occurrence In contact metasomatic iron deposits, in volcanic ejecta, in sanidinites.
Accessory minerals Magnetite, pyrite, ilvaite, andradite, hematite, quartz.
Similar minerals Its paragenesis makes hedenbergite unmistakable; ilvaite is black; actinolite exhibits a different cleavage.

3 Augite

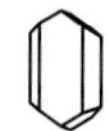

Chem. formula $(Ca,Mg,Fe)_2[(Si,Al)_2O_6]$
Hardness 6, **Sp. gr.** 3.3–3.5
Color Dark green, black
Streak Blackish green
Luster Vitreous
Cleavage Distinct, prismatic, angle between the cleavage faces (cleavage angle) about 90°
Fracture Conchoidal
Tenacity Brittle
Crystal form Monoclinic

Morphology Short to long prismatic, acicular, granular, uneven.
Origin and occurrence In volcanic rocks as a rock constinuent part, well formed crystals, especially in volcanic tuffs in, for example , the Eifel mountain range in Germany or Lanzarote.
Accessory minerals Biotite, olivine, hornblende, sanidine, nosean, sodalite.
Similar minerals Hornblende has a different cleavage with a 120° cleavage angle and a distinct hexagonal cross section in contrast to the distinct quadrilateral or octagonal cross section of augite.

4–5 Gadolinite

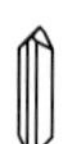

Chem. formula $Y_2FeBe_2[O/SiO_4]_2$
Hardness 6½, **Sp. gr.** 4–4.7
Color Black opaque, green transparent
Streak Greenish
Luster Pitchy to vitreous
Cleavage Mainly indiscernible
Fracture Conchoidal
Tenacity Brittle
Crystal form Monoclinic

Morphology Uneven masses anhedral (opaque, pitchy luster), prismatic, euhedral (transparent, vitreous luster).
Origin and occurrence Anhedral in pegmatites, euhedral on alpine fissures.
Accessory minerals Synchisite, aeschynite, xenotime, monazite, feldspar, quartz.
Similar minerals The green euhedral gadolinite is unmistakable; the black, anhedral mineral can be distinguished from other black minerals by its green streak.

Localities		
1 Dara-i-Pioz, Tajikistan	**3** Predazzo, South Tyrol, Italy	**5** Gastein Valley, Austria
2 Rio Marina, Elba, Italy	**4** Birkelund, Norway	

1
2
3
4
5

1 Graphite

Chem. formula C
Hardness 1, **Sp. gr.** 2.1–2.3
Color Dark to light steel gray, opaque
Streak Black
Luster Metallic to dull
Cleavage Basal perfect
Fracture Foliated
Tenacity Flexible, non-brittle
Crystal form Hexagonal

Morphology Tabular crystals, foliated, flaky aggregates, encrustations, dense.
Origin and occurrence In crystalline schists, marbles, pegmatites.
Accessory minerals Calcite, wollastonite, spinel, pyrrhotite, olivine, garnet.
Similar minerals Molybdenite is harder; its streak, when rubbed against a streak plate, is slightly greenish; that of graphite is more brownish; hematite has a red streak and, like ilmenite, is harder and brittle.

2 Ozocerite

Chem. formula Naturally occurring paraffin
Hardness 1, **Sp. gr.** 0.85–0.95
Color Light brown to black
Streak Light brown to black
Luster Pitchy
Cleavage None
Fracture Uneven
Tenacity Non-brittle
Crystal form Amorphic

Morphology Waxy, uneven, often conchoidal masses, botryoidal aggregates, inclusions, vein fillings, rock impregnations, for example in sandstone.
Origin and occurrence On hydrothermal veins, on fissures in rocks.
Accessory minerals Quartz, calcite, siderite.
Distinguishing feature Ozokerite is soluble in organic solvents, such as alcohol, acetone.
Similar minerals The color and low degree of hardness as well as the waxy tenacity are very characteristic.

3 Nagyagite

Chem. formula $Au(Pb,Sb,Fe)_8(Te,S)_{11}$
Hardness 1–1½, **Sp. gr.** 7.4–7.6
Color Dark lead gray
Streak Gray-black
Luster Metallic
Cleavage Basal perfect
Fracture Hackly
Tenacity Flexible flakes
Crystal form Orthorhombic

Morphology Pseudotetragonal crystals, tabular, foliated.
Origin and occurrence In subvolcanic gold veins on fissures and in cavities.
Accessory minerals Krennerite, sylvanite, native gold, tetradymite, quartz, pyrite.
Similar minerals Molybdenite has a different streak; graphite writes on paper and rubs off on other materials. Hematite has a red streak and, like ilmenite, is harder and brittle. The paragenesis with gold and other tellurium minerals is very characteristic.

4 Molybdenite *Molybdenum glance*

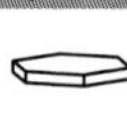

Chem. formula MoS_2
Hardness 1–1½, **Sp. gr.** 4.7–4.8
Color Lead gray with blue streak, purple, opaque
Streak Dark gray
Luster Metallic
Cleavage Perfect
Fracture Foliated
Tenacity Inelastically flexible, non-brittle
Crystal form Hexagonal

Morphology Rarely tabular crystals, foliated, scaly, uneven.
Origin and occurrence In pegmatites, pneumatolytic formations, quartz veins, garnet rocks, contact metasomatic deposits.
Accessory minerals Quartz, pyrite, wolframite.
Distinguishing feature Exhibits a dirty greenish color upon rubbing the streak with a second streak plate.
Similar minerals The streak of graphite produced by rubbing is more metallic and rather brownish; hematite has a red streak, and ilmenite a black streak; both are much harder and brittle.

Localities

1 Windhoek, Namibia	**3** Nagyag, Romania
2 Pribram, Czech Republic	**4** Alpeiner Scharte, Zillertal Alps, Austria

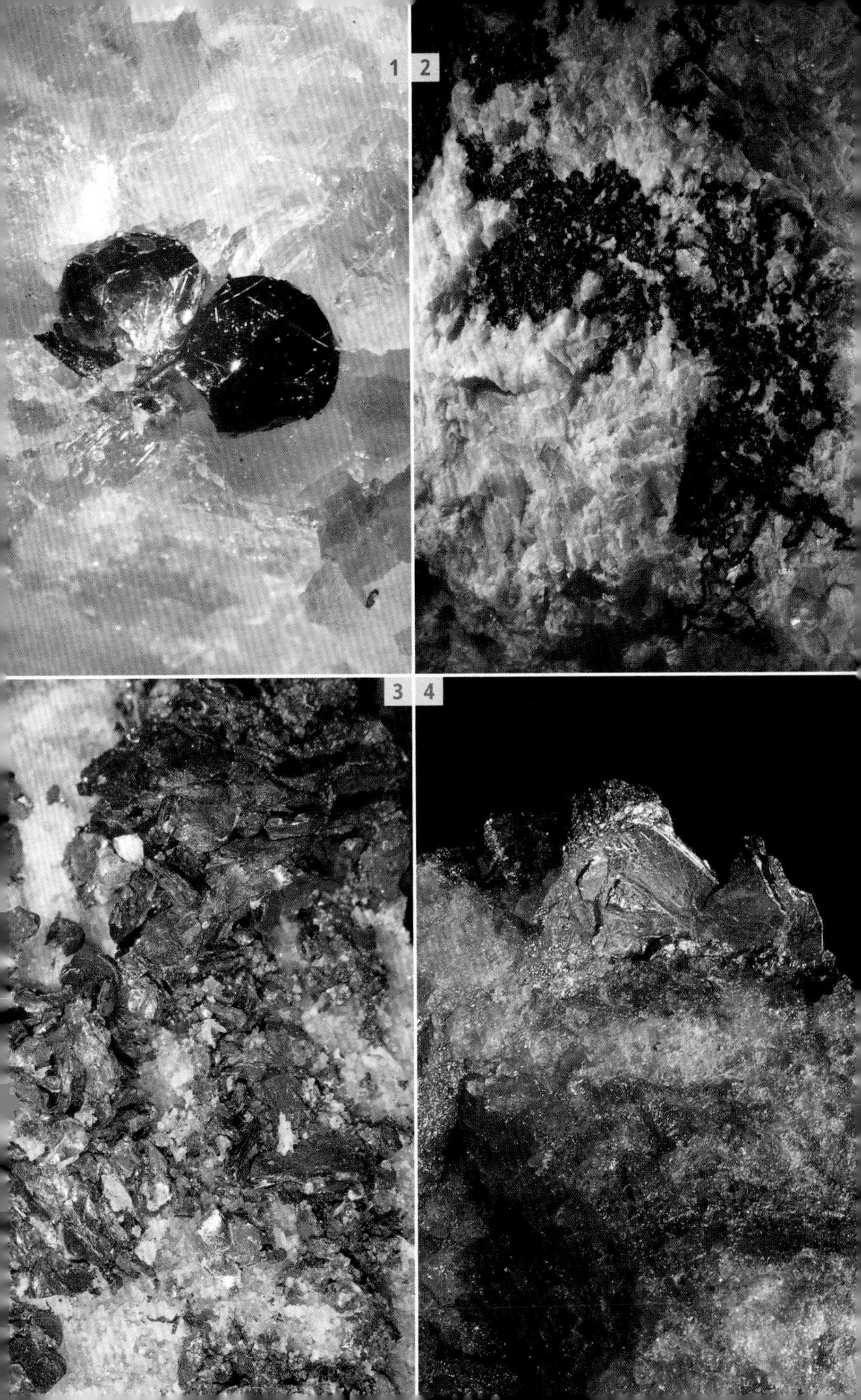
1
2
3
4

1 Tetradymite

Chem. formula Bi_2Te_2S
Hardness 1½–2, **Sp. gr.** 7.1–7.5
Color Steel gray
Streak Gray
Luster Metallic
Cleavage Perfect
Fracture Uneven
Tenacity Non-brittle
Crystal form Hexagonal

Morphology Tabular crystals, anhedral, foliated aggregates, granular, uneven.
Origin and occurrence In hydrothermal veins, in subvolcanic gold deposits.
Accessory minerals Gold, quartz, arsenopyrite, sylvanite, nagyagite, native tellurium.
Similar minerals Molybdenite and graphite have a different color; sylvanite has a different crystal form; nagyagite has different crystal form.

2 Lead

Chem. formula Pb
Hardness 1½, **Sp. gr.** 11.4
Color Lead gray, often darker tarnishing
Streak Gray
Luster Dull
Cleavage None
Fracture Hackly
Tenacity Non-brittle, sectile
Crystal form Cubic

Morphology Cubic and octahedral, usually just sheets, grains, wire-like.
Origin and occurrence In metamorphic manganese deposits, in euhedral form on fissures.
Accessory minerals Manganophyllite, braunite, lithargite, calcite, cerussite.
Similar minerals Taking into consideration its paragenesis and tenacity, lead is unmistakable; silver has a bright streak and is silvery white, at least when not tarnished.

3 Polybasite

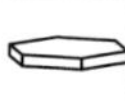

Chem. formula $(Ag,Cu)_{16}Sb_2S_{11}$
Hardness 1½–2, **Sp. gr.** 6–6.2
Color Iron black, reddish translucent on the edges
Streak Black to slightly reddish
Luster Metallic
Cleavage Basal perfect
Fracture Uneven
Tenacity Non-brittle
Crystal form Monoclinic

Morphology Pseudohexagonal crystals, hexagonal plates with triangular striation, foliated aggregates, uneven.
Origin and occurrence In hydrothermal silver veins.
Accessory minerals Argentite, native silver, pyrargyrite, stephanite, quartz, rhodochrosite, dolomite.
Similar minerals Stephanite is slightly harder and shows no triangular striation and scarcely any cleavage; molybdenite and graphite are softer; hematite and ilmenite are much harder than polybasite.

4 Pearceite

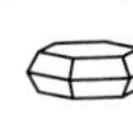

Chem. formula $Ag_{16}As_2S_{11}$
Hardness 1½–2, **Sp. gr.** 6.13
Color Black
Streak Black
Luster Metallic
Cleavage None
Fracture Conchoidal
Tenacity Brittle
Crystal form Monoclinic

Morphology Tabular crystals, foliated and radial aggregates, uneven.
Origin and occurrence In hydrothermal veins.
Accessory minerals Argentite, fluorite, barite, quartz, polybasite, stephanite.
Similar minerals Polybasite cannot be distinguished from pearceite by simple means; stephanite is harder; argentite has a different crystal form; hematite and ilmenite are much harder; molybdenite is much softer.

Localities	
1 Oravica, Romania	**3** Freiberg, Saxony, Germany
2 Langban, Sweden	**4** Rudnui, Kazakhstan

1
2
3
4

1 Covellite *Blue copper*

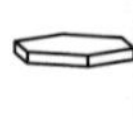

Chem. formula CuS
Hardness 1½–2, **Sp. gr.** 4.68
Color Blue-black
Streak Blue-black, rubbed hard dark blue
Luster Metallic to dull
Cleavage Basal perfect
Fracture Foliated
Tenacity Non-brittle, thin flexible flakes
Crystal form Hexagonal

Morphology Tabular crystals, foliated aggregates, usually uneven, drusy, earthy, coatings.
Origin and occurrence In hydrothermal veins, as a coating on other sulfides, especially pyrite, formed during weathering of primary copper sulfides.
Accessory minerals Pyrite, chalcopyrite, chalcocite.
Distinguishing feature Color turns purple when wetted with water.
Similar minerals The blue-black color and color change when wetted prevent confusion with other minerals.

2 Sylvanite *Schrifterz*

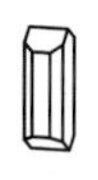

Chem. formula $AgAuTe_4$
Hardness 1½–2, **Sp. gr.** 8–8.3
Color Silver gray, whitish, often darker tarnishing
Streak Gray
Luster Metallic
Cleavage Perfect
Fracture Uneven
Tenacity Non-brittle
Crystal form Monoclinic

Morphology Prismatic to tabular crystals, often striated, frequently intergrown to form graphic texture aggregates (second name!), rarely uneven.
Origin and occurrence In subvolcanic and hydrothermal gold ore veins together with other tellurium minerals.
Accessory minerals Nagyagite, krennerite, calaverite, gold, quartz, pyrite.
Similar minerals Tetradymite has a different crystal form; nagyagite is softer; krennerite and calaverite are harder; the graphic texture intergrowths of sylvanite are very characteristic.

3–4 Stibnite *Antimony glance, gray antimony*

Chem. formula Sb_2S_3
Hardness 2, **Sp. gr.** 4.6–4.7
Color Lead gray, opaque
Streak Black
Luster Metallic
Cleavage Perfect
Fracture Crystalline, foliated
Tenacity Thin flakes and crystals inelastically flexible, non-brittle
Crystal form Orthorhombic

Morphology Prismatic to acicular crystals, usually euhedral, often bent, columnar, stellate aggregates, granular, uneven, dense.
Origin and occurrence In hydrothermal, especially stibnite-quartz veins, more rarely among other sulfides in gold, silver and lead ore veins, rarely metasomatic in limestone.
Accessory minerals Gold, arsenopyrite, realgar, cinnabar, kermesite, fluorite, barite, calcite.
Distinguishing feature Stibnite often transforms into antimony oxides, for example cervantite or stibiconite, while retaining the crystal form (pseudomorphs).
Similar minerals Bismuthhinite is much heavier and more yellowish white; arsenopyrite is harder and distinctly brittle; galena has a different cleavage. Emplectite is not inelastically flexible; rutile is much harder and not metallic gray. The perfect cleavage and the often bent crystals are very characteristic.

Localities	
1 Leogang, Austria	**3** Siegerland Region, Germany
2 Baia de Aries, Romania	**4** Shikoku, Japan

1
2
3
4

1 Emplectite

Chem. formula $CuBiS_2$
Hardness 2, **Sp. gr.** 6.38
Color Steel gray, tarnishes yellow
Streak Black
Luster Metallic
Cleavage Sometimes distinct
Fracture Uneven
Tenacity Non-brittle
Crystal form Orthorhombic

Morphology Acicular to prismatic crystals, radial aggregates, uneven, anhedral.
Origin and occurrence In hydrothermal veins, especially the bismuth-cobalt-nickel formation.
Accessory minerals Wittichenite, skutterudite, chloanthite, barite, quartz.
Similar minerals Distinguishing emplectite from other sulfo-salts is not usually possible using simple means; wittichenite is slightly blacker and has no cleavage. Stibnite and bismuthinite are inelastically flexible.

2 Bismuthinite *Bismuth glance*

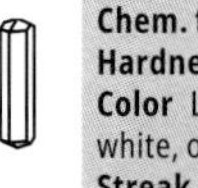

Chem. formula Bi_2S_3
Hardness 2, **Sp. gr.** 6.8–7.2
Color Lead gray to yellowish white, opaque
Streak Gray
Luster Metallic
Cleavage Perfect
Fracture Foliated
Tenacity Thin crystals inelastically flexible, non-brittle
Crystal form Orthorhombic

Morphology Prismatic to acicular crystals, euhedral, often anhedral, columnar and parallel radial aggregates, uneven.
Origin and occurrence In veins of the tin-cobalt and silver-cobalt formations, less frequently in contact deposits and pegmatites.
Accessory minerals Gold, bismuth, chalcopyrite, arsenopyrite, pyrite, stibnite.
Similar minerals Stibnite is much lighter and somewhat grayer; emplectite is not inelastically flexible; boulangerite and jamesonite are considerably more brittle.

3–4 Argentite *Silver glance, acanthite*

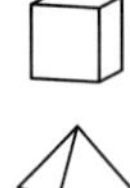

Chem. formula Ag_2S
Hardness 2, **Sp. gr.** 7.3
Color Lead gray
Streak Black
Luster Metallic, quickly tarnishes to dull
Cleavage Mainly indiscernible
Fracture Conchoidal
Tenacity Malleable, sectile
Crystal form Above 354° F cubic (argentite), below monoclinic (acanthite)

Morphology Cubic, octahedral crystals, often in parallel intergrowths (argentite 3), elongated prismatic, acicular crystals (acanthite 4), uneven.
Origin and occurrence In hydrothermal silver ore veins in the cementation zone, as a component of silver-rich ores in masses up to several tons, together with other silver minerals.
Accessory minerals Silver, pyrargyrite, proustite, stephanite, galena, calcite, rhodochrosite.
Distinguishing feature The cubic and octahedral crystals all originated as argentite at a temperature greater than 354° F, but then transformed into acanthite while retaining their shape, so they are actually pseudomorphs of acanthite after argentite.
Similar minerals Galena is neither malleable nor cuttable; stephanite has a different crystal form; the same applies to hessite. Native silver is a lighter silver and more ductile. Polybasite and pearceite primarily form tabular crystals.

Localities

1 Schwarzenberg, Saxony, Germany	**3** Freiberg, Saxony, Germany
2 Llallagua, Bolivia	**4** Freiberg, Saxony, Germany

1
2
3
4

1 Meneghinite

Chem. formula $Pb_{13}CuSb_7S_{24}$
Hardness 2½, **Sp. gr.** 6.6
Color Lead gray to yellowish white, opaque
Streak Gray
Luster Metallic
Cleavage Perfect
Fracture Uneven
Tenacity Brittle
Crystal form Orthorhombic

Morphology Prismatic to acicular crystals, euhedral, often anhedral, columnar and parallel radial aggregates, uneven.
Origin and occurrence In hydrothermal veins, in contact metasomatic deposits.
Accessory minerals Bournonite, galena, boulangerite, jamesonite, tetrahedrite, pyrite, pyrrhotite.
Similar minerals Stibnite is lighter and inelastically flexible; bismuthinite is not brittle; the same applies for emplectite (occurs more in bismuth-rich parageneses).

2 Bismuth

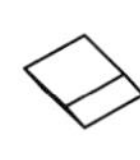

Chem. formula Bi
Hardness 2–2½, **Sp. gr.** 9.7–9.8
Color Silver white with a reddish tinge, often tarnishes darker or yellow
Streak Lead gray, metallic
Luster Metallic
Cleavage Perfect
Fracture Hackly to uneven
Tenacity Brittle but sectile
Crystal form Trigonal

Morphology Well-formed crystals rare, uneven, foliated, skeletal, usually anhedral.
Origin and occurrence In pegmatites, tin ore veins, hydrothermal veins of bismuth-cobalt-nickel formation, in contact metasomatic deposits.
Accessory minerals Bismuth glance, tinstone, safflorite, native silver, chloanthite, skutterudite.
Similar minerals The low hardness, color and striation on the cleavage faces unmistakably indicate this as native bismuth.

3 Tellurium

Chem. formula Te
Hardness 2–2½, **Sp. gr.** 6.1–6.3
Color Silver white, often tarnishes darker or yellow
Streak Pewter white, metallic
Luster Metallic
Cleavage Perfect
Fracture Hackly to uneven
Tenacity Brittle
Crystal form Hexagonal

Morphology Well-formed crystals rare, uneven, crystalline, foliated, skeletal, usually anhedral.
Origin and occurrence In hydrothermal veins, especially subvolcanic gold ore veins, as a formation of volcanic exhalations.
Accessory minerals Sylvanite, tellurite, gold, pyrite, galena, alabandite, quartz.
Similar minerals The low hardness, color and typical paragenesis make tellurium distinctive; bismuth is much heavier and always has a reddish streak.

4 Falkmanite

Chem. formula $Pb_{5,4}Sb_{3,6}S_{11}$
Hardness 2½, **Sp. gr.** 5.8–6.2
Color Lead gray
Streak Black
Luster Metallic, in very fine aggregates silky
Cleavage None
Fracture Uneven
Tenacity Brittle
Crystal form Monoclinic

Morphology Acicular to filiform crystals, radial and fibrous aggregates, fine-grained, dense.
Origin and occurrence On hydrothermal antimony-lead deposits, in metamorphic pyrrhotite deposits.
Accessory minerals Sphalerite, galena, arsenopyrite, pyrrhotite, pyrite.
Similar minerals Jamesonite cannot be distinguished from falkmanite by simple means; the same applies for boulangerite. Stibnite, bismuthinite and emplectite are not brittle.

Localities

1 Bottino, Italy	**3** Emperor Mine, Fiji
2 Hartenstein, Saxony, Germany	**4** Bayerland Mine, Waldsassen, Bavaria, Germany

1
2
3
4

1 Jamesonite *Feather ore*

Chem. formula $Pb_4FeSb_6S_{14}$
Hardness 2½, **Sp. gr.** 5.63
Color Lead gray
Streak Black-gray
Luster Metallic
Cleavage Hardly ever discernible
Tenacity Brittle
Crystal form Monoclinic

Morphology Acicular to filiform crystals, acicular clusters, brush-type intergrowths, fibrous masses, radial aggregates, anhedral and euhedral.
Origin and occurrence In hydrothermal veins of antimony-bearing deposits.
Accessory minerals Sphalerite, arsenopyrite, pyrite, quartz, rhodochrosite, dolomite, calcite.
Similar minerals Distinguishing jamesonite from boulangerite is not possible using simple means. Stibnite, emplectite and bismuthinite are not brittle.

2 Argyrodite

Chem. formula Ag_8GeS_6
Hardness 2½, **Sp. gr.** 6.2–6.3
Color Steel gray with reddish tone, often tarnishes black
Streak Gray-black
Luster Metallic
Cleavage None
Fracture Conchoidal
Tenacity Brittle
Crystal form Cubic

Morphology Octahedral, rhombic dodecahedral, euhedral crystals, botryoidal aggregates, reniform encrustations.
Origin and occurrence In hydrothermal veins of bismuth-cobalt-nickel formations and in subvolcanic deposits.
Accessory minerals Argentite, pyrite.
Similar minerals Argentite is not brittle; galena differs in its perfect cleavage; chloanthite and skutterudite are distinctly harder.

3 Cylindrite

Chem. formula $Pb_3Sn_4Sb_2S_{14}$
Hardness 2½, **Sp. gr.** 5.4
Color Black-gray
Streak Gray-black
Luster Metallic
Cleavage None
Fracture Conchoidal to uneven
Tenacity Brittle
Crystal form Indiscernible

Morphology Tubular individuals with radial-shelled structure, usually anhedral.
Origin and occurrence In subvolcanic tin ore deposits.
Accessory minerals Tinstone, franckeite, teallite, sphalerite, pyrite.
Similar minerals The typical structure of the cylindrite tubes prohibits confusion; argentite is not brittle; galena exhibits perfect cubic cleavage.

4 Diaphorite

Chem. formula $Pb_2Ag_3Sb_3S_8$
Hardness 2½–3, **Sp. gr.** 6.04
Color Steel gray, often tarnishes black
Streak Black
Luster Metallic
Cleavage None
Fracture Uneven
Tenacity Brittle
Crystal form Monoclinic

Morphology Prismatic crystals, often longitudinally striated, occasionally a very large number of faces, euhedral, uneven, anhedral.
Origin and occurrence In silver-bearing, hydrothermal deposits.
Accessory minerals Galena, pyrargyrite, proustite, miargyrite, siderite, calcite, quartz, pyrite.
Similar minerals Bournonite is not as brittle. Stephanite is non-brittle; miargyrite has a reddish streak; galenite exhibits perfect cubic cleavage; argentite is ductile; pyrargyrite can be very dark, but always has a red streak.

Localities	
1 Oruro, Bolivia	**3** Poopó, Bolivia
2 Freiberg, Saxony, Germany	**4** Pribram, Czech Republic

1 2
3 4

1 Calaverite

Chem. formula $AuTe_2$
Hardness 2½, **Sp. gr.** 9.3
Color Silver-white with yellow tinge
Streak Yellow-gray
Luster Metallic
Cleavage None
Fracture Conchoidal
Tenacity Brittle to non-brittle
Crystal form Monoclinic

Morphology Prismatic crystals, longitudinally striated, usually a very large number of faces, euhedral and anhedral, often unevenly intergrown with gold and other gold tellurides.
Origin and occurrence In hydrothermal gold ore veins and subvolcanic gold deposits.
Accessory minerals Nagyagite, sylvanite, krennerite, native gold, pyrite, quartz.
Similar minerals Sylvanite differs from calaverite due to its good cleavage; pyrite is much harder.

2 Boulangerite

Chem. formula $Pb_5Sb_4S_{11}$
Hardness 2½, **Sp. gr.** 5.8–6.2
Color Lead gray
Streak Black
Luster Metallic, in very fine aggregates silky
Cleavage None
Fracture Uneven
Tenacity Brittle
Crystal form Monoclinic

Morphology Acicular to filiform crystals, radial and fibrous aggregates, fine-grained, filiform masses, annular structures, dense.
Origin and occurrence On hydrothermal antimony-lead deposits.
Accessory minerals Sphalerite, galena, arsenopyrite, pyrrhotite.
Similar minerals Jamesonite cannot be distinguished from boulangerite by simple means. Stibnite, bismuthinite, and emplectite are not brittle.

3 Stephanite

Chem. formula Ag_5SbS_4
Hardness 2½, **Sp. gr.** 6.2–6.3
Color Lead gray, iron black, often tarnishes black
Streak Black
Luster Metallic, tarnishes dull
Cleavage Scarcely discernible
Fracture Conchoidal to uneven
Tenacity Non-brittle
Crystal form Orthorhombic

Morphology Pseudohexagonal crystals by twin formation, prismatic, thick tabular, intergrown to rose-shaped aggregates, rarely uneven.
Origin and occurrence In hydrothermal silver ore veins in the cementation zone.
Accessory minerals Argentite, silver, pyrargyrite, proustite, calcite, quartz, polybasite, galena.
Similar minerals Polybasite is relatively softer; its crystals almost always exhibit the characteristic triangular striation; argentite has a different crystal form; galena has a clearly distinct cleavage; hessite has a considerably different crystal form.

4 Gratonite

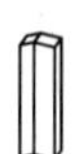

Chem. formula $Pb_9As_4S_{15}$
Hardness 2½, **Sp. gr.** 6.22
Color Dark lead gray
Streak Black
Luster Metallic
Cleavage None
Fracture Conchoidal
Tenacity Brittle
Crystal form Trigonal

Morphology Prismatic crystals with characteristic trigonal end faces, radial aggregates, uneven.
Origin and occurrence In hydrothermal deposits, in subvolcanic tin-silver deposits.
Accessory minerals Jordanite, cerussite, pyrite, enargite, tinstone, argentite.
Similar minerals Its characteristic crystal form makes gratonite unmistakable; tourmaline does not have a metallic luster; prismatic tinstone is tetragonal.

Localities

1 Cripple Creek, Colorado, USA	**3** Freiberg, Saxony, Germany
2 Trepca, Kosovo	**4** Cerro de Pasco, Peru

1 2
3 4

1 Hessite

Chem. formula Ag_2Te
Hardness 2½, **Sp. gr.** 8.2–8.4
Color Lead gray
Streak Black
Luster Metallic
Cleavage Indiscernible
Fracture Uneven
Tenacity Sectile, non-brittle
Crystal form Monoclinic

Morphology Pseudocubic, prismatic, euhedral crystals, uneven, fine-grained.
Origin and occurrence In hydrothermal silver and gold deposits, in subvolcanic deposits.
Accessory minerals Gold, tellurium, quartz, silver, sylvanite.
Similar minerals Argentite is difficult to distinguish from the much rarer hessite, but the latter is somewhat harder; galena has good distinct cleavage; stephanite has a different crystal form; miargyrite has a different streak.

2 Chalcocite *Copper glance*

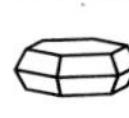

Chem. formula Cu_2S
Hardness 2½–3, **Sp. gr.** 5.7–5.8
Color Dark lead gray to blackish
Streak Blackish to dark gray, shiny
Luster Metallic, often tarnishes dull
Cleavage Indistinct
Fracture Conchoidal
Tenacity Non-brittle
Crystal form Under 217° F monoclinic, including hexagonal

Morphology Tabular to prismatic twins with orthorhombic symmetry, also pseudohexagonal triplets, euhedral crystals, often uneven.
Origin and occurrence In hydrothermal veins, especially in the cementation zone.
Accessory minerals Covelline, enargite, bornite, fahlore, chalcopyrite, pyrite.
Similar minerals Tenacity differentiates copper glance from other copper sulfides; digenite is slightly bluer but often difficult to distinguish. When freshly fractured, bornite is more purple; its tarnish colors are much more variegated.

3–4 Galena *Galenite*

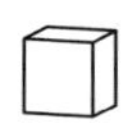

Chem. formula PbS
Hardness 2½–3, **Sp. gr.** 7.2–7.6
Color Lead gray
Streak Black
Luster Bright metallic, often tarnished dull or blue
Cleavage Perfect cubic
Fracture Crystalline
Tenacity Non-brittle
Crystal form Cubic

Morphology Euhedral crystals, mainly cubic, octahedral or combinations of the two, skeletal crystals, dendritic formations, uneven crystalline masses, anhedral and intergrown with other sulfides.
Origin and occurrence In pegmatites, in high to low temperature hydrothermal veins, as replacement in limestone, in sedimentary and resultant metamorphic sulfide deposits.
Accessory minerals Sphalerite, chalcopyrite, pyrite, barite, calcite, quartz, argentite, pyrargyrite, proustite, stephanite, arsenopyrite, pyrrhotite, siderite.
Distinguishing feature Twins can be flattened and then resemble hexagonal plates.
Similar minerals Taking color, luster and perfect cleavage into consideration, it is difficult to mistake galena; argentite is much softer and sectile; stephanite and hessite have scarcely discernible cleavage; stibnite and bismuthinite have perfect cleavage in only one direction and, in contrast to galena, are inelastically flexible; arsenopyrite is much harder.

Localities	
1 Botes, Romania	**3** Siegerland Region, Germany
2 Redruth, Cornwall, Great Britain	**4** Siegerland Region, Germany

1
2
3
4

1 Krennerite

Chem. formula $AuTe_2$
Hardness 2–3, **Sp. gr.** 8.63
Color Silver white, often tarnished slightly yellowish
Streak Gray
Luster Metallic
Cleavage Perfect
Fracture Uneven
Tenacity Brittle
Crystal form Orthorhombic

Morphology Short prismatic crystals, striated, rarely euhedral, usually uneven.
Origin and occurrence In subvolcanic gold deposits, along with other gold tellurides.
Accessory minerals Sylvanite, calaverite, nagyagite, native tellurium, native gold.
Similar minerals Pyrite is much harder; calaverite has no cleavage; sylvanite has a different crystal form; nagyagite is more foliated; galena has perfect cubic cleavage.

2 Wittichenite

Chem. formula Cu_3BiS_3
Hardness 2½, **Sp. gr.** 6–6.2
Color Steel gray, often tarnished darker
Streak Black
Luster Metallic
Cleavage None
Fracture Conchoidal
Tenacity Brittle
Crystal form Orthorhombic

Morphology Prismatic, frequently longitudinally striated to blocky crystals are very rare, usually anhedral form as uneven masses.
Origin and occurrence In hydrothermal deposits with higher bismuth content, in uranium ore veins.
Accessory minerals Pyrite, bornite, calcopyrite, bismuth, emplectite, calcite, quartz.
Similar minerals Galena exhibits perfect cleavage; emplectite is always more acicular; when just fractured, bismuth has a distinctive red color.

3 Semseyite

Chem. formula $Pb_9Sb_8S_{21}$
Hardness 2½, **Sp. gr.** 6.1
Color Steel gray
Streak Black
Luster Metallic
Cleavage Perfect
Fracture Uneven
Tenacity Brittle
Crystal form Monoclinic

Morphology Tabular, crystals often intergrown parallelly into twisted groups, radial aggregates, uneven anhedral masses.
Origin and occurrence In hydrothermal lead-antimony deposits.
Accessory minerals Pyrite, stibnite, bournonite, boulangerite, calcite, quartz.
Similar minerals The characteristic aggregate form of semseyite is unmistakable; bournonite has no distinct cleavage; galena has a different cleavage.

4 Bournonite

Chem. formula $PbCuSbS_3$
Hardness 2½–3, **Sp. gr.** 5.7–5.9
Color Steel gray, lead gray, iron black
Streak Black
Luster Metallic, often tarnishes dull
Cleavage Scarcely distinct
Fracture Conchoidal
Tenacity Brittle to slightly non-brittle
Crystal form Orthorhombic

Morphology Thick tabular to prismatic crystals, often twins, reminiscent of gears (wheel ore), often uneven.
Origin and occurrence In hydrothermal lead veins and antimony ore veins.
Accessory minerals Siderite, galena, chalcopyrite, sphalerite, quartz, calcite.
Similar minerals Fahlore has a different crystal form but is not easily distinguished from bournonite in coarse aggregates; unlike bournonite, galena has excellent cleavage; stephanite and hessite have a different crystal form.

Localities	
1 Baia de Aries, Romania	**3** Baia Sprie, Romania
2 Wittichen, Black Forest, Germany	**4** Georg Mine, Horhausen, Siegerland Region, Germany

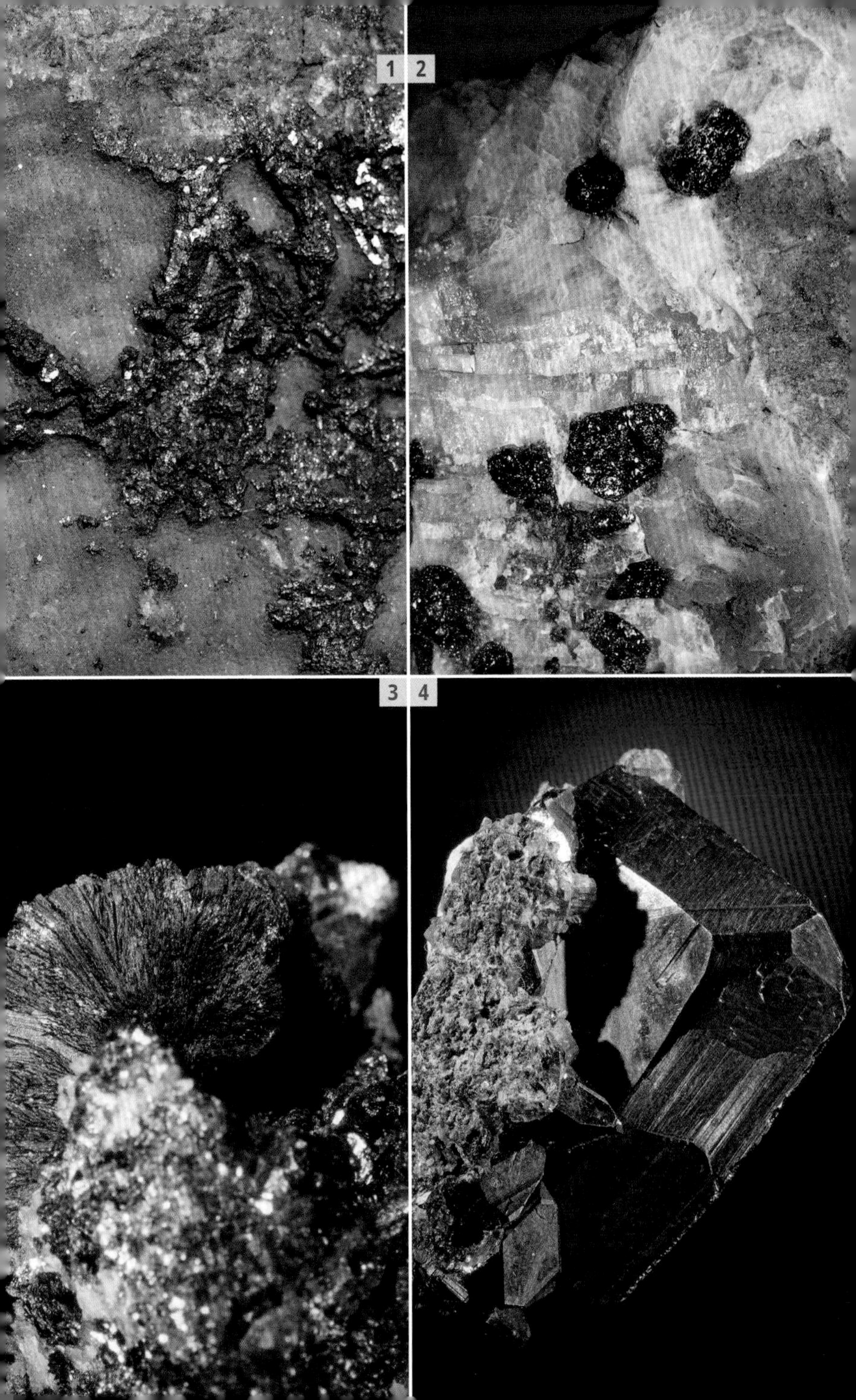
1
2
3
4

1 Andorite

Chem. formula $AgPbSb_3S_6$
Hardness 3–3½, **Sp. gr.** 5.38
Color Dark steel gray
Streak Black
Luster Metallic
Cleavage None
Fracture Conchoidal
Tenacity Brittle
Crystal form Orthorhombic

Morphology Prismatic to thick tabular crystals, striated along the c-axis, uneven.
Origin and occurrence In hydrothermal veins, in subvolcanic deposits.
Accessory minerals Stibnite, tinstone, pyrite, sphaerite, fahlore, bournonite.
Similar minerals The typical crystal form and striation of andorite are characteristic; bournonite has a different crystal form; galena has perfect cubic cleavage.

2 Lautite

Chem. formula CuAsS
Hardness 3–3½, **Sp. gr.** 4.9
Color Dark steel gray with light reddish tone
Streak Black
Luster Metallic
Cleavage Perfect
Fracture Uneven
Tenacity Brittle
Crystal form Orthorhombic

Morphology Prismatic crystals, tabular crystals, striated, uneven anhedral.
Origin and occurrence In hydrothermal veins, in arsenic-rich silver deposits, often intergrown with or well-formed on native arsenic.
Accessory minerals Native arsenic, proustite, pyrargyrite, native silver.
Similar minerals Lautite is distinguished from similar minerals by its cleavage and color; native arsenic has a different crystal form.

3 Bornite *Variegated copper ore*

Chem. formula Cu_5FeS_4
Hardness 3, **Sp. gr.** 4.9–5.3
Color Fresh reddish silver gray with a purple tinge, quickly exhibits variegated tarnished
Streak Black
Luster Metallic
Cleavage Scarcely distinct
Fracture Conchoidal
Tenacity Non-brittle
Crystal form Above 442° F cubic, below trigonal

Morphology Very rarely cubic or octahedral crystals, usually uneven, anhedral.
Origin and occurrence In pegmatites, hydrothermal veins, especially also in the cementation zone, in alpine fissures in beautiful, euhedral crystals.
Accessory minerals Chalcocite, chalcopyrite, magnetite, gold.
Similar minerals The typical tarnish colors distinguish bornite from almost all other sulfides; likewise colorful tarnished chalcopyrite is always yellow in a fresh fracture; chalcocite exhibits a different crystal form.

4 Jordanite

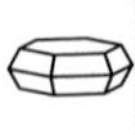

Chem. formula $Pb_4As_2S_7$
Hardness 3, **Sp. gr.** 6.4
Color Dark lead gray
Streak Black
Luster Metallic
Cleavage Perfect
Fracture Uneven
Tenacity Brittle to non-brittle
Crystal form Monoclinic

Morphology Tabular crystals, often hexagonal, often a large number of faces, often strongly striated due to formation of twins, uneven, botryoidal, conchoidal masses.
Origin and occurrence In arsenic-rich lead-zinc deposits, in metamorphic dolomites.
Accessory minerals Sphalerite (especially fibrous blende), galena, sartorite, baumhauerite, realgar.
Similar minerals Gratonite has a different crystal form; galena has perfect cubic cleavage; bournonite has a different crystal form.

Localities	
1 Oruro, Bolivia	**3** Bou Skour, Morocco
2 Mackenheim, Odenwald, Germany	**4** Lengenbach, Valais, Switzerland

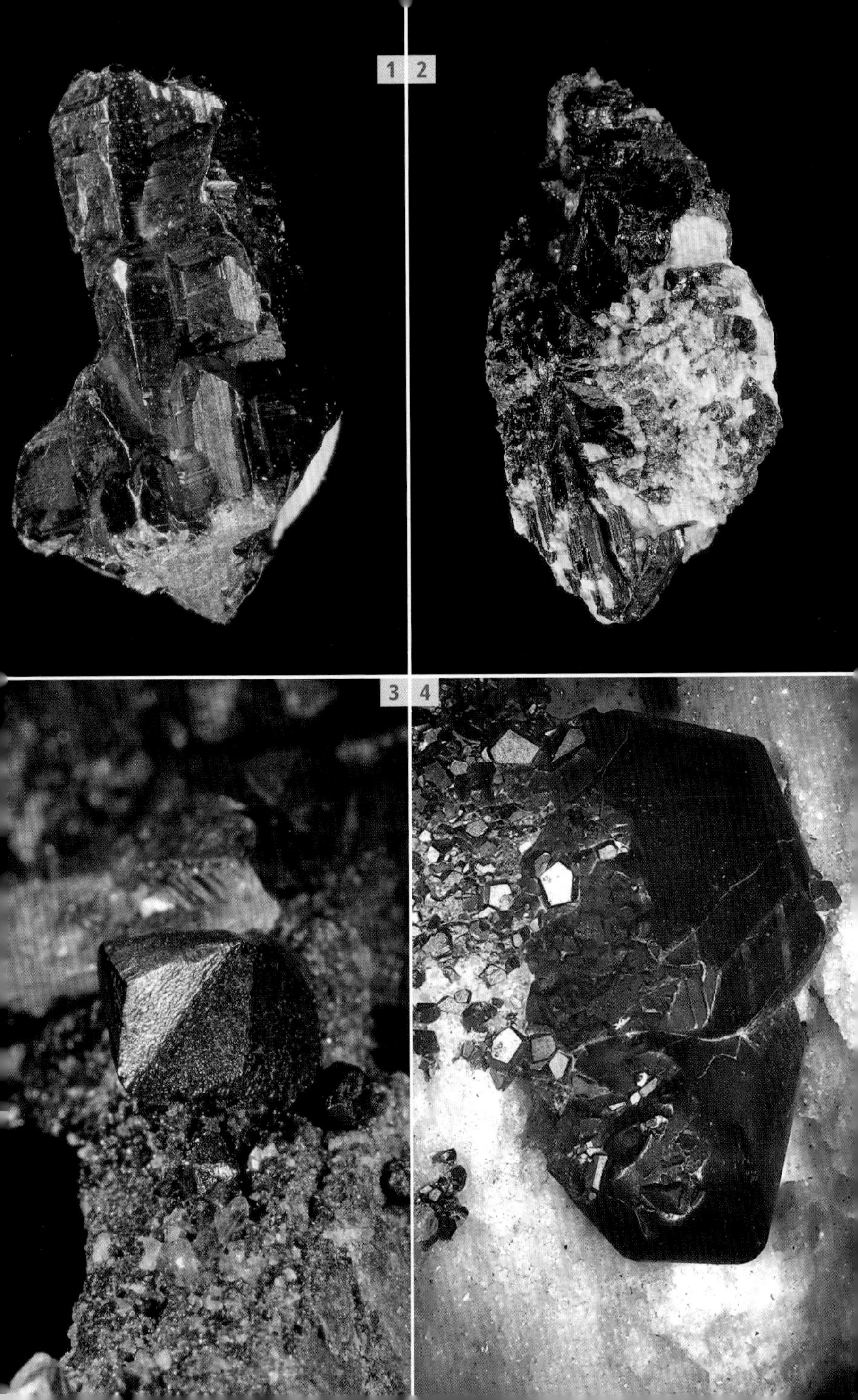
1
2
3
4

1–2 Dyskrasite

Chem. formula Ag_3Sb
Hardness 3½, **Sp. gr.** 9.4–10
Color Fresh silver white, but usually tarnished darker
Streak Black
Luster Metallic
Cleavage Mainly difficult to discern
Fracture Hackly
Tenacity Non-brittle
Crystal form Orthorhombic

Morphology Prismatic, longitudinally striated crystals, usually anhedral and poorly formed, uneven, V-shaped twins, dendritic aggregates.
Origin and occurrence In hydrothermal silver ore deposits, particularly in the cementation zone.
Accessory minerals Native silver, native arsenic, pyrargyrite, calcite, argentite, barite.
Similar minerals Argentite is softer; silver does not tarnish so quickly; the crystal form is quite different in each case. The V-shaped twins are highly typical for dyscrasite. Galena has perfect cubic cleavage.

3–4 Tennantite *Arsenfahlerz*

Chem. formula $Cu_3AsS_{3.25}$
Hardness 3–4, **Sp. gr.** 4.6–5.2
Color Steel gray, reddish translucent in thinnest splinters
Streak Black, brownish red when rubbed
Luster Metallic, often dull
Cleavage None
Fracture Conchoidal
Tenacity Brittle
Crystal form Cubic

Morphology Tetrahedral crystals, sometimes regular botryoidal due to abundance of faces (binnite), euhedral, granular masses, uneven.
Origin and occurrence In hydrothermal veins, in subvolcanic deposits, in contact metasomatic deposits.
Accessory minerals Pyrite, chalcopyrite, arsenopyrite, enargite, galena, sphalerite.
Similar minerals Arsenopyrite is harder; galena has excellent cleavage; tetrahedrite is slightly lighter and does not have a reddish streak when rubbed but is nevertheless difficult to distinguish from tennantite using simple means; enargite has perfect cleavage. Chalcopyrite, at least as a fresh fracture, is always shiny metallic yellow; bournonite is not so brittle; sphalerite never shines as metallically as fahlore.

5–6 Tetrahedrite *Gray copper ore*

Chem. formula $Cu_3SbS_{3.25}$
Hardness 3–4, **Sp. gr.** 4.6–5.2
Color Steel gray to iron black
Streak Black
Luster Metallic, but frequently also dull
Cleavage None
Fracture Conchoidal
Tenacity Brittle
Crystal form Cubic

Morphology Mainly only tetrahedral, rarely more multi-faced crystals, often uneven.
Origin and occurrence Rarely in pegmatites, primarily in hydrothermal veins.
Accessory minerals Pyrite, sphalerite, chalcopyrite, arsenopyrite, galena, silver ores.
Similar minerals Sphalerite and galena differ from tetrahedrite in their cleavage; chalcopyrite has a different color; tennantite has a somewhat reddish streak when rubbed but is difficult to distinguish from tetrahedrite using simple means. Enargite has perfect cleavage. Chalcopyrite, at least as a fresh fracture, is always shiny metallic yellow; bournonite is not so brittle; sphalerite never shines as metallically as fahlore.

Localities		
1 Pribram, Czech Republic	**3** Mackenheim, Odenwald, Germany	**5** Georg Mine, Horhausen, Siegerland Region, Germany
2 St. Andreasberg, Harz, Germany	**4** Brixlegg, Tirol, Austria	**6** Bad Grund, Harz, Germany

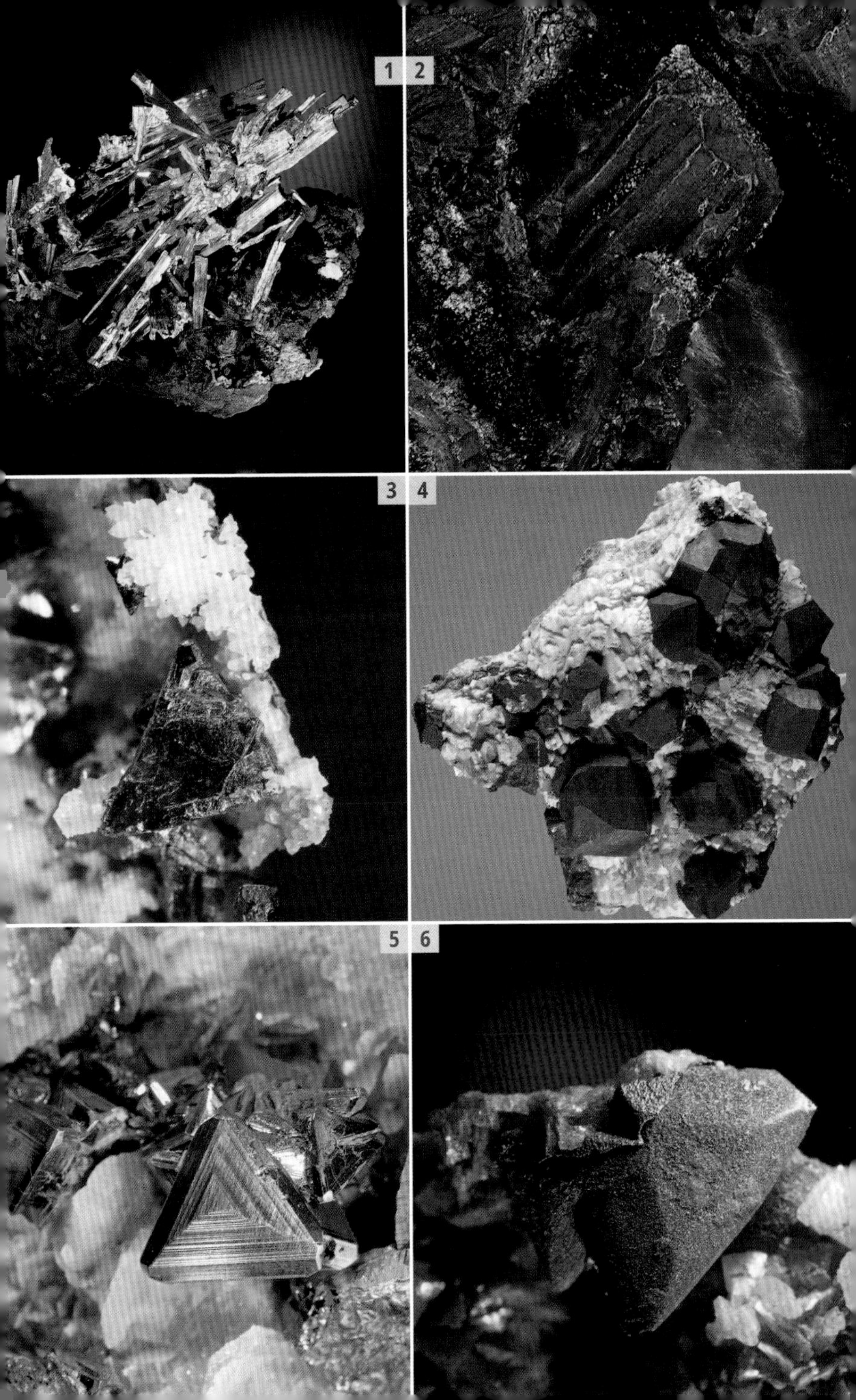
1
2
3
4
5
6

1 Antimony

Chem. formula Sb
Hardness 3–3½, **Sp. gr.** 6.7
Color Silver white
Streak Gray
Luster Metallic
Cleavage Perfect
Fracture Uneven
Tenacity Brittle
Crystal form Trigonal

Morphology Cube-like to thick tabular crystals, crystalline aggregates, uneven.
Origin and occurrence In hydrothermal veins.
Accessory minerals Stibnite, cervantite, stibiconite, quartz, calcite.
Similar minerals Stibnite and bismuthinite are not brittle; native silver has no cleavage; dyscrasite has a different cleavage; galena has perfect cubic cleavage .

2 Millerite *Nickel pyrites, hair pyrites*

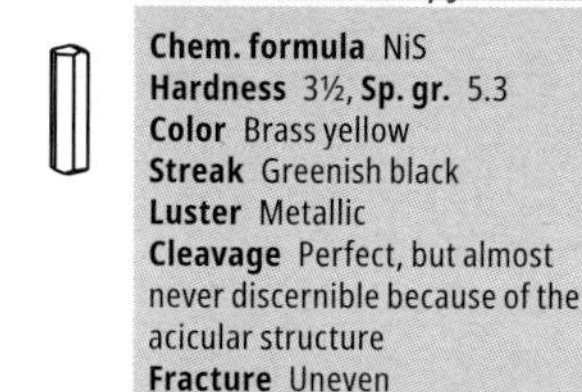

Chem. formula NiS
Hardness 3½, **Sp. gr.** 5.3
Color Brass yellow
Streak Greenish black
Luster Metallic
Cleavage Perfect, but almost never discernible because of the acicular structure
Fracture Uneven
Tenacity Brittle
Crystal form Trigonal

Morphology Acicular crystals, usually filiform, often intergrown into sheaves, stellate aggregates, very seldom uneven.
Origin and occurrence In nickel deposits, here formed from other nickel ores, in coal deposits in vugs in country rock.
Accessory minerals Gersdorffite, bravoite, calcite, chalcopyrite.
Similar minerals The typical acicular to filiform structure and the brass-yellow color of millerite preclude confusion. Rare acicular pyrite is much harder.

3 Enargite

Chem. formula Cu_3AsS_4
Hardness 3½, **Sp. gr.** 4.4
Color Steel gray to iron black with a tinge of purple
Streak Black
Luster Metallic
Cleavage Perfect prismatic
Fracture Uneven
Tenacity Brittle
Crystal form Orthorhombic

Morphology Pseudohexagonal crystals, prismatic, often longitudinally striated, also star-shaped triplets, often radial, granular, uneven.
Origin and occurrence In arsenic-rich copper ore veins, in subvolcanic deposits.
Accessory minerals Tennantite, chalcocite.
Similar minerals Arsenopyrite is harder; fahlore has a different crystal form and no cleavage. Chalcosite is not brittle; bournonite has a different crystal form.

4 Cubanite

Chem. formula $CuFe_2S_3$
Hardness 3½–4, **Sp. gr.** 4.1
Color Bronze yellow
Streak Black
Luster Metallic
Cleavage Mainly indiscernible
Fracture Conchoidal
Tenacity Brittle
Crystal form Orthorhombic

Morphology Crystals prismatic, longitudinally striated, acicular, pseudohexagonal tabular triplets, but usually uneven.
Origin and occurrence Lamellar intergrowth with chalcopyrite in almost all copper deposits of higher temperatures.
Accessory minerals Chalcopyrite, pyrrhotite, siderite.
Similar minerals The fine intergrowths with chalcopyrite are indistinguishable using simple means; cubanite crystals differ from elongated pyrite crystals because of the darker color and longitudinal striation.

Localities	
1 Seinäjoki, Finland	**3** Butte, Montana, USA
2 Wissen, Siegerland Region, Germany	**4** Morro Velho, Brazil

1
2
3
4

1–2 Chalkopyrite *Yellow copper ore*

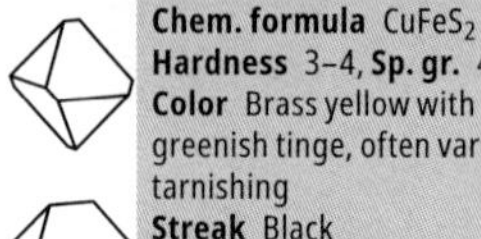

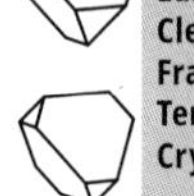

Chem. formula $CuFeS_2$
Hardness 3–4, **Sp. gr.** 4.2–4.3
Color Brass yellow with greenish tinge, often variegated tarnishing
Streak Black
Luster Metallic
Cleavage Scarcely discernible
Fracture Conchoidal
Tenacity Brittle
Crystal form Tetragonal

Morphology Tetrahedral and octahedral-like crystals, often twinned, however, the major part of the chalcopyrite is uneven.
Origin and occurrence In granites and gabbros, in pegmatites and tin ore veins, in hydrothermal veins and black shales.
Accessory minerals Pyrite, sphalerite, pyrrhotite, fahlore, fluorite, calcite, barite, dolomite, quartz.
Distinguishing feature Chalcopyrite is the most important copper ore mineral. Even relatively low levels can, for example, make an intrinsically worthless pyrite deposit worth mining.
Similar minerals Pyrite is much harder; magnetic pyrite is browner; gold is softer and can be cut and hammered. Yellow tarnished bismuth displays its true color when scratched.

3 Moschellandsbergite

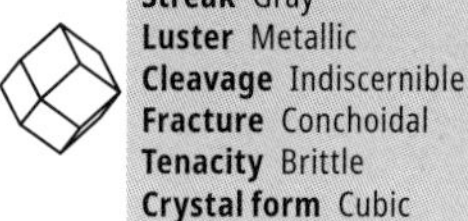

Chem. formula Ag_2Hg_3
Hardness 3½, **Sp. gr.** 13.7
Color Silver white
Streak Gray
Luster Metallic
Cleavage Indiscernible
Fracture Conchoidal
Tenacity Brittle
Crystal form Cubic

Morphology Rhombic dodecahedral, often with rounded edges, botryoidal aggregates, anhedral uneven.
Origin and occurrence In mercury deposits and hydrothermal silver deposits.
Accessory minerals Mercury, calomel, pyrite, cinnabar, quartz, calcite.
Distinguishing feature Moschellandsbergite and related minerals are also simply commonly referred to as amalgams. This is a name for alloys of, in particular, silver with mercury, which we are familiar with from its use in dentistry for fillings.
Similar minerals Argentite is not brittle and is significantly softer; galena has excellent cubic cleavage. Globules of native mercury may resemble botryoidal crystals of moschellandsbergite due to the high surface tension of mercury, but they are actually liquid.

4 Schneiderhöhnite

Chem. formula $Fe_4AsO_3(As_2O_5)_2$
Hardness 3, **Sp. gr.** 4.3
Color Black
Streak Black
Luster Metallic
Cleavage Perfect
Fracture Crystalline
Tenacity Brittle
Crystal form Triclinic

Morphology Thick tabular crystals, flakes, foliated aggregates, uneven.
Origin and occurrence In the oxidation zone of arsenic-rich hydrothermal deposits.
Accessory minerals Stottite, scorodite.
Similar minerals Perfect cleavage distinguishes schneiderhöhnite from similar minerals; hematite is much harder and has a red streak; ilmenite is harder and has no cleavage; magnetite has no cleavage and has a different crystal form. Galena has perfect cubic cleavage; enargite has a different crystal form.

Localities

1 Wissen, Siegerland Region, Germany	**3** Moschellandsberg, Pfalz, Germany
2 Dreislar, Sauerland, Germany	**4** Tsumeb, Namibia

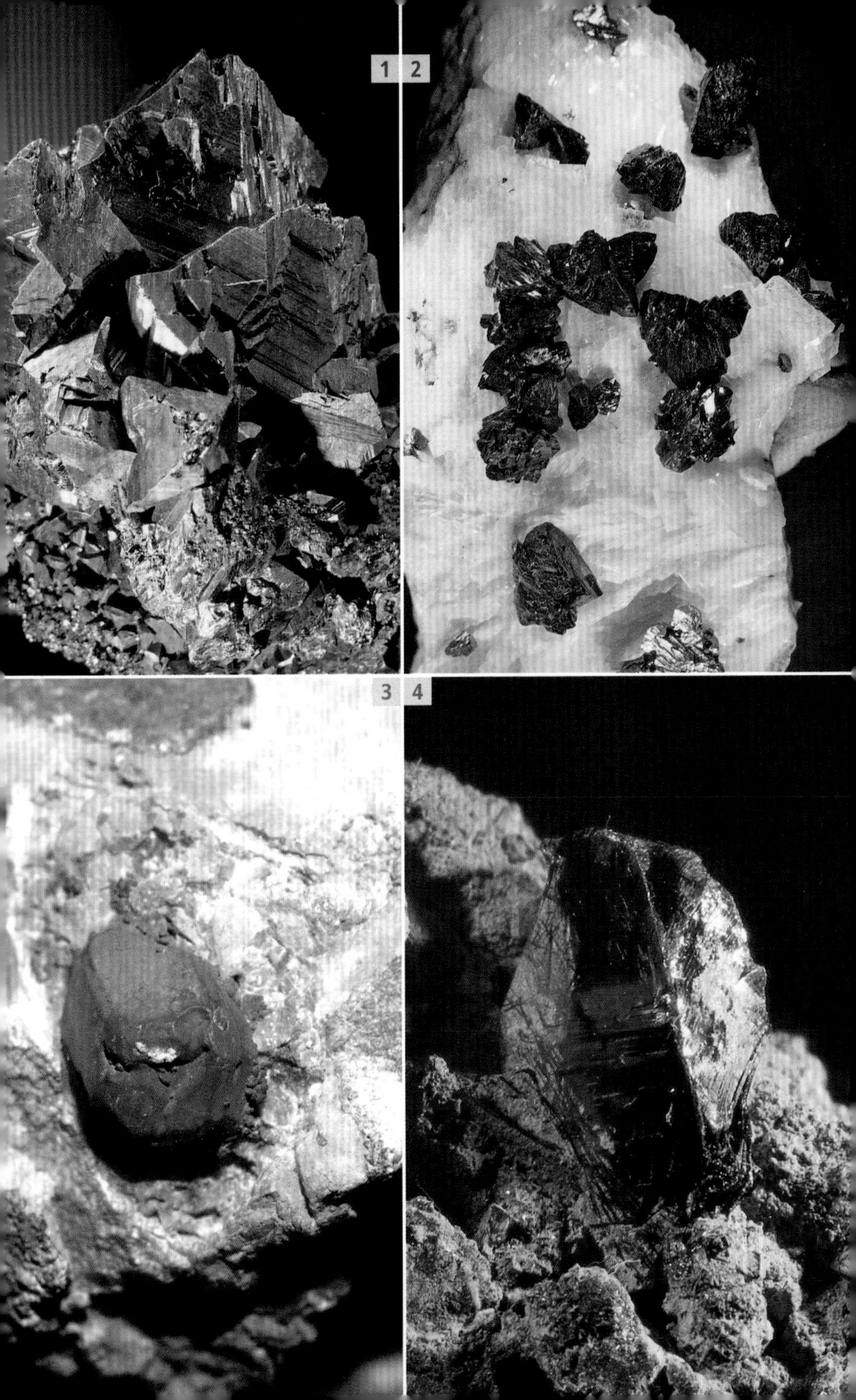
1
2
3
4

1 Arsenic, native

Chem. formula As
Hardness 3–4, **Sp. gr.** 7.06
Color Black to black-gray
Streak Black
Luster Fresh metallic, tarnishes dark and dull very quickly (even after just a few hours)
Cleavage Indistinct
Fracture Uneven
Tenacity Brittle
Crystal form Trigonal

Morphology Rarely cube-like to acicular crystals, usually conchoidal, botryoidal, hematite-like, radial, dense.
Origin and occurrence In arsenic-bearing silver and cobalt veins, in hydrothermal veins.
Accessory minerals Native silver, dyscrasite, polybasite, löllingite, safflorite.
Similar minerals Colloform pyrite and marcasite are much harder; goethite has a brown streak; galenite has excellent cubic cleavage; dyscrasite has a different crystal form and is not brittle.

2 Linneite

Chem. formula Co_3S_4
Hardness 4½–5½, **Sp. gr.** 4.8–5.8
Color Silver white to steel gray
Streak Black-gray
Luster Metallic
Cleavage Discernible
Fracture Conchoidal
Tenacity Brittle
Crystal form Cubic

Morphology Usually octahedral crystals, euhedral, crystal groups, uneven.
Origin and occurrence In hydrothermal veins and replacements, on fissures and in cavities.
Accessory minerals Siderite, cobaltite, pyrite, erythrite, quartz, calcite.
Similar minerals Skutterudite and cobaltite are not easily differentiated from linneite using simple means; pyrite is more yellowish; arsenopyrite has a different crystal form; galena has perfect cleavage.

3 Pyrrhotite *Magnetic pyrites*

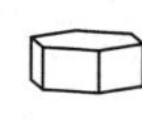

Chem. formula FeS
Hardness 4, **Sp. gr.** 4.6
Color Bronze color with a tinge of brown (= red brass color)
Streak Black
Luster Metallic
Cleavage Seldom distinct
Fracture Uneven
Tenacity Brittle
Crystal form Hexagonal

Morphology Rarely prismatic to thick and thin tabular crystals, sometimes intergrown to roses, but usually dense and uneven.
Origin and occurrence In hydrothermal veins and metamorphic gravel deposits, in gold quartz veins and subvolcanic deposits.
Accessory minerals Pyrite, pentlandite, sphalerite, chalcopyrite, quartz, calcite, siderite.
Similar minerals Pyrite and chalcopyrite are much more yellow; pyrite is harder; sphalerite has perfect cleavage.

4 Iron, native

Chem. formula Fe
Hardness 4–5, **Sp. gr.** 7.88
Color Steel gray, shiny
Streak Gray-black
Luster Metallic
Cleavage None
Fracture Hackly
Tenacity Ductile
Crystal form Cubic

Structure Anhedral flakes, drops, irregular masses, no well-formed crystals, never euhedral.
Origin and occurrence Terrestrially anhedral in basalts, as a component of meteorites; iron meteorites consist almost entirely of nickel-bearing iron.
Accessory minerals Wüstite, olivine, chromite.
Similar minerals Paragenesis in basalts and the tenacity of iron make confusion difficult; magnetite is harder. Native iron is unmistakable in iron meteorites.

Localities	
1 St. Andreasberg, Harz, Germany	**3** Dalnegorsk, Russia
2 Victoria Mine, Siegerland Region, Germany	**4** Siberia, Russia

1
2
3
4

1 Siegenite

Chem. formula $(Co,Ni)_3S_4$
Hardness 4½–5½, **Sp. gr.** 4.5–4.8
Color Steel gray, silvery, often tarnishes brown
Streak Gray
Luster Metallic
Cleavage Indiscernible
Fracture Uneven
Tenacity Brittle
Crystal form Cubic

Morphology Octahedral crystals, often botryoidal, euhedral, uneven masses.
Origin and occurrence In hydrothermal deposits, in deposits of bismuth-cobalt-nickel formation.
Accessory minerals Chalcopyrite, pyrite, linneite, dolomite, calcite, siderite.
Similar minerals The brownish tarnishing is characteristic of this mineral; pyrite is much more yellowish; galena has perfect cubic cleavage; linneite is almost indistinguishable using simple means.

2 Tenorite *Black copper*

Chem. formula CuO
Hardness 3–4, **Sp. gr.** 6
Streak Black
Color Black
Luster Vitreous to metallic, but mainly dull
Cleavage Not identifiable
Tenacity Thin flakes, flexible
Crystal form Monoclinic

Morphology Seldom tabular crystals, thin flakes, earthy encrustations, uneven.
Origin and occurrence At volcanic gas outlets, in the oxidation zone of copper deposits.
Accessory minerals Cuprite, chrysocolla, malachite, azurite, quartz, calcite.
Similar minerals Tenorite is indistinguishable from other earthy black minerals by simple means; however, its paragenesis with chrysocolla and cuprite is very characteristic, as are the thin flakes from fumaroles. Hematite is harder and not flexible.

3 Platinum, native

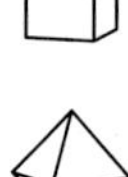

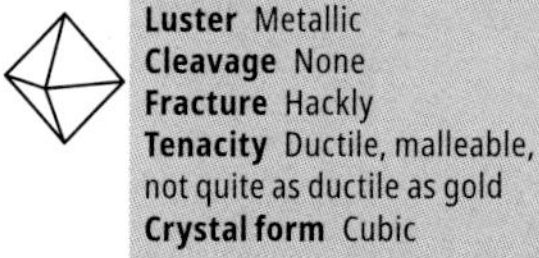

Chem. formula Pt
Hardness 4–4½, **Sp. gr.** 21.4
Color Silver gray
Streak Gray
Luster Metallic
Cleavage None
Fracture Hackly
Tenacity Ductile, malleable, not quite as ductile as gold
Crystal form Cubic

Morphology Cubic crystals, unrolled round nuggets up to several kilograms, small plates, grains, mostly loose, rarely anhedral.
Origin and occurrence In placers and quartz veins, intergrown in basic to ultrabasic rocks.
Accessory minerals Gold, chromite.
Similar minerals Silver is softer; unlike platinum, iron is magnetic; sperrylite is not as ductile and noticeably harder.

4 Germanite

Chem. formula $Cu_{13}Fe_2Ge_2S_{16}$
Hardness 4, **Sp. gr.** 4.46–4.59
Color Reddish gray, tarnishes brown
Streak Black
Luster Metallic, often dull
Cleavage None
Fracture Conchoidal
Tenacity Brittle
Crystal form Cubic

Morphology Tiny crystals are very rare, granular masses, uneven.
Origin and occurrence In hydrothermal deposits.
Accessory minerals Pyrite, chalcopyrite, enargite, galena, sphalerite, bornite.
Similar minerals Arsenopyrite is harder; galena has excellent cleavage; fahlores are not as reddish gray; enargite has perfect cleavage; the color of germanite when freshly fractured is highly characteristic.

Localities	
1 Siegen, Siegerland Region, Germany	**3** Urals, Russia
2 Vesuvius, Italy	**4** Tsumeb, Namibia

1
2
3
4

1 Heterogenite

Chem. formula CoOOH
Hardness 3–5, **Sp. gr.** 3.5–4.5
Color Black
Streak Brown-black
Luster Metallic, often dull
Cleavage None
Fracture Conchoidal
Tenacity Brittle
Crystal form Trigonal and hexagonal

Morphology Reniform, stellate masses, encrustations, coatings, granular masses, uneven.
Origin and occurrence In the oxidation zone of cobalt-rich deposits.
Accessory minerals Chloanthite, erythrite, clinotirolite, malachite, pharmacosiderite, calcite.
Similar minerals Ozokerite is much softer, as is tenorite; romanechite is harder; an association with cobalt minerals is typical.

2 Coronadite

Chem. formula $Pb(Mn^{4+},Mn^{2+})_8O_{16}$
Hardness 4½–5½, **Sp. gr.** 5.2–5.5
Color Light to steel gray
Streak Brown-black
Luster Metallic to dull
Cleavage Poor
Fracture Conchoidal
Tenacity Brittle
Crystal form Monoclinic

Morphology Stellate aggregates, reniform, fibrous, banded with other manganese minerals.
Origin and occurrence In the oxidation zone of lead-rich and manganese-rich deposits.
Accessory minerals Hollandite, pyrolusite, manganite, romanechite, calcite.
Similar minerals Romanechite is distinctly harder, as is hollandite; manganite and pyrolusite have a different crystal form.

3 Hauchecornite

Chem. formula $Ni_9Bi(Sb, Bi)S_8$
Hardness 5, **Sp. gr.** 6.58
Color Yellowish gray, tarnishes darker
Streak Black
Luster Metallic, often dull
Cleavage None
Fracture Conchoidal
Tenacity Brittle
Crystal form Tetragonal

Morphology Tabular crystals, rarely short prismatic or dipyramidal, usually euhedral, granular masses, uneven.
Origin and occurrence In hydrothermal deposits with nickel and bismuth content.
Accessory minerals Pyrite, chalcopyrite, millerite, siderite, galena, sphalerite.
Similar minerals Arsenopyrite is harder; galena has excellent cleavage; the fahlores have a quite different crystal form; unlike hauchecornite, enargite has perfect cleavage.

4 Safflorite

Chem. formula $CoAs_2$
Hardness 4½–5½, **Sp. gr.** 6.9–7.3
Color Pewter white, darkens in air before long
Streak Black
Luster Metallic
Cleavage Scarcely distinct
Fracture Conchoidal
Tenacity Brittle
Crystal form Monoclinic

Morphology Crystals very small, tabular, often intergrown into star-shaped triplets, uneven.
Origin and occurrence In hydrothermal cobalt-nickel-silver veins.
Accessory minerals Native arsenic, calcite, red cobalt, löllingite.
Similar minerals Arsenopyrite is harder; chloanthite and skutterudite have a different crystal form; löllingite is indistinguishable by simple means although the presence of the weathering product red cobalt may give an indication.

Localities	
1 Molvizar, Spain	**3** Wissen, Siegerland Region, Germany
2 Broken Hill, Australia	**4** St. Andreasberg, Harz, Germany

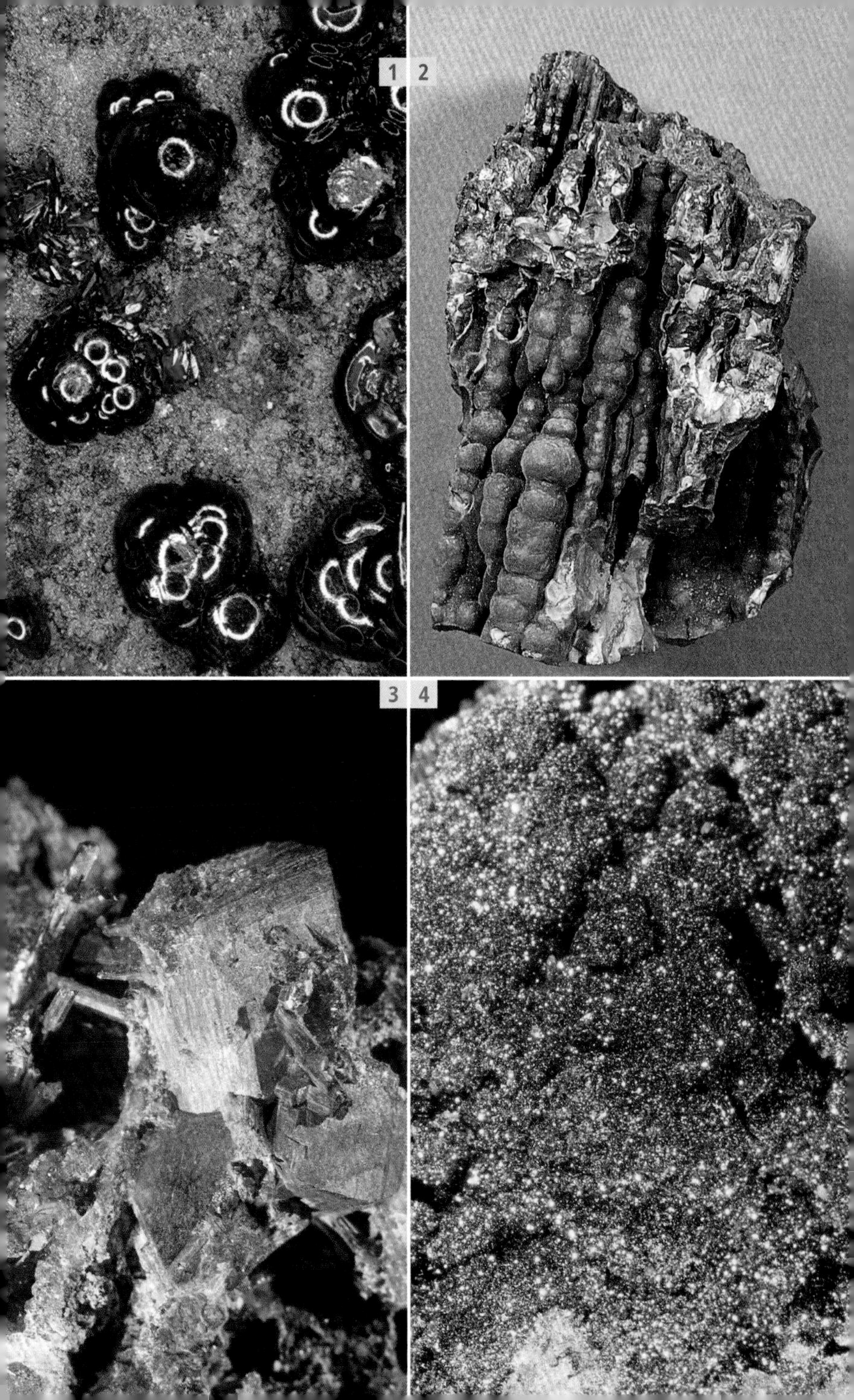
1
2
3
4

1 Ludwigite

Chem. formula $(Mg,Fe)_2Fe[O_2/BO_3]$
Hardness 5, **Sp. gr.** 3.7–4.2
Color Black
Streak Blue-green to black
Luster Silky
Cleavage None
Fracture Radial
Tenacity Brittle
Crystal form Orthorhombic

Morphology Radial to fibrous aggregates, granular, uneven, dense.
Origin and occurrence In boracic, contact metasomatic deposits.
Accessory minerals Magnetite, tinstone, vonsenite.
Similar minerals Tourmaline is harder and has a different crystal form; hedenbergite is more greenish; ilvaite is slightly harder and has a different luster; hornblende and actinolite exhibit cleavage with a 120° cleavage angle.

2 Maucherite

Chem. formula $Ni_{11}As_8$
Hardness 5, **Sp. gr.** 8
Color Reddish silver white, often tarnishes darker
Streak Brownish to blackish
Luster Metallic
Cleavage None
Fracture Conchoidal
Tenacity Brittle
Crystal form Tetragonal

Morphology Rarely tabular or pyramidal crystals, intergrown into whorled aggregates, foliated, columnar, mainly anhedral, uneven.
Origin and occurrence In hydrothermal cobalt-nickel-arsenic veins.
Accessory minerals Niccolite, calcite, cobaltite, chloantite.
Similar minerals Niccolite has more prismatic crystals and, in its rough state, is indistinguishable from maucherite by simple means.

3 Hollandite

Chem. formula $Ba(Mn,Fe)_8O_{16}$
Hardness 6, **Sp. gr.** 4.95
Color Black, black-brown
Streak Black
Luster Metallic to dull
Cleavage Poor
Fracture Uneven
Tenacity Brittle
Crystal form Monoclinic

Morphology Rarely prismatic crystals, mainly columnar, fibrous and reniform aggregates, uneven.
Origin and occurrence In metamorphic manganese deposits.
Accessory minerals Romanechite, pyrolusite, braunite, manganite, calcite, quartz.
Similar minerals Romanechite cannot be distinguished from hollandite by simple means. Manganite is softer and has a different streak; braunite has a different crystal form, as does pyrolusite.

4 Carrollite

Chem. formula $CuCo_2S_4$
Hardness 4½–5½, **Sp. gr.** 4.5–4.8
Color Light to steel gray
Streak Gray
Luster Metallic
Cleavage Poor
Fracture Conchoidal
Tenacity Brittle
Crystal form Cubic

Morphology Octahedral crystals, euhedral and anhedral, more rarely uneven.
Origin and occurrence In hydrothermal deposits, in cobalt-nickel deposits.
Accessory minerals Calcite, pyrite.
Similar minerals Carrollite is hardly distinguishable from linneite and siegenite by simple means. Pyrite is yellower and harder; cobaltine is harder; arsenopyrite has a different crystal form; galenite has perfect cubic cleavage.

Localities

1 Brosso, Piedmont, Italy	**3** Tangen, Norway
2 Zinkwand, Schladming, Austria	**4** Kolwezi, Zaire

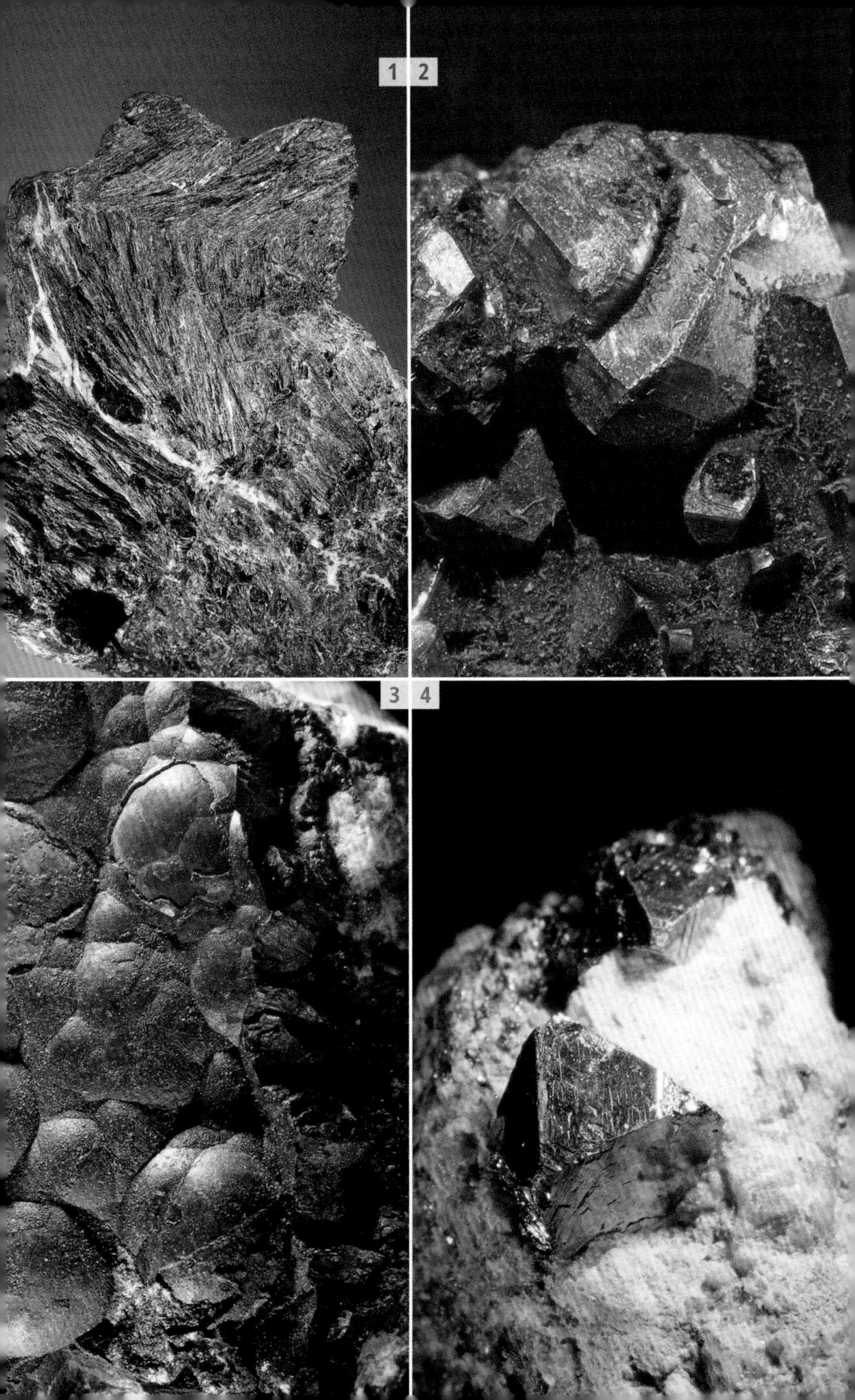
1
2
3
4

1 Loparite-(Ce)

Chem. formula (Ce,Na, Ca)(Ti,Nb)O_3
Hardness 5½–6, **Sp. gr.** 4.6–4.89
Color Black
Streak Brown-black
Luster Metallic to greasy
Cleavage Poor
Fracture Conchoidal
Tenacity Brittle
Crystal form Cubic

Structure Cubic, more rarely octahedral crystals, euhedral and anhedral, often interpenetration twins of two cubes (see image), more rarely uneven.
Origin and occurrence In alkaline rocks or pegmatites in alkaline rocks.
Accessory minerals Nepheline, aegirine, perovskite, ilmenite.
Similar minerals Considering its paragenesis, the typical interpenetration twins are very characteristic; perovskite does not exhibit such formations; magnetite is magnetic; ilmenite has a different crystal form.

2 Jacobsite

Chem. formula $MnFe_2O_4$
Hardness 6, **Sp. gr.** 4.7–5
Color Black
Streak Brown-black
Luster Metallic to dull
Cleavage None
Fracture Conchoidal
Tenacity Brittle
Crystal form Cubic

Morphology Octahedral crystals, mainly distorted, crystalline masses, granular, uneven.
Origin and occurrence In metamorphic manganese deposits together with other manganese minerals.
Accessory minerals Braunite, hausmannite, biotite, calcite, quartz, rhodonite.
Similar minerals Magnetite has a pure black streak and, unlike jacobsite, is strongly magnetic; hematite has a red streak and a different crystal form.

3 Cobaltite *Cobalt glance*

Chem.Chem. formula CoAsS
Hardness 5½, **Sp. gr.** 6–6.4
Color Silver white with reddish tinge
Streak Gray-black
Luster Metallic
Cleavage Scarcely distinct
Fracture Conchoidal
Tenacity Brittle
Crystal form Cubic

Morphology Cubic, often striped, octahedral and rhombic dodecahedral, often anhedral, uneven.
Origin and occurrence In hydrothermal veins, regional metamorphic deposits.
Accessory minerals Chalcopyrite, pyrite, skutterudite, chloanthite, quartz, arsenopyrite.
Similar minerals Blooms of red cobalt simplify distinction from nickel ores; safflorite has a different crystal form; skutterudite and chloanthite are harder; pyrite is more yellowish; arsenopyrite has a different crystal form.

4 Ilmenite *Titanic iron ore*

Chem. formula $FeTiO_3$
Hardness 5–6, **Sp. gr.** 4.5–5
Color Iron black
Streak Black
Luster Metallic, but often tarnishes dull
Cleavage None
Fracture Conchoidal to uneven
Tenacity Brittle
Crystal form Trigonal

Morphology Rhombohedral, thick to thin tabular crystals, sometimes intergrown into roses (ilmenite roses), often granular, uneven.
Origin and occurrence Anhedral in igneous rocks, pegmatites, unrolled grains in placers, tabular crystals and ilmenite roses on alpine fissures.
Accessory minerals Hematite, magnetite, epidote, apatite, rutile.
Similar minerals Magnetite has a different crystal form (usually octahedral); hematite has a red streak; using simple means, ilmenite is indistinguishable from titaniferous hematite, which likewise has a black streak.

Localities	
1 Kola, Russia	**3** Siegerland Region, Germany
2 Jakobshyttan, Sweden	**4** Froland, Norway

1
2
3
4

1 Löllingite

Chem. formula $FeAs_2$
Hardness 5, **Sp. gr.** 7.1–7.4
Color Silver white, tarnishes darker
Streak Gray-black
Luster Metallic
Cleavage Distinct basal
Fracture Uneven
Tenacity Brittle
Crystal form Orthorhombic

Morphology Acicular, prismatic, tabular crystals, often intergrown into star-shaped triplets, columnar, radial, granular, anhedral, uneven.
Origin and occurrence In tin ore veins, pegmatites, hydrothermal veins, in metasomatic deposits.
Accessory minerals Siderite, arsenopyrite.
Similar minerals Arsenopyrite is lighter, somewhat darker when freshly fractured, slightly harder; safflorite cannot be distinguished from löllingite by simple means; nevertheless, the frequent appearance of red cobalt bloom in association with safflorite gives an indication.

2 Allanite *Orthite*

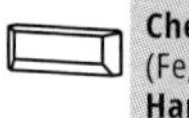

Chem. formula $Ca(Ce,Th)(Fe,Mg)Al_2[O/OH/SiO_4/Si_2O_7]$
Hardness 5½, **Sp. gr.** 3–4.2
Color Pitch black, translucent purple-brown
Streak Green-gray to brown-black
Luster Greasy vitreous
Cleavage Indiscernible
Fracture Conchoidal
Tenacity Brittle
Crystal form Monoclinic

Morphology Rarely tabular crystals, prismatic, elongated tabular to acicular, often unevenly anhedral.
Origin and occurrence In granites, syenites, diorites, gneisses, pegmatites, on alpine fissures, in volcanic ejecta.
Accessory minerals Monazite, xenotime, sanidine, quartz, nosean, apatite.
Similar minerals Black allanite is almost indistinguishable from other black, uneven pegmatite minerals by simple means; rutile never has purple tones.

3 Gersdorffite

Chem. formula NiAsS
Hardness 5½, **Sp. gr.** 5.9
Color Steel gray, mainly tarnishes black
Streak Black
Luster Metallic
Cleavage Perfect
Fracture Uneven
Tenacity Brittle
Crystal form Cubic

Morphology Octahedral, cubic, cubooctahedral, euhedral crystals, uneven.
Origin and occurrence In nickel-bearing hydrothermal veins along with other nickel ores.
Accessory minerals Siderite, uraninite, chalcopyrite, pyrite, calcite, quartz.
Similar minerals Galena has a different color and is considerably softer; pyrite is more yellowish and harder; marcasite has a different crystal form; cobaltite is slightly softer; arsenopyrite has a different crystal form.

4 Groutite

Chem. formula MnOOH
Hardness 5½, **Sp. gr.** 4.2
Color Black
Streak Brown-black
Luster Vitreous to metallic
Cleavage Perfect
Fracture Uneven
Tenacity Brittle
Crystal form Orthorhombic

Morphology Thick tabular, prismatic to acicular, often also lenticular crystals, radial, uneven.
Origin and occurrence In the oxidation zone of manganese-rich deposits, in limonite concretions, on cracks in silicified wood.
Accessory minerals Rhodochrosite, limonite, pyrolusite, romanechite, quartz.
Similar minerals Manganite and pyrolusite have a different crystal form; romanechite is harder; tourmaline has a different crystal form.

Localities

1 St. Andreasberg, Harz, Germany	**3** Mitterberg, Salzburg, Austria
2 New Mexico, USA	**4** Woodruff, Arizona, USA

1
2
3
4

1 Arsenopyrite *Mispickel*

Chem. formula FeAsS
Hardness 5½–6, **Sp. gr.** 5.9–6.2
Color Pewter white to steel gray, often tarnishes darker
Streak Black
Luster Metallic
Cleavage Indiscernible
Fracture Uneven
Tenacity Brittle
Crystal form Orthorhombic

Morphology Octahedral-like to prismatic or tabular crystals, often twins, sometimes intergrown to six-pointed stars, often uneven, anhedral.
Origin and occurrence In pegmatites and tin ore veins, but especially in hydrothermal veins.
Accessory minerals Pyrite, gold, pyrrhotite, siderite, chalcopyrite, quartz, calcite, rhodochrosite.
Similar minerals Pyrite and marcasite have a golden yellow color; magnetite is slightly softer; löllingite is slightly softer but remains hard to distinguish by simple means.

2 Chloanthite *Nickelskutterudite*

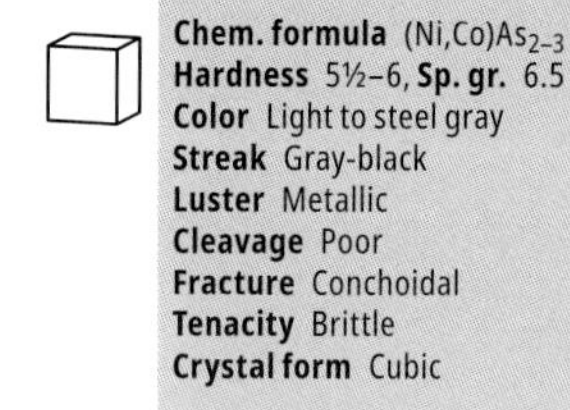

Chem. formula $(Ni,Co)As_{2-3}$
Hardness 5½–6, **Sp. gr.** 6.5
Color Light to steel gray
Streak Gray-black
Luster Metallic
Cleavage Poor
Fracture Conchoidal
Tenacity Brittle
Crystal form Cubic

Morphology Octahedral and cubic crystals, also cubic in combination with rhombic dodecahedral, euhedral and anhedral, uneven.
Origin and occurrence In hydrothermal deposits.
Accessory minerals Cobaltite, barite, quartz, calcite, native bismuth, native silver.
Similar minerals Almost impossible to distinguish from linneite and siegenite using simple means. Pyrite is more yellow and harder; arsenopyrite has a different crystal form; galenite has perfect cubic cleavage.

3 Niobite

Chem. formula $(Fe,Mn)Nb_2O_6$
Hardness 6, **Sp. gr.** 5.3–8.1
Color Brown-black to black
Streak Brown to black
Luster Pitchy
Cleavage Scarcely distinct
Fracture Conchoidal
Tenacity Brittle
Crystal form Orthorhombic

Morphology Tabular to acicular crystals, radial, mainly anhedral.
Origin and occurrence In pegmatites.
Accessory minerals Pitchblende, quartz, feldspar.
Distinguishing feature The following end members of the solid solutions of niobite $(Fe,Mn)Nb_2O_6$ and tantalite $(Fe,Mn)Ta_2O_6$ are referred to as columbites.
Similar minerals Hematite has a different streak; ilmenite has a different crystal form; niobite and tantalite are indistinguishable using simple means.

4 Tantalite

Chem. formula $(Fe,Mn)Ta_2O_6$
Hardness 6, **Sp. gr.** 5.3–8.1
Color Brown-black to black
Streak Brown to black
Luster Pitchy
Cleavage Scarcely distinct
Fracture Conchoidal
Tenacity Brittle
Crystal form Orthorhombic

Morphology Tabular to acicular crystals, radial, mainly anhedral.
Origin and occurrence In pegmatites.
Accessory minerals Pitchblende, quartz, feldspar.
Distinguishing feature The following end members of the solid solutions of niobite $(Fe,Mn)Nb_2O_6$ and tantalite $(Fe,Mn)Ta_2O_6$ are referred to as columbites.
Similar minerals Hematite has a different streak; ilmenite has a different crystal form; niobite and tantalite are indistinguishable using simple means.

Localities	
1 Freiberg, Saxony, Germany	**3** Bendada, Portugal
2 Schneeberg, Saxony, Germany	**4** Minas Gerais, Brazil

1
2
3
4

1 Ilvaite *Lievrite*

Chem. formula $CaFe_2^{2+}Fe^{3+}[OH/O/Si_2O_7]$
Hardness 5½–6, **Sp. gr.** 4.1
Color Black
Streak Black
Luster Vitreous, slightly resinous, often dull
Cleavage Scarcely discernible
Fracture Conchoidal
Tenacity Brittle
Crystal form Orthorhombic

Morphology Prismatic crystals anhedral, radial, columnar aggregates, anhedral granular or uneven.
Origin and occurrence In iron-rich contact deposits.
Accessory minerals Hedenbergite, magnetite, pyrite, hematite, arsenopyrite, garnet (andradite), quartz.
Similar minerals Tourmaline is harder; strahlstein (actinolite) has a different paragenesis and the typical cleavage of members of the amphibole group (cleavage planes at an angle of about 120°).

2 Uraninite *Pitchblende*

Chem. formula UO_2
Hardness 6, often lower if uneven, **Sp. gr.** 9.1–10.6
Color Black, gray, brownish
Streak Black
Luster Greasy, often dull
Cleavage Mainly indistinct
Fracture Conchoidal
Tenacity Brittle
Crystal form Cubic

Morphology Cubic, octahedral crystals, reniform, botryoidal, earthy, uneven.
Origin and occurrence In pegmatites, microscopically in granites, in hydrothermal veins, in sandstones and Precambrian placers.
Accessory minerals Torbernite, zeunerite, saleite, autunite and numerous other uranium oxidation minerals, barite.
Similar minerals Magnetite has a different luster, is magnetic and non-radioactive.
Caution! Pitchblende is highly radioactive!

3 Thorianite

Chem. formula ThO_2
Hardness 6, often lower if uneven, **Sp. gr.** 9.1–10.6
Color Black, gray, brownish
Streak Black
Luster Greasy, often dull
Cleavage Mainly indistinct
Fracture Conchoidal
Tenacity Brittle
Crystal form Cubic

Morphology Cubic crystals, mainly anhedral, uneven.
Origin and occurrence In pegmatites, microscopically in granites, in hydrothermal veins, rarely in alpine fissures.
Accessory minerals Torbernite, zeunerite, saleite, autunite and numerous other uranium oxidation minerals, barite.
Similar minerals Magnetite has a different luster, is magnetic and non-radioactive; pitchblende is indistinguishable using simple means.
Caution! Thorianite is highly radioactive!

4 Ullmannite

Chem. formula NiSbS
Hardness 5–5½, **Sp. gr.** 6.65
Color Steel gray
Streak Black
Luster Metallic
Cleavage Perfect
Fracture Uneven
Tenacity Brittle
Crystal form Cubic

Morphology Cuboidal and octahedral crystals, anhedral and euhedral, botryoidal aggregates, uneven.
Origin and occurrence In nickel-bearing hydrothermal veins.
Accessory minerals Siderite, linneite, siegenite, chalcopyrite, pyrite, galena.
Similar minerals Ullmannite is indistinguishable from gersdorffite using simple means; magnetite occurs in a different paragenesis; siegenite and linneite are more silvery; galenite is much softer.

Localities	
1 Serifos, Greece	**3** Antsirabé, Madagascar
2 Hagendorf, East Bavaria, Germany	**4** Siegerland Region, Germany

1
2

3
4

1 Rammelsbergite

Chem. formula $NiAs_2$
Hardness 5½–6, **Sp. gr.** 6.97
Color Pewter white with reddish tinge, usually tarnishes yellowish
Streak Gray
Luster Metallic
Cleavage None
Fracture Uneven
Tenacity Brittle
Crystal form Orthorhombic

Morphology Tabular crystals, often intergrown into cockscomb aggregates, botryoidal aggregates, anhedral massive, uneven.
Origin and occurrence In nickel-bearing hydrothermal deposits.
Accessory minerals Skutterudite, löllingite, chloanthite, annabergite, quartz, calcite.
Similar minerals Löllingite and safflorite in crystals cannot be distinguished from rammelsbergite using simple means; nevertheless, the nickel-rich paragenesis gives an indication.

2 Skutterudite *Smaltite*

Chem. formula $(Co,Ni)As_3$
Hardness 6, **Sp. gr.** 6.8
Color Pewter white
Streak Black
Luster Metallic
Cleavage None
Fracture Conchoidal
Tenacity Brittle
Crystal form Cubic

Morphology Octahedral crystals, euhedral and anhedral, often uneven.
Origin and occurrence In cobalt-nickel deposits.
Accessory minerals Chloanthite, cobaltite, erythrite, calcite, barite.
Similar minerals Chloanthite is indistinguishable from skutterudite using simple means; coatings of red cobalt or nickel bloom provide indications; safflorite and rammelsbergite have a different crystal form. Ullmannite is blacker; galena has perfect cubic cleavage.

3 Pyrolusite *Manganese dioxide*

Chem. formula MnO_2
Hardness 6, but in aggregates often appears significantly lower, **Sp. gr.** 4.9–5.1
Color Silver gray to black
Streak Black
Luster Metallic to dull
Cleavage None
Fracture Conchoidal, in aggregates brittle to fibrous
Tenacity Brittle
Crystal form Tetragonal

Morphology Prismatic to thick tabular crystals, stellate aggregates, earthy, drusy.
Origin and occurrence In hydrothermal veins, in the oxidation zone, in sediments as small globules (oolites).
Accessory minerals Manganite, romanechite, quartz, barite, rhodochrosite, hausmannite.
Similar minerals Manganite has a brown streak; stibnite is not as brittle and is much softer; romanechite is slightly harder.

4 Crocidolite

Chem. formula $Na_2[(Fe^{2+}Mg)_3Fe_2{}^{3+}]Si_8O_{22}(OH)_2$
Hardness 6, **Sp. gr.** 3.4
Color Black, steel blue
Streak Gray
Luster Metallic
Cleavage Excellent, with a cleavage angle of 120°
Fracture Fibrous
Tenacity Brittle
Crystal form Monoclinic

Morphology Prismatic to acicular crystals, fibrous, asbestos-type aggregates.
Origin and occurrence In alkali granites and syenites, in iron deposits of types of banded iron stones as asbestos.
Accessory minerals Limonite, quartz.
Similar minerals The blue fibrous aggregates are unmistakable.
Caution! Crocydolite (blue asbestos) is carcinogenic when inhaled!

Localities	
1 Bou Azzer, Morocco	**3** Ilfeld, Harz, Germany
2 Schneeberg, Saxony, Germany	**4** Transvaal, South Africa

1
2
3
4

1 Magnetite *Magnetic iron ore, lodestone*

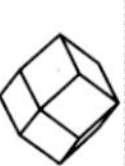

Chem. formula Fe_3O_4
Hardness 6–6½, **Sp. gr.** 5.2
Color Iron black
Streak Black
Luster Dull metallic
Cleavage Scarcely discernible
Fracture Conchoidal
Tenacity Brittle
Crystal form Cubic

Morphology Octahedral, rhombic dodecahedral, euhedral and anhedral, uneven in large masses.
Origin and occurrence Anhedral in igneous rocks, in large masses in pneumatolytic replacement deposits and metamorphic deposits, anhedral crystals in chlorite and talc schists, in hydrothermal veins, beautiful euhedral crystals in alpine fissures.
Accessory minerals Pyrite, ilmenite, hematite, apatite, epidote.
Distinguishing feature Magnetite is, as the name already states, magnetic. This means that it is not only attracted by a magnet, but can also act like a magnet itself and, for example, attract smaller iron objects.
Similar minerals All similar minerals are non-magnetic or only weakly magnetic; chromite has a light brown streak; hematite has a red streak.

2 Ixiolite

Chem. formula $(Ta,Fe,Sn,Nb,Mn)_4O_8$
Hardness 6–6½, **Sp. gr.** 7–7.2
Color Black
Streak Black
Luster Greasy metallic
Cleavage None
Tenacity Brittle
Crystal form Orthorhombic

Morphology Prismatic, tabular crystals, mainly anhedral, uneven.
Origin and occurrence In pegmatites, almost always anhedral.
Accessory minerals Feldspar, niobite, tantalite, beryl, quartz, uraninite.
Similar minerals Niobite and tantalite are indistinguishable from ixiolite using simple means; magnetite has a different crystal form and is magnetic; hematite and ilmenite have a different crystal form; moreover, hematite has a red streak.

3–4 Epidote

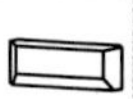

Chem. formula $Ca_2(Fe,Al)Al_2[O/OH/SiO_4/Si_2O_7]$
Hardness 6–7, **Sp. gr.** 3.3–3.5
Color Yellow-green, dark green, black-green
Streak Greenish black
Luster Vitreous
Cleavage Poorly distinct
Fracture Conchoidal
Tenacity Brittle
Crystal form Monoclinic

Morphology Prismatic, rarely thick tabular crystals, radial aggregates, uneven anhedral in rocks.
Origin and occurrence In vugs and cavities of pegmatites, in epidote schists, on fissures of granites and metamorphic rocks.
Accessory minerals Actinolite, diopside, albite, apatite, quartz, garnet, magnetite.
Distinguishing feature Tight intergrowths of greenish epidote and reddish potassium feldspar are sometimes cut into gemstones and given the special name unakite.
Similar minerals Unlike epidote, augite, hornblende and actinolite have perfect cleavage; tourmaline has a different crystal form.

Localities	
1 Binntal, Switzerland	**3** Skardu, Pakistan
2 Viitaniemi, Finland	**4** Prince of Wales Island, Alaska, USA

1
2
3
4

1–4 Pyrite *Fool's gold*

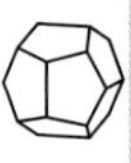

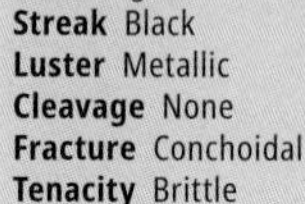

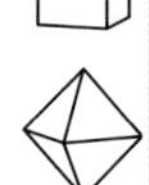

Chem. formula FeS_2
Hardness 6–6½, **Sp. gr.** 5–5.2
Color Light brass colors
Streak Black
Luster Metallic
Cleavage None
Fracture Conchoidal
Tenacity Brittle
Crystal form Cubic

In strongly schistose sedimentary rocks, pyrite does not form spheres but, depending on the position between the schistose surfaces, it forms flat, circular aggregates, called pyrite suns.

Flat pyrite crystals from Huanzalá, Peru.

Morphology Cubic with striated faces, octahedral, pentagon-dodecahedral, stellate and reniform aggregates, rarely spheres or disk-shaped aggregates (pyrite suns), often also uneven.

Origin and occurrence Pyrite is a very common and widespread mineral. It is found intergrown in rocks of all kinds, in intramagmatic deposits, in hydrothermal veins, as concretion in sediments such as limestones or argillaceous shales (here often spheres or round disks, so-called pyrite suns, Fig. 5), in metamorphic deposits. Frequently euhedral crystals in sizes up to many centimeters and crystal specimens up to several tons in weight. Pyrite is not in itself a sought-after ore mineral; it is useless as an iron ore because of its sulfur content. Frequently, however, pyrite deposits contain some copper content. Then this pyrite is mined as copper ore.

Caution! When poorly ventilated, old mine tunnels in pyrite-rich rock may sometimes no longer contain breathable air.

Pyrite has been cut for jewelry purposes, particularly during the Art Deco period. These faceted stones are usually called marcasite although they are always pyrite, not the mineral marcasite.

Accessory minerals Sphalerite, galena, arsenopyrite, quartz, calcite.

Distinguishing feature Pyrite can transform into goethite through oxidation. In the process, it frequently retains its original external shape. This results in pseudomorphs from limonite to pyrite, which still exhibit the typical shape of pyrite, for example a pentagonal dodecahedral, cubic or octahedral crystal, but differ due to their brown to black color. Then such a pseudomorph often still contains remnants of the former golden yellow pyrite within it.

Heat is formed during the weathering of pyrite, drawing oxygen from the air. This leads to heating of the rocks and, in cases where oxidation of pyrite-rich coals occurs, can even lead to spontaneous combustion of coal seams.

Similar minerals Marcasite has a different crystal form (tabular crystals, cockscomb aggregates) and is a shade greener but, in uneven or in reniform, radial aggregates, is often indistinguishable by simple means; chalcopyrite is noticeably softer; native gold is much softer and not brittle like pyrite.

Localities	
1 Rettigheim, Heidelberg, Germany	**3** Logrono, Spain
2 Poona, India	**4** Siegerland Region, Germany

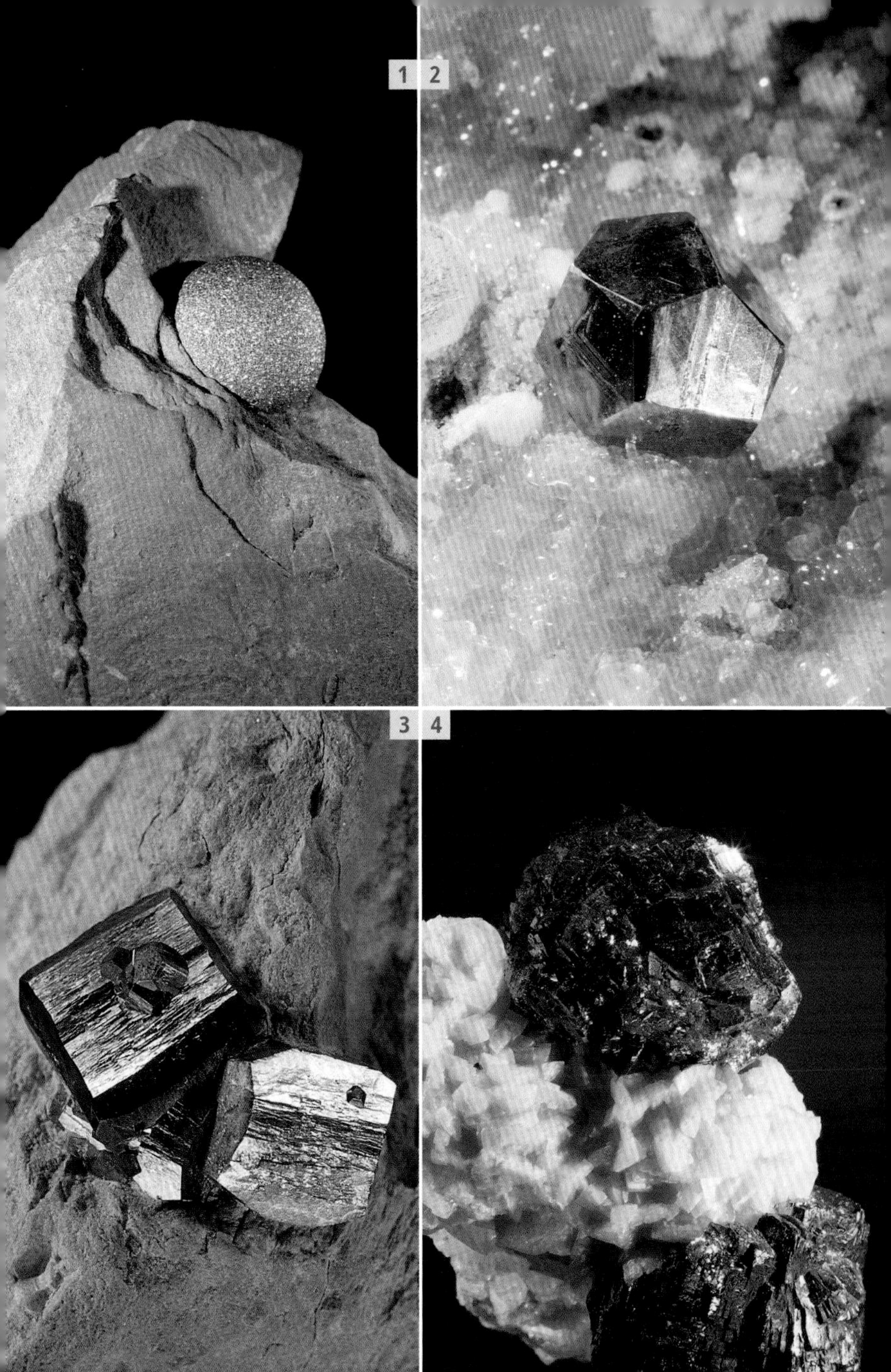
1
2
3
4

1–2 Marcasite *White iron pyrite, cockscomb pyrites*

Chem. formula FeS_2
Hardness 6–6½, **Sp. gr.** 4.8–4.9
Color Brass yellow with green tinge
Streak Black
Luster Metallic
Cleavage Poor
Fracture Uneven
Tenacity Brittle
Crystal form Orthorhombic

Morphology Tabular crystals are often intergrown into serrated, comb-shaped groups, radial and conchoidal, reniform aggregates, botryoidal aggregates, uneven.
Origin and occurrence As concretions in hydrothermal, low-temperature replacement deposits, but also in the form of anhedral crystals in sediments, particularly limestones and marls.
Accessory minerals Pyrite, pyrrhotite, calcite, arsenopyrite, chalcopyrite.
Distinguishing feature Marcasite is not actually stable under the conditions at the Earth's surface. Therefore, it often transforms. Radial aggregates in particular are often already pyrites when examined more closely. Marcasite can also transform to limonite when exposed to air, but such pseudomorphs of limonite after marcasite are much rarer than those of pyrite.
Similar minerals Pyrite does not have a greenish tinge and has a different crystal form (cubic, pyritohedron), but is, however, difficult to distinguish from marcasite when in a uneven, radial aggregate form; chalcopyrite is softer; magnetopyrite and arsenopyrite have a different color.

3–4 Romanechite *Psilomelane*

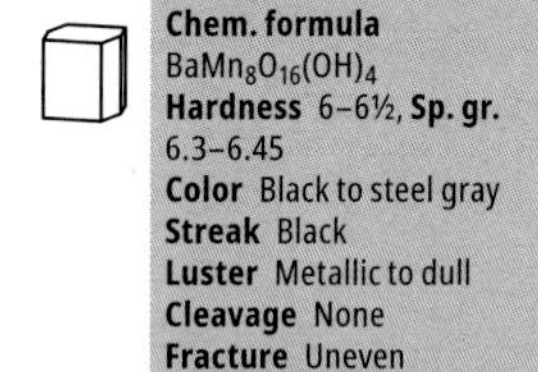

Chem. formula $BaMn_8O_{16}(OH)_4$
Hardness 6–6½, **Sp. gr.** 6.3–6.45
Color Black to steel gray
Streak Black
Luster Metallic to dull
Cleavage None
Fracture Uneven
Tenacity Brittle
Crystal form Monoclinic

Morphology Reniform, stalactitic aggregates, radial, earthy, uneven.
Origin and occurrence As concretions in sediments in weathering deposits, as replacements in limestones, as encurstations on limonite.
Accessory minerals Pyrolusite, manganite, barite, quartz, calcite, hausmannite.
Distinguishing feature The specific gravity varies greatly depending on the aggregate form; it can even fall almost as low as 1, therefore the hardness is not necessarily a diagnostic characteristic for this mineral. Significantly soft masses, which may in some cases also comprise other manganese oxides, are called wads.
Similar minerals Pyrolusite has a different crystal form but is difficult to distinguish in uneven or reniform aggregates. Coronadite cannot be distinguished by simple means, but its paragenesis with lead minerals provides an indication.

Localities	
1 Meggen, Sauerland, Germany	**3** Siegerland Region, Germany
2 Torrelarega, Spain	**4** Siegerland Region, Germany

1
2
3
4

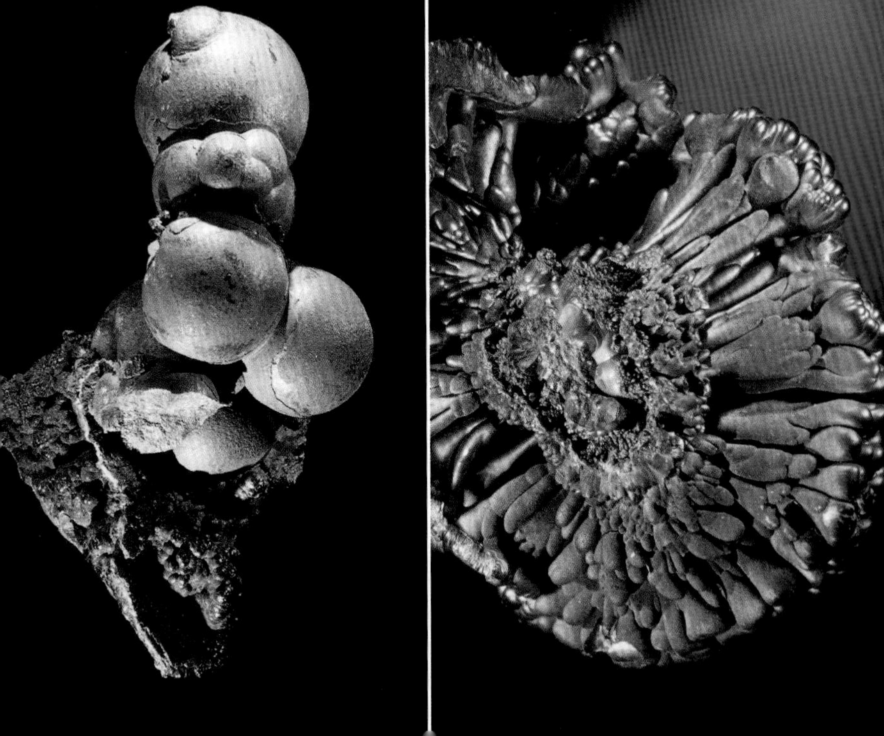

1 Sperrylite

Chem. formula $PtAs_2$
Hardness 6–7, **Sp. gr.** 10.4–10.6
Color Pewter white
Streak Black
Luster Metallic
Cleavage Indiscernible
Fracture Conchoidal
Tenacity Brittle
Crystal form Cubic

Morphology Cubic, cuboctahedral, usually anhedral crystals in pyrrhotine or chalcopyrite.
Origin and occurrence In intramagmatic, platinum-bearing sulfide deposits.
Accessory minerals Chalcopyrite, pyrrhotite, native platinum, pyrite, pentlandite.
Similar minerals Cobaltine is softer; pyrite is more yellowish; galena has perfect cubic cleavage. The paragenesis and the type of occurrence are highly typical.

2 Hibonite

Chem. formula $(Ca,Ce)(Al,Ti,Mg)_{12}O_{19}$
Hardness 7½–8, **Sp. gr.** 3.84
Color Black to black-brown
Streak Brown-black
Luster Vitreous to slightly metallic
Cleavage Discernible
Fracture Conchoidal
Tenacity Brittle
Crystal form Hexagonal

Morphology Prismatic to thick tabular crystals, anhedral and euhedral.
Origin and occurrence In metamorphic limestone, rarely anhedral in meteorites.
Accessory minerals Thorianite, corundum, spinel, calcite, phlogopite.
Similar minerals Corundum is never black; tourmaline has a different streak form and a white streak color; hematite and ilmenite have a much more metallic luster and a different streak color.

3 Bixbyite

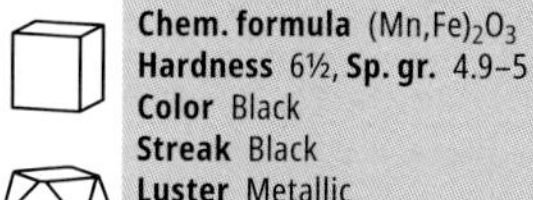

Chem. formula $(Mn,Fe)_2O_3$
Hardness 6½, **Sp. gr.** 4.9–5
Color Black
Streak Black
Luster Metallic
Cleavage Octahedral distinct
Fracture Uneven
Tenacity Brittle
Crystal form Cubic

Morphology Cubic crystals, often with beveled corners, often uneven.
Origin and occurrence In metamorphic manganese deposits and in volcanic rocks and their cavities.
Accessory minerals Topaz, spessartine, braunite, hausmannite, hollandite.
Similar minerals Magnetite has no cleavage and almost never forms cubes; moreover, it is distinctly magnetic. Garnet almost never forms cubes.

4 Gahnite *Kreittonite*

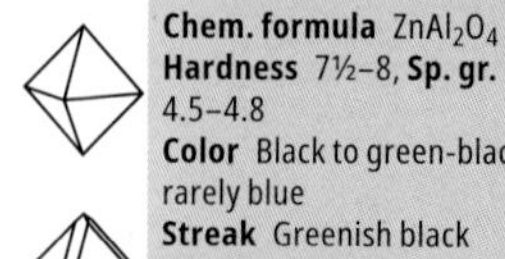

Chem. formula $ZnAl_2O_4$
Hardness 7½–8, **Sp. gr.** 4.5–4.8
Color Black to green-black, rarely blue
Streak Greenish black
Luster Vitreous to greasy
Cleavage Poor
Fracture Conchoidal
Tenacity Brittle
Crystal form Cubic

Morphology Octahedral crystals, partially with rhombic dodecahedral faces, euhedral and anhedral, more rarely uneven.
Origin and occurrence Accessory mineral in granites and pegmatites, in metamorphic rocks, in metamorphic sulfide deposits.
Accessory minerals Pyrrhotine, pyrite, cordierite, andesine, hypersthene, rhodonite, franklinite.
Similar minerals Magnetite is pure black and strongly magnetic; spinel is significantly lighter; franklinite is softer.

Localities	
1 Norilsk, Russia	**3** Thomas Range, Utah, USA
2 Fort Dauphin, Madagascar	**4** Silberberg Mine, Bodenmais, Bavarian Forest, Germany

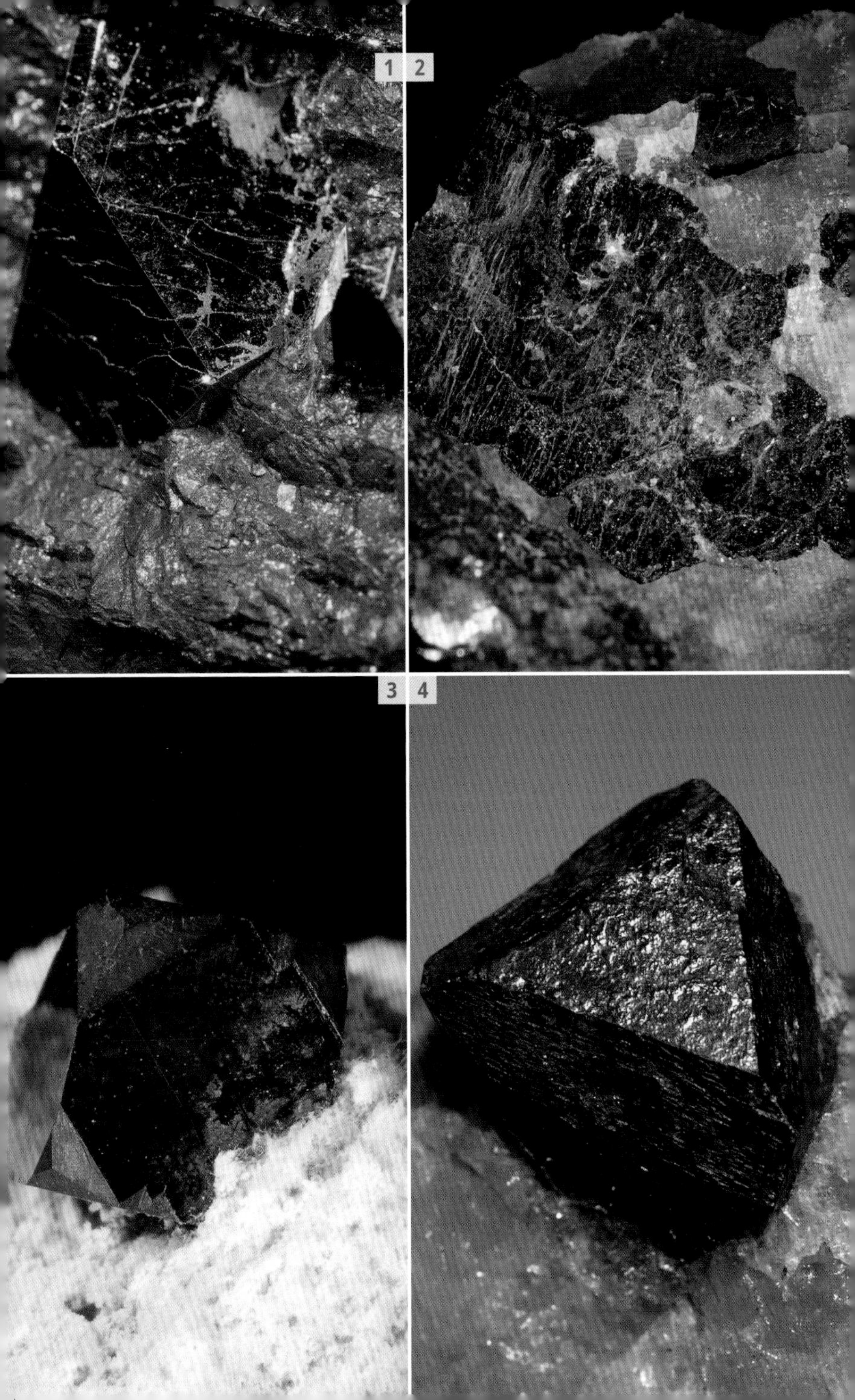
1
2
3
4

1

Mercury

Chem. formula Hg
Hardness –, **Sp. gr.** 13.6
Color Pewter white
Luster Metallic
Cleavage None
Crystal form Liquid

Morphology Forms droplets in cavities in cinnabar-rich ore.
Origin and occurrence On mercury deposits formed by oxidation of cinnabar.
Accessory minerals Cinnabar, mercury fahlore, calcite, fluorite.
Similar minerals Mercury is unmistakable as the only liquid mineral; moschellandsbergite may look like a droplet, but it is solid.

2

Kaolinite

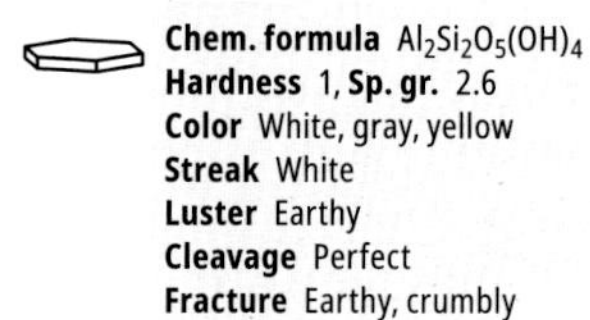

Chem. formula $Al_2Si_2O_5(OH)_4$
Hardness 1, **Sp. gr.** 2.6
Color White, gray, yellow
Streak White
Luster Earthy
Cleavage Perfect
Fracture Earthy, crumbly
Tenacity Non-brittle, plastic
Crystal form Triclinic

Morphology Crystals only microscopic, earthy, powdery, in plastic masses, uneven.
Origin and occurrence Develops through the weathering of silicates, especially feldspar.
Accessory minerals Quartz, feldspar, muscovite, biotite, calcite, limonite.
Similar minerals The low hardness and plastic behavior make kaolin quite unmistakable, but other clay minerals cannot be distinguished by simple means.

3

Talc *Steatite, soapstone*

Chem. formula $Mg_3[(OH)_2/Si_4O_{10}]$
Hardness 1, **Sp. gr.** 2.7–2.8
Color White, gray, yellow, brown, green, translucent to opaque
Streak White
Luster Pearly to greasy
Cleavage Basal perfect
Fracture Uneven to foliated
Tenacity Flexible, non-brittle
Crystal form Monoclinic

Morphology Very rarely well-formed crystals, foliated, dense with a reniform surface; often pseudomorphs after other minerals, for example after quartz crystals.
Origin and occurrence Anhedral in metamorphic rocks, as main component of talc schist, potstone; foliated aggregates as fissure filling in serpentines.
Accessory minerals Dolomite, magnesite, serpentine, calcite, magnetite.
Similar minerals The low hardness and greasy feel make talc quite unmistakable.

4

Glaucocerinite

Chem. formula $(Zn,Cu)_{10}Al_4SO_4(OH)_{30} \cdot 2\,H_2O$
Hardness 1, **Sp. gr.** 2.75
Color White to blue
Streak White
Luster Dull
Cleavage Indiscernible
Fracture Uneven
Tenacity Non-brittle
Crystal form Monoclinic

Morphology Drusy, dense with a reniform surface, stellate aggregates.
Origin and occurrence In the oxidation zone of zinc-copper deposits.
Accessory minerals Azurite, adamite, cuprian adamite, spangolite, serpierite, gibbsite, calcite.
Similar minerals Glaucocerinite is unmistakable. Gibbsite is harder; aurichalcite is more acicular and harder; chrysocolla is harder; smithsonite is harder.

Localities	
1 Almaden, Spain	**3** Arkansas, USA
2 Hirschau-Schnaittenbach, Bavaria, Germany	**4** Lavrion, Greece

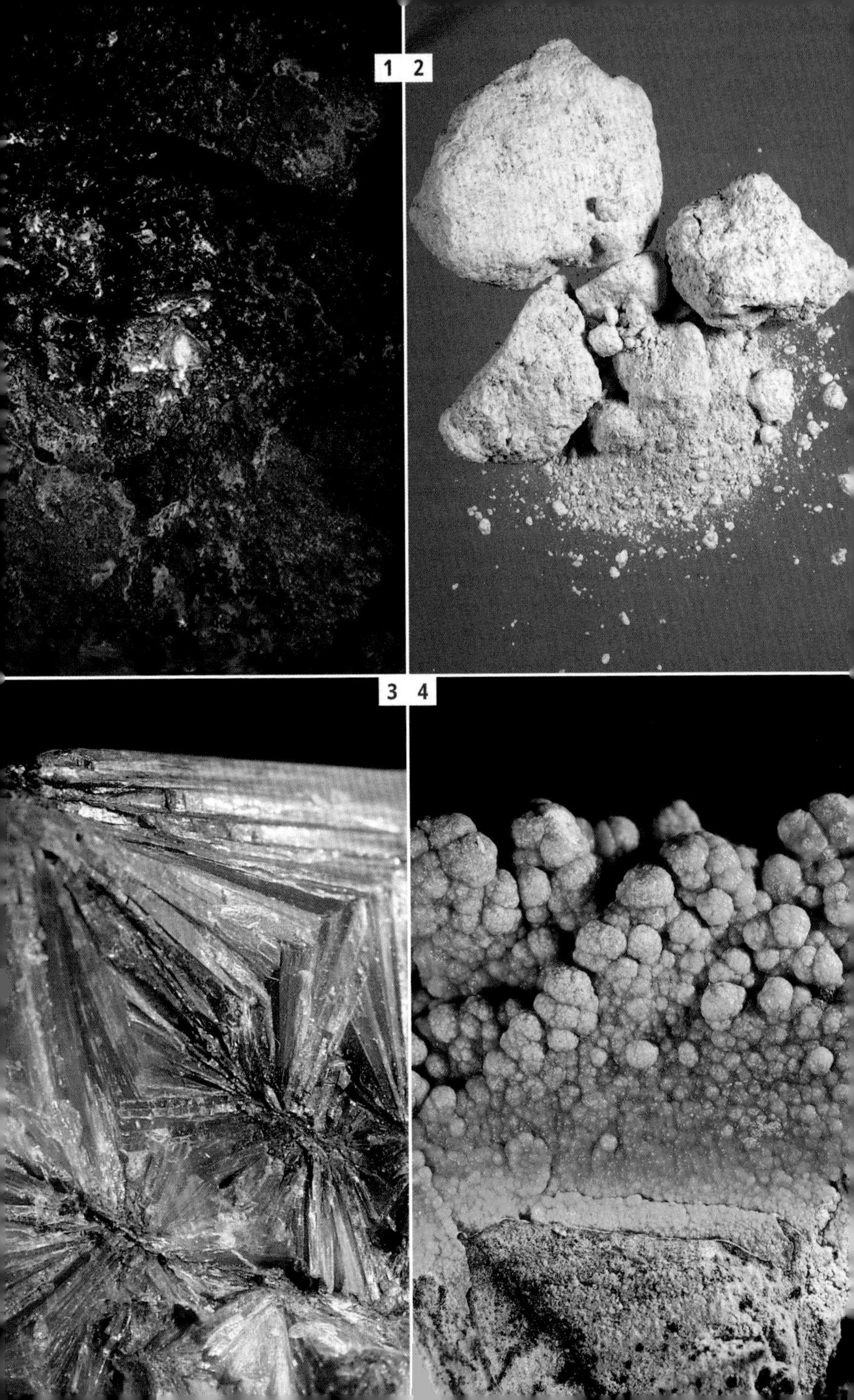
1 2
3 4

1

Larderellite

Chem. formula $NH_4B_5O_6(OH)_4$
Hardness 1, **Sp. gr.** 1.9
Streak White
Color White
Luster Dull
Cleavage Perfect
Fracture Uneven
Tenacity Non-brittle
Crystal form Monoclinic

Morphology Drusy coatings, foliated aggregates, earthy, uneven.
Origin and occurrence As deposition from boron-bearing waters in volcanic areas.
Accessory minerals Calcite, aragonite, opal and other boron minerals.
Similar minerals Its paragenesis is very characteristic; talc occurs with very different minerals and rocks; calcite and aragonite are much harder, and both effervesce when dabbed with diluted hydrochloric acid.

2

Leiteite

Chem. formula $(Zn,Fe)As_2O_4$
Hardness 1½, **Sp. gr.** 4.3
Color White, pink
Streak White
Luster Pearly
Cleavage Perfect
Fracture Foliated
Tenacity Non-brittle, inelastically flexible
Crystal form Monoclinic

Morphology Tabular to long tabular crystals, foliated cleavage pieces, often bent and crumpled, euhedral and anhedral.
Origin and occurrence In the oxidation zone of arsenic-bearing zinc deposits.
Accessory minerals Schneiderhöhnite, scorodite, dolomite, calcite, adamite.
Similar minerals High density, tenacity and cleavability make leiteite unmistakable. Gypsum is lighter and harder.

3

Thermonatrite

Chem. formula $Na_2CO_3 \cdot H_2O$
Hardness 1–1½, **Sp. gr.** 2.25
Color White, gray, pale yellow
Streak White
Luster Vitreous
Cleavage Perfect
Fracture Foliated
Tenacity Non-brittle
Crystal form Orthorhombic

Morphology Extremely rarely microscopic crystals, mainly as efflorescence, powdery encrustations and coatings.
Origin and occurrence As an alteration product of natrite, in salt lakes, as soil efflorescence.
Accessory minerals Rock salt, borax, trona, ulexite, sylvite.
Distinguishing feature Thermonatrite is water soluble.
Similar minerals Borax and trona are harder; calcite is harder and has perfect rhombohedral cleavage.

4

Vermiculite

Chem. formula $(Mg,Fe,Al)_3[(OH)_2/(Al,Si)_2Si_2O_{10}] \cdot 4\,H_2O$
Hardness 1, **Sp. gr.** 2.4–2.7
Color White, gray, yellow, brown, green, translucent to opaque
Streak White
Luster Pearly to dull
Cleavage Basal perfect
Fracture Uneven to foliated
Tenacity Flexible, non-brittle
Crystal form Monoclinic

Morphology Tabular crystals, foliated, scaly, worm-shaped curvature, aggregates of individual leaves folded like a money roll.
Origin and occurrence Created by hydrothermal alteration of igneous rocks, especially from biotite, by metamorphic alteration in the bordering area of serpentines.
Accessory minerals Biotite, serpentine, calcite, magnetite.
Distinguishing feature When heated (by a lighter!), swells up to 50 times its volume.
Similar minerals The low hardness and swelling when heated make vermiculite unmistakable.

Localities	
1 Larderello, Tuscany, Italy	**3** Salar de Atacama, Chile
2 Tsumeb, Namibia	**4** Phalaborwa, South Africa

1 2
3 4

1 Salmiac *Salammoniac*

Chem. formula NH_4Cl
Hardness 1–2, **Sp. gr.** 1.52
Color White, colorless
Streak White
Luster Greasy to dull
Cleavage Indiscernible
Fracture Uneven to earthy
Tenacity Brittle
Crystal form Cubic

Morphology Octahedral crystals, often skeletal, dendritic aggregates, earthy, drusy.
Origin and occurrence On volcanic rocks and burning coal, at volcanic gas outlets (fumaroles).
Accessory minerals Sulfur, alum.
Similar minerals Alum is indistinguishable from salammoniac by simple means. Gypsum is harder; calcite and aragonite are harder and effervesce when dabbed with diluted hydrochloric acid.

2 Hannayite

Chem. Chem. formula $(NH_4)_2Mg_3H_4(PO_4)4 \cdot 8\ H_20$
Hardness 1–2, **Sp. gr.** 2.03
Color White
Streak White
Luster Vitreous
Cleavage Perfect
Fracture Uneven
Tenacity Brittle
Crystal form Triclinic

Morphology Prismatic crystals, acicular sheaves, curly aggregates, fibrous, uneven.
Origin and occurrence In bat caves, formed by reaction of bat guano with the cave rock.
Accessory minerals Gypsum, struvite, newberyite.
Similar minerals Gypsum has a different tenacity; the occurrence in bat caves is not very aesthetic but very characteristic. Aragonite and calcite are much harder. Newberyite is also notably harder than hannayite.

3 Metasideronatrite

Chem. formula $Na_2Fe^{3+}(SO_4)_2(OH) \cdot 1\text{–}2\ H_2O$
Hardness 2, **Sp. gr.** 2.68
Color Yellow, straw yellow
Streak Yellowish white
Luster Silky
Cleavage Perfect
Fracture Foliated
Tenacity Brittle
Crystal form Orthorhombic

Morphology Tabular, prismatic crystals, stellate and sheaved aggregates, planar crystal intergrowth, powdery, uneven.
Origin and occurrence As an oxidation product of pyrite in desert environments, particularly in deposits near the sea coast.
Accessory minerals Pyrite, sulfur, natrojarosite, jarosite, gypsum, copiapite.
Similar minerals The silky luster is very characteristic; copiapite is harder but hardly distinguishable when in a powdery state.

4 Aurichalcite *Blue calamine*

Chem. formula $(Zn,Cu)_5[(OH)_3/CO_3]_2$
Hardness 2, **Sp. gr.** 3.6–4.3
Color Light blue, bluish, greenish blue
Streak White to light blue
Luster Silky to pearly
Cleavage Perfect
Fracture Foliated
Tenacity Non-brittle
Crystal form Orthorhombic

Morphology Foliated, acicular, stellate and sheaved aggregates, planar crystal intergrowth.
Origin and occurrence In the oxidation zone of copper-zinc deposits.
Accessory minerals Hemimorphite, smithsonite, rosasite, duftite, calcite, adamite.
Distinguishing feature Effervesces when dabbed with diluted hydrochloric acid.
Similar minerals Rosasite is harder and never flaky; serpierite is harder and does not effervesce when dabbed with diluted hydrochloric acid.

Localities	
1 Paricutin, Mexico	**3** Chuquicamata, Chile
2 Skipton Caves, Ballarat, Australia	**4** Albunol, Spain

1 2
3 4

1 Liskeardite

Chem. formula $(Al,Fe)_3AsO_4(OH)_6 \cdot 5\,H_2O$
Hardness 1–2, **Sp. gr.** 3.01
Color White, greenish, bluish
Streak White
Luster Silky to dull
Cleavage Discernible
Fracture Fibrous
Tenacity Brittle
Crystal form Monoclinic

Morphology Fibrous encrustations, acicular, radial aggregates, no single crystals.
Origin and occurrence In the oxidation zone of arsenic-bearing deposits.
Accessory minerals Scorodite, pharmacosiderite, jarosite, alunite, gibbsite.
Similar minerals Gibbsite is harder; glaucocerinite is indistinguishable from liskeardite by simple means; alunite is slightly harder; aragonite effervesces when dabbed with diluted hydrochloric acid.

2 Chlorargyrite *Cerargyrite*

Chem. formula $AgCl$
Hardness 1½, **Sp. gr.** 5.5–5.6
Color Colorless, white, yellowish, brownish, gray, black
Streak White to gray, shiny
Luster Adamantine to greasy
Cleavage None
Fracture Hackly
Tenacity Sectile
Crystal form Cubic

Morphology Rarely cubic crystals, mainly drusy, reniform coatings, uneven.
Origin and occurrence In the oxidation zone and cementation zone of silver deposits, particularly in desert environments.
Accessory minerals Argentite, native silver.
Similar minerals Color and tenacity are highly characteristic. Calcite crystals effervesce when dabbed with diluted hydrochloric acid; cerussite crystals are not sectile.

3 Guerinite

Chem. formula $Ca_5H_2(AsO_4)_4 \cdot 9\,H_2O$
Hardness 1½, **Sp. gr.** 2.68
Color White, pink
Streak White
Luster Pearly
Cleavage Perfect
Fracture Fibrous
Tenacity Brittle
Crystal form Monoclinic

Morphology Tabular crystals, acicular, botryoidal aggregates, encrustations.
Origin and occurrence In the oxidation zone of arsenic-bearing deposits.
Accessory minerals Pharmacolite, picropharmacolite, vladimirite, calcite, aragonite, native arsenic.
Similar minerals Pharmacolite and picropharmacolite have a different crystal form; vladimirite is harder; sainfeldite is glassier; calcite and aragonite effervesce when dabbed with diluted hydrochloric acid.

4 Vivianite *Blue iron ore*

Chem. formula $Fe_3[PO_4]_2 \cdot 8\,H_2O$
Hardness 2, **Sp. gr.** 2.6–2.7
Color Green to blue, white with the absence of air
Streak White
Luster Pearly
Cleavage Perfect
Fracture Foliated
Tenacity Thin flexible flakes, non-brittle
Crystal form Monoclinic

Morphology Prismatic to tabular crystals, botryoidal aggregates, uneven, powdery, earthy, encrustations.
Origin and occurrence In pegmatites, in the oxidation zone of ore deposits, in sediments.
Accessory minerals Triphyline, siderite, limonite, ludlamite, pyrite, pyrrhotine, quartz.
Similar minerals Azurite effervesces when dabbed with diluted hydrochloric acid; lazulite has a greasy luster and is harder; neither mineral has flexible tenacity; unlike vivianite, chalcanthite is soluble in water.

Localities	
1 Liskeard, Cornwall, Great Britain	**3** Richelsdorf, Hesse, Germany
2 Broken Hill, Australia	**4** Kertsch, Ukraine

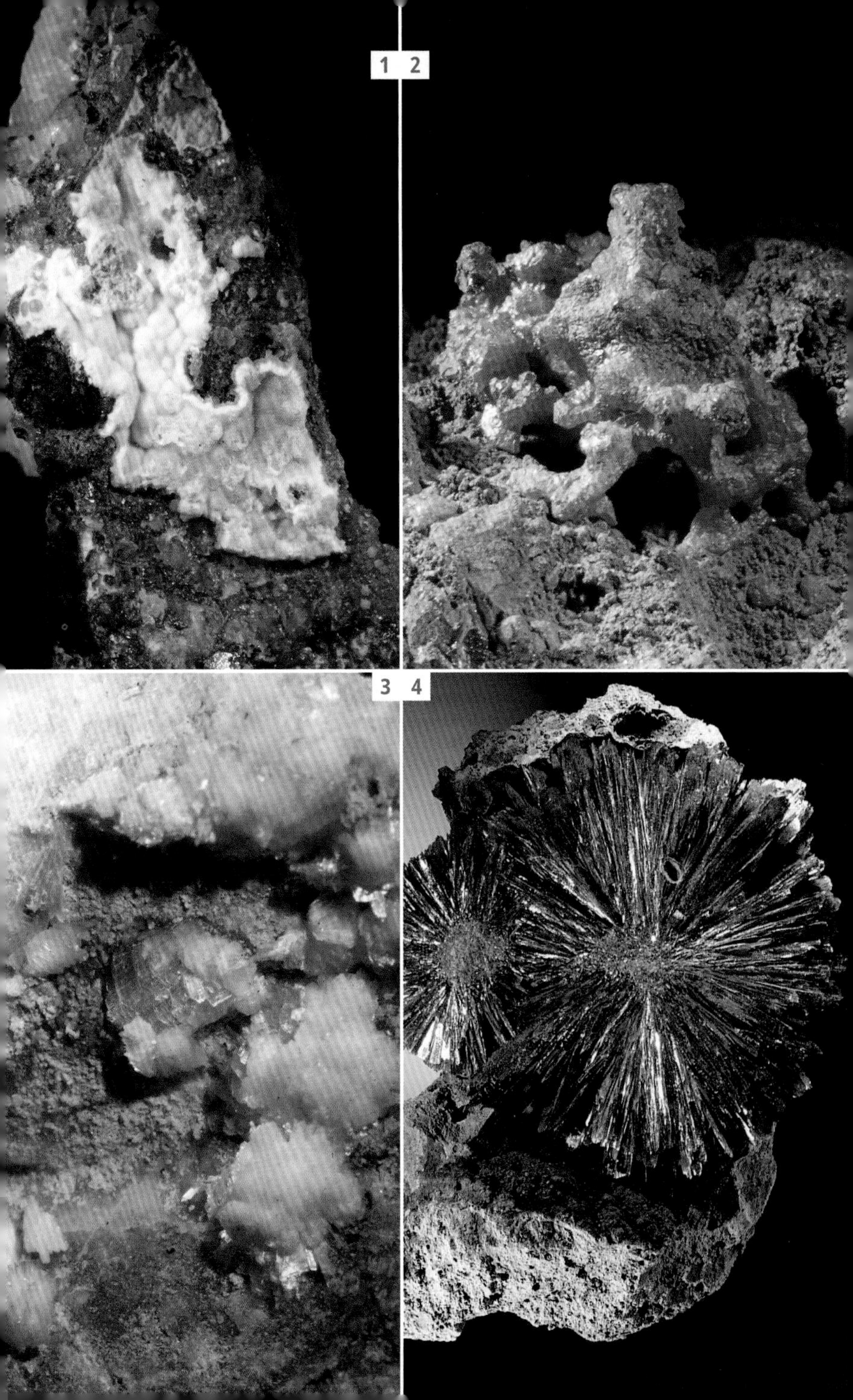

1 2
3 4

1 Pyrophyllite

Chem. formula $Al_2[(OH)_2/Si4O_{10}]$
Hardness 1½, **Sp. gr.** 2.8
Streak White
Color White, yellow, green, brown
Luster Pearly
Cleavage Basal perfect
Fracture Uneven
Tenacity Flexible, non-brittle
Crystal form Monoclinic

Morphology Foliated, stellate aggregates, reniform aggregates, uneven, dense.
Origin and occurrence In crystalline schists, in ore veins.
Accessory minerals Quartz, kyanite.
Similar minerals Talc is indistinguishable from pyrophyllite by simple means; hydroboracite is brittle; aragonite effervesces when dabbed with diluted hydrochloric acid; stilbite is harder.

2 Annabergite *Nickel bloom*

Chem. formula $Ni_3[AsO_4]_2 \cdot 8\,H_2O$
Hardness 2, **Sp. gr.** 3–3.1
Color Light green to apple green
Streak White
Luster Vitreous
Cleavage Perfect
Fracture Foliated
Tenacity Non-brittle, thin flexible flakes
Crystal form Monoclinic

Morphology Prismatic to tabular crystals, always with obliquely truncated end faces, acicular aggregates, usually uneven, earthy, drusy.
Origin and occurrence In the oxidation zone of nickel deposits, primarily as encrustations on nickel ores.
Accessory minerals Nickelite, millerite, dolomite, quartz, adamite.
Similar minerals Malachite and other green copper minerals are darker; the unique green of annabergite is very characteristic; malachite effervesces when dabbed with diluted hydrochloric acid.

3 Autunite *Calco-uranite*

Chem. formula $Ca[UO_2/PO_4]_2 \cdot 8\text{–}12\,H_2O$
Hardness 2–2½, **Sp. gr.** 3.2
Color Yellow with green tinge
Streak White to yellowish
Luster Vitreous, pearly on cleavage faces
Cleavage Perfect basal
Fracture Uneven
Tenacity Brittle to non-brittle
Crystal form Tetragonal

Morphology Tabular to thin tabular crystals, rarely dipyramidal, scaly, coatings, earthy, uneven.
Origin and occurrence In the oxidation zone of uranium deposits, on pegmatite fissures, on granitic rock fissures.
Accessory minerals Torbernite, zeunerite, pitchblende.
Distinguishing feature Autunite fluoresces under UV light.
Similar minerals Torbernite is green and does not fluoresce; uranocircite has a more yellow streak but is often indistinguishable using simple means.
Caution! Autunite is radioactive!

4 Halotrichite

Chem. formula $FeAl_2[SO_4]_4 \cdot 22\,H_2O$
Hardness 1½, **Sp. gr.** 1.73–1.79
Color White with slightly yellowish tinge
Streak White
Luster Silky to vitreous
Cleavage None
Fracture Fibrous
Tenacity Brittle
Crystal form Monoclinic

Morphology Acicular, fibrous, fibrous aggregates, bent curls, powdery, earthy.
Origin and occurrence As efflorescence at the outcrop of aluminum-rich rocks, in old mine workings, often weathering product of pyrite.
Accessory minerals Pickingerite, copiapite, pyrite, quartz, goethite.
Similar minerals Pickingerite, the corresponding magnesium mineral, is indistinguishable from halotrichite by simple means. Otherwise the structure is very typical.

Localities	
1 Beresowsk, Russia	**3** Hagendorf-Süd, East Bavaria, Germany
2 Lavrion, Greece	**4** Rodalquilar, Spain

1 2
3 4

1 Thomsenolite

Chem. formula $CaNaAlF_6 \cdot H_2O$
Hardness 2, **Sp. gr.** 2.98
Color Colorless, white, yellowish, brownish due to limonite
Streak White
Luster Vitreous
Cleavage Perfect
Fracture Uneven
Tenacity Brittle
Crystal form Monoclinic

Morphology Long to short prismatic crystals, often transversely striated.
Origin and occurrence As an alteration product in vugs in decomposed cryolite, in pegmatites, in vugs in alkaline rocks.
Accessory minerals Pachnolite, ralstonite, cryolite, jarlite, siderite, quartz, galena.
Similar minerals Pachnolite crystals have a diamond-shaped cross-section and are not striated; ralstonite has a different crystal form and is harder.

2 Sulfur

Chem. formula S
Hardness 2, **Sp. gr.** 2–2.1
Color Yellow, brownish yellow, greenish yellow, transparent to opaque
Streak White
Luster Resinous to greasy, adamantine on crystal surfaces
Cleavage Rarely present
Fracture Conchoidal
Tenacity Very brittle
Crystal form Orthorhombic

Morphology Euhedral crystals often dipyramidal, pointed pyramidal, rarely tabular, granular, fibrous, reniform, stalactitic, earthy, powdery.
Origin and occurrence Near volcanic gas leaks, veins, natural beds, accumulated veins, impregnations in sedimentary rocks, in salt deposits, on ore deposits with sulfide ores, as fillings in fossil cavities, on vugs in marbles.
Accessory minerals Calcite, celestine, aragonite, pyrite.
Similar minerals The rare yellow sphalerite is immediately distinguishable from sulfur by its good cleavage.

3 Sylvite

Chem. formula KCl
Hardness 2, **Sp. gr.** 1.99
Color Colorless, white, yellowish, orange, brownish
Streak White
Luster Vitreous
Cleavage Cubic, perfect
Fracture Uneven
Tenacity Brittle
Crystal form Cubic

Morphology Cubic crystals with corners beveled by octahedral crystals, granular, uneven.
Origin and occurrence In salt deposits, as efflorescence in steppes, rarely on volcanic rocks at gas outlets.
Accessory minerals Rock salt, carnallite, anhydrite.
Distinguishing feature Sylvite tastes bitter.
Similar minerals Rock salt does not taste bitter; carnallite has no cleavage; kieserite has a completely different crystal form.

4 Parasymplesite

Chem. formula $Fe_3(AsO_4)_2 \cdot 8\,H_2O$
Hardness 2, **Sp. gr.** 3.1
Color Green, gray-green, blue-green
Streak White
Luster Vitreous
Cleavage Perfect
Fracture Uneven
Tenacity Brittle to non-brittle
Crystal form Monoclinic

Morphology Long tabular, acicular crystals, acicular sheaves, stellate aggregates.
Origin and occurrence As a weathering product of arsenopyrite, in particular, in the oxidation zone of arsenic-bearing ore deposits.
Accessory minerals Köttigite, pyrite.
Similar minerals Symplesite is indistinguishable by simple means; annabergite is softer and exhibits a lighter green; malachite is more emerald green and effervesces when dabbed with diluted hydrochloric acid.

Localities	
1 Ivigtut, Greenland	**3** Wathingen, Celle, Lower Saxony, Germany
2 Agrigento, Sicily, Italy	**4** Saubach, Vogtland, Germany

1 2
3 4

1 Rock Salt *Halite*

Chem. formula NaCl
Hardness 2, **Sp. gr.** 2.1–2.2
Color Colorless, white, reddish, pink, yellow, gray, blue, transparent to opaque
Streak White
Luster Vitreous
Cleavage Cubic, perfect
Fracture Conchoidal
Tenacity Non-brittle to brittle
Crystal form Cubic

Morphology Almost exclusively cubic, very rarely octahedral, often euhedral, uneven, granular, fibrous, dense.
Origin and occurrence In rock salt deposits in large dense masses, in steppes and deserts in thin encrustations on the Earth's surface, at volcanic gas outlets.
Accessory minerals Gypsum, anhydrite, boracite.
Similar minerals Fluorite is harder and not water-soluble; it does not taste salty; nor does calcite, which also has a different crystal form.

2 Heliophyllite

Chem. formula $Pb_6As_2Cl_4O_7$
Hardness 2, **Sp. gr.** 6.9
Color Yellow
Streak White
Luster Vitreous
Cleavage Perfect
Fracture Uneven
Tenacity Brittle
Crystal form Orthorhombic

Morphology Tabular to thin tabular crystals, botryoidal aggregates, drusy.
Origin and occurrence In metamorphic deposits and old lead slags.
Accessory minerals Ecdemite, laurionite, paralaurionite, phosgenite, anglesite, aragonite, cerussite.
Similar minerals Paragenesis and color make heliophyllite unmistakable; calcite and aragonite effervesce when dabbed with diluted hydrochloric acid.

3 Dundasite

Chem. formula $Pb_2Al_4(CO_3)(OH)_8 \cdot 3\,H_2O$
Hardness 2, **Sp. gr.** 3.5
Color White
Streak White
Luster Vitreous to silky
Cleavage Perfect
Fracture Uneven
Tenacity Brittle
Crystal form Orthorhombic

Morphology Acicular crystals, planar crystal intergrowths, fibrous encrustations, coatings.
Origin and occurrence In the oxidation zone of lead deposits.
Accessory minerals Crocoite, cerussite, smithsonite, calcite, aragonite, goethite.
Similar minerals If the paragenesis is considered, dundasite is difficult to confuse; aragonite is harder; aurichalcite is more foliated and usually bluish.

4 Mellite *Honey-stone*

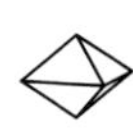

Chem. formula $C_{12}Al_2O_1 \cdot 18\,H_2O$
Hardness 2–2½, **Sp. gr.** 1.64
Color Brown, black
Streak White
Luster Vitreous to resinous
Cleavage None
Fracture Conchoidal
Tenacity Slightly brittle
Crystal form Tetragonal

Morphology Bipyramidal crystals, euhedral and anhedral, uneven, nodular.
Origin and occurrence In coal deposits, anhedral in clay, euhedral on fissures.
Accessory minerals Coal, clay minerals.
Similar minerals The low density and paragenesis of mellite do not allow for confusion; calcite exhibits perfect cleavage and effervesces when dabbed with diluted hydrochloric acid.

Localities	
1 Searles Lake, California, USA	**3** Dundas, Tasmania, Australia
2 Lavrion, Greece	**4** Tatabanya, Hungary

1 2
3 4

1–2 Gypsum *Selenite*

Chem. formula $CaSO_4 \cdot 2\,H_2O$
Hardness 2, **Sp. gr.** 2.3–2.4
Color Colorless, white, yellowish, pink, transparent to opaque
Streak White
Luster Pearly
Cleavage Perfect
Fracture Uneven
Tenacity Inelastically flexible, non-brittle to brittle
Crystal form Monoclinic

Morphology Prismatic to tabular crystals, lenticular, acicular, often twins with re-entrant angles (dovetail twins Fig. 2), fibrous (fibrous gypsum with silky luster), scaly, granular, dense (alabaster), rose-shaped (desert rose).
Origin and occurrence As crystals and concretions in clays and marls, on ore deposits, as a new formation in old mines, tunnels and deserts (here as so-called desert roses), in salt deposits.
Accessory minerals Anhydrite, rock salt, calcite, sulfur, pyrite, marcasite.
Distinguishing feature Gypsum crystals are inelastically flexible, which means that the crystals can be bent, but do not then return to their original shape after the pressure is released. Such bent crystals (see Fig. p. 9) can be found time and again in nature; they are a characteristic feature of the mineral gypsum. However, curly crystal aggregates, which are not uncommon in gypsum, were not formed by bending but rather grew into this shape.
Similar minerals Its cleavage and hardness distinguish gypsum from all other minerals.

3 Borax

Chem. formula $Na_2[B_4O_5(OH)_4] \cdot 8\,H_2O$
Hardness 2–2½, **Sp. gr.** 1.7–1.8
Color Colorless, white, yellowish, gray
Luster Greasy
Cleavage Sometimes distinct
Fracture Conchoidal
Tenacity Brittle
Crystal form Monoclinic

Morphology Short prismatic to tabular crystals, crystal aggregates, encrustations, powdery, uneven.
Origin and occurrence In borax lakes, particularly in arid areas, in deserts.
Accessory minerals Rock salt, soda.
Similar minerals Soda is softer; trona has excellent cleavage; calcite effervesces when dabbed with diluted hydrochloric acid; colemanite has a different crystal form; ulexite is always fibrous.

4 Hydrozincite *Zinc bloom*

Chem. formula $Zn_5[(OH)_3/CO_3]_2$
Hardness 2–2½, **Sp. gr.** 3.2–3.8
Color White to yellowish
Streak White
Luster Dull
Cleavage Mainly indiscernible due to the mineral morphology.
Fracture Earthy to fibrous
Tenacity Non-brittle
Crystal form Monoclinic

Morphology Rarely acicular crystals, mainly radial, reniform encrustations and coatings, earthy.
Origin and occurrence In the oxidation zone of zinc deposits.
Accessory minerals Smithsonite, hemimorphite, wulfenite, sphalerite, aragonite, calcite.
Distinguishing feature Hydrozincite fluoresces intensely with an orange color under UV light.
Similar minerals Its paragenesis, together with other zinc minerals, makes hydrozincite unmistakable.

Localities	
1 Salamanca, Spain	**3** Boron, California, USA
2 Montmartre, Paris, France	**4** Mittenwald, Bavaria, Germany

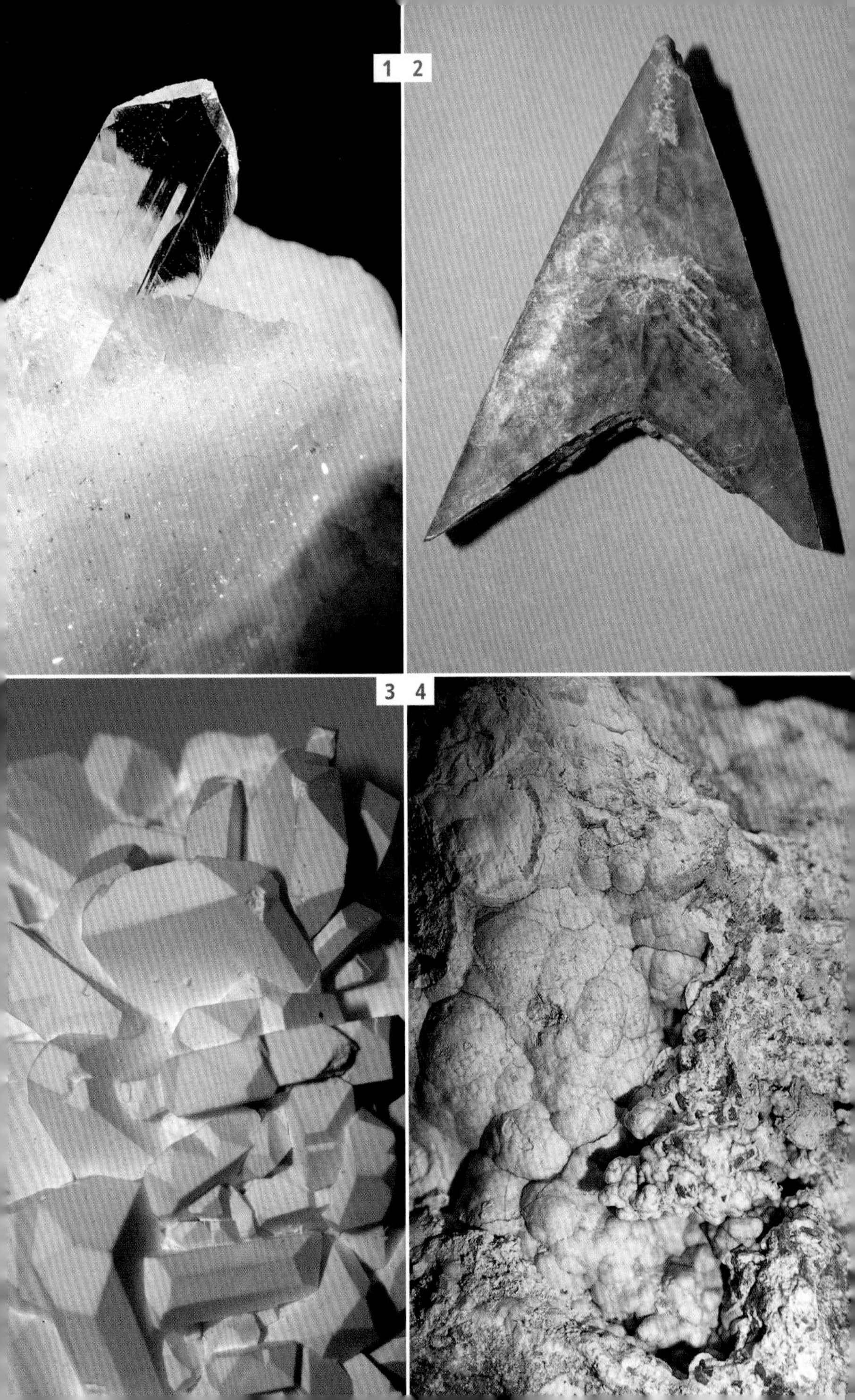
1
2
3
4

1–2 Ettringite

Chem. formula $Ca_6Al_2(SO_4)_3(OH)_{12} \cdot 24\,H_2O$
Hardness 2–2½, **Sp. gr.** 1.77
Color Colorless, yellow, white
Streak White
Luster Vitreous
Cleavage Scarcely discernible
Fracture Uneven
Tenacity Brittle
Crystal form Hexagonal

Morphology Prismatic, tabular and acicular crystals, fibrous, stellate.
Origin and occurrence In volcanic rocks in calcium-rich inclusions, in metamorphic manganese deposits.
Accessory minerals Calcite, afwillite, phillipsite, thaumasite, aragonite.
Distinguishing feature Ettringite is artificially formed when poor concrete is exposed to weathering. Its growth causes crumbling and fretting of the concrete, which thus loses its strength. This process is even called "concrete disease." Sometimes, however, ettringite is deliberately added to the concrete because it can be used to change its setting behavior, in particular its setting time.
Similar minerals Calcite and afwillite have a different crystal form; calcite has perfect cleavage and effervesces when dabbed with diluted hydrochloric acid; aragonite also effervesces when dabbed with diluted hydrochloric acid; apatite is significantly harder than ettringite.

3 Senarmontite

Chem. formula Sb_2O_3
Hardness 2–2½, **Sp. gr.** 5.5
Color Colorless, white
Streak White
Luster Vitreous to resinous
Cleavage None
Fracture Conchoidal
Tenacity Brittle
Crystal form Cubic

Morphology Octahedral crystals, planar crystal intergrowths, granular, drusy, uneven.
Origin and occurrence In the oxidation zone of antimony-rich deposits.
Accessory minerals Stibnite, valentinite, stibiconite, nadorite, calcite.
Similar minerals The octahedral crystal form and occurrence with other antimony minerals do not allow for confusion with senarmontite; arsenolite is softer and water soluble; unlike senarmontite, arsenolite is softer and water soluble; fluorite is significantly harder.

4 Pharmacosiderite *Cubic ore*

Chem. formula $KFe_4[(OH)_4/(AsO_4)_3] \cdot 7\,H_2O$
Hardness 2½, **Sp. gr.** 2.8–2.9
Color Green, yellow, brown, red
Streak White
Luster Vitreous, greasy on fracture surfaces
Cleavage Scarcely discernible
Fracture Conchoidal
Tenacity Brittle
Crystal form Cubic

Morphology Crystals always euhedral, mainly cubic, rarely with corners beveled by octahedra, granular masses, uneven.
Origin and occurrence In the oxidation zone of ore deposits with arsenic-bearing minerals.
Accessory minerals Olivenite, clinoclase, cornwallite, agardite, goethite.
Similar minerals Fluorite is harder and differs due to its good cleavage; jarosite and natrojarosite crystals are not cubic but rhombohedral; the same applies to beudantite.

Localities	
1 Hotazel, South Africa	**3** Djebel Nador, Algeria
2 Hotazel, South Africa	**4** Schöllkrippen, Spessart, Germany

1 2
3 4

1 Phlogopite

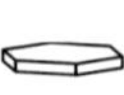

Chem. formula $KMg_3[(F,OH)_2/AlSi_3O_{10}]$
Hardness 2–2½, **Sp. gr.** 2.75–2.97
Color Dark brown, reddish yellowish, greenish, black
Streak White
Luster Vitreous
Cleavage Basal perfect
Fracture Foliated
Tenacity Flexible
Crystal form Monoclinic

Morphology Tabular hexagonal crystals, pseudohexagonal, rarely prismatic, foliated, flaky, anhedral and euhedral, slabs up to a square meter in size.
Origin and occurrence In marbles, metamorphic dolomites and pegmatites, in contact metasomatic formations, on fissures of volcanic rocks.
Accessory minerals Graphite, calcite, diopside.
Similar minerals Biotite occurs in a different paragenesis; muscovite is always lighter; clinochlore is considerably softer.

2 Muskovite

Chem. formula $KAl_2[(OH,F)_2/AlSi_3O_{10}]$
Hardness 2–2½, **Sp. gr.** 2.78–2.88
Color Colorless, white, silver gray, greenish, yellowish, brown
Streak White
Luster Pearly
Cleavage Basal perfect
Fracture Foliated
Tenacity Non-brittle leaves elastically flexible
Crystal form Monoclinic

Morphology Tabular hexagonal crystals euhedral, rarely prismatic, flakes, scales, rose-shaped, mainly anhedral essential mineral.
Origin and occurrence Essential mineral in granites, pegmatites (here, slabs up to several square meters), gneisses, mica schists, sandstones, marbles, not in volcanic rocks; euhedral crystals, for example, in alpine fissures or in vugs in pegmatites.
Accessory minerals Quartz, feldspar, biotite, tourmaline, rutile.
Similar minerals Talc and chlorite are softer; their leaves are not elastically flexible; biotite and phlogopite are almost always significantly darker.

3 Baricite

Chem. formula $Mg_3(PO_4)_2 \cdot 8\,H_2O$
Hardness 2–2½, **Sp. gr.** 2.42
Color Colorless, often blue
Streak White
Luster Vitreous
Cleavage Perfect
Fracture Foliated
Tenacity Flexible
Crystal form Monoclinic

Morphology Tabular crystals, foliated aggregates, uneven.
Origin and occurrence On fissures and in cavities of phosphate-rich rocks.
Accessory minerals Siderite, lazulite, wardite, augelite, quartz, kulanite, gormanite.
Similar minerals Vivianite cannot be distinguished from baricite using simple means; gormanite is more radial; kulanite is notably greener.

4 Mendipite

Chem. formula $Pb_3Cl_2O_2$
Hardness 2½, **Sp. gr.** 7.2
Color White, pink, gray
Streak White
Luster Resinous
Cleavage Perfect
Fracture Conchoidal
Tenacity Brittle
Crystal form Orthorhombic

Morphology Rarely tabular crystals, bladed, fibrous, uneven.
Origin and occurrence In the oxidation zone of lead deposits with a chlorine supply, in ancient lead slags.
Accessory minerals Cerussite, pyromorphite, diaboleite, anglesite, paralaurionite.
Similar minerals Cerussite has no cleavage; mendipite differs from other white minerals due to its very high density; barite and celestine are harder.

Localities	
1 Madagascar	**3** Rapid Creek, Yukon Territory, Canada
2 Minas Gerais, Brazil	**4** Mendip Hills, Great Britain

1 2
3 4

1 Cowlesite

Chem. formula $CaAl_2Si_3O_{10} \cdot 6\,H_2O$
Hardness 2½, **Sp. gr.** 2.1
Color White, gray
Streak White
Luster Vitreous
Cleavage Perfect
Fracture Uneven
Tenacity Brittle
Crystal form Orthorhombic

Morphology Rarely long tabular crystals, mainly stellate, botryoidal aggregates, fibrous, uneven.
Origin and occurrence In cavities in basalts and lava.
Accessory minerals Characteristically, cowlesite is always the only zeolite in its cavities, apophyllite, calcite.
Similar minerals Natrolite and scolecite are much harder; mordenite does not form characteristic spheres; calcite effervesces when dabbed with diluted hydrochloric acid.

2 Chromian clinochlore

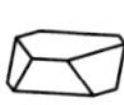

Chem. formula $(Fe,Mg,Al,Cr)_6[(OH)_2/(Si,Al)_4O_{10}]$
Hardness 2, **Sp. gr.** 2.9–3.3
Color Pink purple
Streak White to pale pink
Luster Vitreous, pearly on cleavage faces
Cleavage Perfect
Fracture Foliated
Tenacity Non-brittle, inelastically flexible
Crystal form Monoclinic

Morphology Thick to thin tabular crystals, granular, foliated, uneven.
Origin and occurrence As an alteration product of chromite on fissures in serpentine and in rough chromite ore.
Accessory minerals Chromite, serpentine, titanite.
Similar minerals Micas are harder and elastically flexible; clinochlore is green; the pink-purple color associated with its chromium-rich paragenesis makes chromian clinochlore unmistakable.

3 Switzerite

Chem. formula $(Mn,Fe)_3(PO_4)_2 \cdot 4\,H_2O$
Hardness 2½, **Sp. gr.** 2.95
Color White, pink, brown
Streak White
Luster Pearly to silky
Cleavage Perfect
Fracture Fibrous
Tenacity Brittle
Crystal form Monoclinic

Morphology Tabular to thin tabular crystals, acicular crystal sheaves, fibrous to stellate aggregates, flat roses.
Origin and occurrence In phosphate pegmatites, formed by alteration of primary phosphates.
Accessory minerals Rockbridgeite, hureaulite, apatite, keckite, strengite, phosphosiderite.
Similar minerals Its paragenesis makes switzerite unmistakable; strunzite is more straw yellow; cacoxenite is more golden yellow.

4 Tellurite

Chem. formula TeO_2
Hardness 2½, **Sp. gr.** 5.9
Color White, yellow white, straw yellow, yellow
Streak White
Luster Vitreous to adamantine
Cleavage Perfect
Fracture Foliated
Tenacity Flexible
Crystal form Orthorhombic

Morphology Acicular, long prismatic to lath-shaped crystals, acicular crystal sheaves, fibrous to stellate aggregates, earthy, uneven.
Origin and occurrence In the oxidation zone of tellurium-rich deposits.
Accessory minerals Native tellurium, nagyagite, tetradymite, quartz, calcite.
Similar minerals Its paragenesis with other tellurium minerals is very characteristic; sulfur is rarely so elongated and has a different luster.

Localities	
1 Oregon, USA	**3** Foote Mine, North Carolina, USA
2 Guleman, Turkey	**4** Moctezuma, Sonora, Mexico

1 2
3 4

1–4

Amber *Amber*

Chem. formula ~ $C_{10}H_{16}O+(H_2S)$
Hardness 2½, **Sp. gr.** 1.05–1.09
Color Yellow, white, brown, honey yellow, blue, transparent to opaque
Streak White
Luster Vitreous to greasy
Cleavage None
Fracture Conchoidal
Tenacity Brittle
Crystal form Amorphic

Morphology Amber does not form crystals. It is found in coarse, unrolled lumps, drop-shaped or botryoidal aggregates, bladed pieces, elongated, almost rod-like drops, granular, usually coated with an opaque weathered crust, often translucent to opaque inside. Frequent inclusions of plant parts and living organisms, especially insects.
Origin and occurrence Amber is a fossil resin, produced by a wide range of trees. While Baltic amber originates from conifers.Dominican amber is produced by deciduous trees. Amber is found both in primary deposits (i.e. where it originated as resin) or transported further by water or even glaciers to form secondary deposits (sands, gravels, etc.).
Accessory minerals Rarely pyrite, other resins, in pebbles, for example, in secondary occurrences.
Distinguishing feature Freshly fractured amber fluoresces intensely when irradiated with UV light.
Similar minerals Fluorite and calcite have perfect cleavage; quartz is much harder; calcite effervesces when dabbed with diluted hydrochloric acid.

Amber

Gemstone

Shape and cut Amber is cut into spheres and cabochons, but primarily into free shapes to match the original shape of the piece; it is often processed raw or partially raw while retaining parts of the weathered crust.
Use As solitaire stones in rings, brooches, pendants, beads for necklaces, also for handicraft items, figurines, boxes, knife handles, etc.
Treatment Amber is often clarified, which means it is heated to a temperature at which the many bubbles making it cloudy are expelled, so that it becomes clear. Amber treated in this way contains flat shiny crack structures similar to fish scales, which are formed during the heating and rapid cooling process. Such amber is traded as "genuine amber," while untreated amber is called raw or natural amber. The latter does not exhibit these characteristic structures.
Pressed amber is compressed together under heat and pressure from small pieces of amber and cutting waste. This man-made product is also sold as genuine amber.
Possibilities of Confusion Similarly colored minerals (calcite, quartz, carnelian) are always much harder and, in particular, heavier. Amber floats on saltwater because of its low density, but not on fresh water (plastic also floats on fresh water!). When lit, it smells pleasantly (like incense), similar plastic imitations smell bad (be careful, their smoke is also poisonous!).
Unlike amber, copal (not yet fossilized, tree resin that is a few hundred years old, also with many insect inclusions) becomes sticky after a short time when dabbed with alcohol or acetone; the same is true of synthetic resin. In most cases, plastics do not fluoresce under UV light.

Localities	
1 Lithuania	**3** Lithuania
2 Lithuania	**4** Romania

1 Epsomite

Chem. formula $MgSO4 \cdot 7\,H_2O$
Hardness 2½, **Sp. gr.** 1.68
Color White, pale pink, pale green
Streak White
Luster Vitreous to adamantine
Cleavage Perfect
Fracture Foliated
Tenacity Flexible
Crystal form Orthorhombic

Morphology Rarely acicular, long-prismatic crystals, mainly stellate, fibrous encrustations, reniform aggregates, earthy, uneven.
Origin and occurrence Efflorescence in old tunnels, on pyrite-bearing rocks, in salt lakes, alteration product of kieserite.
Accessory minerals Gypsum, halotrichite, pyrite.
Distinguishing feature Epsomite is soluble in water and tastes bitter.
Similar minerals Its water solubility and bitter taste are very characteristic.

2 Pharmacolite

Chem. formula $CaH[AsO_4] \cdot 2\,H_2O$
Hardness 2–2½, **Sp. gr.** 2.5–2.7
Color Colorless, white, sometimes reddish or green
Streak White
Luster Vitreous, pearly on cleavage faces
Cleavage Perfect
Tenacity Flexible
Crystal form Monoclinic

Morphology Rarely tabular to acicular crystals; stellate sheaves, roses, reniform aggregates, encrustations, earthy.
Origin and occurrence In the oxidation zone of arsenic-rich deposits as often very young formations.
Accessory minerals Gypsum, red cobalt, picropharmacolite, guerinite, sainfeldite, aragonite.
Similar minerals Picropharmacolite does not have good cleavage and is brittle; aragonite effervesces when dabbed with diluted hydrochloric acid; gypsum exhibits different cleavage; the paragenesis with arsenic minerals is characteristic.

3 Sepiolite

Chem. formula $Mg_4Si_6O_{15}(OH)_2 \cdot 6\,H_2O$
Hardness 2–2½, **Sp. gr.** 2.26
Color Colorless, white, gray, brown
Streak White
Luster Dull
Cleavage Indiscernible
Fracture Uneven
Tenacity Flexible
Crystal form Orthorhombic

Morphology Seldom fibrous, usually dense, uneven, reniform nodules, similar to "mountain leather."
Origin and occurrence In serpentinites, particularly on fissures as "mountain leather."
Accessory minerals Opal, calcite, magnetite, olivine, serpentine, ilmenite, dolomite.
Similar minerals The "mountain leather"-like variety is very characteristic; nevertheless, it is can be distinguished from palygorskite by simple means.

4 Strashimirite

Chem. formula $(Cu,Zn)_8(AsO_4)_4(OH)_4 \cdot 5\,H_2O$
Hardness 2–2½, **Sp. gr.** 3.67
Color White, pale green
Streak White
Luster Dull to silky
Cleavage Indiscernible
Fracture Fibrous
Tenacity Brittle
Crystal form Monoclinic

Morphology Rarely long tabular single crystals, mainly stellate aggregates, reniform, fibrous, silky encrustations, coatings, uneven.
Origin and occurrence In the oxidation zone of arsenic-rich copper deposits, the botryoidal aggregates are often covered with a thin layer of grass-green parnauite.
Accessory minerals Parnauite, azurite, malachite, olivenite.
Similar minerals The fibrous structure with green parnauite coatings is very characteristic.

Localities	
1 Lake Bumbunga, Australia	**3** Sunk, Trieben, Austria
2 Richelsdorf, Hesse, Germany	**4** Leogang, Austria

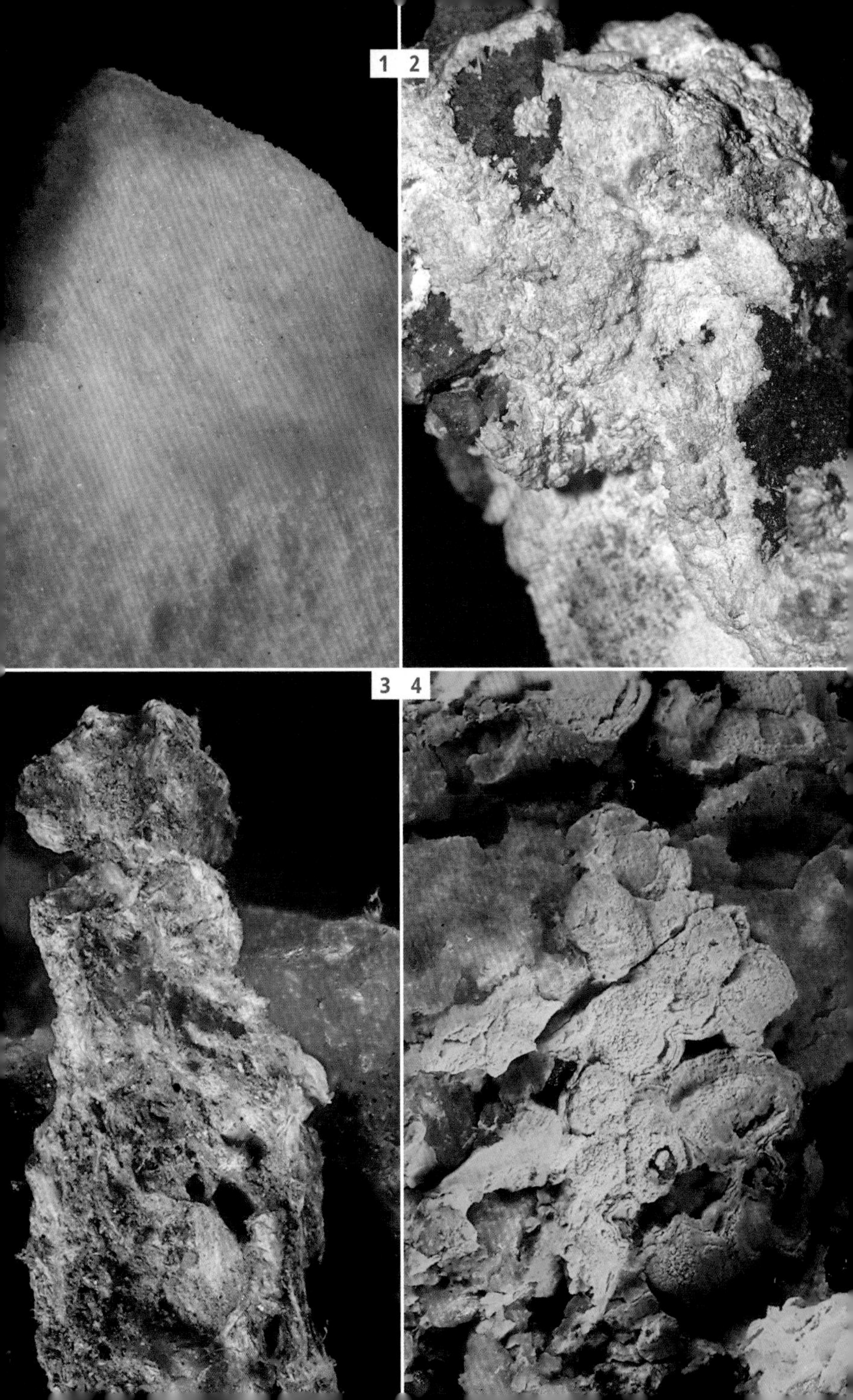
1 2
3 4

1

Carnallite

Chem. formula $KMgCl_3 \cdot 6\,H_2O$
Hardness 2½, **Sp. gr.** 1.6
Color White, yellowish
Streak White
Luster Greasy
Cleavage Indiscernible
Fracture Uneven to conchoidal
Tenacity Brittle
Crystal form Orthorhombic

Morphology Rarely isometric crystals, mainly granular, uneven, in beds, in interdigitation with rock salt.
Origin and occurrence Forms alternating layers with rock salt and other potassium salts in salt deposits, as volcanic efflorescence.
Accessory minerals Sylvite, rock salt, kieserite, gypsum, anhydrite.
Distinguishing feature Carnallite is soluble in water and tastes bitter.
Similar minerals Sylvite and rock salt have a different crystal form.

2

Coquimbite

Chem. formula $Fe_2^{3+}(SO_4)_3 \cdot 9\,H_2O$
Hardness 2½, **Sp. gr.** 2.11
Color Pale purple, amethyst hues, yellowish
Streak White
Luster Vitreous
Cleavage Indiscernible
Fracture Uneven to conchoidal
Tenacity Brittle
Crystal form Hexagonal

Morphology Seldom pyramidal to prismatic crystals, mainly granular, uneven, in reniform aggregates.
Origin and occurrence In the oxidation zone of sulfide deposits, particularly in desert environments, rarely as a fumarole formation.
Accessory minerals Copiapite, chalcanthite, gypsum, pyrite, epsomite.
Distinguishing feature Coquimbite is soluble in water and tastes astringent.
Similar minerals Taking the paragenesis into consideration, the purple color is very characteristic.

3

Ulexite

Chem. formula $NaCaB_5O_6(OH)_6 \cdot 5\,H_2O$
Hardness 2½, **Sp. gr.** 1.955
Color White, gray
Streak White
Luster Silky
Cleavage Perfect
Fracture Fibrous
Tenacity Brittle
Crystal form Triclinic

Morphology Rarely acicular crystals, mainly in parallel-fibered aggregates, uneven, in cotton-like balls.
Origin and occurrence In salt deposits in borax lakes, often in large deposits here.
Accessory minerals Colemanite, borax, hydroboracite, glauberite.
Distinguishing feature If you look at an image through a ulexite aggregate cut perpendicular to the fiber direction, the image is projected onto the surface; ulexite is therefore also called TV rock.
Similar minerals The unique structure of ulexite is very characteristic.

4

Copiapite

Chem. formula $Fe^{2+}Fe_4^{3+}(SO_4)_6(OH)_2 \cdot 20\,H_2O$
Hardness 2½–3, **Sp. gr.** 2.11
Color Pale yellow to yellow
Streak Yellowish white
Luster Vitreous to pearly
Cleavage Perfect
Fracture Uneven
Tenacity Brittle
Crystal form Triclinic

Morphology Rarely prismatic crystals, mainly granular, uneven, in reniform aggregates, powdery, earthy.
Origin and occurrence In the oxidation zone of sulfide deposits, particularly in desert environments, rarely as a fumarole formation.
Accessory minerals Coquimbite, chalcantite, gypsum, pyrite, epsomite.
Distinguishing feature Copiapite is soluble in water and tastes metallic.
Similar minerals Taking the paragenesis into consideration, the yellow color is very characteristic.

Localities	
1 Stassfurt, Saxony-Anhalt, Germany	**3** Boron, California, USA
2 Emery County, Utah, USA	**4** Copiapó, Chile

1 2
3 4

1 Whewellite

Chem. formula $Ca(C_2O_4) \cdot (H_2O)$
Hardness 2½–3, **Sp. gr.** 2.21
Color Colorless, white, brown, yellow, blackish
Streak White
Luster Vitreous to pearly
Cleavage Poor
Fracture Uneven
Tenacity Brittle
Crystal form Monoclinic

Morphology Prismatic to tabular crystals, sometimes V-shaped twins, granular, uneven, in radial aggregates, powdery, earthy.
Origin and occurrence In hydrothermal sulfide veins with carbonate matrix, in septarian nodules, in combination with coal deposits, in uranium deposits.
Accessory minerals Calcite, barite, celestine, pyrite, sphalerite, ozokerite.
Similar minerals Calcite effervesces when dabbed with diluted hydrochloric acid; barite and celestine are considerably heavier.

2 Trona

Chem. formula $Na_3(CO_3)(HCO_3) \cdot 2\,H_2O$
Hardness 2½–3, **Sp. gr.** 2.11
Color White, gray, pale yellow, brown
Streak White
Luster Vitreous
Cleavage Perfect
Fracture Uneven
Tenacity Non-brittle to brittle
Crystal form Monoclinic

Morphology Prismatic to tabular crystals, columnar aggregates, rose-shaped intergrowths.
Distinguishing feature Trona is water soluble.
Origin and occurrence As a deposition in salt lakes, as soil efflorescence, rarely in volcanic fumaroles.
Accessory minerals Rock salt, borax, ulexite, thermonatrite.
Similar minerals Borax has a different crystal form; calcite is slightly harder and has perfect rhombohedral cleavage; rock salt and sylvite have a different crystal form and are much softer.

3 Bloedite *Astrakhanite*

Chem. formula $Na_2Mg(SO_4)_2 \cdot 4\,H_2O$
Hardness 2½–3, **Sp. gr.** 2.22–2.24
Color White, colorless, gray
Streak White
Luster Vitreous
Cleavage None
Fracture Conchoidal
Tenacity Brittle
Crystal form Monoclinic

Morphology Thick tabular to isometric crystals, partially very large, anhedral, granular, uneven.
Origin and occurrence In salt deposits, in nitrate deposits, as volcanic efflorescence, in salt lakes, as efflorescence on the ground.
Accessory minerals Cainite, carnallite, polyhalite, gypsum, sylvite.
Similar minerals The crystals are very characteristic; calcite effervesces when dabbed with diluted hydrochloric acid; rock salt and sylvite are softer and have excellent cleavage.

4 Leonite

Chem. formula $K_2Mg(SO_4)_2 \cdot 4\,H_2O$
Hardness 2½–3, **Sp. gr.** 2.2
Color White opaque, colorless, yellowish
Streak White
Luster Vitreous
Cleavage None
Fracture Conchoidal
Tenacity Brittle
Crystal form Monoclinic

Morphology Thick tabular to prismatic crystals, euhedral, anhedral, granular, uneven.
Distinguishing feature Leonite quickly becomes coated with a white encrustation and is then completely opaque.
Origin and occurrence In salt deposits, formed secondarily from kieserite or carnallite.
Accessory minerals Cainite, carnallite, polyhalite, sylvite, rock salt.
Similar minerals The chalky white crystals are very characteristic; calcite effervesces when dabbed with diluted hydrochloric acid. Rock salt and sylvite are softer.

Localities	
1 Hartenstein, Saxony, Germany	**3** Searles Lake, California, USA
2 Searles Lake, California, USA	**4** Siegmundshall, Lower Saxony, Germany

1 2
3 4

1 Uralolite

Chem. formula $Ca_2Be_4(PO_4)_3(OH)_3 \cdot 5\,H_2O$
Hardness 2½–3, **Sp. gr.** 2.05–2.14
Color White, colorless, yellowish
Streak White
Luster Vitreous
Cleavage None
Fracture Conchoidal
Tenacity Brittle
Crystal form Monoclinic

Morphology Long tabular to acicular crystals, euhedral, forming radial suns, granular, uneven.
Origin and occurrence In pegmatites on cracks and fissures.
Accessory minerals Spodumene, beryl, lepidolite, albite.
Distinguishing feature Uralolite fluoresces with a greenish color when irradiated with UV light.
Similar minerals Natrolite and scolecite are harder; stilbite and heulandite exhibit excellent cleavage; bavenite is harder and has a different crystal form.

2 Lindackerite

Chem. formula $(Cu, Co)_5(AsO_4)_2(AsO_3OH)_2 \cdot 10\,H_2O$
Hardness 2–2½, **Sp. gr.** 3.37
Color Pale green to pale blue, colorless
Streak White
Luster Vitreous
Cleavage Perfect
Fracture Uneven
Tenacity Brittle
Crystal form Triclinic

Morphology Long tabular crystals, acicular, intergrown to form roses or sheaves, encrustations, coatings.
Origin and occurrence In the oxidation zone of arsenic-rich copper deposits.
Accessory minerals Erythrite, annabergite, freirinite, olivenite, chalcanthite, antlerite.
Similar minerals Calcite and aragonite effervesce when dabbed with diluted hydrochloric acid; annabergite is more emerald green; chalcanthite is more intensely blue and water soluble.

3 Artinite

Chem. formula $Mg_2[(OH)_2/CO_3] \cdot 3\,H_2O$
Hardness 2–3, **Sp. gr.** 2.03
Color White
Streak White
Luster Vitreous to silky
Cleavage Indiscernible due to the acicular character
Fracture Fibrous
Tenacity Brittle
Crystal form Monoclinic

Morphology Acicular crystal sheaves, stellate aggregates, suns.
Origin and occurrence As a secondary formation on fissures and in cavities of serpentinites.
Accessory minerals Hydromagnesite, brucite, dolomite, chromian clinochlore, calcite.
Similar minerals Hydromagnesite has tabular crystals; aragonite usually has thicker crystals; very thin acicular aggregates are, however, difficult to distinguish from artinite; aragonite is slightly harder than artinite.

4 Cryolite

Chem. formula Na_3AlF_6
Hardness 2½–3, **Sp. gr.** 2.97
Color White, colorless, yellowish, rarely purple
Streak White
Luster Vitreous, greasy
Cleavage None, sometimes distinct scoria
Fracture Conchoidal
Tenacity Brittle
Crystal form Monoclinic

Morphology Cubic crystals, euhedral or as outgrowth of uneven cryolite, large, uneven masses, inclusions, granular, uneven.
Origin and occurrence In pegmatites, in carbonatites, on fractures and in vugs of fluorine-rich rhyolites.
Accessory minerals Ralstonite, thomsenolite, pachnolite, jarlite.
Distinguishing feature Cryolite fluoresces with a greenish color when irradiated with UV light.
Similar minerals Fluorite has excellent cleavage; quartz is much harder; ralstonite is genuinely cubic.

Localities	
1 Koralpe, Styria, Austria	**3** Kraubath, Styria, Austria
2 Jachymov, Czech Republic	**4** Ivigtut, Greenland

1 2
3 4

1

Schulenbergite

Chem. formula $(Cu,Zn)_7(SO_4,CO_3)_2(OH)_{10} \cdot 3\,H_2O$
Hardness 2, **Sp. gr.** 3.4
Color Light blue
Streak White
Luster Vitreous to pearly
Cleavage Perfect
Fracture Foliated
Tenacity Brittle
Crystal form Trigonal

Morphology Thin tabular crystals, hexagonal flakes, often curved, scaly, botryoidal aggregates, thin encrustations and coatings.
Origin and occurrence In the oxidation zone of copper deposits.
Accessory minerals Serpierite, linarite, ktenasite, claringbullite, aurichalcite.
Similar minerals Devilline is indistinguishable from schulenbergite using simple means; serpierite is more acicular or elongated tabular; aurichalcite forms elongated crystals not hexagonal leaves.

2

Garnierite

Chem. formula $(Ni,Mg)_6Si_4O_{10}(OH)_8$
Hardness 2–3, **Sp. gr.** 2.2–2.7
Color Green, yellow-green, blue-green
Streak White
Luster Greasy to dull
Cleavage None
Fracture Conchoidal
Tenacity Brittle
Crystal form Monoclinic

Morphology Uneven, reniform aggregates, thin coatings, powdery, earthy masses, no single crystals.
Origin and occurrence In serpentine rocks as a weathering product of nickel content.
Accessory minerals Serpentine, limonite, chlorite, calcite, magnesite.
Distinguishing feature In abundant deposits, particularly in tropical climates, garnierite can be mined as nickel ore.
Similar minerals Serpentine is usually less intensely green, not as brittle and never earthy, powdery; nevertheless, it is often indistinguishable from garnierite using simple means.

3–4

Wulfenite *Yellow lead ore*

Chem. formula $PbMoO_4$
Hardness 3, **Sp. gr.** 6.7–6.9
Color Yellow to orange-red, blue, gray
Streak White
Luster Adamantine to resinous
Cleavage Weak pyramidal
Fracture Conchoidal
Tenacity Brittle
Crystal form Tetragonal

Morphology Pointed pyramids, thick to thin tabular crystals, often sandwich-like structure, acicular, almost always euhedral, rarely uneven.
Origin and occurrence In the oxidation zone of lead deposits, wherever a molybdenum source (for example, black shales) is present in the country rock.
Accessory minerals Galena, cerussite, hydrozincite, pyromorphite, smithsonite, mimetesite, hemimorphite, calcite.
Distinguishing feature Some wulfenite crystals are hemimorphic, i.e. they exhibit different crystal faces at the top and bottom crystal ends. Thus, they sometimes exhibit pointed pyramids at the top, while they are quite flat at the bottom and bound only by the basal surface. When present in large quantities, wulfenite was previously even mined as molybdenum ore.
Similar minerals Confusion is not possible due to its appearance (particularly, the crystal form and orange color) and the occurrence of wulfenite with other lead and zinc oxidation minerals.

Localities	
1 Friedrichssegen Mine, Bad Ems, Germany	**3** Bleiberg, Carinthia, Austria
2 Frankenstein, Poland	**4** Los Lamentos, Mexico

1 2
3 4

1–2 Vanadinite

Chem. formula $Pb_5[Cl/(VO_4)_3]$
Hardness 3, **Sp. gr.** 6.8–7.1
Color Yellow, brown, orange, red
Streak White to yellowish
Luster Adamantine to greasy
Cleavage None
Fracture Conchoidal
Tenacity Brittle
Crystal form Hexagonal

Morphology Prismatic to tabular crystals with hexagonal cross-section, euhedral, stellate and botryoidal aggregates, rarely uneven.
Origin and occurrence In the oxidation zone of lead deposits in the simultaneous presence of vanadium-rich weathering solutions. The Moroccan deposits are particularly well-known with their large, intensely red vanadinite crystals on a brown or black substrate.
Accessory minerals Wulfenite, calcite, descloizite, limonite, mimetesite, mottramite, quartz.
Similar minerals Apatite is harder; pyromorphite and mimetesite are not red; brown or yellow vanadinite cannot be distinguished from mimetesite or pyromorphite by simple means; red wulfenite does not form hexagonal crystals.

3 Kainite

Chem. formula $KMgSO_4Cl \cdot H_2O$
Hardness 3, **Sp. gr.** 2.1–2.2
Color White, reddish, yellowish, gray, blue, purple
Streak White
Luster Vitreous
Cleavage Perfect
Fracture Splintery
Tenacity Brittle
Crystal form Monoclinic

Morphology Thick tabular to isometric crystals, often planar, uneven.
Origin and occurrence In salt deposits, particularly in the uppermost layers.
Accessory minerals Sylvite, rock salt, carnallite, gypsum, anhydrite, kieserite.
Distinguishing feature Kainite tastes bitter and salty and is soluble in water.
Similar minerals Its crystal form and taste distinguish kainite from rock salt and sylvite; gypsum and anhydrite are not soluble in water. The same applies to calcite and aragonite; both of which effervesce when dabbed with diluted hydrochloric acid.

4 Hydroboracite

Chem. formula $CaMgB_6O_{11} \cdot H_2O$
Hardness 2–3, **Sp. gr.** 2.2
Color White, brownish
Streak White
Luster Vitreous
Cleavage Perfect
Fracture Uneven
Tenacity Brittle
Crystal form Monoclinic

Morphology Acicular crystals, stellate, sun-shaped aggregates, granulitic, uneven.
Origin and occurrence In salt deposits containing boron minerals.
Accessory minerals Rock salt, anhydrite.
Similar minerals Its paragenesis makes acicular hydroboracite unmistakable; colemanite is more tabular; aragonite has no cleavage and effervesces when dabbed with diluted hydrochloric acid, as does radial calcite, which, unlike hydroboracite, cleaves obliquely relative to the fiber alignment.

Localities	
1 Arizona, USA	**3** Aschersleben, Saxony-Anhalt, Germany
2 Mibladen, Morocco	**4** Niedersachswerfen, Thuringia, Germany

1 2
3 4

1 Valentinite *Antimony bloom*

Chem. formula Sb_2O_3
Hardness 2–3, **Sp. gr.** 5.6–5.8
Color Colorless, white, yellowish, gray
Streak White
Luster Adamantine, pearly on cleavage faces
Cleavage Perfect
Fracture Uneven
Tenacity Non-brittle, fragile
Crystal form Orthorhombic

Morphology Prismatic to acicular crystals, stellate and sun-shaped aggregates, granular and fibrous masses, uneven.
Origin and occurrence In the oxidation zone of antimony deposits.
Accessory minerals Stibnite, senarmontite.
Similar minerals The notable luster and the acicular structure as well as its paragenesis with stibnite make valentinite unmistakable; aragonite effervesces when dabbed with diluted hydrochloric acid.

2 Phosgenite *Horn lead*

Chem. formula $Pb_2[Cl_2/CO_3]$
Hardness 2½–3, **Sp. gr.** 6-6.3
Color Colorless, white, gray, brown, yellow
Streak White
Luster Greasy to adamantine
Cleavage Perfect
Fracture Conchoidal
Tenacity Non-brittle
Crystal form Tetragonal

Morphology Short-columned, tabular, long-prismatic crystals, sometimes planar, acicular.
Origin and occurrence In the oxidation zone of lead deposit, in ancient lead slags.
Accessory minerals Cerussite, anglesite, galenite, nealite, laurionite, paralaurionite, fiedlerite.
Similar minerals Cerussite and anglesite have a different crystal form; calcite has different cleavage and crystal form; the same applies to aragonite and willemite; leadhillite is more tabular.

3 Stolzite *Lead tungstate*

Chem. formula $PbWO_4$
Hardness 3, **Sp. gr.** 7.9-8.2
Color Yellow, brown, gray
Streak White to yellowish
Luster Greasy
Cleavage None
Fracture Conchoidal
Tenacity Brittle
Crystal form Tetragonal

Morphology Dipyramidal crystals, edges often curved, planar crystal intergrowths, uneven.
Origin and occurrence In the oxidation zone of plumbiferous tungsten deposits and tungsten-bearing lead deposits.
Accessory minerals Quartz, raspite, fluorite, ferberite, hubnerite, scorodite.
Similar minerals Unlike stolzite, scheelite fluoresces in UV light; wulfenite is not readily distinguished by simple means.

4 Anglesite

Chem. formula $PbSO_4$
Hardness 3, **Sp. gr.** 6.3
Color Colorless, white, yellowish, brownish, gray
Streak White
Luster Vitreous to greasy
Cleavage Basal visible
Fracture Conchoidal
Tenacity Brittle
Crystal form Orthorhombic

Morphology Euhedral tabular crystals, prismatic, dipyramidal, acicular, in addition also granular, drusy, uneven.
Origin and occurrence In the oxidation zone of lead deposits, often as the first formation during the weathering of galena.
Accessory minerals Cerussite, galena, phosgenite, calcite, quartz, wulfenite.
Similar minerals Barite exhibits considerably better cleavage; unlike anglesite, cerussite often exhibits knee-shaped twins and star-shaped triplets.

Localities	
1 Pribram, Czech Republic	**3** Zinnwald, Czech Republic
2 Monte Poni, Sardinia, Italy	**4** Siegerland Region, Germany

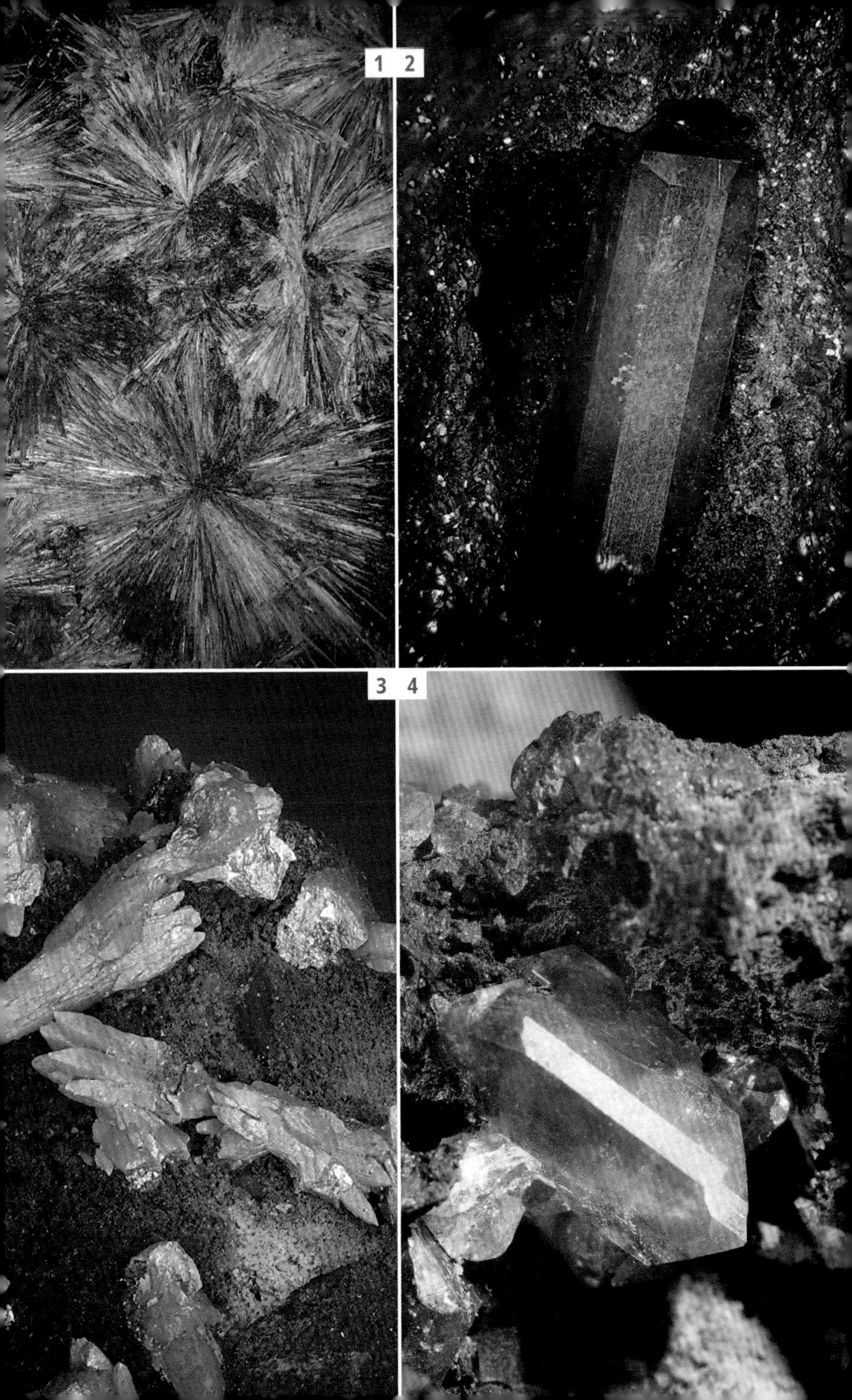
1
2
3
4

1–2 Silver, native

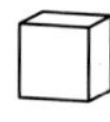

Chem. formula Ag
Hardness 2½–3, **Sp. gr.** 9.6-12
Color Silver white, often tarnishes yellowish to blackish
Streak Metallic white
Luster Metallic, sometimes tarnishes dull
Cleavage None
Fracture Hackly
Tenacity Non-brittle, very ductile, can be hammered into small plates
Crystal form Cubic

Morphology Rare as crystals, predominantly cubic, skeletal, dendritic, sheet- and wire-like aggregates, often curly, uneven, anhedral.
Origin and occurrence In hydrothermal veins at different temperatures; rarely primary, mainly secondary as cementation formation, on fissure surfaces in black shales. The most well-known deposit in Europe is the Kongsberg deposit, where native silver was found in large masses and in wiry aggregates as thick as an arm. In Germany, the most beautiful grades of solid silver come from Freiberg in Saxony and from Wittichen in the Black Forest.
Accessory minerals Argentite, pyrargyrite, proustite, stephanite, galena, calcite, rhodochrosite.
Similar minerals Galena and other silver-gray minerals, with the exception of argentite, cannot be hammered into small plates; argentite has a dark streak.

3 Freieslebenite

Chem. formula $AgPbSbS_3$
Hardness 3, **Sp. gr.** 6.22
Color Lead gray to silver white
Color Silver white
Luster Metallic
Cleavage Mainly indiscernible
Fracture Uneven
Tenacity Brittle
Crystal form Monoclinic

Morphology Tabular to long tabular, characteristic longitudinally striated crystals, granular, uneven.
Origin and occurrence In hydrothermal silver veins.
Accessory minerals Argentite, silver, pyrargyrite, proustite, stephanite, galena, calcite, barite, andorite.
Similar minerals Galena has perfect cubic cleavage; stephanite exhibits a different crystal form; the same applies to hessite. Native silver is a lighter silver and more ductile; argentite is not brittle.

4 Leadhillite

Chem. formula $Pb_4[(OH)_2/SO_4/(CO_3)_2]$
Hardness 2½, **Sp. gr.** 6.45–6.55
Color Colorless, white, yellowish, brownish, gray
Streak White
Luster Greasy to pearly
Cleavage Basal perfect
Fracture Conchoidal
Tenacity Brittle
Crystal form Monoclinic

Morphology Pseudohexagonal plates, thick to thin tabular, granular, drusy, shelly.
Origin and occurrence In the oxidation zone of lead deposits, in ancient lead slags.
Accessory minerals Galena, anglesite, cerussite, phosgenite, calcite, aragonite.
Distinguishing feature Leadhillite effervesces when dissolved in concentrated hydrochloric acid (**Caution! Dangerous, highly corrosive**); however, it does not dissolve in cold diluted hydrochloric acid.
Similar minerals Cerussite is harder and has much poorer cleavage; anglesite is sometimes difficult to distinguish from leadhillite, but it exhibits a different crystal form; calcite immediately effervesces strongly when dabbed with diluted hydrochloric acid.

Localities	
1 Freiberg, Saxony, Germany	**3** Freiberg, Saxony, Germany
2 Hartenstein, Saxony, Germany	**4** Leadhills, Scotland

1 2
3 4

1 Raspite

Chem. formula $PbWO_4$
Hardness 2½–3, **Sp. gr.** 8.5
Color Yellow, yellow brown
Streak White
Luster Adamantine
Cleavage Perfect
Fracture Uneven
Tenacity Brittle
Crystal form Monoclinic

Morphology Thick tabular to prismatic, elongated crystals, uneven.
Origin and occurrence In the oxidation zone of plumbiferous tungsten deposits and tungsten-bearing lead deposits.
Accessory minerals Stolzite, scheelite, ferberite, hubnerite, quartz, scorodite, beudantite.
Similar minerals Stolzite and scheelite are clearly tetragonal; beudantite and scorodite exhibit a different crystal form.

2 Biotite

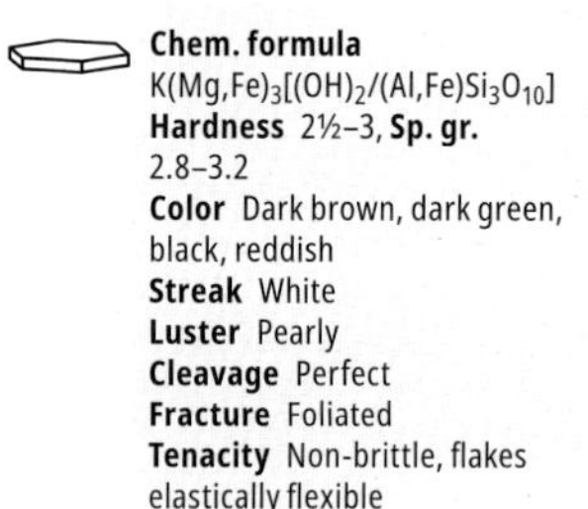

Chem. formula $K(Mg,Fe)_3[(OH)_2/(Al,Fe)Si_3O_{10}]$
Hardness 2½–3, **Sp. gr.** 2.8–3.2
Color Dark brown, dark green, black, reddish
Streak White
Luster Pearly
Cleavage Perfect
Fracture Foliated
Tenacity Non-brittle, flakes elastically flexible
Crystal form Monoclinic

Morphology Hexagonal tabular crystals, rarely prismatic, rose-shaped aggregates, flakes, scales.
Origin and occurrence Anhedral as a rock essential mineral in granites, pegmatites, gneisses, mica schists, diorites, hornfels, volcanic rocks, rarely euhedral crystals on fissures of the cited rocks, in vugs in volcanic ejecta.
Accessory minerals Quartz, muscovite, feldspar.
Similar minerals Chlorite and talc are softer; muscovite has a different color, as does lepidolite.

3 Lepidolite

Chem. formula $KLi_2Al[(F,OH)_2/Si_4O_{10}]$
Hardness 2½–3, **Sp. gr.** 2.8–3.2
Color Pink, pink-purple, reddish
Streak White
Luster Pearly
Cleavage Basal perfect
Fracture Foliated
Tenacity Non-brittle, flakes elastically flexible
Crystal form Monoclinic

Morphology Hexagonal tabular crystals, rarely prismatic, rose-shaped aggregates, flakes, scaly to dense aggregates and masses.
Origin and occurrence Mainly anhedral in pegmatites and in pneumatolytic veins, rarely euhedral crystals, mainly in pegmatites.
Accessory minerals Tourmaline (for example, rubellite, verdelite, often of gemstone quality), beryl, topaz, apatite, feldspar, quartz.
Similar minerals The color of lepidolite is characteristic; manganese-bearing muscovite (alurgite) can also be pink to reddish, but it only occurs in metamorphic rocks.

4 Duftite

Chem. formula $CuPbAsO_4OH$
Hardness 3, **Sp. gr.** 6.4
Color Green, yellow-green
Streak Whitish
Luster Vitreous, greasy
Cleavage Indiscernible
Fracture Uneven
Tenacity Brittle
Crystal form Orthorhombic

Morphology Thick tabular crystals, planar crystal intergrowths, botryoidal aggregates, drusy coatings.
Origin and occurrence In the oxidation zone of lead-copper deposits.
Accessory minerals Cerussite, azurite, chrysocolla, mimetesite, aurichalcite, calcite, olivenite.
Similar minerals Olivenite has a different crystal form; conichalcite is more apple green; cornwallite is more emerald green; chrysocolla is more blue-green; pyromorphite and mimetesite have a different crystal form.

Localities	
1 Broken Hill, Australia	**3** Himalaya Mine, California, USA
2 Miask, Urals, Russia	**4** Tsumeb, Nambia

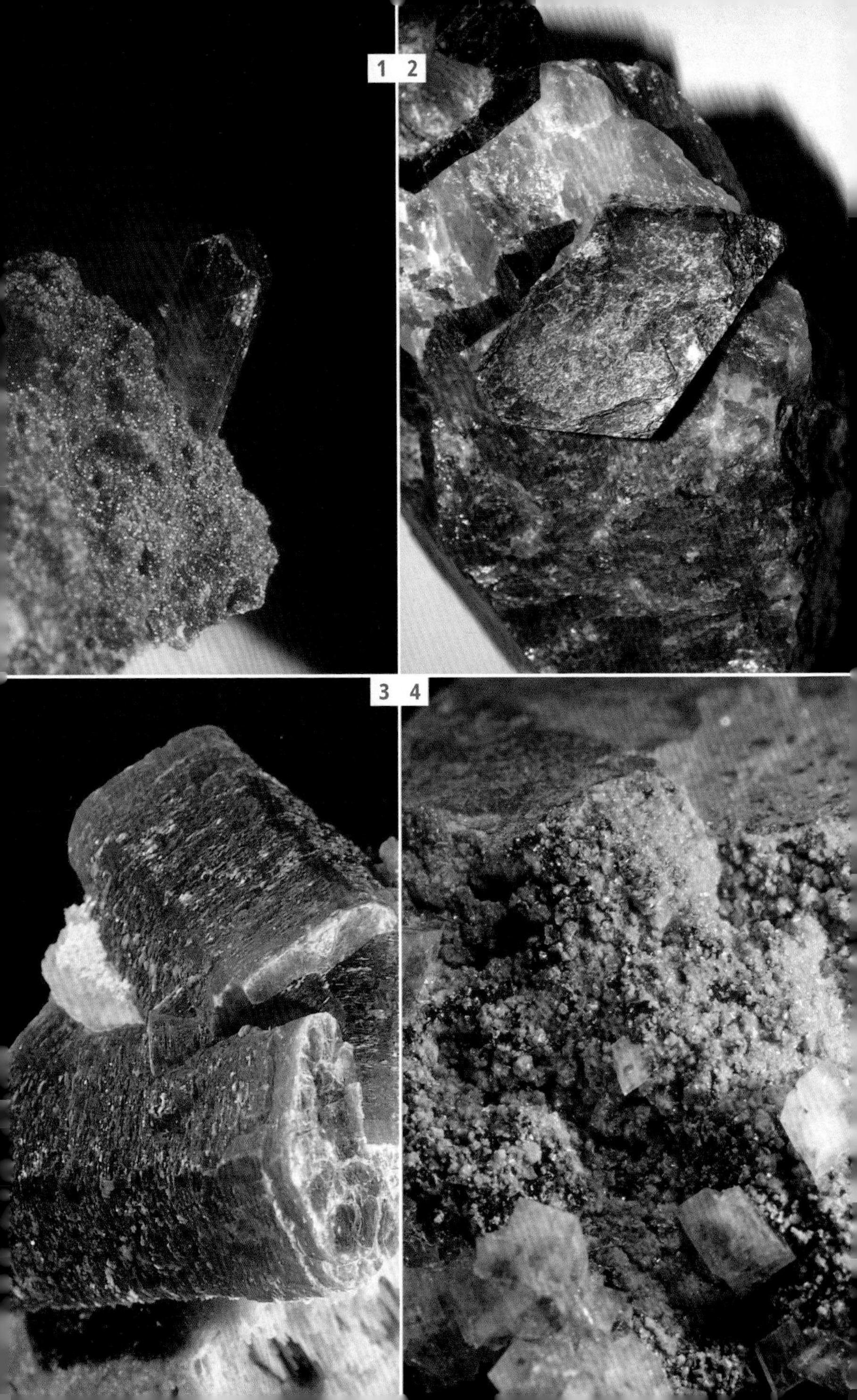
1 2
3 4

1

Whitmoreite

Chem. formula $Fe^{2+}Fe_2^{3+}(PO_4)_2(OH)_2 \cdot 4\,H_2O$
Hardness 3, **Sp. gr.** 2.85
Color Brown, yellow-brown
Streak Whitish
Luster Vitreous
Cleavage Indiscernible
Fracture Uneven
Tenacity Brittle
Crystal form Monoclinic

Morphology Long tabular to acicular crystals, stellate crystal sheaves, botryoidal aggregates, coatings.
Origin and occurrence In phosphate pegmatites, by alteration of the primary phosphates.
Accessory minerals Strunzite, laueite, pseudolaueite, stewartite, mitridatite, rockbridgeite.
Similar minerals Laueite, pseudolaueite, stewartite, childrenite and eosphorite have a different crystal form; cacoxenite is more golden yellow; strunzite more straw yellow.

2

Embolite

Chem. formula Ag(Cl,Br)
Hardness 2–3, **Sp. gr.** 5.6–5.8
Color Green, yellow-green, yellow-brown, gray
Streak Whitish
Luster Greasy
Cleavage Indiscernible
Fracture Uneven
Tenacity Non-brittle
Crystal form Cubic

Morphology Distorted crystals, rounded aggregates, drusy coatings.
Origin and occurrence In the oxidation zone of silver deposits, particularly in arid climates.
Accessory minerals Chlorargyrite, native silver, argentite, calcite, limonite.
Similar minerals Chlorargyrite is not distinguishable using simple means; the paragenesis with other silver minerals is otherwise quite characteristic.

3

Gibbsite

Chem. formula $Al(OH)_3$
Hardness 2½–3½, **Sp. gr.** 2.4
Color White, light blue, greenish, gray
Streak White
Luster Vitreous
Cleavage Mainly indiscernible
Fracture Uneven
Tenacity Brittle
Crystal form Monoclinic

Morphology Tabular crystals very rare, mainly uneven, reniform, drusy.
Origin and occurrence In the oxidation zone of hydrothermal deposits, particularly in country rock rich in aluminum.
Accessory minerals Azurite, hydrozincite, aurichalcite, limonite, gypsum.
Similar minerals Glaucocerinite is much softer; aurichalcite is more fibrous; chalcedony is much harder; chrysocolla is more blue-green.

4

Zinnwaldite

Chem. formula $K(Li,Al,Fe)_3(Al,Si)_4O_{10}(OH,F)_2$
Hardness 2½–4, **Sp. gr.** 2.9–3.3
Color Silver gray to greenish
Streak Whitish
Luster Vitreous
Cleavage Perfect
Fracture Foliated
Tenacity Flexible
Crystal form Monoclinic

Morphology Tabular crystals with hexagonal cross-section, foliated aggregates.
Origin and occurrence In pegmatites and tin deposits.
Accessory minerals Topaz, tinstone, feldspar, fluorite, zinnwaldite, scheelite.
Similar minerals Muscovite is indistinguishable from stannwaldite using simple means; nevertheless, its paragenesis gives an indication; biotite and phlogopite are browner or black; lepidolite is pinker.

Localities	
1 Hagendorf-Süd, East Bavaria, Germany	**3** Lavrion, Greece
2 Broken Hill, Australia	**4** Zinnwald, Czech Republic

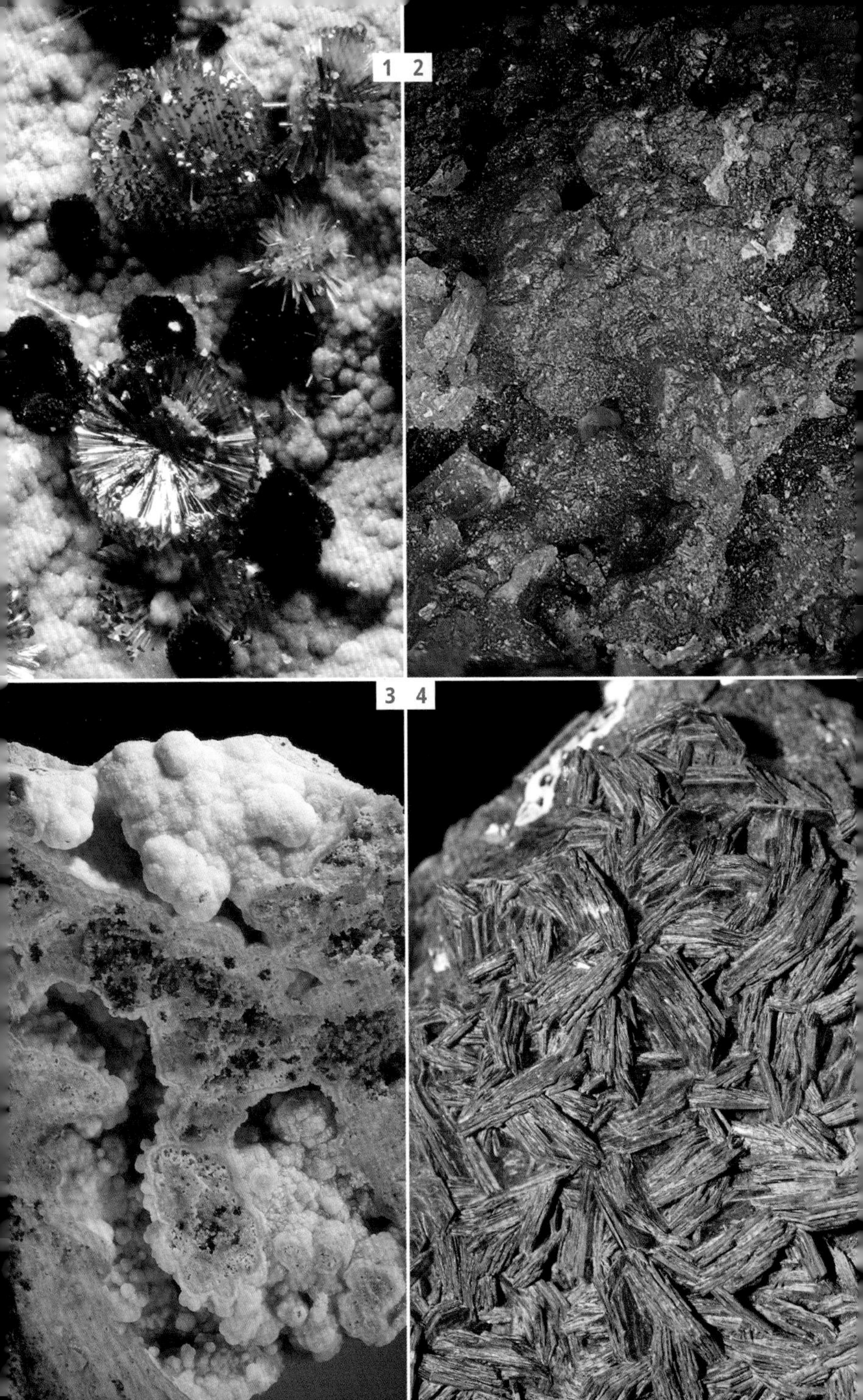
1 2
3 4

1 Kapellasite

Chem. formula $Cu_3Zn(OH)_6Cl_2$
Hardness 3, **Sp. gr.** 3.55
Color Blue to green-blue
Streak Blueish white
Luster Vitreous to silky
Cleavage Perfect
Fracture Uneven
Tenacity Brittle
Crystal form Trigonal

Morphology Acicular to long tabular crystals, crystal sheaves, radial aggregates, coatings.
Origin and occurrence In the oxidation zone of copper-zinc deposits.
Accessory minerals Gypsum, serpierite, claringbullite, spangolite, devilline, schulenbergite, aragonite, calcite.
Distinguishing feature Kapellasite crystals are often typically scraggy at the edges and appear completely white in this area.
Similar minerals Linarite turns white when dabbed with hydrochloric acid; devilline is more foliated or foamy; serpierite is more acicular and deeper blue; schulenbergite is foliated.

2 Zalesiite

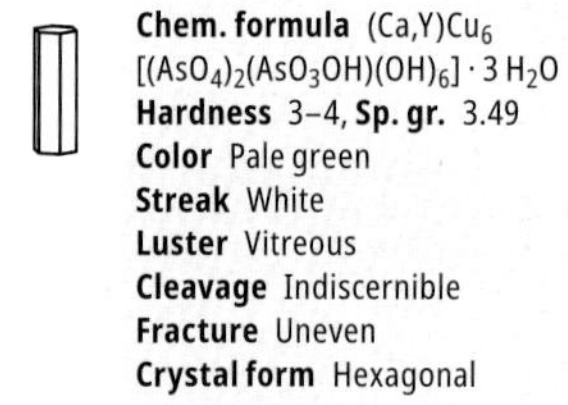

Chem. formula $(Ca,Y)Cu_6[(AsO_4)_2(AsO_3OH)(OH)_6] \cdot 3\,H_2O$
Hardness 3–4, **Sp. gr.** 3.49
Color Pale green
Streak White
Luster Vitreous
Cleavage Indiscernible
Fracture Uneven
Crystal form Hexagonal

Morphology Acicular, fibrous, felty, sheaved crystal aggregates.
Origin and occurrence In the oxidation zone of arsenic-rich copper deposits.
Accessory minerals Adamite, olivenite, limonite, malachite, azurite.
Similar minerals Distinction from individual agardite minerals and from mixite is not possible using simple means; apart from this, zalesiite is very characteristic; malachite effervesces when dabbed with hydrochloric acid; the same applies to aragonite, which is rarely so finely acicular.

3 Astrophyllite

Chem. formula $(K,Na)_3(Fe,Mn)_7Ti_2[(O,OH)_7/Si_8O_{24}]$
Hardness 3, **Sp. gr.** 3.3–3.4
Color Yellowish, greenish olive
Streak White
Luster Metallic vitreous
Cleavage Perfect
Fracture Foliated
Tenacity Brittle
Crystal form Triclinic

Morphology Tabular crystals, foliated aggregates, often radially intergrown.
Origin and occurrence In alkaline rocks and their pegmatites.
Accessory minerals Quartz, feldspar, aegirine, lorenzenite, phlogopite.
Similar minerals Mica minerals are not brittle and do not have such a metallic luster; aegirine has a different cleavage with a cleavage angle of about 90°.

4 Stewartite

Chem. formula $MnFe_2[OH/PO_4]_2 \cdot 8\,H_2O$
Hardness 3, **Sp. gr.** 2.46
Color Yellow, orange, greenish yellow
Streak White
Luster Vitreous
Cleavage None
Fracture Uneven
Tenacity Brittle
Crystal form Monoclinic

Morphology Thin tabular elongated crystals, pointed with oblique end faces, parallel intergrowths, stellate aggregates, crystal sheaves.
Origin and occurrence In phosphate pegmatites as a formation during alteration of primary phosphate minerals.
Accessory minerals Laueite, strunzite, pseudolaueite, beraunite, rockbridgeite, apatite.
Similar minerals Laueite always exhibits a thicker tabular form and has a different crystal form; strunzite is acicular; pseudolaueite is thick tabular with a hexagonal outline.

Localities	
1 Almeria, Spain	**3** Mt. St. Hilaire, Montreal, Canada
2 Mina Dolores, Pastrana, Spain	**4** Hagendorf-Süd, East Bavaria, Germany

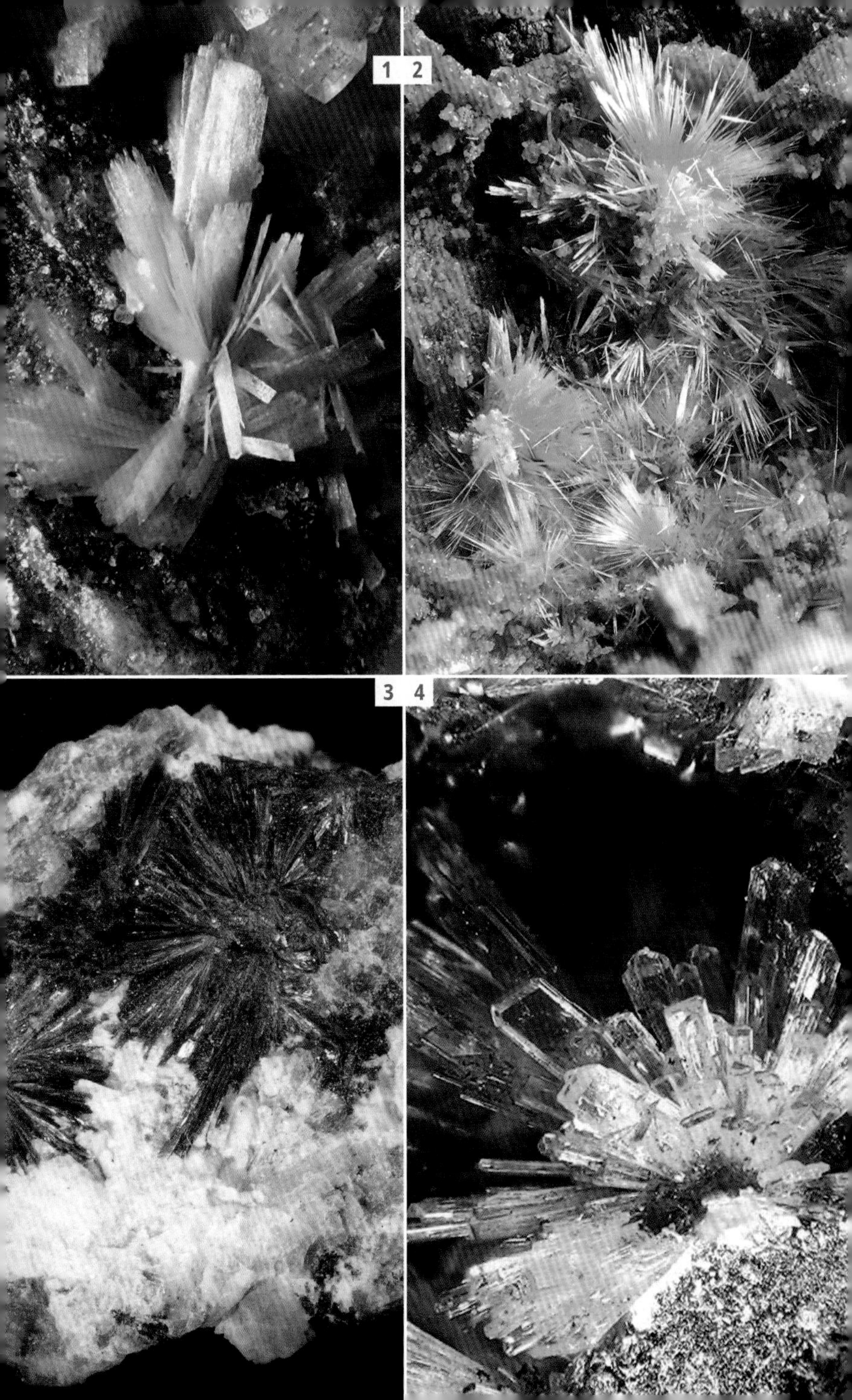
1 2
3 4

1 Weinschenkite *Churchite*

Chem. formula $(Y,Er)PO_4 \cdot H_2O$
Hardness 3, **Sp. gr.** 3.3
Color White
Streak White
Luster Vitreous to silky
Cleavage Indiscernible
Fracture Fibrous
Tenacity Brittle
Crystal form Monoclinic

Morphology Acicular crystals, mainly intergrown to sheaves, rarely prismatic, fibrous and stellate aggregates.
Origin and occurrence In phosphate deposits, particularly in phosphate-rich iron deposits.
Accessory minerals Limonite, cacoxene, beraunite, strengite, dufrenite, rockbridgeite.
Similar minerals Wavellite is almost never as finely fibrous as churchite; it usually still exhibits end faces; crandallite also forms thicker crystals, often exhibiting a triangular end face.

2 Kernite

Chem. formula $Na_2B_4O_7 \cdot 4\,H_2O$
Hardness 2½–3, **Sp. gr.** 1.9
Color Colorless, white
Streak White
Luster Vitreous to silky
Cleavage Perfect
Tenacity Brittle
Crystal form Monoclinic

Morphology Rarely thick tabular crystals, uneven, radial, bladed masses.
Origin and occurrence In borate deposits, in the sediments of salt lakes.
Accessory minerals Colemanite, borax, ulexite, trona, rock salt, gypsum, bloedite.
Similar minerals Kernite distinguishes itself from other borate minerals in its perfect cleavage; colemanite exhibits a different crystal form; ulexite is always more radial and fibrous.

3 Picropharmacolite

Chem. formula $CaH[AsO_4] \cdot 2\,H_2O$
Hardness 2–2½, **Sp. gr.** 2.6
Color Colorless, white, due to cobalt or nickel sometimes reddish or green
Streak White
Luster Vitreous
Cleavage Indiscernible due to the acicular structure
Fracture Fibrous
Tenacity Brittle
Crystal form Monoclinic

Morphology Acicular to filiform crystals, stellate sheaves, roses.
Origin and occurrence In the oxidation zone of arsenic-rich deposits as often very young formations.
Accessory minerals Gypsum, red cobalt, pharmacolite, guerinite, sainfeldite, aragonite.
Similar minerals Pharmacolite has good cleavage; the same applies to gypsum; aragonite effervesces when dabbed with diluted hydrochloric acid. Natrolite and scolecite occur in a quite different paragenesis.

4 Köttigite

Chem. formula $Zn_3(AsO_4)_2 \cdot 8\,H_2O$
Hardness 2½–3, **Sp. gr.** 3.3
Color White, gray, brown, reddish
Streak White
Luster Vitreous
Cleavage Perfect
Fracture Uneven
Tenacity Slightly flexible
Crystal form Monoclinic

Morphology Prismatic, long tabular crystals with mainly oblique end face, stellate, uneven.
Origin and occurrence In the oxidation zone of arsenic-bearing zinc deposits.
Accessory minerals Adamite, cuprian adamite, paradamite, legrandite.
Similar minerals The paragenesis and crystal form of köttigite make confusion very unlikely. Parasymplesite is more greenish; vivianite is blue to blue-green; annabergite is grass green; ery-thrite is intense red-purple.

Localities	
1 Leonie Mine, Auerbach, Bavaria, Germany	**3** Richelsdorf, Hesse, Germany
2 Kern County, California, USA	**4** Mina Ojuela, Mapimi, Mexico

1 2
3 4

1–4 Calcite *Calcareous spar, lime spar*

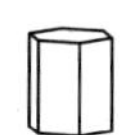

Chem. formula $CaCO_3$
Hardness 3, **Sp. gr.** 2.6–2.8
Color Colorless, white, yellow, brown; variegated due to foreign inclusions: red, blue, green, black
Streak Whitish
Luster Vitreous
Cleavage Basic rhombohedral perfect
Fracture Crystalline to conchoidal
Tenacity Brittle
Crystal form Trigonal

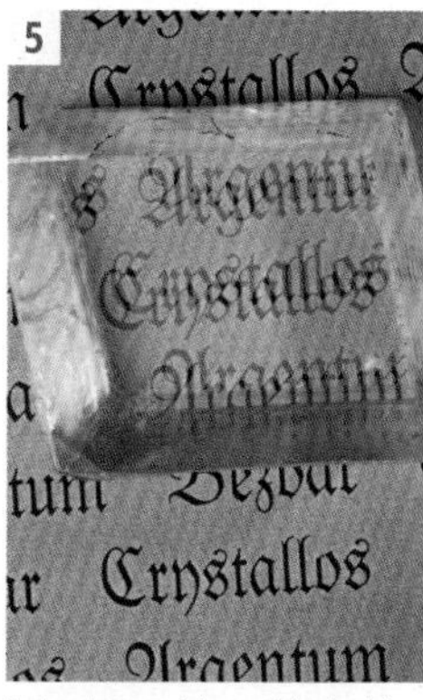

Iceland spar with notable double refraction

Prismatic calcite crystals from St. Andreasberg in Harz, Germany

Morphology Crystals very diverse as scalenohedra, rhombohedra, prism with base; habit prismatic, isometric, lenticular, acicular, thick and thin tabular; often twins with re-entrant angles, heart- or butterfly-shaped, often also radial, botryoidal and reniform aggregates, in the form of dripstones, as gangue fillings, essential mineral as limestone and marble uneven. Clear cleavage pieces of calcite enable a special feature, namely double refraction, to be observed. If such cleavage pieces are placed on lined paper, all the lines appear duplicated (Fig. 5). Among minerals, calcite has the largest number of different forms. More than 2000 different combinations of crystal forms are known. As an essential mineral in the form of limestones, calcite forms entire mountain ranges such as the Limestone Alps or parts of the Himalayas.

Origin and occurrence Crystals in vugs of ore veins, bubble cavities of volcanic rocks, on fissures and in vugs of carbonate rocks, as gangue of many hydrothermal veins; magmatic essential mineral in carbonatites, sedimentary essential mineral in limestones, in lime tuffs, in marls, as binder in sandstones, metamorphic in marbles.

Accessory minerals Dolomite, quartz, galena, chalcopyrite, pyrite, arsenopyrite, sphalerite and many other ore minerals.

Distinguishing feature Clear cleavage pieces of calcite enable a special feature to be observed: double refraction. If such cleavage pieces are placed on lined paper or written text, all lines or letters appear duplicated (see Fig. 5). Technically, this property is used in various pieces of optical equipment, particularly in polarizing microscopes. The best and clearest specimens of this calcite originate from Iceland, where they were found in the cavities of volcanic rock. They are called double refraction calcspar on account of this feature and also Iceland spar based on their origin.

Similar minerals Calcite effervesces when dabbed with cold diluted hydrochloric acid; unlike calcite, dolomite effervesces only with hot hydrochloric acid; quartz is harder; gypsum is softer; anhydrite has a cleavage with right-angle cleavage and does not effervesce with hydrochloric acid. Aragonite has no cleavage and exhibits a different crystal form; rock salt and sylvite are soluble in water; barite and celestine are much heavier, have a different cleavage and do not effervesce when dabbed with diluted hydrochloric acid; the same applies to strontianite and witherite. Cerussite is much heavier, has a different cleavage and almost always exhibits its typical twinning.

Localities	
1 St. Andreasberg, Harz, Germany	**3** Blaubeuren, Ulm, Germany
2 Schneeberg, Saxony, Germany	**4** Richelsdorf, Hesse, Germany

1 2
3 4

1 Laueite

Chem. formula $MnFe_2[OH/PO_4] \cdot 8\, H_2O$
Hardness 3, **Sp. gr.** 2.49
Color Yellow, orange-yellow, honey brown
Streak White to yellowish
Luster Vitreous
Cleavage Slightly distinct
Fracture Conchoidal
Tenacity Brittle
Crystal form Triclinic

Morphology Prismatic to thick tabular crystals, planar crystal intergrowths, encrustations.
Origin and occurrence In phosphate pegmatites, as an alteration product of the primary phosphates.
Accessory minerals Strunzite, stewartite, pseudolauite, apatite, beraunite.
Similar minerals Stewartite has a different crystal form and exhibits a much thinner tabular appearance; pseudolaueite also has a different crystal form; paravauxite has a color other than orange-brown.

2 Paralaurionite

Chem. formula PbClOH
Hardness 3, **Sp. gr.** 6.2
Color Colorless, white, yellow
Streak White
Luster Vitreous to adamantine
Cleavage Perfect
Fracture Fibrous
Tenacity Non-brittle, inelastically flexible
Crystal form Monoclinic

Morphology Long tabular crystals, prismatic, thin tabular, acicular, often bent.
Origin and occurrence In the oxidation zone of lead deposit and in ancient lead slags.
Accessory minerals Phosgenite, laurionite, fiedlerite, anglesite, georgiadesite, nealite, aragonite, calcite.
Similar minerals Laurionite is brittle; fiedlerite has a different crystal form; the same applies to anglesite and cerussite; cerussite differs in particuar due to its characteristic twinning.

3 Polyhalite

Chem. formula $K_2MgCa_2(SO_4)_4 \cdot 2\, H_2O$
Hardness 3, **Sp. gr.** 2.78
Color Reddish, white, gray
Streak White
Luster Vitreous to resinous
Cleavage Perfect
Fracture Fibrous
Tenacity Brittle
Crystal form Triclinic

Morphology Fibrous, granular, uneven.
Origin and occurrence In salt deposits, particularly in alpine deposits in Europe.
Accessory minerals Gypsum, rock salt, sylvite, anhydrite, hematite, calcite.
Similar minerals Gypsum has a different crystal form and is softer; rock salt is considerably softer; the reddish color often caused by finely divided hematite is very characteristic; anhydrite exhibits a different cleavage; calcite effervesces when dabbed with diluted hydrochloric acid.

4 Shortite

Chem. formula $Na_2Ca_2(CO_3)_3$
Hardness 3, **Sp. gr.** 2.6
Color White, colorless, pale yellow
Streak White
Luster Vitreous
Cleavage Poor
Fracture Conchoidal
Tenacity Brittle
Crystal form Orthorhombic

Morphology Thick tabular to short prismatic crystals, mainly anhedral.
Origin and occurrence Euhedral in argillaceous rocks, in sediments of saline lakes.
Accessory minerals Calcite, pyrite.
Similar minerals Calcite has a different crystal form and rhombohedral cleavage; anhydrite exhibits different cleavage; rock salt has cubic cleavage.

Localities	
1 Hagendorf-Süd, East Bavaria, Germany	**3** Berchtesgaden, Bavaria, Germany
2 Lavrion, Greece	**4** Uintah County, Utah, USA

1 2
3 4

1 Klebelsbergite

Chem. formula $Sb_4O_4[(OH)_2|SO_4]$
Hardness 3, **Sp. gr.** 3.5
Color White to yellow
Streak White
Luster Vitreous
Cleavage Indiscernible
Fracture Uneven
Tenacity Brittle
Crystal form Orthorhombic

Morphology Acicular, long tabular crystals, often longitudinally striated, stellate.
Origin and occurrence In the oxidation zone of antimonic deposits as a weathering product of stibnite.
Accessory minerals Stibnite, valentinite, senarmontite.
Similar minerals Taking its paragenesis with stibnite into consideration, klebelsbergite is unmistakable; valentinite crystals are thicker and not longitudinally striated; aragonite effervesces when dabbed with diluted hydrochloric acid.

2 Pseudolaueite

Chem. formula $MnFe_2(PO_4)_2(OH)_2 \cdot 8\,H_2O$
Hardness 3, **Sp. gr.** 2.5
Color Yellow to yellow-brown
Streak White
Luster Vitreous
Cleavage None
Fracture Uneven
Tenacity Brittle
Crystal form Monoclinic

Morphology Thick tabular crystals with a mainly hexagonal outline, almost always euhedral single crystals, planar crystal intergrowths, rarely botryoidal aggregates.
Origin and occurrence In phosphate pegmatites as an alteration formation of primary phosphate minerals.
Accessory minerals Laueite, strunzite, stewartite, rockbridgeite.
Similar minerals The crystal form exhibited by pseudolaueite is unmistakable; laueite and stewartite are more elongated and never have a hexagonal outline; strunzite is acicular.

3 Pachnolite

Chem. formula $CaNaAlF_6 \cdot H_2O$
Hardness 3, **Sp. gr.** 2.98
Streak White
Color Colorless, white, brownish due to limonite
Luster Vitreous
Cleavage Scarcely discernible
Fracture Conchoidal
Tenacity Brittle
Crystal form Monoclinic

Morphology Prismatic crystals with pointed pyramidal end faces, rarely tabular, sometimes right-angled intergrowths.
Origin and occurrence On vugs in pegmatites, mainly as an alteration product of cryolite.
Accessory minerals Thomsenolite, ralstonite, cryolite, siderite, galenite, jarlite.
Similar minerals Thomsenolite has better cleavage and usually exhibits distinctly monoclinic, unilaterally oblique crystals.

4 Glauberite

Chem. formula $Na_2Ca(SO_4)_2$
Hardness 3, **Sp. gr.** 2.8
Color Colorless, white, gray, yellowish
Streak White
Luster Vitreous to silky
Cleavage Perfect
Tenacity Brittle
Crystal form Monoclinic

Morphology Tabular, prismatic crystals, pseudomorphs of calcite after glauberite crystals are common, often intergrown to form radial aggregates.
Origin and occurrence In salt deposits and sediments, primarily anhedral.
Accessory minerals Rock salt, sylvite, gypsum, calcite, anhydrite.
Similar minerals Gypsum is softer; anhydrite has a different cleavage; the pseudomorphs of calcite to glauberite are always dull and opaque and effervesce when dabbed with diluted hydrochloric acid.

Localities	
1 Pereta, Tuscany, Italy	**3** Ivigtut, Greenland
2 Hagendorf-Süd, East Bavaria, Germany	**4** Camp Verde, Arizona, USA

1 2
3 4

1 Paravauxite

Chem. formula $FeAl_2(PO_4)_2(OH)_2 \cdot 8\,H_2O$
Hardness 3, **Sp. gr.** 2.38
Color Colorless to greenish white
Streak White
Luster Vitreous
Cleavage Perfect
Fracture Conchoidal
Tenacity Brittle
Crystal form Triclinic

Morphology Tabular to short prismatic crystals with oblique end faces, mainly euhedral, planar crystal intergrowths, rarely stellate aggregates.
Origin and occurrence In the oxidation zone of subvolcanic deposits, in phosphate pegmatites during the alteration of primary phosphates.
Accessory minerals Wavellite, quartz, vauxite, apatite, tinstone, pyrite.
Similar minerals Laueite has a different color and is always more intense yellow-brown; stewartite exhibits a thinner tabular form; its end faces have a steeper angle, and the color is always yellow; vauxite has a different crystal form and is almost always blue.

2 Zeophyllite

Chem. formula $Ca_4(Si_3O_7)(OH)_4F_2$
Hardness 3, **Sp. gr.** 2.6–2.7
Color White
Streak White
Luster Pearly
Cleavage Perfect
Fracture Foliated
Tenacity Brittle
Crystal form Triclinic

Morphology Tabular crystals, botryoidal aggregates, reniform coatings, drusy.
Origin and occurrence In cavities of volcanic rocks, always euhedral.
Accessory minerals Calcite, phillipsite, gonnardite, natrolite, aragonite.
Similar minerals Gonnardite and natrolite are more fibrous; phillipsite does not have foliated cleavage. Calcite has a different crystal form and different cleavage and effervesces when dabbed with diluted hydrochloric acid. Aragonite does not exhibit a foliated fracture and effervesces when dabbed with diluted hydrochloric acid; spheres of colorless to white opal exhibit no internal structure.

3–4 Barite

Chem. formula $BaSO_4$
Hardness 3–3½, **Sp. gr.** 4.48
Color Colorless, white, yellowish, reddish, blue
Streak White
Luster Vitreous, pearly on cleavage faces
Cleavage Basal perfect
Fracture Crystalline to conchoidal
Tenacity Brittle
Crystal form Orthorhombic

Morphology Crystals tabular, rarely prismatic; fan-shaped and cockscomb aggregates, in sands also flower-shaped aggregates (barite roses), crystalline, often uneven.
Origin and occurrence As gangue in hydrothermal veins, in vugs often forming beautiful crystals, as concretions in sandstones and other sedimentary rocks.
Accessory minerals Calcite, quartz, fluorite, pyrite, chalcopyrite, galena, cinnabar, sphalerite.
Distinguishing feature Because of its high specific gravity, barite is used to weight paper (barite paper) and drilling muds; it improves radiation protection as an additive to concrete.
Similar minerals Quartz and feldspar are harder; gypsum, calcite and aragonite are much lighter; uneven celestine often cannot be distinguished from barite by simple means.

Localities	
1 Llallagua, Bolivia	**3** Touissit, Morocco
2 Radzein, Czech Republic	**4** Cumberland, Great Britain

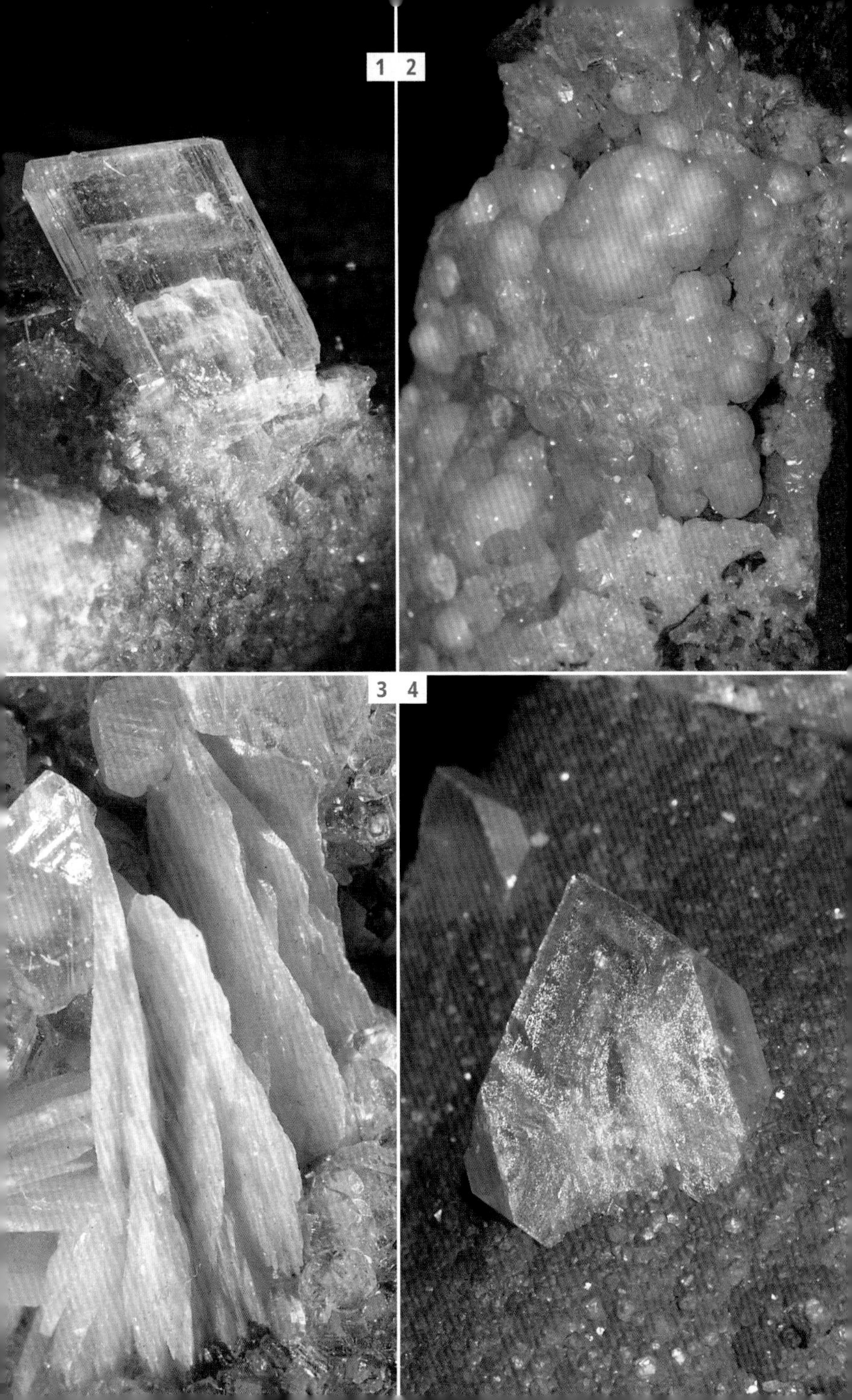
1 2
3 4

1 Scholzite

Chem. formula $CaZn_2[PO_4] \cdot 2\,H_2O$
Hardness 3–4, **Sp. gr.** 3.11
Color Colorless, white, yellowish
Streak White
Luster Vitreous
Cleavage Scarcely distinct
Fracture Conchoidal
Tenacity Brittle
Crystal form Orthorhombic

Morphology Tabular to acicular crystals, short prismatic, fibrous, radial.
Origin and occurrence In phosphate pegmatites by alteration of primary phosphates in the presence of sphalerite, in iron deposits with zinc and phosphorus content.
Accessory minerals Phosphophyllite, hopeite, parahopeite, tarbuttite.
Similar minerals Considering its paragenesis with zinciferous minerals and phosphates, confusion is almost impossible.

2 Hydromagnesite

Chem. formula $Mg_5(CO_3)_4(OH)_2 \cdot 4\,H_2O$
Hardness 3–3½, **Sp. gr.** 2.25
Color Colorless, white
Streak White
Luster Vitreous
Cleavage Perfect
Fracture Uneven
Tenacity Brittle
Crystal form Monoclinic

Morphology Tabular to acicular crystals, fibrous, stellate aggregates, sun-like structures, encrustations, planar crystal intergrowths, uneven.
Origin and occurrence On fissures of serpentinite and altered ultrabasic rocks, in caves, as a component of dolomite xenoliths.
Accessory minerals Serpentine, artinite, aragonite, calcite, dolomite, magnesite.
Similar minerals Artinite is more acicular; aragonite has no cleavage.

3 Fuchsite

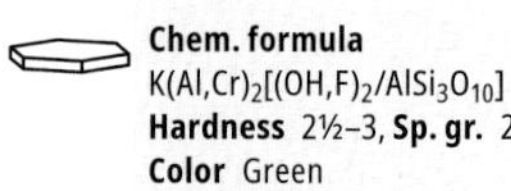

Chem. formula $K(Al,Cr)_2[(OH,F)_2/AlSi_3O_{10}]$
Hardness 2½–3, **Sp. gr.** 2.8–3
Color Green
Streak White
Luster Pearly
Cleavage Basal perfect
Fracture Foliated
Tenacity Non-brittle flakes elastically flexible
Crystal form Monoclinic

Morphology Tabular, hexagonal crystals euhedral extremely rare, mainly flakes, scales, largely anhedral essential mineral.
Origin and occurrence Essential mineral in metamorphic rocks, gneisses, mica schists, marbles.
Accessory minerals Quartz, feldspar, calcite, pyrite, muscovite, tourmaline, rutile.
Similar minerals Talc and chlorite are softer; their leaves are not elastically flexible; biotite and phlogopite are always significantly darker.

4 Nordstrandite

Chem. formula $Al(OH)_3$
Hardness 3-3½, **Sp. gr.** 2.41–2.43
Streak White
Color White, colorless
Luster Vitreous, pearly on cleavage faces
Cleavage Perfect
Fracture Foliated
Tenacity Brittle
Crystal form Monoclinic

Morphology Thick to thin tabular crystals, blocky, foliated, stellate, drusy.
Origin and occurrence In pegmatites, in xenoliths in nepheline syenites, in oil shales, limestones, clays.
Accessory minerals Quartz, kaolinite, goethite, analcime, sodalite, natrolite, albite, microcline.
Similar minerals Albite exhibits a different cleavage; muscovite is not brittle; calcite effervesces when dabbed with diluted hydrochloric acid.

Localities	
1 Hagendorf-Süd, East Bavaria, Germany	**3** Minas Gerais, Brazil
2 San Benito County, California, USA	**4** Kola, Russia

1 2

3 4

1

Alunite

Chem. formula $KAl_3(SO_4)_2(OH)_6$
Hardness 3½–4, **Sp. gr.** 2.6–2.9
Color White, colorless, gray
Streak White
Luster Vitreous
Cleavage Perfect
Fracture Uneven
Tenacity Brittle
Crystal form Hexagonal

Morphology Pseudo-octahedral crystals, fibrous aggregates, encrustations, earthy, uneven.
Origin and occurrence During the reaction of sulfate-rich weathering solutions with aluminum-rich rocks.
Accessory minerals Pyrite, gypsum, quartz, kaolinite, calcite, jarosite.
Similar minerals Gypsum has a different crystal form; calcite effervesces when dabbed with diluted hydrochloric acid; jarosite is yellow to brown; kaolinite is much softer; quartz is much harder than alunite.

2

Witherite

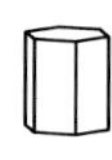

Chem. formula $BaCO_3$
Hardness 3½, **Sp. gr.** 4.28
Color Colorless, white, gray, yellow-white
Streak White
Luster Vitreous to dull
Cleavage Discernible
Fracture Uneven
Tenacity Brittle
Crystal form Orthorhombic

Morphology Apparently hexagonal dipyramids, radial, reniform, fibrous, foliated, uneven.
Origin and occurrence In hydrothermal veins as rare gangue mineral.
Accessory minerals Calcite, galena, barite, celestine, sphalerite.
Similar minerals Witherite has a different crystal form to strontianite; distinction is sometimes not possible with uneven pieces; aragonite and calcite effervesce even with cold, undiluted hydrochloric acid; barite and celestine have much better cleavage.

3

Phosphophyllite

Chem. formula $Zn_2Fe[PO_4]_2 \cdot 4\,H_2O$
Hardness 3½, **Sp. gr.** 3.1
Color Colorless, white, green, blue-green
Streak White
Luster Vitreous
Cleavage Perfect
Fracture Uneven
Tenacity Brittle
Crystal form Monoclinic

Morphology Scalenohedral crystals, often intergrown to V-shaped twins, rarely tabular crystals, uneven, crystalline masses.
Origin and occurrence In phosphate pegmatites as an alteration product of primary phosphates and sphalerite, in the oxidation zone of ore veins.
Accessory minerals Hopeite, parahopeite, scholzite, rockbridgeite.
Similar minerals Calcite effervesces when dabbed with diluted hydrochloric acid; hopeite and parahopeite have a different crystal form.

4

Anhydrite

Chem. formula $CaSO_4$
Hardness 3–3½, **Sp. gr.** 2.98
Color Colorless, white, gray, blue
Streak White
Luster Vitreous
Cleavage Perfect, cuboid cleavage body with right angles
Fracture Crystalline
Tenacity Brittle
Crystal form Orthorhombic

Morphology Tabular, isometric to prismatic crystals, granular, crystalline, uneven.
Origin and occurrence In salt deposits, sedimentary rocks, as separate rock bodies, in hydrothermal veins as gangue, on alpine fissures.
Accessory minerals Gypsum, rock salt.
Similar minerals Characteristic right-angle cleavage makes anhydrite unmistakable; calcite effervesces when dabbed with diluted hydrochloric acid; gypsum is much softer and has significantly different cleavage.

Localities	
1 Tolfa, Tuscany, Italy	**3** Hagendorf-Süd, East Bavaria, Germany
2 Cumberland, Great Britain	**4** Berchtesgaden, Bavaria, Germany

1 2
3 4

1–2 Celestine

Chem. formula $SrSO_4$
Hardness 3–3½, **Sp. gr.** 3.9-4
Color Colorless, white, blue, reddish, greenish, brownish
Streak White
Luster Vitreous, pearly on cleavage faces
Cleavage Basal perfect, two other cleavage directions are much harder to discern
Fracture Uneven
Tenacity Brittle
Crystal form Orthorhombic

Morphology Crystals thin to thick tabular, prismatic, aggregates stellate, columnar, fibrous, granular, earthy.
Origin and occurrence In hydrothermal veins and bubble cavities of volcanic rocks, as fissure and vug fillings in limestones and marls, in sedimentary layers in limestones.
Accessory minerals Calcite, pyrite, barite.
Similar minerals Barite is denser and uneven, but often difficult to distinguish using simple means; calcite has perfect rhombohedral cleavage and effervesces when dabbed with diluted hydrochloric acid; aragonite has no cleavage and also effervesces when dabbed with diluted hydrochloric acid. Gypsum is much softer; quartz and feldspar are harder; strontianite and witherite have a different crystal form; dolomite has perfect rhombohedral cleavage.

3 Ferrierite

Chem. formula $(Na,K)_2MgAl_3Si_{15}O_{36}OH \cdot 9\,H_2O$
Hardness 3–3½, **Sp. gr.** 2.1
Color White, reddish
Streak White
Luster Vitreous
Cleavage Indiscernible
Fracture Uneven
Tenacity Brittle
Crystal form Orthorhombic

Morphology Acicular crystals, stellate aggregates, fibrous vug fillings.
Origin and occurrence In cavities of volcanic rocks.
Accessory minerals Calcite, heulandite, chabazite, stilbite, quartz, calcite.
Similar minerals Ferrierite cannot be distinguished from natrolite and scolecite by simple means; the same applies to mordenite; calcite and aragonite effervesce when dabbed with diluted hydrochloric acid.

4 Newberyite

Chem. formula $MgHPO_4 \cdot 3\,H_2O$
Hardness 3–3½, **Sp. gr.** 2.1
Color Colorless, gray, brown
Streak White
Luster Vitreous
Cleavage Perfect
Fracture Uneven
Tenacity Brittle
Crystal form Orthorhombic

Morphology Tabular, prismatic crystals, foliated aggregates, powdery, uneven.
Origin and occurrence In bat caves, formed by reaction of bat guano with the cave rock.
Accessory minerals Gypsum, struvite, hannayite.
Similar minerals Gypsum has different tenacity; the type of gypsum that occurs in bat caves as a formation from bat guano is not very aesthetic but very characteristic; aragonite and calcite effervesce when dabbed with diluted hydrochloric acid; hannayite, occurring in the same paragenesis, is much softer than newberyite.

Localities	
1 Tarnobrzeg, Poland	**3** Sassari, Sardinia, Italy
2 Rüdersdorf, Berlin, Germany	**4** Skipton Cave, Ballarat, Australia

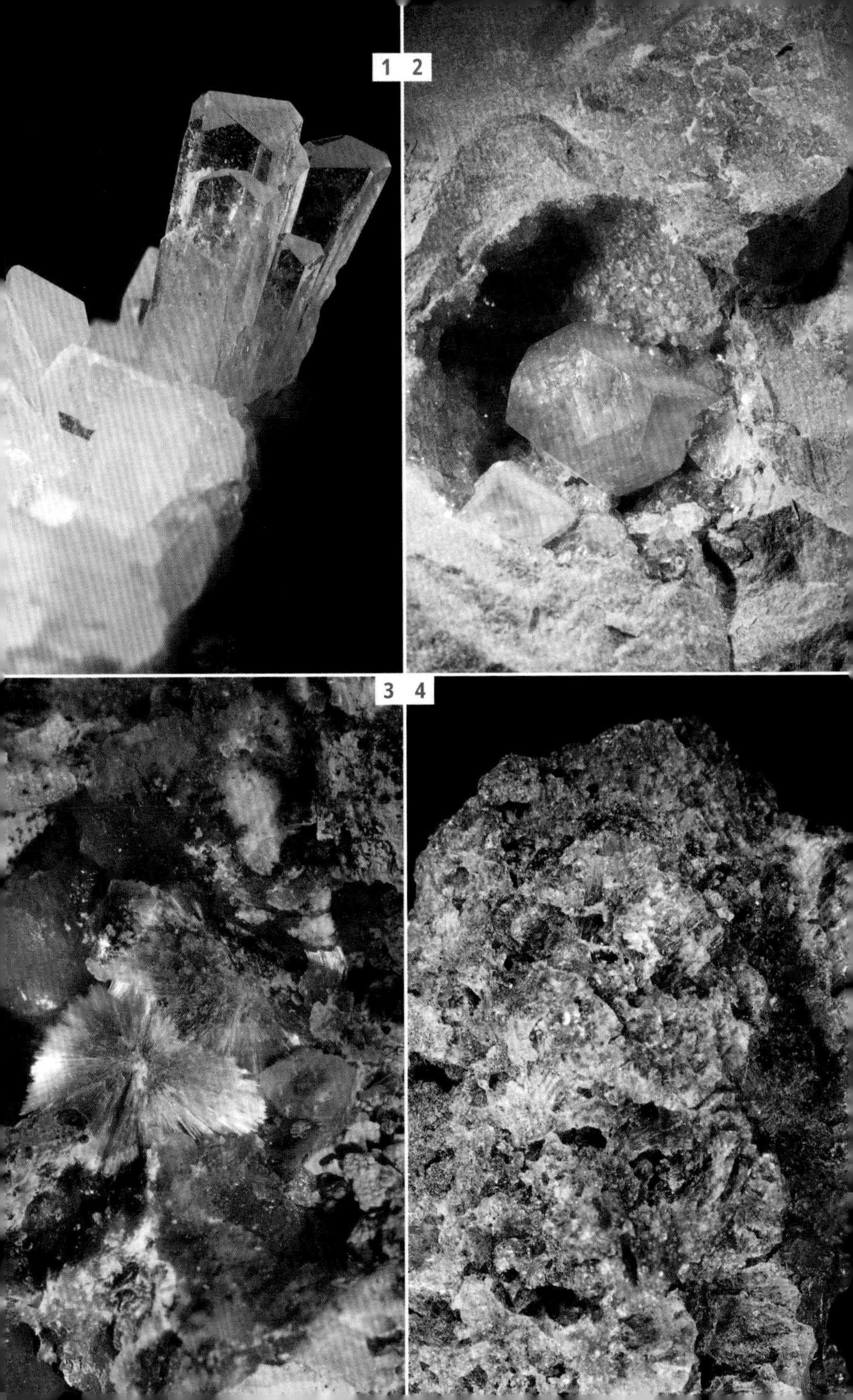
1 2
3 4

1–2 Cerussite *Lead spar*

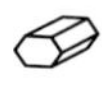

Chem. formula $PbCO_3$
Hardness 3–3½, **Sp. gr.** 6.4–6.6
Color Colorless, white, gray, yellow, brown, blackish
Streak White
Luster Greasy to adamantine
Cleavage Poorly discernible
Fracture Conchoidal
Tenacity Brittle
Crystal form Orthorhombic

Morphology Crystals prismatic, isometric, tabular, often knee-shaped twins, multiple twinning produces star-shaped and lattice-like structures, reniform aggregates, drusy, earthy.
Origin and occurrence In the oxidation zone of lead deposits.
Accessory minerals Galena, pyromorphite, smithsonite, anglesite, calcite, quartz, sphalerite.
Distinguishing feature Cerussite dissolves in concentrated hydrochloric acid (**Caution! Highly corrosive!**) while effervescing, while it does not effervesce in cold diluted hydrochloric acid. Cerussite colored black by residual unconverted galena is called black lead ore.
Similar minerals Calcite and aragonite, in contrast to cerussite, effervesce even with diluted hydrochloric acid; the characteristic twinning distinguishes cerussite from anglesite. Barite has a distinct cleavage and also does not effervesce in concentrated hydrochloric acid; the same is true for celestine; unlike celestine, cerussite is never blue.

3 Weloganite

Chem. formula $Na_2(Sr,Ca)_3(CO_3)_4 \cdot 3\,H_2O$
Hardness 3½, **Sp. gr.** 3.2
Color White, yellowish
Streak White
Luster Vitreous
Cleavage Perfect
Fracture Conchoidal
Crystal form Hexagonal

Morphology Tapered to one end, hexagonal crystals.
Origin and occurrence In vugs and cavities of alkaline rocks.
Accessory minerals Strontianite, dawsonite, pyrite, calcite, aragonite, quartz.
Similar minerals The characteristic crystal form of weloganite does not allow for any confusion; calcite has perfect rhombohedral cleavage; strontianite exhibits a different crystal form.

4 Laumontite

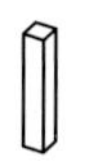

Chem. formula $CaAl_2Si_4O_{12} \cdot 4H_2O$
Hardness 3–3½, **Sp. gr.** 2.25–2.35
Color Colorless, white (in the event of water loss)
Streak White
Luster Vitreous, pearly on cleavage faces
Cleavage Perfect in the longitudinal direction of the crystal
Fracture Uneven
Tenacity Brittle
Crystal form Monoclinic

Morphology Prisms with characteristic oblique end faces; radial, powdery, uneven.
Origin and occurrence In vugs in pegmatites, granites, in bubble cavities of volcanic rocks, on alpine fissures.
Accessory minerals Apophyllite, stilbite, chabazite.
Distinguishing feature Fresh laumontite loses part of its crystal water very quickly and then becomes white and powdery.
Similar minerals The crystal form of laumontite precludes any confusion; potassium feldspar can sometimes form pseudomorphs after laumontite, but these are much harder.

Localities	
1 Arizona, USA	**3** Francon Quarry, Montreal, Canada
2 Siegerland Region, Germany	**4** Pune, India

1 2
3 4

1 Vauxite

Chem. formula $FeAl_2(PO_4)_2(OH)_2 \cdot 6 H_2O$
Hardness 3½, **Sp. gr.** 2.4
Color Blue
Streak White
Luster Vitreous
Cleavage None
Fracture Conchoidal
Tenacity Brittle
Crystal form Triclinic

Morphology Mainly very small tabular crystals, planar crystal intergrowths, stellate botryoidal aggregates, crystal encrustations, coatings, uneven.
Origin and occurrence In the oxidation zone of subvolcanic tin deposits.
Accessory minerals Paravauxite, wavellite, tinstone, apatite.
Similar minerals The color and characteristic paragenesis of vauxite prevent any confusion; paravauxite has a different crystal form and is never blue; apatite is always hexagonal.

2 Phosphoferrite

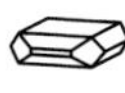

Chem. formula $(Fe,Mn)_3(PO_4)_2 \cdot 3 H_2O$
Hardness 3–3½, **Sp. gr.** 3.29
Color Colorless, greenish, brown
Streak White
Luster Vitreous
Cleavage Poor
Fracture Conchoidal
Tenacity Brittle
Crystal form Orthorhombic

Morphology Octahedral, isometric to thick tabular crystals, uneven.
Origin and occurrence In phosphate pegmatites as an alteration product of primary phosphate minerals.
Accessory minerals Ludlamite, vivianite, siderite, strengite, rockbridgeite.
Similar minerals Taking its paragenesis into consideration, it is not possible to confuse this with other minerals; rockbridgeite is significantly blacker and always radial; frondelite is radial; strengite is never brown.

3 Thaumasite

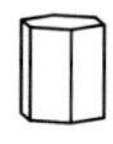

Chem. formula $Ca_3Si(OH)_6(CO_3)(SO_4) \cdot 12 H_2O$
Hardness 3½, **Sp. gr.** 1.91
Color White, colorless
Streak White
Luster Vitreous to silky
Cleavage None
Fracture Conchoidal
Tenacity Brittle
Crystal form Hexagonal

Morphology Fine-acicular, fibrous, sheaved aggregates, rarely prismatic crystals with hexagonal cross section, uneven.
Origin and occurrence In cavities of volcanic rocks in calcium-rich xenoliths, in metamorphic manganese deposits.
Accessory minerals Ettringite, aragonite, tobermorite, afwillite.
Similar minerals Ettringite is usually not as finely acicular but is often difficult to distinguish from thaumasite; the rare hexagonal prisms are difficult to confuse when considering the paragenesis; apatite is distinctly harder.

4 Kovdorskite

Chem. formula $Mg_2(PO4)(OH) \cdot 3 H_2O$
Hardness 3½–4, **Sp. gr.** 2.28
Color White, colorless, pink, pale blue
Streak White
Luster Vitreous
Cleavage None
Fracture Conchoidal
Tenacity Brittle
Crystal form Monoclinic

Morphology Prismatic crystals, planar crystal intergrowths, stellate aggregates.
Origin and occurrence In veins in ultrabasic to alkaline rock complexes, euhedral on fissures or as cavity linings.
Accessory minerals Collinsite, magnesite, apatite, dolomite, magneitite, forsterite.
Similar minerals Apatite is distinctly harder and has a different crystal form; collinsite has a different crystal form; calcite effervesces when dabbed with diluted hydrochloric acid.

Localities	
1 Llallagua, Bolivia	**3** Hatrurim, Israel
2 Hagendorf-Süd, East Bavaria, Germany	**4** Kovdor, Kola, Russia

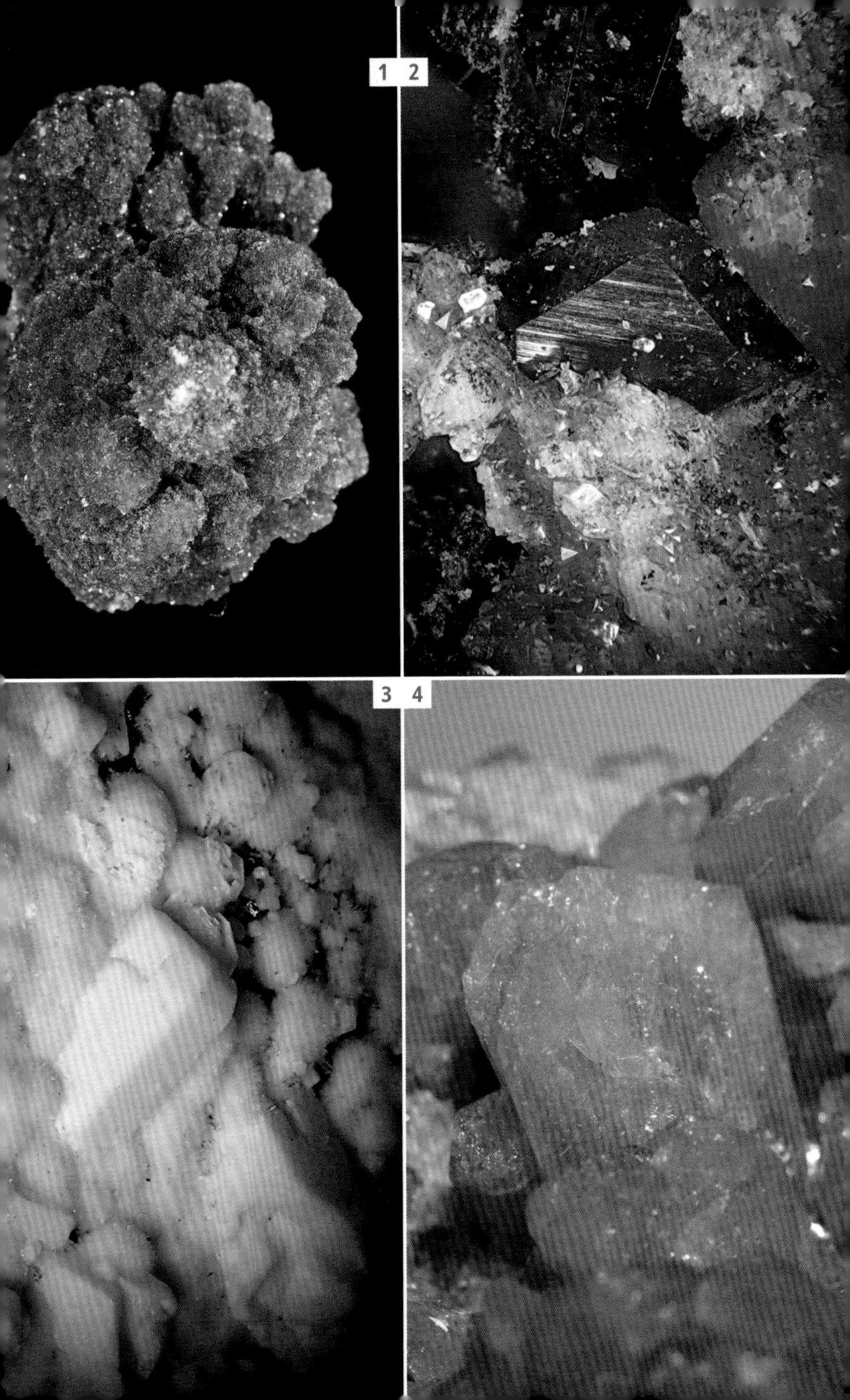
1 2
3 4

1 Adamite

Chem. formula $Zn_2[OH/AsO_4]$
Hardness 3½, **Sp. gr.** 4.3–4.5
Color Colorless, white, yellow, pink to purple (cobalt-bearing = cobalt adamite)
Streak White
Luster Vitreous
Cleavage Perfect but mainly indiscernible
Fracture Conchoidal
Tenacity Brittle
Crystal form Orthorhombic

Morphology Prismatic to acicular crystals, stellate aggregates, drusy, uneven.
Origin and occurrence In the oxidation zone of zinc deposits that also contain arsenical primary minerals.
Accessory minerals Smithsonite, azurite, hemimorphite, aurichalcite.
Similar minerals Cuprian adamite has various green shades; olivenite is always dark green; anglesite and cerussite have a different crystal form.

2 Cuprian adamite

Chem. formula $(Zn,Cu)_2[OH/AsO_4]$
Hardness 3½, **Sp. gr.** 4.3–4.5
Color Light to dark green, blue-green
Streak White
Luster Vitreous
Cleavage Perfect but mainly indiscernible
Fracture Conchoidal
Tenacity Brittle
Crystal form Orthorhombic

Morphology Prismatic to acicular crystals, stellate aggregates, drusy, uneven.
Origin and occurrence In the oxidation zone of zinc deposits that also contain arsenical and cupriferous primary minerals.
Accessory minerals Smithsonite, azurite, hemimorphite, agardite, aurichalcite.
Similar minerals Olivenite is always dark green; malachite effervesces when dabbed with diluted hydrochloric acid.

3 Strontianite

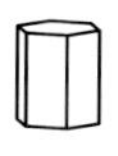

Chem. formula $SrCO_3$
Hardness 3½, **Sp. gr.** 3.7
Color Colorless, white, yellowish, greenish, gray
Streak White
Luster Vitreous, on fracture surfaces greasy
Cleavage Discernible
Fracture Conchoidal
Tenacity Brittle
Crystal form Orthorhombic

Morphology Acicular, spiky crystals, often intergrown to sheaves, sometimes curved, rarely prismatic or bipyramidal, stellate, uneven.
Origin and occurrence In hydrothermal veins, as fissure filling in limestones, on alpine fissures.
Accessory minerals Calcite, barite, galena, sphalerite, calcite, pyrite.
Similar minerals Calcite and aragonite readily effervesce when dabbed with cold diluted hydrochloric acid; barite and colestine are distinctly heavier.

4 Burkeite

Chem. formula $Na_6CO_3(SO_4)_2$
Hardness 3½, **Sp. gr.** 2.56
Color White, gray, pink
Streak White
Luster Vitreous
Cleavage None
Fracture Conchoidal
Tenacity Brittle
Crystal form Orthorhombic

Morphology Tabular crystals, botryoidal, reniform aggregates, encrustations.
Origin and occurrence In borax lakes.
Accessory minerals Rock salt, borax.
Distinguishing feature The frequent pink color of burkeite is caused by inclusions of pink-red colored bacteria that only live in salt lakes.
Similar minerals Rock salt and kernite have good cleavage; borax is softer; sylvite has good cleavage and a different crystal form.

Localities	
1 Mina Ojuela, Mapimi, Mexico	**3** Oberdorf, Styria, Austria
2 Tsumeb, Namibia	**4** Searles Lake, California, USA

1 2
3 4

1

Parahopeite

Chem. formula
$Zn_3(PO_4)_2 \cdot 4\,H_2O$
Hardness 3½, **Sp. gr.** 3.3
Color White, colorless
Streak White
Luster Vitreous
Cleavage Perfect
Fracture Uneven
Tenacity Brittle
Crystal form Triclinic

Morphology Tabular crystals, foliated and stellate aggregates.
Origin and occurrence In phosphate deposits as an alteration product of primary phosphates and sphalerite, in the oxidation zone of zinc deposits.
Accessory minerals Hopeite, scholzite, rockbridgeite, apatite, keckite, goethite.
Similar minerals Hopeite and parahopeite exhibit a different crystal form; calcite effervesces when dabbed with diluted hydrochloric acid.

2

Ludlamite

Chem. formula
$Fe_3[PO_4]_2 \cdot 4\,H_2O$
Hardness 3–4, **Sp. gr.** 3.1
Color Light green to green
Streak White
Luster Vitreous
Cleavage Basal perfect
Fracture Uneven
Tenacity Brittle
Crystal form Monoclinic

Morphology Octahedral to thick and thin tabular crystals, rose-like aggregates and uneven, crystalline, easily cleavable masses.
Origin and occurrence In phosphate pegmatites, on hydrothermal ore deposits.
Accessory minerals Vivianite, pyrite, siderite, marcasite.
Similar minerals The color and cleavage of ludlamite prevent any confusion. Vivianite is bluer; greenish gypsum is clearly softer.

3

Georgiadesite

Chem. formula $Pb_3AsO_4Cl_3$
Hardness 3½, **Sp. gr.** 7.1
Color White to colorless
Streak White
Luster Vitreous
Cleavage None
Tenacity Brittle
Crystal form Monoclinic

Morphology Thick tabular to prismatic, longitudinally striated crystals, always euhedral.
Origin and occurrence In ancient lead slags.
Accessory minerals Phosgenite, paralaurionite, laurionite, anglesite, cerussite.
Similar minerals Phosgenite has a different crystal form and no striation; laurionite and paralaurionite are never as thick tabular; cerussite has a different crystal form and usually exhibits its characteristic twinning; calcite effervesces when dabbed with diluted hydrochloric acid.

4

Collinsite

Chem. formula
$Ca_2(Mg,Fe)(PO_4)_2 \cdot 2\,H_2O$
Hardness 3½, **Sp. gr.** 2.99
Color Colorless, white, brownish, occasionally red
Streak White
Luster Vitreous
Cleavage Perfect
Fracture Uneven
Tenacity Brittle
Crystal form Triclinic

Morphology Short prismatic to thin tabular crystals, stellate aggregates, drusy.
Origin and occurrence In phosphate pegmatites as an alteration product of primary phosphate minerals, in phosphate-rich limonite deposits.
Accessory minerals Apatite, scholzite, goethite, rockbridgeite, parahopeite.
Similar minerals Scholzite has a different crystal form; apatite always has clearly recognizable hexagonal forms; parahopeite has a different crystal form.

Localities	
1 Hagendorf-Süd, East Bavaria, Germany	**3** Lavrion, Greece
2 Santa Eulalia, Mexico	**4** Kovdor, Kola, Russia

1 2
3 4

1

Fairfieldite

Chem. formula $Ca_2(Mn,Fe)(PO_4)_2 \cdot 2\,H_2O$
Hardness 3½, **Sp. gr.** 3.08
Color Colorless, white, beige, yellowish
Streak White
Luster Vitreous
Cleavage Perfect
Fracture Uneven
Tenacity Brittle
Crystal form Triclinic

Morphology Tabular prismatic crystals, stellate aggregates, botryoidal aggregates, suns.
Origin and occurrence In phosphate pegmatites as an alteration product of primary phosphate minerals.
Accessory minerals Apatite, eosphorite, rockbridgeite, strunzite, siderite, messelite.
Similar minerals Scholzite and laueite have a different crystal form; apatite is harder; parahopeite has a different crystal form but is difficult to distinguish using simple means; its paragenesis with sphalerite gives an indication.

2

Fiedlerite

Chem. formula $Pb_3Cl_4(OH)_2$
Hardness 3½, **Sp. gr.** 5.8
Color Colorless, white
Streak White
Luster Adamantine
Cleavage Poorly discernible
Fracture Conchoidal
Tenacity Brittle
Crystal form Monoclinic

Morphology Tabular crystals, never uneven.
Origin and occurrence In ancient lead slags.
Accessory minerals Paralaurionite, laurionite, phosgenite, anglesite, cerussite.
Similar minerals Considering the occurrence of fiedlerite and its characteristic crystal form (photo), there is no possibility of confusion; the small bevel of the end face of fiedlerite crystals is characteristic; paralaurionite is not brittle, rather inelastically flexible; laurionite has a different crystal form.

3

Kieserite

Chem. formula $MgSO_4 \cdot H_2O$
Hardness 3½, **Sp. gr.** 2.57
Color Colorless, white, gray, yellowish
Streak White
Luster Vitreous
Cleavage Perfect
Fracture Uneven
Tenacity Brittle
Crystal form Monoclinic

Morphology Rare dipyramidal crystals, mainly granular, powdery, uneven.
Origin and occurrence In salt deposits.
Accessory minerals Rock salt, kainite, sylvite.
Distinguishing feature Kieserite tastes bitter and salty and is soluble in water.
Similar minerals Kieserite cannot be distinguished from kainite using simple means; rock salt and sylvite do not taste bitter; calcite effervesces when dabbed with diluted hydrochloric acid and is not soluble in water.

4

Hopeite

Chem. formula $Zn_3(PO_4)_2 \cdot 2\,H_2O$
Hardness 3½, **Sp. gr.** 3.05
Color Colorless, white, gray, brown
Streak White
Luster Vitreous
Cleavage Perfect
Fracture Uneven
Tenacity Brittle
Crystal form Orthorhombic

Morphology Prismatic to tabular crystals, stellate aggregates, drusy.
Origin and occurrence In phosphate deposits, in the oxidation zone of zinc deposits.
Accessory minerals Tarbuttite, parahopeite, goethite, scholzite, sphalerite, apatite.
Similar minerals Parahopeite has a different crystal form; the same applies to tarbuttite; scholzite is normally more acicular; apatite is harder and hexagonal.

Localities	
1 Foote Mine, North Carolina, USA	**3** Stassfurt, Saxony-Anhalt, Germany
2 Lavrion, Greece	**4** Broken Hill, Zambia

1 2
3 4

1–2 Siderite *Iron spar*

Chem. formula $FeCO_3$
Hardness 4–4½, **Sp. gr.** 3.7–3.9
Color Yellow-white, yellow-brown to dark brown, sometimes with a bluish tarnish
Streak White
Luster Vitreous
Cleavage Perfect rhombohedral
Fracture Crystalline
Tenacity Brittle
Crystal form Trigonal

Morphology Rhombohedral crystals, often saddle-shaped, rarely scalenohedra, reniform aggregates and encrustations, often uneven.
Origin and occurrence In pegmatites and bubble cavities of volcanic rocks, as gangue in hydrothermal veins, in stocks and lenses in metasomatically altered limestones, as concretions or in layers in sediments, in peat bogs.
Accessory minerals Chalcedony, barite, calcite, pyrite, bournonite, chalcopyrite.
Distinguishing feature Siderite is an important iron ore. In the oxidation zone, it transforms into goethite or limonite. This can result in pseudomorphs of limonite after siderite crystals. The calcium contents released during weathering of the siderite lead to the formation of aragonite, frequently in the form of "iron flowers" (see Fig. p. 232/2). Manganese contents lead to the formation of pyrolusite crystals in cavities in limonite.
Similar minerals Unlike siderite, calcite effervesces readily with diluted hydrochloric acid; sphalerite has a different cleavage; it is not possible to distinguish siderite from ferruginous dolomite, which may have a similar color, using simple means.

3 Rhodesite

Chem. formula $(Ca,Na_2,K_2)Si_{16}O_{40} \cdot 11\ H_2O$
Hardness 3–4, **Sp. gr.** 2.36
Color White
Streak White
Luster Silky
Cleavage Indiscernible
Fracture Fibrous
Tenacity Brittle
Crystal form Orthorhombic

Morphology Acicular, fibrous, stellate and sun-shaped aggregates, uneven.
Origin and occurrence In volcanic rocks, on fissures of contact metasomatic, silicic sedimentary inclusions (for example, sandstone).
Accessory minerals Ettringite, heulandite, quartz, apophyllite, dachiardite, calcite.
Similar minerals Rhodesite cannot be distinguished from natrolite and scolecite using simple means; aragonite effervesces when dabbed with diluted hydrochloric acid.

4 Minyulite

Chem. formula $KAl_2(PO_4)_2(OH,F) \cdot 4\ H_2O$
Hardness 3½, **Sp. gr.** 2.45
Streak White
Color Colorless, white, yellowish
Luster Silky
Cleavage Perfect
Fracture Uneven, fibrous
Tenacity Brittle
Crystal form Orthorhombic

Morphology Acicular, stellate aggregates, crystal sheaves, fibrous, uneven.
Origin and occurrence In phosphate deposits in phosphate-rich sediments.
Accessory minerals Limonite, cacoxenite, strengite, fluellite, quartz, calcite.
Similar minerals Cacoxenite and beraunite are always much more intensely colored; aragonite effervesces when dabbed with diluted hydrochloric acid.

Localities	
1 Siegerland Region, Germany	**3** Maroldsweisach, Lower Franconia, Bavaria, Germany
2 Neudorf, Harz Mountains, Germany	**4** Pereta, Tuscany, Italy

1 2
3 4

1–2 Magnesite

Chem. formula $MgCO_3$
Hardness 4–4½, **Sp. gr.** 3
Color Colorless, white, yellowish, brownish, gray
Luster Vitreous
Cleavage Perfect rhombohedral
Fracture Crystalline
Tenacity Brittle
Crystal form Trigonal

Morphology Rarely rhombohedral crystals, hexagonal plates, mainly uneven, granular, crystalline masses, dense.
Origin and occurrence Large replacement bodies in dolomites, in talc schists, on fissures and in veins in serpentine.
Accessory minerals Aragonite, calcite, dolomite, apatite, talc, serpentine, quartz.
Distinguishing feature During the transformation of limestone into magnesite in replacement deposits, coarsely crystalline black and white striped masses are formed (Fig. 1), called pinolite or pinolite-magnesite. Because of their visual attractiveness, they are used as decorative stone or for the production of craft items.
Similar minerals Unlike magnesite, calcite readily effervesces with cold diluted hydrochloric acid; dolomite is somewhat softer, but it often cannot be distinguished from magnesite by simple means.

3 Paradamite

Chem. formula $Zn_2[OH/AsO_4]$
Hardness 3½, **Sp. gr.** 4.55
Color Yellowish to orange-yellow
Streak White
Luster Vitreous
Cleavage Perfect
Fracture Uneven
Tenacity Brittle
Crystal form Triclinic

Morphology Tabular crystals, often rounded, mainly euhedral, rarely uneven.
Origin and occurrence In the oxidation zone of zinc deposits that also contain arsenical primary minerals.
Accessory minerals Limonite, adamite, mimetesite, calcite.
Similar minerals Adamite has a different crystal form; unlike paradamite, yellowish calcite effervesces when dabbed with diluted hydrochloric acid; barite has a different crystal form; mimetesite crystals always have a hexagonal cross section.

4 Leucophosphite

Chem. formula $KFe_2(OH)(PO_4)2 \cdot H_2O$
Hardness 3½, **Sp. gr.** 2.95
Color Colorless, white, yellow, pink, greenish
Streak White
Luster Vitreous
Cleavage Perfect
Fracture Uneven
Tenacity Brittle
Crystal form Monoclinic

Morphology Tabular rhombic crystals, botryoidal, cockscomb aggregates, usually euhedral in cavities of other phosphates, particularly rockbridgeite.
Origin and occurrence In phosphate pegmatites, as an alteration product of the primary phosphates.
Accessory minerals Strengite, rockbridgeite, cyrilovite, laueite, apatite.
Similar minerals Strengite has a different crystal form but is not easily distinguished from leucophosphite in botryoidal aggregates; the applies to phosphosiderite; cyrilovite is browner and exhibits a different crystal form.

Localities	
1 Sunk, Trieben, Austria	**3** Mina Ojuela, Mapimi, Mexico
2 Bahia, Brazil	**4** Hagendorf-Süd, East Bavaria, Germany

1 2
3 4

1 Penfieldite

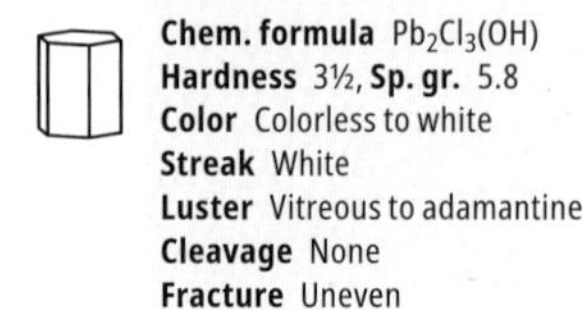

Chem. formula $Pb_2Cl_3(OH)$
Hardness 3½, **Sp. gr.** 5.8
Color Colorless to white
Streak White
Luster Vitreous to adamantine
Cleavage None
Fracture Uneven
Tenacity Brittle
Crystal form Hexagonal

Morphology Elongated, prismatic crystals of hexagonal cross-section, often with typical transverse striation.
Origin and occurrence In cavities of ancient lead slags, rarely in the oxidation zone of lead deposits.
Accessory minerals Fiedlerite, paralaurionite, cerussite, anglesite, phosgenite.
Similar minerals Paralaurionite and laurionite as well as anglesite and cerussite have a different crystal form; aragonite effervesces when dabbed with diluted hydrochloric acid; quartz is much harder.

2 Cyrilovite

Chem. formula $NaFe_3^{3+}(PO_4)_2(OH)_4 \cdot 2\,H_2O$
Hardness 3½, **Sp. gr.** 3.1
Color Yellow, brownish
Streak Yellowish white
Luster Vitreous
Cleavage None
Fracture Uneven
Tenacity Brittle
Crystal form Tetragonal

Morphology Octahedral, tetragonal bipyramids, thick tabular crystals, planar crystal intergrowths, crystal encrustations, stellate, botryoidal aggregates.
Origin and occurrence In phosphate pegmatites through the alteration of primary phosphates, in phosphatic brown iron deposits.
Accessory minerals Leucophosphite, strengite, phosphosiderite, apatite, rockbridgeite.
Similar minerals Wardite is more white to green; strengite is always purple.

3 Serpierite

Chem. formula $Ca(Cu,Zn)_4[(OH)_6/(SO_4)_2] \cdot 3\,H_2O$
Hardness 3½–4, **Sp. gr.** 3.08
Color Blue
Streak White
Luster Vitreous
Cleavage Perfect
Fracture Uneven
Tenacity Brittle
Crystal form Monoclinic

Morphology Acicular to long tabular crystals, acicular sheaves, radial aggregates, crystal encrustations, coatings.
Origin and occurrence In the oxidation zone of copper-zinc deposits.
Accessory minerals Gypsum, spangolite, devilline, schulenbergite, aragonite, calcite.
Similar minerals Unlike serpierite, linarite turns white when dabbed with hydrochloric acid; devilline is more foliated or foamy; schulenbergite is foliated.

4 Variscite

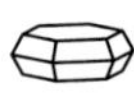

Chem. formula $Al[PO_4] \cdot 2\,H_2O$
Hardness 4–5, **Sp. gr.** 2.52
Color Colorless, white, light green to green
Streak White
Luster Vitreous to waxy
Cleavage None
Fracture Conchoidal
Tenacity Brittle to non-brittle
Crystal form Orthorhombic

Morphology Rarely crystals, mainly stellate, botryoidal, drusy in uneven, dense masses.
Origin and occurrence On fissures of aluminum-rich rocks.
Accessory minerals Wavellite, strengite, clinovariscite.
Similar minerals Strengite is hardly ever green; wavellite exhibits a different crystal form.

Localities	
1 Lavrion, Greece	**3** Friedrichsegen Mine, Bad Ems, Germany
2 Hagendorf-Süd, East Bavaria, Germany	**4** Lucin, Box Elder County, Utah, USA

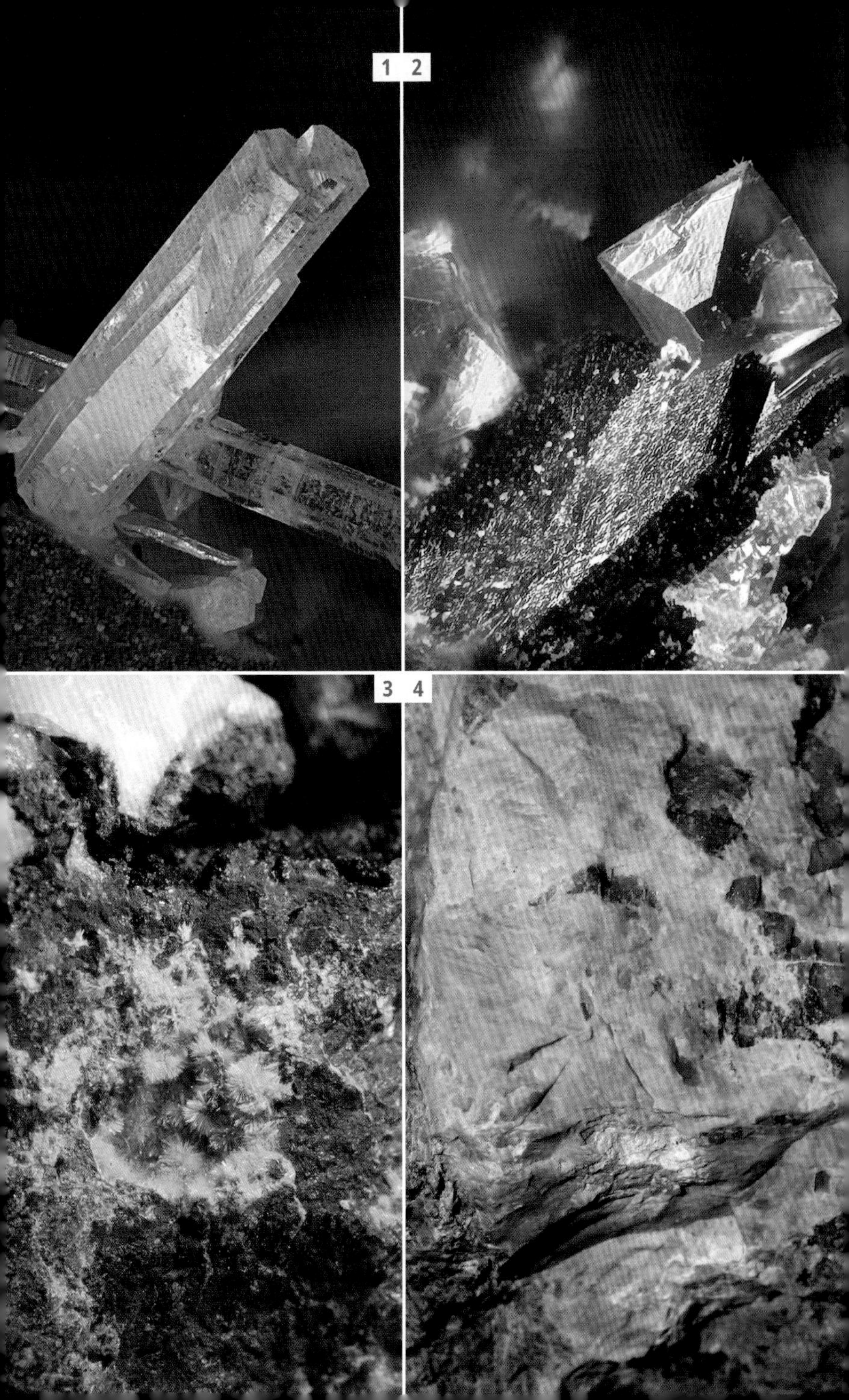
1 2
3 4

1–3 Aragonite

Chem. formula $CaCO_3$
Hardness 3½–4, **Sp. gr.** 2.95
Color Colorless, white, gray, red to red-purple
Streak White
Luster Vitreous
Cleavage Only indiscernible
Fracture Conchoidal
Tenacity Brittle
Crystal form Orthorhombic

Morphology Crystals mainly acicular, prismatic, spatulate, triplets resemble hexagonal prisms; radial, granular aggregates, worm-like, coral-like structures are called iron blooms.
Origin and occurrence In the oxidation zone, in vugs and on fissures of extrusive igneous rocks, anhedral in clays (mostly triplets here), in the deposits of hot springs.
Accessory minerals Heulandite, stilbite, phillipsite, quartz, calcite, siderite, limonite.
Distinguishing feature The actually orthorhombic aragonite often forms triplets, which are extremely similar to hexagonal prisms. However, the curved prism faces and small re-entrant angles indicate that these are not true hexagonal prisms. Worldwide, the best known occurrences of such triplets are at the Spanish sites of Minglanilla and Molina de Aragon, where they are found in large quantities and often intergrown into aggregates and in anhedral form in argillaceous rocks. Aragonite fluoresces with a distinct yellow or orange color when irradiated with ultraviolet light (in particular, short wave UV). The aragonite of some deposits, for example, those from the sulfur deposits in Agrigento in Sicily, still exhibit a clear afterglow for a few seconds after switching the UV light off. This phenomenon is called phosphorescence.
Similar minerals Calcite differs from aragonite on account of its cleavage and differs from all other minerals in the hydrochloric acid test: unlike aragonite, they do not effervesce when dabbed with diluted hydrochloric acid.

4 Kulanite

Chem. formula $Ba(Fe,Mn,Mg)_2Al_2(PO_4)_3(OH)_3$
Hardness 3½–4, **Sp. gr.** 3.92
Color Green to blue
Streak Greenish white
Luster Vitreous
Cleavage Poorly discernible
Fracture Uneven
Tenacity Brittle
Crystal form Monoclinic

Morphology Tabular crystals, often intergrown to form rose-shaped aggregates.
Origin and occurrence On fissures and in cavities of phosphate-rich schists, in granite pegamtites.
Accessory minerals Lazulite, wardite, augelite, siderite, quartz, brazilianite, gormanite.
Similar minerals Lazulite is clearer blue; wardite and augelite exhibit a different crystal form; brazilianite is yellower; gormanite is acicular; siderite has perfect rhombohedral cleavage.

Localities	
1 Minglanilla, Spain	**3** Kamsdorf, Thuringia, Germany
2 Erzberg, Styria, Austria	**4** Rapid Creek, Yukon Territory, Canada

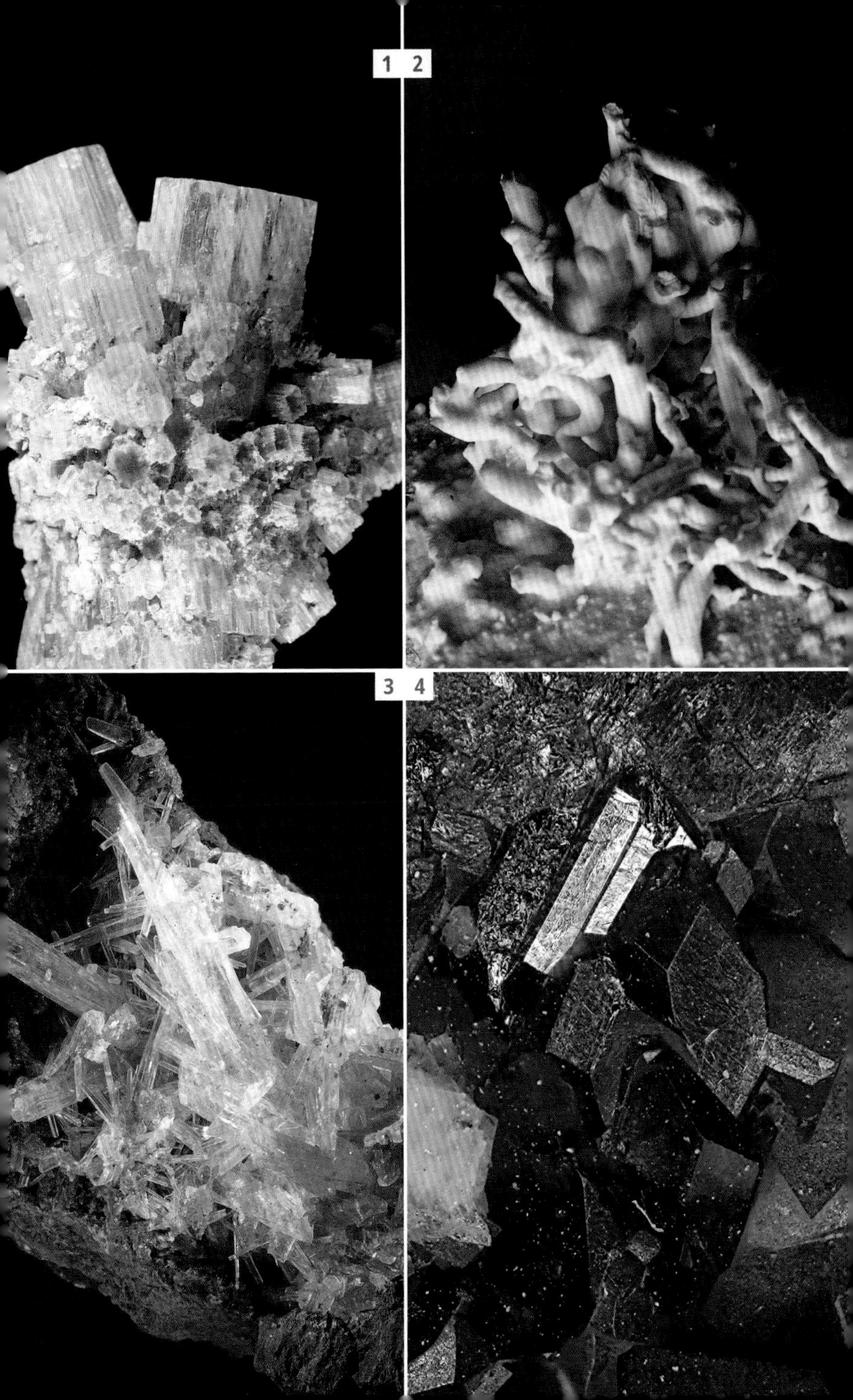
1 2
3 4

1 Laurionite

Chem. formula PbOHCl
Hardness 3–3½, **Sp. gr.** 6.1-6.24
Color Colorless to white
Streak White
Luster Vitreous to adamantine
Cleavage Scarcely discernible
Fracture Uneven
Tenacity Brittle
Crystal form Orthorhombic

Morphology Long tabular to acicular crystals, often with typical V-shaped striation.
Origin and occurrence In cavities of ancient lead slags, in the oxidation zone of lead deposits.
Accessory minerals Fiedlerite, paralaurionite, cerussite, anglesite, phosgenite.
Similar minerals Paralaurionite is not brittle and can be inelastically bent; anglesite and cerussite have a different crystal form; aragonite effervesces when dabbed with diluted hydrochloric acid.

2 Gyrolite

Chem. formula $NaCa_{16}(Si_{23}Al)O_{60}(OH)_8 \cdot 14\ H_2O$
Hardness 3–4, **Sp. gr.** 3–4
Color Colorless, white, greenish, brown, black
Streak White
Luster Vitreous
Cleavage Perfect
Fracture Uneven
Tenacity Brittle
Crystal form Hexagonal

Morphology Botryoidal aggregates, extremely thin flakes, stellate.
Origin and occurrence In cavities of volcanic rocks.
Accessory minerals Prehnite, apophyllite, laumontite, stilbite, heulandite.
Similar minerals Prehnite always forms much thicker crystal tablets; stilbite has a different crystal form and also forms much thicker crystals, as does heulandite.

3 Strunzite

Chem. formula $MnFe_2[OH/PO_4]_2$
Hardness 4, **Sp. gr.** 2.52
Color Straw yellow
Streak White
Luster Vitreous
Cleavage None
Fracture Uneven
Tenacity Brittle
Crystal form Triclinic

Morphology Acicular to filiform crystals, very rarely prismatic, fibrous to stellate aggregates.
Origin and occurrence In phosphate pegmatites, in phosphorus-rich brown iron deposits.
Accessory minerals Beraunite, rockbridgeite, laueite, strengite, pseudolaueite, apatite.
Similar minerals Cacoxenite is more golden yellow but often indistinguishable from strunzite by simple means; beraunite is more orange and not as straw yellow; switzerite is more whitish.

4 Wavellite

Chem. formula $Al_3[(OH)_3/(PO_4)_2] \cdot 5\ H_2O$
Hardness 4, **Sp. gr.** 2.3-2.4
Color Colorless, white, yellow, green
Streak White
Luster Vitreous
Cleavage Indistinct due to the acicular structure
Fracture Uneven
Tenacity Brittle
Crystal form Monoclinic

Morphology Acicular crystals, radial, botryoidal to sun-shaped aggregates on narrow fissures in the rock.
Origin and occurrence On fissures of siliceous shale, decomposed granite, limestone.
Accessory minerals Strengite, cacoxene, quartz, calcite, strengite, crandallite.
Similar minerals Natrolite and prehnite are harder; unlike wavellite, calcite and aragonite effervesce when dabbed with diluted hydrochloric acid.

Localities	
1 Lavrion, Greece	**3** Hagendorf-Süd, East Bavaria, Germany
2 Pune, India	**4** Filleigh Quarry, Devon, Great Britain

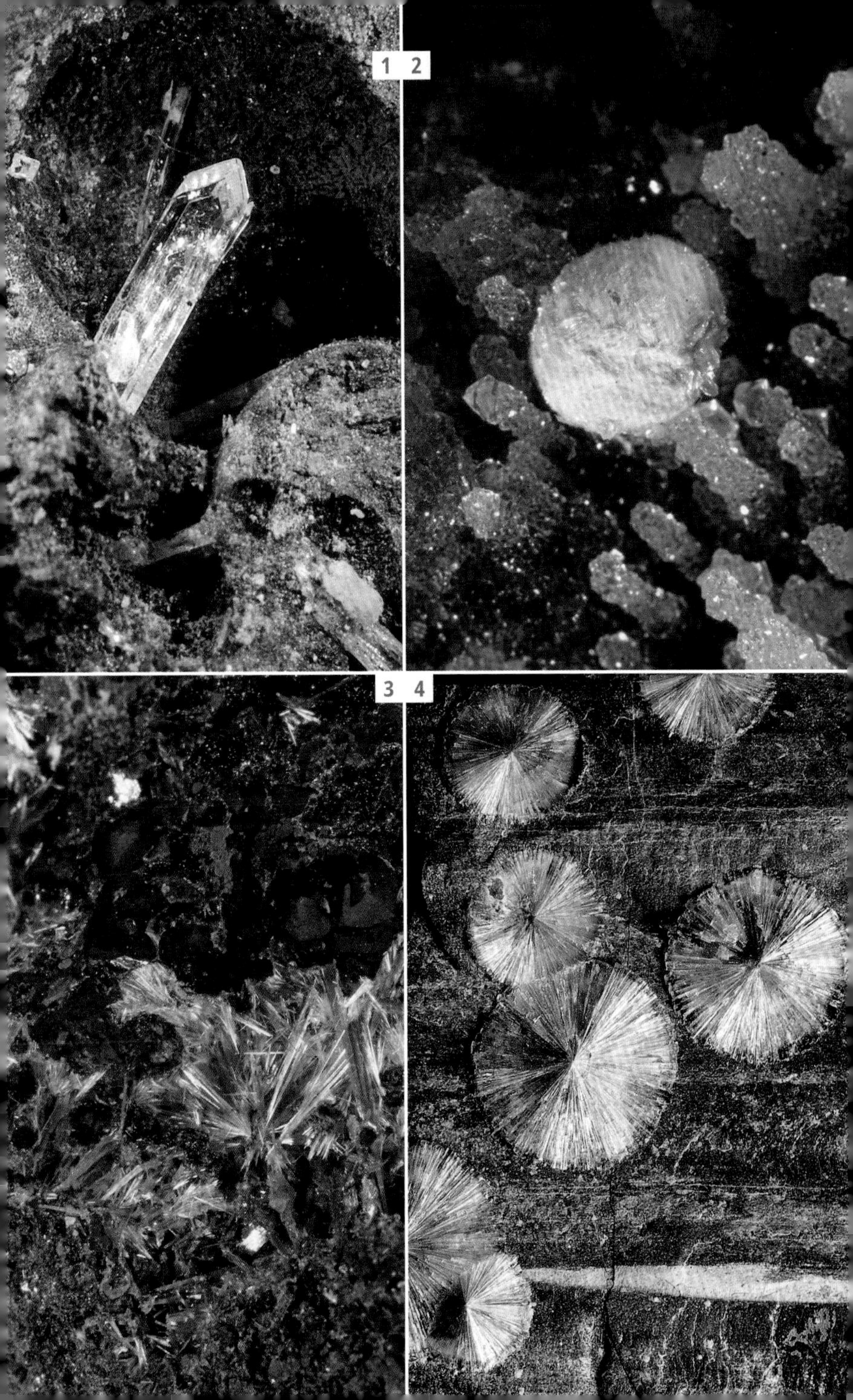
1 2
3 4

1 Ankerite *Brown spar*

Chem. formula $CaFe[CO_3]_2$
Hardness 3½–4, **Sp. gr.** 2.95–3.02
Color White, ivory colors, brownish
Streak White
Luster Vitreous
Cleavage Perfect basic rhombohedral
Fracture Crystalline
Tenacity Brittle
Crystal form Trigonal

Morphology Rhombohedral crystals, often saddle-shaped curved, uneven, crystalline.
Origin and occurrence In siderite deposits and hydrothermal veins, on alpine fissures.
Accessory minerals Dolomite, calcite, siderite, chlorite, quartz, galena, sphalerite.
Similar minerals Calcite effervesces when dabbed with cold hydrochloric acid; dolomite and siderite are often difficult to distinguish from ankerite; the same applies to brownish, ferruginous magnesite.

2 Scorodite

Chem. formula $Fe[AsO_4] \cdot 2\,H_2O$
Hardness 3½–4, **Sp. gr.** 3.1–3.3
Color Colorless, white, yellow, greenish, blue, brown
Streak White
Luster Greasy vitreous
Cleavage Scarcely distinct
Fracture Conchoidal
Tenacity Brittle
Crystal form Orthorhombic

Morphology Tabular to bipyramidal crystals, stellate aggregates, drusy, as a coating.
Origin and occurrence In the oxidation zone of arsenic-rich deposits, often as a direct alteration product of arsenopyrite.
Accessory minerals Arseniosiderite, olivenite, adamite, beudantite, jarosite, natrojarosite.
Similar minerals Considering its crystal form and paragenesis with other arsenical minerals, there is no possibility of confusion.

3 Nadorite

Chem. formula $PbSbO_2Cl$
Hardness 3½–4, **Sp. gr.** 7.02
Color White, yellow, brown
Streak White
Luster Resinous
Cleavage Perfect
Fracture Conchoidal
Tenacity Brittle
Crystal form Orthorhombic

Morphology Thin tabular crystals, often lenticular in shape, botryoidal aggregates.
Origin and occurrence In the oxidation zone of antimony deposits.
Accessory minerals Stibiconite, valentinite, stibnite, cervantite, senarmontite.
Similar minerals Considering its paragenesis, nadorite is unmistakable; siderite exhibits rhombohedral cleavage; calcite effervesces when dabbed with diluted hydrochloric acid.

4 Phosphosiderite *Clinostrengite*

Chem. formula $Fe[PO_4] \cdot 2\,H_2O$
Hardness 3½–4, **Sp. gr.** 2.76
Color Colorless, white, pink, purple
Streak White
Luster Vitreous
Cleavage Perfect
Fracture Uneven
Tenacity Brittle
Crystal form Monoclinic

Morphology Thick to thin tabular crystals, stellate aggregates, drusy, warty.
Origin and occurrence In phosphate pegmatites as an alteration product of primary phosphate minerals.
Accessory minerals Strengite, rockbridgeite.
Similar minerals Strengite exhibits a different crystal form; in stellate aggregates, the two minerals are indistinguishable by simple means; cyrilovite is yellower, as are laueite, stewartite and pseudolaueite; leucophosphite has characteristic diamond-shaped crystals.

Localities	
1 Siegerland Region, Germany	**3** Djebel Nador, Algeria
2 Gestoso, Portugal	**4** Pleystein, East Bavaria, Germany

1 2
3 4

1 Powellite

Chem. formula $CaMoO_4$
Hardness 3½–4, **Sp. gr.** 4.23
Color Gray, brown
Streak White
Luster Vitreous to greasy
Cleavage Poor
Fracture Uneven
Tenacity Brittle
Crystal form Tetragonal

Morphology Bipyramidal crystals, mainly euhedral, drusy, uneven.
Origin and occurrence In the oxidation zone of ore deposits, in cavities of volcanic rocks.
Accessory minerals Molybdenite, stilbite, heulandite, laumontite, apophyllite.
Distinguishing feature Powellite fluoresces with a yellow to orange color.
Similar minerals Scheelite fluoresces in a different color; wulfenite does not fluoresce at all; apophyllite exhibits excellent basal cleavage.

2 Stilbite *Desmine*

Chem. formula $Ca[Al_2Si_7O_{18}] \cdot 7\,H_2O$
Hardness 3½–4, **Sp. gr.** 2.1–2.2
Color Colorless, yellow, white, brown
Streak White
Luster Vitreous, pearly on cleavage faces
Cleavage Perfect
Fracture Uneven
Tenacity Brittle
Crystal form Monoclinic

Morphology Prismatic to tabular crystals, often grown into sheaf structures, botryoidal, stellate aggregates, almost always euhedral.
Origin and occurrence In bubble cavities of volcanic rocks, vugs and fissures of pegmatites, granites, in alpine fissures, in ore veins.
Accessory minerals Heulandite, chabazite, scolecite, calcite.
Similar minerals The characteristic crystal form of stilbite makes confusion highly unlikely; however, the much rarer stellerite cannot be distinguished by simple means.

3 Strengite

Chem. formula $Fe[PO_4] \cdot 2\,H_2O$
Hardness 3–4, **Sp. gr.** 2.87
Color Colorless, white, yellow, pink, purple
Streak White
Luster Vitreous
Cleavage Basal perfect
Fracture Conchoidal
Tenacity Brittle
Crystal form Orthorhombic

Morphology Tabular to isometric, often planar crystals, stellate, botryoidal aggregates, encrustations, coatings.
Origin and occurrence In phosphoric brown iron deposits and phosphate pegmatites, where it is formed by weathering of other phosphate minerals.
Accessory minerals Phosphosiderite, strunzite, rockbridgeite.
Similar minerals Phosphosiderite has a different crystal form but is not easily distinguished from strengite in stellate aggregates; amethyst, which has a very similar color, is much harder.

4 Sainfeldite

Chem. formula $H_2Ca_6(AsO_4)_4 \cdot H_2O$
Hardness 4, **Sp. gr.** 3
Color Colorless, white, pink
Streak White
Luster Vitreous
Cleavage None
Fracture Uneven
Tenacity Brittle
Crystal form Monoclinic

Morphology Prismatic, thick tabular crystals, rose-shaped aggregates.
Origin and occurrence In the oxidation zone of arsenic-rich deposits.
Accessory minerals Pharmacolite, guerinite, picropharmacolite, calcite, aragonite.
Similar minerals Pharmacolite and guerinite have perfect cleavage; picropharmacolite is always acicular; calcite and aragonite effervesce when dabbed with diluted hydrochloric acid.

Localities	
1 Pune, India	**3** Svappavaara, Sweden
2 Hollersbach Valley, Austria	**4** Richelsdorf, Hesse, Germany

1
2
3
4

1–3 Pyromorphite *Green lead ore, brown lead ore*

Chem. formula $Pb_5[Cl/(PO_4)_3]$
Hardness 3½–4, **Sp. gr.** 6.7–7
Color Green, brown, orange, white, colorless
Streak White
Luster Greasy
Cleavage None
Fracture Conchoidal
Tenacity Brittle
Crystal form Hexagonal

Morphology Prismatic crystals, often barrel-shaped due to curved prism faces, acicular, stellate, reniform aggregates, drusy, earthy.
Origin and occurrence In the oxidation zone of various types of lead deposits, especially in their upper weather-exposed parts; the phosphorus necessary for formation is often of animal and vegetable origin.
Accessory minerals Galena, cerussite, wulfenite, hemimorphite.
Similar minerals Mimetesite is often difficult to distinguish from pyromorphite by simple means; nevertheless, arsenical minerals as accessory minerals may give an indication of the presence of mimetesite. Vanadinite is usually red; this color is extremely rare in pyromorphite.

4–5 Mimetesite

Chem. formula $Pb_5[Cl/(AsO_4)_3]$
Hardness 3½–4, **Sp. gr.** 7.1
Color Colorless, white, brown, orange, yellow, green, gray
Streak White
Luster Adamantine to greasy
Cleavage None
Fracture Conchoidal
Tenacity Brittle
Crystal form Hexagonal

Morphology Crystals prismatic, often barrel-shaped due to curvature of prism faces, acicular, tabular to thick tabular, botryoidal aggregates, reniform encrustations, stellate aggregates, earthy.
Origin and occurrence In the oxidation zone of lead deposits that also contain arsenical minerals. While pyromorphite usually occurs only in the uppermost zones, mimetesite can also occur in deeper deposit areas.
Accessory minerals Galena, cerussite, duftite, anglesite, wulfenite, pyromorphite, calcite, quartz, vanadinite.
Similar minerals Apatite is harder; vanadinite and pyromorphite cannot be distinguished by simple means, but mimetesite's paragenesis with arsenical minerals gives an indication; vanadinite is usually red which is a very rare color in mimetesite.

6 Clinomimetesite

Chem. formula $Pb_5[Cl/(AsO_4)_3]$
Hardness 3½–4, **Sp. gr.** 7.1
Color Colorless, white, brown, orange, yellow, green, gray
Streak White
Luster Adamantine to greasy
Cleavage None
Fracture Conchoidal
Tenacity Brittle
Crystal form Monoclinic

Morphology Pseudohexagonal, crystals prismatic, tabular to thick tabular.
Origin and occurrence In the oxidation zone of lead deposits that also contain arsenical minerals.
Accessory minerals Galena, cerussite.
Similar minerals Apatite is harder; vanadinite and pyromorphite cannot be distinguished by simple means; clinomimetesite can only be distinguished from mimetesite using X-ray techniques. Vanadinite is usually red; clinomimetesite is never red.

Localities		
1 Badenweiler, Black Forest, Germany	**3** Siegerland Region, Germany	**5** Cumberland, Great Britain
2 Siegerland Region, Germany	**4** Tsumeb, Namibia	**6** Johanngeorgenstadt, Saxony, Germany

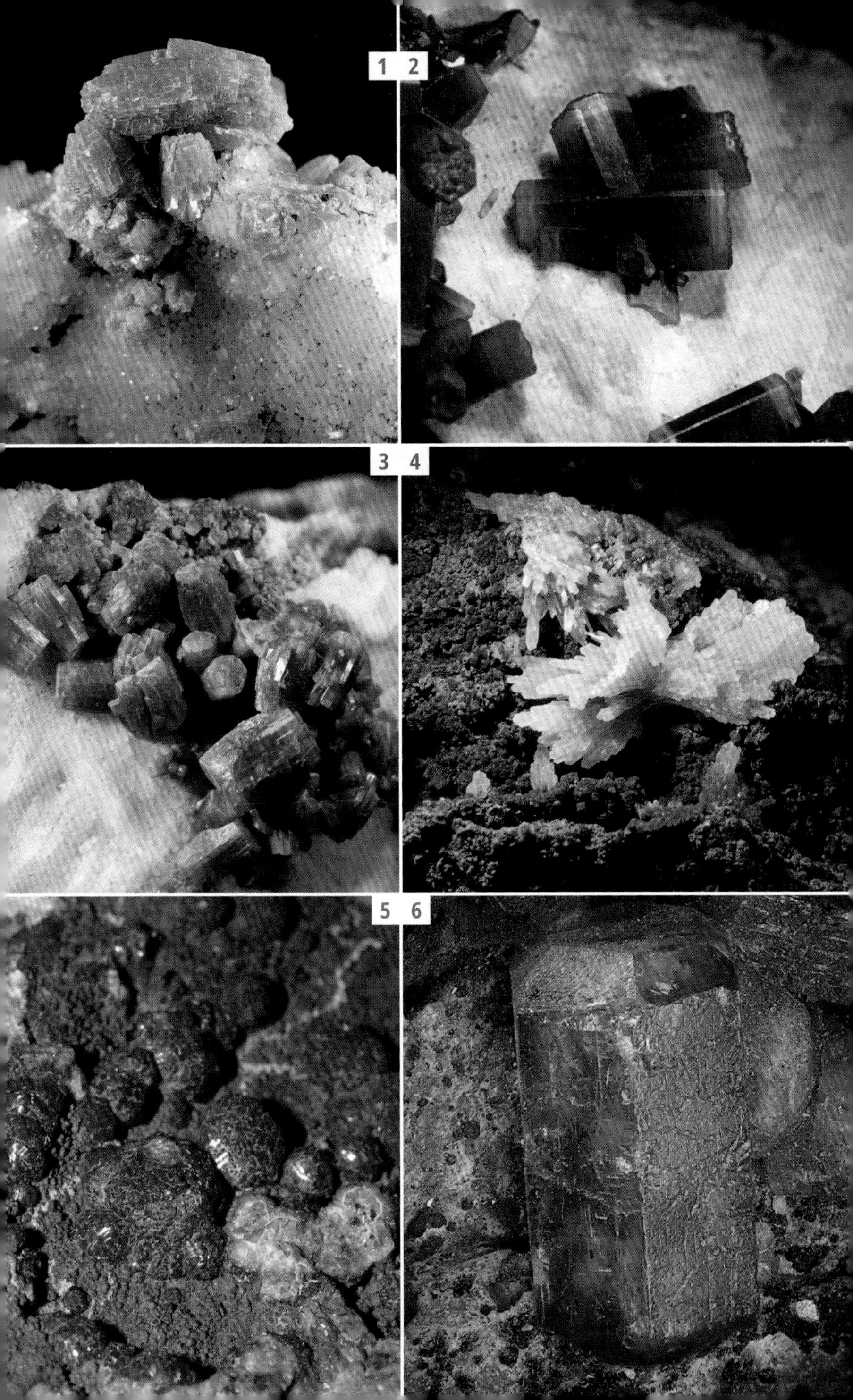
1 2
3 4
5 6

1–2 Rhodochrosite *Raspberry spar, manganese spar*

Chem. formula $MnCO_3$
Hardness 3½–4, **Sp. gr.** 3.3–3.6
Color Pink colors in varying tones, light red, deep red, yellow-gray, brownish
Streak White
Luster Vitreous
Cleavage Rhombohedral perfect
Fracture Uneven
Tenacity Brittle
Crystal form Trigonal

Morphology Rhombohedra, scalenohedra, often rounded, frequently botryoidal, reniform and stellate aggregates, stalactitic, drusy, uneven.
Origin and occurrence In hydrothermal veins, in the oxidation zone of iron-manganese deposits, as lenses and deposits in metamorphic rocks.
Accessory minerals Quartz, limonite, pyrolusite, rhodonite.
Distinguishing feature Dense, beautifully striped rhodochrosites from the stalactitic deposits are used for jewelry purposes. In particular, beads for necklaces and cabochons for brooches and pendants are produced, along with decorative art objects. Very clear stones are sometimes faceted; however, they are used only for collections of cut stones because of their low hardness and high sensitivity.
Similar minerals Unlike rhodochrosite, calcite effervesces with cold diluted hydrochloric acid; rhodochrosite is sometimes indistinguishable from manganiferous dolomite, which can also be pink, by simple means.

3 Dolomite *Bitter spar*

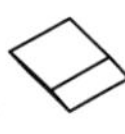

Chem. formula $CaMg(CO_3)_2$
Hardness 3½–4, **Sp. gr.** 2.85-2.95
Color Colorless, white, pink, gray, brownish, blackish
Streak White
Luster Vitreous
Cleavage Perfect rhombohedral
Fracture Crystalline
Tenacity Brittle
Crystal form Trigonal

Morphology Primarily only the basal rhombohedral present, often saddle-shaped curvature, very rarely pointed rhombohedral or planar, often uneven.
Origin and occurrence In hydrothermal veins as gangue and in vugs, essential mineral, crystals frequently on fissures of dolomite rock.
Accessory minerals Quartz, calcite, pyrite, chalcopyrite, siderite.
Similar minerals Calcite readily effervesces with cold, diluted hydrochloric acid; quartz is harder, and gypsum is softer; anhydrite has different cleavage and also does not effervesce even with hot hydrochloric acid.

4 Edingtonite

Chem. formula $BaAl_2Si_3O_{10} \cdot 4\,H_2O$
Hardness 4, **Sp. gr.** 2.8
Color Colorless, white
Streak White
Luster Vitreous
Cleavage Perfect
Fracture Uneven
Tenacity Brittle
Crystal form Orthorhombic

Morphology Prismatic to thick tabular crystals, usually euhedral, uneven.
Origin and occurrence In cavities of volcanic rocks, rarely on hydrothermal veins.
Accessory minerals Heulandite, stilbite, manganite, calcite, quartz, chabazite.
Similar minerals Stilbite, harmotome and phillipsite have a different crystal form; calcite and aragonite effervesce when dabbed with diluted hydrochloric acid; heulandite also has a different crystal form and characteristic cleavage on a face.

Localities	
1 Wolf Mine, Siegerland Region, Germany	**3** Siegerland Region, Germany
2 Wolf Mine, Siegerland Region, Germany	**4** Ice River, Canada

1 2
3 4

1 Otavite

Chem. formula $CdCO_3$
Hardness 4, **Sp. gr.** 5
Color White
Streak White
Luster Adamantine
Cleavage Good
Fracture Uneven
Tenacity Brittle
Crystal form Trigonal

Morphology Rhombohedral crystals, crystal encrustations, coatings.
Origin and occurrence In the oxidation zone of hydrothermal lead-zinc deposits.
Accessory minerals Cerussite, azurite, dolomite, calcite, duftite, malachite.
Similar minerals Dolomite and calcite have a different luster, not adamantine; cerussite has a different crystal form.

2 Epistilbite

Chem. formula
$CaAl_2Si_6O_{16} \cdot 5\,H_2O$
Hardness 4, **Sp. gr.** 2.25
Color Colorless, white, reddish
Streak White
Luster Vitreous
Cleavage Perfect
Fracture Uneven
Tenacity Brittle
Crystal form Monoclinic

Morphology Prismatic to thick tabular crystals, stellate aggregates.
Origin and occurrence In cavities of volcanic rocks, on alpine fissures.
Accessory minerals Quartz, yugawaralite, stilbite, heulandite, fluorite.
Similar minerals Yugawaralite and stilbite have a different crystal form; calcite effervesces when dabbed with diluted hydrochloric acid; celestine and barite exhibit a different cleavage.

3 Heulandite

Chem. formula
$Ca[Al_2Si_7O_{18}] \cdot 6\,H_2O$
Hardness 3½–4, **Sp. gr.** 2.2
Color Colorless, white, yellowish, red, brown
Streak White
Luster Vitreous, pearly on cleavage faces
Cleavage Perfect
Fracture Uneven
Tenacity Brittle
Crystal form Monoclinic

Morphology Thin to thick tabular crystals, stellate to botryoidal aggregates, always euhedral.
Origin and occurrence In vugs of pegmatites, on ore veins, in bubble cavities of volcanic rocks.
Accessory minerals Stilbite, chabazite, scolecite, calcite, quartz, apophyllite.
Similar minerals Stilbite, phillipsite and chabazite have a different crystal form; unlike heulandite, calcite effervesces when dabbed with diluted hydrochloric acid; apophyllite also has a different crystal form.

4 Volborthite

Chem. formula
$Cu_3V_2O_7(OH)_2 \cdot 2\,H_2O$
Hardness 3½–4, **Sp. gr.** 3.5–3.8
Color Olive green, green, yellow-green
Streak Greenish white
Luster Vitreous, pearly on cleavage faces
Cleavage Perfect, one cleavage face
Fracture Uneven
Tenacity Brittle
Crystal form Monoclinic

Morphology Thin to thick tabular crystals, hexagonal, rose-like to botryoidal aggregates, always euhedral, earthy, drusy.
Origin and occurrence In the oxidation zone of hydrothermal, vanadium-rich deposits.
Accessory minerals Calcite, brochantite, malachite, atacamite, chrysocolla.
Similar minerals Mica is flexible; chlorite is softer and has a green streak; chloritoid is much harder; occurrence with other vanadium minerals is characteristic.

Localities	
1 Tsumeb, Namibia	**3** Fassa Valley, South Tyrol, Italy
2 Osilo, Sardinia, Italy	**4** Beresowsk, Russia

1 2
3 4

1–4 Fluorite *Fluorspar*

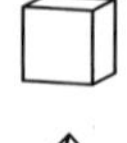

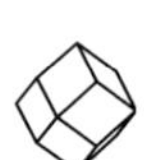

Chem. formula CaF_2
Hardness 4, **Sp. gr.** 3.1–3.2
Color Colorless, white, pink, yellow, brown, green, blue, purple, black, sometimes also multiple colors in a crystal
Streak White
Luster Vitreous
Cleavage Perfect octahedral
Fracture Uneven
Tenacity Brittle
Crystal form Cubic

Cubic fluorite from China.

Green octahedral fluorite crystal from the Gastein Valley, Austria

Morphology Cubic, octahedral, also in combination with each other or with other crystal forms, rarely rhombic dodecahedral or scalenohedral crystals, radial, reniform aggregates, rarely botryoidal, uneven.

Origin and occurrence In hydrothermal veins as gangue where they partially occur in cavities as very large crystals, crystals in vugs and on fissures in limestones, on fissures of silicate rocks, in alpine fissures, uneven in layers in sedimentary rocks.

Accessory minerals Calcite, barite, quartz, pyrite, galena, sphalerite, cinnabar.

Distinguishing feature Fluorite glows intensely when irradiated with ultraviolet light. The property of fluorescence derives its name from the mineral fluorite.

Very clear, colorless fluorite, or fluorspar, was used for optical purposes for a long time and was mined as "optical spar." Today fluorite crystals are produced artificially for this purpose. They are used for the production of particularly high-quality lenses for astronomical telescopes. However, the main use of synthetic fluorite crystals today is in the manufacture of lenses, which are used in the attachment of very small miniaturized circuits to computer chips. Unlike fluorite, glass is unsuitable for this task because it is no longer transparent to the short wavelengths of light required for the miniaturization.

In the past, a large proportion of fluorite was used in enamel production, but today one of its main uses is as a flux agent, particularly in steel production.

Deep purple to black radiation-dyed fluorite is found in the area of uranium deposits, for example, in Wölsendorf in Bavaria. When struck, it gives off a peculiar odor, which is why it is called decaying fluorspar.

Fluorescence Fluorite can glow in various colors when irradiated with short-wave or long-wave ultraviolet light. Frequently, the colors are blue or yellow. The internationally recognized name fluorspar, fluorite is used for the name for the property of fluorescence. Phosphorescent, or photoluminescent, fluorites are also not uncommon.

Similar minerals Fluorite differs from apatite in crystal form and cleavage and from calcite and quartz in hardness; rock salt is soluble in water and tastes salty.

Localities	
1 Göscheneralp, Switzerland	**3** China
2 Hocharn, High Tauern, Austria	**4** Ribadisella, Spain

1 2
3 4

1 Levyne

Chem. formula $(Na,Ca)_2(Al,Si)_9O_{18} \cdot 8\ H_2O$
Hardness 4–4½, **Sp. gr.** 2.1
Color Colorless, white, yellowish
Streak White
Luster Vitreous
Cleavage None
Fracture Uneven
Tenacity Brittle
Crystal form Hexagonal

Morphology Thin tabular, rarely thick tabular with typical hexagonal outline, foliated.
Origin and occurrence In cavities of volcanic rocks, always euhedral.
Accessory minerals Chabazite, thomsonite, phillipsite, calcite, aragonite.
Similar minerals Calcite has perfect cleavage and effervesces when dabbed with diluted hydrochloric acid, as does aragonite, which is always more acicular to prismatic; heulandite has good cleavage.

2 Creedite

Chem. formula $Ca_3Al_2SO_4(F,OH)_{10} \cdot 2\ H_2O$
Hardness 4, **Sp. gr.** 2.7
Color Colorless, white, purple
Streak White
Luster Vitreous
Cleavage Perfect
Fracture Uneven
Tenacity Brittle
Crystal form Monoclinic

Morphology Prismatic, acicular crystals, stellate aggregates, botryoidal, reniform, uneven.
Origin and occurrence In hydrothermal veins as young formations with ore minerals.
Accessory minerals Quartz, fluorite, barite, galena, sphalerite, calcite.
Similar minerals Gypsum is much softer; calcite effervesces readily when dabbed with diluted hydrochloric acid; barite and celestine are much heavier; in its amethyst variety, quartz is much harder.

3 Phillipsite

Chem. formula $KCa[Al_3Si_5O_{16}] \cdot 6\ H_2O$
Hardness 4–4½, **Sp. gr.** 2.2
Color Colorless, white, yellowish, reddish
Streak White
Luster Vitreous
Cleavage Discernible
Fracture Uneven
Tenacity Brittle
Crystal form Monoclinic

Morphology Always twinned, mainly prismatic twins and quads, but also dodecahedra that look like rhombic dodecahedra, stellate, botryoidal aggregates, almost always euhedral.
Origin and occurrence Euhedral in bubble cavities of volcanic rocks.
Accessory minerals Chabazite, natrolite, heulandite, stilbite, calcite, aragonite, opal, quartz.
Similar minerals Stilbite/heulandite have perfect cleavage with a pearly luster on the cleavage faces.

4 Ganophyllite

Chem. formula $NaMn_3(OH)_4(Si,Al)_4O_{10}$
Hardness 4–4½, **Sp. gr.** 2.85
Color Brown, yellowish
Streak White
Luster Vitreous
Cleavage Perfect
Fracture Foliated
Tenacity Brittle
Crystal form Monoclinic

Morphology Tabular crystals, foliated aggregates, micaceous roses.
Origin and occurrence In metamorphic manganese deposits.
Accessory minerals Rhodonite, sursassite, axinite, rhodochrosite, spessartine.
Similar minerals The paragenesis of ganophyllite with other manganese minerals is very characteristic and hinders confusion; biotite and phlogopite are not brittle; mcgovernite has a brown streak.

Localities	
1 Brattabrekka, Iceland	**3** Siegerland Region, Germany
2 Santa Elalia, Mexico	**4** Franklin, New Jersey, USA

1 2
3 4

1 Triphyline

Chem. formula $Li(Fe,Mn)[PO_4]$
Hardness 4, **Sp. gr.** 3.4–3.6
Color Gray-green
Streak Gray-white
Luster Vitreous
Cleavage Perfect in three directions
Fracture Splintery
Tenacity Brittle
Crystal form Orthorhombic

Morphology Rarely thick tabular to prismatic crystals, always anhedral, usually uneven, crystalline masses.
Origin and occurrence In phosphate pegmatites as a primary mineral, as an accessory mineral in granites.
Accessory minerals Zwieselite, heterosite, graftonite and other primary phosphates.
Similar minerals Taking its cleavage and color into consideration, there is no mineral in the same paragenesis that could be confused with triphyline; graftonite is pinker; lithiophilite is more brownish yellowish.

2 Bastnäsite

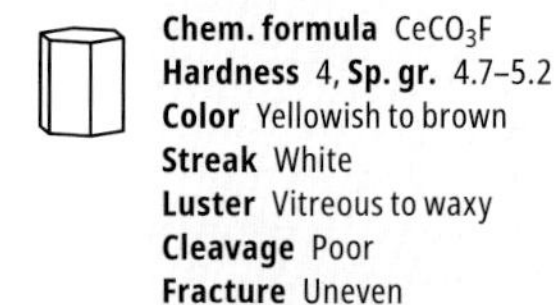

Chem. formula $CeCO_3F$
Hardness 4, **Sp. gr.** 4.7–5.2
Color Yellowish to brown
Streak White
Luster Vitreous to waxy
Cleavage Poor
Fracture Uneven
Tenacity Brittle
Crystal form Hexagonal

Morphology Thick to thin tabular crystals, often intergrown to roses, rarely prismatic crystals, mainly euhedral, uneven.
Origin and occurrence In pegmatites, on alpine fissures, in hydrothermal deposits.
Accessory minerals Barite, monazite.
Similar minerals Synchisite and parisite are difficult to distinguish from bastnäsite by simple means; calcite has a different cleavage; monazite has a different crystal form and cleavage.

3 Tarbuttite

Chem. formula $Zn_2[OH/PO_4]$
Hardness 4, **Sp. gr.** 4.15
Color Colorless, white, yellowish, brownish
Streak White
Luster Vitreous
Cleavage Perfect
Fracture Uneven
Tenacity Brittle
Crystal form Triclinic

Morphology Planar crystals, isometric to thick tabular, encrustations, uneven.
Origin and occurrence In the oxidation zone of hydrothermal zinc deposits.
Accessory minerals Scholzite, hopeite, parahopeite, goethite, calcite.
Similar minerals Calcite and smithsonite have a different cleavage; calcite effervesces when dabbed with diluted hydrochloric acid; hemimorphite has a different crystal form, as do hopeite and parahopeite.

4 Goosecreekite

Chem. formula $CaAl_2Si_6O_{16} \cdot 5\,H_2O$
Hardness 4–4½, **Sp. gr.** 2.45
Color Colorless, white
Streak White
Luster Vitreous
Cleavage Indiscernible
Fracture Uneven
Tenacity Brittle
Crystal form Monoclinic

Morphology Prismatic crystals, often parallel intergrowths with curved faces.
Origin and occurrence In cavities of volcanic rocks.
Accessory minerals Quartz, epistilbite, yugawaralite, heulandite, stilbite.
Similar minerals The characteristic morphology (photo) distinguishes goosecreekite from all similar minerals; sharply formed crystals without the characteristic curved faces are indistinguishable from epistilbite.

Localities	
1 Hagendorf-Süd, East Bavaria, Germany	**3** Broken Hill, Zambia
2 Trimouns, France	**4** Pune, India

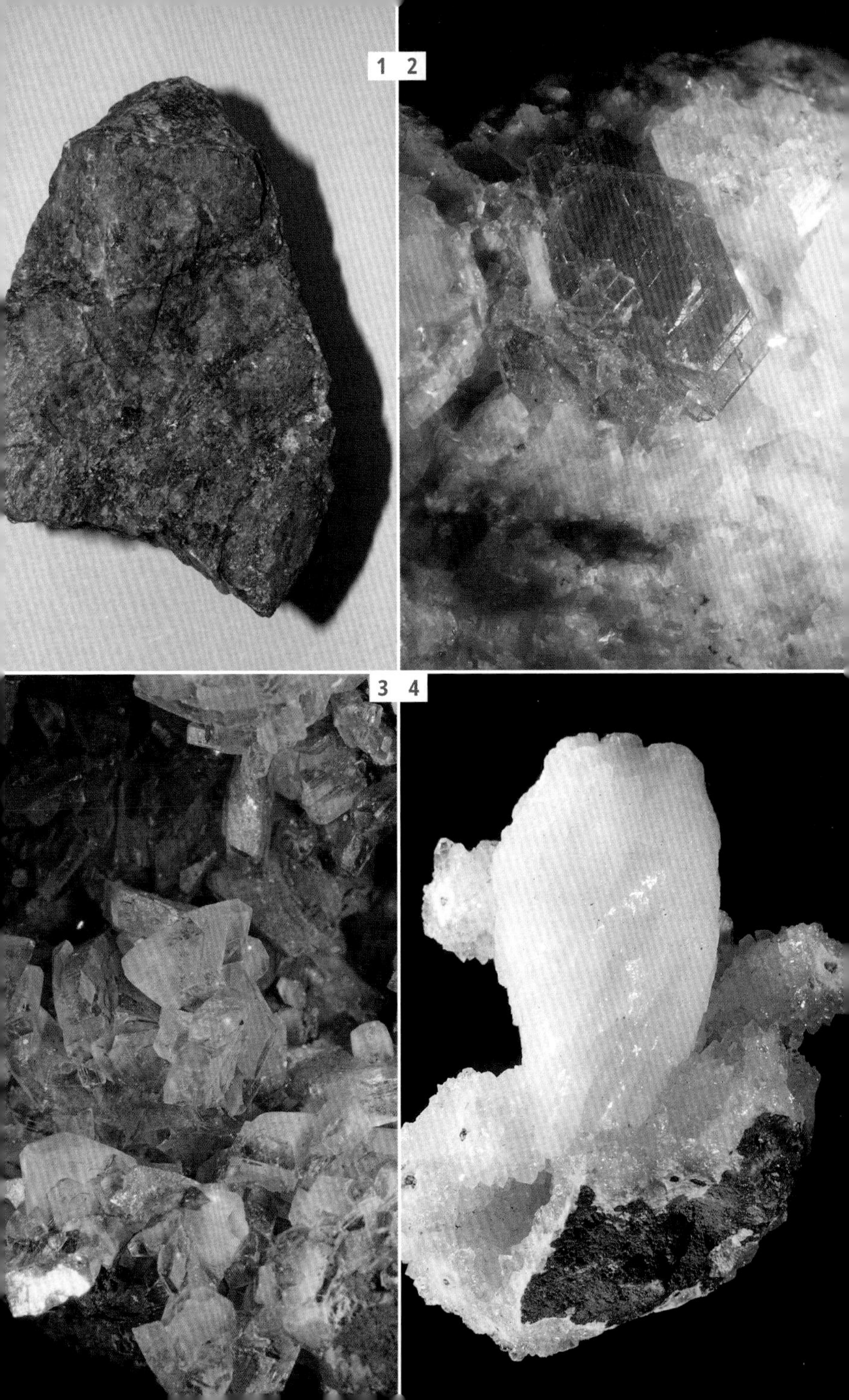
1 2
3 4

1 Eulytine *Agricolite, bismouth blende*

Chem. formula $Bi_4[SiO_4]_3$
Hardness 4–4½ Sp. gr.
Color Light to dark brown
Streak White
Luster Vitreous to adamantine
Cleavage Indiscernible
Fracture Uneven
Tenacity Brittle
Crystal form Cubic

Morphology Tetrahedral and tristetrahedral crystals, often interpenetration twins, botryoidal aggregates, planar crystal intergrowths, encrustations.
Origin and occurrence In the oxidation zone of bismuth-bearing hydrothermal deposits.
Accessory minerals Quartz, native bismuth, bismuthite, pucherite, calcite.
Similar minerals The characteristic morphology (photo) distinguishes eulytine from all other minerals in bismuth-rich parageneses.

2 Parisite-(Ce)

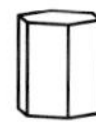

Chem. formula $Ca(Ce,La)_2(CO_3)_3F_2$
Hardness 4½, **Sp. gr.** 4.33
Color Yellowish to brown
Streak White
Luster Vitreous to waxy
Cleavage Poor
Fracture Uneven
Tenacity Brittle
Crystal form Hexagonal

Morphology Thick to thin tabular crystals, often intergrown into roses, often prismatic upward tapering crystals, often transversely striated, euhedral, anhedral, uneven.
Origin and occurrence In pegmatites, on alpine fissures, in hydrothermal deposits.
Accessory minerals Monazite, synchisite, bastnäsite, apatite.
Similar minerals Synchisite and bastnäsite are difficult to distinguish using simple means; calcite has a different cleavage; monazite has a different crystal form.

3 Tobermorite

Chem. formula $Ca_5Si_6O_{16}(OH)_2 \cdot 4\,H_2O$
Hardness 4½, **Sp. gr.** 2.4
Color White
Streak White
Luster Vitreous to silky
Cleavage Poorly discernible
Fracture Fibrous
Tenacity Brittle
Crystal form Monoclinic

Morphology Acicular crystals, crystal sheaves, fibrous, stellate aggregates.
Origin and occurrence In calcareous xenoliths in volcanic rocks, in vugs in basalts, in metamorphic manganese deposits.
Accessory minerals Natrolite, thaumasite, afwillite, ettringite, calcite.
Similar minerals Natrolite usually has thicker crystals, often with end faces; aragonite effervesces when dabbed with diluted hydrochloric acid.

4 Stibiconite

Chem. formula $Sb^{3+}Sb_2^{5+}O_6(OH)$
Hardness 4½–7, **Sp. gr.** 3.3–4.5
Color White, yellowish, orange, gray, brown
Streak White
Luster Dull
Cleavage None
Fracture Fibrous, uneven
Tenacity Brittle
Crystal form Cubic

Morphology Reniform aggregates, uneven masses, shelly aggregates, powdery, earthy, uneven.
Origin and occurrence In the oxidation zone of antimony-rich hydrothermal deposits.
Accessory minerals Senarmontite, stibnite, native antimony, valentinite.
Distinguishing feature Stibiconite forms pseudomorphs after stibnite crystals.
Similar minerals Uneven stibiconite is difficult to identify; existing stibnite residues provide an indication.

Localities	
1 Schneeberg, Saxony, Germany	**3** N'Chwaning, Hotazel, South Africa
2 Trimouns, France	**4** Zacatecas, Mexico

1 2
3 4

1

Lithiophilite

Chem. formula $Li(Mn,Fe)[PO_4]$
Hardness 4, **Sp. gr.** 3.43
Color Light brown, translucent
Streak White
Luster Vitreous
Cleavage Perfect in three directions
Fracture Splintery
Tenacity Brittle
Crystal form Orthorhombic

Morphology Rarely thick tabular to prismatic crystals, always anhedral, mainly uneven, crystalline masses, sometimes up to a meter in size.
Origin and occurrence In phosphate pegmatites as a primary mineral, as an accessory mineral in granites.
Accessory minerals Zwieselite, heterosite, graftonite and other primary phosphates.
Similar minerals Taking cleavage and color into consideration, there is no mineral in the same paragenesis that could be confused with lithiophilite; graftonite is pinker; triphyline is greener to green-gray, however, iron-rich lithiophilite is also greener but cannot be distinguished from triphyline without analysis.

2

Margarite

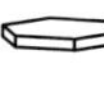

Chem. formula $CaAl_4Si_2O_{10}(OH)_2$
Hardness 4–4½, **Sp. gr.** 3.0–3.1
Color White, pink, yellowish
Streak White
Luster Pearly
Cleavage Perfect
Fracture Foliated
Tenacity Brittle
Crystal form Monoclinic

Morphology Tabular, foliated aggregates and intergrowths, rarely euhedral crystals.
Origin and occurrence In metamorphic rocks and deposits, particularly emerald deposits.
Accessory minerals Emerald, staurolite, tourmaline, biotite, actinolite, phenakite.
Distinguishing feature Margarite belongs to the brittle micas, which, in contrast to the classical micas, are not elastically flexible, rather notably brittle. When bent, these micas break by splintering. Characteristic of all brittle mica, of which margarite is by far the most common, is that they do not contain alkali metals, such as sodium or potassium, but rather alkaline earth metals, in particular calcium, as cations.
Similar minerals Muscovite is not brittle, the same applies for biotite and phlogopite; clinochlore and other chlorite minerals are much softer; albite usually forms thicker tabular crystals and exhibits a different cleavage.

3–4

Smithsonite *Zinc spar*

Chem. formula $ZnCO_3$
Hardness 5, **Sp. gr.** 4.3–4.5
Color Colorless, white, yellow, brown, red, green, blue, gray
Streak White
Luster Vitreous
Cleavage Rhombohedral perfect
Fracture Uneven
Tenacity Brittle
Crystal form Trigonal

Morphology Scalenohedra and rhombohedra, often rounded, rice-grain shaped, aggregates reniform, stalactitic, shelly, uneven.
Origin and occurrence In the oxidation zone of zinc deposits.
Accessory minerals Hydrozincite, wulfenite, hemimorphite, aurichalcite, cerussite, anglesite, willemite.
Similar minerals Unlike smithsonite, calcite effervesces with diluted hydrochloric acid; dolomite does not normally occur in the oxidation zone of zinc deposits; it does not have the same color (yellow, red, green, blue) as smithsonite.

Localities	
1 Owl Creek Mine, Arizona, USA	**3** Tsumeb, Namibia
2 Takowaja, Urals, Russia	**4** Rush Creek, Arkansas, USA

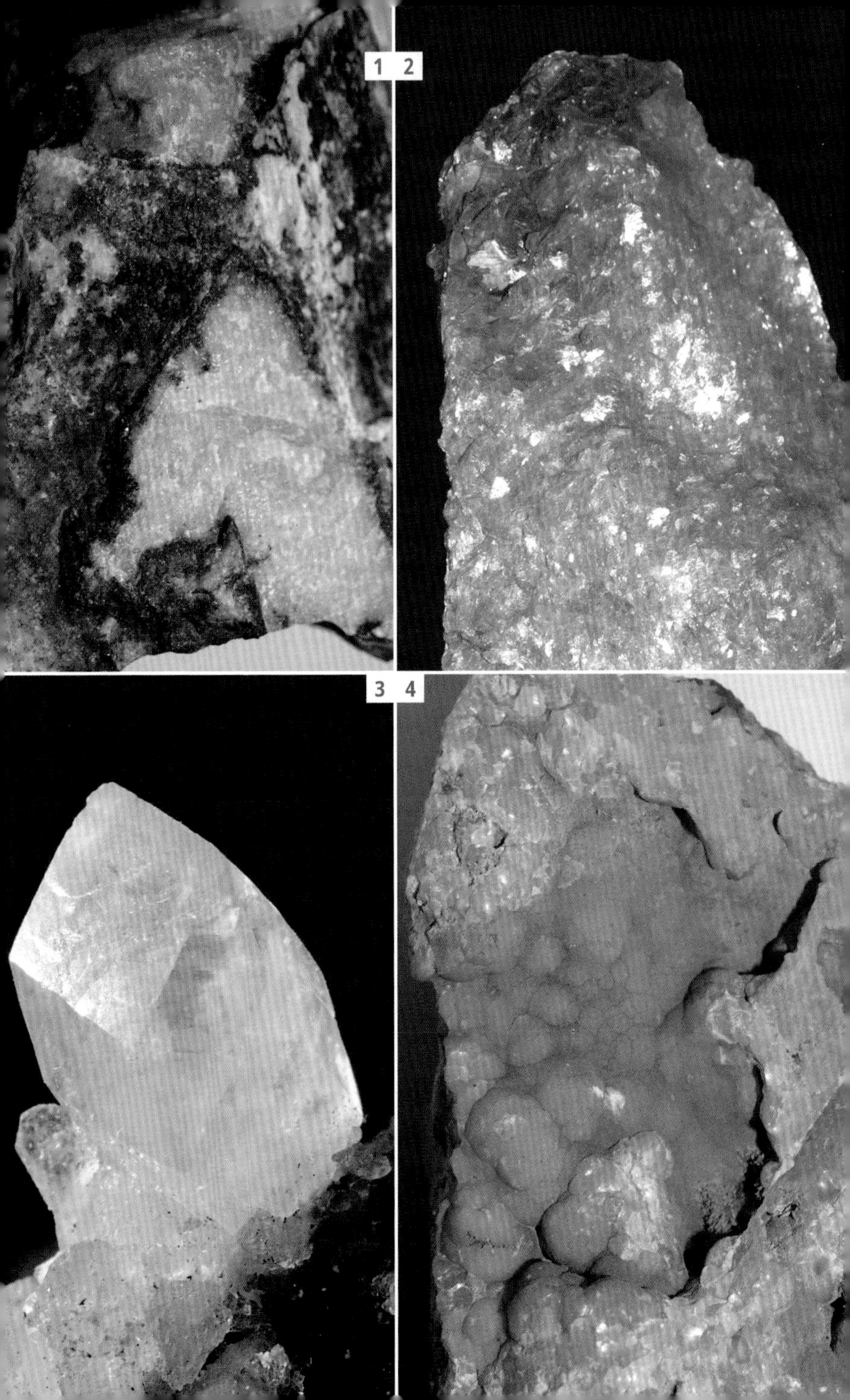
1 2
3 4

1 Woodhouseite

Chem. formula $CaAl_3PO_4SO_4(OH)_6$
Hardness 4–4½, **Sp. gr.** 3
Color White, brownish, pale pink
Streak White
Luster Vitreous
Cleavage Perfect
Fracture Uneven
Tenacity Brittle
Crystal form Trigonal

Morphology Thick tabular crystals, crystal encrustations, stellate aggregates, uneven.
Origin and occurrence In hydrothermal veins, anhedral crystals on alpine fissures.
Accessory minerals Quartz, lazulite, augelite, topaz, apatite, calcite.
Similar minerals Augelite has a different crystal form; calcite effervesces when dabbed with diluted hydrochloric acid and is softer; topaz and quartz are clearly harder; jarosite and natrojarosite are always brown.

2 Austinite

Chem. formula $CaZnAsO_4OH$
Hardness 4–4½, **Sp. gr.** 4.3
Color Colorless, white, greenish (cuproaustinite)
Streak White
Luster Vitreous
Cleavage Poor
Fracture Uneven
Tenacity Brittle
Crystal form Orthorhombic

Morphology Prismatic to tabular crystals, stellate aggregates, reniform, drusy.
Origin and occurrence In the oxidation zone of cobalt-rich deposits.
Accessory minerals Adamite, limonite, smithsonite, wulfenite, mimetesite.
Similar minerals Adamite has a different crystal form; calcite effervesces when dabbed with diluted hydrochloric acid; smithsonite has good cleavage.

3 Jarlite

Chem. formula $NaSr_3Al_3F_{16}$
Hardness 4–4½, **Sp. gr.** 3.8
Color White, colorless, yellowish
Streak White
Luster Vitreous
Cleavage None
Fracture Uneven
Tenacity Brittle
Crystal form Monoclinic

Morphology Tabular crystals, stellate, botryoidal aggregates, uneven.
Origin and occurrence As a weathering and alteration product of cryolite.
Accessory minerals Thomsenolite, ralstonite, pachnolite, fluorite, topaz, cryolite.
Similar minerals The characteristic crystal form of jarlite is unmistakable; thomsenolite and pachnolite are clearly prismatic; ralstonite forms cubic crystals; topaz is much harder.

4 Synchisite

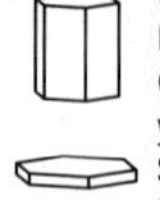

Chem. formula $CeCa[F/(CO_3)_2]$
Hardness 4½, **Sp. gr.** 4.35
Color Colorless, whiteish, yellow, orange, greenish, gray
Streak White
Luster Vitreous
Cleavage Scarcely distinct
Fracture Conchoidal
Tenacity Brittle
Crystal form Monoclinic

Morphology Pseudohexagonal crystals, prismatic, tapering towards the ends, transversely striated, thin tabular, flower-shaped aggregates, practically always euhedral.
Origin and occurrence In alpine fissures and cavities of magmatic rocks.
Accessory minerals Anatase, brookite, titanite.
Similar minerals Titanite has a different crystal form; bastnäsite and parisite are indistinguishable using simple means; however, they are much rarer, at least in alpine fissures; calcite has perfect cleavage.

Localities	
1 White Mountains, California, USA	**3** Ivigtut, Greenland
2 Mina Ojuela, Mapimi, Mexico	**4** Adra, Spain

1
2
3
4

1 Yugawaralite

Chem. formula $CaAl_2Si_6O_{16} \cdot 4\ H_2O$
Hardness 4½, **Sp. gr.** 2.25
Color Colorless, white
Streak White
Luster Vitreous
Cleavage Poor
Fracture Uneven
Tenacity Brittle
Crystal form Monoclinic

Morphology Thin to rarely thick tabular crystals, always euhedral.
Origin and occurrence Euhedral in cavities of volcanic rocks.
Accessory minerals Quartz, heulandite, stilbite, goosecreekite, epistilbite.
Similar minerals Epistilbite has a different crystal form and exhibits perfect cleavage; goosecreekite differs because of its characteristic aggregate form; stilbite and heulandite have perfect cleavage.

2 Ralstonite

Chem. formula $NaMgAl(F,OH)_6 \cdot H_2O$
Hardness 4½, **Sp. gr.** 2.56
Color Colorless, white, yellowish
Streak White
Luster Vitreous
Cleavage None
Fracture Uneven
Tenacity Brittle
Crystal form Cubic

Morphology Cubic, octahedral crystals, often cubes with chamfered corners, planar crystal intergrowths, encrustations, usually euhedral.
Origin and occurrence As an alteration product of cryolite in pegmatites.
Accessory minerals Thomsenolite, pachnolite, cryolite, fluorite, topaz, siderite, quartz.
Similar minerals Thomsenolite and pachnolite have a significantly different crystal form; jarlite is more tabular; topaz is harder, as is quartz.

3 Tunisite

Chem. formula $NaHCa_2Al_4(CO_3)_4(OH)_{10}$
Hardness 4½, **Sp. gr.** 2.5
Color Colorless, white
Streak White
Luster Vitreous
Cleavage Good
Fracture Uneven
Tenacity Brittle
Crystal form Tetragonal

Morphology Mainly very small, tabular crystals, radial aggregates, granular, uneven.
Origin and occurrence In hollow concretions and vugs in sedimentary rocks.
Accessory minerals Calcite, celestine, quartz, barite, calcite.
Similar minerals Celestine and calcite have a different crystal form; calcite and aragonite effervesce when dabbed with diluted hydrochloric acid; barite has a different crystal form and a much higher density.

4 Gmelinite

Chem. formula $(Na_2,Ca)Al_2Si_4O_{12} \cdot 6\ H_2O$
Hardness 4½, **Sp. gr.** 2.1
Color Colorless, white, pink, yellowish
Streak White
Luster Vitreous
Cleavage None
Fracture Uneven
Tenacity Brittle
Crystal form Hexagonal

Morphology Thick tabular to bipyramidal crystals with a hexagonal plan.
Origin and occurrence In cavities of volcanic rocks, on cavities and fissures of hydrothermal veins, always euhedral.
Accessory minerals Philippsite, chabazite.
Similar minerals The characteristic crystal form of gmelinite does not allow for any confusion; calcite and aragonite effervesce when dabbed with diluted hydrochloric acid.

Localities	
1 Pune, India	**3** Condorcet, France
2 Ivigtut, Greenland	**4** St. Andreasberg, Harz, Germany

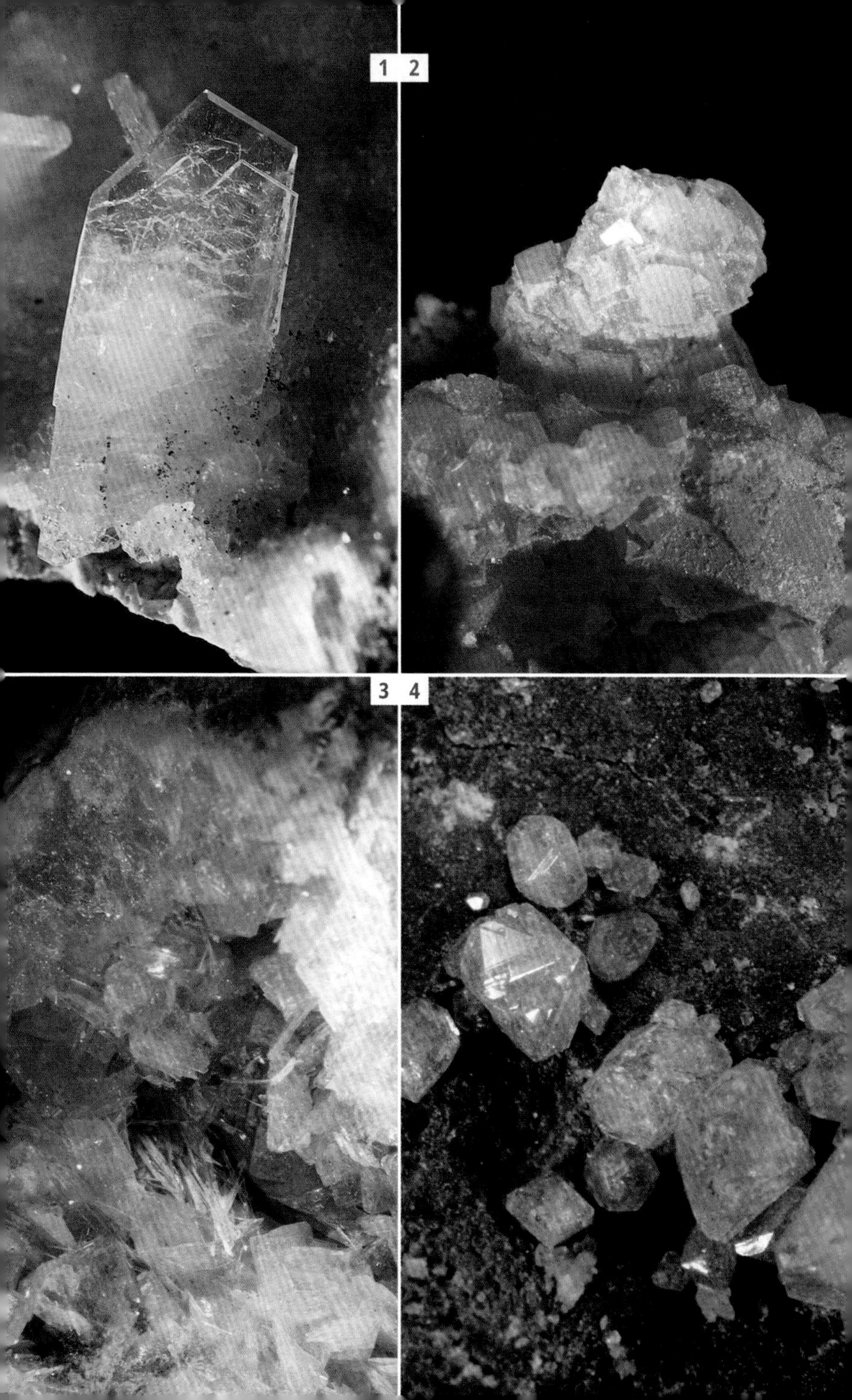
1 2
3 4

1–2 Kyanite *Disthene, Cyanite*

Chem. formula $Al_2[O/SiO_4]$
Hardness 4 (longitudinal) up to 7 (transverse), **Sp. gr.** 3.6–3.7
Color Blue, gray, whiteish, black
Streak White
Luster Vitreous
Cleavage Perfect
Fracture Uneven
Tenacity Brittle
Crystal form Triclinic

Morphology Columnar, lath-shaped crystals, stellate aggregates, always anhedral.
Origin and occurrence Anhedral in metamorphic rocks, gneisses, mica schists.
Accessory minerals Staurolite, quartz, biotite, muscovite, actinolite, garnet, andalusite.
Distinguishing feature Kyanite exhibits a significantly different hardness in two different directions. While this occurs in many minerals, kyanite is the only mineral in which this direction-dependent hardness can be easily detected without the use of complicated equipment. Kyanite exhibits hardness 4 on the Mohs hardness scale in the longitudinal direction of the crystals and hardness 7 perpendicular to that, i.e. transversely. If a steel needle (hardness about 6) is used for testing, it is notable that you can easily score the kyanite longitudinally but not at all transversely.
Similar minerals The difference in hardness in two different directions in kyanite distinguishes it from all other minerals; in addition, actinolite has a distinctly recognizable cleavage with a cleavage angle of about 120°.

3 Hidalgoite

Chem. formula $PbAl_3AsO_4SO_4(OH)_6$
Hardness 4½, **Sp. gr.** 4
Color White, gray, greenish
Streak White
Luster Vitreous
Cleavage None
Fracture Uneven
Tenacity Brittle
Crystal form Trigonal

Morphology Tiny rhombohedral crystals, reniform aggregates, drusy, uneven.
Origin and occurrence In the oxidation zone of lead-bearing deposits.
Accessory minerals Pyromorphite, beudantite, mimetesite, wulfenite, duftite, calcite.
Similar minerals Hidalgoite is indistinguishable from beudantite by simple means, but the latter, unlike hidalgoite, often forms crystals; calcite effervesces when dabbed with diluted hydrochloric acid.

4 Harmotome

Chem. formula $Ba[Al_2Si_6O_{16}] \cdot 6\ H_2O$
Hardness 4½, **Sp. gr.** 2.44–2.5
Color Colorless, white, yellowish
Streak White
Luster Vitreous
Fracture Conchoidal
Tenacity Brittle
Crystal form Monoclinic

Morphology Almost always cruciform twins, prismatic, euhedral.
Origin and occurrence In cavities of volcanic rocks, in hydrothermal additions and gravel deposits.
Accessory minerals Stilbite, heulandite, brewsterite, barite, calcite.
Similar minerals Harmotome cannot be distinguished from phillipsite using simple means; the latter, however, does not occur in ore deposits; the characteristic twin crystals with cruciform re-entrant angles distinguish harmotome from all other minerals.

Localities	
1 Alpe Sponda, Ticino, Switzerland	**3** Sylvester Mine, Australia
2 Ziller Valley, Austria	**4** Idar-Oberstein, Palatinate, Germany

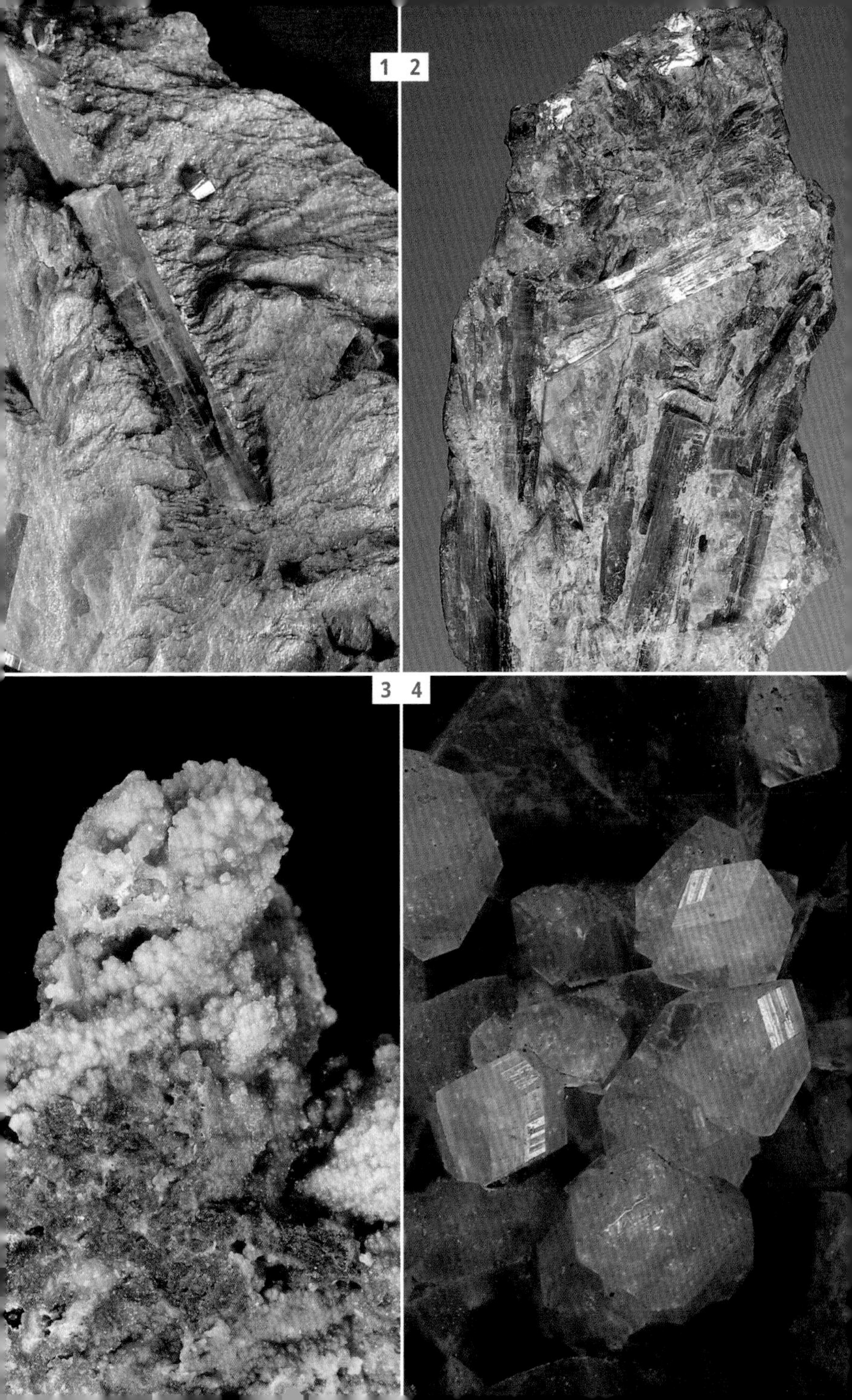
1 2
3 4

1 Gismondine

Chem. formula $CaAl_2Si_2O_8] \cdot 4\,H_2O$
Hardness 4½, **Sp. gr.** 2.3
Color Colorless, white
Streak White
Luster Vitreous
Cleavage None
Fracture Uneven
Tenacity Brittle
Crystal form Monoclinic

Morphology Octahedral crystals, planar crystal intergrowths, encrustations, stellate aggregates.
Origin and occurrence In cavities of volcanic rocks, always euhedral.
Accessory minerals Phillipsite, thomsonite, natrolite, calcite.
Similar minerals Taking its paragenesis into account, the characteristic crystal form of gismondine does not allow for any confusion; calcite effervesces when dabbed with diluted hydrochloric acid; chabazite has a different crystal form and forms characteristic cube-like rhombohedra.

2 Colemanite

Chem. formula $Ca[B_3O_4(OH)_3] \cdot H_2O$
Hardness 4½, **Sp. gr.** 2.4
Color Colorless, white
Streak White
Luster Vitreous
Cleavage Perfect
Fracture Uneven
Tenacity Brittle
Crystal form Monoclinic

Morphology Prismatic to tabular crystals, granular, columnar, uneven.
Origin and occurrence In borax lakes and corresponding sediments.
Accessory minerals Realgar, hydroboracite, pandermite, realgar, calcite.
Similar minerals Borax and soda are softer; calcite and aragonite effervesce when dabbed with diluted hydrochloric acid; barite and celestine are much heavier; anhydrite exhibits right-angle cleavage.

3 Xenotime

Chem. formula $Y[PO_4]$
Hardness 4–5, **Sp. gr.** 4.5–5.1
Color Yellow, brown, opaque
Streak White
Luster Greasy (opaque) to vitreous (transparent)
Cleavage Perfect but often indistinct
Fracture Conchoidal
Tenacity Brittle
Crystal form Tetragonal

Morphology Prismatic to tabular crystals, anhedral and euhedral, sometimes oriented intergrowths with zircon.
Origin and occurrence Microscopically in granites, in pegmatites (large crystals, opaque, greasy luster, anhedral); on alpine fissures (small crystals, transparent, vitreous luster, euhedral).
Accessory minerals Zircon, monazite, anatase.
Similar minerals Zircon is harder; anatase only very rarely has prism faces and is harder.

4 Wollastonite

Chem. formula $Ca_3[Si_3O_9]$
Hardness 4½–5, **Sp. gr.** 2.8–2.9
Color Colorless, white, gray
Streak White
Luster Vitreous
Cleavage Perfect, but almost never distinct due to its fibrous structure
Fracture Fibrous
Tenacity Brittle
Crystal form Triclinic

Morphology Rarely tabular crystals, mainly fibrous, radial aggregates, coarsely crystalline, dendritic growths on joint faces.
Origin and occurrence In metamorphic limestones, in skarn deposits.
Accessory minerals Grossular, vesuvianite, diopside, calcite, graphite.
Similar minerals Tremolite is harder and acid resistant and exhibits cleavage with a 120° cleavage angle; lighter colored diopside has a cleavage angle of about 90°.

Localities	
1 Capo di Bove, Rome, Italy	**3** Ziller Valley, Austria
2 Boron, California, USA	**4** Saxony, Germany

1
2
3
4

1 Serpentine *Antigorite, Chrysotile*

Chem. formula $Mg_6[(OH)_8/Si_4O_{10}]$
Hardness 3–4, **Sp. gr.** 2.5–2.6
Color White, all shades of green, yellow
Streak White
Luster Greasy to silky
Cleavage Mainly indiscernible due to its fine granular structure
Fracture Conchoidal to fibrous
Tenacity Non-brittle
Crystal form Monoclinic

Morphology Antigorite is flaky, usually very granulitic, dense; chrysotile (asbestos) is fibrous, filiform.
Origin and occurrence Essential mineral in serpentinites, chrysotile on the fissures of this rock.
Accessory minerals Olivine, talc, magnetite, dolomite, magnesite, annabergite, calcite.
Similar minerals Talc is softer; unlike chrysotile, hornblende asbestos (fine fibrous hornblende minerals) is brittle.
Caution! If inhaled, chrysotile asbestos is carcinogenic due to its fine fibers.

2 Serpentine

Gemstone

Color Yellowish, greenish
Luster Greasy
Shape and cut Cabochon cut, spheres

Use Cabochons for brooches, pendants, spheres or beads for stone necklaces, also often as handicraft items.
Differentiating Jadeite and nephrite are harder and not quite as yellowish.

3 Whiteite

Chem. formula $Ca(Fe,Mn)Mg_2Al_2(OH)_2(H_2O)_8(PO_4)_4$
Hardness 3–4, **Sp. gr.** 2.6
Color Brown
Streak White
Luster Vitreous
Streak White
Cleavage Perfect
Fracture Uneven
Tenacity Brittle
Crystal form Monoclinic

Morphology Thick tabular, prismatic crystals, stellate aggregates.
Origin and occurrence In sedimentary phosphate deposits and in phosphate pegmatites as an alteration formation of primary phosphates.
Accessory minerals Lazulite, siderite, childrenite, eosphorite, zanazziite, quartz, kulanite.
Similar minerals Siderite exhibits a different crystal form and rhombohedral cleavage; childrenite and eosphorite also have different cleavage.

4 Chabazite

Chem. formula $Ca[Al_2Si_4O_{12}]$
Hardness 4½, **Sp. gr.** 2.08
Color Colorless, white, yellow, orange, brown
Luster Vitreous
Cleavage Indiscernible
Fracture Uneven
Tenacity Brittle
Crystal form Trigonal

Morphology Cubic rhombohedra, often twins, always euhedral, rarely also in the form of flat, hexagonal pyramids known as phacolite.
Origin and occurrence In bubble cavities of volcanic rocks and cavities of pegmatites, in vugs and fissures on ore veins, on alpine fissures.
Accessory minerals Stilbite, heulandite, scolecite, natrolite, phillipsite, calcite, opal, quartz, aragonite.
Similar minerals Calcite differs from chabazite in its cleavage and effervesces when dabbed with diluted hydrochloric acid; unlike chabazite, fluorite also exhibits discernible cleavage.

Localities	
1 Connemara, Ireland	**3** Rapid Creek, Yukon Territory, Canada
2 Asbestos, Canada	**4** Striegau, Poland

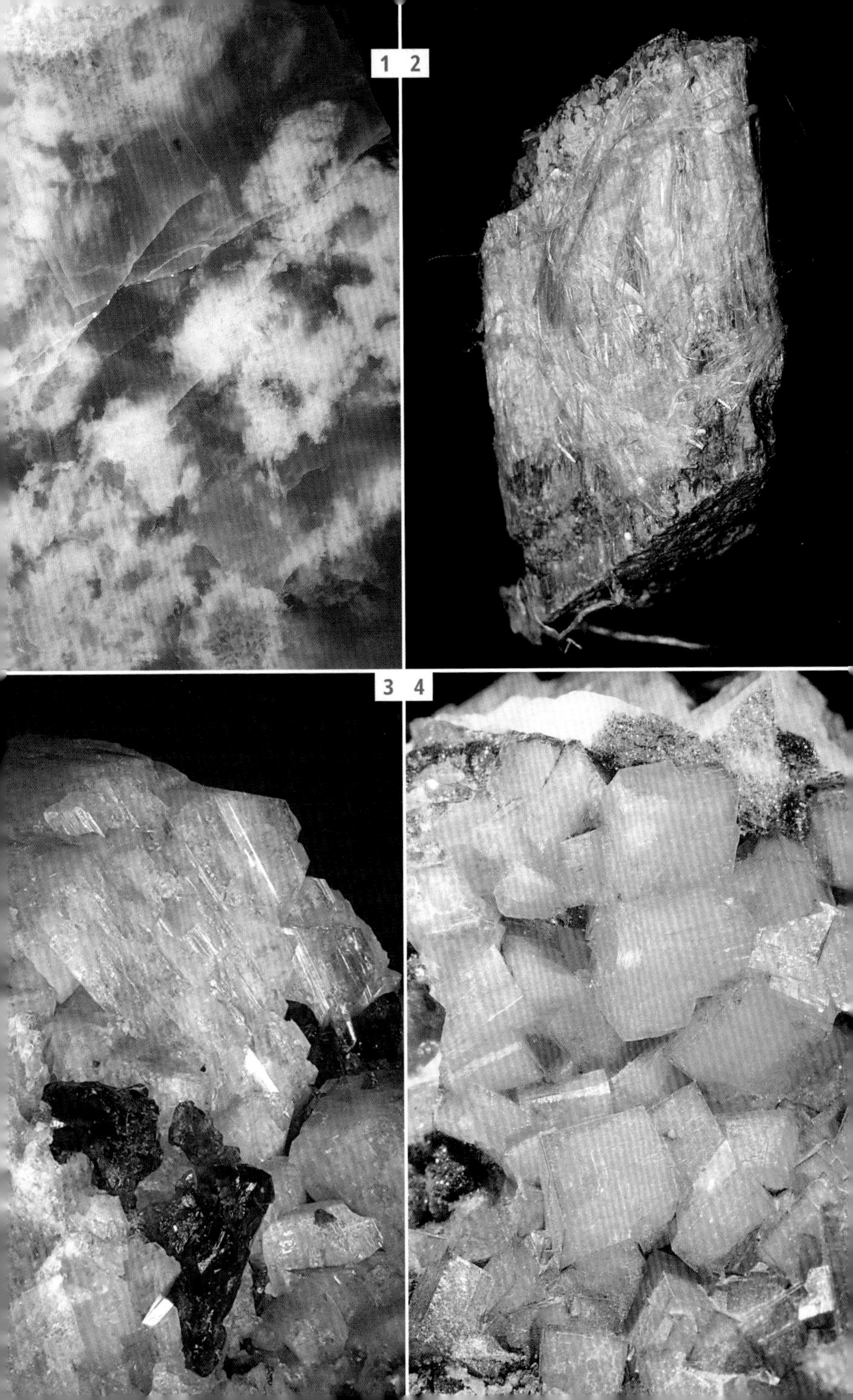
1 2
3 4

1 Apophyllite

Chem. formula $KCa_4[(F,OH)/(Si_4O_{10})_2] \cdot 8\,H_2O$
Hardness 4½–5, **Sp. gr.** 2.3–2.4
Color Colorless, white, yellow, green, blue-green, brown, pink
Streak White
Luster Vitreous, basal pronounced pearly luster
Cleavage Perfect
Fracture Uneven
Tenacity Brittle
Crystal form Tetragonal

Morphology Crystals tabular, cubic-like, prismatic, also bipyramidal, aggregates foliated, granular, uneven.
Origin and occurrence In bubble cavities of volcanic rocks, in vugs and on fissures of ore veins, on alpine fissures.
Accessory minerals Stilbite, heulandite, calcite, quartz, harmotome.
Similar minerals Crystal form and the pronounced pearly luster on the basal face distinguish apophyllite from all other minerals of these parageneses.

2 Graftonite

Chem. formula $(Fe,Mn,Ca)_3(PO_4)_2$
Hardness 5, **Sp. gr.** 3.7–3.8
Color Pink brown
Streak White
Luster Vitreous to resinous
Cleavage Discernible
Fracture Splintery
Tenacity Brittle
Crystal form Monoclinic

Morphology Rarely thick tabular to prismatic crystals, always anhedral, mainly uneven, crystalline masses, sometimes intergrown in a lamellar manner with triphyline.
Origin and occurrence In phosphate pegmatites as a primary mineral, as an accessory mineral in granites.
Accessory minerals Zwieselite, heterosite, triphyline and other primary phosphates.
Similar minerals Taking into consideration its cleavage and color, no mineral in the same paragenesis can be confused with graftonite; triphyline is greenish; lithiophilite more brownish-yellowish.

3 Pectolite

Chem. formula $Ca_2NaH[Si_3O_9]$
Hardness 5, **Sp. gr.** 2.8
Color Colorless, white, blue, yellowish
Streak White
Luster Vitreous, silky in aggregates
Cleavage None
Fracture Conchoidal, fibrous in aggregates
Tenacity Brittle
Crystal form Triclinic

Morphology Rarely prismatic crystals, mainly fibrous, stellate aggregates.
Origin and occurrence On fissures of basic extrusive rocks.
Accessory minerals Prehnite, diopside, thomsonite, grossular, xonotlite is not distinguishable by simple means.
Similar minerals Wollastonite occurs in a very different paragenesis; tobermorite is usually more finely fibrous.

4 Larimar

Gemstone

Color Blue, blue-white, stellate
Luster Vitreous
Shape and cut Cabochon cut, spheres

Distinguishing feature The blue, stellate pectolite is called larimar; other varieties of pectolite are not used for jewelry purposes.
Use Cabochons as ring stones and for brooches, pendants; spheres or beads for stone necklaces.
Differentiating The blue stellate aggregates are very characteristic and cannot be confused with any other gemstone or semiprecious stone.

Localities	
1 Pune, India	**3** Paterson, New Jersey, USA
2 Brissago, Ticino, Switzerland	**4** Dominican Republic

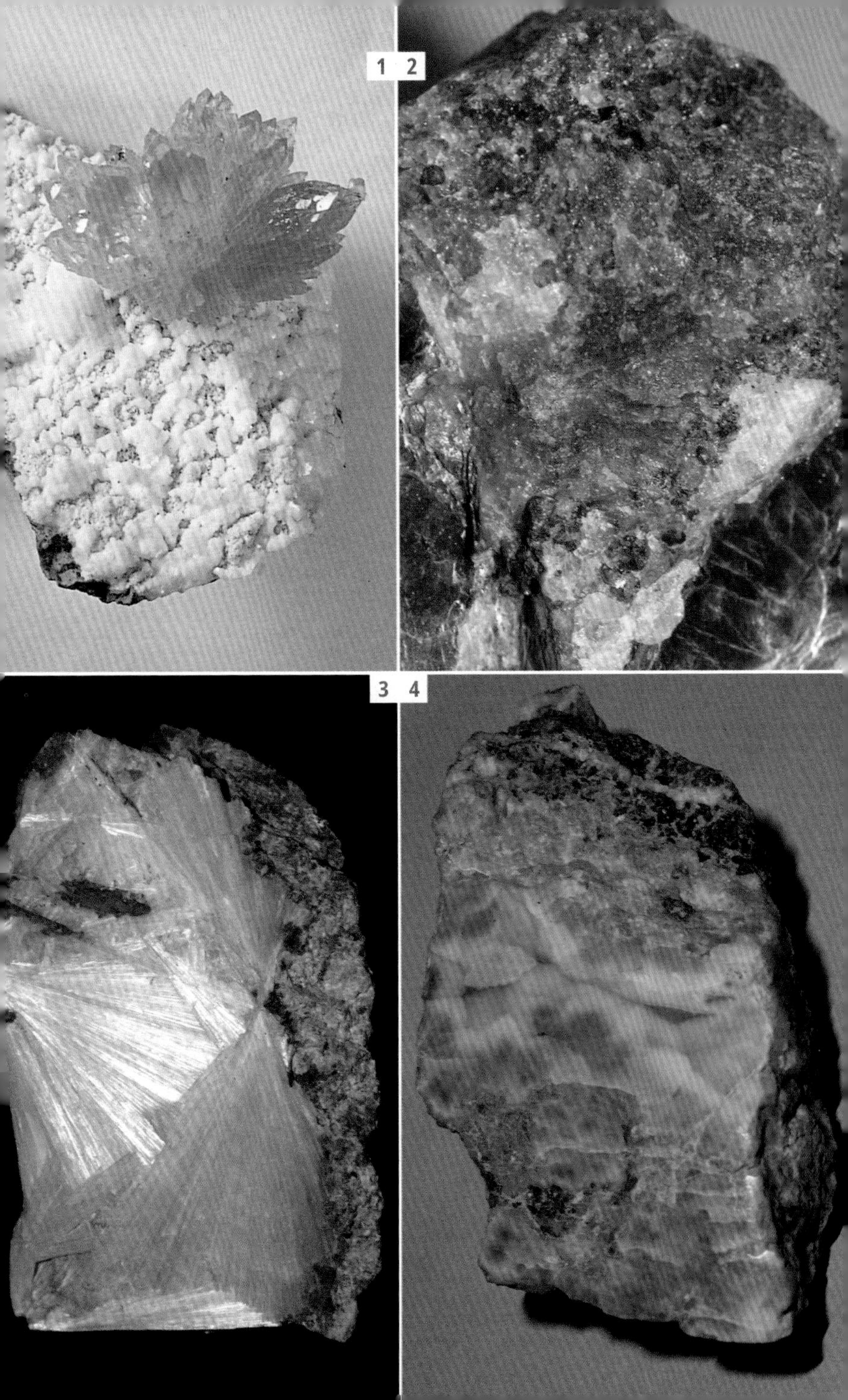
1 2
3 4

1 Serandite

Chem. formula $Na(Mn,Ca)_2Si_3O_8(OH)$
Hardness 5, **Sp. gr.** 3.34
Color Pink, orange, brown, black
Streak White
Luster Vitreous, silky in aggregates
Cleavage Perfect
Fracture Conchoidal, fibrous in aggregates
Tenacity Brittle
Crystal form Triclinic

Morphology Prismatic to blocky crystals, fibrous, stellate aggregates.
Origin and occurrence In alkaline rocks and pegmatites in alkaline rocks, for example nepheline syenites, in cavities in rhyolites.
Accessory minerals Sodalite, aegirine, nepheline, astrophyllite, analcime, eudialyte.
Similar minerals Feldspar has a different crystal form; eudialyte is redder; nepheline does not have perfect cleavage; rhodochrosite has perfect rhombohedral cleavage and is softer.

2 Senegalite

Chem. formula $Al_2(PO_4)(OH)_3] \cdot H_2O$
Hardness 5, **Sp. gr.** 2.55
Color White, colorless, yellowish
Streak White
Luster Vitreous
Cleavage None
Fracture Uneven
Tenacity Brittle
Crystal form Orthorhombic

Morphology Tabular crystals, euhedral, stellate aggregates and encrustations, botryoidal, reniform.
Origin and occurrence In the oxidation zone of an iron deposit.
Accessory minerals Turquoise, augelite, limonite, wavellite, crandallite, calcite.
Similar minerals Augelite has a different crystal form; wavellite and crandallite are more acicular; calcite and aragonite effervesce when dabbed with diluted hydrochloric acid.

3 Gonnardite

Chem. formula $Na_2Ca[Al_2Si_3O_{10}]_2] \cdot 6\ H_2O$
Hardness 4½–5, **Sp. gr.** 2.25
Color White, colorless
Streak White
Luster Vitreous
Cleavage None
Fracture Fibrous
Tenacity Brittle
Crystal form Orthorhombic

Morphology Stellate aggregates and encrustations, fibrous, botryoidal, reniform.
Origin and occurrence Euhedral in cavities of volcanic rocks.
Accessory minerals Phillipsite, calcite, thomsonite, aragonite, chabazite.
Similar minerals Gonnardite cannot be distinguished from natrolite and scolecite using simple means; calcite and aragonite effervesce when dabbed with diluted hydrochloric acid.

4 Goyazit *Hamlinite*

Chem. formula $SrAl_3[(OH)_6/PO_4/PO_3OH]$
Hardness 4½, **Sp. gr.** 3.2
Color Colorless, white, yellow
Streak White
Luster Vitreous
Cleavage Basal perfect
Fracture Uneven
Tenacity Brittle
Crystal form Trigonal

Morphology Rhombohedral, more rarely pseudohexagonal crystals, euhedral.
Origin and occurrence In vugs of pegmatites and dolomites; on alpine fissures.
Accessory minerals Sphalerite, sulfosalt minerals, topaz, palermoite, goedkenite, apatite.
Similar minerals Whitlockite is softer; topaz and apatite harder; dolomite and calcite have different cleavage; calcite effervesces when dabbed with diluted hydrochloric acid.

Localities	
1 Mt. St. Hilaire, Montreal, Canada	**3** Schellkopf, Eifel Mountains, Germany
2 Diakouma, Senegal	**4** Minas Gerais, Brazil

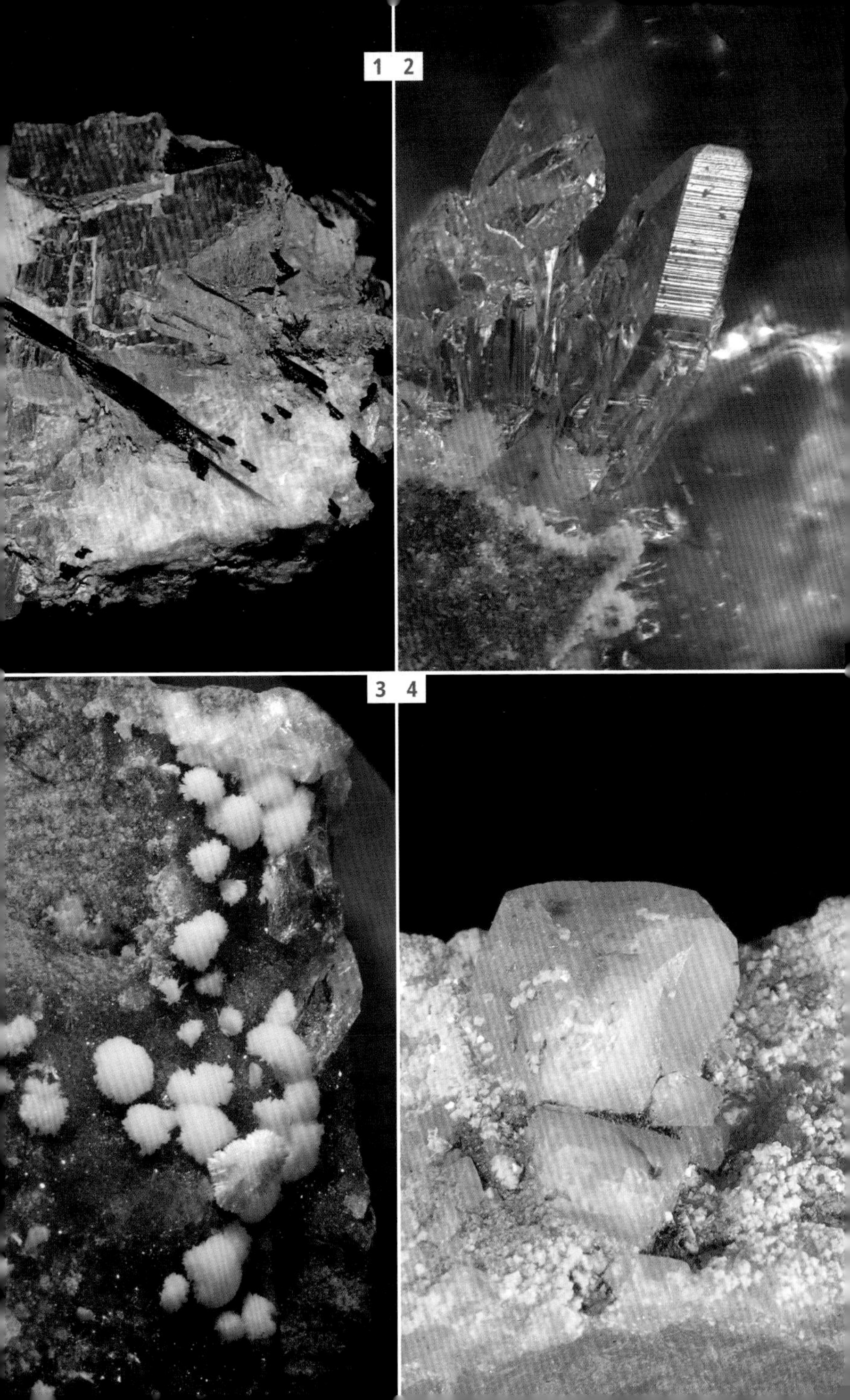
1 2
3 4

1 Okenite

Chem. formula $CaSi_2O_4(OH)_2 \cdot H_2O$
Hardness 4½–5, **Sp. gr.** 2.3
Color Colorless, white
Streak White
Luster Vitreous
Cleavage Indiscernible
Fracture Uneven, fibrous
Tenacity Brittle
Crystal form Triclinic

Morphology Acicular, rarely long tabular crystals, fine-acicular spheres (“cotton balls”) and stellate aggregates, botryoidal sheaves and aggregates.
Origin and occurrence In cavities of volcanic rocks.
Accessory minerals Prehnite, gyrolite, quartz, heulandite, stilbite, calcite.
Similar minerals The botryoidal acicular sheaves (photo) are characteristic, but otherwise okenite is indistinguishable from natrolite using simple means.

2 Hemimorphite *Calamine*

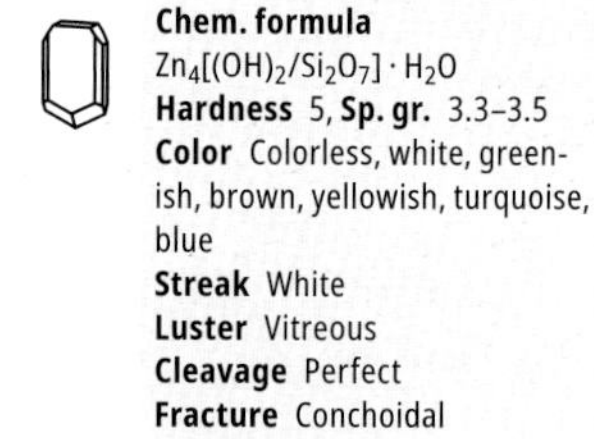

Chem. formula $Zn_4[(OH)_2/Si_2O_7] \cdot H_2O$
Hardness 5, **Sp. gr.** 3.3–3.5
Color Colorless, white, greenish, brown, yellowish, turquoise, blue
Streak White
Luster Vitreous
Cleavage Perfect
Fracture Conchoidal
Tenacity Brittle
Crystal form Orthorhombic

Morphology Crystals prismatic to acicular, tabular, aggregates radial, reniform, stalactitic, drusy.
Origin and occurrence In the oxidation zone of zinc deposits, where there is sufficient silica.
Accessory minerals Smithsonite, hydrozincite, aurichalcite, willemite, cerussite, limonite.
Similar minerals Barite is notably heavier; cerussite and anglesite have a different crystal form; unlike hemimorphite, aragonite effervesces when dabbed with diluted hydrochloric acid.

3 Mordenite

Chem. formula $(Ca,Na_2K_2)Al_2Si_{104} \cdot 7\ H_2O$
Hardness 4–5, **Sp. gr.** 2.15
Color Colorless, white
Streak White
Luster Vitreous
Cleavage Indiscernible
Fracture Fibrous
Tenacity Brittle
Crystal form Orthorhombic

Morphology Acicular crystals, acicular sheaves, fibrous, stellate aggregates, dense.
Origin and occurrence Euhedral in cavities of volcanic rocks.
Accessory minerals Chabazite, phillipsite, natrolite calcite, aragonite.
Similar minerals Natrolite is indistinguishable from mordenite by simple means; calcite and aragonite effervesce when dabbed with diluted hydrochloric acid.

4 Wardite

Chem. formula $NaAl_3[(OH)_4/(PO_4)_2] \cdot 2\ H_2O$
Hardness 5, **Sp. gr.** 2.81
Color Colorless, white, yellowish
Streak White
Luster Vitreous
Cleavage Basal perfect
Fracture Uneven
Tenacity Brittle
Crystal form Tetragonal

Morphology Octahedral bipyramids, euhedral, stellate aggregates.
Origin and occurrence In vugs of pegmatites, on fissures of phosphate-bearing sediments.
Accessory minerals Lazulite, variscite, whiteite, augelite, kulanite, gormanite, siderite.
Similar minerals Taking into consideration its phosphorus-rich paragenesis, the characteristic crystal form of wardite does not allow for any confusion; calcite effervesces when dabbed with diluted hydrochloric acid.

Localities	
1 Pune, India	**3** Coromandel, New Zealand
2 Mina Ojuela, Mapimi, Mexico	**4** Rapid Creek, Yukon Territory, Canada

1 2
3 4

1 Scheelite

Chem. formula $CaWO_4$
Hardness 4½–5, **Sp. gr.** 5.9–6.1
Color Colorless, white, yellowish gray, orange, brown, blue
Luster Greasy
Cleavage Mainly difficult to discern
Fracture Conchoidal
Tenacity Brittle
Crystal form Tetragonal

Morphology Mainly dipyramids, rarely basal, often uneven, granular aggregates.
Origin and occurrence In pegmatites, pneumatolytic veins, hydrothermal gold ore veins, on alpine fissures.
Accessory minerals Fluorite, quartz, tinstone, wolframite, molybdenite, beryl, topaz.
Distinguishing feature Scheelite fluoresces intensely when irradiated with ultraviolet light. The fluorescence color is dependent on the molybdenum content in scheelite. Scheelite without molybdenum fluoresces blue-white; a low molybdenum content produces a yellow fluorescent color, while a higher content can be recognized by an intense orange fluorescent color. Scheelite is an important tungsten ore with UV lamps often used in prospecting because they can detect even low scheelite content in the rock.
Similar minerals Anatase does not fluoresce and has a different luster; unlike scheelite, fluorite has perfect octahedral cleavage.

2–3 Apatite

Chem. formula $Ca_5[(F,Cl)/(PO_4)_3]$
Hardness 5, **Sp. gr.** 3.16–3.22
Color Colorless, yellow, blue, green, purple, red
Streak White
Luster Vitreous
Cleavage Basal sometimes distinct
Fracture Conchoidal
Tenacity Brittle
Crystal form Hexagonal

Morphology Crystals prismatic, long to short columnar, sometimes botryoidally anhedral and euhedral on many faces, aggregates acicular, radial, botryoidal, also uneven.
Origin and occurrence Microscopically in all igneous rocks, in unimpeded euhedral crystals on their fissures and in cavities, in pegmatites, alpine fissures, as concretions and deposits in sediments.
Accessory minerals Magnetite, anatase, rutile, leucite, beryl, muscovite, feldspar, calcite.
Distinguishing feature Sedimentary apatite deposits are often mined for fertilizer production.
Similar minerals Quartz, beryl and phenakite are harder; calcite, pyromorphite and mimetesite are softer.

4 Wolfeite

Chem. formula $(Fe,Mn)_2PO_4OH$
Hardness 5, **Sp. gr.** 3.79
Color Brown
Streak White
Luster Resinous
Cleavage Poor
Fracture Uneven
Tenacity Brittle
Crystal form Monoclinic

Morphology Radial aggregates, rarely prismatic crystals, uneven, anhedral.
Origin and occurrence In phosphate pegmatites as a primary formation with other primary phosphates.
Accessory minerals Hagendorfite, zwieselite, vivianite, arrojadite, triphyline.
Similar minerals Zwieselite is never radial; nevertheless, it is sometimes indistinguishable from wolfeite by simple means; the same applies to triplite; unlike wolfeite, graftonite exhibits good cleavage.

Localities	
1 Tae-Wha, Korea	**3** Kovdor, Kola, Russia
2 Nagar, Pakistan	**4** Hagendorf-Süd, East Bavaria, Germany

1
2
3
4

1

Triplite

Chem. formula $(Mn,Fe)_2(PO_4)F$
Hardness 5, **Sp. gr.** 3.5–3.8
Color Brown
Streak White
Luster Resinous
Cleavage Poor
Fracture Uneven
Tenacity Brittle
Crystal form Monoclinic

Morphology Uneven, anhedral, dense masses, extremely rarely anhedral crystals.
Origin and occurrence In phosphate pegmatites and pneumatolytic deposits.
Accessory minerals Feldspar, heterosite, quartz, triphyline, lithiophilite, wolfeite.
Similar minerals Wolfeite is often radial but otherwise difficult to distinguish from triplite by simple means; zwieselite can only be distinguished chemically; lithiophilite and triphyline exhibit good cleavage.

2

Goedkenite

Chem. formula $(Sr,Ca)_2Al(PO_4)_2(OH)$
Hardness 5, **Sp. gr.** 3.83
Color White, colorless
Streak White
Luster Vitreous
Cleavage Poorly discernible
Fracture Uneven
Tenacity Brittle
Crystal form Monoclinic

Morphology Tabular, sharp-edged crystals, often euhedral in rows on other phosphates.
Origin and occurrence In phosphate pegmatites as a late formation.
Accessory minerals Feldspar, childrenite, strunzite, siderite, whitlockite, quartz, apatite.
Similar minerals The wedge-shaped, sharp-edged crystal form and the parallel arrangement of the crystals of goedkenite are very characteristic.

3

Isokite

Chem. formula $CaMg(PO_4)F$
Hardness 5, **Sp. gr.** 3.15–3.28
Color Brown
Streak White
Luster Resinous
Cleavage Poor
Fracture Uneven
Tenacity Brittle
Crystal form Monoclinic

Morphology Uneven, anhedral, dense masses, white coatings on triplite.
Origin and occurrence In phosphate pegmatites and pneumatolytic deposits.
Accessory minerals Feldspar, heterosite, quartz, triphyline, lithiophilite, apatite, fluorite.
Similar minerals Isokite is indistinguishable from zwieselite and triplite using simple means; triphyline and lithiophilite have easily discernible cleavage.

4

Sellaite

Chem. formula MgF_2
Hardness 5, **Sp. gr.** 3.15
Color Colorless, white
Streak White
Luster Vitreous to silky
Cleavage Perfect
Fracture Uneven, fibrous
Tenacity Brittle
Crystal form Tetragonal

Morphology Prismatic to acicular crystals, acicular sheaves, stellate aggregates, encustations.
Origin and occurrence In evaporitic rocks, in volcanic ejecta, in hydrothermal fluorite deposits.
Accessory minerals Fluorite, topaz, jeremejevite, gypsum, magnesite, quartz, barite.
Similar minerals Sheaf-type topaz crystals always exhibit orthorhombic crystal symmetry; aragonite effervesces when dabbed with diluted hydrochloric acid.

Localities	
1 Branchville, Connecticut, USA	**3** Assuncao, Portugal
2 Palermo Mine, New Hampshire, USA	**4** Clara Mine, Black Forest, Germany

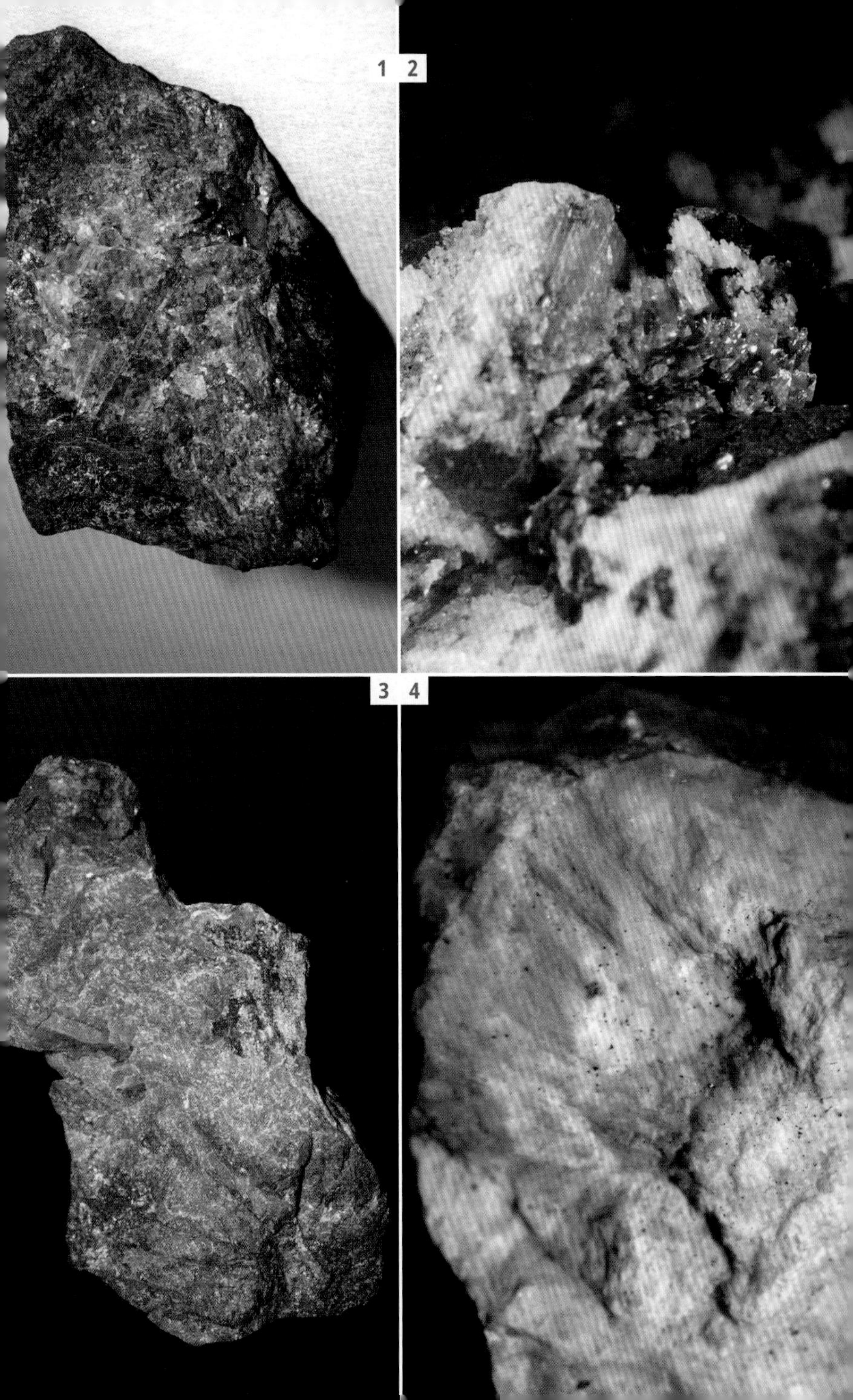
1
2
3
4

1 Vladimirite

Chem. formula $Ca_5H_2(AsO_4)_4 \cdot 5\,H_2O$
Hardness 5, **Sp. gr.** 3.15
Color Colorless, white
Streak White
Luster Vitreous to silky
Cleavage Indiscernible
Fracture Uneven, fibrous
Tenacity Brittle
Crystal form Monoclinic

Morphology Acicular crystals, acicular sheaves, stellate aggregates, encrustations.
Origin and occurrence In the oxidation zone of arsenic-rich deposits.
Accessory minerals Erythrite, talmessite, asenopyrite, löllingite, chloanthite.
Similar minerals Picropharmacolite is indistinguishable from vladimirite using simple means but is much more common; pharmacolite has good cleavage; aragonite effervesces when dabbed with diluted hydrochloric acid.

2 Talmessite

Chem. formula $Ca_2Mg(AsO_4)_2 \cdot 2\,H_2O$
Hardness 5, **Sp. gr.** 3.5
Color White, greenish, pink
Streak White
Luster Vitreous to dull
Cleavage None
Fracture Uneven
Tenacity Brittle
Crystal form Triclinic

Morphology Fibrous, stellate aggregates, reniform encrustations, dense, rarely long tabular crystals with oblique end faces.
Origin and occurrence In the oxidation zone of arsenic-rich deposits.
Accessory minerals Pharmacolite, picropharmacolite, erythrite, annabergite.
Similar minerals Picropharmacolite is difficult to distinguish from talmessite using simple means, but it has a brighter luster and is much softer.

3 Crandallite

Chem. formula $CaAl_3H[(OH)_6/(PO_4)_2] \cdot H_2O$
Hardness 5, **Sp. gr.** 2.78
Color Colorless, white, beige, yellowish
Streak White
Luster Vitreous
Cleavage Basal perfect but often indiscernible
Fracture Uneven
Tenacity Brittle
Crystal form Trigonal

Morphology Prismatic to acicular crystals with triangular end faces, stellate aggregates, suns.
Origin and occurrence On fissures of phosphorus-bearing sediments, in phosphorus-rich iron deposits.
Accessory minerals Fluellite, wavellite, strengite, rockbridgeite, cacoxenite, goethite.
Similar minerals Crandallite differs from wavellite due to its triangular end face; strengite has a different crystal form and is usually pink to purple; aragonite effervesces when dabbed with diluted hydrochloric acid.

4 Analcime

Chem. formula $Na[AlSi_2O_6] \cdot H_2O$
Hardness 5½, **Sp. gr.** 2.2–2.3
Color Colorless, white, reddish, orange, yellow
Streak White
Luster Vitreous
Cleavage Indiscernible
Fracture Conchoidal
Tenacity Brittle
Crystal form Cubic

Morphology Almost exclusively deltoid icositetrahedron, rarely cubic with beveled corners, also uneven, mainly euhedral.
Origin and occurrence In bubble cavities of volcanic rocks, on ore veins, in syenites and basalts also anhedral.
Accessory minerals Calcite, apophyllite, quartz, natrolite, heulandite, phillipsite.
Similar minerals Leucite in euhedral crystals is indistinguishable using simple means; apophyllite exhibits excellent cleavage.

Localities	
1 Irhtem, Morocco	**3** Blaton, Belgium
2 Markirch, Alsace, France	**4** Seiser Alm, South Tyrol, Italy

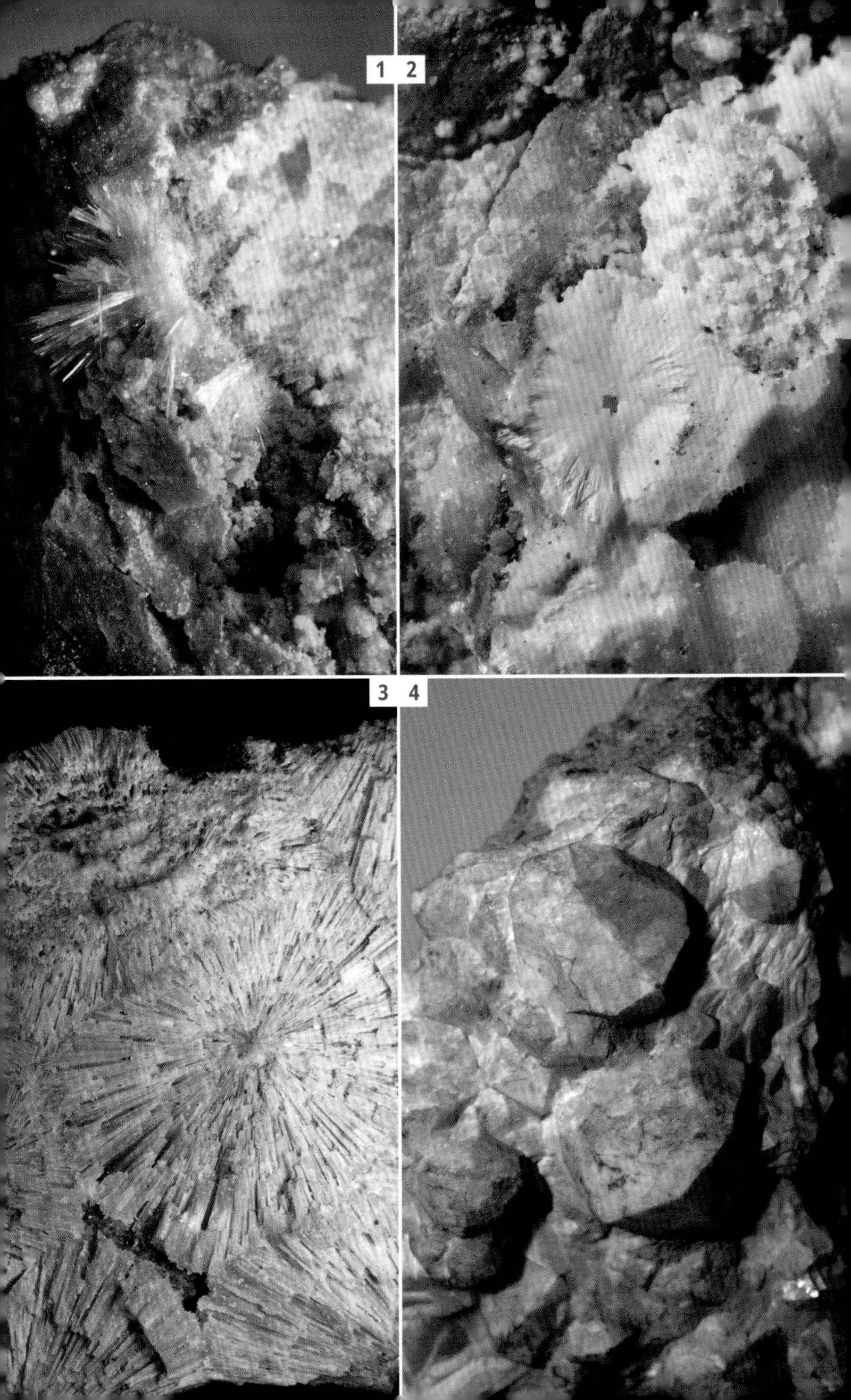
1
2
3
4

1 Eosphorite

Chem. formula $(Mn,Fe)AlPO_4(OH)_2 \cdot H_2O$
Hardness 5, **Sp. gr.** 3
Color Colorless, yellowish, brown
Streak White
Luster Vitreous
Cleavage None
Fracture Conchoidal
Tenacity Brittle
Crystal form Monoclinic

Morphology Prismatic, long tabular to acicular crystals, crystal sheaves, stellate aggregates.
Origin and occurrence In phosphate pegmatites, mainly euhedral in vugs.
Accessory minerals Quartz, feldspar, fairfieldite, zanazziite, siderite, apatite.
Similar minerals Eosphorite is indistinguishable from childrenite using simple means, otherwise unmistakable. Apatite is always distinctly hexagonal; aragonite effervesces when dabbed with diluted hydrochloric acid.

2 Childrenite

Chem. formula $(Fe,Mn)Al[(OH)_2/PO_4] \cdot H_2O$
Hardness 4½, **Sp. gr.** 3
Color Yellow to brown
Streak White
Luster Vitreous
Cleavage Mainly indiscernible
Fracture Conchoidal
Tenacity Brittle
Crystal form Monoclinic

Morphology Prismatic, long tabular crystals, stellate aggregates, crystal sheaves.
Origin and occurrence In phosphate pegmatites as a young formation in vugs.
Accessory minerals Quartz, feldspar, zanazziite, muscovite, apatite, siderite.
Similar minerals The manganese-rich end member eosphorite is indistinguishable by simple means; however, the two do not occur together; the crystals of apatite are clearly hexagonal.

3 Wagnerite

Chem. formula $(Mg,Fe)_2(PO_4)F$
Hardness 5, **Sp. gr.** 3.15
Color Yellowish, honey colors, orange, gray
Streak White
Luster Vitreous to resinous
Cleavage Indiscernible
Fracture Uneven, fibrous
Tenacity Brittle
Crystal form Monoclinic

Morphology Prismatic, elongated crystals, longitudinally striated, massive, uneven.
Origin and occurrence In metamorphic rocks in pegmatites.
Accessory minerals Lazulite, quartz, siderite, gypsum, cordierite, corundum, sillimanite.
Similar minerals Quartz is harder; gypsum is considerably softer; siderite has perfect rhombohedral cleavage; unlike wagnerite, aragonite effervesces when dabbed with diluted hydrochloric acid.

4 Thomsonite

Chem. formula $NaCa_2[Al_5Si_5O_{20}] \cdot 6\ H_2O$
Hardness 5–5½, **Sp. gr.** 2.3–2.4
Color Colorless, white
Streak White
Luster Vitreous
Cleavage Perfect
Fracture Uneven
Tenacity Brittle
Crystal form Orthorhombic

Morphology Prismatic, tabular, long tabular crystals, stellate, fibrous, botryoidal aggregates, often with a highly lustrous and smooth surface.
Origin and occurrence In bubble cavities of volcanic rocks.
Accessory minerals Natrolite, chabazite, phillipsite, apophyllite, calcite.
Similar minerals Unlike thomsonite, natrolite crystals have a square cross-section, but, nevertheless, they are often not easily distinguishable from thomsonite.

Localities	
1 Taquaral, Minas Gerais, Brazil	**3** Werfen, Salzburg, Austria
2 Linopolis, Minas Gerais, Brazil	**4** Marienberg, Aussig, Czech Republic

1 2
3 4

1

Carpholite *Straw stone*

Chem. formula $MnAl_2Si_2O_6(OH)_4$
Hardness 5–5½, **Sp. gr.** 3
Color Straw yellow, greenish yellow
Streak White
Luster Vitreous
Cleavage Perfect
Fracture Fibrous
Tenacity Brittle
Crystal form Orthorhombic

Morphology Fibrous, stellate aggregates, always anhedral, no unimpeded euhedral crystals.
Origin and occurrence In hydrothermal veins, in tin deposits.
Accessory minerals Quartz, fluorite.
Similar minerals The properties color and crystal form contribute to unmistakable identification of the mineral; tremolite is whiter, as is wollastonite; actinolite is intensely green; epidote is never as fibrously radial as carpholite; pectolite occurs in an entirely different paragenesis.

2

Datolite

Chem. formula $CaB[OH/SiO_4]$
Hardness 5–5½, **Sp. gr.** 2.9–3
Color Colorless, white, yellowish
Streak White
Luster Vitreous, on fracture surfaces greasy
Cleavage None
Fracture Conchoidal
Tenacity Brittle
Crystal form Monoclinic

Morphology Short prismatic to thick tabular crystals, granular, fibrous, reniform, uneven.
Origin and occurrence In bubble cavities of volcanic rocks, on ore veins, alpine fissures, in boron-rich skarn deposits.
Accessory minerals Apophyllite, stilbite, heulandite, pectolite.
Similar minerals Calcite is softer and effervesces when dabbed with diluted hydrochloric acid; apophyllite is softer and has a different luster as well as perfect cleavage; danburite exhibits a different cleavage.

3

Microlite

Chem. formula $(Na,Ca)_2Ta_2O_6(O,OH,F)$
Hardness 5–5½, **Sp. gr.** 5.9–6.4
Color Yellow, orange, reddish
Streak White
Luster Vitreous
Cleavage None
Fracture Conchoidal
Tenacity Brittle
Crystal form Cubic

Morphology Mainly octahedral, rarely cubic, anhedral and euhedral.
Origin and occurrence In carbonatites, pegmatites and volcanic ejecta.
Accessory minerals Biotite, cancrinite, nepheline, lepidolite.
Similar minerals Its typical paragenesis makes microlite unmistakable; anatase has mainly euhderal crystals and exhibits steeper pyramidal faces; magnetite is black and very magnetic; pyrochlore is indistinguishable by simple means.

4

Zwieselite

Chem. formula $(Fe,Mn)_2(PO_4)F$
Hardness 5, **Sp. gr.** 3.89–3.97
Color Brown
Streak White
Luster Resinous
Cleavage Poor
Fracture Uneven
Tenacity Brittle
Crystal form Monoclinic

Morphology Uneven, anhedral, dense masses, extremely rarely anhedral crystals.
Origin and occurrence In phosphate pegmatites and pneumatolytic deposits.
Accessory minerals Feldspar, heterosite, quartz, triphyline, lithiophilite, wolfeite.
Similar minerals Wolfeite is often radial, but otherwise difficult to distinguish from zwieselite by simple means; triplite can only be distinguished chemically; lithiophilite and triphyline exhibit good cleavage.

Localities	
1 Wippra, Saxony, Germany	**3** Minas Gerais, Brazil
2 Teis, South Tyrol, Italy	**4** Hagendorf-Süd, East Bavaria, Germany

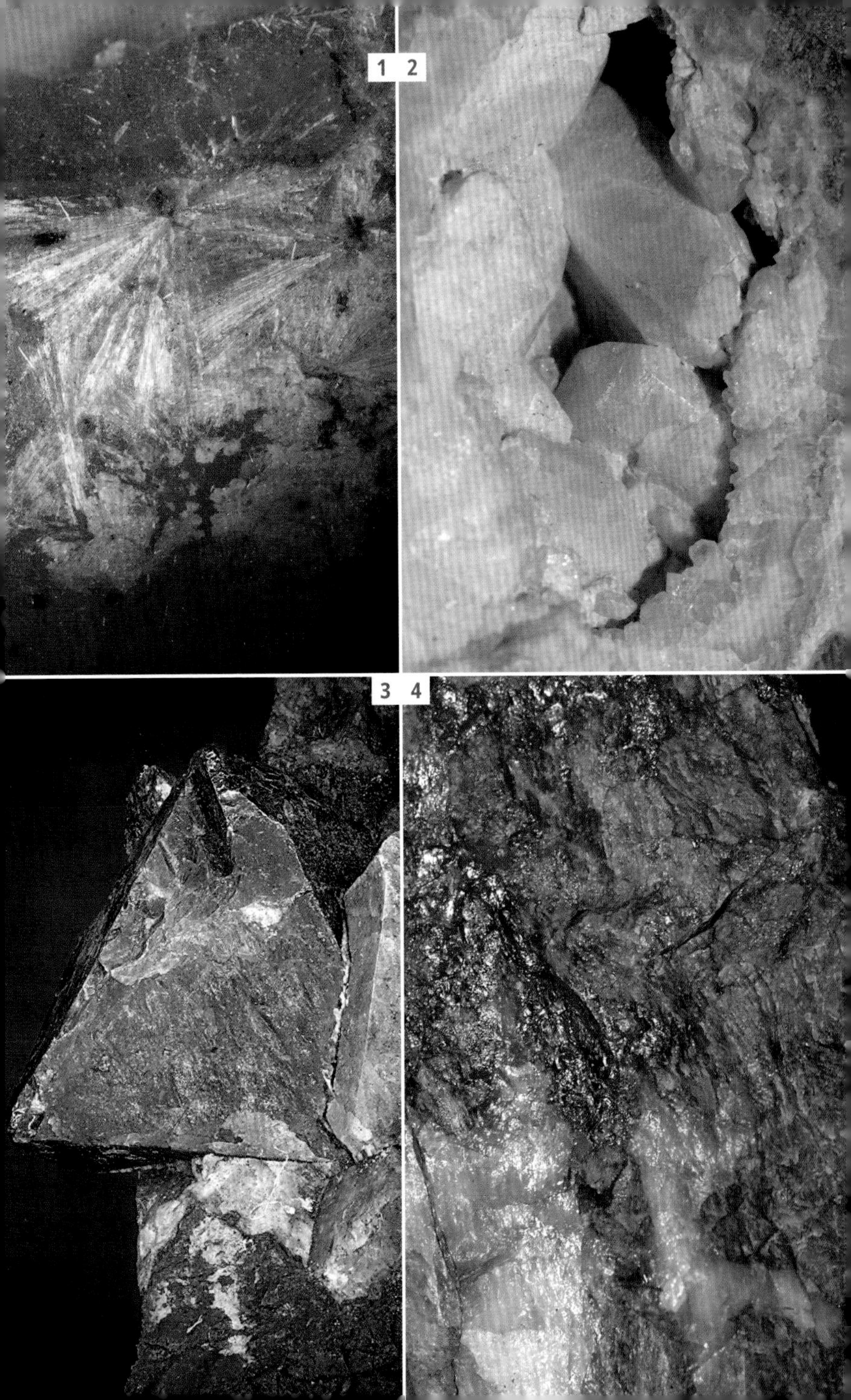
1 2
3 4

1–2 Titanite *Sphene*

Chem. formula $CaTi[O/SiO_4]$
Hardness 5–5½, **Sp. gr.** 3.4–3.6
Color Colorless, white, yellow, greenish, red, brown, black-brown, blue
Streak White
Luster Resinous
Cleavage Difficult to discern
Fracture Conchoidal
Tenacity Brittle
Crystal form Monoclinic

Morphology Euhedral crystals tabular to prismatic, often cruciform twins with re-entrant angles, more rarely isometric, envelope-shaped anhedral crystals.
Origin and occurrence Anhedral in many igneous rocks and crystalline schists, euhedral crystals in alpine fissures, particularly in amphibolites, in pegmatites, anhedral in marbles.
Accessory minerals Quartz, feldspar, anatase, rutile, brookite, calcite, graphite, hornblende, apatite.
Distinguishing feature The name sphene (ancient Greek word for wedge) was given to the mineral because its euhedral crystals on alpine fissures are often wedge-shaped.
Similar minerals Anatase is clearly tetragonal; monazite glows green when irradiated with unfiltered UV light.

3 Scolezite

Chem. formula $Ca[Al_2Si_3O_{10}] \cdot 3\,H_2O$
Hardness 5½, **Sp. gr.** 2.26–2.4
Color Colorless, white
Streak White
Luster Vitreous
Cleavage Perfect, but poorly discernible on acicular crystals
Fracture Conchoidal
Tenacity Brittle
Crystal form Monoclinic

Morphology Crystals acicular to prismatic, sheaved to stellate aggregates, almost always euhedral, rarely anhedral.
Origin and occurrence On fissures of granites and syenites, on alpine fissures, in bubble cavities of volcanic rocks.
Accessory minerals Apophyllite, laumontite, stilbite, heulandite, calcite, quartz, prehnite.
Similar minerals Natrolite is generally slightly more finely fibrous and more restricted to volcanic rocks, but otherwise almost indistinguishable from scolecite by simple means; aragonite effervesces when dabbed with diluted hydrochloric acid.

4 Natrolite

Chem. formula $Na_2[Al_2Si_3O_{10}] \cdot 2\,H_2O$
Hardness 5–5½, **Sp. gr.** 2.2–2.4
Color Colorless, white, yellowish
Streak White
Luster Vitreous
Cleavage Perfect, but almost never discernible due to its structure
Fracture Conchoidal
Tenacity Brittle
Crystal form Orthorhombic

Morphology Crystals prismatic, rarely with easily visible end faces, often long prismatic to acicular, stellate to botryoidal aggregates, fibrous encrustations, mainly euhedral, rarely anhedral.
Origin and occurrence In bubble cavities of volcanic rocks, in syenites and nepheline syenites.
Accessory minerals Phillipsite, analcime, chabazite, calcite, aragonite.
Similar minerals Scolecite is difficult to distinguish from natrolite, but it is rarer and often occurs in a different paragenesis; unlike natrolite, aragonite effervesces when dabbed with diluted hydrochloric acid.

Localities	
1 Habach Valley, Austria	**3** Hollersbach Valley, Austria
2 Dodo, Polar Urals, Russia	**4** Salesel, Aussig, Czech Republic

1 2
3 4

1

Herderite

Chem. formula $CaBe[(F,OH)/PO_4]$
Hardness 5, **Sp. gr.** 2.8–3
Color Colorless, white, yellowish, purple
Streak White
Luster Vitreous
Cleavage None
Fracture Conchoidal
Tenacity Brittle
Crystal form Monoclinic

Morphology Prismatic, thick tabular crystals, usually euhedral, rarely uneven.
Origin and occurrence Euhedral in the vugs of pegmatites.
Accessory minerals Topaz, tourmaline, apatite, feldspar, quartz, euclase.
Similar minerals Apatite has a distinct hexagonal symmetry; topaz and quartz are harder; feldspar has a different cleavage; tourmaline has a different crystal form, as does euclase.

2

Eudialyte

Chem. formula $Na_4(Ca,Fe,Ce)_2ZrSi_6O_{17}(OH)_2$
Hardness 5–5½, **Sp. gr.** 2.8
Color Yellowish brown, red-brown, pink, red
Streak White
Luster Vitreous to greasy
Cleavage None
Fracture Conchoidal
Tenacity Brittle
Crystal form Trigonal

Morphology Thick tabular, prismatic to isometric crystals, mainly anhedral, often uneven.
Origin and occurrence In alkaline rocks, also as an essential mineral.
Accessory minerals Zircon, nepheline, feldspar, aegirine, apatite, astrophyllite.
Distinguishing feature Rocks with a high content of intensely red eudialyte are visually very attractive and are sometimes used to make handicraft items.
Similar minerals Considering the paragenesis and characteristic color of eudialyte, there is no possibility of confusion; garnet is much harder; feldspar has perfect cleavage; nepheline usually has a different color.

3–4

Monazite

Chem. formula $CePO_4$
Hardness 5–5½, **Sp. gr.** 4.9–5.5
Color Colorless, orange, brown transparent, brown to dark brown opaque
Streak White
Luster Vitreous to greasy
Cleavage Sometimes distinct
Fracture Conchoidal
Tenacity Brittle
Crystal form Monoclinic

Morphology Thick tabular to prismatic crystals, rarely uneven, euhedral and anhedral.
Origin and occurrence Distributed microscopically in magmatites, large crystals and inclusions in pegmatites, in placers, on alpine fissures (in this case, clear transparent crystals).
Accessory minerals Quartz, feldspar, xenotime, rutile, zircon, hematite.
Distinguishing feature Monazite, particularly the enriched monazite sand found in placers, is often industrially mined. It serves as a raw material for cerium and also thorium, which is present in small amounts in many monazites, particularly those found in pegmatites and igneous rocks.
Similar minerals Titanite has a different crystal form; xenotime is clearly tetragonal; rutile has very good cleavage and is more metallic; gadolinite has a greenish streak.
Caution! Monazite, particularly monazite sand and monazite from pegmatites, may be radioactive!

Localities	
1 Zufurt Quarry, Fichtel Mountains, Bavaria, Germany	**3** Sweden
2 Ilimaussaq, Greenland	**4** Binntal, Valais, Switzerland

1
2
3
4

1 Nosean

Chem. formula $Na_8(Al_6Si_6O_{24})(SO_4) \cdot H_2O$
Hardness 5½, **Sp. gr.** 2.3
Color White, beige, gray, brown, black
Streak White
Luster Vitreous to greasy
Cleavage None
Fracture Conchoidal
Tenacity Brittle
Crystal form Cubic

Morphology Rhombic dodecahedral, hexagonal columns (twins), uneven, anhedral.
Origin and occurrence Essential mineral of volcanic rocks, in volcanic ejecta.
Accessory minerals Sanidine, biotite, zircon, allanite, hauyne, apatite, pyroxene.
Similar minerals Zircon is clearly tetragonal; hauyne is usually blue; apatite is never so characteristically gray; calcite effervesces when dabbed with diluted hydrochloric acid.

2 Milarite

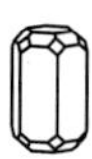

Chem. formula $K_2Ca_4Al_2Be_4Si_{24}O_{60} \cdot H_2O$
Hardness 5½–6, **Sp. gr.** 2.52
Color Colorless, white, yellow
Streak White
Luster Vitreous
Cleavage None
Fracture Uneven
Tenacity Brittle
Crystal form Hexagonal

Morphology Well-formed hexagonal prisms, often planar, euhedral, stellate aggregates.
Origin and occurrence In pegmatites as an alteration product of beryl, on alpine fissures, in low-temperature hydrothermal deposits.
Accessory minerals Feldspar, quartz, bavenite, bertrandite, fluorite, phenakite, muscovite.
Similar minerals The crystal form is very characteristic; beryl is distinctly harder, as is quartz, which also has a different crystal form.

3 Hureaulite

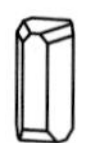

Chem. formula $(Mn,Fe)_5H_2[PO_4]_4 \cdot 4\,H_2O$
Hardness 5, **Sp. gr.** 3.2
Color Pink, reddish, brownish, yellow, white, colorless
Streak White
Luster Vitreous
Cleavage None
Fracture Uneven
Tenacity Brittle
Crystal form Monoclinic

Morphology Crystals prismatic, with oblique end faces, tabular, aggregates radial, uneven.
Origin and occurrence In phosphate pegmatites, in vugs and cavities.
Accessory minerals Rockbridgeite, phosphoferrite, reddingite, strengite, mitridatite, phosphosiderite.
Similar minerals Strengite and phosphosiderite have a different crystal form, as does apatite; quartz and feldspar are harder than hureaulite.

4 Soerensenite

Chem. formula $Na_4SnBe_2Si_6O_{16}(OH)_4$
Hardness 5½, **Sp. gr.** 2.9
Color White, pink
Streak White
Luster Vitreous
Cleavage Poor
Fracture Uneven
Tenacity Brittle
Crystal form Monoclinic

Morphology Long tabular crystals, mainly anhedral, radial aggregates.
Origin and occurrence Anhedral in alkaline rocks.
Accessory minerals Analcime, nepheline, neptunite, aegirine, eudialyte.
Similar minerals Considering its paragenesis, it is difficult to mistake soerensenite for another mineral; actinolite is always greenish and has perfect cleavage with a 120° cleavage angle; the same applies to tremolite which is rather white.

Localities	
1 In den Dellen Quarries, Eifel Mountains, Germany	**3** Mangualde, Portugal
2 Habach Valley, Austria	**4** Ilimaussaq, Greenland

1 2
3 4

1 Willemite

Chem. formula $Zn_2[SiO_4]$
Hardness 5½, **Sp. gr.** 4
Color Colorless, white, yellow, greenish, gray, brown
Streak White
Luster Greasy vitreous
Cleavage None
Fracture Splintery
Tenacity Brittle
Crystal form Trigonal

Morphology Short to long prismatic crystals, stellate, reniform aggregates, granular, uneven.
Origin and occurrence In the oxidation zone of zinc deposits, in metamorphic zinc deposits.
Distinguishing feature Willemite fluoresces with a yellow-green color under UV light.
Accessory minerals Zincite, franklinite, hydrozincite, cerussite.
Similar minerals Calcite, pyromorphite, mimetesite and vanadinite are softer; the same applies to cerussite; calcite effervesces when dabbed with diluted hydrochloric acid.

2 Bavenite

Chem. formula $Ca_4Al_2Be_2[(OH)_2/Si_{96}]$
Hardness 5½, **Sp. gr.** 2.7
Color Colorless, white
Streak White
Luster Vitreous, pearly on cleavage faces
Cleavage Perfect
Fracture Foliated
Tenacity Brittle
Crystal form Orthorhombic

Morphology Thick and thin tabular to acicular crystals, often grouped into roses, felty, foliated, powdery, uneven, euhedral, as pseudomorphs after beryl.
Origin and occurrence In vugs of pegmatites, on alpine fissures.
Accessory minerals Milarite, bityite, bertrandite, stilbite, feldspar, quartz.
Similar minerals Stilbite and laumonite have a different crystal form; tremolite is harder; the paragenisis of bavenite with other beryllium minerals is characteristic.

3 Perovskite

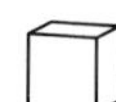

Chem. formula $CaTiO_3$
Hardness 5½, **Sp. gr.** 4–4.8
Color Pitch black, various brown tones ranging from black- to yellow-brown, opaque to translucent
Streak White to gray
Luster Greasy, metallic
Cleavage Moderate to good
Fracture Uneven to conchoidal
Tenacity Brittle
Crystal form Orthorhombic

Morphology Pseudocubic crystals, sometimes crystal skeletons, dendritic aggregates, anhedral and euhedral, also uneven, fine crystalline masses.
Origin and occurrence As an accessory mineral in alkaline rocks and their pegmatites, in carbonatites, in many basalts, on their fissures and in cavities, at the contact of the cited rocks with limestones, in crystalline schists, on fissures of serpentinites.
Accessory minerals Nepheline, melilite, magnetite, clinochlore.
Similar minerals Magnetite is magnetic and has a black streak; black garnet (melanite) is harder.

4 Brazilianite

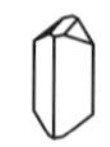

Chem. formula $NaAl_3[(OH)_2/PO_4]_2$
Hardness 5½, **Sp. gr.** 2.98
Color Yellow to whiteish
Streak White
Luster Vitreous
Cleavage Perfect, parallel to the longitudinal extension
Fracture Uneven
Tenacity Brittle
Crystal form Monoclinic

Morphology Prismatic to thick tabular crystals, euhedral, uneven, anhedral.
Origin and occurrence In vugs of pegmatites, as an alteration product of primary phosphates.
Accessory minerals Muscovite, albite, microcline, quartz, apatite, augelite, lazulite.
Similar minerals Topaz and albite are harder; the cleavage parallel to its longitudinal extension is very characteristic; euclase is much harder; herderite has a different crystal form; calcite effervesces when dabbed with diluted hydrochloric acid.

Localities	
1 Berg Aukas, Namibia	**3** Urals, Russia
2 Madrid, Spain	**4** Consolheiro Pena, Minas Gerais, Brazil

1
2
3
4

1 **Turquoise**

Chem. formula $CuAl_6[(OH)_2/PO_4]_4 \cdot H_2O$
Hardness 6, **Sp. gr.** 2.91
Color Turquoise blue, more rarely greenish, often with black veining; opaque
Streak White
Luster Waxy to dull
Fracture Uneven
Crystal form Triclinic

Morphology Tiny crystals, mainly reniform, nodular, uneven.
Origin and occurrence In the oxidation zone of copper deposits, as seams and veins in phosphorus-rich shales.
Accessory minerals Quartz, limonite, malachite, chrysocolla.
Similar minerals Its color and paragenesis make turquoise unmistakable; malachite and chrysocolla are more greenish; magnesite is white.

2 **Turquoise**

Gemstone

Shape and cut Cabochon cut, spheres, baroque stones

Use Cabochons are used for ring stones as well as for brooches and pendants. Baroque stones and spheres, or beads, are used to make necklaces.
Treatment Turquoise is often porous and crumbly; it is solidified by impregnation with synthetic resin. Tiny turquoise particles and powder can be used to make stones through compression with synthetic resin. Nodular magnesite can be transformed into a turquoise-like material through coloring.
Differentiating possibilities Turquoise impregnated or solidified with synthetic resin has a distinct scratch mark and a distinct resin odor when scratched with a red-hot needle. Colored magnesite is softer and changes color when dabbed with hydrochloric acid.

3 **Cancrinite**

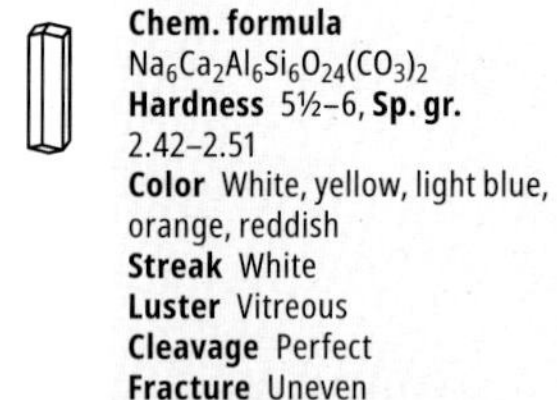

Chem. formula $Na_6Ca_2Al_6Si_6O_{24}(CO_3)_2$
Hardness 5½–6, **Sp. gr.** 2.42–2.51
Color White, yellow, light blue, orange, reddish
Streak White
Luster Vitreous
Cleavage Perfect
Fracture Uneven
Tenacity Brittle
Crystal form Hexagonal

Morphology Rarely long prismatic crystals with pyramidal ends, usually crystalline, uneven, massive, almost always anhedral.
Origin and occurrence In alkaline rocks and their pegmatites, also an alteration product of nepheline.
Accessory minerals Nepheline, sodalite, feldspar, zircon, natrolite, melanite.
Similar minerals Feldspar has a different cleavage; nepheline exhibits almost no cleavage.

4 **Tremolite** *Grammatite*

Chem. formula $Ca_2Mg_5[OH/Si_4O_{11}]_2$
Hardness 5½–6, **Sp. gr.** 2.9–3.1
Streak White
Color White to pale green
Luster Vitreous
Cleavage Indiscernible
Fracture Fibrous
Tenacity Brittle
Crystal form Monoclinic

Morphology Long prismatic crystals, columnar, radial, almost always anhedral.
Origin and occurrence In marbles, dolomites, talc schists.
Accessory minerals Calcite, dolomite.
Similar minerals Unlike tremolite, wollastonite decomposes upon contact with hydrochloric acid; actinolite is always notably green; strontianite is softer; aragonite effervesces when dabbed with diluted hydrochloric acid.

Localities	
1 Isfahan, Iran	**3** Urals, Russia
2 Arizona, USA	**4** Campolungo, Ticino, Switzerland

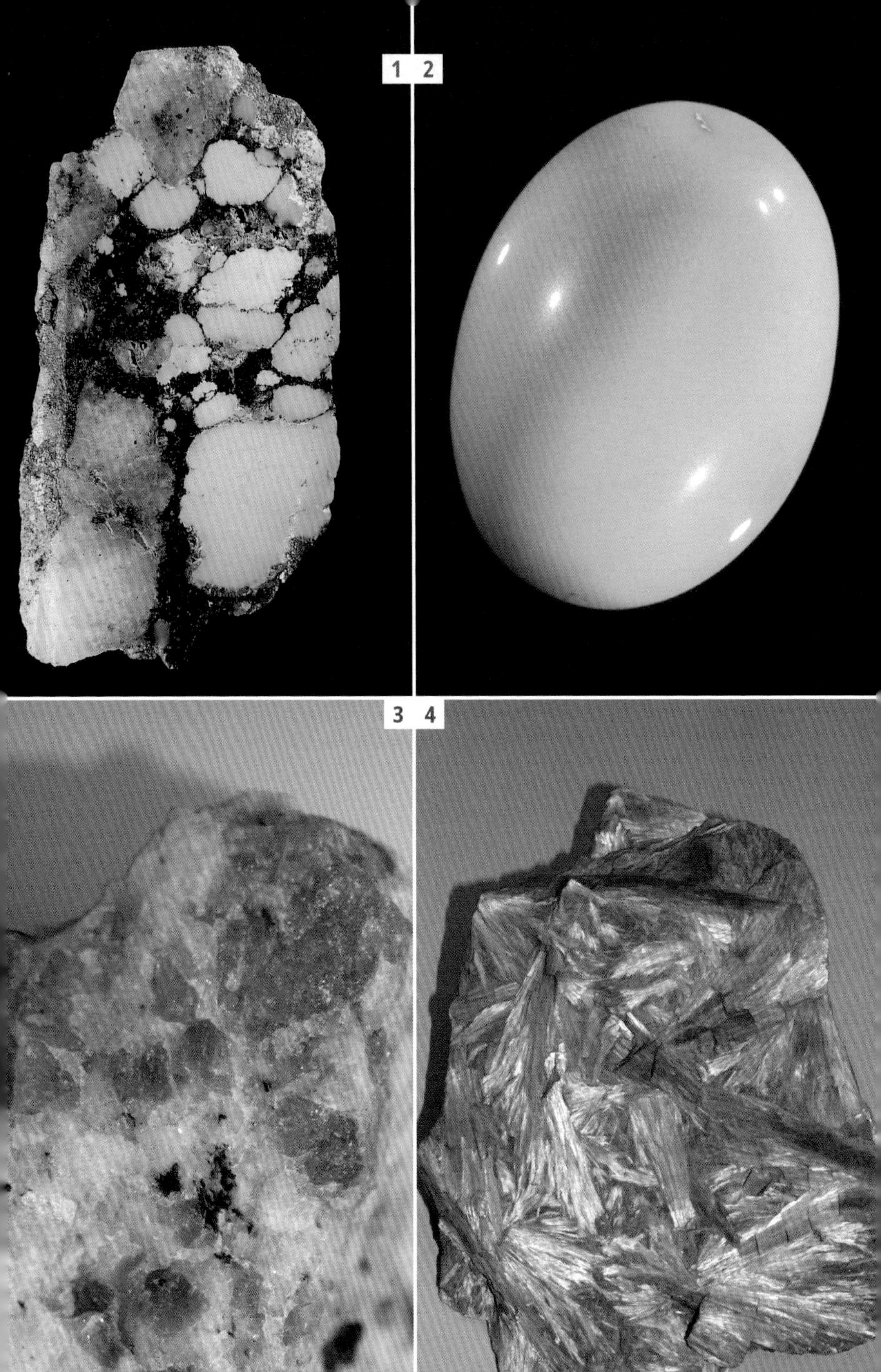
1 2
3 4

1 Pyrochlore

Chem. formula $(Na,Ca,U)_2(Nb,Ti,Ta)_2O_6(OH,F,O)$
Hardness 5½–6, **Sp. gr.** 4.3–6.4
Color Yellow, orange, reddish
Streak White
Luster Vitreous
Cleavage None
Fracture Conchoidal
Tenacity Brittle
Crystal form Cubic

Morphology Mainly octahedral, rarely cubic, anhedral and euhedral.
Origin and occurrence In carbonatites, pegmatites and volcanic ejecta.
Accessory minerals Calcite, biotite, cancrinite, feldspar, nepheline, lepidolite.
Similar minerals Its typical paragenesis makes pyrochlore unmistakable; anatase has mainly euhderal crystals and exhibits steeper pyramidal faces; magnetite is black and very magnetic.

2 Beryllonite

Chem. formula $NaBePO_4$
Hardness 5½–6, **Sp. gr.** 2.8
Color Colorless, white
Streak White
Luster Vitreous
Cleavage Perfect
Fracture Conchoidal
Tenacity Brittle
Crystal form Monoclinic

Morphology Thick tabular crystals, often lenticular-rounded, almost always hexagonal triplet structures.
Origin and occurrence In pegmatites, euhedral and anhedral, in beryllium-rich skarns.
Accessory minerals Tourmaline, albite, quartz, beryl, phenakite, muscovite.
Similar minerals Apatite does not have perfect cleavage; phenakite is harder, as is beryl; quartz exhibits no cleavage; calcite effervesces when dabbed with diluted hydrochloric acid.

3 Anatase

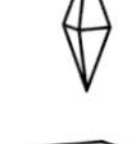

Chem. formula TiO_2
Hardness 5½–6, **Sp. gr.** 3.8–3.9
Color Colorless, pink, red, yellow, blue, brown, black, green
Streak White
Luster Metallic to adamantine
Cleavage Mainly indistinct
Fracture Uneven
Tenacity Brittle
Crystal form Tetragonal

Morphology Pointed to flat bipyramids, tabular crystals, almost exclusively euhedral, often horizontally striated.
Origin and occurrence Euhedral in alpine fissures, anhedral in argillaceous rocks, sandstones.
Accessory minerals Brookite, rutile, titanite, quartz, feldspar, magnetite, calcite, chlorite.
Similar minerals Magnetite and hematite have a black or red streak; brookite exhibits a different crystal form; scheelite fluoresces intensely when irradiated with ultraviolet light.

4 Amblygonite

Chem. formula $(Li,Na)Al[(F,OH)/PO_4]$
Hardness 6, **Sp. gr.** 3–3.1
Color White, yellow, bluish, greenish, gray
Streak White
Luster Vitreous
Cleavage Good in four different directions
Fracture Uneven
Tenacity Brittle
Crystal form Triclinic

Morphology Euhedral crystals rare, mainly crystalline, radial, granular, anhedral.
Origin and occurrence Almost always anhedral in pegmatites, rarely euhedral, in pneumatolytic tin ore veins.
Accessory minerals Apatite, tinstone, feldspar, spodumene.
Similar minerals Uneven feldspar is sometimes indistinguishable from amblygonite by simple means; spodumene has a different cleavage; apatite is softer; calcite effervesces when dabbed with diluted hydrochloric acid.

Localities	
1 Minas Gerais, Brazil	**3** Grieswies, Rauris, Austria
2 Newry, Maine, USA	**4** Viitaniemi, Finland

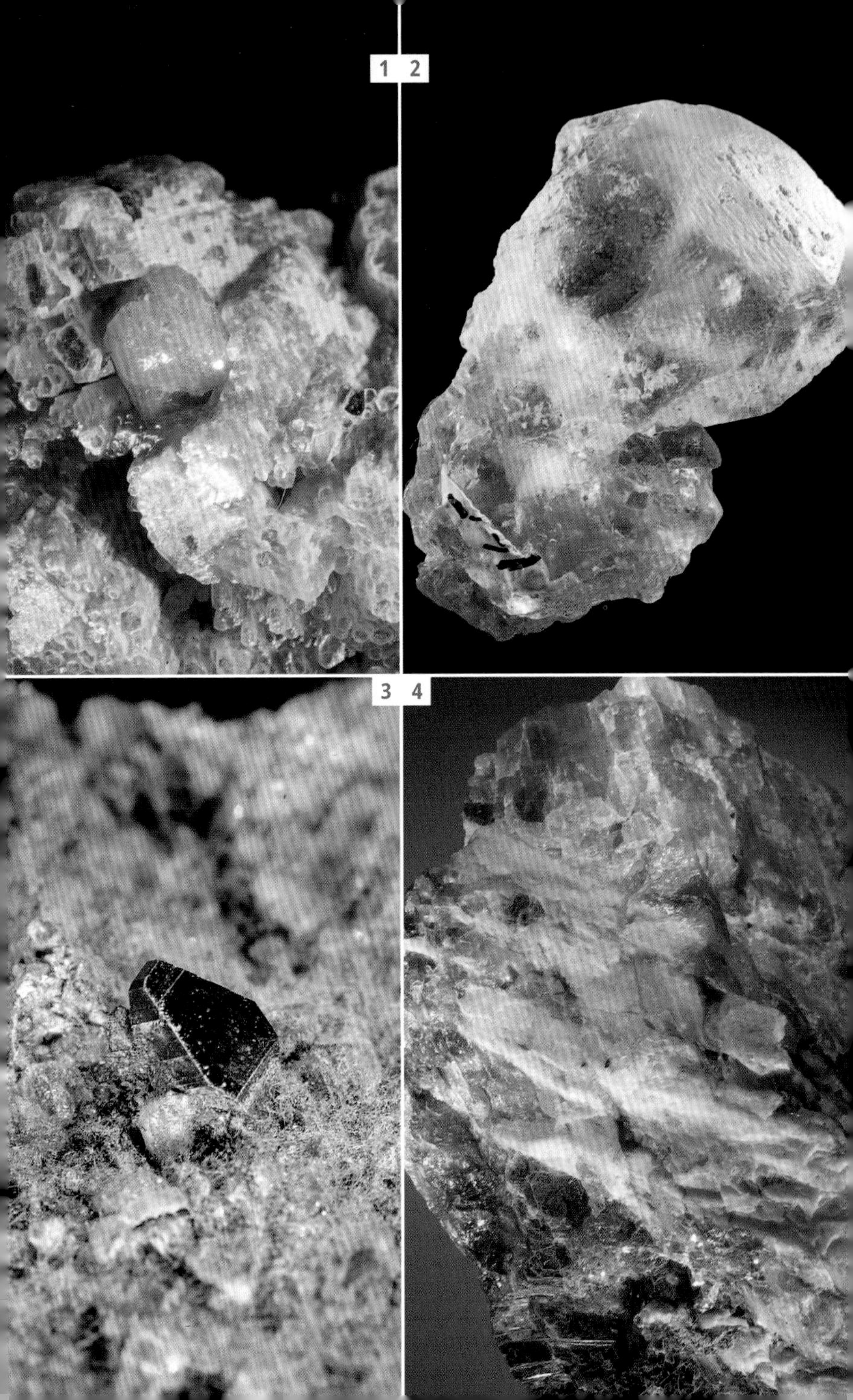
1 2
3 4

1 Anthophyllite

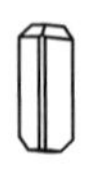

Chem. formula $(Mg,Fe)_7Si_{82}(OH)_2$
Hardness 5½–6, **Sp. gr.** 2.8–3.6
Color White, gray, greenish
Streak White
Luster Vitreous
Cleavage Perfect
Fracture Fibrous
Tenacity Brittle
Crystal form Orthorhombic

Morphology Prismatic crystals very rare, mainly stellate, fibrous aggregates, asbestiform.
Origin and occurrence Anhedral in metamorphic rocks or as fissure filling.
Accessory minerals Feldspar, mica.
Similar minerals Actinolite is indistinguishable from anthophyllite using simple means; the same applies to tremolite; the asbestos form differs from chrysotile due to its brittleness.

2 Diopside

Chem. formula $CaMg[Si_2O_6]$
Hardness 6, **Sp. gr.** 3.3
Color Colorless, white, green, blue, yellow, brown
Streak White
Luster Vitreous
Cleavage Discernible, cleavage angle about 90°
Fracture Uneven
Tenacity Brittle
Crystal form Monoclinic

Morphology Prismatic crystals, columnar, radial, columnar aggregates, uneven.
Origin and occurrence In intrusive igneous rocks, marbles, calc-silicate country rocks, on alpine fissures.
Accessory minerals Calcite, grossular, olivine, feldspar, quartz.
Similar minerals Hornblende has a different cleavage angle; epidote has a different crystal form and a very characteristic color; carpholite is always characteristically radial and clearly softer.

3 Inesite

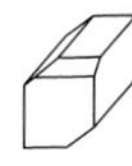

Chem. formula $Ca_2Mn_7Si_{10}O_{28}(OH)_2 \cdot 5\,H_2O$
Hardness 5½, **Sp. gr.** 3
Color Pink to red
Streak White
Luster Vitreous
Cleavage Perfect
Fracture Uneven
Tenacity Brittle
Crystal form Triclinic

Morphology Sharp-edged tabular to acicular crystals, stellate aggregates.
Origin and occurrence In metamorphic manganese deposits together with other manganese minerals.
Accessory minerals Rhodochrosite, rhodonite, spessartine, hausmannite, braunite.
Similar minerals Rhodochrosite does not have such sharp-edged crystals; rhodonite is often indistinguishable by simple means; however, it is never acicular.

4 Hiortdahlite

Chem. formula $(Ca,Na)_{13}Zr_3Si_9(O,OH)_{33}$
Hardness 5½, **Sp. gr.** 3.2
Streak White
Color Yellow, yellow brown
Luster Vitreous
Cleavage Poor
Fracture Uneven
Tenacity Brittle
Crystal form Triclinic

Morphology Tabular to long tabular crystals and columns, anhedral, very rarely euhedral.
Origin and occurrence In alkaline rocks, in volcanic ejecta.
Accessory minerals Feldspar, nepheline.
Similar minerals Melinophane and woehlerite are indistinguishable from hiortdahlite by simple means; feldspar has good cleavage; aegirine has perfect cleavage with a 120° cleavage angle.

Localities	
1 Paala, Finland	**3** Trinity County, California, USA
2 Skardu, Pakistan	**4** Risöya, Norway

1 2
3 4

1–2 Brookite *Arkansite*

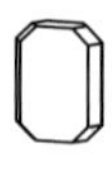

Chem. formula TiO_2
Hardness 5½–6, **Sp. gr.** 4.1
Color Brown, greenish to blackish, usually translucent
Streak Light brownish to white
Luster Adamantine
Cleavage Indiscernible
Fracture Uneven
Tenacity Brittle
Crystal form Orthorhombic

Morphology Thin tabular crystals, longitudinally striated, often with a dark hourglass pattern (1), rarely apparently hexagonal dipyramids (2).
Origin and occurrence On alpine fissures, in cavities of alkaline rocks.
Accessory minerals Anatase, rutile, quartz, feldspar, hematite, titanite.
Distinguishing feature Brookite exhibits two completely different structures. Thin tabular brown, mainly longitudinally striated crystals occur on alpine fissures, often exhibiting a characteristic hourglass pattern (Fig. 1). In other deposits, brookite forms jet-black crystals resembling hexagonal bipyramids (Fig. 2). This variety is called arkansite.
Similar minerals Hematite has a different streak; anatase is always clearly tetragonal; the thin tabular crystals with hourglass markings are unmistakable.

3 Lazulite *Blue spar*

Chem. formula $(Mg,Fe)Al_2[OH/PO_4]_2$
Hardness 5–6, **Sp. gr.** 3
Color Light to dark blue
Streak White
Luster Vitreous to greasy
Cleavage Mainly indiscernible
Fracture Splintery
Tenacity Brittle
Crystal form Monoclinic

Morphology Prismatic, pointed pyramdial tabular crystals, anhedral and euhedral, uneven.
Origin and occurrence In quartzites, more rarely in pegmatites.
Accessory minerals Quartz, wagnerite.
Distinguishing feature Due to its beautiful blue color, massive deposits are locally cut into jewelry (cabochons) or made into handicraft items.
Similar minerals Vivianite is softer; azurite is a darker blue and occurs in a very different paragenesis; it also has a blue streak; blue beryl is significantly harder; kulanite is greener; cordierite is significantly harder; lasurite occurs in a very different paragenesis.

4 Leucite

Chem. formula $KAlSi_2O_6$
Hardness 5½–6, **Sp. gr.** 2.5
Color Colorless, white
Streak White
Luster Vitreous
Cleavage None
Fracture Uneven
Tenacity Brittle
Crystal form Tetragonal

Morphology Pseudocubic, deltoid icositetrahedron, almost always anhedral, sometimes transformed into feldspar or argillaceous minerals while retaining its crystal form (pseudomorphs after leucite).
Origin and occurrence In volcanic rocks, basalts, tephrites, leucitites, often formed in beautiful euhedral crystals.
Accessory minerals Augite, biotite.
Similar minerals Analcime has mainly euhedral crystals but is otherwise difficult to distinguish; leucite is never pink; nepheline has a different crystal form; sanidine exhibits perfect cleavage; quartz is harder and has a different crystal form.

Localities	
1 Maderaner Tal, Switzerland	**3** Werfen, Salzburg, Austria
2 Magnet Cove, Arkansas, USA	**4** Vesuvius, Italy

1 2
3 4

1

Sodalite

Chem. formula $Na_8[Cl_2/(AlSiO_4)_6]$
Hardness 5–6, **Sp. gr.** 2.3
Color Colorless, white, gray, blue
Streak White
Luster Vitreous, on the fracture greasy
Cleavage Mainly indistinct
Fracture Conchoidal
Tenacity Brittle
Crystal form Cubic

Morphology Rarely rhombic dodecahedral, anhedral and euhedral, mainly uneven, massive, granular.
Origin and occurrence Essential mineral in syenites, basalts, phonolites, tephrites, in volcanic ejecta, crystals on fissures of the mentioned rocks.
Accessory minerals Nepheline, hematite, pseudobrookite, augite, hornblende.
Similar minerals Leucite and analcime exhibit a different crystal form; hauyne and lasurite are always a lighter blue than blue sodalite.

2

Sodalite

Gemstone

Color Colorless, white, gray, dark blue, with purple tinges; opaque.
Luster Vitreous; greasy on fractures.
Shape and cut Cabochon cut, spheres, baroque pearls

Use Cabochons as ring stones or for brooches and pendants, spheres, necklaces. Arts and crafts items, rocks with blue sodalite as the essential mineral are used as decorative stones in architecture.
Differentiating possibilities Lapis lazuli is more inky blue and almost always exhibits golden yellow pyrite inclusions, which sodalite lacks; azurite is distinctly softer and effervesces when dabbed with diluted hydrochloric acid.

3

Nepheline *Elaeolite*

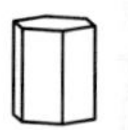

Chem. formula $KNa_3[AlSiO_4]_4$
Hardness 5½–6, **Sp. gr.** 2.6–2.65
Color Colorless, white, yellowish
Streak White
Luster Vitreous
Cleavage Mainly indiscernible
Fracture Conchoidal
Tenacity Brittle
Crystal form Hexagonal

Morphology Prismatic to short columnar crystals, granular masses, uneven.
Origin and occurrence In low-silica rocks and volcanic ejecta, on fissures of volcanic rocks.
Accessory minerals Melilite, apatite, augite, magnetite, phlogopite, feldspar.
Similar minerals Apatite is somewhat softer, located in the fissures of volcanic rocks; it is clearly more acicular than nepheline; calcite effervesces when dabbed with diluted hydrochloric acid.

4

Hauyne

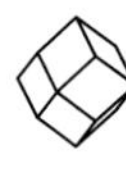

Chem. formula $(Na,Ca)_{8-4}[(SO_4)_{2-1}/(AlSiO_4)_6]$
Hardness 5–6, **Sp. gr.** 2.5
Color Colorless, white, gray, mainly deep blue, transparent to translucent
Streak White
Luster Vitreous
Cleavage Poorly distinct
Fracture Conchoidal
Tenacity Brittle
Crystal form Cubic

Morphology Crystals mainly rhombic dodecahedra, anhedral and euhedral, rarely hexagonal prisms (formation of twins), granular, uneven.
Origin and occurrence Essential mineral in phonolites, basalts, in volcanic ejecta.
Accessory minerals Sanidine, nepheline, leucite, augite, hornblende, biotite, titanite.
Similar minerals Sodalite, in the same paragenesis, is not usually blue; hauyne is barely distinguishable from lapis lazuli in the same paragenesis, but, in volcanic rocks, blue hauyne is unmistakable.

Localities	
1 Kaokoveld, Namibia	**3** Langesundfjord, Norway
2 Brazil	**4** Tayarapu, Tahiti

1 2
3 4

1

Franzinite

Chem. formula $(Na,Ca)_7(Si,Al)_{12}O_{24}(SO_4,CO_3,OH,Cl)_3 \cdot H_2O$
Hardness 5, **Sp. gr.** 2.5
Color White
Streak White
Luster Vitreous
Cleavage None
Fracture Uneven
Tenacity Brittle
Crystal form Hexagonal

Morphology Crystals lenticular, tabular, anhedral and euhedral, granular, uneven.
Origin and occurrence In volcanic ejecta and inclusions.
Accessory minerals Pyroxene, grossular, vesuvianite, feldspar, pyroxene, fassaite.
Similar minerals Sanidine has perfect cleavage; leucite and analcime have a different crystal form; calcite effervesces when dabbed with diluted hydrochloric acid.

2

Humite

Chem. formula $(Mg,Fe)_7(SiO_4)_3(F,OH)_2$
Hardness 6, **Sp. gr.** 3.3–3.32
Color Orange to brown
Streak White
Luster Vitreous
Cleavage Poor
Fracture Uneven
Tenacity Brittle
Crystal form Orthorhombic

Morphology Planar, isometric crystals, uneven, granular, anhedral.
Origin and occurrence In metamorphic limestone, in volcanic ejecta.
Accessory minerals Spinel, forsterite, graphite, diopside, calcite, chondrodite.
Similar minerals Humite is indistinguishable from clinohumite and chondrodite by simple means; otherwise its color and paragenesis are very characteristic.

3

Clinohumite

Chem. formula $Mg_9Si_4O_{16}(F,OH)_2$
Hardness 6, **Sp. gr.** 3.3
Color Orange
Streak White
Luster Vitreous
Cleavage Poor
Fracture Uneven
Tenacity Brittle
Crystal form Monoclinic

Morphology Planar, isometric crystals, uneven, granular, anhedral.
Origin and occurrence In metamorphic limestone, in volcanic ejecta.
Accessory minerals Spinel, forsterite, graphite, diopside, calcite, chondrodite.
Similar minerals Humite is indistinguishable from clinohumite and chondrodite by simple means; otherwise its color and paragenesis are very characteristic.

4

Chondrodite

Chem. formula $(Mg,Fe)_5(SiO_4)_2(F,OH)_2$
Hardness 6–6½, **Sp. gr.** 3.16–3.26
Color Orange to brown
Streak White
Luster Vitreous
Cleavage Poor
Fracture Uneven
Tenacity Brittle
Crystal form Monoclinic

Morphology Planar, isometric crystals, uneven, granular, anhedral.
Origin and occurrence In metamorphic limestone, in volcanic ejecta.
Accessory minerals Spinel, forsterite, graphite, diopside, calcite, clinohumite.
Similar minerals Chondrodite is indistinguishable from clinohumite and humite by simple means; otherwise its color and paragenesis are very characteristic.

Localities	
1 Pitigliano, Tuscany, Italy	**3** Juanar, Marbella, Spain
2 Monte Somma, Vesuvius, Italy	**4** Franklin, New Jersey, USA

1
2
3
4

1

Opal

Chem. formula $SiO_2 \cdot n\, H_2O$
Hardness 5–6½, **Sp. gr.** 1.9–2.2
Color Colorless, transparent (hyalite), whiteish, bluish with a play of colors (precious opal), red to orange, translucent (fire opal), green, red, brown, yellow, opaque (common opal)
Streak White
Luster Waxy to vitreous, sometimes an iridescent play of colors
Cleavage None
Fracture Conchoidal
Tenacity Brittle
Crystal form Amorphic

Morphology Uneven anhedral, as vug filling, reniform, botryoidal, drop-shaped aggregates.
Origin and occurrence In cavities of volcanic rocks, in sediments at the water table level, as deposition from hot springs (geyserite).
Accessory minerals Zeolites, chalcedony, agate, quartz, calcite.
Distinguishing feature In contrast to the almost chemically identical quartz, opal is amorphous and does not have a regular crystal structure. It consists of tiny silica spherules arranged in a more or less regular pattern. If the spherules are irregularly arranged, they form what is known as the "common opal," which does not exhibit any color play; if it is colorless and transparent, it is called hyalite. If spherules are arranged in a very regular pattern, the light hitting the opal scatters from them, creating a multi-colored color play.
Similar minerals Chalcedony can be formed in a similar manner and is then indistinguishable by simple means; precious opal is distinguished by its play of colors.

2–4

Opal

Gemstone

Color Colorless, white, red (fire opal), brown, black, often with a colorful play of colors (precious opal); transparent to opaque
Luster Vitreous
Cut shape Cabochon cut, often with free shaping to display the valuable precious opal in the best possible manner; transparent fire opal is also facet cut

Precious opal from Australia

Use Due to its high value and the sensitivity of the stone, it is used mainly as a center stone in brooches and pendants, in doublets or triplets also for rings.
Treatment Thin small layers are cut from small pieces and are then underlaid with a layer of other, normally dark, material. The stones produced in this way are called doublets. They are significantly less valuable than pure opals. If these doublets are then further glued over with a flat, transparent cabochon, for example of rock crystal, to protect them against damage, the resulting product is called a triplet. An extraordinarily valuable, untreated precious opal is very delicate. Opals are sensitive to heat, which means that opal jewelry should never be exposed to the sun, nor kept in the glove compartment of a car, for example. In heat or drought, the opal loses its water content and, with it, its color play. It can be restored by placing it in water, but, once removed from the water, it disappears again. This is why inexpensive precious opals are often presented in small water bowls; once back at home, it is considerably disappointing when the main part of the color play disappears as the stone dries.
Differentiating possibilities Common opal is often indistinguishable from jasper; precious opals are distinctive on account of their color play; rhodochrosite is much softer than fire opal.

Localities	
1 Valec, Czech Republic	**3** Australia
2 Australia	**4** Australia

1 2
3 4

1 Rhodonite

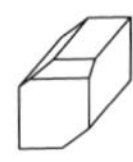

Chem. formula $CaMn_4[Si_5O_{15}]$
Hardness 5½–6½, **Sp. gr.** 3.73
Color Pink, blood red, brown-red, deep red
Streak White
Luster Vitreous
Cleavage Perfect
Fracture Uneven
Tenacity Brittle
Crystal form Triclinic

Morphology Tabular (often sharply tabular) to prismatic crystals, crystalline, uneven.
Origin and occurrence In metamorphic manganese deposits, ore veins.
Accessory minerals Rhodochrosite, quartz, spessartine, galena.
Similar minerals Rhodochrosite is softer; feldspar has a different cleavage and is never so intensely red; spessartine has no cleavage and exhibits browner to orange tones; axinite is never red but more brown-purple; babingtonite is always black.

2 Rhodonite

Gemstone

Color Pink, red, deep red, often with black veins
Luster Vitreous
Shape and cut Cabochon cut, spheres

Use Cabochons as ring stones and for brooches, pendants, spheres for stone necklaces, also often as handicraft items.
Differentiation Due to its color and typical black veining, it is impossible to confuse rhodonite with any other gemstone or semi-precious stone.

3 Gorceixite

Chem. formula $BaAl_3(PO_4)_2(OH)_5 \cdot H_2O$
Hardness 6, **Sp. gr.** 3.3
Color White, brown
Streak White
Luster Vitreous
Cleavage None
Fracture Conchoidal
Tenacity Brittle
Crystal form Trigonal

Morphology Tabular crystals, reniform, stellate aggregates, granular, uneven.
Origin and occurrence In sedimentary phosphate deposits, in pegmatites.
Accessory minerals Lazulite, wardite, goyazite, feldspar, augelite, brazilianite.
Similar minerals Augelite has a different crystal form; goyazite is slightly softer; calcite effervesces when dabbed with diluted hydrochloric acid and is much softer.

4 Scapolite

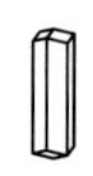

Solid solution series with end members
Marialite $Na_8[(Cl_2,SO_4,CO_3)/(AlSi_3O_8)_6]$ und
Mejonite $Ca_8[(Cl_2,SO_4,CO_3)_2/(Al_2Si_2O_8)_6]$
Hardness 5–6½, **Sp. gr.** 2.54–2.77
Color Colorless, white, yellowish, greenish, bluish, reddish, purple
Streak White
Luster Vitreous
Cleavage Perfect
Fracture Conchoidal
Tenacity Brittle
Crystal form Tetragonal

Morphology Prismatic crystals, columnar, stellate aggregates, granular.
Origin and occurrence In contact deposits and volcanic ejecta, on alpine fissures, in metamorphic rocks.
Accessory minerals Muscovite, calcite, sanidine, biotite, apatite, titanite.
Similar minerals Calcite is trigonal and softer; it effervesces when dabbed with diluted hydrochloric acid; zircon is harder; vesuvianite has no cleavage; apatite is clearly hexagonal; quartz is harder; feldspar has a different crystal form and exhibits a different cleavage; nepheline has a different crystal form; tremolite has perfect cleavage with a cleavage angle of 120°.

Localities	
1 Harstigen, Sweden	**3** Rapid Creek, Yukon Territory, Canada
2 Australia	**4** New York, USA

1 2

3 4

1–2 Potassium feldspar *Sanidine, orthoclase, microcline*

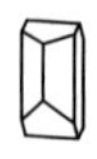

Chem. formula $K[AlSi_3O_8]$
Hardness 6, **Sp. gr.** 2.53–2.56
Color Colorless, white, yellow, brown, blood-red, green
Streak White
Luster Vitreous
Cleavage Basal pinacoidal perfect, transverse pinacoidal less perfect
Fracture Conchoidal
Tenacity Brittle
Crystal form Monoclinic (sanidine and orthoclase) and triclinic (microcline)

Audular coated with chlorite

Morphology Prismatic, thick and thin tabular (sanidine), also rhombohedral (adularia), often twins with re-entrant angles, often uneven in large masses, euhedral crystals in pegmatites (microcline).
Origin and occurrence Essential mineral in granites, syenites, trachytes, rhyolites, gneisses, arkoses, graywackes, pegmatites, euhedral crystals on alpine fissures (especially adularia) and as gangue in hydrothermal veins (paradoxite).
Accessory minerals Quartz, muscovite, biotite, plagioclase, garnet, tourmaline and many others.
Distinguishing feature Potassium feldspar often forms intergrown twin crystals. Interpenetration twins with re-entrant angles, often anhedral in porphyritic granites, are called Carlsbad twins after one of their localities, which was where Johann Wolfgang von Goethe first described them. Other twin types are named after the traditionally accepted discovery locality, Manebach (after Manebach in Thuringia) (see Fig. 1) and Baveno twins (after Baveno in Northern Italy).
Similar minerals When uneven, potassium feldspar and plagioclase are difficult to distinguish; the crystals are unmistakable. Quartz exhibits no cleavage; calcite, barite, gypsum and dolomite are softer.

3–4 Potassium feldspar

Gemstone

Color Blood red, green (amazonite), orange iridescent (sunstone), white, partly milky with bluish glint (moonstone)
Luster Vitreous, silky
Shape and cut Cabochon cut, spheres

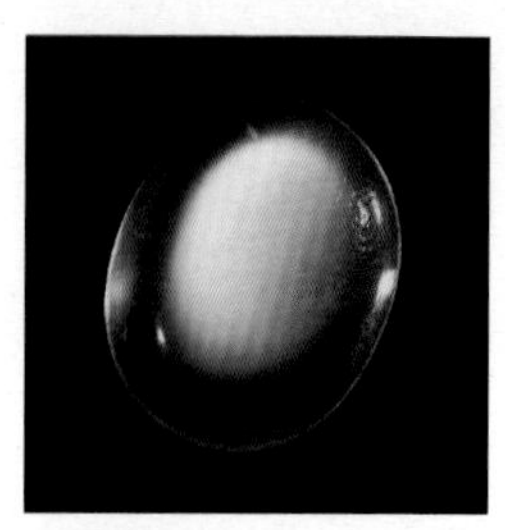

Moonstone as a cabochon

Use Cabochons as ring stones and for brooches, pendants, spheres for stone necklaces, also often as handicraft items, particularly from amazonite.
Distinguishing feature For a long time, the reason behind the green coloring of amazonite was disputed. Now we know that a tiny amount of lead is responsible. Amazonite is found almost exclusively in pegmatites. The characteristically oriented flame-shaped solid solution lamellae of white albite (see Fig. 4) clearly shows that amazonite is a potassium feldspar.
Differentiation The color of amazonite and the iridescent hue of moonstone are very characteristic, preventing any confusion.

Localities	
1 Baveno, Italy	**3** Striegau, Poland
2 Pikes Peak, Colorado, USA	**4** Minas Gerais, Brazil

1 2
3 4

1–2 Plagioclase

Chem. formula $(Na,Ca)[(Al,Si)_2Si_2O_8]$
Hardness 6–6½, **Sp. gr.** 2.61–2.77
Color Colorless, white, greenish, reddish, gray
Streak White
Luster Vitreous
Cleavage Perfect, cleavage angle 90°
Fracture Conchoidal
Tenacity Brittle
Crystal form Triclinic

Cabochon of spectrolite

Morphology Prismatic to tabular, often twinned, often uneven.
Origin and occurrence Essential mineral in igneous and metamorphic rocks, depending on the silicon content of the rocks in different albite-orthite mixture ratios; in pegmatites, however, much more rarely than potassium feldspar here, in volcanic ejecta, in contact rocks, on alpine fissures, in ore veins, in meteorites.
Accessory minerals Potassium feldspar, quartz, biotite, muscovite, augite, hornblende, epidote, diopside, actinolite.
Distinguishing feature The plagioclases form a solid solution series with the two end members albite $Na[Al_{S}i_3O_8]$ (Fig. 1) and anorthite $Ca[Al_2Si_2O_8]$ (Fig. 2). The intermediate members have different names depending on the mixing ratio:

Oligoclase	70–90 % albite
Andesine	50–70 % albite
Labradorite	30–50 % albite
Bytownite	10–30 % albite

Porcelain white albite twinned according to a specific twin law, the Pericline Law, is called pericline (Fig. 4). It occurs almost exclusively on alpine crevasses.
Similar minerals Quartz exhibits no cleavage; calcite, barite, gypsum and dolomite are softer; potassium feldspar has different crystal forms and the typical Carlsbad twinning that does not occur in plagioclase.

3–4 Plagioclase

Gemstone

Color Blue to variegated hue on dark background (labradorite and spectrolite).
Luster Vitreous
Shape and cut Cabochon cut, spheres

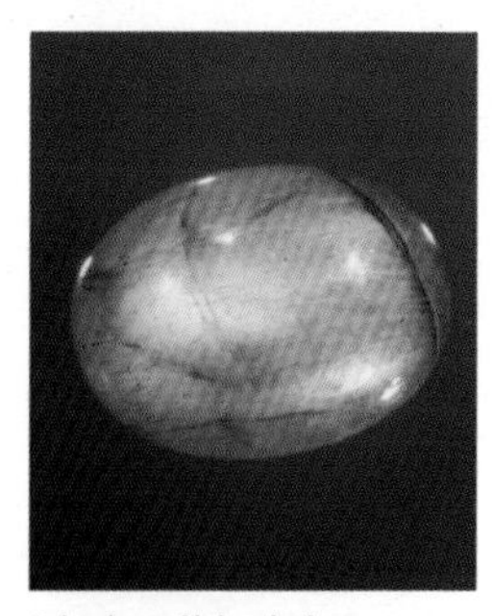

Cabochon of labradorite

Use Cabochons as ring stones and for brooches, pendants, spheres for stone necklaces, also often as handicraft items, particularly from labradorite. Rocks rich in iridescent feldspars, such as larvikite from Norway, are used as decorative rocks in construction and for the manufacturing of headstones.
Distinguishing feature Labradorite gets its name from its occurrence on the Labrador Peninsula. However, the varying color shimmer, or iridescence, is not limited to plagioclases of labra-dorite composition. Other plagioclases, for example andesine or bytownite, can also exhibit this iridescent color play. It is created by the interference of light on extremely thin twin lamellae.
Differentiation The iridescent colors on a dark background are high characteristic, preventing any confusion.

Localities	
1 Val Bedretto, Switzerland	**3** Madagascar
2 Monzoni, South Tyrol, Italy	**4** Pfitschtal, South Tyrol, Italy

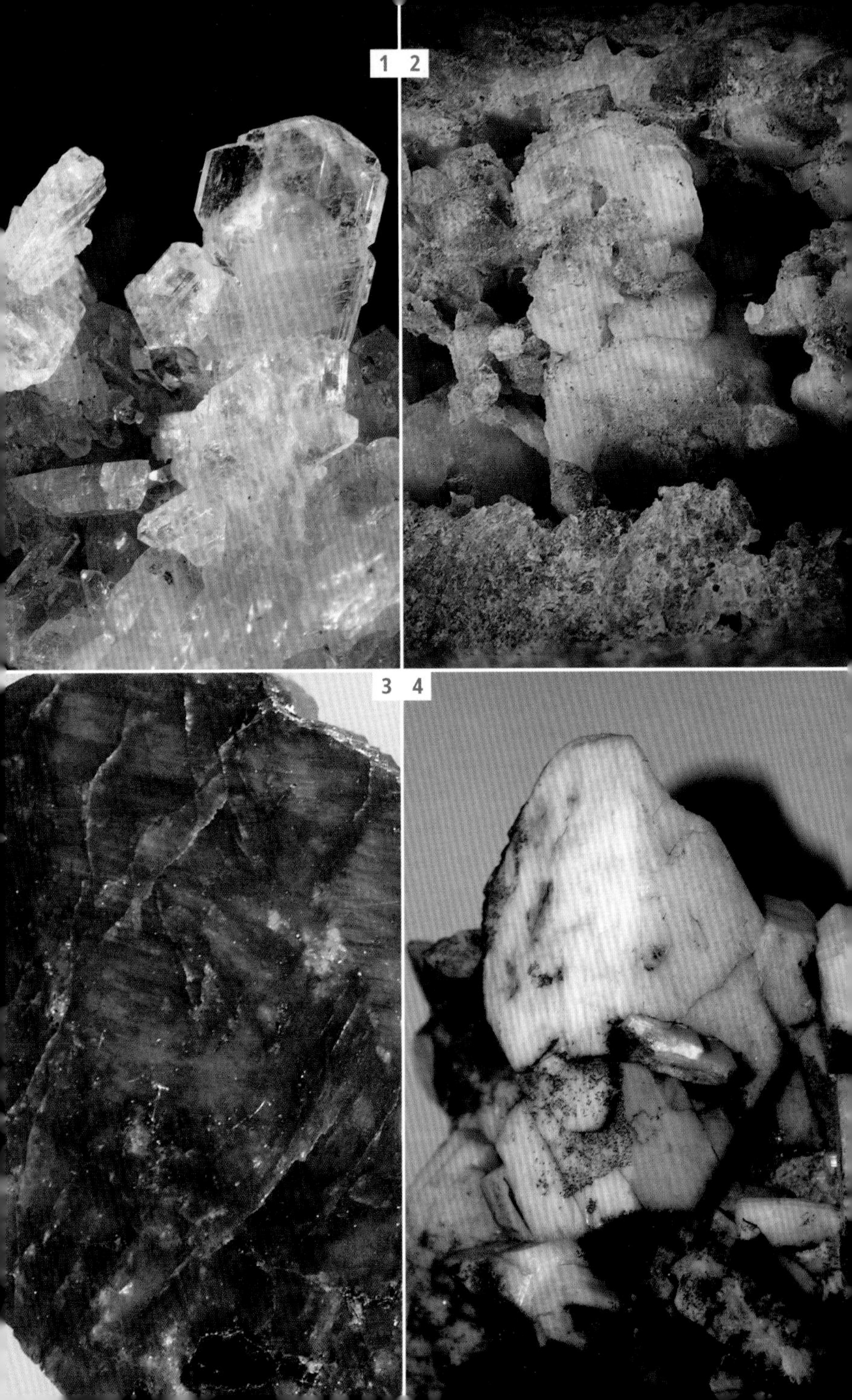
1 2
3 4

1 Melilite

Chem. formula $(Ca,Na)_2(Mg,Al,Fe)[Si_2O_7]$
Hardness 5–5½, **Sp. gr.** 2.9–3
Color Colorless, yellow, brown, red
Streak Whitish
Luster Vitreous on fresh fractures and greasy in weathered state
Cleavage Indiscernible
Fracture Conchoidal
Tenacity Brittle
Crystal form Tetragonal

Morphology Cubic-like to tabular crystals, euhedral, often uneven, anhedral.
Origin and occurrence Essential mineral in many volcanic rocks, on their fissures also as euhedral crystals.
Accessory minerals Nepheline, magnetite, augite, apatite, perovskite, olivine, pseudobrookite.
Similar minerals The paragenesis makes melilite unmistakable; chabazite is softer; calcite effervesces when dabbed with diluted hydrochloric acid.

2 Benitoite

Chem. formula $BaTi[Si_3O_9]$
Hardness 6½, **Sp. gr.** 3.7
Color Pale to deep blue, occasionally pink
Streak White
Luster Vitreous
Cleavage None
Fracture Conchoidal
Tenacity Brittle
Crystal form Trigonal

Morphology Flat dipyramidal crystals, anhedral, often artificially free-etched.
Origin and occurrence Anhedral in hydrothermal natrolite veins.
Accessory minerals Natrolite, neptunite, joaquinite, andradite, actinolite.
Similar minerals The color and crystal form of benitoite prevent any confusion; its paragenesis in natrolite veins together with neptunite is absolutely unmistakable.

3 Hyalophane

Chem. formula $(K,Ba)(Al,Si)_2Si_2O_8$
Hardness 6½, **Sp. gr.** 2.6–2.9
Color White, yellow
Streak White
Luster Vitreous
Cleavage Perfect
Fracture Uneven
Tenacity Brittle
Crystal form Monoclinic

Morphology Tabular to prismatic crystals, crystalline masses, uneven.
Origin and occurrence In volcanic rocks, hydrothermal deposits.
Accessory minerals Dolomite, barite, quartz, muscovite, goyazite, titanite.
Similar minerals Hyalophane is indistinguishable from potassium feldspar by simple means; quartz exhibits no cleavage; calcite effervesces when dabbed with diluted hydrochloric acid.

4 Prehnite

Chem. formula $Ca_2Al[(OH)_2/AlSi_3O_{10}]$
Hardness 6–6½, **Sp. gr.** 2.8–3
Color Colorless, white, yellowish, green
Streak White
Luster Vitreous
Cleavage Discernible
Fracture Uneven
Tenacity Brittle
Crystal form Orthorhombic

Morphology Tabular, rarely prismatic crystals, stellate aggregates with a reniform surface, botryoidal, uneven.
Origin and occurrence In bubble cavities of volcanic rocks, in vugs of pegmatites, on alpine fissures.
Accessory minerals Pectolite, stilbite, heulandite, laumontite, quartz, apatite.
Similar minerals Wavellite occurs in a different paragenesis and crystal form; stilbite and heulandite have different hardness, crystal form and much better cleavage.

Localities	
1 Capo di Bove, Rome, Italy	**3** Busovaca, Bosnia and Herzegovina
2 San Benito County, California, USA	**4** Namibia

1 2
3 4

1 Tinstone *Cassiterite*

Chem. formula SnO_2
Hardness 7, **Sp. gr.** 6.8–7.1
Streak Yellowish to white
Color Colorless, reddish, brown, brown-black
Luster Pitch-type luster to greasy
Cleavage Scarcely distinct
Fracture Conchoidal
Tenacity Brittle
Crystal form Tetragonal

Morphology Prismatic to acicular crystals, elbow-shaped twins, stellate aggregates ("Cornish tin ore"), uneven.
Origin and occurrence In pegmatites, pneumatolytic veins and replacements, hydrothermal veins, placers.
Accessory minerals Fluorite, topaz, wolframite.
Similar minerals Tinstone can be distinguished from almost all other minerals by its crystalline form and high density; rutile is lighter in color or, if dark, much more metallic and also exhibits a more obvious cleavage.

2 Bertrandite

Chem. formula $Be_4[(OH)_2/Si_2O_7]$
Hardness 6½–7, **Sp. gr.** 2.6
Color Colorless, white, yellowish, transparent
Streak White
Luster Vitreous, pearly on the base
Cleavage Basal perfect
Fracture Conchoidal
Tenacity Brittle
Crystal form Orthorhombic

Morphology Tabular crystals, V-shaped twins, almost always euhedral.
Origin and occurrence In vugs of pegmatites, particularly in cavities of former beryl crystals, on alpine fissures, in pneumatolytic tin-tungsten deposits together with beryl.
Accessory minerals Bavenite, milarite, phenakite, beryl, rhodochrosite.
Similar minerals Albite has a different crystal form; barite and muscovite are much softer; tabular quartz crystals are sometimes difficult to distinguish from bertrandite.

3 Thortveitite

Chem. formula $(Sc,Y)_2Si_2O_7]$
Hardness 6–7, **Sp. gr.** 3.27–3.58
Color Gray-green to black
Streak Greenish white
Luster Vitreous
Cleavage Poor
Fracture Uneven to conchoidal
Tenacity Brittle
Crystal form Monoclinic

Morphology Long to short prismatic crystals, almost always anhedral, uneven.
Origin and occurrence Anhedral in granite pegmatites in feldspar.
Accessory minerals Feldspar, quartz, monazite, euxenite, biotite, zircon, fergusonite.
Similar minerals Fergusonite is very difficult to distinguish by simple means; monazite has a different crystal form; the same applies to euxenite.

4 Mullite

Chem. formula $Al_8[O_3(O_{0,5},OH,F)/AlSi_3O_{16}]$
Hardness 6–7, **Sp. gr.** 3.2–3.3
Color Colorless, white, purple
Streak White
Luster Vitreous
Cleavage Indistinct due to the acicular structure
Fracture Fibrous
Tenacity Brittle
Crystal form Orthorhombic

Morphology Acicular crystals, acicular sheaves, stellate aggregates, fibrous, uneven.
Origin and occurrence In volcanic ejecta and inclusions in basalts.
Accessory minerals Topaz, pyroxene, hornblende, pseudobrookite, sillimanite.
Similar minerals Sillimanite is indistinguishable from mullite by simple means, but it rarely forms free sheaves and is never pink; natrolite and scolecite are softer.

Localities	
1 Minas Gerais, Brazil	**3** Iveland, Norway
2 Lohning Quarry, Rauris, Austria	**4** Bellerberg, Eifel Mountains, Germany

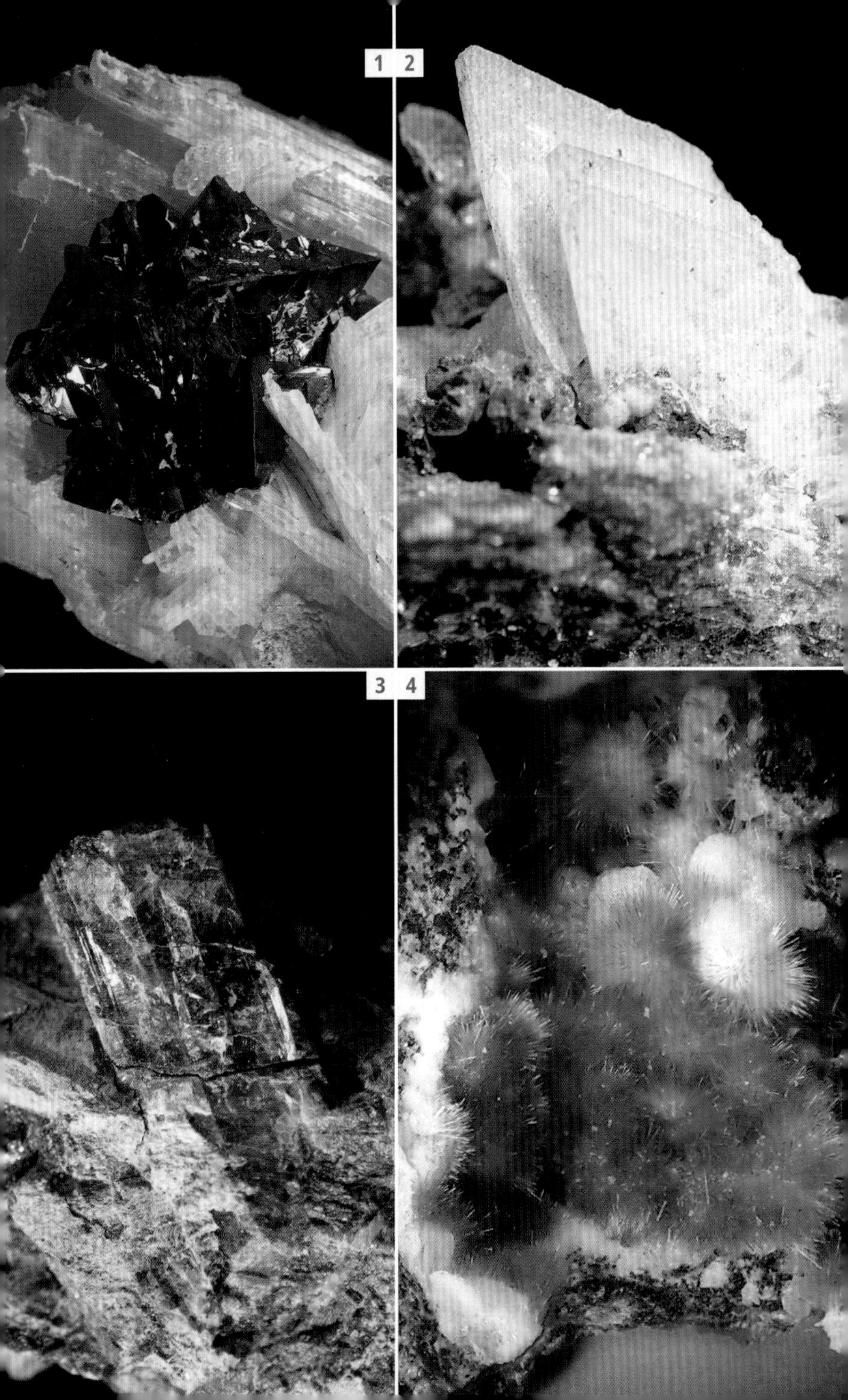
1
2
3
4

1 Jadeite

Chem. formula $NaAl[Si_2O_6]$
Hardness 6½, **Sp. gr.** 3.2–3.3
Color White, yellowish, green, purple
Streak White
Luster Vitreous
Cleavage Indistinct due to the acicular structure
Fracture Conchoidal
Tenacity Tough
Crystal form Monoclinic

Purple jade

Morphology Rarely short prismatic crystals, mainly dense, finely felted, granular.
Origin and occurrence In crystalline schists, formed by regional metamorphism from basaltic source rocks, very resistant to weathering due to its toughness and therefore as cobbles, pebbles and even large boulders in river debris.
Accessory minerals Diopside, albite.
Distinguishing feature Growths of albite with about 20% of an intense green jadeite colored by chromium content are called jade albite or by the Burmese local name Maw-sit-sit. A solid solution of diopside, jadeite and aegirine is called chloromelanite. On account of its toughness, jadeite was used in various cultures to make prehistoric stone tools.
Similar minerals Nephrite is slightly softer but only difficult to distinguish from jadeite.

2–4 Jadeite

Gemstone

Color White, pink, red, orange, purple, black, green, brown; translucent to opaque
Luster Vitreous
Shape and cut Cabochon cut, tabular cut, spheres, baroque stones

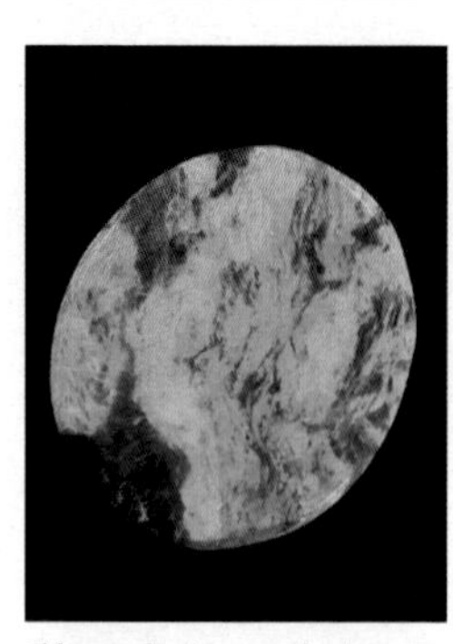

Chloromelanite as a cabochon

Use Cabochons and tabular-cut stones are used for ring stones as well as for brooches and pendants. Baroque stones and spheres, or beads, are used to make necklaces. Larger irregularly cut stones serve as worry stones. In addition, jadeite is also used to make handicraft items such as figurines, ashtrays, inlays, boxes, etc.
Distinguishing feature Jade is the typical Chinese gemstone. Therefore, particularly valuable jade is often called Chinese jade or Yunnan jade. However, this is misleading in that genuine jadeite was not found in China at all but was imported from Myanmar (Burma). In China itself, no distinction was made between jadeite and nephrite. While yellowish jade (the color of the emperor) was at one time considered particularly valuable in China, extraordinarily intense green shades are the most expensive in Western culture.
Differentiating possibilities Nephrite is usually more yellowish green; the green of grossular (transvaal jade) is darker than jadeite; serpentine is much softer.

Localities	
1 Myanmar	**3** Myanmar
2 Myanmar	**4** Myanmar

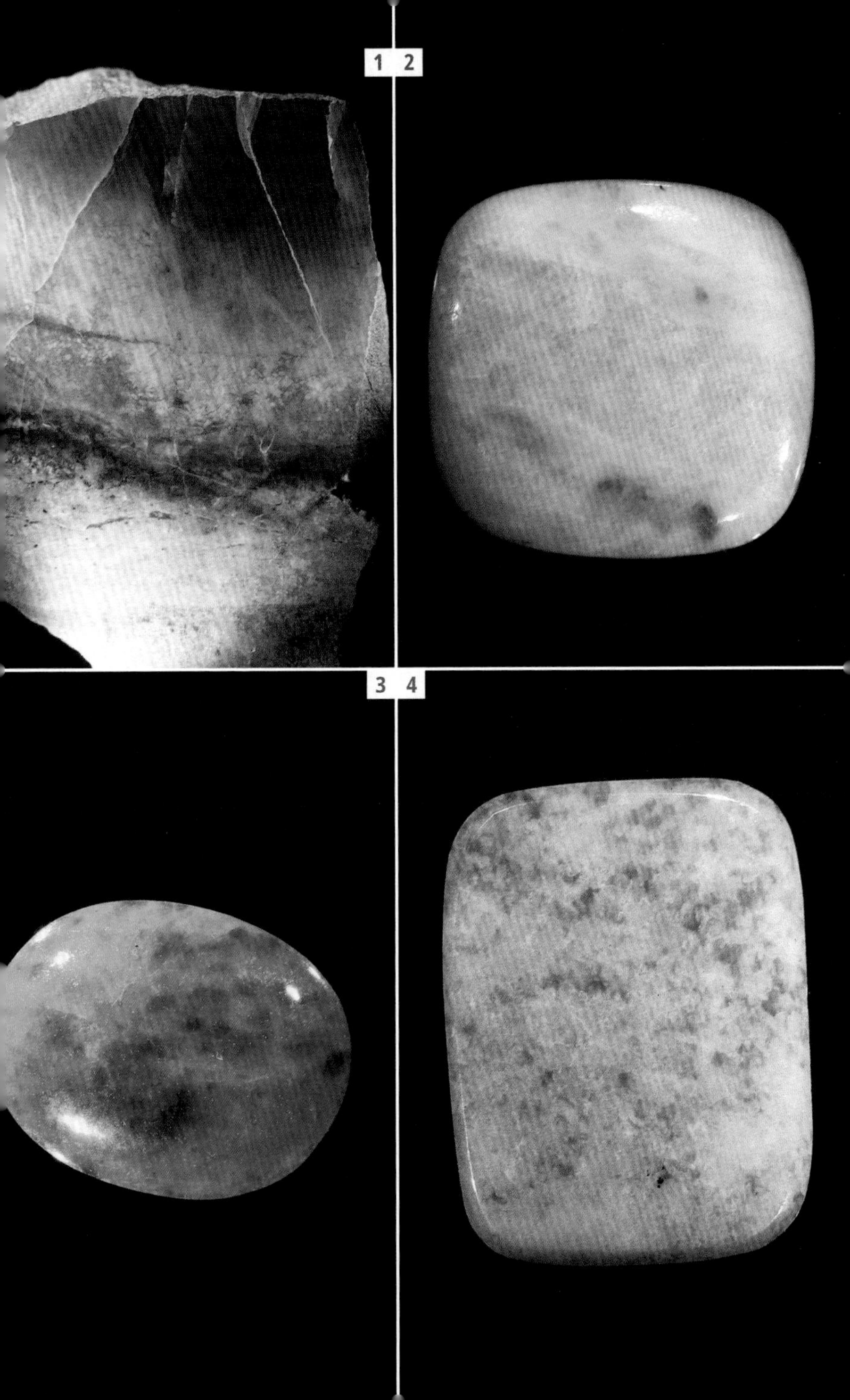
1 2
3 4

1–2 Vesuvianite *Idocrase*

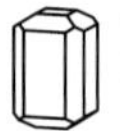

Chem. formula $Ca_{10}(Mg,Fe)_2Al_4[(OH)_4/(SiO_4)_5/(Si_2O_7)_2]$
Hardness 6½, **Sp. gr.** 3.27–3.45
Color Yellow, brown, green
Streak White
Luster Vitreous to greasy
Cleavage None
Fracture Conchoidal
Tenacity Brittle
Crystal form Tetragonal

Morphology Long to short prismatic crystals, columnar, radial (versuvianite (egeran)), granular, uneven.
Origin and occurrence In metamorphic limestone, on alpine fissures, in volcanic ejecta.
Accessory minerals Grossular, wollastonite, diopside, olivine.
Distinguishing feature Vesuvianite earned its name because it was first found in the volcanic ejecta from Mount Vesuvius in Italy.
Similar minerals Grossular is cubic, but often difficult to distinguish from short-prismatic vesuvianite; zircon is heavier and harder; chondrodite, humite and clinohumite have a different crystal form.

3 Wiluite

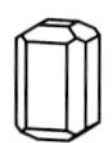

Chem. formula $Ca_{19}(Al,Mg,Fe,Ti)_{13}(B,Al)_5Si_{18}O_{68}(O,OH)_{10}$
Hardness 6½, **Sp. gr.** 3.27–3.45
Color Brown, green
Streak White
Luster Vitreous to greasy
Cleavage None
Fracture Conchoidal
Tenacity Brittle
Crystal form Tetragonal

Morphology Long to short prismatic crystals, anhedral, granular, uneven.
Origin and occurrence In a serpentinized skarn rock.
Accessory minerals Grossular, diopside, calcite, serpentine.
Distinguishing feature Wiluite was long thought to be vesuvianite and is still displayed under that name in many existing collections. It was not until modern investigation methods were available that boron could be established as a significant component of this mineral, and it is the occurrence of this that distinguishes wiluite from vesuvianite. It was named after its only occurrence in the world up until that date. This was on the Wilui River in Siberia, Russia.
Similar minerals Grossular is cubic, but often difficult to distinguish from short-prismatic wiluite; zircon is heavier and harder; chondrodite, humite and clinohumite have a different crystal form; vesuvianite is indistinguishable by simple means.

4 Ussingite

Chem. formula $Na_2AlSi_3O_8(OH)$
Hardness 6½–7, **Sp. gr.** 2.51
Color Pale pink, purple, pink
Streak White
Luster Vitreous to greasy
Cleavage Perfect
Fracture Uneven
Tenacity Brittle
Crystal form Triclinic

Morphology Very rarely cubic, tabular crystals, euhedral, mainly granular, uneven, sometimes in large masses, anhedral.
Origin and occurrence In pegmatites in sodalite-bearing nepheline syenites, in sodalite-bearing xenoliths in syenites.
Accessory minerals Aegirine, quartz, feldspar, pectolite, calcite, natrolite, sodalite, eudialyte.
Similar minerals The occurrence and color are very characteristic; fluorite and calcite are much softer; quartz has a different crystal form; calcite effervesces when dabbed with diluted hydrochloric acid.

Localities	
1 Asbestos, Canada	**3** Wilui, Siberia, Russia
2 Asbestos, Canada	**4** Kola, Russia

1 2
3 4

1

Narsarsukite

Chem. formula $Na_2(Ti,Fe^{3+})Si_4(O,F)_{11}$
Hardness 6½–7, **Sp. gr.** 2.64–2.83
Color Yellow, honey yellow, green-yellow, brownish
Streak White
Luster Vitreous to greasy
Cleavage Poorly discernible
Fracture Conchoidal
Tenacity Brittle
Crystal form Tetragonal

Morphology Tabular crystals, rarely isometric or prismatic, mainly anhedral, radial aggregates, granular, uneven masses.
Origin and occurrence In alkaline rock pegmatites, in veins in syenites, in xenoliths in syenitic rocks.
Accessory minerals Aegirine, quartz, feldspar, pectolite, calcite, galena.
Similar minerals The occurrence with syenitic rocks is very characteristic; fluorite and calcite are much softer; quartz has a different crystal form; calcite effervesces when dabbed with diluted hydrochloric acid.

2

Lavenite

Chem. formula $(Na,Ca,Mn)_3(Zr,Ti,Fe)(SiO_4)_2F$
Hardness 6, **Sp. gr.** 3.5
Color Colorless, yellow, brown
Streak White
Luster Vitreous
Cleavage Perfect
Fracture Uneven
Tenacity Brittle
Crystal form Monoclinic

Morphology Prismatic to acicular crystals, rarely tabular, often uneven.
Origin and occurrence In volcanic ejecta and as an essential mineral in alkaline rocks, such as nepheline syenite, and their pegmatites.
Accessory minerals Woehlerite, feldspar, zircon, astrophyllite, aegirine, apatite.
Similar minerals Woehlerite is more tabular; astrophyllite is always more foliated.

3

Chkalovite

Chem. formula $Na_2BeSi_2O_6$
Hardness 6, **Sp. gr.** 2.7
Color Colorless, white
Streak White
Luster Vitreous
Cleavage Poorly discernible
Fracture Uneven
Tenacity Brittle
Crystal form Orthorhombic

Morphology Isometric crystals, rarely euhedral, often anhedral, uneven.
Origin and occurrence In alkaline rock pegmatites, in sodalite xenoliths in syenites.
Accessory minerals Sodalite, eudialyte, neptunite, pectolite, feldspar, aegirine.
Similar minerals Quartz is harder; feldspar has perfect cleavage; the crystal form of nepheline differs from that of chkalovite.

4

Petalite

Chem. formula $LiAlSi_4O_{10}$
Hardness 7, **Sp. gr.** 2.4
Color Colorless, white, pink
Streak White
Luster Vitreous
Cleavage Perfect
Fracture Crystalline
Tenacity Brittle
Crystal form Monoclinic

Morphology Tabular crystals, rarely euhedral, often anhedral, cleavage pieces, uneven.
Origin and occurrence In granite pegmatites, partly extracted as lithium ore.
Accessory minerals Pollucite, beryl, feldspar, quartz, tourmaline, lepidolite.
Similar minerals Quartz has no cleavage; feldspar is slightly softer and has a different cleavage; spodumene has cleavage with a 120° cleavage angle.

Localities	
1 Kola, Russia	**3** Kola, Russia
2 Kola, Russia	**4** Varuträsk, Sweden

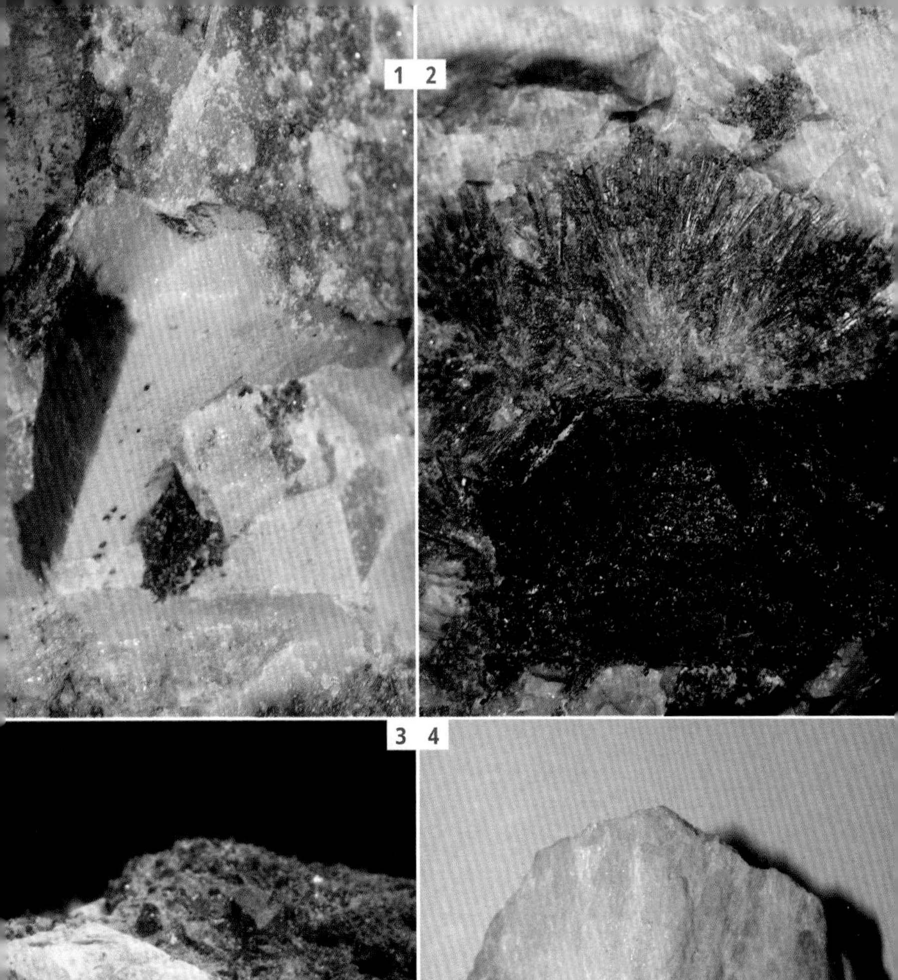
1 2

3

4

1

Sugilite

Chem. formula $(K,Na)(Na,Fe)_2(Li_2Fe)[Si_{12}O_{30}]$
Hardness 6–7, **Sp. gr.** 2.74
Color Light to dark purple
Streak White
Luster Vitreous to dull
Cleavage Indiscernible
Crystal form Hexagonal

Morphology Prismatic, longitudinally striated crystals, dense masses, granular, uneven.
Origin and occurrence In metamorphic manganese deposits.
Accessory minerals Hausmannite, braunite, pyrolusite, quartz, pectolite, apophyllite.
Similar minerals The characteristic color makes sugilite unmistakable.

2

Sugilite

Gemstone

Shape and cut Cabochon cut, spheres, baroque stones

Use Cabochons are cut for ring stones or for brooches and pendants. Baroque stones and spheres, or beads, are used to make necklaces. Larger irregularly cut stones serve as worry stones. In addition, sugilite is also used to make handicraft items such as figurines, ashtrays, inlays, boxes, etc.
Differentiating possibilities The rare charoite from Siberia is always unmistakable and also visible with the naked eye, fibrous and not granular like sugilite. It is also usually more distinctly blue-purple. Otherwise, the color of the sugilite is extraordinarily characteristic and unmistakable.

3

Xonotlite

Chem. formula $Ca_6Si_6O_{17}(OH)_2$
Hardness 6½, **Sp. gr.** 2.7
Color White
Streak White
Luster Vitreous to silky
Cleavage Poorly discernible
Fracture Fibrous
Tenacity Brittle
Crystal form Monoclinic

Morphology Acicular crystals, crystal sheaves, fibrous, stellate aggregates.
Origin and occurrence In calcareous xenoliths in volcanic rocks, in vugs in basalts, in metamorphic manganese deposits, on fissures in altered basic rocks.
Accessory minerals Tobermorite, thaumasite, afwillite, ettringite, calcite.
Similar minerals Natrolite usually has thicker crystals, often with end faces; aragonite effervesces when dabbed with diluted hydrochloric acid; tobermorite is much softer.

4

Clinozoisite

Chem. formula $Ca_2Al_3(O/OH/SiO_4/Si_2O_7)$
Hardness 6–7, **Sp. gr.** 3.3–3.5
Color Gray, light brown, gray-brown
Streak Gray to white
Luster Vitreous
Cleavage Perfect
Tenacity Brittle
Fracture Uneven
Crystal form Monoclinic

Morphology Long tabular to prismatic crystals, radial aggregates, columnar, uneven.
Origin and occurrence In hydrothermal veins and metamorphic rocks.
Accessory minerals Axinite, hornblende asbestos, albite, calcite, quartz.
Similar minerals Epidote is always slightly green; zoisite is sometimes difficult to distinguish from clinozoisite; actinolite and hornblende have perfect cleavage with a 120° cleavage angle.

Localities	
1 Hotazel, South Africa	**3** N'Chwaning, Hotazel, South Africa
2 Hotazel, South Africa	**4** Ahrntal, South Tyrol, Italy

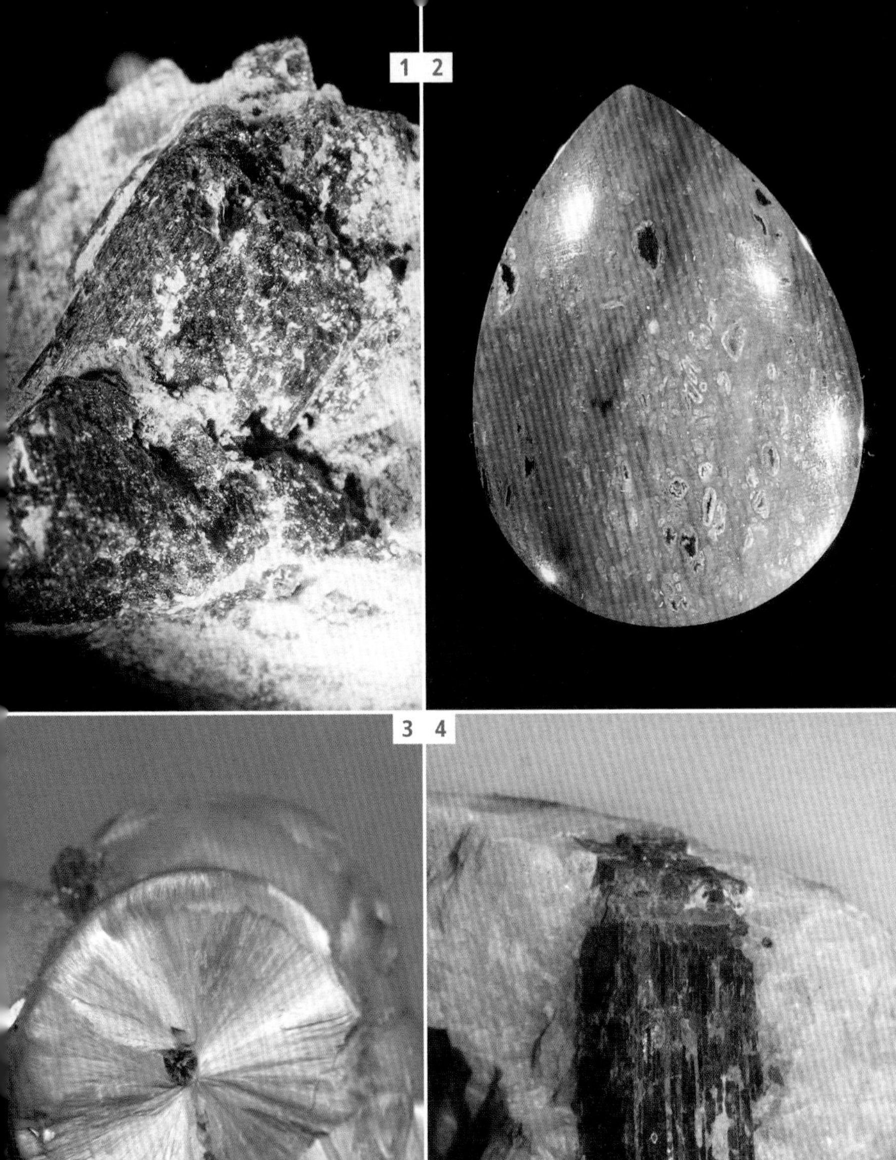
1 2

3 4

1 Zoisite

Chem. formula $Ca_2Al_3(SiO_4)(Si_2O_7)O(OH)$
Hardness 6–7, **Sp. gr.** 3.15–3.36
Color Gray, light brown, gray-brown, blue
Streak Gray to white
Luster Vitreous
Cleavage Perfect
Tenacity Brittle
Fracture Uneven
Crystal form Orthorhombic

Morphology Long tabular to prismatic crystals, radial aggregates, columnar, uneven.
Origin and occurrence In metamorphic rocks, particularly blueschist facies, in pegmatites.
Accessory minerals Albite, biotite, quartz, plagioclase, grossular, calcite.
Similar minerals Epidote is always slightly green; clinozoisite is sometimes difficult to distinguish from zoisite; actinolite and hornblende have perfect cleavage with a 120° cleavage angle.

2 Zoisite

Gemstone

Color Green, blue, deep blue (tanzanite)
Shape and cut Facet cut

Use Primarily cut for ring stones or for brooches and pendants.
Treatment The mostly brownish to greenish tanzanites are fired to produce the sapphire blue color.
Distinguishing feature The deep blue variety is called tanzanite because of its origin, since sectile material is only found in one single locality in the world, Tanzania. It is the only locality where the stones are processed into jewelry in large volumes.
Differentiating possibilities Sapphire is notably harder and rarely exhibits such a deep blue.

3 Chloritoide

Chem. formula $(Fe,Mg,Mn)_2Al_4Si_2O_{10}(OH)_4$
Hardness 6–7, **Sp. gr.** 3.56
Color Gray-green, green
Streak Gray to white
Luster Vitreous
Cleavage Perfect
Tenacity Brittle
Fracture Uneven
Crystal form Monoclinic

Morphology Pseudohexagonal, tabular crystals, foliated aggregates, uneven.
Origin and occurrence In metamorphic rocks, in hydrothermally altered rocks.
Accessory minerals Albite, biotite, quartz, plagioclase, kyanite, staurolite.
Similar minerals Chlorite and mica are much softer; feldspar exhibits a different cleavage; quartz exhibits no cleavage whatsoever.

4 Osumilite

Chem. formula $(K,Na)(Mg,Fe^{2+})_2(Al,Fe^{3+})_3(Si,Al)_{12}O_{30}$
Hardness 7, **Sp. gr.** 2.6–2.8
Color Gray, light brown, gray-brown, blue, black, green
Streak Gray to white
Luster Vitreous
Cleavage Poor
Tenacity Brittle
Fracture Uneven
Crystal form Hexagonal

Morphology Thick tabular to prismatic crystals, usually euhedral, uneven.
Origin and occurrence In volcanic ejecta, in cavities in volcanic rocks.
Accessory minerals Sanidine, tridymite, biotite, quartz, pyroxene, amphibole.
Similar minerals Cordierite occurs in a different paragenesis; apatite is softer, the same applies to nepheline; hematite has a red streak.

Localities	
1 Passeier Valley, South Tyrol, Italy	**3** East Tyrol, Austria
2 Tanzania	**4** Funtanafigu, Sardinia, Italy

1
2
3
4

1 Asbecasite

Chem. formula $Ca_3(Ti,Sn)As_6Si_2Be_2O_{20}$
Hardness 6½–7, **Sp. gr.** 3.7
Color Yellow
Streak White
Luster Vitreous
Cleavage Good
Fracture Uneven
Tenacity Brittle
Crystal form Trigonal

Morphology Thick tabular crystals, euhedral, uneven, powdery masses.
Origin and occurrence Euhedral on alpine fissures.
Accessory minerals Cafarsite, torbernite, tilasite, synchisite, adularia, quartz, agardite.
Similar minerals Based on its paragenesis, asbecasite is unmistakable; titanite is intensely yellow; calcite effervesces when dabbed with diluted hydrochloric acid.

2 Cordierite *Dichroite*

Chem. formula $Mg_2Al_3[AlSi_5O_{18}]$
Hardness 7, **Sp. gr.** 2.6
Color Gray, blue, purple, greenish to yellow
Streak White
Luster Vitreous to greasy
Cleavage Indiscernible
Fracture Conchoidal
Tenacity Brittle
Crystal form Orthorhombic

Morphology Hexagonal and dodecahedral prisms, mainly anhedral, often uneven.
Origin and occurrence In gneisses and contact rocks, in metamorphic gravel deposits, in volcanic ejecta.
Accessory minerals Garnet, sillimanite, gahnite, pyrrhotine, quartz, feldspar, biotite.
Similar minerals Tourmaline in a similar paragenesis is always shiny black; distinguishing uneven cordierite from quartz by simple means is not always possible.

3 Axinite

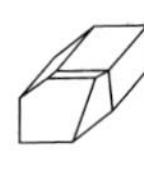

Chem. formula $Ca_2(Fe,Mg,Mn)Al_2[OH/BO_3/Si_4O_{12}]$
Hardness 6½–7, **Sp. gr.** 3.3
Color Brown, gray, purple, blue, greenish
Luster Vitreous
Streak White
Cleavage Poorly distinct
Fracture Conchoidal
Tenacity Brittle
Crystal form Triclinic

Morphology Tabular crystals, very sharp edged, mainly euhedral, uneven, crystalline, columnar.
Origin and occurrence In calc-silicate rocks, contact metasomatic deposits, on alpine fissures, in vugs in pegmatites.
Accessory minerals Clinozoisite, chlorite, apatite, scheelite, tinstone, quartz.
Similar minerals The sharp-edged crystals of axinite are unmistakable; rhodonite is always more or less red; adularia and albite never have such sharp edges.

4 Sillimanite

Chem. formula $Al_2[O/SiO_4]$
Hardness 6–7, **Sp. gr.** 3.2
Color Colorless, white, yellowish, gray
Streak White
Luster Vitreous, silky in aggregates
Cleavage Perfect but mainly indiscernible
Fracture Uneven
Tenacity Brittle
Crystal form Orthorhombic

Morphology Scarcely prismatic to acicular single crystals, mainly fibrous, radial, columnar.
Origin and occurrence In gneisses, mica schists, eclogites, granulites, in pegmatites within these rocks, in metamorphic gravel deposits.
Accessory minerals Cordierite, gahnite, garnet, quartz, kyanite, andalusite.
Similar minerals Asbestos fibers are flexible; beryl is hexagonal; kyanite always exhibits marked differences in hardness; diopside has a different cleavage.

Localities	
1 Cherbadung, Valais, Switzerland	**3** Harz, Germany
2 Silberberg Mine, Bodenmais, Bavarian Forest, Germany	**4** Pleystein, East Bavaria, Germany

1
2
3
4

1 Almandine

Chem. formula $Fe_3Al_2[SiO_4]_3$
Hardness 6½–7½, **Sp. gr.** 4.32
Color Red, red-brown, brown
Streak White
Luster Vitreous
Cleavage None
Fracture Conchoidal
Tenacity Brittle
Crystal form Cubic

Morphology Rhombic dodecahedral and deltoid icositetrahedron, almost always anhedral.
Origin and occurrence In mica schists, gneisses, granulites, more rarely in pegmatites.
Accessory minerals Staurolite, mica, quartz, feldspar.
Similar minerals The paragenesis of almandine in mica schists and gneisses is characteristic.

Almandine

Gemstone

Color Red, red-brown
Luster Vitreous
Shape and cut Facet cut

Use Mainly as jewelry, as ring stones, for brooches and pendants, usually combines typically multi-faceted stones, rarely cabochons.

2 Pyrope

Chem. formula $Mg_3Al_2[SiO_4]$
Hardness 7–7½, **Sp. gr.** 3.58
Color Dark red, blood red
Streak White
Luster Vitreous
Cleavage None
Fracture Conchoidal
Tenacity Brittle
Crystal form Cubic

Morphology Rhombic dodecahedral, deltoid icositetrahedron, often roundish grains, always anhedral.
Origin and occurrence In ultrabasic rock, serpentinites and placers.
Accessory minerals Diamond, phlogopite, olivine.
Similar minerals The paragenesis of pyrope is characteristic; almandine is always slightly browner, never a pure dark red.

3 Pyrope

Gemstone

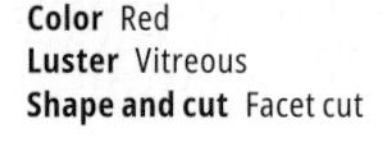

Color Red
Luster Vitreous
Shape and cut Facet cut

Use Mainly for jewelry, as ring stones, nearly always faceted for brooches and pendants, very rarely as cabochons.

4–5 Grossular

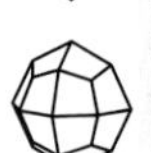

Chem. formula $Ca_3Al_2[SiO_4]_3$
Hardness 6½–7, **Sp. gr.** 3.59
Color Colorless, yellow, green
Streak White
Luster Vitreous
Cleavage None
Fracture Conchoidal
Tenacity Brittle
Crystal form Cubic

Morphology deltoid icositetrahedron and rhombic dodecahedral, anhedral and euhedral, uneven, granular.
Origin and occurrence In contact marbles, on fissures of serpentinites and rodingites.
Accessory minerals Vesuvianite, diopside, calcite.
Distinguishing feature Reddish brown, iron-rich grossular is called hessonite.
Similar minerals The paragenesis of grossular is very characteristic; vesuvianite is usually clearly prismatic; when uneven, it is difficult to distinguish using simple means.

6 Hessonite

Gemstone

Color Colorless, white, pink, yellow, brown, green, red
Luster Vitreous
Shape and cut Facet cut

Use Mainly for jewelry, as ring stones, for brooches, pendants.

Localities		
1 Stillup Valley, Austria	**3** India	**5** Transvaal, South Africa
2 Alpe Arami, Ticino, Switzerland	**4** Asbestos, Canada	**6** Strzelce Krajeńskie, Poland

1
2
3
4
6
5

1 Andradite

Chem. formula $Ca_3Fe_2[SiO_4]_3$
Hardness 6½–7½, **Sp. gr.** 3.86
Color Colorless, brown, green, black
Streak White
Luster Vitreous
Cleavage None
Fracture Conchoidal
Tenacity Brittle
Crystal form Cubic

Morphology Rhombic dodecahedral and deltoid icositetrahedron, anhedral and euhedral.
Origin and occurrence In metamorphic deposits, on fissures of serpentine and skarn rocks, in volcanic rocks (particularly melanite).
Accessory minerals Chlorite, diopside, hedenbergite, magnetite.
Distinguishing feature Yellow translucent andradite is called demantoid; black titanium-bearing andradite is called melanite.
Similar minerals Grossular is often indistinguishable from andradite by simple means.

2 Andradite

Gemstone

Color Colorless, white, pink, yellow, brown, green, red
Luster Vitreous
Shape and cut Facet cut

Use Mainly for jewelry, as ring stones, for brooches and pendants.

3 Uwarowite

Chem. formula $Ca_3Cr_2[SiO_4]_3$
Hardness 6½–7½, **Sp. gr.** 3.85
Color Emerald green
Streak White
Luster Vitreous
Cleavage None
Fracture Conchoidal
Tenacity Brittle
Crystal form Cubic

Morphology Rhombic dodecahedral and deltoid icositetrahedron, anhedral and euhedral.
Origin and occurrence In chromium-rich, metamorphic deposits, on fissures of chromite-bearing rocks and chromite ores.
Accessory minerals Chromite, chromian clinochlore, titanite.
Similar minerals The color is very characteristic; its paragenesis makes uwarowite unmistakable.

Uwarowite

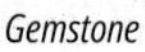

Gemstone

Color Emerald green
Luster Vitreous
Shape and cut Facet cut

Use Mainly for jewelry, as ring stones, for brooches and pendants.

4 Spessartine

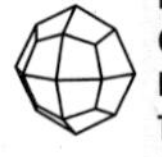

Chem. formula $Mn_3Al_2[SiO_4]_3$
Hardness 7, **Sp. gr.** 4.19
Color Pink, orange, brown
Streak White
Luster Vitreous
Cleavage None
Fracture Conchoidal
Tenacity Brittle
Crystal form Cubic

Morphology deltoid icositetrahedron, anhedral and euhedral.
Origin and occurrence In metamorphic manganese deposits, in pegmatites and granites.
Accessory minerals Rhodonite, feldspar, quartz.
Similar minerals Almandine is more reddish brown; unlike spessartine, it often exhibits rhombic dodecahedral crystals.

Spessartine

Gemstone

Color Orange, red
Luster Vitreous
Shape and cut Facet cut

Use Mainly for jewelry, as ring stones, for brooches, pendants.

Localities	
1 Serifos, Greece	**3** Saranyi, Urals, Russia
2 Val Malenco, Piemont, Italy	**4** Gilgit, Pakistan

1 2
3 4

1

Andalusite *Chiastolite*

Chem. formula $Al_2[O/SiO_4]$
Hardness 7½, **Sp. gr.** 3.1–3.2
Color Various gray tones, yellowish, reddish, green, brown, sometimes also multi-colored
Streak White
Luster Vitreous, but mainly clouded
Cleavage Mainly indiscernible
Fracture Uneven
Tenacity Brittle
Crystal form Orthorhombic

Morphology Thick columnar crystals with nearly square cross-section, stellate aggregates, almost always anhedral. Some andalusites are called chiastolite because, when sectioned, they exhibit a cross-shaped pattern similar to the Greek letter chi.
Origin and occurrence Anhedral in gneisses and mica schists, in quartz nodules of metamorphic rocks, in clay schists and pegmatites. The most beautiful and largest andalusites of German origin are found in the Bavarian Forest.
Accessory minerals Quartz, feldspar, tourmaline, mica, corundum, sillimanite.
Similar minerals Tourmaline has a different crystal form with a triangular or hexagonal cross-section; hornblende, augite and actinolite exhibit a different cleavage.

2

Andalusite

Gemstone

Color Yellowish with black cross (chiastolite)
Shape and cut Tabular cut or cabochon, rarely facet cut

Use As ring stones, for pendants. Due to chiastolite's distinct cruciform shape and its occurrence near the pilgrimage site of Santiago de Compostela in Spain, chiastolite pendants were often worn as religious amulets.

3

Melanophlogite

Chem. formula SiO_2
Hardness 6½–7, **Sp. gr.** 2.0
Color Colorless, white
Streak White
Luster Vitreous
Cleavage None
Fracture Conchoidal
Tenacity Brittle
Crystal form Cubic

Morphology Cubic, botryoidal aggregates with a parquett-type surface, water drop-like aggregates with a smooth surface.
Origin and occurrence In sedimentary rocks containing many organic substances, in sulfur deposits.
Accessory minerals Sulfur, calcite, aragonite.
Similar minerals Fluorite and calcite are much softer; quartz has a different crystal form; paragenesis with sulfur is very characteristic; calcite effervesces when dabbed with diluted hydrochloric acid.

4

Lawsonite

Chem. formula $CaAl_2Si_2O_7(OH)_2 \cdot H_2O$
Hardness 7, **Sp. gr.** 3.09
Color White, pink, gray, blue
Streak White
Luster Vitreous to greasy
Cleavage Perfect
Fracture Conchoidal
Tenacity Brittle
Crystal form Orthorhombic

Morphology Long to short prismatic and tabular crystals, euhedral on fissures and anhedral in rocks, granular, uneven.
Origin and occurrence In rocks of subsidence metamorphism, for example, in glaucophane schists.
Accessory minerals Glaucophane, quartz.
Similar minerals Its paragenesis in high pressure rocks is very characteristic; feldspar has a different crystal form; quartz exhibits no cleavage.

Localities	
1 Lisens-Alm, Stubai Valley, Austria	**3** Livorno, Italy
2 Spain	**4** Berkeley, California

1 2
3 4

1 Tridymite

Chem. formula SiO_2
Hardness 6½–7, **Sp. gr.** 2.27
Color Colorless, white
Streak White
Luster Vitreous
Cleavage Seldom distinct
Fracture Conchoidal
Tenacity Brittle
Crystal form Hexagonal formed at high temperatures

Morphology Thin to rarely thick tabular crystals, fan-like triplets, uneven.
Origin and occurrence On fissures and in vugs in acidic, volcanic rocks, in the contact zone of acidic inclusions, in volcanic rocks, often pseudomorphs from quartz to tridymite.
Accessory minerals High temperature quartz, hornblende, augite.
Similar minerals Sanidine is usually a thicker tabular crystal and exhibits a different crystal form; tridymite differs from most other thin tabular white minerals due to its characteristic paragenesis.

2 Cristobalite

Chem. formula SiO_2
Hardness 6½–7, **Sp. gr.** 2.2
Color Cloudy milky white
Streak White
Luster Vitreous
Cleavage None
Fracture Conchoidal
Tenacity Brittle
Crystal form Cubic, tetragonal

Morphology Cubically formed at higher temperatures, altered to the tetragonal modification during cooling; mainly octahedral, often distorted bladed, rarely cubic.
Origin and occurrence On fissures and vugs in acidic, volcanic rocks, in obsidian rocks.
Accessory minerals Tridymite, high temperature quartz, hematite, pseudobrookite, augite, hornblende.
Similar minerals The paragenesis, crystal form and color distinguish cristobalite from all other minerals; tridymite is tabular; sanidine has a different crystal form.

3–4 Spodumene *Kunzite, hiddenite*

Chem. formula $LiAl[Si_2O_6]$
Hardness 6½–7, **Sp. gr.** 3.1–3.2
Color Colorless, white, pink and purple (kunzite), green (hiddenite), yellow, brown
Streak White
Luster Vitreous
Cleavage Perfect prismatic
Fracture Crystalline
Tenacity Brittle
Crystal form Monoclinic

Morphology Crystals tabular, rarely prismatic, radial, crystalline, uneven, anhedral and euhedral.
Origin and occurrence Radial, tabular anhedral in pegmatites, turbid, in vugs in these pegmatites transparent and beautifully colored anhedral crystals, prismatic to tabular.
Accessory minerals Feldspar, quartz, beryl, muscovite.
Distinguishing feature If you look at pink colored kunzite from all sides, it exhibits a special feature: pleochroismos. Depending on the direction of the view, the color changes in intensity and its color also changes from pink to yellow.
Similar minerals Feldspar exhibits a different cleavage; quartz exhibits no cleavage at all; pink beryl has a very different hexagonal crystal form; apatite is softer and has a different crystal form, also hexagonal.

5 Spodumene

Gemstone

Color Colorless, white, pink and purple (kunzite), green (hiddenite), yellow, brown
Shape and cut Facet cut

Use As a ring stone, for brooches and pendants.
Differentiating possibilities Morganite cannot be distinguished by simple means; nevertheless, the color intensity in kunzite changes significantly depending upon the direction of the view; morganite does not have this property.

Localities		
1 Colli Euganei, Italy	**3** Nuristan, Afghanistan	**5** Minas Gerais, Brazil
2 Bellerberg, Eifel Mountains, Germany	**4** Minas Gerais, Brazil	

1 2
3 4
5

1–2 Quartz

Chem. formula SiO_2
Hardness 7, **Sp. gr.** 2.65
Color Colorless or varied colors (see under the varieties)
Streak White
Luster Vitreous to greasy
Cleavage None
Fracture Conchoidal
Tenacity Brittle
Crystal form Trigonal (low-temperature quartz), the high-temperature quartz formed above 1063° F is hexagonal

Morphology Crystals mainly hexagonal, distinctly trigonal (three-sided) crystals are formed at particularly low temperatures. Frequent twinning, also exhibiting re-entrant angles. Such twins are called Japan Law Twin crystals. Crystals can be distorted laminates, acicular, short prismatic or bipyramidal. Aggregates are stellate (star quartz), columnar or granular.
Origin and occurrence As a component of intrusive igneous rocks (for example, granite), volcanic rocks (for example, rhyolite, quartz porphyry), of sedimentary rocks (for example, sandstone) and metamorphic rocks (for example, gneiss). Beautiful crystals on vugs in pegmatites, in pneumatolytic veins, in ore veins, in hydrothermal quartz veins, on alpine fissures, in the cavities of marble, in septarian nodules, anhedral in sedimentary rocks.
Accessory minerals Calcite, feldspar, ores, tourmaline, garnet and many others.
Distinguishing feature Left and right variants can occur in quartz crystals. They can be recognized by the fact that small triangular areas at the corners of the prism occur either only on the left or only on the right.
Similar minerals Quartz is distinguished from other similar minerals by its hardness and resistance to acids.

Facetted smoky quartz

Varieties:
Rock crystal Colorless, clear, transparent.
Smoky quartz Smoky brown to deep black (morion).
Amethys Purple.
Citrine Pale yellow, yellow.
Rose quartz Pink; rarely crystals.
Ferruginous quartz Opaque red due to hematite inclusions.
Milk quartz Appearance is milky white, clouded by liquid inclusions.
Prase Opaque green due to mineral inclusions, for example, hedenbergite.

Facetted amethyst

3–4 Quartz

Gemstone

Color Colorless (rock crystal), white, pink (rose quartz), purple (amethyst), yellow (citrine), brown (smoky quartz)
Shape and cut Facet cut, cabochon

Distinguishing feature When cut as a cabochon or bead, some rose quartz exhibits a clearly visible light star.
Use As a ring stone, for brooches and pendants.
Treatment Natural citrine is very rare; most material used for cutting is produced by burning amethyst.
Differentiating possibilities Amethyst is distinctive; rose quartz is usually paler than morganite and kunzite; it is almost never faceted.

Localities	
1 Corinto, Diamantina, Brazil	**3** Oravica, Romania
2 Las Vigas, Mexico	**4** St. Gotthard, Switzerland

1 2
3 4

1–2 Agate

Chem. formula SiO_2
Hardness 7, **Sp. gr.** 2.65
Color Colorless or varied colors, frequently striped or with multi-color bands
Streak White
Luster Vitreous to greasy
Cleavage None
Fracture Conchoidal to uneven
Tenacity Brittle
Crystal form Trigonal

Dendritic agate

Morphology Agate is microcrystalline quartz and therefore does not form visible crystals, but only reniform aggregates, fillings in cavities, stalactitic structures. The various agates are named after the images they exhibit when the nodules are sectioned. Thus, there are band, ring and fortification agates, but also rubble agates or landscape agates (Fig. 4).
Origin and occurrence In hydrothermal veins, in fossilized wood, most commonly in cavities of volcanic rocks. Due to their weathering resistance, agate nodules are often found in the bed loads of rivers and streams and in gravel deposits. The most beautiful and famous agates in Germany originate from the area of Idar-Oberstein in the Palatinate; today, the largest quantities of agate come from Brazil, where the deposits were discovered by emigrants from Idar-Oberstein.
Accessory minerals Rock crystal, amethyst, calcite, chabazite and other zeolite minerals, hematite.
Similar minerals Shape and coloring are unmistakable; similar formations of calcite differ slightly in hardness and in the resulting effervescence when dabbed with diluted hydrochloric acid.

3–4 Agate

Gemstone

Color Multi-colored with a wide range of patterns
Shape and cut Tabular cut and cabochon cut

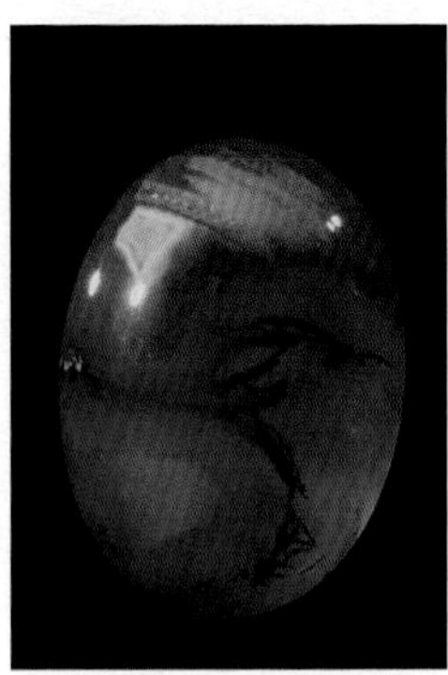

Moss agate, Cabochon

Treatment Agates have been artificially colored since Roman times. By soaking in honey followed by treatment with sulfuric acid, it was possible to produce black and white layered stones. These, just like natural layered stones, are used to make multicolored carved gems and cameos. With today's modern dyes, agates can be dyed in a wide variety of colors. There are also many colors, such as intense green, intense blue or pink and purple, that do not appear at all on natural stones.
Use As ring stones, for brooches and pendants, for necklaces and for handicraft items, as bookends, for making carved gems and cameos. Due to its toughness, agate is also used industrially for the production of mortars, of rollers for painting or for spinning nozzles in the textile industry.
Differentiating possibilities The shape and color of cut stones are distinctive.

Localities	
1 Rio Grande do Sul, Brazil	**3** Rio Grande do Sul, Brazil
2 St. Egidien, Saxony, Germany	**4** Brazil

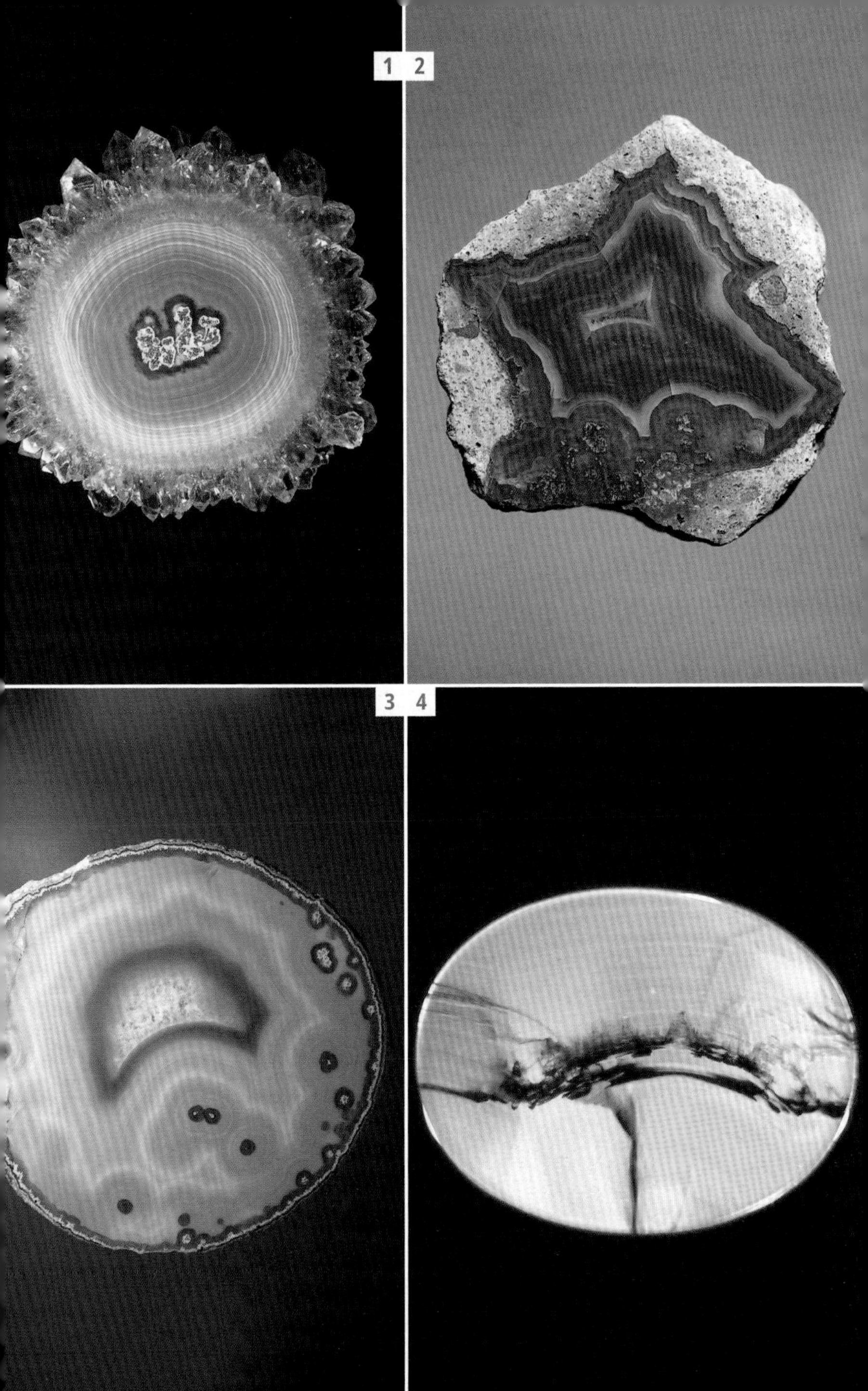
1 2
3 4

1–2 Chalcedony

Chem. formula SiO_2
Hardness 7, **Sp. gr.** 2.65
Color Colorless or varied colors (see under the varieties)
Streak White
Luster Vitreous to greasy
Cleavage None
Fracture Conchoidal to uneven
Tenacity Brittle
Crystal form Trigonal

Morphology Chalcedony is microcrystalline quartz and only forms reniform aggregates, fillings in cavities, stalactitic structures.
Origin and occurrence In hydrothermal veins, cavities of volcanic rocks, layers and nodules in sedimentary rocks.
Accessory minerals Rock crystal, calcite, siderite, fluorite.
Similar minerals Fluorite and calcite are softer.

Varieties:
Chalcedony (in the strictest sense) Colorless, white, gray, blue, single-color and striped.
Carnelian Red to red-brown translucent, green.
Chrysoprase Green due to nickel mineral inclusions.
Onyx Only alternating black and white layers.
Flint, chert Gray to brown colored nodules in sedimentary rocks.
Heliotrope Green with red flecks.

3–4 Chalcedony

Gemstone

Color Blue, brown, green, red
Shape and cut Tabular cut and cabochon cut, spherical cut

Use As ring stones, for brooches and pendants, for necklaces and for handicraft items.
Differentiating possibilities The shape and color of cut stones are distinctive.

5 Jasper

Chem. formula SiO_2
Hardness 7, **Sp. gr.** 2.65
Color Varied color, opaque (see under the varieties)
Streak White
Luster Vitreous to greasy
Cleavage None
Fracture Conchoidal to uneven
Tenacity Brittle
Crystal form Trigonal

Morphology Jasper is microcrystalline quartz that is completely opaque due to inclusions of foreign minerals.
Origin and occurrence In hydrothermal veins, cavities of volcanic rocks, as layers and nodules in sedimentary rocks.
Accessory minerals Rock crystal, agate, chalcedony, calcite.
Similar minerals Fluorite and calcite are distinctly softer; chalcedony and its varieties are always translucent at least at the edges.

Varieties:
Jasper (in the strictest sense) Brown, red or yellow.
Green jasper Also called plasma; heliotrope is green with red flecks (hematite).
Carnelian Red to red-brown translucent, green.

6 Jasper

Gemstone

Color Brown, yellow, green, red
Shape and cut Tabular cut and cabochon cut, spherical cut

Use As ring stones, for brooches and pendants, for necklaces and for handicraft items.
Differentiating possibilities Chalcedony and its varieties are not completely opaque.

Localities		
1 Transylvania, Romania	**3** Namibia	**5** Frankenstein, Poland
2 Iceland	**4** South Africa	**6** India

1 2
3 4
5 6

1 **Staurolite**

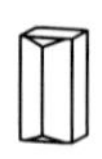

Chem. formula $(Fe,Mg,Zn)_2Al_9[O_6/(OH)_2/(SiO_4)_4]$
Hardness 7–7½, **Sp. gr.** 3.7–3.8
Color Red to black-brown
Streak White
Luster Vitreous
Cleavage Scarcely distinct
Fracture Conchoidal
Tenacity Brittle
Crystal form Monoclinic

Morphology Prismatic to tabular crystals, often cruciform twins (right-angled or intergrown at about 60°), always anhedral.
Origin and occurrence Anhedral in mica schists and gneisses.
Accessory minerals Quartz, mica, kyanite.
Similar minerals Tourmaline always clearly exhibits trigonal symmetry and does not form cruciform twins; kyanite is never dark brown; garnet has a distinct cubic crystal form; unlike staurolite, andalusite has an almost square cross-section.

2 **Hambergite**

Chem. formula $Be_2BO_3(OH,F)$
Hardness 7½, **Sp. gr.** 2.35–2.37
Color White-gray, yellow, colorless
Streak White
Luster Vitreous
Cleavage Perfect
Fracture Uneven
Tenacity Brittle
Crystal form Orthorhombic

Morphology Prismatic to long tabular, also bipyramidal crystals, usually euhedral.
Origin and occurrence In granite pegmatites, anhedral as late formation in vugs.
Accessory minerals Feldspar, quartz, tourmaline (elbaite), spodumene, beryl, beryllonite, herderite.
Similar minerals Feldspar has a different crystal form, as does quartz; spodumene has a different crystal form; calcite effervesces when dabbed with diluted hydrochloric acid and is much softer.

3 **Boracite**

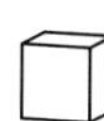

Chem. formula $Mg_3[Cl/B_7O_{13}]$
Hardness 7, **Sp. gr.** 2.9–3
Streak White
Color Colorless, white, yellowish, greenish, bluish
Luster Vitreous
Cleavage None
Fracture Conchoidal
Tenacity Brittle
Crystal form Above 514° F cubic, below orthorhombic

Morphology Cubic, tetrahedral crystals, anhedral, uneven, fibrous.
Origin and occurrence Anhedral in salt deposits in anhydrite or gypsum.
Accessory minerals Gypsum, anhydrite, rock salt.
Distinguishing feature Fibrous boracite is called stassfurtite.
Similar minerals Rock salt is much softer and has good cleavage, as does fluorite; however, it is also soluble in water. Fluorite has excellent octahedral cleavage and occurs in quite different parageneses.

4 **Rhodizite**

Chem. formula $(K,Cs)Al_4Be_4(B,Be)_{12}O_{28}$
Hardness 8, **Sp. gr.** 3.2–3.6
Color White-gray, yellow
Streak White
Luster Vitreous to greasy
Cleavage Indiscernible
Fracture Conchoidal
Tenacity Brittle
Crystal form Cubic

Morphology Rhombic dodecahedral and tetrahedral crystals, anhedral.
Origin and occurrence In alkali-rich pegmatites as a late formation.
Accessory minerals Feldspar, quartz, tourmaline (elbaite), spodumene, beryl.
Similar minerals Feldspar has a different crystal form; the same applies to quartz; garnet is usually more brown or red; spinel forms almost only octahedral crystals.

Localities	
1 Brittany, France	**3** Bernburg, Thuringia, Germany
2 Skardu, Pakistan	**4** Sahatany, Madagascar

1 2
3 4

1–4 Tourmaline

Chem. formula Tourmalines are a group of solid solutions with the following end members:
Elbaite
$Na(Li,Al)_3Al_6[OH)_4/(BO_3)_3/Si_6O_{18}]$
Dravite
$NaMg_3(Al,Fe^{3+})_3Al_6[OH)_4/(BO_3)_3/Si_6O_{18}]$
Schorl
$NaFe_3^{2+}(Al,Fe)_6[OH)_4/(BO_3)_3/Si_6O_{18}]$
Buergerite
$NaFe_3^{3+}Al_6[F/O_3/(BO_3)_3/Si_6O_{18}]$
Tsilaisite
$NaMn_3Al_6[OH)_4/(BO_3)3/Si_6O_{18}]$
Uvite
$CaMg_3(Al_5Mg)[OH)_4/(BO_3)_3/Si_6O_{18}]$
Liddicoatite
$Ca(Li,Al)_3Al_6[OH)_4/(BO_3)_3/Si_6O_{18}]$
Povondraite $(Na,K)(Fe^{2+},Fe^{3+})_3(Fe^{3+},Mg,Al)_6[OH)_4/(BO_3)_3/Si_6O_{18}]$

Hardness 7, **Sp. gr.** 3–3.25
Color Colorless, pink (rubellite), green (verdelite), blue (indigolite), yellow, brown, black, transparent to opaque. Tourmalines that have black ends with yellowish or pinkish crystal are called moor's heads
Streak White
Luster Vitreous
Cleavage None
Fracture Conchoidal
Tenacity Brittle
Crystal form Trigonal

Morphology Crystals prismatic to acicular, mainly with triangular cross-section, euhedral and anhedral, radial, columnar, uneven.
Origin and occurrence Anhedral and euhedral in granites, pegmatites, pneumatolytic veins, hydrothermal veins, euhedral crystals of gemstone quality in vugs in pegmatites, anhedral in mica schists and gneisses, euhedral on alpine fissures. The variegated tourmalines, also extracted as gemstones, are mainly elbaites, more rarely dravites or liddicoatites. The main country supplying gemstone tourmalines is Brazil, where rubellites of up to one meter in size have been found. Particularly beautiful grades with black schorl on white albite originate from Pakistan; large dravites have been found in Australia. In Germany, particularly lovely tourmalines have been found in the Bavarian Forest.
Accessory minerals Quartz, feldspar, beryl, mica.
Distinguishing feature Tourmaline crystals do not have a mirror plane perpendicular to their normal longitudinal extension. Consequently, the two ends of the crystals, top and bottom, do not consist of the same crystal faces. Thus, for example, a tourmaline crystal may exhibit the typical three end faces at the top, while only the horizontal basal face forms the bottom. This property is called hemimorphism, and, with the exception of tourmaline, its occurrence is limited to a very small number of minerals, such as hemimorphite. This fact gives tourmaline another of its properties, that of being piezo-electric. If a tourmaline crystal is subjected to a directional pressure perpendicular to its longitudinal extension, it becomes differently charged at each of its two ends and an electric current flows. This effect can also be produced by rubbing or heating; in the latter case, it is referred to as pyroelectricity. If you rub a tourmaline crystal vigorously so that each of its two ends receives a different electrical charge, it can attract small pieces of paper. The Dutch, therefore, used it to clean their pipes and called it aschentrekker, which translates to pipe cleaner. Today, on account of its piezoelectricity, small disks of tourmaline are used in measuring devices to check the operation of jet engines.
Similar minerals The usually distinctly triangular cross-section distinguishes tourmaline from all other minerals.

Localities	
1 Schorl: Hörlberg, Bavarian Forest, Germany	**3** Elbaite: Minas Gerais, Brazil
2 Elbaite: San Piero, Elba, Italy	**4** Elbaite: Salinas, Minas Gerais, Brazil

1 2
3 4

5–8

Tourmaline

Gemstone

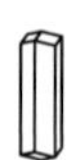

Color Colorless, pink, red, green, blue, black, brown; transparent to translucent
Luster Vitreous
Shape and cut Facet cut, due to the elongated crystals often trepan cut, rarely cabochon cut

Elbaite crystal from the Island of Elba

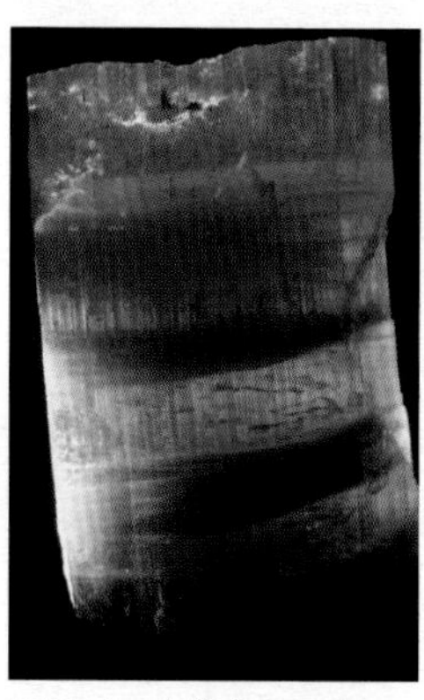

Multi-colored elbaite crystal

Color varieties of tourmaline

Among the tourmaline group, elbaite, in its diverse color varieties, is almost the only mineral used for making jewelry. Much rarer are yellow varieties of dravite or exceptionally liddicoatite, uvite and tsilaisite. However, tourmalines used for jewelry purposes are not normally analyzed, so it is usually unknown whether the stone in question is a color variety of elbaite or one of the rarer tourmaline species of the same color.

In the jewelry trade, people are much more likely to determine the stone based on its color and adapt the names of the color varieties: Rubellite is a pink to occasionally intense red tourmaline. Rubellites measuring up to a meter in diameter have been found in Brazil. Verdelite is a tourmaline ranging from blue-green to grass green. Indigolite is a normally rather dark blue tourmaline, often with a tinge of green. Among tourmalines, blue is by far the rarest color. Paraiba tourmaline is the name given to an intense blue elbaite, colored by its low copper content and found near Paraíba, Brazil. Black schorl is rarely cut; however, it is more often processed as a raw crystal for esoteric reasons when used in jewelry.

Tourmalines are often multi-colored. Crystals that are colored at the bottom (pink, yellow or green) and have a black end at the top, or head, are called moor's heads. Such tourmalines are found exclusively in the pegmatites found on the Italian island of Elba, where exceptional crystal growth conditions resulted in this particular coloring.

Individual tourmaline crystals can have up to eight different color zones perpendicular to the longitudinal extension between the top and bottom ends. However, other crystals are green on the outside and have a red core. Due to this coloring, they are called watermelon tourmalines.

Tourmaline crystals with a fibrous structure are occasionally made into cabochons and have a distinct cat's eye effect. The most common of these is the rubellite cat's eye.

Localities	
5 Elbaite: Minas Gerais, Brazil	**7** Elbaite: Minas Gerais, Brazil
6 Elbaite: Skardu, Pakistan	**8** Elbaite: Minas Gerais, Brazil

5 6

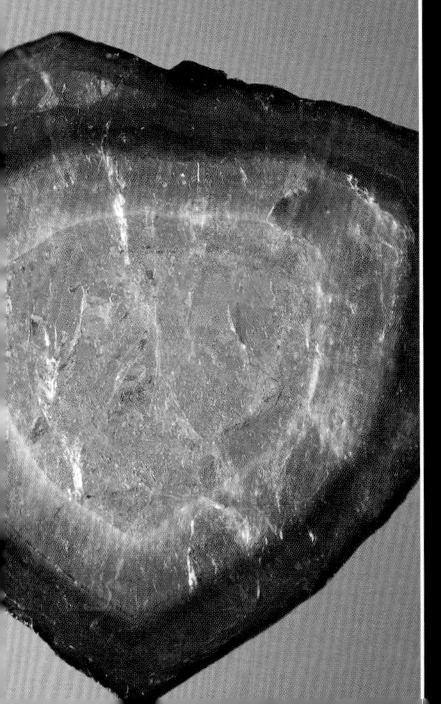
7 8

11–14 Tourmaline

Dravite crystal from Dobrava, Slovenia

Tabular povondraite crystals from Alto Chaparé, Bolivia

Processing Tourmaline is usually processed in facet cut; due to the elongated crystals, particularly with smaller rough stones, the material-saving trepan cut is also used. The cabochon cut is only selected for more impure stones and the very rare cat's eye stones. Watermelon stones and other tourmaline cross-sections with beautiful markings are no longer usually cut, but they are processed as pure cross-sections to create jewelry, in particular pendants.
Use As a center stone in valuable jewelry. Different colored stones in multi-colored necklaces. Tourmaline is also used to make handicraft items, in particular sculptures. Multi-colored rough stones are particularly suitable for this purpose because their different color zones offer a wide design scope if they are selected and oriented skillfully.
Treatment Because tourmaline attracts dust and dirt particles particularly easily due to its pyroelectric property, jewelry containing tourmaline must be cleaned much more frequently than jewelry containing other gemstones.
Distinguishing feature Stones that exhibit a multi-colored center under a dark, often black outer shell present a special feature of tourmaline. Unlike watermelon tourmaline, which is purely red inside, the cross-sections of these crystals exhibit multi-colored geometric shapes, in particular, a wide range of triangles. While the raw crystal appears rather unremarkable, only the thin-cut slices exhibit the variety of shapes and colors of these tourmalines. Only a few tourmalines, mainly those from the Anjanabonoina locality in Madagascar, display this particular characteristic. Large crystals from there have supplied beautiful slabs measuring up to almost half a meter in diameter. If cross-sections of black schorl are cut thinly to a few hundredths of a millimeter, then they often also display beautiful colors and markings in transmitted light.
Differentiating possibilities Tourmaline exhibits a very high birefringence and strong pleochroism. Therefore, when viewed through a tabular crystal, the back edges of a cut stone appear doubled. This property clearly distinguishes tourmaline from other stones. Rubellite is softer than pink topaz and does not have the same cleavage. Green glass, unlike verdelite, always has air bubbles, while peridot is more of a yellow-green. Green garnet is always a lighter green. Emerald is harder and is always the characteristic emerald green, which does not occur with verdelite.

Localities	
11 Rubellite: Minas Gerais, Brazil	**13** Elbaite: Minas Gerais, Brazil
12 Dravite: Gouverneur, New York, USA	**14** Uvite: Brumado, Brazil

11 12
13 14

1

Danburite

Chem. formula $Ca[B_2Si_2O_8]$
Hardness 7–7½, **Sp. gr.** 2.9–3
Color Colorless, white
Streak White
Luster Vitreous
Cleavage None
Fracture Conchoidal
Tenacity Brittle
Crystal form Orthorhombic

Morphology Prismatic crystals with roof-shaped end faces, sometimes vertically striated, crystals mainly euhedral.
Origin and occurrence On alpine fissures, in ore veins, in boron-bearing skarn deposits.
Accessory minerals Quartz, datolite, pyrite.
Similar minerals Quartz has a different crystal form; topaz is harder and has good cleavage; datolite has a different crystal form.

2

Olivine *Peridote*

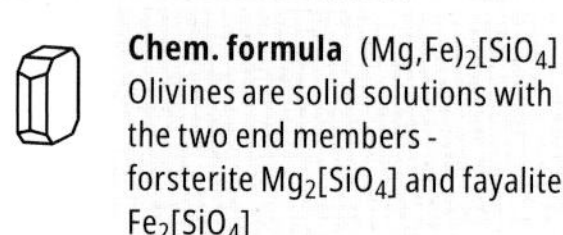

Chem. formula $(Mg,Fe)_2[SiO_4]$
Olivines are solid solutions with the two end members - forsterite $Mg_2[SiO_4]$ and fayalite $Fe_2[SiO_4]$
Hardness 6½–7, **Sp. gr.** 3.27–4.2
Color Yellowish green to bottle green, red, brownish
Streak White
Luster Vitreous, somewhat greasy
Cleavage Scarcely discernible
Fracture Conchoidal
Tenacity Brittle
Crystal form Orthorhombic

Morphology Euhedral crystals are thick tabular to prismatic, often granular, uneven, anhedral.
Origin and occurrence As an essential mineral anhedral in gabbros, diabases, basalts, peridotites, forms as a monomineral the rock dunite, euhedral crystals on fissures of the cited rocks, crystals and grains in crystalline limestones, in meteorites (particularly beautiful in pallasites).
Accessory minerals Spinel, diopside, augite, hornblende.
Similar minerals Apatite is softer, as is serpentine; beryl is harder and always has a hexagonal cross-section.

3

Olivine

Gemstone

Farbe Intense green with a clear tinge of yellow-green, translucent
Luster Vitreous, somewhat greasy
Shape and cut Facet cut

Use Facetted stones as center stones in valuable jewelry, baroque stones or beads are made into necklaces.
Distinguishing feature Peridote has a particularly high birefringence. If you look through the polished tabular crystal to the back facet edges of cut stones, you will see them doubled.
Differentiating possibilities Chrysoberyl is always notably more yellow; it does not have a high birefringence.

4

Euclase

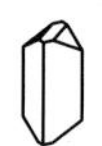

Chem. formula $AlBe[OH/SiO_4]$
Hardness 7½, **Sp. gr.** 3–3.1
Color Colorless, light green, blue, brown
Streak White
Luster Vitreous
Cleavage Perfect prismatic
Fracture Conchoidal
Tenacity Brittle
Crystal form Monoclinic

Morphology Crystals prismatic to tabular, usually strongly striated longitudinally, almost exclusively euhedral crystals, very rarely uneven.
Origin and occurrence In vugs in pegmatites, on alpine fissures, always euhedral crystals.
Accessory minerals Bertrandite, quartz, topaz, microcline, pericline, muscovite, anatase, rutile.
Similar minerals Unlike the longitudinally striated euclase, quartz crystals are always transversely striated; they also have no cleavage; albite has a different crystal form.

Localities	
1 Potosi, Mexico	**3** Pakistan
2 Seberget, Egypt	**4** Mwami, Zambia

1 2

3 4

1 Spinel

Chem. formula $MgAl_2O_4$
Hardness 8, **Sp. gr.** 3.6
Color Red, purple, blue, black, yellow, colorless
Streak White
Luster Vitreous
Cleavage Scarcely discernible
Fracture Conchoidal
Tenacity Brittle
Crystal form Cubic

Morphology Mainly octahedral crystals, twins, anhedral, unrolled.
Origin and occurrence Anhedral in metamorphic rocks, particularly in marbles and calc-silicate rocks and in placers. In Germany, purple anhedral spinel crystals in marble are found especially in the graphite area of Kropfmühl in the Bavarian Forest. Beautiful red spinel crystals measuring up to more than a centimeter in size are found near Marbella, Spain.
Accessory minerals Graphite, olivine, calcite, diopside.
Distinguishing feature Depending on its composition, spinel changes color. Iron contents produce a violet to black color; zinc contents create a greenish hue; pure magnesium spinel is colorless to red; it is also called precious spinel.
Similar minerals Corundum has a different crystal form.

2 Spinel

Gemstone

Color Red, purple, transparent
Luster Vitreous
Shape and cut Facet cut

Color varieties The red variety, also called ruby spinel, is mainly used for jewelry. Very bright red spinels are also erroneously called balas ruby. Dark green to almost black spinel is called ceylanite because of its occurrence on the island of Ceylon (now Sri Lanka).
Use Facetted stones as center stones in precious jewelry.
Differentiating possibilities Ruby is indistinguishable from red spinel by simple methods; the same applies to synthetic ruby and spinel.

3–4 Phenakite

Chem. formula $Be_2[SiO_4]$
Hardness 8, **Sp. gr.** 3
Color Colorless, yellowish, pink, white
Streak White
Luster Vitreous
Cleavage None
Fracture Conchoidal
Tenacity Brittle
Crystal form Trigonal

Morphology Crystals prismatic to tabular, lenticular, prisms vertically striated, anhedral and euhedral. Phenakite often forms twins in which the crystals are intergrown in such a way that the corners of one crystal project over the end faces of the other. Because of this appearance, they are also called “drill-bit twins.”
Origin and occurrence Anhedral in mica schists together with emerald, in vugs and on fissures in pegmatites and granites, on alpine fissures. The largest phenakites were found together with emeralds in Takovaya in the Urals.
Accessory minerals Emerald, bertrandite, chrysoberyl, apatite.
Similar minerals Quartz is slightly softer and always transversely striated over the prisms; apatite is softer; beryl is not trigonal but hexagonal.

Localities	
1 Hunzatal, Pakistan	**3** Spitzkoppe, Namibia
2 Mogok, Myanmar	**4** Gastein Valley, Austria

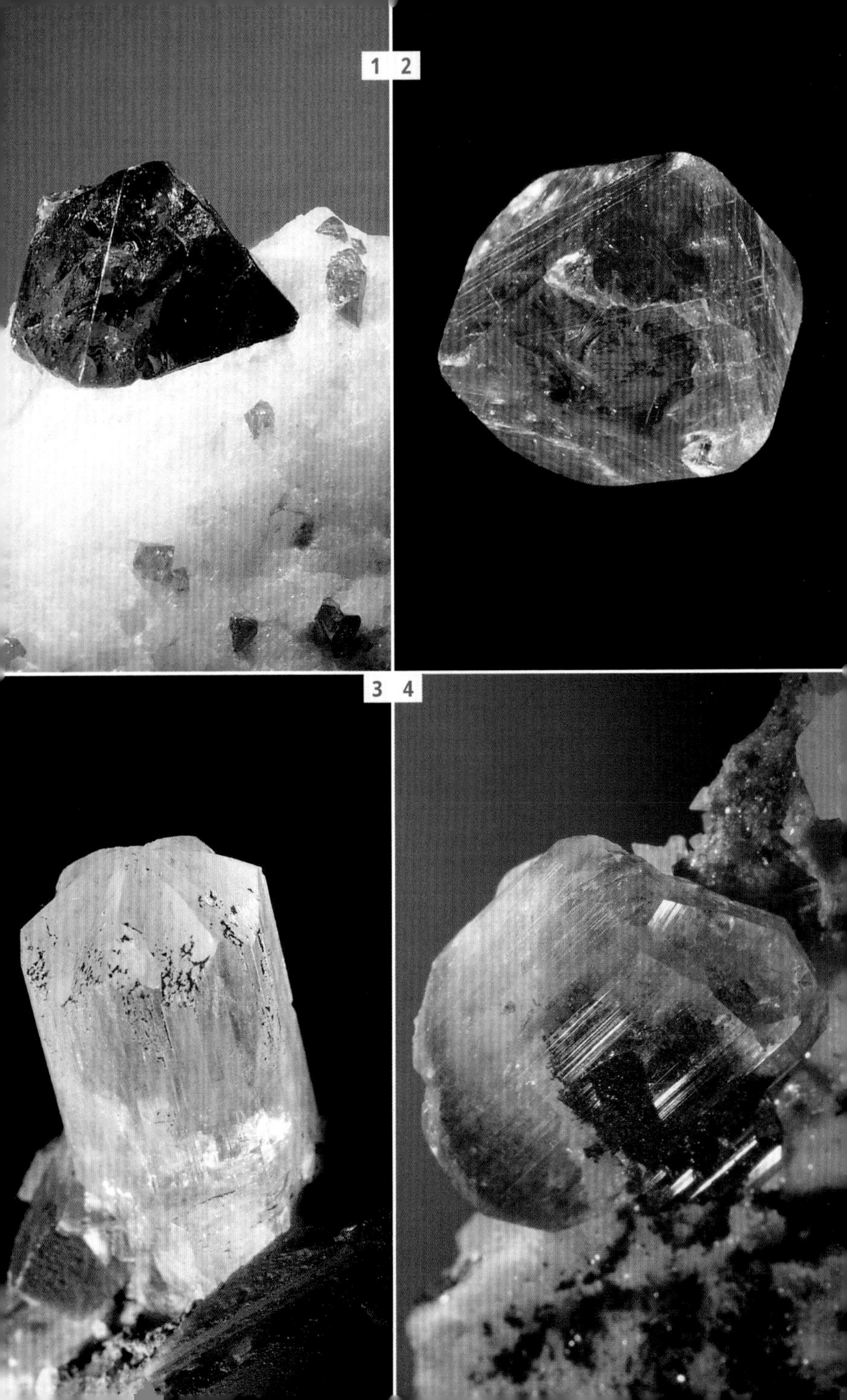
1 2
3 4

1

Zircon

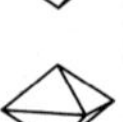

Chem. formula $Zr[SiO_4]$
Hardness 7½, **Sp. gr.** 4.55–4.67
Color Colorless, white, pink, yellow, green, blue, brown, brown-red
Streak White
Luster Adamantine-type luster, greasy on fracture surfaces
Cleavage Scarcely discernible
Fracture Conchoidal
Tenacity Brittle
Crystal form Tetragonal

Morphology Prismatic to bipyramidal crystals, euhedral, more often anhedral, almost never uneven, always in crystals.
Origin and occurrence In granites, syenites, rhyolites, trachytes, volcanic ejecta, in placers, pegmatites, on alpine fissures.
Accessory minerals Xenotime, monazite.
Distinguishing feature Some zircons may contain small amounts of uranium or thorium. As a result, they become dark green or dark brown, and their crystal lattice is destroyed. Minerals affected in this way are called metamicts.
Similar minerals Vesuvianite is softer; tinstone is heavier.

2

Zircon

Gemstone

Color Green, brown, red, blue colorless
Luster Vitreous, somewhat greasy
Shape and cut Facet cut

Use Facetted stones as center stones in precious jewelry.
Distinguishing feature Zircon exhibits a particularly high birefringence. If you look through the polished tabular crystal to the back facet edges of cut stones, you will see them doubled.
Treatment White and blue zircons are produced by burning and irradiation.
Differentiating possibilities Sapphires do not have a high birefringence; diamond produces a much higher fire.

3

Chrysoberyl *Alexandrite*

Chem. formula Al_2BeO_4
Hardness 8½, **Sp. gr.** 3.7
Color Yellow, green (alexandrite)
Streak White
Luster Vitreous
Cleavage Basal discernible
Fracture Conchoidal
Tenacity Brittle
Crystal form Orthorhombic

Morphology Crystals prismatic to thick tabular, heart-shaped to V-shaped twins, triplets resemble hexagonal dipyramids, anhedral and euhedral.
Origin and occurrence In pegmatites and mica schists, anhedral and euhedgral, rarely uneven, almost always crystals.
Accessory minerals Emerald, feldspar, mica, phenakite.
Distinguishing feature Alexandrite changes color; in daylight, its green color changes to red under incandescent light.
Similar minerals The high hardness of chrysoberyl almost allows for no confusion; topaz always has very good cleavage; beryl exhibits a different hexagonal crystal form.

4

Chrysoberyl

Gemstone

Color Yellow, brown, green; transparent to translucent
Luster Vitreous
Shape and cut Facet cut for chrysoberyl and alexandrite, cabochon cut for chrysoberyl cat's eye

Use As a center stone in valuable jewelry.
Differentiating possibilities Chrysoberyl: yellow sapphire is usually more intense and a purer yellow; zircon has a high birefringence. Synthetic spinel: fluoresces strongly with a green color. Topaz: is a purer yellow. Glass and yellow orthoclase: are much softer. Alexandrite: synthetic color-changing corundum and synthetic alexandrite exhibit a much purer color change than natural stones.

Localities	
1 Gilgit, Pakistan	**3** Orissa, India
2 Sri Lanka	**4** Sri Lanka

1 2
3 4

1–4 Beryl

Chem. formula $Al_2Be_3[Si_6O_{18}]$
Hardness 7½–8, **Sp. gr.** 2.63–2.8
Color Colorless, yellow (gold beryl, heliodor), pink (morganite), intense pink-red (the cesium beryl pezzottaite), red, blue (aquamarine), green (emerald)
Streak White
Luster Vitreous
Cleavage Basal sometimes discernible
Fracture Conchoidal to uneven
Tenacity Brittle
Crystal form Hexagonal

Aquamarine crystals from Pakistan

The trapiche emerald gets its name from its shape, which resembles the wheels of old sugar cane mills

Morphology Crystals prismatic to tabular, rarely planar, anhedral (cloudy) and euhedral (transparent), to some extent giant crystals up to several meters in size and several tons in weight.
Origin and occurrence Anhedral in pegmatites (common beryl and aquamarine), euhedral in vugs in pegmatites (morganite, pezzottaite, aquamarine, gold beryl), in mica schists and hydrothermal calcite veins (emerald). The best European emeralds come from the famous Leckbachscharte deposit in Habach Valley in the High Tauern mountains in Austria. Anhedral crystals form in mica schists here. The emeralds from the deposits in the Urals, by Takovaya, are also well-known. Large crystals are found in the mica schist together with alexandrite and phenakite at this locality.
The most beautiful Morganite crystals (tabular crystals up to 20 cm) come from Brazil, while pezzottaite is found almost exclusively in pegmatites on the island of Madagascar.
Accessory minerals Feldspar, quartz, calcite, pyrite, muscovite, biotite, phenakite.
Distinguishing feature For a long time, Russian deposits in the Urals were the only suppliers of larger quantities of emerald. Cleopatra's classic emerald mines had been forgotten, as had the Colombian emerald mines of the Incas. Both occurrences were only rediscovered in the 20th century. However, while the Egyptian deposit is exhausted and only of scientific interest, the Colombian sites, such as Muzo or Chivor, still deliver the world's best crystals and crystal grades.
Similar minerals Apatite is much softer; quartz only very rarely forms anhedral crystals and is never blue or green, otherwise the structure of hexagonal crystals is very characteristic; dioptase always has triangular end faces and is much softer; topaz has excellent cleavage and distinct orthorhombic crystals. Green tourmaline never exhibits the beautiful emerald color, rather it is usually darker and more yellow-green; vanadinite occurs in a different paragenesis to red beryl and is much softer.

Localities	
1 Nagar, Pakistan	**3** Wah-Wah Mountains, Utah, USA
2 Muzo, Columbia	**4** Muzo, Columbia

1 2
3 4

1–4 Beryl

Gemstone

Color Emerald green (emerald), blue (aquamarine), pink (morganite), transparent
Luster Vitreous
Shape and cut Facet cut, often trepan cut due to the elongated shape of the rough stones, translucent stones with many inclusions also as cabochon

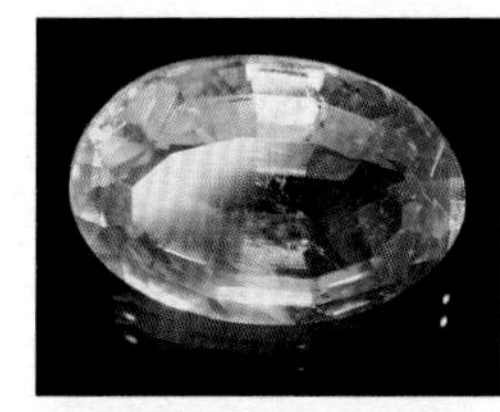

Facetted aquamarine

Facetted gold beryl

Facetted emerald

Color varieties Beryl occurs in many different color varieties, almost all of which are cut for jewelry purposes.
Aquamarine is a light to dark blue, also greenish beryl. Poorly colored specimens can be transformed into beautiful blue stones by firing at 752° F.
Emerald is an intensely green-colored beryl due to low levels of chromium; a similar color can also be produced by low levels of vanadium.
Golden beryl, or heliodor, is a golden yellow-colored beryl in which its color occurs as a result of natural radioactive irradiation.
Goshenite is called a colorless beryl; it is only rarely cut.
Morganite, or worobieffite, is an intensely pink beryl.
Pezzotaite is a cesium beryl that stands out for its intense pink color; as it is very rare, it is not often made into jewelry.
Red beryl or bixbite is an intense dark red; large sectile crystals are very rare.
Use Primarily as a center stone in rings and pendants. In a few cases, particularly large emeralds or aquamarines were processed to make handicraft items, such as small bowls or small boxes. Today these pieces are priceless.
Treatment Emeralds are often oiled to improve their color. Some emerald doublets exist; the top of which is colorless beryl affixed with an intensely green glue to the bottom section, for example rock crystal, so that the doublet appears emerald green. Aquamarine is fired for color enhancement.
Distinguishing feature Due to the high value of good emeralds, the trepan or emerald cut, a particularly material-saving cut, was developed for elongated rough pieces.
Differentiating possibilities Duplicates can be recognized by the separating layer when viewed from the side; the color of emeralds is very characteristic; aquamarine is softer than blue topaz. Unlike aquamarine, blue zircon has a notable birefringence. Chrysoberyl is harder than heliodor; unlike heliodor, yellow zircon has a significant birefringence; natural citrine is a paler yellow and softer. Unlike morganite, kunzite exhibits a clear pleochroism; pink sapphire is distinctly harder. Colorless topaz has a much higher density than goshenite and exhibits distinct cleavage.

Localities	
1 Hühnerkobel, Bavarian Forest, Germany	**3** Urals, Russia
2 Habach Valley, Austria	**4** Wolodarsk, Ukraine

1 2
3 4

1–4 **Topaz**

Chem. formula $Al_2[F_2/SiO_4]$
Hardness 8, **Sp. gr.** 3.5–3.6
Color Colorless, white, yellow, blue, green, red, pink, purple, brown
Streak White
Luster Vitreous
Cleavage Perfect basal
Fracture Conchoidal
Tenacity Brittle
Crystal form Orthorhombic

Red topaz from Russia

Morphology Crystals short or long columnar, euhedral and anhedral, giant crystals up to many hundreds of kilograms in weight, uneven, radial.
Origin and occurrence Anhedral and euhedral crystals in pegmatites, euhedral in pneumatolytic formations and in radial aggregates and unrolled on placers. Well-formed crystals are found in cavities of quartz-rich, rhyolitic rocks. The main occurrences of this species are in Utah, USA and San Luis Potosí, Mexico. Beautiful gemstone-quality yellow crystals come from Schneckenstein in Vogtland, Saxony, Germany.
Accessory minerals Tinstone, fluorite, tourmaline, quartz, feldspar, mica, beryl.
Distinguishing feature Yellow, radial topaz from pneumatolytic deposits is also called pyknite. Sherry brown topaz, particularly found near Ouro Preto in Brazil, is called imperial topaz (Fig. 6).
Pink and brown topaz quickly loses its color with prolonged exposure to sunlight. Such crystals as well as the gemstones cut from them should be stored away from the sun.
Due to its high value, other minerals are often erroneously called topaz. Thus, quartz topaz or Madeira topaz is nothing but burnt amethyst, and smoky topaz is actually common smoky quartz.
Similar minerals Quartz is lighter and has no cleavage; fluorite is much softer; beryl has a very different crystal form and its cleavage is not as distinct.

Topaz *Gemstone*

Color Colorless, yellow, brown, blue, pink, red, green; transparent
Luster Vitreous
Shape and cut Facet cut

Facetted imperial topaz

Use Facetted stones as a center stones in rings, brooches, etc. Spheres, or beads, and baroque stones in necklaces.
Treatment Irradiation and subsequent firing often lends a desired blue color to colorless topaz. Stones treated in this way are worth much less than the naturally blue ones and also sometimes fade over time. In trade, these must always be marked as "treated." They are also frequently described as "color-enhanced."
Differentiating possibilities Fired amethyst and natural citrine are softer than brown to yellow topaz and exhibit no cleavage; aquamarine is almost indistinguishable from blue topaz using simple means; blue zircon has a high birefringence; glass is much softer.

Localities	
1 Thomas Range, Utah, USA	**3** Mursinka, Urals, Russia
2 Mursinka, Urals, Russia	**4** Schneckenstein, Vogtland, Germany

1 2
3 4

1 Dumortierite

Chem. formula $Al_7(BO_3)(SiO_4)_3O_3$
Hardness 8–8½, **Sp. gr.** 3.3–3.5
Color Purple, crimson, blue, brown
Streak White
Luster Vitreous
Cleavage Poorly discernible
Fracture Fibrous
Tenacity Brittle
Crystal form Orthorhombic

Morphology Long prismatic to acicular crystals, almost always anhedral, uneven, radial, fibrous, stellate.
Origin and occurrence Anhedral crystals in pegmatites, in aluminum-rich metamorphic rocks and quartz veins in these rocks.
Accessory minerals Tourmaline, quartz, feldspar, mica, cordierite, andalusite, corundum.
Distinguishing feature Submicroscopic inclusions of dumortierite are the reason behind the rose color of rose quartz.
Similar minerals Tourmaline is never as purple, likewise andalusite; cordierite is neither fibrous or acicular.

2–4 Corundum

Chem. formula Al_2O_3
Hardness 9, **Sp. gr.** 3.9–4.1
Color Many color varieties, some of which have received their own names, for example, blue (sapphire), red (ruby), also yellow, orange, green, brown, purple, white, colorless
Streak White
Luster Vitreous
Cleavage Poor, sometimes basal scoria
Fracture Conchoidal
Tenacity Brittle
Crystal form Trigonal

Morphology Crystals prismatic, bipyramidal, tabular, often barrel-shaped, spindle-shaped, uneven.
Origin and occurrence Anhedral in pegmatites, peridotites, amphibolites, gneisses, marbles, as foreign inclusions in volcanic rocks euhedral crystals in volcanic ejecta, unrolled in placers. Corundum-rich rocks are called emery or corundite rocks.
Accessory minerals Spinel, magnetite, calcite, biotite, feldspar, quartz.
Similar minerals Hardness and crystal form distinguish corundum from all other minerals; spinel is softer and exhibits distinct octahedral crystals; unlike corundum, dumortierite usually has a radial morphology.

5–6 Corundum

Gemstone

Color Red (ruby), pink, blue (sapphire), yellow, orange (padparadscha)
Shape and cut Facet cut; specimens that are only translucent due to multiple inclusions, and the star stones, in particular, are cut as cabochons

Distinguishing feature Some rubies and sapphires exhibit a six-rayed light star when cut as a cabochon.
Treatment Sapphire is usually fired to bring out the beautiful blue color.
Use As a faceted stone or cabochon mainly used as a ring stone or for pendants, usually as a center stone. Less commonly, opaque stones are cut into spheres for stone necklaces.
Differentiating possibilities The correspondingly colored glasses are much softer; synthetic star rubies and star sapphires have a much sharper star than natural stones and have a much too uniform, opaque groundmass; spinel is softer but difficult to distinguish using simple means; in rough stones, the respective crystal shape is characteristic; garnet is clearly softer and usually has a different shade of red than a ruby.

Localities		
1 California, USA	**3** Hunzatal, Pakistan	**5** Pakistan
2 Madagascar	**4** Campolungo, Switzerland	**6** Kashmir

1
2
3
4
5
6

1–2 Diamond

Chem. formula C
Hardness 10, **Sp. gr.** 3.52
Color Colorless, white, yellow, brown, reddish, greenish, blue, gray, black
Streak White
Luster Adamantine
Cleavage Octahedral perfect
Fracture Conchoidal
Tenacity Brittle
Crystal form Cubic

Octahedral diamond crystals from Brazil

Morphology Most common are octahedral, rhombic dodecahedral, less common cubic, often strongly etched, rounded crystals, stellate aggregates (bort), crystals always anhedral, never euhedral.
Origin and occurrence In basic, volcanic rocks, especially kimberlites, which form pipes, in eclogites, eroded in placers, re-consolidated in conglomerates and metamorphic shales, in meteorites.
Accessory minerals Pyrope, olivine, phlogopite, chromite, diopside, spinel.
Distinguishing feature Diamond deposits are usually heavily guarded; as a layperson or collector, you are not allowed to visit them. However, in the USA, there is a locality near Dumfriesboro, Arkansas, where you can prospect for diamonds for just a small charge. They also quite rare here, but individual collectors have found stones weighing many carats.
Similar minerals Its high hardness distinguishes the diamond from all other minerals. Rock crystal and zircon have much lower refraction; zircon also has a very high birefringence. Colorless sapphire is softer than diamond; colorless topaz has perfect cleavage and is much softer.

3–4 Diamond

Gemstone

Color Colorless, white, yellow, green, blue, red, pink, brown, black; transparent to opaque
Luster Adamantine
Shape and cut Facet cut
Diamond is always facet cut because this accentuates its high light refraction. The classic form of diamond cut is called brilliant cut. In common parlance, diamonds cut in this way are also simply called brilliants although this type of cut is also used for other gemstones

Use Diamonds are processed into all types of high quality jewelry; small diamonds are also often used to encircle a main stone of another type of gemstone, for example, an emerald, sapphire or ruby.
Treatment Diamond is very hard, but it is still very sensitive to impact and can chip or jump relatively easily.

Localities	
1 South Africa	**3** Kimberley, South Africa
2 South Africa	**4** South Africa

1 2
3 4

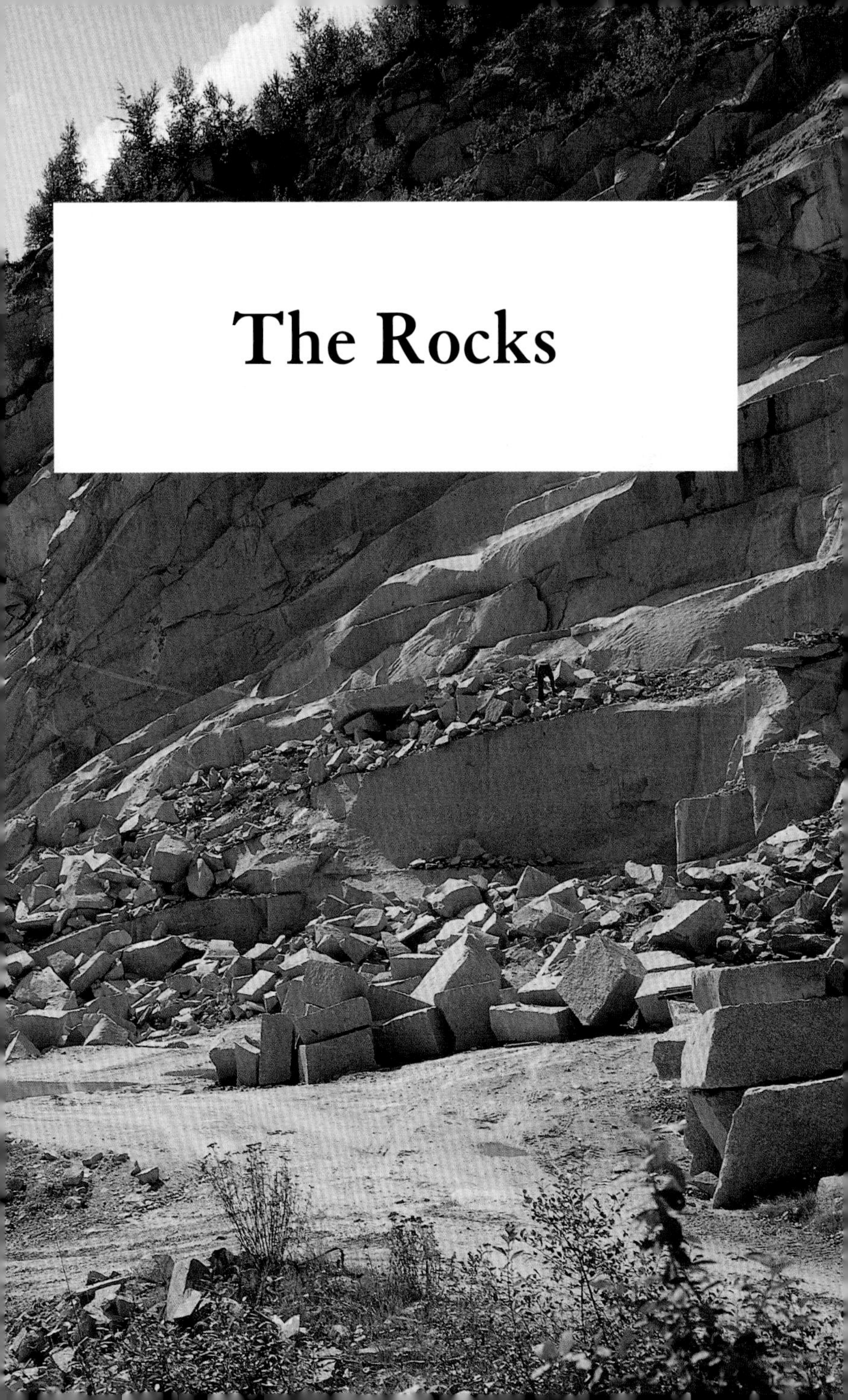

The Rocks

1 Granite

Intrusive igneous rock

Essential minerals Potassium feldspar, plagioclase, quartz
Accessory minerals Muscovite, hornblende, tourmaline
Color White, gray, reddish, greenish, yellowish
Structure Medium- to coarse-grained, often inclusions of foreign rocks, often heavily fissured

Origin By melting of rocks of granitic composition as the final stage of metamorphism.
Occurrence Smaller and larger intrusions, stocks, laccoliths, dikes.
Use As building stone, for decorative purposes, as a gravestone, curbstone, as crushed stone in road construction.
Similar rocks In granodiorite, plagioclase outweighs potassium feldspar; gneiss exhibits significant schistosity.

2 Binary granite

Intrusive igneous rock

Essential minerals Potassium feldspar, plagioclase, quartz
Accessory minerals Muscovite, biotite, hornblende, tourmaline
Color White, gray, reddish, greenish, yellowish
Structure Medium- to coarse-grained, often inclusions of foreign rocks, often heavily fissured

Origin By melting of rocks of granitic composition as the final stage of metamorphism.
Occurrence Smaller and larger intrusions, stocks, laccoliths, dikes.
Use As building stone, for decorative purposes, as a gravestone, curbstone, as crushed stone in road construction.
Similar rocks In granodiorite, plagioclase outweighs potassium feldspar; gneiss exhibits significant schistosity; ordinary granite only contains one type of mica.

3 Porphyritic granite

Intrusive igneous rock

Essential minerals Potassium feldspar, plagioclase, quartz
Accessory minerals Biotite, muscovite, hornblende, tourmaline
Inclusions Potassium feldspar, plagioclase, hornblende, tourmaline
Color White, gray, reddish, greenish, yellowish
Structure Medium- to coarse-grained groundmass, porphyritic with large potassium feldspars, often inclusions of foreign rocks, often heavily fissured

Origin By melting of rocks of granitic composition as the final stage of metamorphism.
Occurrence Smaller and larger intrusions, stocks, laccoliths, dikes.
Use As building stone, for decorative purposes, as a gravestone, curbstone, as crushed stone in road construction.
Similar rocks In granodiorite, plagioclase outweighs potassium feldspar; gneiss exhibits significant schistosity.

4 Biotite granite

Intrusive igneous rock

Essential minerals Potassium feldspar, plagioclase, quartz
Accessory minerals Biotite, hornblende
Inclusions Potassium feldspar, plagioclase, hornblende
Color White, gray, reddish, greenish, yellowish
Structure Medium- to coarse-grained groundmass, rarely porphyritic

Origin By melting of rocks of granitic composition as the final stage of metamorphism.
Occurrence Smaller and larger intrusions, stocks, laccoliths, dikes.
Use As building stone, for decorative purposes, as a gravestone, curbstone, as crushed stone in road construction.
Similar rocks In granodiorite, plagioclase outweighs potassium feldspar; gneiss exhibits significant schistosity.

Localities

1 Gavorrano, Italy	**3** Höhenberg, Bavaria, Germany
2 Leuchtenberg, Bavaria, Germany	**4** Wegscheid, Bavaria, Germany

1 2
3 4

1 Graphic granite

Dike rock

Essential minerals Potassium feldspar, quartz
Accessory minerals Muscovite, plagioclase
Color White, gray, reddish, greenish, yellowish
Structure Graphic texture intergrowth of potassium feldspar and quartz

Origin Formation in the border area of pegmatites or in their intermediate zone.

Occurrence In the area of pegmatite dikes and pegmatite stocks.

Use As building stone, for decorative purposes, as a gravestone, curbstone, as crushed stone in road construction.

Similar rocks In granodiorite, plagioclase outweighs potassium feldspar; gneiss exhibits significant schistosity.

2 Orbicular granite

Intrusive igneous rock

Essential minerals Potassium feldspar, plagioclase, quartz
Accessory minerals Biotite, muscovite, hornblende, tourmaline
Inclusions Potassium feldspar, plagioclase, hornblende, tourmaline
Color White, gray, reddish, greenish, yellowish
Structure Botryoidal aggregates in medium- to coarse-grained groundmass

Origin The method of formation of the botryoidal structure has not yet been reliably clarified through melting of rocks with granitic composition.

Occurrence Smaller and larger intrusions, stocks, laccoliths, dikes.

Use As building stone, for decorative purposes, as a gravestone, curbstone, as crushed stone in road construction.

Similar rocks In granodiorite, plagioclase outweighs potassium feldspar; gneiss exhibits significant schistosity.

3 Tonalite

Intrusive igneous rock

Essential minerals Plagioclase (oligoclase andesine), quartz, hornblende
Accessory minerals Biotite, muscovite, pyroxene
Inclusions Hornblende, biotite
Color Light to dark gray, often light with dark inclusions
Structure Medium- to coarse-grained, often with inclusions in a finer groundmass

Origin The first product of the differentiation of granitic magma bodies during the melting of rocks at great depths.

Occurrence Inside large, granitic magma bodies, for example, on Adamello in South Tyrol, Italy.

Use As building stone, road gravel, as decorative stone.

Similar rocks Granite and granodiorite differ from tonalite through the presence of potassium feldspar; the same applies to syenite; pegmatite is much coarser-grained; nepheline syenite contains nepheline.

4 Aplite

Dike rock

Essential minerals Quartz, potassium feldspar
Accessory minerals Biotite, muscovite, hornblende, tourmaline
Inclusions Tourmaline, hornblende
Color White to light gray
Structure Fine-grained, sometimes zoned, dike-type, often also as a fine-grained zone adjacent to or around pegmatite

Origin At the end of the crystallization process of a magma body, dike rocks such as aplite form in cracks and fissures.

Occurrence As dikes in granites and their surrounding country rocks, common in all granitic areas.

Use Aplite is extracted from granite during crushed stone production; otherwise it is considered an undesirable country rock.

Similar rocks Occurrence as a vein is typical and, together with the light color, makes aplite unmistakable; pegmatite is much coarser-grained.

Localities	
1 Bodenmais, Bavaria, Germany	**3** Zillertal, Austria
2 Finland	**4** Tittling, Bavaria, Germany

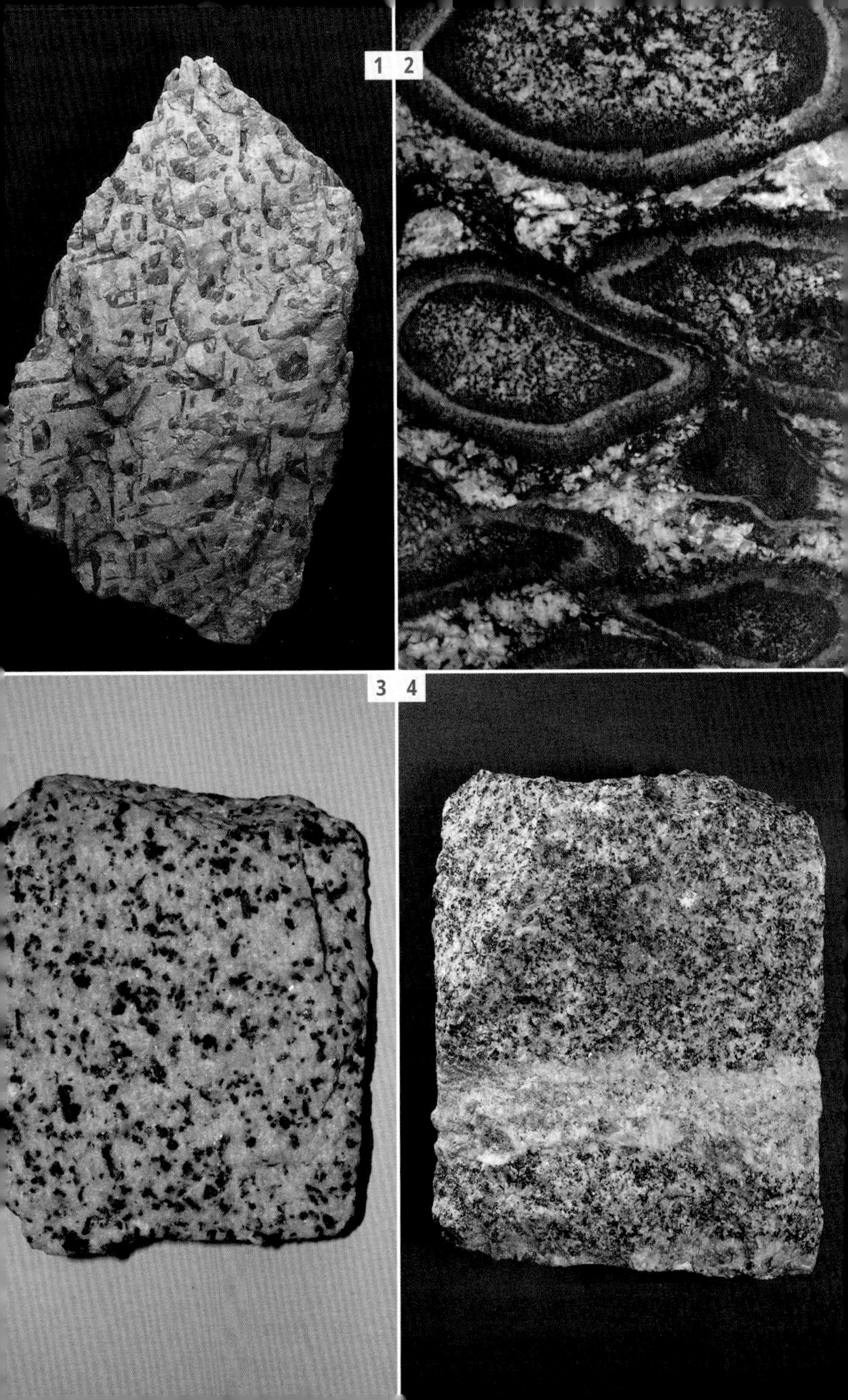
1 2
3 4

1 Lamprophyre
Dike rock

Essential minerals Biotite, hornblende, potassium feldspar
Accessory minerals Pyroxene, olivine
Inclusions Hornblende
Color Dark gray to brown
Structure Fine-grained, dike-type, sometimes porphyritic

Origin At the end of the crystallization process of larger intrusive bodies.

Occurrence As dikes in granites and gabbros and their surrounding country rocks.

Use Lamprophyre is extracted during crushed stone production; otherwise it is considered an undesirable country rock with no intended use.

Similar rocks Occurrence as a vein is typical; alpite is much lighter; pegmatite is much coarser-grained.

2 Pegmatite
Dike rock

Essential minerals Quartz, potassium feldspar
Accessory minerals Plagioclase, muscovite
Inclusions Tourmaline, columbite, beryl, topaz, lepidolite and many other rare minerals
Color White, gray, pink, variegated
Structure Coarse to giant grains (grain sizes in the meter range)

Origin At the end of rock crystallization, volatile phases remain, which also contain all the elements that do not fit into the normal rock-forming minerals. From these, pegmatites are formed in fissures, cracks and other cavities.

Occurrence As dikes, schlieren, stocks, usually together with granites.

Use The potassium feldspar of the pegmatites is extracted as raw material for the porcelain industry.

Similar rocks The very large grain size of the pegmatite does not allow for any confusion.

3 Syenite
Intrusive igneous rock

Essential minerals Potassium feldspar, plagioclase (andesine oligoclase), hornblende
Accessory minerals Biotite, pyroxene, quartz
Inclusions Hornblende, pyroxene, titanite
Color Light to dark gray
Structure Medium- to coarse-grained, rarely porphyritic, sometimes drusy, porous

Origin By differentiation from more basic magmas.

Occurrence In smaller, distinct intrusive bodies, as part of large, differentiated gabbroid rock bodies. In Germany, near Seußen and Wölsau in the Fichtelgebirge (Fichtel Mountains) and in the Plauenschen Grund in Saxony.

Use Locally as building stone, for crushed stone production.

Similar rocks Unlike syenite, granite has quartz as a main component and hornblende as an accessory mineral at best; unlike syenite, diorite does not contain potassium feldspar as an essential mineral.

4 Nepheline syenite
Intrusive igneous rock

Essential minerals Potassium feldspar, albite, nepheline
Accessory minerals Pyroxene, amphibole, sodalite
Inclusions Hornblende, pyroxene, titanite
Color Light to dark gray
Structure Medium- to coarse-grained, rarely porphyritic, sometimes drusy, porous

Origin From very alkaline magmas.

Occurrence In smaller, distinct intrusive bodies, as part of large, differentiated alkaline rock bodies.

Use Locally as building stone, for crushed stone production.

Similar rock Unlike nepheline syenite, granite has quartz as its main component and does not contain nepheline. The presence of nepheline is characteristic.

Localities	
1 Kropfmühl, Bavaria, Germany	**3** Vosges, France
2 Naabburg, Bavaria, Germany	**4** Langesundfjord, Norway

1
2
3
4

1 Essexite

Intrusive igneous rock

Essential minerals Plagioclase (labradorite), potassium feldspar, pyroxene
Accessory minerals Nepheline, leucite, sodalite
Inclusions Plagioclase
Color Light to dark gray
Structure Fine- to medium-grained, rarely porphyritic

Origin From very alkali-rich and low-silicon magmas.
Occurrence In smaller distinct intrusive bodies, often together with other alkaline rocks.
Use Locally as building stone for wall construction.
Similar rocks Unlike essexite, granite has quartz as its main component; nepheline syenite does not contain labradorite; monzonite does not contain nepheline, nor do diorite and granodiorite; all volcanic rocks of similar composition are much finer-grained than essexite.

2 Monzonite

Intrusive igneous rock

Essential minerals Plagioclase (labradorite), potassium feldspar, pyroxene
Accessory minerals Quartz, biotite
Inclusions Plagioclase
Color Light to dark gray
Structure Fine- to medium-grained, often flow structures

Origin Through local remelting.
Occurrence In small intrusive bodies, stocks, lenses.
Use Locally as building stone, for crushed stone production.
Distinguishing feature Monzonite is named after its occurrence in the Monzoni Massif in South Tyrol.
Similar rocks Unlike monzonite, granite has quartz as a major component; norite and gabbro contain no potassium feldspar; essexite, unlike monzonite, contains the feldspar representatives nepheline, leucite and sodalite; diorite contains hornblende and does not contain nepheline.

3 Diorite

Intrusive igneous rock

Essential minerals Plagioclase (oligoclase andesine), hornblende
Accessory minerals Quartz, biotite, pyroxene
Inclusions Hornblende, quartz, titanite
Color Medium to dark gray
Structure Fine- to medium-grained, rarely botryoidal structures

Origin As first segregation during differentiation of granitic magmas.
Occurrence At the boundary area of large, silicon-rich rock complexes, also in smaller, discrete rock complexes.
Use Locally as building stone, for crushed stone production, attractively colored variants as decorative stone.
Similar rocks Unlike diorite hornblende, gabbro contains more anorthite-rich plagioclase and pyroxenes as main components.

4 Granodiorite

Intrusive igneous rock

Essential minerals Plagioclase (oligoclase andesine), hornblende, quartz
Accessory minerals Biotite, pyroxene
Inclusions Hornblende, quartz
Color Medium to dark gray
Structure Fine- to medium-grained, rarely porphyritic

Origin As first segregation during differentiation of granitic magmas.
Occurrence At the boundary area of large, silicon-rich rock complexes, also in smaller, discrete rock complexes.
Use Locally as building stone, for crushed stone production, attractively colored variants as decorative stone.
Similar rocks Unlike diorite hornblende, gabbro contains more anorthite-rich plagioclase and pyroxenes as main components.

Localities	
1 Scotland, Great Britain	**3** Fürstenstein, Bavaria, Germany
2 Monzoni, South Tyrol, Italy	**4** Fürstenstein, Bavaria, Germany

1
2
3
4

1 Titanite-speckled diorite

Intrusive igneous rock

Essential minerals Plagioclase (oligoclase andesine), hornblende
Accessory minerals Quartz, biotite, pyroxene
Inclusions Hornblende, quartz, titanite
Color Medium to dark gray
Structure Fine- to medium-grained groundmass, porphyritic with titanite inclusions, each with a plagioclase-rich white aureole

Origin As first segregation during differentiation of granitic magmas, with high titanium contents.

Occurrence At the boundary area of large, silicon-rich rock complexes, also in smaller, discrete rock complexes.

Use Locally as building stone, for crushed stone production, attractively colored variants as decorative stone.

Similar rocks Unlike diorite hornblende, gabbro contains more anorthite-rich plagioclase and pyroxenes as main components; the mottled appearance is typical.

2 Gabbro

Intrusive igneous rock

Essential minerals Plagioclase (labradorite-bytownite), pyroxene (monoclinal)
Accessory minerals Hornblende, magnetite, ilmenite
Inclusions Plagioclase, pyroxene
Color Medium to dark gray, dark green, black-brown
Structure Medium- to coarse-grained, sometimes porphyritic, often banded, flow structures

Origin By differentiation from ultrabasic magmas of the Earth's mantle.

Occurrence In large, stratified, basic intrusions, as independent rock bodies.

Use Locally as building stone, for crushed stone production, more attractive variants as decorative stone in architecture, for gravestones.

Similar rocks Diorite contains hornblende as an essential mineral instead of pyroxene; norite contains prismatic pyroxenes; pyroxenite does not contain any feldspar.

3 Norite

Intrusive igneous rock

Essential minerals Plagioclase (labradorite-bytownite), pyroxene (orthorhombic)
Accessory minerals Hornblende, magnetite, ilmenite
Inclusions Plagioclase, pyroxene
Color Medium to dark gray, dark green, black-brown
Structure Medium- to coarse-grained, sometimes porphyritic, often banded, flow structures

Origin By differentiation from ultrabasic magmas of the Earth's mantle.

Occurrence In large, stratified, basic intrusions, as independent rock bodies.

Use Locally as building stone, for crushed stone production, more attractive variants as decorative stone in architecture, for gravestones.

Similar rocks Diorite contains hornblende as an essential mineral instead of pyroxene; gabbro contains monoclinal pyroxenes; pyroxenite does not contain any feldspar.

4 Anorthosite

Intrusive igneous rock

Essential minerals Plagioclase (labradorite-bytownite)
Accessory minerals Pyroxene, olivine, chromite, magnetite
Color White, gray, black, greenish, reddish
Structure Medium- to coarse-grained, always uniformly grained, rarely interspersed with magnetite or chromite layers

Origin During the differentiation of basic magmas.

Occurrence As layers and strata within basic rock complexes. In Europe, there is hardly any anorthosite. Large occurrences are found in South Africa and the USA, in particular.

Use Mined for chromite extraction if there is sufficient chromite content, attractively colored and textured varieties as decorative stones in architecture, for gravestones.

Similar rocks Granite and aplite always contain quartz and potassium feldspar instead of plagioclase; pegmatite always has coarse to giant grains and consists of potassium feldspar.

Localities

1 Fürstenstein, Bavaria, Germany	**3** South Africa
2 Harzburg, Harz, Germany	**4** Labrador Peninsula, Canada

3 4

1 Peridotite

Intrusive igneous rock

Essential minerals Olivine, pyroxene
Accessory minerals Spinel, hornblende, pyrope, phlogopite, chromite
Inclusions Pyrope, pyroxene
Color Light to dark green
Structure Medium-grained, partly porphyritic with large pyroxene or pyrope inclusions, sometimes clearly zoned

Origin During the differentiation of basic magmas, by transport up from the upper mantle. It is thought that the mantle is partly comprised of peridotite rocks. The olivine nodules from volcanic rocks are parts of such rocks of the Earth's mantle that have been torn out and brought to the surface.
Occurrence As smaller, discrete rock complexes, in ophiolite complexes, in basic rock complexes.
Use Sometimes as decorative rock.
Similar rocks Gabbro always contains feldspar.

2 Kimberlite

Intrusive igneous rock

Essential minerals Olivine, pyroxene, biotite, phlogopite
Accessory minerals Pyrope, ilmenite, melilite
Inclusions Pyrope, pyroxene, olivine, phlogopite, diamond
Color Light to dark green, gray-green, blue-green
Structure Fine- to medium-grained, partly porphyritic with large olivine inclusions, often brecciated

Origin During explosive penetration of pipes. In the process, rocks from the mantle and country rocks are also brought to the surface. The associated pressures are so high that diamonds can be formed.
Occurrence As vents and sills in geologically ancient areas of the Earth's crust.
Distinguishing feature Kimberlite pipes are important diamond deposits.
Similar rocks Gabbro always contains feldspar; peridotite does not contain mica; Occurrence in the form of pipes is typical.

3 Dunite

Intrusive igneous rock

Essential minerals Olivine
Accessory minerals Spinel, hornblende, pyrope, phlogopite, chromite
Inclusions Pyrope
Color Light to dark green
Structure Medium-grained, partly porphyritic with large pyrope inclusions

Origin During the differentiation of basic magmas, by transport up from the upper mantle.
Occurrence As smaller, discrete rock complexes, in ophiolite complexes, in basic rock complexes.
Use Sometimes as decorative rock, especially in the case of a porphyritic formation with pyrope.
Similar rocks Gabbro always contains feldspar, peridotite contains pyroxenes as an additional essential mineral.

4 Carbonatite

Intrusive igneous rock

Essential minerals Calcite, dolomite
Accessory minerals Phlogopite, apatite, nepheline, perovskite, barite, pyrochlore
Inclusions Pyrochlore, apatite
Color White, yellowish, gray, brown
Structure Medium-grained to very coarse-grained

Origin From carbonate melts originating from the lower mantle.
Occurrence As smaller, independent rock complexes, in alkali rock complexes, very rarely as extrusive rocks.
Use Sometimes as decorative rock, for lime extraction, sometimes as niobium-tantalum ore.
Similar rocks Marble does not occur in alkali rock complexes.

Localities

1 Alpe Arami, Ticino, Switzerland	**3** Kraubath, Styria, Austria
2 Sweden	**4** Sud As, Sweden

1
2
3
4

1 Rhyolite

Volcanic rock

Essential minerals Quartz, potassium feldspar
Accessory minerals Plagioclase (albite), biotite
Inclusions Potassium feldspar
Color Very light gray to whitish, light brown
Structure Groundmass very fine-grained, sometimes large inclusions of sanidine (potassium feldspar)

Origin When silicon-rich magmas escape, this is the volcanic rock corresponding to the intrusive igneous rock granite.
Occurrence In vents, stocks, dikes, rarely forming uniform rock strata. Localities are, for example, on the Lipari Islands in Italy, where the rock is also called liparite, or in the French Massif Central.
Use Locally as building stone, for crushed stone production.
Similar rocks Granite never has such a fine-grained groundmass as rhyolite; it never occurs in areas that have been volcanically active.

2 Quartz porphyry

Volcanic rock

Essential minerals Quartz, potassium feldspar
Accessory minerals Plagioclase (albite), biotite
Inclusions Quartz, potassium feldspar
Color Brown, reddish brown, the groundmass is colored by iron oxides
Structure Fine-grained groundmass with quartz and potassium feldspar inclusions

Origin When silicic magmas escape, which could cover large areas because of their high mobility. Quartz porphyry is the name for geologically ancient rhyolite.
Occurrence As huge lava fields, particularly from the Permian and Triassic periods roughly 200 million years ago.
Use Locally as building stone, for the production of paving stones, floor slabs, ballast.
Similar rocks Rhyolite does not have a reddish colored groundmass; granite does not have such a fine-grained groundmass.

3 Dacite

Volcanic rock

Essential minerals Plagioclase (labradorite), quartz, potassium feldspar
Accessory minerals Biotite, hornblende, pyroxene
Inclusions Plagioclase, biotite, quartz
Color Light to medium gray, light brown
Structure Groundmass very fine-grained, often vitreous, sometimes large inclusions of plagioclase or quartz

Origin When silicon-rich magmas escape, dacite is the volcanic rock corresponding to the intrusive igneous rock tonalite.
Occurrence In vents, stocks, dikes, rarely forming uniform rock strata.
Use Locally as building stone, for crushed stone production.
Similar rocks Granite never has such a fine-grained groundmass as dacite; it never occurs in areas that have been volcanically active; rhyolite and quartz porphyry have potassium feldspar as an essential mineral.

4 Latite

Volcanic rock

Essential minerals Plagioclase, sanidine, pyroxene
Accessory minerals Hornblende, biotite
Inclusions Plagioclase, sanidine
Color Light to medium gray, light brown
Structure Very fine-grained groundmass, often vitreous, sometimes large inclusions of sanidine, plagioclase, pyroxene

Origin When monzonitic magmas escape, latite is the volcanic rock corresponding to monzonite.
Occurrence In flows, dikes, rarely forming uniform rock strata.
Use Locally as building stone, for crushed stone production.
Similar rocks Granite never has such a fine-grained groundmass as latite; it never occurs in areas that have been volcanically active; rhyolite and quartz porphyry have potassium feldspar as an essential mineral.

Localities

1 Massif Central, France	**3** Deva, Hungary
2 Bozen, South Tyrol, Italy	**4** Lazio, Italy

1 2

3 4

1 Andesite

Volcanic rock

Essential minerals Plagioclase, pyroxene, hornblende
Accessory minerals Biotite, magnetite
Inclusions Plagioclase, pyroxene, hornblende
Color Brown to brown-black
Structure Very fine-grained groundmass, sometimes vitreous, sometimes large inclusions

Origin During the melting of oceanic crust in subduction zones, where the melted material then returns to the surface in volcanoes.
Occurrence In flows, effusions, laccoliths.
Use Locally as building stone, for crushed stone production.
Similar rocks Dacite and rhyolite contain quartz; trachybasalt contains sanidine; unlike andesite, phonolite contains nepheline and olivine; unlike andesite, basalt contains olivine as an accessory mineral.

2 Phonolite

Volcanic rock

Essential minerals Nepheline, potassium feldspar, aegirine (a sodium pyroxene)
Accessory minerals Olivine, sodalite, haüyne, sodium hornblende
Inclusions Haüyn, potassium feldspar, nepheline
Color Light to dark gray, greenish, brown
Structure Fine-grained with inclusions of nepheline, potassium feldspar, typical conchoidal fracture, often flow structures, sometimes columnar scoria

Origin The volcanic rock corresponding to the intrusive igneous rock nepheline syenite is from alkali-rich magmas.
Occurrence As volcanic stocks, also the form of dikes, in which case it is called tinguaite. Occurrence at the Kaiserstuhl hill range in Germany, tinguaite dikes with anhedral melanite crystals (titan garnet) also occur.
Use As building stone, for crushed stone extraction.
Distinguishing feature Phonolite got its name, which translates to "clinkstone," because phonolite slabs produce a distinct bell-like sound when struck.
Similar rocks Unlike phonolite, tephrite also contains leucite, often in large inclusions.

3 Basalt

Volcanic rock

Essential minerals Plagioclase (labradorite-bytownite), augite
Accessory minerals Olivine, hornblende, biotite
Inclusions Plagioclase, augite, olivine
Color Black to gray-black, brown-black
Structure Dense with conchoidal fracture, sometimes scoriaceous, very fine-grained groundmass, columnar scoria

Origin When gabbro-like magmas escape, basalt is the volcanic rock corresponding to the intrusive igneous rock, gabbro.
Occurrence In lava flows, as rock strata, stocks, dikes.
Use As road gravel, as paving stone.
Similar rocks All principally similar intrusive igneous rocks are much finer-grained; rhyolite contains quartz as an essential mineral; tephrite contains leucite as an essential mineral.

4 Melaphyre

Volcanic rock

Essential minerals Plagioclase (labradorite-bytownite), augite
Accessory minerals Olivine, hornblende, biotite
Inclusions Plagioclase, augite, olivine
Color Black to gray-black, brown-black
Structure Groundmass dense, fine-grained, cavities

Origin When basaltic to andesitic lavas escape, often subvolcanic formation as well.
Occurrence In lava flows, as rock strata, stocks, dikes.
Use Rarely used as road gravel; unsuitable as building material due to its many cavities; interesting for mineral collectors on account of the minerals in its cavities.
Similar rocks The numerous mineral-filled cavities are characteristic.

Localities	
1 Bulgaria	**3** Fichtel Mountains, Bavaria, Germany
2 Kaiserstuhl Hills, Germany	**4** Kaiserstuhl Hills, Germany

1
2
3
4

1 Trachyte

Volcanic rock

Essential minerals Plagioclase (andesine), sanidine
Accessory minerals Pyroxene, hornblende, biotite
Inclusions Sanidine
Color White to light gray
Structure Fine-grained groundmass with often large inclusions, these are often arranged in parallel, flow structures, porous with rough surface

Origin When syenitic magmas escape, trachyte is the volcanic rock corresponding to the intrusive igneous rock syenite.
Occurrence In lava flows, as rock strata, stocks, dikes, laccoliths.
Use As road gravel, as paving stone.
Similar rocks Trachybasalt contains anorthite-rich plagioclase; dacite and rhyolite contain quartz as an essential mineral; tephrite contains leucite; andesine does not contain any sanidine.

2 Obsidian

Volcanic rock

Essential minerals Rock glass
Accessory minerals Cristobalite, magnetite
Inclusions Cristobalite
Color Black to gray-black, brown-black, with white banding, white-spotted, brown-spotted.
Structure Dense with conchoidal fracture, sometimes scoriaceous with rough surface, translucent to opaque

Origin During very rapid cooling of silicic magmas.
Occurrence In lava flows, lava crusts, ejecta.
Use Used in the past for making stone tools, in ancient times for mirrors, rarely as a gemstone (rainbow obsidian).
Distinguishing feature Botryoidal obsidian inclusions found in volcanic tuffs in Arkansas are called Apache tears. White-flecked obsidian is called snowflake obsidian; brown-banded obsidian is called mahogany obsidian.
Similar rocks The vitreous property renders confusion impossible.

3 Pumice

Volcanic rock

Essential minerals Rock glass
Accessory minerals Sanidine, hornblende, pyroxene
Inclusions Hauyne, titanite
Color White, light green, light brown
Structure Porous, unconsolidated, extremely light (floats on water)

Origin During very gassy volcanic eruptions.
Occurrence In layers in the ejecta of silica-rich volcanoes.
Use In the production of lightweight building materials, as aggregate, as planting material.
Similar rocks The vitreous, highly porous composition renders confusion impossible; no other rock floats on water.

4 Ignimbrite

Volcanic rock

Essential minerals Rock glass, crystal fragments, rock fragments
Accessory minerals Sanidine, hornblende, pyroxene
Color White, light green, light brown
Structure Dense, with dark "flames" that are fused, vitreous scoria

Origin As deposits from clouds of volcanic ash.
Occurrence In layers in the ejecta of silica-rich volcanoes.
Use Rarely as building stone, as aggregate for concrete.
Similar rocks The vitreous composition with the typical "flames" renders confusion impossible; pumice is more porous and, unlike ignimbrite, floats on water.

Localities	
1 Sieben Mountains in Rhine Region, Germany	**3** Azores
2 Georgia	**4** Tuscany, Italy

1 2
3 4

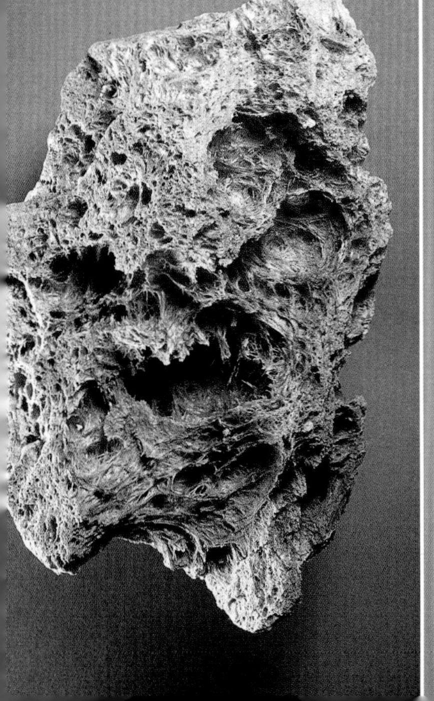

1 Volcanic tuff

Volcanic rock

Essential minerals Ejecta, volcanic ash, rock glass
Inclusions Augite, hornblende, sanidine, olivine
Color Black to gray-black, brown, gray
Structure Very diversely grained, porous, often attractively stratified

Origin By deposition and compaction of the loose masses ejected by volcanoes.

Occurrence In the surroundings of volcanoes.

Use Sometimes as building stone, for cement production, for concrete.

Similar rocks Tufa effervesces when dabbed with diluted hydrochloric acid.

2 Tephrite

Volcanic rock

Essential minerals Plagioclase (labradorite-bytownite), pyroxene
Accessory minerals Nepheline, leucite
Inclusions Leucite crystals, plagioclase
Color Gray to black
Structure Fine-grained groundmass, often porous, feldspar and leucite inclusions

Origin From basic, low-silica lava that has often incorporated carbonate country rocks.

Occurrence In volcanic effusions, rock strata. In Germany, for example, at the Kaiserstuhl Hills; often in Lazio, Italy, for example at Lago Bracciano.

Use Locally as ballast material.

Similar rocks Unlike tephrite, phonolite contains potassium feldspar, as does rhyolite.

3 Leucite-tephrite

Volcanic rock

Essential minerals Leucite, plagioclase (labradorite-bytownite)
Accessory minerals Nepheline, pyroxene
Inclusions Leucite crystals, plagioclase
Color Gray to black
Structure Fine-grained groundmass, often porous, with large leucite inclusions

Origin From basic, low-silica lava that has often incorporated carbonate country rocks.

Occurrence In volcanic effusions, rock strata. In Germany, for example, at the Kaiserstuhl Hills; often in Lazio, Italy, for example at Lago Bracciano.

Use Locally as ballast material.

Similar rocks Phonolite contains potassium feldspar, as does rhyolite; tephrite does not contain leucite as an essential mineral.

4 Lava

Volcanic rock

Essential minerals Plagioclase, pyroxene
Accessory minerals Olivine, hornblende, biotite
Inclusions Olivine, augite, hornblende, biotite
Color Black, gray, brown
Structure Hackly, pancake-like, ropy solidification forms with diverse flow structures, dense to porous, fine-grained, with various types of inclusions

Origin The term lava describes quite superficially solidified volcanic rocks of more or less basaltic composition. Lava is often found in the form of lava flows.

Occurrence In the area of young, partly still active volcanoes, for example in the Eifel Mountains in Germany, on Iceland, Hawaii, at Vesuvius and Etna in Italy and on the Aeolian Islands and Stromboli in the Mediterranean.

Use As an aggregate for concrete, in horticulture, in ornamental plant cultivation as a substrate.

Similar rocks Lava rock is unmistakable in its surface structure.

Localities	
1 Argentina	**3** Trevignano, Italy
2 Limburg, Kaiserstuhl Hills, Germany	**4** Tenerife, Canary Islands

1 2

3 4

1 Argillaceous schist

Metamorphic rock

Essential minerals Argillaceous minerals
Accessory minerals Grains of quartz, mica, calcite, feldspar
Color Gray to black
Structure Extremely fine-grained, individual grains visible only under the microscope, schistose, cleavable into slabs

Origin By deposition of argillaceous minerals in water bodies, especially in the sea.
Occurrence As layers between other sedimentary rocks, in salt water deposits, but also in lake deposits, for example during ice ages.
Use Roof slates for roofing, for table tops, as floor tiles.
Similar rocks Phyllites exhibit abundant silvery mica on the stratification planes.

2 Chiastolite slate

Metamorphic rock

Essential minerals Argillaceous minerals
Accessory minerals Grains of quartz, mica
Inclusions Columnar andalusite, known as chiastolite
Color Gray to black
Structure Extremely fine-grained groundmass, individual grains visible only under the microscope, schistose, cleavable into slabs

Origin By contact metamorphism from argillaceous rocks.
Occurrence In the contact aureole around intrusive rock bodies in sedimentary rocks.
Use When the chiastolites are large, as decorative stone, for arts and crafts purposes.
Similar rocks Phyllites exhibit abundant silvery mica on the stratification planes; clay schists exhibit no andalusite inclusions.

3 Hornfels

Metamorphic rock

Essential minerals Diopside, biotite, cordierite
Accessory minerals Garnet, cordierite, biotite, sillimanite
Inclusions Garnet, biotite, spinel, andalusite
Color Gray to black
Structure Extremely fine-grained groundmass, dense, structureless

Origin By contact metamorphism from argillaceous rocks, dolomites.
Occurrence Formed in the contact aureole around intrusive rock bodies in sedimentary rocks, close to intrusive rock.
Use As ballast.
Similar rocks Basalts occur in quite different geologic settings; obsidian is much glassier. Amphibolite is much coarser.

4 Phyllite

Metamorphic rock

Essential minerals Quartz, mica
Accessory minerals Graphite, feldspar, chlorite, chloritoid
Color Gray, yellowish, greenish, silvery, often silky luster
Structure Very fine-grained, the individual mica flakes are not distinct even with a magnifying glass, slaty, folded in layers, often very finely fluted

Origin During low-grade regional metamorphism from argillaceous to sandy sedimentary rocks.
Occurrence In extended metamorphic areas (regional metamorphism).
Use Fine ground for coating highly reflective boards and mats.
Similar rocks Clay schist does not have a silky luster like phyllite; with mica schist, it is possible to distinguish the individual mica flakes using a magnifying glass; also, unlike phyllite, it frequently has inclusions of a wide range of minerals.

Localities

1 Krautheim, Baden-Wuerttemberg, Germany	**3** Kösseine, Fichtel Mountains, Germany
2 Gefrees, Upper Franconia, Germany	**4** Ainet, East Tyrol, Austria

1 2

3 4

1 Mica schist

Metamorphic rock

Essential minerals Mica, quartz
Accessory minerals Feldspar, chlorite, garnet, tourmaline, actinolite
Color Gray, silver gray, black, brown, shiny
Structure Fine- to coarse-grained, often folded, partly with quartz-rich or feldspar-rich layers

Origin During medium- to high-grade metamorphism from sandy to argillaceous parent rocks.
Occurrence Prevalent in regional metamorphic areas, for example, the Alps.
Similar rocks Unlike mica schist, the individual mica flakes of phyllite cannot be seen with a magnifying glass; phyllite also has no inclusions; gneisses also always contain feldspar as a specific mineral.

2 Garnet mica schist

Metamorphic rock

Essential minerals Mica, quartz
Accessory minerals Feldspar, chlorite, garnet, tourmaline, actinolite, hornblende, kyanite
Inclusions Garnet
Color Gray, silver gray, black, brown, shiny
Structure Fine- to coarse-grained, often folded, partly with quartz-rich or feldspar-rich layers, large almandine crystals

Origin During medium- to high-grade metamorphism from sandy to argillaceous parent rocks.
Occurrence Prevalent in regional metamorphic areas, for example, the Alps.
Similar rocks Unlike mica schist, the individual mica flakes of phyllite cannot be seen with a magnifying glass; phyllite also has no inclusions; gneisses also always contain feldspar as an essential mineral; garnet amphibolite does not consist mainly of mica.

3 Hornblende mica schist

Metamorphic rock

Essential minerals Mica, quartz
Accessory minerals Feldspar, chlorite
Inclusions Hornblende
Color Gray, silver gray, black, brown, shiny
Structure Fine- to coarse-grained, often folded, partly quartz-rich or feldspar-rich layers

Origin During medium- to high-grade metamorphism from sandy to argillaceous parent rocks.
Occurrence Prevalent in regional metamorphic areas, for example, the Alps.
Similar rocks Unlike mica schist, the individual mica flakes of phyllite cannot be seen with a magnifying glass; phyllite also has no inclusions; gneisses also always contain feldspar as an essential mineral.

4 Kyanite mica schist

Metamorphic rock

Essential minerals Mica (especially paragonite), quartz
Accessory minerals Feldspar, chlorite
Inclusions Kyanite
Color Gray, silver gray, black, brown, shiny
Structure Fine- to coarse-grained, often folded, partly quartz-rich or feldspar-rich layers

Origin During medium- to high-grade metamorphism from sandy to argillaceous parent rocks.
Occurrence Prevalent in regional metamorphic areas, for example, the Alps.
Similar rocks Unlike mica schist, the individual mica flakes of phyllite cannot be seen with a magnifying glass; phyllite also has no inclusions; gneisses also always contain feldspar as a specific mineral.

Localities	
1 Hohe Tauern, Austria	**3** Zillertal, Austria
2 Zillertal, Austria	**4** Alpe Sponda, Ticino, Switzerland

1 2

3 4

1 Metavulkanite

Metamorphic rock

Essential minerals Chlorite, pyroxene, serpentine
Accessory minerals Magnetite, quartz, hornblende
Color Light to dark green
Structure Fine- to coarse-grained, sometimes botryoidal structures of former lithophyses, the structures of the former volcanic rocks are still recognizable

Origin Created during low-grade metamorphism from lavas and different volcanic rocks.
Occurrence In areas of low-grade metamorphism, involving volcanic rocks.
Use Used as decorative stone and for craft items when it occurs as interesting structures, then often given invented names (for example, Kabamba).
Similar rocks The intense green color due to chlorite and serpentine minerals in the presence of volcanic rock structures is very characteristic.

2 Chlorite schist

Metamorphic rock

Essential minerals Chlorite
Accessory minerals Magnetite, pyrite, hornblende, epidote, albite
Inclusions Magnetite, pyrite
Color Light to dark green
Structure Fine- to coarse-grained, foliated, slaty, often with inclusions of magnetite and pyrite

Origin During low-grade metamorphism from lavas, volcanic tuffs and other basic rocks.
Occurrence In large-scale metamorphic areas, for example, in the Alps.
Use Only of interest to mineral collectors.
Similar rocks Mica schist and phyllite have mica as the main mineral, amphibolites contain hornblende or actinolite as an essential mineral. Its green color and low hardness (hardness 2) make chlorite schist unmistakable.

3 Talc schist

Metamorphic rock

Essential minerals Talc
Accessory minerals Magnetite, pyrite, hornblende, epidote, albite, dolomite, magnesite, serpentine
Inclusions Magnetite, pyrite, dolomite
Color Light to dark green, silvery gray
Structure Fine-grained, foliated, slaty, often with inclusions of magnetite and pyrite

Origin During low-grade metamorphism from peridotites, pyroxenites or dolomitic marls.
Occurrence In large-scale metamorphic areas.
Use As filler in the paint industry, in the cosmetics industry, for refractory products.
Similar rocks Mica schist and phyllite have mica as the main mineral; chlorite schist has chlorite as the main mineral; the low hardness of talc schist is highly characteristic.

4 Amphibolite

Metamorphic rock

Essential minerals Hornblende, actinolite
Accessory minerals Epidote, plagioclase, chlorite, garnet
Color Dark green to black
Structure Coarse-grained, schistose, sometimes with garnet inclusions

Origin During low- to medium-grade metamorphism from basic, primarily volcanic rocks.
Occurrence Amphibolites are widespread in Alpine metamorphic stratigraphic sequences, for example, in the Habach Valley in the Hohe Tauern in Austria and in the St. Gotthard Massif in Switzerland.
Use Rarely locally for crushed stone production.
Similar rocks Serpentinites do not contain amphiboles; chlorite schists have chlorite as the main component and are much softer; eclogite has pyroxenes as the main component.

Localities	
1 Madagascar	**3** Matrei, East Tyrol, Austria
2 Zillertal, Austria	**4** Schobergruppe, Austria

1
2
3
4

1 Garnet amphibolite

Metamorphic rock

Essential minerals Hornblende, actinolite
Accessory minerals Epidote, plagioclase, chlorite, garnet
Inclusions Garnet
Color Dark green to black
Structure Coarse-grained, schistose, sometimes with garnet inclusions

Origin During low- to medium-grade metamorphism from basic, primarily volcanic rocks.
Occurrence Amphibolites are widespread in metamorphic stratigraphic sequences in the Alps.
Use Rarely locally for crushed stone production and as building stone, sometimes decorative stone.
Similar rocks Serpentinites do not contain amphiboles; chlorite schists have chlorite as the main component and are much softer amphibolites; eclogite has pyroxenes as the main component and does not contain any amphiboles.

2 Gneiss

Metamorphic rock

Essential minerals Feldspar, quartz, mica
Accessory minerals Garnet, cordierite, sillimanite, hornblende
Color Light to dark gray, greenish, yellowish, brownish
Structure Medium- to coarse-grained, layered with light and dark layers, streaky, folded

Origin In medium- to high-grade metamorphism from argillaceous sediments (paragneisses) or granitic rocks (orthogneisses).
Occurrence Everywhere in metamorphic areas.
Use Highly schistose, unfolded gneiss as floor tiles and roof slates.
Similar rocks Granite is not schistose.

3 Garnet gneiss

Metamorphic rock

Essential minerals Feldspar, quartz, mica
Accessory minerals Garnet, cordierite, sillimanite, hornblende
Inclusions Garnet
Color Light to dark gray, greenish, yellowish, brownish
Structure Medium- to coarse-grained, layered with light and dark layers, folded, almandine inclusions

Origin In medium- to high-grade metamorphism from argillaceous sediments (paragneisses) or granitic rocks (orthogneisses).
Occurrence Everywhere in metamorphic areas.
Use Highly schistose, unfolded gneiss as floor tiles and roof slates.
Similar rocks Granite is not schistose; garnet amphibolite primarily consists of amphiboles.

4 Hornblende gneiss

Metamorphic rock

Essential minerals Feldspar, quartz, mica
Accessory minerals Garnet, cordierite, sillimanite, hornblende
Inclusions Hornblende
Color Light to dark gray, greenish, yellowish, brownish
Structure Medium- to coarse-grained, layered with light and dark layers, streaky, folded, hornblende inclusions

Origin In medium- to high-grade metamorphism from argillaceous sediments (paragneisses) or granitic rocks (orthogneisses).
Occurrence Everywhere in metamorphic areas.
Use Highly schistose, unfolded gneiss as floor tiles and roof slates.
Similar rocks Granite is not schistose; amphibolite primarily consists of amphiboles; other gneisses do not contain hornblende.

Localities

1 Fichtel Mountains, Bavaria, Germany
2 Zillertal, Austria
3 Kinzigtal, Black Forest, Germany
4 Hohe Tauern, Austria

1 2

3 4

1 Cordierite gneiss
Metamorphic rock

Essential minerals Feldspar, quartz, mica
Accessory minerals Garnet, cordierite, sillimanite, hornblende
Inclusions Cordierite
Color Light to dark gray, greenish, yellowish, brownish
Structure Medium- to coarse-grained, layered with light and dark layers, streaky, folded

Origin During high-grade metamorphism from argillaceous sediments.
Occurrence Everywhere in high-grade metamorphic areas.
Use Rarely as floor tiles.
Similar rocks Granite is not schistose; garnet gneiss contains garnet as inclusion; amphibolite primarily consists of amphiboles.

2 Anatexite
Metamorphic rock

Essential minerals Feldspar, quartz, mica
Accessory minerals Garnet, cordierite, sillimanite, hornblende
Inclusions Garnet
Color Light to dark gray, greenish, yellowish, brownish, banded in light and dark layers, slightly slaty
Structure Medium- to coarse-grained, irregularly layered with light and dark layers, streaky, folded

Origin During high-grade metamorphism from argillaceous sediments or granitic rocks by partial melting of the lighter-colored components.
Occurrence Everywhere in high-grade metamorphic areas.
Use Sometimes as decorative stone.
Similar rocks Granite is not schistose; garnet amphibolite primarily consists of amphiboles; garnet gneiss is more consistent.

3 Eclogite
Metamorphic rock

Essential minerals Pyroxene (omphacite), garnet
Accessory minerals Kyanite, quartz, actinolite
Inclusions Garnet, kyanite
Color Light to dark green, mottled red
Structure Coarse-grained, garnet inclusions, more rarely kyanite inclusions, sometimes stratified, but mainly undirected

Origin During high-grade metamorphism from basic rocks. Minerals of lower temperatures and pressures, such as mica or kyanite, often form during retrograde metamorphism.
Occurrence Lenses and layers in highly metamorphic rock sequences and bodies. More frequent occurrence in the Alps, but also in the Münchberger Gneismasse in Bavaria, Germany.
Use As decorative rock.
Similar rocks The characteristic composition does not leave room for any confusion.

4 Granulite
Metamorphic rock

Essential minerals Potassium feldspar, plagioclase, garnet
Accessory minerals Kyanite, cordierite, sillimanite
Inclusions Garnet
Color White to gray, yellowish, brownish, shaded light purple
Structure Fine- to coarse-grained, without stratification, with garnet inclusions

Origin During high-grade metamorphism from sandy to argillaceous sedimentary rocks.
Occurrence In areas of particularly high-grade regional metamorphism, for example, in the Valle d'Ossola in Italy.
Use With particularly attractive structure as a decorative stone in construction, also for floor tiles or table tops.
Similar rocks Unlike granulite, quartzites do not contain garnet; unlike granulite, gneisses always contain quartz and mica.

Localities

1 Bodenmais, Bavaria, Germany	**3** Weissenstein, Fichtel Mountains, Germany
2 Lam, Bavaria, Germany	**4** Meidling, Lower Austria

1
2
3
4

1 Marble

Metamorphic rock

Essential minerals Calcite
Accessory minerals Dolomite, wollastonite, vesuvianite, graphite, diopside, spinel, corundum
Inclusions Spinel, garnet, wollastonite
Color White, yellowish, brownish
Structure Fine- to coarse-grained, sometimes zoned

Origin From limestone by regional or contact metamorphism.
Occurrence In contact aureole around intrusive igneous rocks, in regional metamorphic rock outcrop series.
Use As building stone, for decorative purposes, for gravestones, for sculpture work, as ornamental stone.
Similar rocks Unlike marble, the cleavage faces of the individual calcite grains cannot be seen in limestone; gypsum rock is softer.

2 Dolomite marble

Metamorphic rock

Essential minerals Dolomite
Accessory minerals Muscovite, calcite, albite
Inclusions Pyrite, dolomite crystals, calcite crystals
Color White, yellowish, brownish
Structure Fine-grained, saccharoidal, crumbly

Origin From dolomite by regional or contact metamorphism.
Occurrence In contact aureole around intrusive igneous rocks, in regional metamorphic rock outcrop series.
Use For sculpture work.
Similar rocks Unlike dolomite marble, the cleavage faces of the individual dolomite grains cannot be seen in dolomite; gypsum rock is softer; marble effervesces when dabbed with diluted hydrochloric acid.

3 Silicate marble

Metamorphic rock

Essential minerals Calcite, forsterite, wollastonite, grossular, vesuvianite
Accessory minerals Graphite, diopside, spinel, corundum
Inclusions Spinel, garnet, wollastonite
Color White, yellowish, brownish
Structure Fine- to coarse-grained, sometimes zoned

Origin From limestone by regional or contact metamorphism.
Occurrence In contact aureole around intrusive igneous rocks, in regional metamorphic rock outcrop series.
Use As building stone, for decorative purposes, for gravestones, as ornamental stone.
Similar rocks Unlike marble, the cleavage faces of the individual calcite crystallites cannot be seen in limestone.

4 Serpentinite

Metamorphic rock

Essential minerals Serpentine as antigorite, more rarely as chrysotile
Accessory minerals Magnetite, chromite, olivine, talc, dolomite, magnesite
Inclusions Olivine
Color Yellow, light to dark green, brown
Structure Fine- to coarse-grained, felty, foliated, dense

Origin By low-grade metamorphism of peridotites.
Occurrence In regional metamorphic areas.
Use As building stone, for decorative purposes, for gravestones, as ornamental stone.
Similar rocks Amphibolites consist of amphiboles as essential minerals; talc schist is distinctly schistose and softer; peridotite and dunite contain fresh, unconverted olivine.

Localities	
1 Obernzell, Bavaria, Germany	**3** Ivrea, Italy
2 Campolungo, Switzerland	**4** Obernzell, Bavaria, Germany

1 2
3 4

1 Limestone

Sedimentary rock

Essential minerals Calcite
Accessory minerals Limonite, dolomite, quartz, argillaceous minerals
Inclusions Pyrite, flint, marcasite, quartz
Color White, yellowish, brownish, gray, black
Structure Fine-grained, stratified, bedded, sometimes folded, rarely completely dense and structureless

Origin Primarily from the remains of living organisms, rarely also inorganically precipitated.
Occurrence Extraordinarily widespread in all sedimentary stratigraphic sequences, often mountain-forming, thus for example in the Swabian and Franconian Alb and in the Limestone Alps.
Use As building stone, as crushed stone, for calcination of limestone, attractively colored and marked varieties also as ornamental stone, for wall coverings, as floor tiles.
Similar rocks Unlike limestone, dolomite does not effervesce when dabbed with diluted hydrochloric acid.

2 Calcareous oolite *Peastone, roestone, pisolite*

Sedimentary rock

Essential minerals Calcite
Accessory minerals Limonite, dolomite, quartz, argillaceous minerals
Inclusions Quartz, sand
Color White, yellowish, brownish
Structure Fine-grained to coarse-grained, stratified, consists of spheroidal, shell-like lime aggregates (oolites) that are densely caked together

Origin Primarily inorganically precipitated, formation in surf areas, in springs.
Occurrence In all sedimentary stratigraphic sequences, in formations of warm, calcareous springs (pisolite, peastone).
Use For decorative purposes, for craft items.
Similar rocks Dolomite does not effervesce when dabbed with diluted hydrochloric acid; limestone does not exhibit any oolites; iron oolite consists mainly of limonite.

3 Iron oolite

Sedimentary rock

Essential minerals Limonite
Accessory minerals Calcite, quartz, argillaceous minerals
Inclusions Fossils
Color Brownish, brown
Structure Fine- to coarse-grained, stratified, consists of spheroidal, shell-like limonite aggregates (oolites)

Origin Primarily inorganically precipitated, formation in surf areas.
Occurrence In many sedimentary stratigraphic sequences, especially of the Brown Jurassic.
Use As iron ore when content is sufficiently high (for example, Lorraine minette).
Similar rocks Calcarous oolite effervesces when dabbed with diluted hydrochloric acid.

4 Ammonite limestone

Sedimentary rock

Essential minerals Calcite
Accessory minerals Limonite, dolomite, quartz, argillaceous minerals
Inclusions Pyrite, flint, marcasite, quartz
Color White, yellowish, brownish, gray, black
Structure Fine-grained, stratified, bedded, sometimes folded, contains, sometimes very abundantly, remains of ammonites

Origin By filling and cementation of ammonite shells with lime and argillaceous minerals.
Occurrence Widely distributed in all sedimentary stratigraphic sequences from the Palaeozoic to the Cretaceous eras.
Use As building stone, as crushed stone, attractively colored and marked varieties also as ornamental stone, for wall coverings, as floor tiles, for ornamental objects, table tops.
Similar rocks Dolomite does not effervesce when dabbed with diluted hydrochloric acid.

Localities

1 Mörnsheim, Franconia, Germany	**3** Haverlahwiese, Lower Saxony, Germany
2 Weserbergland, Germany	**4** Dorset, Great Britain

1 2
3 4

1 Coralline limestone

Sedimentary rock

Essential minerals Calcite
Accessory minerals Limonite, dolomite, quartz, argillaceous minerals
Inclusions Pyrite, flint, marcasite, quartz
Color White, yellowish, brownish, gray, black, often with white coral structures
Structure Fine-grained, stratified, bedded, contains, sometimes very abundantly, coral remains

Origin By filling and cementation of corals with lime and argillaceous minerals.

Occurrence Widely distributed in all sedimentary stratigraphic sequences from the Palaeozoic era to the present.

Use As building stone, as crushed stone, attractively colored and marked varieties also as ornamental stone, for wall coverings, as floor tiles, for ornamental objects, table tops.

Similar rocks Unlike limestone, dolomite does not effervesce when dabbed with diluted hydrochloric acid and only rarely contains fossils.

2 Snail shell limestone

Sedimentary rock

Essential minerals Calcite
Accessory minerals Limonite, dolomite, quartz, argillaceous minerals
Inclusions Pyrite, flint, marcasite, quartz
Color White, yellowish, brownish, gray, black
Structure Fine-grained, stratified, bedded, sometimes folded, contains, sometimes very abundantly, snail remains

Origin By filling and cementation of snail shells with lime and argillaceous minerals, in both fresh and salt water.

Occurrence Occurring in all sedimentary stratigraphic sequences from the Palaeozoic era to the present.

Use As building stone, as crushed stone, attractively colored and marked varieties also as ornamental stone, for wall coverings, as floor tiles, for ornamental objects.

Similar rocks Unlike limestone, dolomite does not effervesce when dabbed with diluted hydrochloric acid and only rarely contains fossils.

3 Solnhofen limestone

Sedimentary rock

Essential minerals Calcite
Accessory minerals Limonite, dolomite, quartz, argillaceous minerals
Inclusions Pyrite, flint, marcasite, quartz
Color White, yellowish, brownish, gray, black
Structure Fine-grained, stratified, bedded, sometimes folded, contains, sometimes very abundantly, fossils

Origin By laminar precipitation especially in lagoonal areas.

Occurrence Occurring in all sedimentary stratigraphic sequences from the Palaeozoic era to the present.

Use As building stone, for wall coverings, as floor tiles, for ornamental objects.

Similar rocks Unlike limestone, dolomite does not effervesce when dabbed with diluted hydrochloric acid and only rarely contains fossils.

4 Tufa *Calc-sinter*

Sedimentary rock

Essential minerals Calcite
Accessory minerals Limonite, organic substances
Color White, yellowish, brownish
Structure Fine-grained, fibrous, stratified, very porous, often encrusting organic substances (for example, reed stems)

Origin Through precipitation from highly calcareous water.

Occurrence At the outlet of hot springs, in rivers and streams through which calcareous water flows.

Use As building stone because the soft stone hardens within a short period after freshly extracting from a mountain.

Similar rocks Volcanic tuff does not effervesce when dabbed with diluted hydrochloric acid.

Localities

1 Adnet, Salzburg, Austria	**3** Solnhofen, Bavaria, Germany
2 Liesberg, Basel, Switzerland	**4** Murnau, Bavaria, Germany

1 2

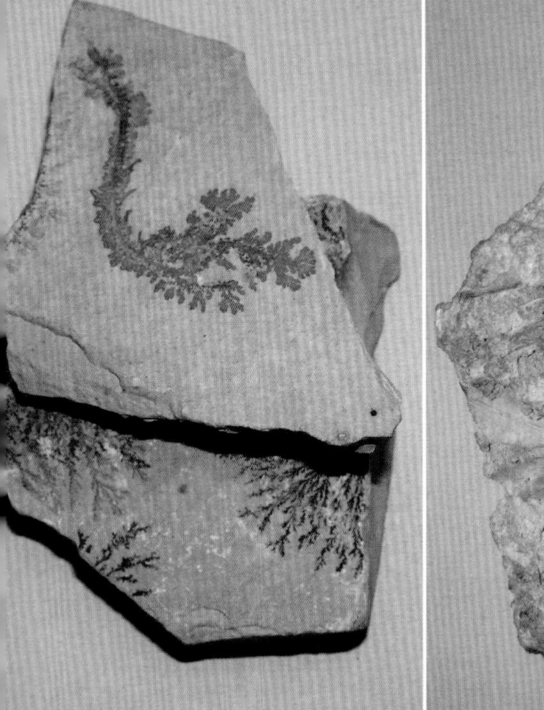
3 4

1 Chalk

Sedimentary rock

Essential minerals Calcite
Accessory minerals Limonite, dolomite, quartz, argillaceous minerals
Inclusions Pyrite, flint, marcasite
Color White, yellowish, brownish
Structure Fine-grained, stratified, bedded, sometimes folded, contains, sometimes very abundantly, remains of organisms, such as sea urchins.

Origin From the remains of tiny single-cell organisms.
Occurrence Particularly in the Cretaceous, the youngest of the Mesozoic periods.
Use For calcination of limestone, for making blackboard chalk, as a filler for paper.
Similar rocks Unlike limestone, dolomite does not effervesce when dabbed with diluted hydrochloric acid and only rarely contains fossils.

2 Marl

Sedimentary rock

Essential minerals Calcite, argillaceous minerals
Accessory minerals Limonite, dolomite, quartz
Inclusions Pyrite
Color White, yellowish, gray
Structure Fine-grained, stratified, bedded, sometimes folded, contains, sometimes very abundantly, fossils, relatively unconsolidated and soft

Origin In the combined deposition of calcarous ooze and argillaceous minerals especially in shallow water areas.
Occurrence Particularly prevalent in the younger stratigraphic sequences.
Use For soil improvement, as an aggregate in cement production.
Similar rocks In contrast to marl, dolomite does not effervesce when dabbed with diluted hydrochloric acid and rarely contains fossils; limestone is denser and more solid.

3 Clay

Sedimentary rock

Essential minerals Argillaceous minerals
Accessory minerals Grains of quartz, mica
Color White, light gray to black
Structure Extremely fine-grained, individual grains only visible under a microscope, directionless, plastic

Origin In the deposition of argillaceous minerals in water bodies of all types.
Occurrence As layers between other sedimentary rocks, in salt water deposits, but also in lake deposits, for example, during ice ages.
Use As a raw material for ceramics production, brick making, stoneware and earthenware production, refractory materials.
Similar rocks Clay schists are bedded; marls are not so plastic.

4 Dolomite

Sediment

Essential minerals Dolomite
Accessory minerals Calcite, quartz, limonite
Inclusions Dolomite only rarely contains fossils
Color White, yellow, beige, gray, brownish
Structure Fine to medium-grained, stratified, bedded, less frequently folded

Origin Primarily formed from limestone through magnesium exchange with magnesian water or rock, rarely formed primarily as dolomite.
Occurrence In many sedimentary stratigraphic sequences.
Use As building stone, for crushed stone production, as floor tiles, in the production of dolomite bricks for blast furnaces, as an aggregate in steel smelting.
Similar rocks Unlike dolomite, limestone effervesces when dabbed with diluted hydrochloric acid.

Localities	
1 Rügen, Germany	**3** Westerwald, Germany
2 Rosenheim, Bavaria, Germany	**4** Eschenlohe, Bavaria, Germany

1 2
3 4

1 Sandstone

Sediment

Essential minerals Quartz grains
Accessory minerals Mica, feldspar, calcite
Inclusions Feldspar, mica
Color White, light to dark gray, red, red-brown, brown, purple, black
Structure Fine- to medium-grained, stratified, bedded. The sand grains may be cemented by quartz, calcite or clay

Origin During the deposition of the erosion residues of silicate rocks, by solidification of sand.
Occurrence Formed in all sedimentary stratigraphic sequences, always near the mainland. There are sandstones from all periods, for example, from the Triassic (mottled sandstone, reed sandstone) or the Tertiary (molasse sandstone from the foothills of the Alps).
Use Wide variety of uses as building stone, as floor tiles, for sculpting.
Similar rocks Breccias and conglomerates consist of rock fragments.

2 Arkose

Sediment

Essential minerals Quartz grains, feldspar
Accessory minerals Mica
Inclusions Feldspar, mica
Color White, light to dark gray, red, red-brown, brown, purple, black
Structure Fine- to medium-grained, stratified, bedded

Origin During the deposition of the erosion residues of silicate rocks, for example, granites, through solidification of sand with feldspar grains.
Occurrence Formed in all sedimentary stratigraphic sequences, always near the mainland.
Use Rarely as building stone, crushed stone, filling material.
Similar rocks Breccias and conglomerates consist of rock fragments.

3 Sand

Sediment

Essential minerals Quartz grains, grain size up to a few millimeters
Accessory minerals Mica, calcite
Inclusions Mica, calcareous shells
Color White, gray, red, red-brown, brown, purple, black
Structure Fine- to medium-grained, stratified, without binder, sand is loose rock

Origin During the deposition of the erosion residues of silicate rocks, without solidification.
Occurrence In all sedimentary stratigraphic sequences, both freshwater and saltwater deposition.
Use For construction purposes, road building, multiple other uses, as an additive in concrete production.
Similar rocks Sandstone is solid; gravel has much larger grains.

4 Placers

Sediment

Essential minerals Quartz grains, gravel, argillaceous minerals
Accessory minerals Gemstones, such as ruby, sapphire, diamond and many others, gold, magnetite, monazite, ilmenite
Color White, light to dark gray, red, red-brown, brown, purple, black, multi-colored
Structure Fine- to large-grained, without binder, an unconsolidated rock

Origin During the deposition of the erosion residues of silicate rocks, marbles and sediments, without solidification.
Occurrence There are river, lake, sea or surf placers in all sedimentary stratigraphic sequences. Placers can also be blown together by the wind.
Use For gemstone mining, for the extraction of thorium and cerium (monazite placers), titanium (ilmenite placers).
Similar rocks Sandstone is solid; placers are identified by their characteristic accessory minerals.

Localities

1 Helgoland, Germany	**3** Koroni, Greece
2 Schmidgaden, Upper Palatinate, Bavaria, Germany	**4** Sri Lanka

1
2
3
4

1 Gravel

Sediment

Essential minerals Pebbles, grain size up to several centimeters
Accessory minerals Sand, argillaceous minerals
Color White, light to dark gray, red, red-brown, brown, purple, black
Structure Coarse-grained, stratified, without binder, gravel is loose rock

Origin During the deposition of the erosion residues of silicate rocks and limestone.
Occurrence In younger sedimentary stratigraphic sequences, primarily a continental formation, often resulting from glaciation.
Use For construction purposes, road building, multiple other uses, as an additive in concrete production.
Similar rocks Sandstone is solid; sand has much smaller grains; conglomerates and nagelfluh are consolidated gravels.

2 Breccia

Sediment

Essential minerals Rock fragments
Accessory minerals Calcite, quartz
Inclusions Rock fragments
Color Wide variety in color, also extremely variegated
Structure Coarse-grained, also with widely varying grain sizes, all rock fragments are angular, binding mass sandy, calcareous, clayey

Origin By fracturing of rocks and subsequent re-solidification without transporting the rock fragments away.
Occurrence In areas with strong mechanical stress, in tectonic rift zones, along fault zones, in landslide masses, in ore veins.
Use Mechanically strong and visually attractive breccias are used as decorative stones.
Similar rocks Conglomerates consist of unrolled rounded rock fragments.

3 Conglomerate

Sediment

Essential minerals Rock fragments
Accessory minerals Calcite, quartz, argillaceous minerals
Color Wide variety in color, also extremely variegated
Structure Coarse-grained, also widely varying grain sizes, sometimes stratified, all rock fragments rounded

Origin In the solidification of gravels.
Occurrence In freshwater and seawater sediments, often at the basement. The presence of conglomerates indicates strongly agitated water; in the case of marine sediments, it also indicates very close proximity to the coast.
Use Strongly compacted conglomerates are used as building stones.
Similar rocks Breccias consist solely of angular rock fragments.

4 Nagelfluh

Sediment

Essential minerals Rock fragments
Accessory minerals Calcite, quartz, argillaceous minerals
Color Wide variety in color, also extremely variegated
Structure Coarse-grained, also widely varying grain sizes, mainly stratified, all rock fragments rounded

Origin By solidification of glacial gravels of the alpine uplands.
Occurrence In the Alpine foothills, in the former glacier foreland.
Use As building stone, for crushed stone.
Similar rocks Breccias consist solely of angular rock fragments; unlike nagelfluh, gravel is loose rock.

Localities

1 Isar, Bavaria, Germany
2 Garmisch-Partenkirchen, Bavaria, Germany
3 Traunstein, Bavaria, Germany
4 Grünwald, Munich, Germany

1 2

3 4

1 Quartzite

Metamorphic and sedimentary rock

Essential minerals Quartz
Accessory minerals Mica, feldspar
Inclusions Mica
Color White, yellowish, gray, brownish
Structure Finely-grained, stratified

Origin From highly silicic rocks, as early as the beginning of solidification from sands as sedimentary rocks, then in all metamorphic stages.
Occurrence Interbedded in sand layers, in many metamorphic stratigraphic sequences.
Use As building stone, in the production of silicate stone, as aggregate for ore smelting, for glass production, for glass fiber fabrication, for silicon production.
Similar rocks Unlike quartzite, the individual sand grains can be identified in sandstone.

2 Gypsum rock

Sediment

Essential minerals Gypsum
Accessory minerals Rock salt, calcite, argillaceous minerals
Inclusions Rock salt, quartz crystals, sulfur
Color White, yellowish, brownish, reddish, gray
Structure Fine- to coarse-grained, rarely stratified, sometimes in a crest-like bend

Origin During the evaporation of seawater, often by water absorption from primarily formed anhydrite, resulting in the individual rock layers bending in a worm- or crest-like manner due to the larger volume of the gypsum.
Occurrence In sedimentary stratigraphic sequences, often associated with rock salt deposits.
Use In the production of plaster and other gypsum products.
Similar rocks Unlike gypsum rock, limestone effervesces when dabbed with diluted hydrochloric acid; dolomite is significantly harder.

3 Bituminous coal

Sediment

Essential minerals Carbaceous organic substances, especially plant parts
Accessory minerals Quartz, calcite, pyrite
Inclusions Pyrite
Color Black
Structure Dense with conchoidal fracture, flaky, fibrous, granular

Origin By coalification of vegetable matter in the absence of air. Bituminous coal is usually geologically older. When temperatures rise, for example during mountain-building processes, geologically younger lignite can also be converted into bituminous coal. The resulting product is then also called black coal.
Occurrence In numerous sedimentary sequences, lignite particularly in the Carboniferous period.
Use As fuel for energy production, as a starting product for the organic chemical industry.
Similar rocks Obsidian is much harder.

4 Lignite

Sediment

Essential minerals Carbaceous organic substances, especially plant parts
Accessory minerals Quartz, calcite, pyrite
Inclusions Pyrite
Color Brown to black
Structure Plant parts firmly caked together, but still readily recognizable, granular, fibrous

Origin By coalification of vegetable matter in the absence of air. Lignite (brown coal) is usually geologically younger.
Occurrence In numerous sedimentary sequences of mostly younger age, especially in the Tertiary.
Use As fuel for energy production, as a starting product for the organic chemical industry.
Similar rocks Obsidian is much harder; bituminous coal is much denser, more solid.

Localities	
1 Lienz, East Tyrol, Austria	**3** Peissenberg, Bavaria, Germany
2 Lower Franconia, Bavaria, Germany	**4** Wackersdorf, Bavaria, Germany

1
2

3

4

The Meteorites

1–2 Octahedrite

Type Iron meteorite
Magnetism Strong
Color Encrustation brown to black, inner steel gray metallic
Luster Metallic luster in sections/cuts

Morphology Metallic, very heavy, magnetic, no fractures, sometimes bent, torn pieces (so-called shrapnel) often regmaglypts.
Origin and occurrence Iron meteorites are parts of the iron core of planets originally formed at the start of our Solar System and then quickly destroyed again.
Main components Kamacite, taenite.
Accessory minerals Troilite, schreibersite, chromite.
Distinguishing feature Cut and etched structures from bars of kamacite and lamellae of taenite are apparent; the so-called Widmanstätten patterns, or Thomson structures (see picture).
Similar minerals Hematite is non-magnetic; the same applies to pyrite and limonite. Artificial blast furnace slags always have bubble voids. Widmanstätten patterns are absolutely diagnostic.

3 Pallasite

Type Stony-iron meteorite
Magnetism Strong
Color Encrustation brown to black, inner matrix metallic steel gray , inclusions greenish to brownish
Luster Metallic in sections/cuts, vitreous in inclusions

Morphology Metallic groundmass with embedded, idiomorphic, rounded or fractured crystals.
Origin and occurrence Pallasites are formations from the melting chamber of an asteroid body.
Main components Kamacite, taenite, inclusions of olivine crystals of centimeter size.
Accessory minerals Troilite, chromite.
Distinguishing feature Cut and etched structures from bars of kamacite and lamellae of taenite are apparent, the Widmanstätten patterns or Thomson structures; the inclusions are translucent to transparent in thin sections.
Similar minerals Hematite is non-magnetic; the same applies to pyrite and limonite. Artificial blast furnace slags always have bubble voids. The typical combination of metal and olivine is absolutely diagnostic.

4 Mesosiderite

Type Stony-iron meteorite
Magnetism Strong
Color Encrustation brown to black, inner matrix metallic steel gray, inclusions white, gray, brownish
Luster Metallic in sections/cuts, vitreous in inclusions

Morphology Metallic groundmass with embedded brecciated silicate fragments.
Origin and occurrence Mesosiderites are formed in collisions of highly modified, large asteroids.
Main components Kamazite, taenite, silicate inclusions consisting of olivine, plagioclase and pyroxene.
Accessory minerals Troilite.
Similar minerals Hematite is non-magnetic; the same applies to pyrite and limonite. Artificial blast furnace slags always have bubble voids. The typical combination of metal and silicate fragments is absolutely diagnostic.

Localities	
1 Gibeon, Namibia	**3** Brenham, Texas, USA
2 Gibeon, Namibia	**4** Estherville, Iowa, USA

1 2

3

4

1–4 Chondrite

Type Stone meteorite
Magnetismus Significant
Color Encrustation brown to black, inner matrix whitish, gray, brown, greenish, with metal inclusions
Luster Vitreous in sections/cuts to dull, metallic in inclusions

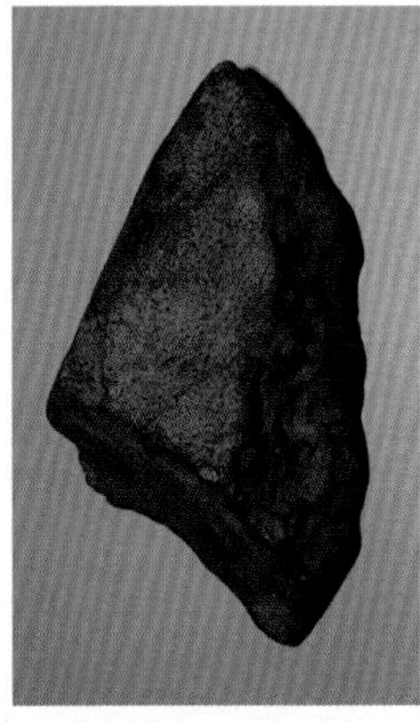

Chondrite from Gao Burkina Faso, Central Africa

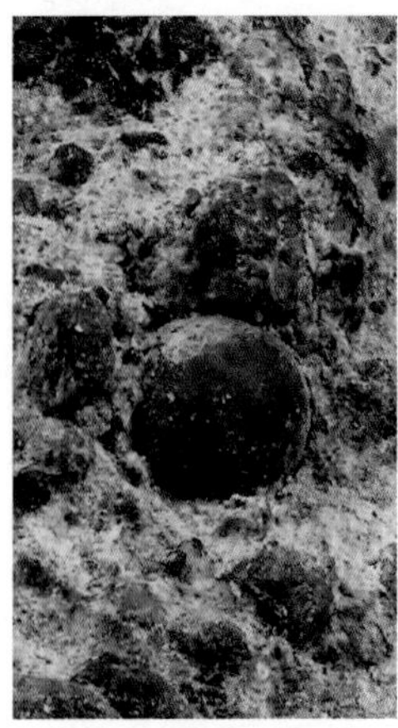

A well-formed, highly visible chondrule in the Bjurböhle chondrite from Finland

Morphology Basic mass of siliceous minerals with more or less numerous and well-formed spheroidal aggregates, the so-called chondrules and metal inclusions, sometimes also breccia-like structures. The chondrules can be composed of different minerals and are classified based on the mineral content and structure of the minerals in the chondrules.
Origin and occurrence Chondrites, which have never been part of a larger planetary body since the beginning of the formation of our planetary system, are matter originating from the solar cloud. Therefore, they represent a highly original substance of our Solar System.
Subdivision The chondrites are subdivided into three groups based on their total iron content (as metal and in the silicates):

H chondrite (High metal, Fe content: 27.5 wt.%)
L chondrite (Low metal, Fe content: 21.5 wt.%)
LL chondrite (Low metal, Low iron, Fe content: 18.5 wt.%)

Moreover, the chondrites of these groups are divided according to their petrological structure. This is particularly recognizable in the structure of the chondrules. Class 3 chondrites (for example, H3 or L3) were only exposed to low temperatures since their formation; therefore the chrondules are numerous and very sharp.
Class 6 chondrites (for example, H6 or L6) were heated up to 1652° F; they are strongly recrystallized; chondritic structures can only be recognized in a blurred manner.
Main components Depending on the chondrite type, the proportions of olivine, pyroxene, plagioclase and frit differ.
Accessory minerals Troilite, kamacite, taenite, schreibersite.
Distinguishing feature The chondrites are 4.5 billion years old and thus represent the oldest matter of our Solar System.
Similar minerals The chondritic structure, together with the metallic inclusions, is highly distinctive; calcareous or iron oolites are softer; calcareous oolite effervesces when dabbed with diluted hydrochloric acid.

Localities	
1 H5 Gao, Burkina Faso	**3** L6 Holbrook, Arizona, USA
2 L6 Alfianello, Italy	**4** L4 Bjurböhle, Finland

1
2
3
4

1 Lunaite

Type Stone meteorite
Magnetism Weak to none
Color Encrustation brown to black, inner groundmass dark, with light inclusions, light colored
Luster Vitreous in sections/cuts

Morphology Siliceous groundmass, partly brecciated, dark with light inclusions, rhegolithic.
Origin and occurrence Moon meteorites represent rocks from the lunar surface that were ejected out into space when large meteorites hit the moon and were subsequently attracted to the Earth. Depending on the type, the rocks resemble terrestrial basalts, anorthosites or are parts of the regolith layer, crushed by meteorite impacts, which does not exist on Earth.
Main components Anorthite, pyroxene, olivine.
Accessory minerals Armstrongite, tranquillityite, pseudobrookite, pyrrhotite.
Similar minerals Similar terrestrial rocks have no fusion crust; Martian meteorites have different rock structures, nevertheless; a definitive identification as lunaite requires more detailed scientific investigations.

2–3 Shergottite

Type Stone meteorite
Magnetism Weak to none
Color Encrustation brown to black, inner groundmass dark to light, gray, brown
Luster Vitreous in sections/cuts

Morphology Siliceous groundmass, partly with vitreous melt veins.
Origin and occurrence Shergottites represent rocks from the surface of Mars that were ejected out into space when large meteorites hit Mars and were subsequently attracted to the Earth. The rocks resemble terrestrial basalts or basalt-like volcanic rocks.
Main components Anorthite, pyroxene, olivine.
Accessory minerals Pyrrhotite, ilmenite, magnetite.
Similar minerals Similar terrestrial rocks have no fusion crust; lunar meteorites have different rock structures; nevertheless, a definitive identification as shergottite requires more detailed scientific investigations.

4 Nakhlite

Type Stone meteorite
Magnetism Weak to none
Color Encrustation brown to black, inner groundmass dark, gray, brown, greenish
Luster Vitreous in sections/cuts

Morphology Siliceous groundmass, partly with vitreous melt veins.
Origin and occurrence Nakhlites represent rocks from the surface of Mars that were ejected out into space when large meteorites hit Mars and were subsequently attracted to the Earth. Nakhlitic rocks resemble terrestrial peridotites.
Main components Pyroxene, olivine.
Accessory minerals Titanomagnetite, ilmenite.
Similar minerals Similar terrestrial rocks have no fusion crust; lunar meteorites have different rock structures; nevertheless, a definitive identification as shergottite requires more detailed scientific investigations.

Localities	
1 Dho 490, Oman	**3** NWA 1068, Northwest Africa
2 Zagami, Nigeria	**4** NWA 998, Northwest Africa

1 2
3 4

1 Eucrite

Type Stone meteorite
Magnetism Weak to none
Color Crust brown to black, inner groundmass dark to light gray, brown, greenish
Luster Vitreous in sections/cuts

Morphology Siliceous groundmass.
Origin and occurrence Eucrites are formed by the palingenesis of chondritic material in large asteroid bodies.
Main components Pyroxene, plagioclase.
Accessory minerals Olivine, ilmenite, magnetite.
Similar minerals Similar terrestrial rocks have no fusion crust; lunar and Martian meteorites have different rock structures; nevertheless, a definitive identification as eucrite requires more detailed scientific investigations.

2 Howardite

Type Stone meteorite
Magnetism Weak to none
Color Crust brown to black, inner groundmass dark to light gray, brown, greenish
Luster Vitreous in sections/cuts

Morphology Siliceous groundmass.
Origin and occurrence Howardites are a brecciated mixture of eucrites and chondritic matter.
Main components Pyroxene, plagioclase.
Accessory minerals Olivine, ilmenite, magnetite.
Similar minerals Similar terrestrial rocks have no fusion crust; lunar and Martian meteorites have different rock structures; the breccia structure differs from eucrite. However, a reliable identification as howardite requires detailed scientific investigations.

3 Carbonaceous chondrite

Type Stone meteorite
Magnetism Weak to none
Color Encrustation brown to black, inner groundmass dark, partially with light inclusions
Luster Vitreous in sections/cuts

Morphology Siliceous groundmass.
Origin and occurrence Carbonaceous chondrites contain carbon (up to 3%) and partially a high level of water.
Main components Pyroxene, plagioclase, olivine.
Accessory minerals Diamond, magnetite, ferronickel-calcium-aluminum silicates, organic carbon compounds (for example amino acids), graphite, carbonates.
Similar minerals Carbonaceous chondrites have no equivalent in terrestrial rocks; however, a reliable identification requires detailed scientific investigations.

4 Enstatite chondrite

Type Stone meteorite
Magnetism Weak
Color Encrustation brown to black, inner groundmass dark to light with metal inclusions
Luster Vitreous in sections/cuts, metallic in inclusions

Morphology Siliceous groundmass with chondrules and metal inclusions.
Origin and occurrence Enstatite chondrites are the most strongly reduced chondrites.
Main components Enstatite, plagioclase, olivine, taenite, troilite.
Accessory minerals Graphite, oldhamite (calcium sulfide), schreibersite, alabandite.
Similar minerals Enstatite chondrites have no equivalent in terrestrial rocks; however, a reliable identification requires detailed scientific investigations.

Localities	
1 Smara, Sahara	**3** CV3 Allende, Mexico
2 Jelica, Serbia	**4** EL6 Yilmia, Australia

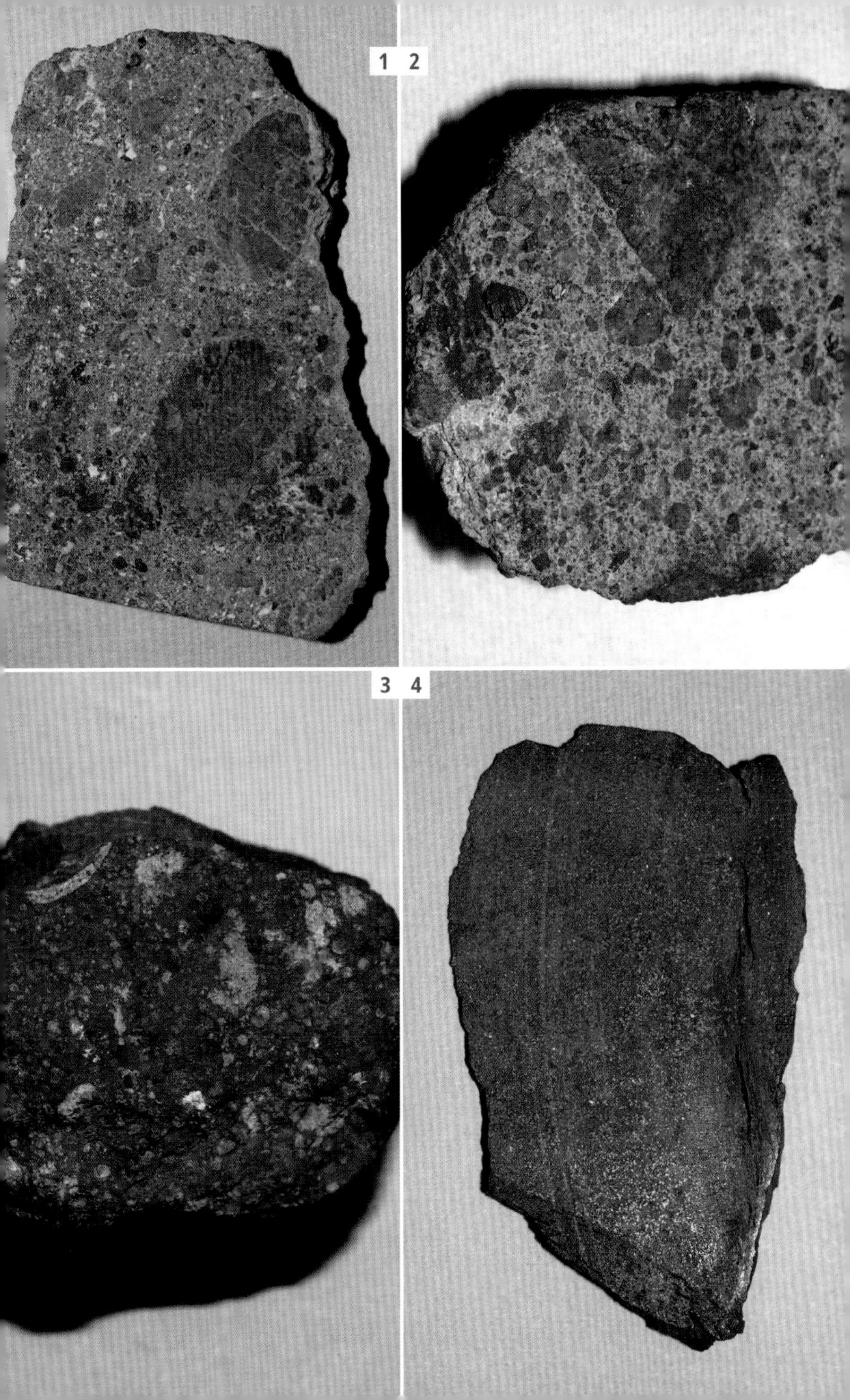
1 2
3 4

1 Moldavite

Type Tektite
Magnetism None
Color Bottle green to olive green, translucent to transparent
Luster Vitreous

Morphology Vitreous aggregates, roundish, shard-like, covered in pits formed by melted-down gas bubbles and etched structures.
Origin and occurrence The moldavites were formed during the impact of the Ries Crater meteorite 15 million years ago.
Main components Glass.
Similar minerals The green color and typical glassy appearance do not leave room for confusion with natural minerals; artificial glasses do not exhibit the typical aerodynamic shapes and surface structures. Indochinites are always black.

2 Indochinite

Type Tektite
Magnetism None
Color Black, opaque
Luster Vitreous

Morphology Vitreous aggregates, with aerodynamic shapes, botryoidal, disk-like, roundish, shard-like, covered in pits formed by melted-down gas bubbles
Origin and occurrence The indochinites were formed by the impact of a large meteorite in Southeast Asia just under a million years ago.
Main components Glass.
Similar minerals The black color and typical glassy appearance do not leave room for confusion with natural minerals; artificial glasses do not exhibit the typical aerodynamic shapes and surface structures. Moldavites are always green.

3 Suevite

Type Impact fused rock
Magnetism None
Color Light to dark gray
Luster Vitreous

Morphology Strongly inhomogeneous rock with light and dark parts, partly holey, with various rock fragments.
Origin and occurrence Suevite was formed through the melting and mixing processes of the underground rock as a result of the impact of the Ries Crater meteorite.
Main components Glass, rock fragments.
Similar minerals The strongly inhomogeneous structure with the high glass content is very characteristic and restricted to impact rocks alone.

4 Shatter cone

Type Impact rock
Magnetism None
Color Light to dark gray
Luster Vitreous to dull

Morphology Rock with typical radial structures that produce cone-shaped fragments.
Origin and occurrence Shatter cones arise in the vicinity of a large meteorite impact as an effect of the strong, directional shock wave.
Similar minerals The typical radial structure is very characteristic.

Localities	
1 Mähren, Czech Republic	**3** Nördlinger Ries, Bavaria, Germany
2 Thailand	**4** Haughton, Devon Island, Canada

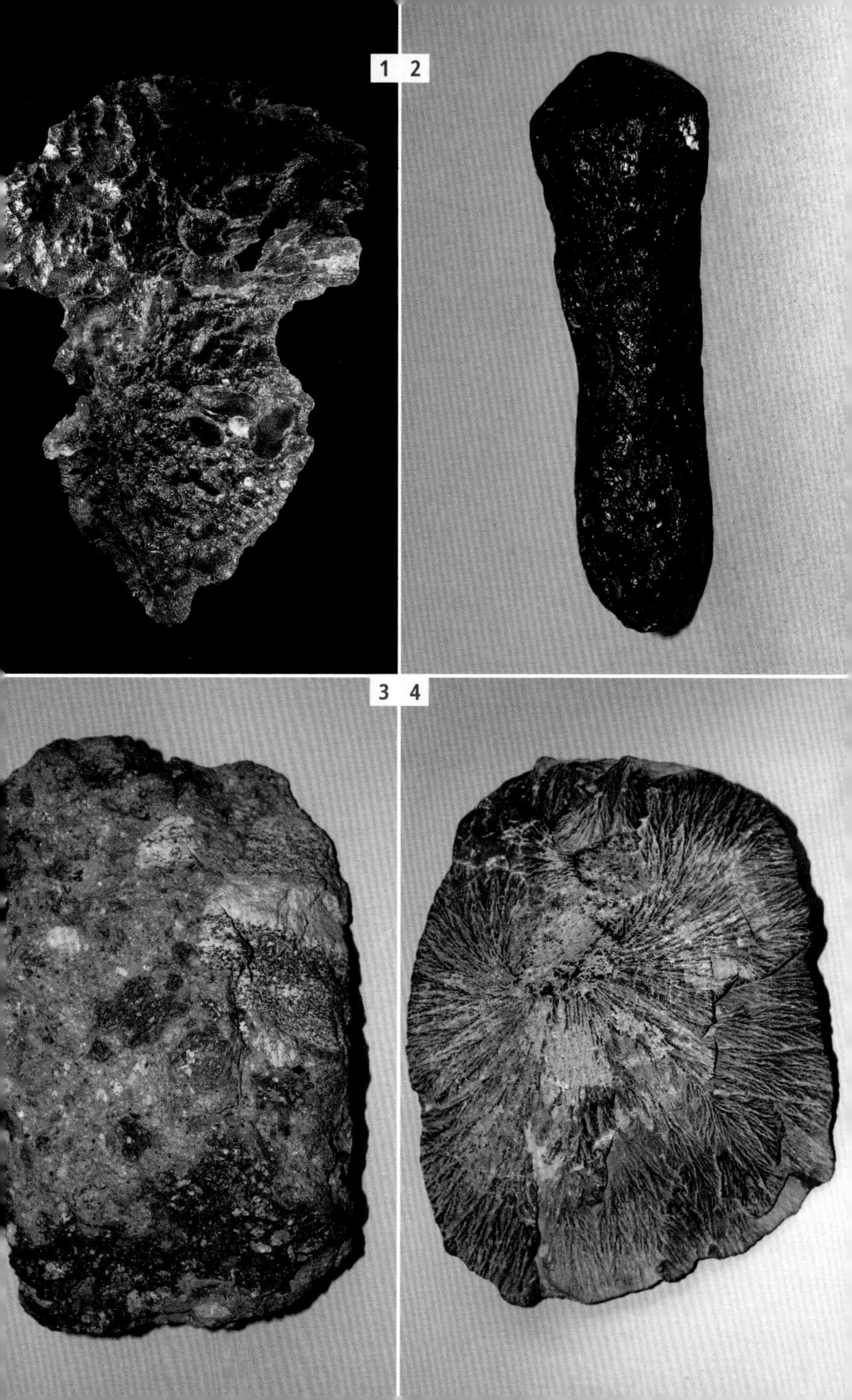
1 2
3 4

Collecting Minerals and Rocks

Collecting minerals is a popular hobby in all corners of the world.

The easiest, but also the most expensive, way to acquire minerals to build up a collection is to buy them. For this purpose, there are specialized stores in all major cities. Additionally, stores in popular vacation areas and tourist resorts often sell minerals. Their wares are sometimes sourced from the area but usually come from all over the world.

Mineral fairs and mineral trade shows where dealers from across the globe exhibit their minerals are of particular interest. Whereas, when you visit a store you can only see what one dealer has to offer, a mineral fair gives you the opportunity to compare the offers of many different dealers. In this setting, it quickly becomes apparent that the same mineral can be offered for a great range of prices by various dealers, even when it comes from the same locality. Therefore, it is essential to compare the offers. If you buy from the first dealer you see, you will often pay a lot more than necessary. At the same time, a dealer at a fair is not necessarily cheaper than the owner of a retail store. The rents for stands at fairs are expensive, and the exhibitor often travels long distances which must be factored in when the buyer sets their prices. However, one thing is beyond comparison at mineral fairs: the range of the selection. Even if you have limited funds and can't actually afford to buy anything, the scope of information and knowledge you can gain from a visit to such a fair is enormous. Large fairs, such as the Munich Mineral Show (Mineralientage Munich), additionally offer special exhibitions, which alone will make a visiting worth your while.

Nevertheless, collecting your own minerals is generally cheaper and more satisfying but also requires considerably more effort. If your want to start a rock collection, then this is essentially the only way, since rocks for collection purposes are almost never offered as retail items. So where is this actually possible? In principle, any area where the top layer of earth has been eroded or is not present at all, where encroachment into the Earth's crust has already taken place. Quarries, spoil heaps from mines, mountains, scree slopes and the beds of mountain streams offer some of the best locations for finding minerals. Of course, the opportunities for discoveries are not always the same; information about particularly good localities is provided, for example, by locality guides published by relevant publishers.

The first important question is: where can I obtain minerals? How do I get pieces like the ones depicted in this book? Looking for minerals in nature is the most fascinating as well as the cheapest method.

Minerals and crystals exist wherever there are exposed rocks. This exposure can be a result of natural causes, for example, on the banks of rivers and streams, on rocky

The spoil heaps of old mines can be interesting places in which rare minerals can be found.

A quarry in which volcanic rock is mined: The Cava Funtanafigu in Sardinia is a locality in which excellent osumilite crystals are found.

slopes or on rockfall piles in the mountains. However, rock segments are also exposed artificially, as in the case of road building, quarries and mines. This is where the opportunities for making good finds are often the best. However, you cannot collect wherever you like.

In Germany and Austria, the hewing of minerals with tools is restricted or even completely prohibited in certain areas (national parks, nature reserves, protected geotopes). Information about such restrictions can be obtained from the relevant municipal or tourist offices and, in Germany, also from the respective federal state geological offices. In many areas of Switzerland, mineral collecting is only possible with a permit. Please contact the relevant municipality. The same is true for South Tyrol, where you have to apply for your collecting permit from the South Tyrolean Mineralogical Association (Landesverband der Mineralien- und Fossilien-Sammelvereine Südtirols) at Ostmarkt 9, 39100 Bozen, Italy. However, permits are only granted to members of mineral collector clubs. In general, it is important to be aware of collecting restrictions when planning an excursion.

Although there are no general collection restrictions, bear in mind that localities are frequently on private property. Do not forget to ask the owner or quarry manager for permission, if not an actual permit. Assuming you carry out your search on non-working days, then you will not impede any workers and will not be disturbed by them during your activities; nevertheless, even then you will need a permit to enter the quarry or locality. However, if you want to purchase your findings, you should also go on a weekday. At mines, it is sometimes possible to collect during working days with an appropriate permit. A particularly good example of this is Clara Mine in the Black Forest, where, for a small fee, collectors are allowed to search the heaps built specifically for them in Oberwolfach.

Find out about such opportunities as early as possible!

Even if there are no obvious prohibitions and the site is freely accessible, you should keep a few things in mind: Hardly anyone will object to simple surface collecting. It's always more problematic once you start smashing blocks or digging holes, which is often necessary, particularly on old spoil heaps. Leave the locality just as you found it. Close up any holes you dug, do not damage any trees or plants, take your trash (drink cans, etc.) with you. Protect the environment during your activities. The best collector is one who other people don't even realize has been there.

Localities, quarries and mine spoil heaps are private property. You must always request a collector's permit before entering them!

If you are lucky enough to be able to go mineral hunting with an experienced collector, you will, in any case, have no trouble finding minerals. One of the best ways to find more experienced collectors is in mineral collector clubs, where you will meet like-minded people happy to take you on a collecting tour. However, if that's not the case or if you simply want to be the first to break new ground, then you need to plan your trip or excursion well in advance.

Literature

The first step is a study of the literature. If your aim is to visit an area unknown to you from a mineralogical point of view, you need to learn about the localities in that area. A good start here are, for example, books from the series *Mineral Localities* (in German, *Mineralfundstellen*), published by the Christian Weise Verlag. These describe the localities in various landscapes of Germany and Europe. Special issues of *Der Aufschluss*, the journal of the German Mineral Collector Association, usually also highlight a specific collecting area. Individual localities are often presented in magazines such as *Lapis* or *Der Aufschluss*. Please also note the literature references provided in these magazines. The more you know about a deposit beforehand, the greater your chances of making a good find are.

Alpine fissures are a special case. By the time such a find is published, the fissure will almost certainly have been depleted. In this case, you should search the literature for areas with a certain density of fissures. Even if you don't find a new fissure, rubble piles or waste heaps in front of cleared fissures often contain nice small minerals; even larger finds are occasionally possible.

If, during your preparatory studies, you come across a mineral you are unfamiliar with, look it up in this *Minerals Encyclopedia*. If you can't find the mineral here because of its great rarity, then look it up in a specialized mineralogy text book. You can find recommended references under the section "For Further Reading" on page 437. In any event, it is important that you already know what the minerals to be found look like.

Maps

You now have enough information about the locality and its minerals. The locality could, for example, often be an old spoil heap somewhere in a forest, so you will need a good map to find it. Unfortunately, unless it is a large mine or a similar setting, road maps will not be detailed enough. Trail maps with a scale of 1:100 000 or, even better, 1:50 000 and ordinance survey maps with a scale of 1:25 000 are ideal. Decide on the precise route on the map in advance. For many countries, such map series can also be purchased digitally now, so that you can even plan your collection trip in advance on your PC, tablet or phone. Likewise, an excellent starting point is Google Earth with its satellite maps, although the quality of the satellite images varies between areas, so that exactly the locality you are interested in often disappears in a blurry section. Also, for individual countries, separate satellite views are accessible on the Internet. These are sometimes better and have a higher resolution than those found on Google Earth. Nevertheless, the offer and accessibility are constantly changing, so careful research before each trip is always necessary.

In addition, you can also contact a collector in the area of the locality (addresses are, for example, available in the Association of Friends of Minerology and Geology (VFMG) member directory) or the author of a magazine article. However, you should of course remember that, for the most part, scientific authors do not live near the locality and usually also do not have enough spare time to conduct guided tours. In contrast, a collector living near the locality will certainly be able to help you a great deal, perhaps even guide you to or show you other interesting localities. You can easily search online for the addresses of, for example, local collector clubs or even clubs located abroad. Perhaps a small mineral exchange fair may even be scheduled during the time of your journey. If so, you should make a point of visiting it. You will easily be able to make contacts at the fair. You can immediately see what is being found, and you can usually acquire interesting local finds at much more affordable prices than at large, international fairs.

You should always treat information about possible findings with skepticism. Nevertheless, localities that a collector of large pieces might consider exploited can be an El Dorado for a more observant collector of small specimens that can be viewed with a microscope. For a collector of beautifully crystallized specimens, a locality with very rare but more or less uneven minerals would perhaps be rather unrewarding. If someone thinks they haven't found a single useful mineral in a spoil heap, it could well be that they just haven't dug in the right place. In quarries that are still active, the conditions often change very quickly. Where you might have found nothing at all a month ago, you might find wonderful pieces in almost the exact same spot now.

Equipment

Of course, for successful collecting, you also need the right equipment. First, you need a standard hammer (a little over a pound) for breaking up small pieces and for finer chiseling. Hammers with a steel handle are preferred. For coarser work, a commercially available miner's hammer is suitable. You will also need a range of chisels, flat chisels and pointed chisels. You will need at least one large chisel for coarse work and a small chisel for fine work. A folding spade and a hammer with an edge as wide as possible are suitable for searching old spoil heaps.

Hammers are the most important equipment items for a mineral collector.

You should always wear safety glasses or goggles to protect your eyes against splinters when working with a hammer and chisel.

To get your pieces safely back home, you will also require some packaging material: Old newspapers for less delicate specimens, soft paper or foam for fragile pieces, pouches or small jars and mineral putty for small finds that would otherwise be easily lost. If you can drive to the locality, a produce crate is much better for holding your finds than a backpack, which is of course indispensable if you will be walking long distances. Once you reach the locality, it is advisable that you first get your bearings based on the spots where other collectors have already hammered or dug. Often, collectors who were previously there may have placed pieces that were of no use to them in one spot. From these, you can see right away what there is to find and what you have to look out for. You may also find a specimen that you need. When you leave the locality, do the same as the previous collectors. Your successor will be pleased!

One final request: Leave the locality as you found it! Even in quarries a certain sense of order prevails. It is irresponsible for collectors to leave prospecting trenches, deep pits and fallen boulders. Forgotten or lost tools can get into mining equipment, resulting in huge financial losses. This hinders work in the quarry, and the owner may be forced to impose a ban on mineral collecting.

Purchasing Minerals

To complete your collection, you will need to buy minerals that you cannot find yourself. As it is impossible to set fixed prices for minerals due to the inherent uniqueness of each piece, pricing is entirely up to the individual dealer. Therefore, there may be very large differences in prices for quite similar pieces. Collectors have the opportunity to view a wide range of minerals of all kinds, compare their prices and buy pieces at many mineral fairs as well as at large and small sales exhibitions. Nevertheless, because of the often very high rents for stands at the large fairs, the minerals sold there are often no cheaper than those in a mineral store. Prices at mineral fairs are often not lower, but rather higher than in specialist shops. While the expensive super specimens, rare systematics and international material from almost every country in the world are more likely to be obtained at the large fairs, smaller local fairs provide an opportunity to procure interesting finds from regional localities or even from the last collecting trip abroad directly from the collector. And, of course, all at much more favorable prices.

Exchanging Minerals

The third possibility for acquiring minerals, is to swap or exchange them. The prerequisite here is that you have spare mineral specimens in your collection that you want to offer in exchange for other minerals of interest to you. Most collector clubs organize monthly member meetings which often include lectures and presentations as well as opportunities for swapping minerals and informative discussions. In-person exchanges are preferable but not always possible, particularly between collectors who live far from each other. However, in precisely such circumstances, an exchange is of particular interest because the greater the distance between the two partners is, the more their respective offers will differ. Thus, a mineral that nobody in Germany wants anymore because everybody already has it can be exotic and very interesting to a collector in the USA and vice versa. Not only that, exchanges can be made via mail. The first step is to send out wish and offer lists. Once the two partners have agreed upon what they would like to exchange as well as the procedure for doing so, the packages are sent. Of course, good packaging is essential here. Anyone who has ever watched the loading of parcels at a train station will know that the packages and parcels are hardly handled with care. Even if parcels are marked "Caution! Contains glass!" or "Fragile — Do not throw!", the instructions are seldom observed. Package your goods so that they can be dropped to the ground from a height of a few feet without concern. If so, the package should survive its postal journey. The sent minerals do not become your property until the exchange partner has agreed to the exchange.

Addresses of possible exchange partners can be found in the VFMG member directory or in the exchange section of the magazine published by the association or in the collector's market of the magazine, *LAPIS*. Various online chat rooms are a particularly good opportunity for connecting with other collectors around the world. For example, at mindat.org, you not only can find comprehensive information on virtually all existing minerals, including locality information, but you can also contact other users of the site, ask questions, answer other members' questions based on your own experience or search for exchange partners.

Collection cabinets with multiple drawers are ideal for storing mineral specimens.

Organizing a Mineral Collection

To begin with, you will probably collect every specimen you can get your hands on. However, the number of minerals in your collection will soon grow to the point where you will need to start thinking about what you want to collect now and how, if at all, you want to limit your collection. There are lots of possibilities here:

A systematic collection, known as a systematic for short, is the most comprehensive. If possible, it should contain all known minerals. However, no one can achieve a complete systematic. Even museums and mineralogical institutes do not have complete collections. You can consider a collection with more than a thousand of the well over four thousand known minerals (additionally, about thirty new minerals are described every year) a reasonably good collection. For a beginner, a collection with three to five hundred mineral species is rather remarkable. Furthermore, a discerning system should document the most important localities, crystal forms, habit types and parageneses of the minerals it contains. Therefore, an analogy for a system is a bottomless barrel; completeness can be strived for but never attained. Admittedly, this is also part of the particular appeal of a system: You can spend your whole life working on it, and you will always still be able to discover something new.

It is easier to achieve a complete collection if you create a special collection, that is, a collection that only focuses on a portion of the vast range of minerals. There are many possibilities; the only limits are those set by your own imagination. Particularly rewarding groups for special collections are, for example, copper oxidation minerals, minerals of the zeolite group, phosphate minerals or minerals from alpine fissures as well as twins or different morphologies of a single mineral such as quartz or fluorite. Particularly beautiful, but extremely expensive, is, for example, a collection of gemstone minerals, possibly also with the respective cut counterpart gem for each uncut mineral.

Another type of special collection that is also of scientific interest is a local collection. It contains the minerals of a single locality or discovery area. This is, however, a complete as possible collection with all the morphologies and associations of the minerals. With this, it is worthwhile to build up a good systematic collection alongside it to compare the minerals found locally with the same minerals from other localities. In most cases, an advanced collector will have a systematic as well as some local and special collections.

Specimen Sizes

As the size of a collection grows, the question of specimen size automatically comes into play. For city dwellers in particular, but also for almost all collectors, the problem of space is a rather important factor, regardless of what a collector happens to collect. The collection should have a good overall appearance, so the specimens should be reasonably equal in size. It is almost impossible for anybody to collect samples of more than 15 × 20 cm in size, from either a space-related or financial point of view. This is the size range addressed by museums or institutes; it is not for nothing that such magnificent specimens are often referred to as museum specimens. Sizes between 5 × 7 cm and 9 × 12 cm present a good compromise. These pieces are just the right size to ensure they are neither too large nor too expensive. However, there are enough mineral species that normally occur in such small dimensions that even such sizes cannot be achieved; you either have to collect them in a smaller size or forego them completely.

Micromounts are small mineral specimens glued into boxes, on the lid of which a label with all the relevant information is attached.

To view micromounts, you need a binocular- or stereo microscope.

In an era when many people often have a lack of space and limited finances, one method of collecting that originated in the USA has become more widely known: The collection of micromounts which are specimens of no more than 2 × 2 cm that are viewed using a stereo microscope. The advantage of these small specimens is that they require less space and are a good deal cheaper that larger samples. When collectors first view their specimens using a stereo microscope, they discover a whole world of previously unimagined beauty. Nevertheless, the purchase of a stereo microscope represents a one-time major expense. Albeit, this is soon returned in the savings on mineral purchases. Before investing in such an expensive device (starting at roughly 330.00 USD), you should first seek advice from collector friends and try out the various microscopes. Today, a stereo microscope is an indispensable tool for almost every advanced collector (not just for micromounts). Many collector clubs have a club microscope, which can also be borrowed. This way, you can find out what suits you best. In principle, it makes more sense to save funds over time so that you can then afford a microscope with better lenses and optics. After all, a stereo microscope may be a once-in-a-lifetime acquisition.

Storing Specimens

The optimum solution is plastic boxes. These are available at many mineral stores. Cardboard boxes are not much cheaper and not as strong. Only buy boxes that allow you to use your available space as efficiently as possible. Since this becomes difficult when using a variety of differently-sized boxes, you should limit yourself to no more than two or three sizes.

Place a label with the name, number and locality of the mineral in the box. Then put a transparent plastic sheet over it to protect it. Then place the specimen on top of this. Alternatively, you can also cover the label with transparent adhesive film or laminate it.

It is essential that you attach the mineral number firmly to the specimen so that it is impossible to confuse them, particularly when taking several pieces out for inspection at the same time. Of course, micromounts are a special case. They are secured in the small boxes using an adhesive putty. The collection is then much tidier and easier to handle. In this case, the labels are adhered to the small boxes. Further marking of the mineral is unnecessary because it is affixed to the labeled box with the adhesive putty. It is important that the adhesive labels are secured firmly in place and do not come loose and fall off after a few years, which is the case with many stick-on labels. In such cases, all the information is lost and the mineral is worthless. Likewise, the pen used for labeling must be permanent and must not fade. Many printer inks do not fulfill this requirement. Some collectors have started to store even larger specimens in lidded boxes, which provides extra protection from dust. However, the larger versions of the small boxes are so expensive that this method of storage has not yet become widespread.

Of course, the optimum solution for arranging the boxes or cases is a custom-made mineral cabinet. However, it is also the most expensive. Therefore, in most cases, an ordinary cupboard must make do as a replacement. Office cabinets with open, shallow drawers for storing forms are highly practical. The drawers should not be so large that they cannot be pulled out easily even if they are fully loaded.

No matter how neatly you store your collection in cabinets, when a collector friend visits, you may find that you can't find a specimen you've been desperate to show them. Moreover, the space on the label in the box is far from adequate for all the required information.

The Collection Index

These problems are resolved with a collection index. Over time, two forms of indexes have proved to be the most practical: The first method creates a separate index card for each mineral. To save space, the optimum size is about half the size of a postcard. The card should contain the following details: number of the mineral, name, chemical formula, color, morphology and habit, locality, date of discovery, finder, origin of the mineral (for example, self-found, exchanged, purchased), accessory minerals, special treatment of the specimen (for example, etched with HCl) and, most importantly, the location in the collection. The necessity of listing other properties of the mineral, such as hardness, density and streak, is the subject of debate. Moreover, your diligence will be tested if you must repeatedly record hardness 3 for twenty calcite specimens.

Perhaps a more practical solution is to write a card for each mineral that lists all its properties and place it in front of the other cards for that mineral in the card file.

The cards are arranged by mineral number to ensure quick retrieval. Some collectors simply number their samples sequentially. This has several disadvantages: First, the number then becomes a mere number and gives no information about the mineral; secondly, a list must also be created containing all numbers for the respective minerals because you may wish to single out all the quartz crystals whose cards would otherwise be scattered all over the card index with this type of numbering. It is better to assign a specimen a number based on a crystal-chemical mineral classification system. The most useful in this respect are the Strunz Mineralogical Tables, which lays out a comprehensive numbering system based on the mineral groups: For example, the phosphates, arsenates, etc. are all assigned Roman numeral VII. "A" means anhydrous without foreign anions, and "1" refers to the berlinite-beryllonite-hurlbutite group. Now, only lowercase letters need to be assigned to the minerals in this group and appended to the number. With that, you have a unique reference number for the mineral. For example, berlinite is then assigned the number VIIA1a. Individual specimens of the same mineral species are sequentially numbered using the standard procedure from 1 to x. The berlinite sample number 1 is then assigned the reference number VIIA1a1. The advantage of this method is that the index cards for all specimens of a mineral species are positioned consecutively in the card index and are thus easily accessible.

The cards are best stored in small wooden index card boxes, which are available in office supply stores. Pre-printed index cards are available in many mineral stores.

For the second index type, you need a ring binder, preferably for 8 1/2 x 11" paper. For this method, you create an index sheet for each mineral species that contains all the consistent properties. Enter the individual specimens on the same sheet in a table that has columns for all the important information (as listed above). The advantage of this method is its ease of use, since all specimens of the same mineral species are listed on a single sheet. One disadvantage is that rare minerals require a large sheet of paper even though there may only be a single specimen. Viewed overall, this system saves space for the common minerals and wastes it on the rare ones. The numbering is the same as described above.

Of course, in this computer era, many collectors manage their collection using a PC; appropriate programs to meet the needs of mineral collectors are available from specialized suppliers. Likewise, anyone with appropriate knowledge and enough spare time can create their own database program tailored to meet their specific needs.

Whatever method of documentation is used, the single most important factor is that the locality is always clearly assigned to the collection item. You can re-identify a mineral at any time, but it is almost always impossible to re-trace the locality. Without its locality information, your mineral is practically worthless for your collection.

Collecting Rocks

Collecting rocks is both easier and more difficult than mineral collecting. It is easier because rocks, as large, geological bodies, are generally easier than tiny crystals to find and discover. One difficulty is that you really have to collect most pieces yourself because purchasing them is rarely possible. Rocks are only rarely sold at mineral fairs. On the other hand, this is also an advantage: in principle, you can find rocks everywhere, while hiking or travelling anywhere; such a collection often has many more individual features than a mineral collection bought from mineral fairs.

Collection specimens of rocks are cut into sizes from 7 x 9 to 9 x 12 cm and stored in appropriate collection boxes.

Collecting rocks is also much cheaper, since, due to the smaller offering, it is difficult to spend a lot of money, at least at mineral fairs.

Rocks are normally collected as hand-sized specimens. These are rectangular pieces of about 7 × 9 to 9 × 12 cm in size, as can also be seen in the rock section of this book. In general, this size is large enough to document the typical features of the rock. Special care must be taken to ensure that the selected rock piece is fresh and has not already been changed by weathering. Where coarse-grained rocks, such as pegmatites or coarse-porphyritic granites, are concerned, this size is inadequate for displaying the characteristics of the rock, so the collection piece must then be larger. This immediately leads to the next quandary: having sufficient space to store them. You can't collect rocks as micromounts; you need space for them. However, you don't need at least 1000 pieces to have a reasonable collection; a collection of 200 different rocks easily indicates your earnest intentions as a collector. Of interest is the collection of special features, for example, beautiful folds, inclusions of foreign rocks, for example, in granites or vulcanites, or a collection of special bedding structures in sedimentary rocks, such as stylolites, schist structures, cementation of cracks and rupture structures, or, for example, cross stratification or wave ripples. Even though hand-sized rock specimens are large, you still need a magnifying glass for field work and a stereo microscope for home use. Many rock components, the identification of which is essential for rock identification, are so small that they can only be determined using adequate magnification. At the end of the day, every rock collector is always a mineral collector as well, and it

Thin-section photograph of a periodotite taken using crossed polarizers, which causes the olivines to show up in various shades of blue, while the pyroxenes are contrasted in brown.

is always advantageous, if not essential, to build up a collection of all the important rock-forming minerals for comparison purposes.

Petrographers, as scientists who deal specifically with rocks and their formation are called, seldom rely solely on visual identification when identifying rocks. Precise classification is normally only possible by means of analyses and thin section examinations. In the latter method, thin rock disks are produced which are then sanded so thin that you could read a newspaper through them. Then they are viewed under a petrographic microscope. The species, morphology and intergrowth ratios of the individual rock-forming minerals can then be precisely determined, as can their proportions relative to each other. Together with a total rock analysis, this then allows for a very precise identification of a rock. There are also rock collectors who produce thin sections and collect them. However, the devices needed to manufacture the sections and the petrographic microscope needed to view them are very costly. It is also necessary to take a course to learn how to operate the microscope and examine the thin sections. Such courses are only offered at corresponding university-level institutes.

Collecting Gemstones

Collecting gemstones has become a popular hobby. Of course, the cut stones are not worn as jewelry but rather are kept in specially made boxes and jewel cases. In this way, it is possible and even particularly worthwhile to also collect minerals in a cut condition that are not normally used for jewelry production for specific reasons, for example, because the gems in question are not hard enough. Thus, for example, faceted calcite can look extraordinarily beautiful although

Typical garnet jewelry is characterized by the use of many relatively small stones.

its low hardness makes it completely unsuitable for jewelry.

However, if you don't own your own cutting machine, you will have to buy such cut stones from a dealer or cutter. There are gem cutters who specialize entirely in such specific "collector's" stones. Their addresses can be found advertised in collector's magazines, and their work can be viewed directly at larger mineral fairs. As for many rare pieces, there are often only a few unique pieces in existence. Furthermore, because cutting material only rarely becomes available on the market, you need to stay in contact with the suppliers as regularly as possible so that you can react to the singular opportunities that arise if you aim to build up a more extensive collection.

If you want to go beyond simply collecting these cut stones but also want to study them more closely, the purchase of gemological literature and the appropriate examination equipment (gemstone microscope, refractometer, diamond tester, etc.) becomes essential in the long term.

There are a few things to bear in mind when buying gemstones, whether for collection purposes or to have them cut later to make jewelry:

Only purchase valuable stones directly from a specialist dealer or directly from the cutter. More so than in the case of other objects, the purchase of gemstones is a matter of trust.

You should always be suspicious of offers that seem too good to be true, especially when vacationing abroad. Inexpensive, synthetic stones are often sold as genuine. Moreover, do not rely on any offered expert opinions. It is almost impossible to ascertain whether a certificate actually refers to the loose stone you are being offered.

Furthermore, do not buy gemstones as an investment. This, if at all, should be left to the experts. As a rule, it is unlikely that, if you choose to sell, you will get back what you paid, let alone an increase in value. There are many much better and, in particular, safer investments available.

Glossary

Accessory minerals Minerals that consistently occur together with the described mineral.
Aggregate Intergrowth of multiple individual crystals that can, for example, be radial, fibrous, botryoidal (grape-like) or reniform (kidney-shaped).
Amorphous Non-crystalline; minerals without any crystal structure are amorphous, such as, for example, opal.
Amphibole Group of silicate minerals with a typical 120° cleavage angle.
Cementation zone In a deposit in the area of the groundwater level, in which certain elements are enriched.
Concretion A nodular, more or less spherical, mineral enrichment in a sedimentary rock.
Cruciform twin Twin in which the two crystal individuals are intergrown in a cross-shaped form.
Density (specific gravity) Weight of a 1 cm cube of a particular mineral.
Deposit Enrichment of minerals in a particular location on our planet.
Double ender Freely grown, fully formed crystal.
Ductile Malleable, deformable, such as, for example, gold.
Essential mineral Mineral species comprising a rock.
Exhalation Escaping of gases from the Earth's interior.
Fissure Cavities or fractures in the rock formed by stress and strain conditions. Fissures in siliceous minerals, particularly in the Alps, are called Alpine fissures.
Fracture Shape of the fracture surface, for example, conchoidal, uneven, crystalline, hackly, granular.
Gangues Minerals that exist alongside the ore minerals in an ore vein, for example, quartz, calcite, barite.
Geode A spherical cavity in volcanic rock that is lined with crystals.
Hydrochloric acid test (HCl test) The mineral being tested is wetted with a drop of cold diluted hydrochloric acid.
Hydrothermal formations are minerals that have formed from warm to hot aqueous solutions.
Impregnation Filling of the smallest cavities in a rock by a subsequently formed mineral species (for example, an ore).
Inclusion Crystal embedded in a fine-grained or granulitic rock.
Metamorphism Transformation of rocks under the influence of pressure and/or temperature.
Native metals A metal that occurs as an element in nature, for example, gold, silver, copper, platinum.
Occurrence The preferred type of appearance of a mineral in certain rocks or deposits.
Ore deposit A deposit in which ore is present in economically recoverable quantities.
Ore Mineral or mineral content that is extracted for the production of metals or other elements.
Ore piece Intergrowth of multiple crystals of the same or different mineral species.
Oxidation zone Area of a deposit that is subject to the influence of weathering.
Paragenesis Characteristic occurrence of minerals resulting from the formation conditions.
Petrography Lithology.
Placer Enrichment of heavy, weathering-resistant minerals; depending on the location and enrichment mechanism, there are river, marine, coastal or surf placers. Typical minerals that are enriched in placers include gold, diamond, corundum, magnetite, ilmenite, monazite, garnet, chromite.
Pneumatolytic formations Minerals that have been formed from the gas phase.
Pseudomorph A mineral in the crystal form of another mineral.
Pyroxenes Group of silicate minerals with a typical 90° cleavage angle.
Radioactive A mineral is radioactive if it emits alpha, beta or gamma rays.
Secondary minerals Minerals newly formed by the alteration of other minerals.

Solid solutions Crystals containing two or more elements in variable proportions, where one element replaces the other element.
Subvolcanic formations Mineral formations, that have developed directly beneath a volcano in the Earth's crust.
Tarnish colors Colors arising from the formation of thin oxidation skins on minerals, particularly sulfides.
Twin Ordered intergrowth of two crystals of the same species of mineral. There are also triplets, quadruplets, quintuplets, etc.
Uneven Mineral pieces that are not delimited by crystalline surfaces but rather by irregular fracture surfaces are uneven.
Varieties Examples of a mineral that differ due to particular properties (color, aggregate form, etc.)
Vein Filling of a fissure in rock with minerals younger than the surrounding rock.
Vug A more or less round cavity in rock in which crystals grow.

Folded structures are typical of metamorphic rocks: Gneiss from the Bavarian Forest.

For further reading

Hochleitner/Philipsborn/Weiner/Rapp
Minerale – Bestimmen nach äußeren Kennzeichen **(Orig. in German, Minerals - Identification Based on External Characteristics)**
The latest edition of the classic textbook from Schweizerbart Science Publishers, frequently reprinted for over 50 years, is also of great use to the interested layperson. Specially prepared identification tables, ordered by hardness and streak, allow quick and reliable field identification of the most important minerals for collections. A special color chart section explains properties that repeatedly occur in the table section, from color striping to twinning, and provides further explanation with characteristic photos.

Weiss
Das große LAPIS-Mineralienverzeichnis **(Orig. in German, The Large LAPIS Directory of Minerals)**
This directory from the Christian Weise Verlag contains the names of all existing and recognized minerals as well as information about their properties: chemistry, crystal system, hardness, color, streak, cleavage, morphology, rarity, systematics.

LAPIS Mineral **Magazine**
Mineral collectors can find the latest information here on new and classic localities, newly discovered minerals and what's happening in the collecting world. Classified advertisements help you find swap partners, contact fellow collectors or buy and sell surplus collection specimens.

Further Literature

Strunz H., Nickel, E. H., *Strunz Mineralogical Tables.* Schweizerbart Science Publishers, Stuttgart, 2001.

Duthaler, R., Weiß, St., *Mineralien reinigen und aufbewahren.* Christian Weise Verlag, Munich, 2008.

Borchardt-Ott, W., *Kristallographie. Springer* Spektrum, 2018.

Dietrich, R. V., Skinner, B. J., *Die Gesteine und ihre Mineralien.* Ott Verlag Thun, 1995.

Wimmenauer, W., *Petrographie der magmatischen und metamorphen Gesteine.* Enke Verlag, 1985.

Anthony, J. W., Bideaux, R. A., *Handbook of Mineralogy,* Volume I–V. 1990–2000.

Eppler, W. F., *Praktische Gemmologie.* Rühle-Diebener Verlag, 1984.

Press, F., Siever, R., *Allgemeine Geologie.* Springer Spektrum, 2016.

Index

Alternative secondary names of minerals and rocks are shown in *italics*

A

B

C

D

E

F

G

H

I

J

K

Author

Rupert Hochleitner holds a doctorate in mineralogy. His area of expertise is systematic mineralogy. His additional research areas include meteorites, in particular, those originating from Mars, oxidation minerals and pegmatitic phosphate minerals. He has published numerous scientific articles on this subject. His mineral identification books have been published in fourteen different languages. For many years, he was the editor-in-chief of the magazine LAPIS, a trade journal for mineral collectors and mineral enthusiasts. He has been active as the Deputy Director of the Mineralogical State Collection of Munich (Mineralogische Staatssammlung) since 1993.

Credits

With 807 color photos taken by Rupert Hochleitner and 41 color photos taken by Christian Rewitzer: 22/4, 24/1, 24/4, 26/2, 40/2, 44/3, 44/4, 48/3, 76/2, 76/3, 86/3, 94/2, 110/3, 112/1, 132/1, 140/3, 142/2, 162/3, 174/4, 184/2, 196/1, 198/1, 198/2, 198/4, 200/4, 204/1, 204/2, 206/2, 212/3, 222/1, 222/3, 224/2, 228/4, 230/1, 230/2, 236/2, 238/4, 252/1, 256/4, 278/1, 288/1, Photograph three (karibibite) on front flap plus 1 photograph by Melanie Kaliwada (423) and 191 black and white drawings by Rupert Hochleitner and 2 black and white drawings by Wolfgang Lang (page 1).

Cover design by Walter Typografie & Grafik GmbH, Würzburg with the use of a photograph from shutterstock © Albert Russ on the front cover, a photograph of Rupert Hochleitner on the back cover and two drawings from shutterstock © Bodor Tivadar.

The photograph on the front shows prase crystals from the Greek island of Serifos; the drawing shows agate. The photograph on the back cover shows rutile from Itabira, Brazil; the drawing shows quartz crystals.

Editor: Lisa Hummel
Production: Markus Schärtlein
Basic layout: eStudio Calamar
Setting: typopoint GbR, Ostfildern

Published by Firefly Books Ltd., 2022

2nd printing, 2023

Library of Congress Control Number: 2022934050

Library and Archives Canada Cataloguing in Publication
"Title: The minerals encyclopedia / Rupert Hochleitner.
Other titles: Kosmos mineralienführer. English
Names: Hochleitner, Rupert, author.
Description: Translation of: Der Kosmos mineralienführer.
Stuttgart: Kosmos, 2019. | Includes index.
Identifiers: Canadiana 20220186324 | ISBN 9780228103622 (softcover)
Subjects: LCSH: Minerals—Encyclopedias. | LCSH: Minerals—Identification. |
LCSH: Rocks—Encyclopedias. | LCSH: Rocks—Identification. |
LCSH: Mineralogy—Encyclopedias. | LCSH: Petrology—Encyclopedias. |
LCGFT: Encyclopedias. | LCGFT: Field guides.
Classification: LCC QE355 .H6313 2022 | DDC 549.03—dc23"

Published in Canada by
Firefly Books Ltd.
50 Staples Avenue, Unit 1
Richmond Hill, Ontario
L4B 0A7

Published in the United States by
Firefly Books (U.S.) Inc.
P.O. Box 1338, Ellicott Station
Buffalo, New York
14205

Translation: Travod International Ltd.

Printed in China | E

Examples of structure types of rocks

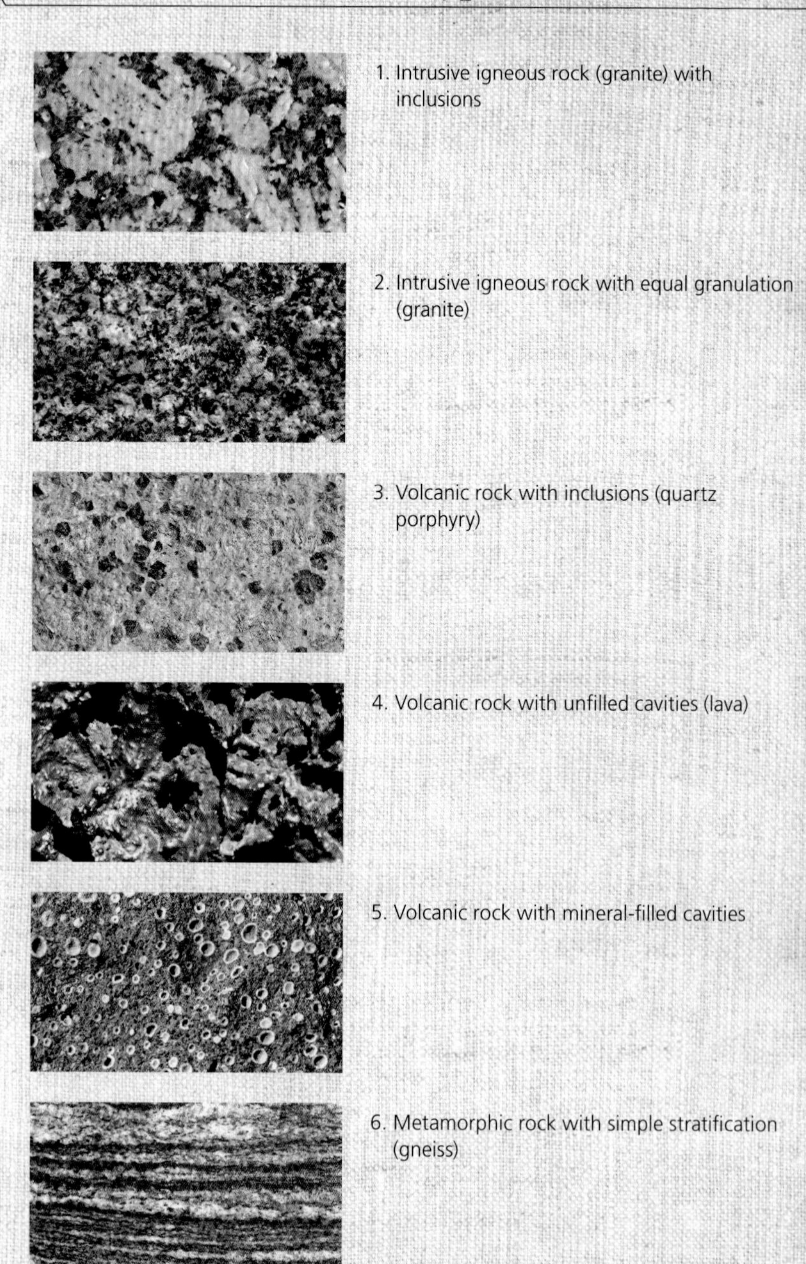

1. Intrusive igneous rock (granite) with inclusions
2. Intrusive igneous rock with equal granulation (granite)
3. Volcanic rock with inclusions (quartz porphyry)
4. Volcanic rock with unfilled cavities (lava)
5. Volcanic rock with mineral-filled cavities
6. Metamorphic rock with simple stratification (gneiss)